The Lonely Planet Story

A beat-up old car, a few dollars in the pocket and a sense of adventure.

That's all Tony and Maureen Wheeler needed for the trip of a lifetime. They met on a park bench in Regent's Park, London and married a year later. For their honeymoon, they decided to attempt what few people thought possible – crossing Europe and Asia overland, all the way to Australia.

It was too amazing an experience to keep to themselves. Urged by their friends, they stayed up nights at their kitchen table writing, typing and stapling together their very first travel guide, *Across Asia on the Cheap*.

Within a week they'd sold 1500 copies and Lonely Planet was born. Two years later, their second journey led to the creation of *Southeast Asia on a Shoestring*, which led to books on Nepal, Australia, Africa and India and, more than 40 years later, to this book...

The
World

A Traveller's Guide to the Planet
SECOND EDITION

The World Contents

Destinations

Africa
America
Antarctica
Asia
Australia/Oceania
Europe

Welcome to the World

While your father is alive, make as many friends as you can; while your horse is alive, visit as many lands as you can. [Mongolian proverb]

Today it is more important than ever to heed this proverb's calling to visit as many lands as you can. Travel is easier and cheaper than ever before...and in a political and social climate which is confused and confronting, it is important to see the world, and all it has to offer, through your own eyes. If you travel – near or far – the world will exhibit its beauty and diversity. Adventure and inspiration await around every corner, so what's stopping you?

APROTT / GETTY IMAGES ©

Natural Wonders

There is so much to discover across seven continents and 221 countries, from rivers deep, like the Nile (snaking 6850km from central Africa to the Mediterranean), and the sunken shores of the Dead Sea (427m below sea level), to mountains high, like the Himalayas (more than 100 peaks over 7200m, including Everest at 8848m), the Andes and the Alps. There are mighty expanses of greenery, like the Amazon basin (7 million sq km of jungle), while beneath the crystal clear Pacific Ocean lies the Great Barrier Reef (stretching 2300km), and the scarred hide of the Grand Canyon is a repository of 2 billion years of geological history.

Wildlife spectacles include the annual wildebeest migration (two million strong) across the Serengeti, the stoic emperor penguins of Antarctica, and the diverse menagerie on the Galápagos Islands, where people seem out of place.

Spectacular Cities

More than half of the world's population now lives in cities. They are the pulsating beacons that attract us and each has its own distinctive character: New York with its skyscrapers and taxicabs; London with its parks, pubs and palaces; İstanbul straddling the border of Europe and Asia; and Jerusalem, holy to Judaism, Islam and Christianity. There are cities with thousands of years of history (Athens, Damascus, Varanasi) and booming new cities mushrooming across Asia, Africa and South America.

Cappadocia (Turkey) p901

Man-Made Marvels

But cities are not necessarily humankind's greatest achievements. These are many and dispersed, assuming myriad physical forms. Mystery clings to many, such as the Great Pyramid of Giza, built in 2560BC, the Terracotta Warriors in Xī'ān and the mighty stone *moai* of Easter Island. Others no less awe-inspiring were built for specific purposes, like St Basil's Cathedral in the Kremlin, the Great Wall of China, and the Taj Mahal, a monument to love. More modern spectacles, like the architectural extravaganzas of Dubai and the Shanghai skyline, may lack the gravity of history but if anything are more dazzling.

We remember that not all of humankind's achievements are tangible. Just as intoxicating and just as worth getting out to see are cultures, festivals and events, from Viennese coffee-house culture to Cuban jazz, from Full Moon Parties on Koh Samui to Maasai warrior dances under an African sunset.

This book can act as inspiration and as a first step on your own voyage of discovery. Listed here is every country; each includes enough of a taste of its top sights and experiences to get your feet itchy, basic practical information to help you start planning and a map to help you plot a rough itinerary.

In the words of Lonely Planet's founder, Tony Wheeler, 'all you've got to do is decide to go and the hardest part is over'. Where exactly you want to go and how you proceed from here is entirely up to you, but we encourage you to get out there and do it.

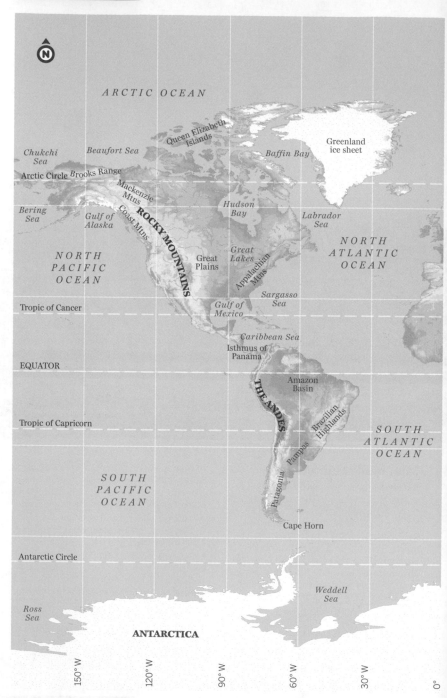

ARCTIC OCEAN

Queen Elizabeth Islands

Greenland ice sheet

Chukchi Sea

Beaufort Sea

Baffin Bay

Arctic Circle Brooks Range

Mackenzie Mtns

Bering Sea

Gulf of Alaska

Coast Mtns

ROCKY MOUNTAINS

Hudson Bay

Labrador Sea

NORTH ATLANTIC OCEAN

NORTH PACIFIC OCEAN

Great Plains

Great Lakes

Appalachian Mtns

Tropic of Cancer

Gulf of Mexico

Sargasso Sea

Caribbean Sea

Isthmus of Panama

EQUATOR

Amazon Basin

THE ANDES

Tropic of Capricorn

Brazilian Highlands

SOUTH ATLANTIC OCEAN

Pampas

SOUTH PACIFIC OCEAN

Patagonia

Cape Horn

Antarctic Circle

Weddell Sea

Ross Sea

ANTARCTICA

150° W

120° W

90° W

60° W

30° W

0°

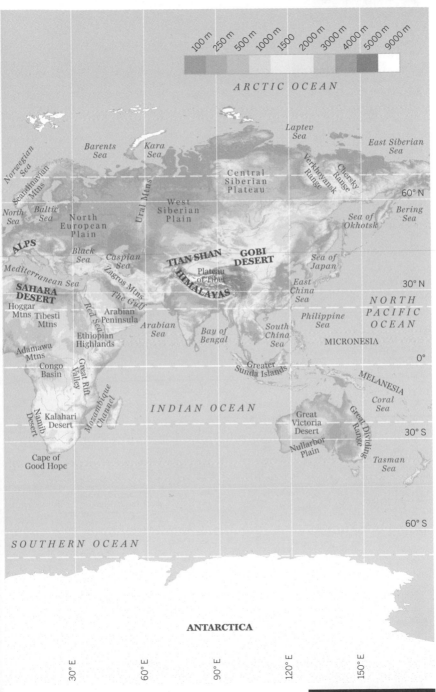

ARCTIC OCEAN

100 m 250 m 500 m 1000 m 1500 2000 m 3000 m 4000 m 5000 m 9000 m

Norwegian Sea

Barents Sea

Kara Sea

Laptev Sea

East Siberian Sea

Scandinavian Mtns

Verkhoyansk Range

Chersky Range

Central Siberian Plateau

60° N

North Sea

Baltic Sea

North European Plain

Ural Mtns

West Siberian Plain

Sea of Okhotsk

Bering Sea

ALPS

Black Sea

Caspian Sea

TIAN SHAN

GOBI DESERT

Sea of Japan

Mediterranean Sea

Zagros Mtns

Plateau of Tibet

HIMALAYAS

East China Sea

30° N

SAHARA DESERT

The Gulf

Arabian Peninsula

Arabian Sea

Bay of Bengal

South China Sea

Philippine Sea

NORTH PACIFIC OCEAN

Hoggar Mtns

Tibesti Mtns

Red Sea

Ethiopian Highlands

MICRONESIA

Adamawa Mtns

Congo Basin

Great Rift Valley

Greater Sunda Islands

0°

Namib Desert

Kalahari Desert

Mozambique Channel

INDIAN OCEAN

MELANESIA

Coral Sea

Great Victoria Desert

Great Dividing Range

Cape of Good Hope

Nullarbor Plain

30° S

Tasman Sea

60° S

SOUTHERN OCEAN

ANTARCTICA

30° E   60° E   90° E   120° E   150° E

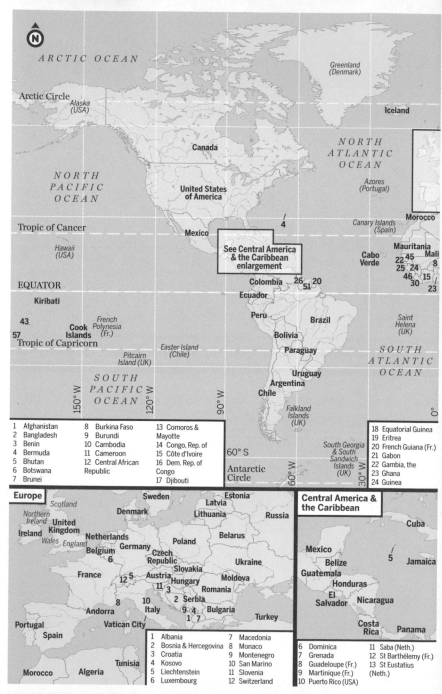

ARCTIC OCEAN

Arctic Circle
Alaska (USA)

Greenland (Denmark)

Iceland

NORTH PACIFIC OCEAN

Canada

NORTH ATLANTIC OCEAN

Azores (Portugal)

Tropic of Cancer

United States of America

Morocco

Canary Islands (Spain)

Hawaii (USA)

Mexico

4

See Central America & the Caribbean enlargement

Cabo Verde

Mauritania
22 45 Mali
25 24 8
46 15
30 23

EQUATOR

Colombia 26 20
51

Kiribati

Ecuador

Peru

Brazil

Saint Helena (UK)

43

French Polynesia (Fr.)

57 Cook Islands

Tropic of Capricorn

Pitcairn Island (UK)

Easter Island (Chile)

Bolivia

Paraguay

SOUTH ATLANTIC OCEAN

SOUTH PACIFIC OCEAN

Uruguay
Argentina
Chile

Falkland Islands (UK)

150° W 120° W 90° W 0°

60° S

South Georgia & South Sandwich Islands (UK)

Antarctic Circle

60° W 30° W

1	Afghanistan	8	Burkina Faso	13	Comoros & Mayotte	18	Equatorial Guinea
2	Bangladesh	9	Burundi	14	Congo, Rep. of	19	Eritrea
3	Benin	10	Cambodia	15	Côte d'Ivoire	20	French Guiana (Fr.)
4	Bermuda	11	Cameroon	16	Dem. Rep. of Congo	21	Gabon
5	Bhutan	12	Central African Republic	17	Djibouti	22	Gambia, the
6	Botswana					23	Ghana
7	Brunei					24	Guinea

Europe

Scotland
Northern Ireland United Kingdom
Ireland
Wales England

Sweden Estonia
Latvia
Denmark Lithuania

Russia

Netherlands Poland Belarus
Belgium Germany
6 Czech Republic Ukraine
France 12 5 Austria Slovakia
11 3 Hungary Moldova
8 10 Italy Romania
Andorra 9 4 Serbia
Vatican City 2 Bulgaria
1 7 Turkey

Portugal
Spain

Tunisia

Morocco Algeria

1	Albania	7	Macedonia
2	Bosnia & Hercegovina	8	Monaco
3	Croatia	9	Montenegro
4	Kosovo	10	San Marino
5	Liechtenstein	11	Slovenia
6	Luxembourg	12	Switzerland

Central America & the Caribbean

Cuba

Mexico
Belize
Guatemala
Honduras
El Salvador Nicaragua

Jamaica

5

Costa Rica Panama

6	Dominica	11	Saba (Neth.)
7	Grenada	12	St Barthélemy (Fr.)
8	Guadeloupe (Fr.)	13	St Eustatius (Neth.)
9	Martinique (Fr.)		
10	Puerto Rico (USA)		

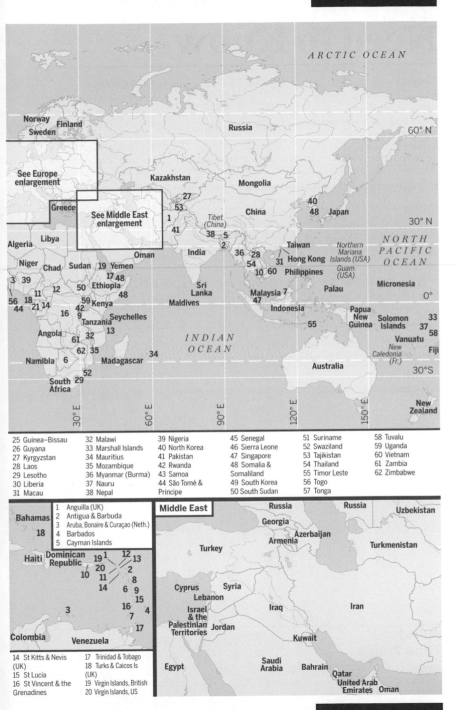

ARCTIC OCEAN

Norway
Finland
Sweden

Russia   60° N

See Europe
enlargement   Kazakhstan   Mongolia

Greece   27
                     See Middle East   53   Tibet   China   40
                     enlargement   1   (China)   48   Japan   30° N

Algeria   Libya   41   38   5
                                              2   Taiwan   Northern   NORTH
                          Oman   India   36 28   Mariana   PACIFIC
Niger   Chad Sudan 19 Yemen   54   31 Hong Kong Islands (USA)   OCEAN
              17 48   10 60 Philippines   Guam
      39   50 Ethiopia   (USA)
3   12   48   Sri   Malaysia 7   Palau   Micronesia
56 18   11   59 Kenya   Lanka   47   0°
44 21 14 42   Maldives   Indonesia   Papua
      16 9   55   New   Solomon   33
          Tanzania Seychelles   Guinea Islands   37
Angola   32   13   Vanuatu   58
        61   INDIAN   New
      62 35   OCEAN   Caledonia   Fiji
Namibia 6   Madagascar   34   Australia   (Fr.)
                                                                                     30°S
South 29
Africa   New
                                                                               Zealand

30° E   60° E   90° E   120° E   150° E

---

25 Guinea–Bissau   32 Malawi   39 Nigeria   45 Senegal   51 Suriname   58 Tuvalu
26 Guyana   33 Marshall Islands 40 North Korea   46 Sierra Leone   52 Swaziland   59 Uganda
27 Kyrgyzstan   34 Mauritius   41 Pakistan   47 Singapore   53 Tajikistan   60 Vietnam
28 Laos   35 Mozambique   42 Rwanda   48 Somalia &   54 Thailand   61 Zambia
29 Lesotho   36 Myanmar (Burma) 43 Samoa   Somaliland   55 Timor Leste   62 Zimbabwe
30 Liberia   37 Nauru   44 São Tomé &   49 South Korea   56 Togo
31 Macau   38 Nepal   Principe   50 South Sudan   57 Tonga

---

	1 Anguilla (UK)	**Middle East**	Russia	Russia	Uzbekistan
Bahamas	2 Antigua & Barbuda		Georgia		
18	3 Aruba, Bonaire & Curaçao (Neth.)		Azerbaijan	Turkmenistan
	4 Barbados	**Turkey**	Armenia	
Haiti **Dominican**	5 Cayman Islands			

Bahamas
18
        Dominican   19 1   12   13
Haiti   Republic   20   2
        10   11   8
              14   6   9
                     15
              16   Iran
        3   7   4
                 17
Colombia
      Venezuela

Cyprus   Syria
Lebanon
Israel
& the   Iraq
Palestinian Jordan
Territories
              Kuwait

14 St Kitts & Nevis   17 Trinidad & Tobago
(UK)   18 Turks & Caicos Is
15 St Lucia   (UK)
16 St Vincent & the   19 Virgin Islands, British
Grenadines   20 Virgin Islands, US

Egypt   Saudi   Bahrain
            Arabia   Qatar
                         United Arab   Oman
                         Emirates

Need to Know

Money

Wherever you go in the world you'll need a fistful of cash (or a credit card). There are around 180 different currencies circulating in the world today. So-called hard currencies – think the US dollar, the British pound, the euro, the yen and the Swiss franc – are widely accepted, so can be handy to carry.

Depending on where you go, and where you come from, you will need to exchange your own currency into that of your destination. How far your money will go depends on exchange rates: they may make you feel like a pauper, or a millionaire.

Money-Saving Tips

➡ Consider low-season travel.

➡ Look for favourable exchange rates; when one currency rises against yours, another may fall.

➡ Book ahead for the best deals.

Languages

It's the babble of Babel out there! There are almost 7000 languages spoken in the world today. These are divided into six major language families, and around 130 smaller ones. The distribution of languages across the globe reflects movements of people through history, and language families include some unlikely relatives: for example, Albanian is related to English, Hindi, Persian and Russian. The size of

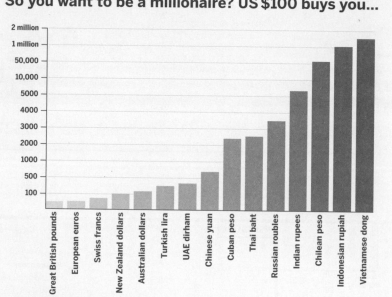

So you want to be a millionaire? US $100 buys you...

	2 million
	1 million
	50,000
	10,000
	5000
	4000
	3000
	2000
	1000
	500
	100

Great British pounds · European euros · Swiss francs · New Zealand dollars · Australian dollars · Turkish lira · UAE dirham · Chinese yuan · Cuban peso · Thai baht · Russian roubles · Indian rupees · Chilean peso · Indonesian rupiah · Vietnamese dong

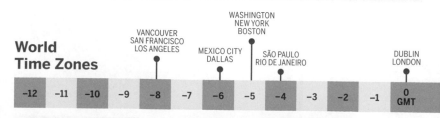

World Time Zones

WASHINGTON NEW YORK BOSTON

VANCOUVER SAN FRANCISCO LOS ANGELES

MEXICO CITY DALLAS

SÃO PAULO RIO DE JANEIRO

DUBLIN LONDON

| −12 | −11 | −10 | −9 | −8 | −7 | −6 | −5 | −4 | −3 | −2 | −1 | 0 GMT |

countries and populations don't necessarily account for numbers of languages, either: in New Guinea almost 450 languages are spoken by a population of only 3.5 million people.

It's estimated that half of the world's population speaks more than one language. Fear not if you don't: a smile can go a long way, even among people you share no language with. That said, learning a few words of the language spoken at your destination can open a lot of doors.

Useful Websites

Lonely Planet (www.lonely planet.com) Travel portal

Time and date (www.timeand date.com) Time differences

XE (www.xe.com) Currency conversion

Time

We all know that as the world orbits the sun, the planet is also spinning, meaning that for some of us the sun is setting, and for others it is rising. So, when it is bedtime in Sydney, locals will be reaching for a late-afternoon chai in Mumbai, lunching in London or getting ready to rise in New York. To make life easier, the world is divided into time zones.

Time Zones

The clever fellows at London's Royal Observatory saw to it that from the 1880s Greenwich Mean Time (GMT) was adopted as the global reference time. Each time zone is designated as either

Most Widely Spoken Languages

If you can speak one or more of the following languages, you can communicate with these percentages of the world's population.

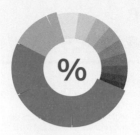

▲ French 1.1%
▲ Japanese 1.9%
▲ Russian 2.3%
▲ Bengali 3.1%
▲ Portuguese 3.3%
△ Arabic 4.4%

△ English 5.4%
△ Hindi/Urdu 5.7%
△ Spanish 6.2%
▲ Mandarin 14.4%
▲ Other 52.2%

being + or − whole numbers of hours (or half hours) from GMT. In 1972, Coordinated Universal Time (UTC) replaced GMT (it works the same way, but UTC accounts for stray 'leap seconds').

Passports & Visas

To leave your own country and to enter any other, you need a passport, a travel document certifying your identity and issued by your government. Regulations and rules regarding visas are many and complex, and vary from country to country. Some countries allow visa-free travel to passport holders of other countries (such as within the EU), while others may allow certain visitors to obtain a visa upon arrival. Still others require aspiring visitors to get a visa before they leave home. Bottom line: investigate visa require-

ments before you book your next trip.

Keeping in Touch

➡ Check with your mobile phone provider if you will be able to use your phone at your destination and if you need to activate international roaming before you leave home.

➡ Check what your provider charges you to make and receive calls and messages and to use data.

➡ Consider buying a local prepaid SIM card.

➡ Search out free wi-fi to avoid big hotel wi-fi charges.

➡ Try free video chat services such as Skype or Facetime. Check which services work with your device and set up an account before you leave.

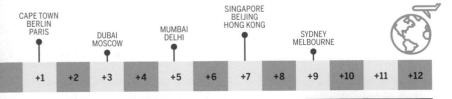

CAPE TOWN
BERLIN
PARIS

DUBAI
MOSCOW

MUMBAI
DELHI

SINGAPORE
BEIJING
HONG KONG

SYDNEY
MELBOURNE

| +1 | +2 | +3 | +4 | +5 | +6 | +7 | +8 | +9 | +10 | +11 | +12 |

If You Like
Beach Paradises

Australia Plunging waterfalls, pristine beaches and reefs (pictured below right). (p68)

Maldives Whiter-than-white powder sand and luminous cyan-blue water. (p552)

Seychelles White-sand beaches lapped by luxuriously warm waters and trees leaning over the shore. (p768)

French Polynesia Bora Bora (pictured below left): a perfect Morse-code ring of small islets. (p324)

Thailand The soaring limestone karsts of Railay (pictured right) are one of Thailand's most famous natural features. (p872)

Senegal Empty swaths of gorgeous sand together with traditional culture make for some of West Africa's finest beaches. (p760)

Turks & Caicos The clearest waters and the most varied marine life in the Caribbean. (p908)

PRETO PEROLA / SHUTTERSTOCK ©

JG PHOTO / SHUTTERSTOCK ©

Grenada Palm-backed white sand and translucent water, to grey-black dunes and rolling breakers. (p364)

Bulgaria Charming seaside towns stand above smaller sandy coves. (p152)

Antigua & Barbuda Hypnotic strips of pristine powdery white sand perfect for strolling, swimming, chilling and picnicking. (p50)

India Goa's cool coastal strip full of bustle and and an easy-going atmosphere. (p418)

Mexico Oaxaca's coast has long golden sands and it's bursting with turtles, dolphins, whales, crocs and birdlife. (p580)

If You Like
Cultural Festivals

HUGH SITTON / SHUTTERSTOCK ©

Carnaval, Brazil Carnaval is nonstop revelry, with nearly 500 street parties happening in every corner of town. (p140)

Día de Muertos, Mexico Day of the Dead; the happy-sad remembrance of departed loved ones at the beginning of November. (p580)

Goroka Show, Papua New Guinea Massive feather headdresses, rustling grass skirts and evocative face and body paint. (p685)

Loi Krathong, Thailand (pictured left) Thousands of lanterns rise into the sky, or float down

waterways, carrying away the sins of the year. (p877)

Naadam, Mongolia (pictured above) Two or three days of serious wrestling, horse racing and archery action. (p589)

New Orleans, United States of America New Orleans' riotous annual Mardi Gras and Jazz Fest are famous the world over. (p927)

Exit Festival, Novi Sad, Serbia Massive music party rocks at the Petrovaradin Fortress each July. (p765)

If You Like Food & Drink

Beer, Czech Republic Czechs claim to have the best *pivo* (beer) in the world and who are we to argue? (p250)

Champagne, France Celebrated around the world for the sparkling wines that have been produced here since the days of Dom Pérignon. (p321)

Copenhagen, Denmark (pictured top) One of the hottest culinary destinations in Europe, with more Michelin stars than any other Scandinavian city. (p253)

Japan (pictured bottom left) Attention to detail, genius for presentation and insistence on the finest ingredients result in memorable cuisine. (p462)

Malaysia Start with Chinese-Malay 'Nonya' fare, move on to Indian curries, Chinese buffets and Malay food stalls. (p546)

San Sebastián, Spain Chefs here have turned *pintxos* (Basque tapas) into an art form. (p811)

Turkey Mezes aren't just a type of dish, they're a whole eating experience. (p903)

Vietnam (pictured bottom right) Essentially it's all about the freshness of the ingredients. The result? Incomparable texture and flavour combinations. (p958)

If You Like History

Brú na Bóinne, Ireland Ireland's finest Stone Age passage tomb, predating the pyramids by some six centuries. (p440)

Flanders Fields, Belgium Manicured graveyards with white memorial crosses bear silent witness in seemingly endless rows. (p104)

Gallipoli, Turkey Memorials and cemeteries mark the spots where young men from far away fought and died in gruelling conditions. (p904)

Machu Picchu, Peru (pictured below) A mysterious lost city backed by steep peaks and Andean ridges. (p691)

Persepolis, Iran The artistic harmony leaves you in little doubt that in its prime Persepolis was at the centre of the known world. (p427)

Petra, Jordan (pictured right) Petra has been drawing the crowds since Jean Louis Burckhardt rediscovered this spectacular site in 1812. (p471)

Pompeii, Italy A once-thriving Roman town frozen in time 2000 years ago in the midst of its death throes. (p449)

Tikal, Guatemala The remarkably restored temples are a testament to the cultural and artistic heights scaled by this jungle civilisation. (p375)

ANTON_IVANOV / SHUTTERSTOCK ©

If You Like Adventure

New Zealand The sublime forests, mountains, lakes, beaches and fiords have made NZ one of the best hiking destinations on the planet. (p638)

Botswana (pictured below) Chobe National Park ranks among the elite of African safari destinations. (p132)

Blue Hole, Belize (pictured right) The sheer walls of the Blue Hole Natural Monument drop more than 400ft into the ocean. (p108)

Dolomites, Italy This tiny pocket of northern Italy takes hiking possibilities to dizzying heights. (p453)

Switzerland (pictured above) This country begs outdoor escapades with its larger-than-life canvas of hallucinatory landscapes. (p850)

Slovenia Slovenia is a mega outdoor destination and fast rivers like the Soča cry out to be rafted. (p782)

Red Sea, Egypt Underwater world of coral cliffs, colourful fish and spookily beautiful wrecks. (p275)

Puerto Rico Rincón boasts some of the most consistent, varied and exciting surf locations in the Caribbean. (p721)

Mérida, Venezuela Myriad options for hiking, canyoning, rafting, mountain biking and Mérida's specialty: paragliding. (p947)

Philippines Wakeboarding, surfing, kitesurfing and snorkelling with whale sharks at this up-and-coming adrenaline destination. (p696)

If You Like Natural Wonders

Cappadocia, Turkey The hard-set honeycomb landscape looks sculpted by a swarm of genius bees. (p901)

Dead Sea, Israel & the Palestinian Territories (pictured top left) Cobalt-blue waters, outlined by snow-white salt deposits, reddish-tan cliffs and tufts of dark-green vegetation. (p443)

Grand Canyon, United States of America It took 6 million years for the canyon to form and some rocks exposed along its walls are 2 billion years old. (p929)

Great Barrier Reef, Australia Stretching more than 2000km along the Queensland coastline, with dazzling coral, languid sea turtles and tropical fish of every colour and size. (p69)

Iguazú Falls, Argentina The roar, the spray and the sheer volume of water live forever in the memory. (p55)

Mt Everest, Nepal/China Tibet has easily the best views of the world's most famous mountain. (p883)

Ngorongoro Crater, Tanzania The magic starts while you're still up on the rim, with the chill air and sublime views over the enormous crater. (p867)

Northern Lights, Iceland Celestial kaleidoscope transforms long winter nights into natural lava lamps. (p409)

Salto Ángel (Angel Falls), Venezuela Witness the cascade of the world's tallest waterfall, as it thunders 979m from the plateau of Auyantepui. (p947)

Fish River Canyon, Namibia Experiencing the enormous scope of this immense canyon is something best done on the monumental five-day hike that traverses half its length. (p615)

Tham Kong Lor, Laos Float beneath the cathedral-high ceiling of stalactites in this extraordinary 7.5km-long underworld in remote Khammuan Province. (p500)

Plitvice Lakes National Park, Croatia Startling forest-fringed waterfalls and turquoise lakes (pictured bottom right; p229)

If You Like Man-Made Wonders

Temples of Angkor, Cambodia The Cambodian 'god-kings' each strove to better their ancestors in size, and scale. (p165)

Eiffel Tower, France Pedal beneath it, skip the lift and hike up, buy a crêpe from a stand here or visit it at night. (p315)

Great Wall, China Perfectly chiselled bricks, overrun with saplings, coil splendidly into the hills. (p193)

Stonehenge, England People have been drawn to this myth-rich ring of boulders for more than 5000 years. (p281)

Pyramids of Giza, Egypt Witness the extraordinary shape, impeccable geometry and sheer bulk of the pyramids. (p273)

Taj Mahal, India This marble mausoleum is the world's most poetic parting gift. (p413)

La Sagrada Família, Spain Barcelona's quirky temple soars skyward with an almost playful majesty. (p811)

Sheikh Zayed Grand Mosque, Abu Dhabi (pictured top right) A monumental and made-to-impress mix of marble, gold, semiprecious stones, crystals and ceramics set amid serene gardens. (p923)

If You Like Wildlife

Okavango Delta, Botswana
(pictured bottom left) There's nowhere quite like it on earth. It's a place where wild creatures roam and rule, where big cats and much bigger elephants walk free in one of the world's last great wildernesses. (p133)

Tanjung Puting National Park, Indonesia Anchor along one of its iconic rivers and watch orang-utans go about their business just metres away. (p423)

Costa Rica (pictured bottom right) Sloths, monkeys, jaguars, toucans and iguanas: Costa Rica's menagerie is a thrill for wildlife enthusiasts. (p218)

Kaikoura, New Zealand Few places in the world are home to such a variety of easily spottable marine wildlife: whales, dolphins, NZ fur seals, penguins, shearwaters, petrels and several species of albatross. (p644)

Galápagos Islands, Ecuador At this showcase of biodiversity you'll rub noses with massive lumbering tortoises, scurrying marine iguanas, prancing blue-footed boobies and a host of other unusual species. (p267)

Tanzania The great wildebeest migration – one of earth's most spectacular natural dramas – plays out in the Serengeti National Park (pictured right). Mahale Mountains and Gombe National Parks are among the best places anywhere to get close to chimpanzees. (p866)

Bwindi Impenetrable National Park, Uganda Trek through the jungle to critically endangered mountain gorillas. (p915)

Itineraries

A Mighty Asian Junket

This is the Asian century, so a jaunt through the great cities and landscapes of Asia is definitely in order.

Start your trip in booming **Tokyo**, a city combining tradition and ultra-modernity, from where you can visit the solemn majesty of **Mt Fuji**. Crossing to the continental landmass of Asia, head for **Shanghai**, the most dynamic city in the world's fastest-changing nation. Then turn your gaze southward to **Hong Kong**, for fantastic shopping and leisurely ferry trips, or lap up the Portuguese ambience in nearby **Macau**. Zip across to historic **Hanoi** to savour its graceful architecture en route to the surreal-looking limestone islands of **Halong Bay**. Returning via Hanoi, hop across to **Luang Prabang**, glistening with temples and on the banks of the **Mekong River**. Move on to the moated old city of **Chiang Mai** to enjoy a meditation retreat, before heading for the awe-inspiring ruins of Angkor near **Siem Reap**. Skipping south it's time for a beachside idyll on the Andaman Sea, either at **Phuket** or **Krabi**. Move on to **Singapore** for shopping and for planning your next moves.

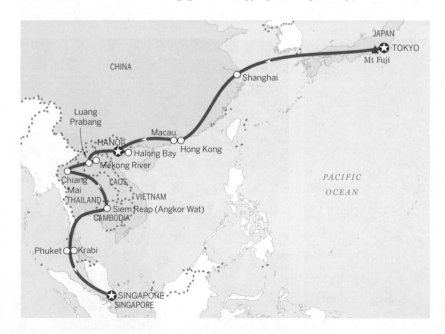

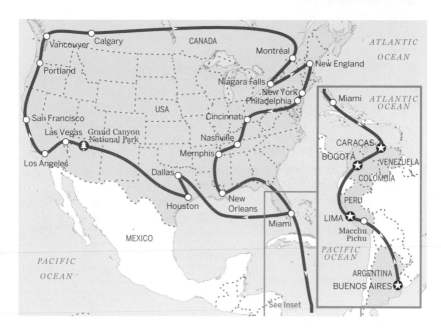

Road Trippin' the Americas

Considering the wide open spaces of America it stands to reason that this was the birthplace of the road trip. Tailor your own adventure, following in the footsteps (or tyre treads) of Jack Kerouac and many more besides.

Start in **New York**, the city that never sleeps, then ramble down to historic **Philadelphia** for a picture of what colonial American cities looked like, then press on to **Cincinnati** on the banks of the Ohio River. From there head south to **Nashville**, country music mecca and home to historic buildings and big-name sports. Continuing the musical theme, roll on to **Memphis** to pay respects to Elvis and Johnny Cash, then follow the Mississippi down to steamy **New Orleans** for southern cooking, ornate architecture and the famous jazz clubs. Then, if you're inclined, you could head to Latin-flavoured **Miami**, and roll on to reverse the tracks of Che Guevara by heading south to **Caracas**, **Bogotá** and **Lima**, en route to the lofty heights of **Macchu Picchu**, before fetching up in **Buenos Aires**, a slice of Europe in the southern hemisphere.

Alternatively, go west from Miami, hitting **Dallas** for cowboys and cheerleaders, then mozy on down to sprawling, boot-scootin' **Houston**. For awesome desert views and iconic landscapes the **Grand Canyon** is a must, before getting a dose of glitz and striking it rich in **Las Vegas**. Cruise on to **Los Angeles** to spot a star in **Hollywood**, then follow Kerouac's footsteps again to **San Francisco**. Head north to counter-culture **Portland**, before crossing the Canadian border and hitting the hip neighbourhoods of **Vancouver**. Don your spurs to drop in at 'cowtown' **Calgary**, then cruise over the seemingly endless prairie and above the Great Lakes to **Montréal** for diverse cuisines and European-style architecture. Complete your loop to New York either via Lake Ontario and the muscular shoals of water plummeting over **Niagara Falls** or through the picturesque landscapes of **New England**.

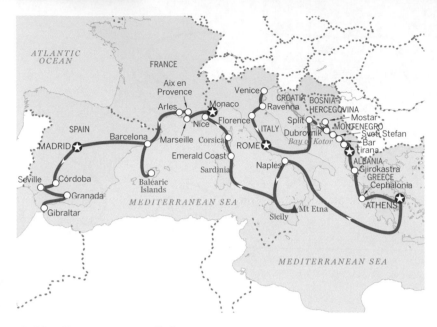

A Mediterranean Odyssey

The Mediterranean has been the scene of countless cultures, empires and civilisations throughout history – come here for a dizzying array of art, culture and natural beauty on show.

Venice, seaboard city of art and maritime endeavour, has been the embarkation point for many an odyssey. Follow in the footsteps of Lord Byron, that swashbuckling romantic, and head towards **Ravenna**, with its Byzantine mosaics, before moving on to the Renaissance time capsule that is **Florence**, then to **Rome**, to gawk at the Colosseum. Ferrying across the Adriatic brings you to Croatia's idyllic Dalmatian coast, dropping in at **Split** and **Dubrovnik**, described by Byron as the 'pearl of the Adriatic'. From here cross into Bosnia & Hercegovina to the slim bridge in **Mostar**. Back on the coast, savour the breathtaking scenery of the **Bay of Kotor**, then push on to gorgeous beachside **Sveti Stefan** and **Bar**. Heading into Albania you'll encounter post-communist **Tirana** with its colourful buildings and the hilltop citadel of **Gjirokastra**. Down on the Ionian coast lie idyllic Corfu, Ithaka, the island home that Odysseus long sought, and **Cephalonia**, where Lord Byron fetched up. From here you can reach **Athens** to see the Acropolis, or catch a ferry onward throughout the Greek islands, or back to Italy.

Naples is Italy's pulsing southern metropolis and is the transit point for **Sicily**, home to Greek temples and slumbering **Mt Etna**. From here aim for Sardinia's crystalline **Emerald Coast** then the quiet fishing villages and rugged interior of **Corsica**. The Corniche at **Nice** and **Monaco** are sun-splashed places to linger. **Marseille** then beckons, with its castle and gritty port ambience. Inland is **Aix en Provence**, and the Provençale landscapes of **Arles** that inspired Van Gogh. Beyond lies **Barcelona**, city of art and architecture and gateway to the **Balearic Islands**. Head for the nightlife in the Spanish capital, **Madrid**, then onward for the Moorish delights of **Córdoba**, **Seville** and **Granada**. Finish in **Gibraltar**, gateway to the Atlantic, and the westernmost point of Hercules' travels.

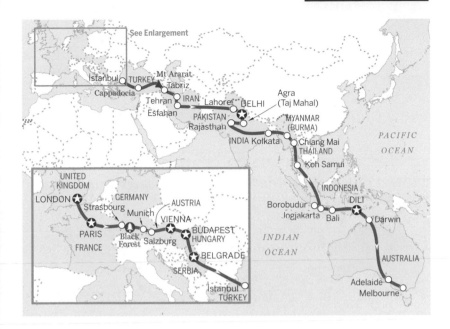

The Hippy Trail: London to Melbourne

6 months

A rite of passage for many, the overland trail from Europe and across Asia has inspired generations of travellers, including Maureen and Tony Wheeler, the founders of Lonely Planet.

Starting from **London**, head to **Paris** for a view of the Eiffel Tower and the Louvre. Motor eastwards to view the half-timbered houses of **Strasbourg**, then trundle through the **Black Forest** en route to the provincial charms of **Munich**. Take in the musical atmosphere and charming architecture of **Salzburg** then head for the operas and coffee houses of **Vienna**. Stately **Budapest** and buzzing **Belgrade** provide spa treatments and throbbing nightlife en route to **İstanbul**, the mighty Turkish city astride two continents. Catch a Bosphorus ferry, then make a bee-line for the otherworldly landscapes of **Cappadocia**. Passing the foothills of **Mt Ararat**, aim for **Tabriz** across the Iranian border. Enjoy the teahouses of **Tehran** before revelling in the breathtaking architecture of **Esfahan** and hitting the desert road. Head to the old city of **Lahore** for its arts scene and serene Mughal gardens.

Cross the Indian frontier and head to thunderous **Delhi**, with its Red Fort and fragrant bazaars, and continue to **Agra** to swoon before the sublime architecture of the **Taj Mahal**. Zip westward to the deserts and dreamy fortresses of **Rajasthan**. Then, passing through the clamour of **Kolkata**, move on to **Myanmar**, now opening up to tourism. From there it's a short hop to a spa retreat in **Chiang Mai**, before zipping in to throbbing Bangkok. **Koh Samui** provides an island idyll in the Gulf of Thailand before you move on to Indonesia. **Jogjakarta** is a centre for Javanese art and puppetry, and is the gateway to the Buddhist monuments at **Borobudur**. Next, hit **Bali** for some sun and surf before skipping to rapidly changing **Dili**. From there it's a short hop to **Darwin**, Australia's most Asian-flavoured city, from where you can drive across the desert to **Adelaide**, before hitting **Melbourne**, the artistic and cultural capital of Australia.

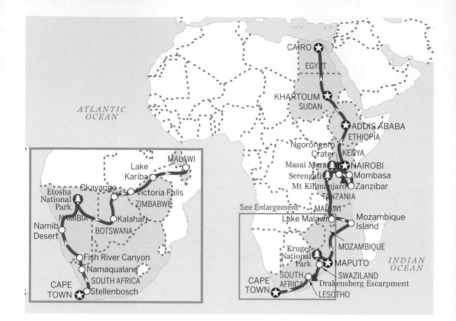

Safari of a Lifetime

4 months

Africa offers vast landscapes, an opportunity to see wildlife on a scale unrivalled anywhere else in the world, and more cultural diversity than you can poke a rhino's horn at.

From **Cape Town**, after climbing Table Mountain and sampling the wineries of **Stellenbosch**, you can choose either of two routes. Enjoy the floral bounty of **Namaqualand** as you proceed to **Fish River Canyon** for fantastic hiking. Continue through the **Namib Desert** and the desolate Skeleton Coast, as you aim for **Etosha National Park**. If you don't spot a lonely rhino there, head east towards the **Kalahari**, where you can walk with bushmen, and then the lush **Okavango** delta, realm of wallowing hippos. Onward in the footsteps of Dr Livingstone to **Victoria Falls**, to spy the endlessly rushing waters of the 'smoke that thunders'. Continue via **Lake Kariba** to **Malawi** to enjoy chilling out on the 'lake of stars', as Livingstone did back in the day.

The alternative route from Cape Town is through the rugged **Drakensberg Escarpment**, to the mountainous kingdom of **Lesotho**, the perfect spot for a pony trek, and then **Swaziland**. Press on to **Kruger National Park**, for a chance to spot the Big Five. Slide into Mozambique to hit **Maputo** for its Portuguese atmosphere and beachside caipirinhas, then proceed up the coast in the wake of Ferdinand Magellan, diving with whale sharks, then stopping in at the faded architectural grandeur of **Mozambique Island**. From there proceed to **Lake Malawi** and north into Tanzania, being sure to visit the premier wildlife areas of the **Serengeti** and **Ngorongoro Crater**. Then strike out for the peak of **Mt Kilimanjaro** and on to the Indian Ocean and enjoy the spice gardens and beaches of **Zanzibar**. Sultry **Mombasa** is an entrepôt of Swahili culture and the gateway to Kenya. Proceed via the **Masai Mara** to **Nairobi**. From there you can head via **Addis Ababa**, **Khartoum** and **Cairo** to the Mediterranean, to complete a mighty trans-continental journey.

Go Forth & Explore

The World

CAPITAL	Kabul
POPULATION	33.3 million
AREA	652,230 sq km
OFFICIAL LANGUAGES	Dari, Pashto

Band-e Amir Lakes, near Bamiyan

Afghanistan

A battered but beautiful country, Afghanistan's road to recovery remains uncertain and ongoing war and instability still render it off-limits to travellers. Yet the resilience of its people and beauty of its landscape endure.

Throughout its history, Afghanistan has been a country united against invaders but divided within itself.

The most recent cycle of violence started with the Soviet invasion of 1979, a bloody 'David and Goliath' conflict, with the underdogs eventually besting the superpower. The war's dividend wasn't peace, but a ruinous civil war – a morass that came back to haunt the West in the shape of the medieval Taliban. The subsequent ousting of the Taliban promised another new start, but Afghanistan's rebirth as an infant democracy has been troubled at best.

Yet before all this bloodshed, Afghanistan formed part of the original overland hippie trail, beguiling its visitors with great mountain ranges, a rich mix of cultures – and the Afghan people themselves, who greeted everyone with an easy charm and ready hospitality.

Snapshot

Kabul

1 Kabul is exciting, frustrating, inspiring and shocking in equal measure. Once a stop on the hippie trail to India, then ruined by the civil war, the city has boomed in recent years, with fancy restaurants and an air thick with the sound of mobile phones. But scratch the surface and things aren't so rosy – Kabul's path to reconstruction continues to be rocky.

Bamiyan

2 Once a site of pilgrimage, Bamiyan is now associated with the destruction visited on Afghanistan's culture by war. The two giant statues of the Buddha that dominated the valley now lie in rubble, victims of the Taliban's iconoclastic rage. Despite this, it remains a beautiful place.

Herat

3 Herat is as much Persian as it is Afghan, and wears an air of independence as the country's old cultural heart. Many of its monuments are in a sorry state, but in its 800 year old Friday Mosque the city still possesses one of Islam's great buildings. A masterclass in the art of tile mosaic, its colours and detailing are an exuberant hymn in praise of Allah.

Seasons

 SEP–NOV

 JUN–AUG

 MAR–MAY

Food & Drink

Pulao Rice with meat, almonds, raisins and grated carrot.

Kebabs Diced or ground lamb, with bread, onion and spice.

Fruit Melons, pomegranates, apples, grapes and mulberries.

Tea Hot green and black tea.

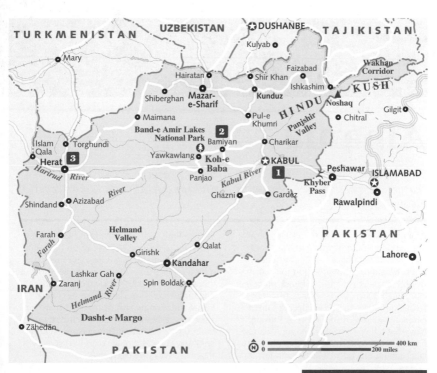

CAPITAL	Tirana
POPULATION	2.8 million
AREA	28,748 sq km
OFFICIAL LANGUAGE	Albanian

Ottoman houses in Berat

Albania

With its stunning mountain scenery, a thriving capital in Tirana and beaches to rival any elsewhere in the Mediterranean, Albania is the sleeper hit of the Balkans.

Albania has natural beauty in such abundance that you might wonder why it took so long to take off as a tourist destination after the end of communism in the country in 1991. So backward was Albania when it emerged blinking into the bright light of freedom that it needed two decades just to catch up with the rest of Eastern Europe. Now that it has arguably done so, Albania offers a remarkable array of attractions: ancient mountain codes of behaviour, forgotten archaeological sites and villages where time seems to have stood still are all on the menu.

Lively, colourful Tirana is where this tiny nation's hopes and dreams coalesce into a vibrant whirl of traffic, brash consumerism and unfettered fun. Having undergone a transformation of extraordinary proportions since the early 1990s, the city centre has buildings painted in primary colours, and public squares and pedestrianised streets that are a pleasure to wander.

Top Experiences

Lake Koman Ferry

1 One of Albania's undisputed highlights is the superb three-hour ferry ride across vast Lake Koman. This lake was created in 1978 when the Drin River was dammed, with the result that you can cruise through spectacular mountain scenery where many incredibly hardy people still live as they have for centuries, tucked away in tiny mountain villages.

Berat

2 Berat weaves its own very special magic, and is easily a highlight of visiting Albania. Its most striking feature is the collection of white Ottoman houses climbing up the hill to its castle, earning it the title of 'town of a thousand windows' and helping it join

Food & Drink

Byrek Pastry with cheese or meat.

Fergesë Baked peppers, egg and cheese, and occasionally meat.

Midhje Wild or farmed mussels, often served fried.

Paçë koke Sheep's head soup, usually served for breakfast.

Qofta Flat or cylindrical minced-meat rissoles.

Sufllaqë Doner kebab.

Tavë Meat baked with cheese and egg.

Konjak Local brandy.

Raki Popular spirit made from grapes.

Raki mani Spirit made from mulberries.

Map of Albania

MONTENEGRO
- Peja (Peć)
- KOSOVO
- Plav **7**
- Valbonë
- PODGORICA
- Theth — Drini
- Lake Fierza — Kukës
- Lake Skadar — Lake Koman **1** — Tetovo
- Shkodra
- Mavrovo National Park
- Peshkopia
- Milot
- Bulqiza — Drini
- Kruja — Zall Gjocaj National Park — MACEDONIA
- **5** TIRANA
- Durrës — Ohrid
- Kavaja — Elbasan — Lake Ohrid — Lake Prespa
- Divjaka National Park — Lushnja
- Lake Prespa National Park
- Fier — Berat **2** — Mt Tomorri National Park — Korça
- Vjosa River
- Sazan — Vlora — Këlcyra
- Karaburun Peninsula
- Llogaraja Pass National Park **3** — Drymades — Gjirokastra **6**
- Ionian Coast — GREECE
- **8** — Kakavija
- Saranda
- IONIAN SEA
- Butrint **4** — Ioannina
- Corfu — Konispoli
- GREECE
- 0 — 50 km / 0 — 25 miles

When to Go

HIGH SEASON (Jul–Aug)

SHOULDER (Apr–Jun & Sep–Oct)

LOW SEASON (Nov–Mar)

The Soundtrack

Blaring from cars, bars, restaurants and mobile phones – music is something you get plenty of in Albania. Most modern Albanian music has clarinet threaded through it and a goatskin drum beat behind it. Polyphony, the blending of several independent vocal or instrumental parts, dates from ancient Illyrian times, and can still be heard, particularly in the south.

IAN BOTTLE / ALAMY STOCK PHOTO ©

Gjirokastra on the list of Unesco World Heritage sites in 2008. Its rugged mountain setting is particularly evocative when the clouds swirl around the tops of the minarets, or break up to show the icy peak of Mt Tomorri. Despite now being a big centre for tourism in Albania, Berat has managed to retain its easy-going charm and friendly atmosphere.

Albanian Riviera

3 Catch some sun at one of the many beaches on the Albanian Riviera. Huge and popular Dhërmi Beach has a busy bar- and restaurant-lined central strip and more secluded areas at either end, gorgeous Drymades is a rocky white beach reached via a sealed road that twists through olive groves, while isolated and pristine Gjipe Beach is backed by towering cliffs and lapped by turquoise waters.

Butrint

4 The ancient ruins of Butrint, 18km south of Saranda, are famed for their size, beauty and tranquillity. Set in forest in a 29-sq-km national park, the remains are from a variety of periods, spanning 2500 years. Greeks from Corfu settled on the hill in Butrint (Buthrotum) in the 6th century BC. As you enter the site the path leads to a 3rd-century-BC Greek theatre, secluded in the forest below the acropolis. Close by are the small public baths and deeper in the forest is a wall covered with crisp Greek inscriptions, and a 6th-century palaeo-Christian baptistry decorated with colourful mosaics. The top of the hill is where the acropolis once was. There's now a castle here, housing an informative museum.

Tirana

5 Tirana's grand boulevards are lined with fascinating relics of its Ottoman, Italian and communist past – from delicate minarets to loud socialist murals – while trendy Blloku buzzes with the well-heeled and flush hanging out in bars and cafes. Add to this some excellent museums and you have a compelling list of reasons to visit. With the traffic doing daily battle with both itself and pedestrians, this city is loud, crazy, colourful and dusty, but never dull.

Gjirokastra

6 Defined by its castle, roads paved with chunky limestone and shale, imposing slate-roofed houses and views out to the Drina Valley, Gjirokastra is a magical hillside town described beautifully by Albania's most famous author, Ismail Kadare (b 1936), in Chronicle in Stone. There has been a settlement here

Getting Around

Buses and *furgon* (privately run minibuses) are the main form of public transport in Albania and fares are low. Municipal buses operate in Tirana, Durrës, Shkodra, Berat, Korça and Vlora.

Road infrastructure is improving; there's an excellent highway from Tirana to Kosovo.

Trains are slow but dirt cheap and travelling on them is an adventure.

for 2500 years, though these days it's the 600 'monumental' Ottoman-era houses in town that attract visitors. The town is also synonymous for Albanians with former dictator Enver Hoxha, who was born here and ensured the town was relatively well preserved under his rule; though he is not memorialised in any way here today. Far less touristy than Berat, the town is equally as charming and has several fascinating sights, as well as some excellent accommodation options.

Accursed Mountains

7 The 'Accursed Mountains' (Bjeshkët e Namuna) offer some of Albania's most impressive scenery, and the area has exploded in recent years as a popular backpacker destination. It's a totally

different side of the country here: that of blood feuds, deep tradition, extraordinary landscapes and fierce local pride. It's absolutely a highlight of any trip to Albania, and indeed, it's quite unusual to get this far removed from modern life in 21st-century Europe.

Blue Eye Spring

8 The Blue Eye Spring is a magical place: a hypnotic pool of deep blue water surrounded by electric-blue edges like the iris of an eye. It's further enveloped in thick woods and is some 22km east of Saranda on the road to Gjirokastra. Bring your swimming gear and towel for a dive into the cold water on a summer's day. If you don't mind a dusty 3km walk, buses between Saranda and Gjirokastra can drop you at the spring's turn-off.

LOKVI / SHUTTERSTOCK ©

CAPITAL	Algiers
POPULATION	40.2 million
AREA	2.4 million sq km
OFFICIAL LANGUAGES	Algerian Arabic, Berber

Camel caravan in the Sahara desert near Timimoun

Algeria

Africa's largest country lies just a short hop from Europe and, with tourists still a novelty, offers attractions as unpeopled as they are varied.

Algeria's capital, Algiers, is one of the Maghreb's most urbane and charismatic cities, with a heady, nostalgic mix of colonial and modernist architecture, and a traditional medina at its vertiginous heart. Across the north are stunning coastlines, lush rural hinterland and a number of well-preserved Roman cities.

The country's trump card is, though, its extraordinary Saharan region. Whether it's a glimpse of the sand seas that surround Timimoun, or a plunge headlong into the far south from Tamanrasset, these are the desert landscapes of dream and legend.

Perhaps best of all, Algerians welcome visitors with warmth and a genuine curiosity. For accessible adventure and a complex, enthralling cultural odyssey, head for Algeria now.

Top Experiences

Timimoun

 The largest oasis in the Grand Erg Occidental, this dusty desert city is an enchanting place. Its red mud buildings studded with spikes hint at sub-Saharan Africa. Its location, at the edge of an escarpment, makes for breathtaking views across a salt lake and out to the dunes. The main street bustles in the morning and evening.

Algiers

 Algiers (Al-Jazaïr) is a city of rare beauty and of thrilling, disorientating, and sometimes brutal, contrast. The country's turbulent history is writ large in the city's richly textured architecture: wide French-built boulevards, socialist-era monuments and an Islamic heart in the steep, hillside Casbah.

Ghardaïa

 In the river valley of the Oued M'Zab is a cluster of five towns often referred to collectively as Ghardaïa. Bargain for a boldly patterned carpet in the main square, peek at a pristine medieval town then swim in the shade of date palms. While locals can be deeply reserved, it's a friendly and surprisingly laid-back place.

When to Go

☁ **HIGH SEASON**
(Nov–Apr)

☀ **SHOULDER**
(May–Jul &
Sep–Oct)

☀ **LOW SEASON**
(Aug)

Food & Drink

Bourek Beef-stuffed pastry rolls.

Tagine Savoury stew with meat, vegetables and spices, often served with couscous.

Drinks Mint tea and coffee.

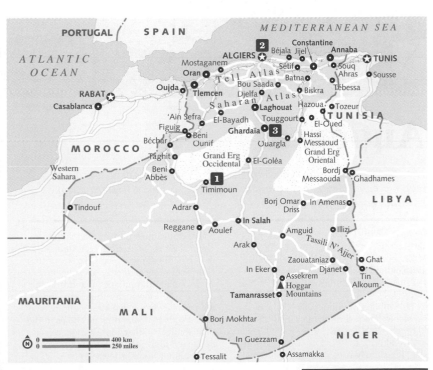

CAPITAL
Andorra la Vella

POPULATION
85,700

AREA
468 sq km

OFFICIAL LANGUAGE
Catalan

Grandvalira ski resort

Andorra

The Thumbelina, Catalan-speaking principality of Andorra, a dramatic realm of mountain scenery amid the Pyrenees, is one of Western Europe's most intriguing corners.

If you're on the lookout for great hiking or skiing, then the curious nation of Andorra is for you. Neatly wedged between France and Spain in the mountainous eastern Pyrenees, it's one of Europe's smallest countries.

This minicountry offers by far the best ski slopes and resort facilities in all the Pyrenees. Racing down snow-packed pistes, mollycoddling après-ski mulled wine and sleeping snug between boutique-hotel ice walls is how most think of this tiny principality. Shake yourself free of Andorra la Vella's tawdry embrace, take one of the state's three secondary roads and you're very soon amid dramatic mountain scenery.

Once the snow melts, there's also an abundance of great walking, ranging from easy strolls to demanding day hikes in the principality's higher, more remote reaches. Strike out above the tight valleys and you can walk for hours, almost alone.

Top Experiences

Skiing

1 Shush your way over the snowfields of Grandvalira. With 193km of runs and a combined lift system that can shift more than 100,000 skiers per hour, it's the largest ski area in the Pyrenees.

Walking Trails

2 Ordino is Andorra's most attractive village and at an elevation of 1300m, it's a good starting point for summer activity holidays. From mid-July to mid-September, the Canillo and Soldeu gondolas whisk you up to the higher reaches, from where you can walk or hire a mountain bike to whizz back down.

La Caldea

3 Steep yourself in the warm mineral waters of space-age La Caldea. All glass and gleaming like some futuristic cathedral, Europe's largest spa complex offers lagoons, giant jacuzzis, vapour baths and saunas, fed by warm thermal springs. It is a blissful experience after a day of high-speed fun on the ski slopes or invigorating summertime walks.

When to Go

 HIGH SEASON
(Dec–Apr)

 SHOULDER
(Jun–Sep)

 LOW SEASON
(May & Oct–Nov)

Food & Drink

Cabrito con picadillo de frutos secos Goat roasted with almonds and pine nuts.

Escudella A thick soup of *albondigas* (meatballs), chickpeas, carrots and potatoes.

Pato con pera de invierno Roast duck with pears.

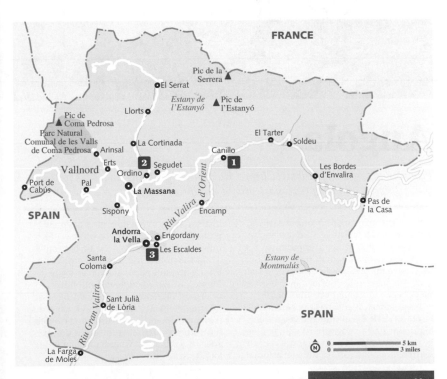

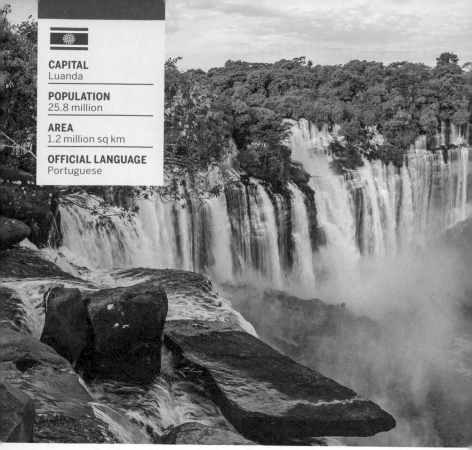

CAPITAL
Luanda

POPULATION
25.8 million

AREA
1.2 million sq km

OFFICIAL LANGUAGE
Portuguese

Kalandula Falls

Angola

Fronting the Atlantic and stretching into Africa's interior, Angola is nothing if not diverse, a land of traumatic history and startling natural treasures.

For most people, Angola is one of Africa's last great travel mysteries. Yet, despite its size and relative economic importance, the country remains closed off to all but the most adventurous travellers thanks to stringent visa policies, high prices and a history that's been more about war than peace.

It's a shame. Angola has the potential to be one of Africa's cultural and geographic highlights. Lurking within its wild borders lie the continent's second largest waterfall, scattered remnants of Portuguese colonial history, a handful of emerging national parks, beaches galore and a diverse and unbelievably stoic cross-section of people.

For the time being, Angola's physical beauty lies untapped, ignored by a government still bogged down with other priorities. The sooner the country tackles nagging political issues such as income disparity and lingering corruption, the quicker it can emerge from its protracted slumber and show the world what it's been missing for 50 years.

Top Experiences

Kalandula Falls

1 Among its varied landscapes, Angola has some unusual and spectacular natural features. Topping the list are the Kalandula Falls on the Lucala River near Malange. These massive waterfalls are as spectacular as any in Africa and one of the continent's largest falls by volume, but get very few visitors.

Parque Nacional da Kissama

2 Kissama (also spelt Quiçama), situated 70km south of Luanda, is Angola's most accessible and well-stocked wildlife park. This huge swathe of coastal savannah punctuated by gnarly baobab trees is home to elephants, water buffalo, indigenous palanca antelopes and a precarious population of nesting sea turtles.

Miradouro da Lua

3 Miradouro da Lua is a magnificent lookout over a canyon of moon-like cliffs that cascade dramatically into the Atlantic Ocean. Angola's most visited tourist site, this bizarre, multicoloured landscape has been shaped by millions of years of wind and rain erosion.

When to Go

HIGH SEASON
(Jun–Aug)

SHOULDER
(May & Sep–Oct)

LOW SEASON
(Nov–Apr)

Food & Drink

Alãos (white coffee) Locals love coffee with milk.

Pastelerias Pastry and coffee shops with a European flavour.

Street food Women sell fruit and baguette-like sandwiches from washing bowls across the city centre.

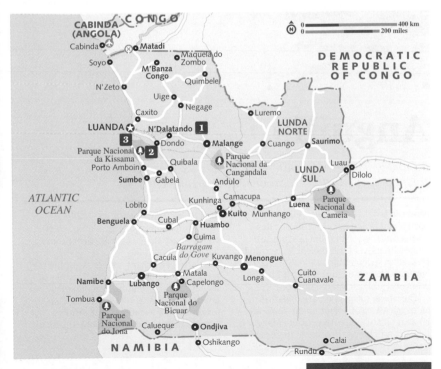

Anguilla

Fringed by shimmering white-sand beaches shaded by coconut palms and sea grape trees, Anguilla is the Caribbean dream come true.

Anguilla is filled with colorfully painted, open-sided beach bars serving sizzling barbecues, feisty rum punches and live reggae tunes. Its crystal-clear waters and reefs offer spectacular snorkeling, glass-bottomed kayaking and sailing to tiny islets and atolls scattered offshore.

The island's rich and varied history dates back to settlement by the Ameridians and Arawaks, with extraordinary rock art still being discovered in sites such as the Fountain Cavern National Park. And unlike many nearby islands, the flat terrain makes it easy to get around by car, bicycle or quad bike.

There's a catch, of course. Anguilla is no shoestring destination and authenticity comes at a premium here. Luxury hotels and private villas cater to jetsetters craving a vacation off the radar. Visit outside high season for a more affordable taste of paradise.

Top Experiences

Prickly Pear Cays

 Sail to this secluded mini-Anguilla, some 6 miles (9.6km) northwest of the mainland, with 360 degrees of flaxen sand and mellow waves. It also has the best diving on Anguilla – an underwater cavern where nurse sharks and barracuda swim through rock formations and sunken shipwrecks.

Shoal Bay East

 Snorkel in the turquoise waters, laze on the sparkling white sand or hang out at one of the laid-back beach bars. This quintessential Caribbean stretch of white sand is 2 miles long, with swaying coconut palms and sea grape trees, reefs and luminous water. Just inland is the Fountain Cavern National Park, with rock art by the Arawaks dating back more than two millennia.

Heritage Collection Museum

 Anguilla's only museum occupies a quaint bungalow next to East End Salt Pond. Anguilla's flag flies out front. Inside, the museum details the island's history through an impressive assortment of artifacts.

When to Go

☀ **HIGH SEASON** (Dec–Jan)

☁ **SHOULDER** (Feb–Apr, Sep–Nov)

☂ **LOW SEASON** (May–Aug)

Food & Drink

Seafood specialties Lobster, crayfish, conch and triggerfish.

Barbecue tents Roadside tents serve smoky ribs and chicken.

Goat The most common meat; often used in curries.

Streetside vendors For organic cassava and lakatan bananas.

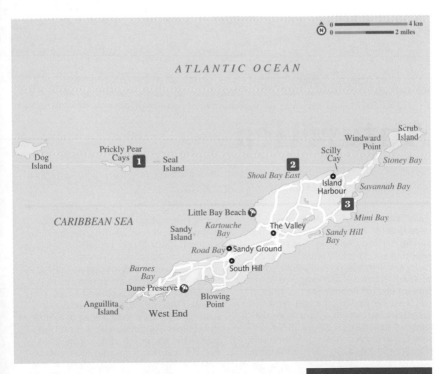

CAPITAL	None
POPULATION	Summer 4490, Winter 1106
AREA	14.2 million sq km
OFFICIAL LANGUAGE	None

Lemaire Channel

Antarctica

No place on Earth compares to this vast white wilderness of elemental forces: snow, ice, water, rock. Antarctica is simply stunning.

Antarctica's remoteness, extreme cold, enormous ice shelves and mountain ranges, and myriad exotic life forms invariably challenge you to embrace life fully. Everyone – scientist, support worker, government official and tourist alike – who comes to this isolated continent, must 'earn' it, whether by sea-voyage or flight. Ice and weather, not clocks and calendars, determine the itinerary and the timetable of all travel here. Expect experiences unlike any other, whether whale-watching across the open sea, spying a penguin rookery, or framing that perfect photograph of an awe-inspiring ice-form. Today, it's even possible for visitors to climb Antarctic peaks, or kayak icy waters. But there is nothing quite like the craggy crevasses of a magnificent glacier or the sheer expanse of the polar ice cap.

Call it inspiration, call it grandeur...it is simply the indescribable feeling of being a small speck in a vast, harshly beautiful land. To let our minds soar in a place nearly free of humankind's imprint: this is magic.

Top Experiences

Amundsen-Scott South Pole Station

1 First reached just 100 years ago by the valiant explorer Roald Amundsen during the Heroic Age of Antarctic exploration, the South Pole still embodies myth, hardship and glory. Today it is topped by a new high-tech station surrounded by cutting edge astrophysical observation equipment (including a neutrino detector array buried approximately 1.9km below the ice). To the visitor, a photo op with the flapping flags and globe-topped pole is, indeed, a once-in-a-lifetime opportunity.

Cruising the Lemaire Channel

2 The sheer-sided Lemaire Channel is a perennial favourite for photography buffs and naturalists alike. Under pale-pink skies, glaciers tumble slow-motion to the sea from the mountains overhead. Your Zodiac glides past a floe topped by basking Weddell seals, another crowded by a noisy group of gentoo penguins. Nearby, an enormous female leopard seal sleeps off a recent meal.

Cape Evans

3 Reaching Ross Island's Cape Evans

When to Go

 HIGH SEASON (Dec–Jan)

 SHOULDER (Nov & Feb–Mar)

 LOW SEASON (Apr–Oct)

isn't easy – but then again, it never was. Dog skeletons bleach on the sand in the Antarctic sun, chiding memento mori of Captain Robert Scott's death march from the Pole. Inside Scott's hut from that ill-fated Terra Nova expedition a collection of sledging pennants, rustling pony harnesses and a sighing

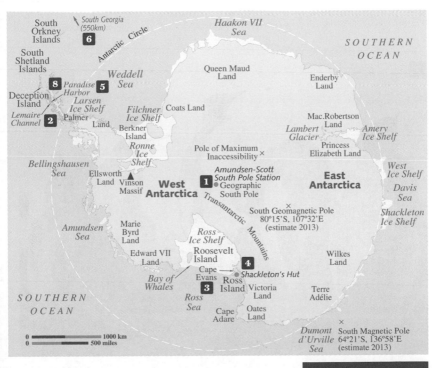

wind evoke the doomed men who left here with high hopes of reaching the pole. Explore the captain's bunkroom, and peer at the perfectly preserved provisions and photographic supplies.

Shackleton's Hut

4 Step inside Ernest Shackleton's Nimrod expedition hut at Cape Royds on Ross Island and enter an eerily preserved world from a century ago. Amazingly intact despite 100 years of blasting Antarctic storms, the wooden house is surprisingly homey. Coloured glass medicine bottles line shelves, a fur sleeping bag rests on one of the bunks and tins of food with unappetising names (boiled mutton, lunch tongue, pea powder) are stacked on the floor, awaiting diners who will never return. Adélie penguins fill the cape now, breeding in summer.

Paradise Harbor

5 The pragmatic whalers who worked in the waters of the Antarctic Peninsula at the beginning of the 20th century were hardly sentimental. Yet they named this harbour Paradise, obviously quite taken with the stunning icebergs and reflections of the surrounding mountains. Gentoos and shags call the area home, and a climb up the hill here offers magnificent glacier views. If you're lucky, perhaps you'll see one calving.

Grytviken, South Georgia

6 A tall granite headstone marking the last resting place of British explorer Ernest Shackleton, known to his loyal men simply as 'the Boss', stands

Getting Around

Nearly all visitors arrive by sea, most of them by ship from Ushuaia.

Zodiacs (small, inflatable boats powered by outboard engines) are ideal for cruising among icebergs and landing in otherwise inaccessible areas once in the Antarctic.

Sightseeing flights over Antarctica, fly-cruise combinations and flights to the interior are all possible.

7

at the rear of the whalers' cemetery at Grytviken. This old whaling station is still strewn with evidence of its past industry, and its South Georgia Museum gives insight into whaling life, as well as South Georgia's history and wildlife. Meanwhile, seals wriggle outside the station's quaint, white-clapboard whalers' church.

Penguin Rookeries

7 When you first lay eyes on these ever-anthropomorphised birds, you'll know you've arrived in the Antarctic. From the tiny tuxedo-clad Adélie and the bushy-browed macaroni, to the world's largest penguin, the fabulously debonair emperor, the Antarctic offers a chance to see these unique creatures on their own turf: sea, ice and shore. Spot them shooting out

Food & Drink

Frozen, dried and canned food form the majority of meals at the South Pole. Cooking is challenging: due to the risk of fire, all stoves are electric, which take much longer than professional gas ranges. Most food is stored outdoors, where it freezes solid, so it can take up to two weeks for meat to defrost in the walk-in refrig-erator! Through the long, dark winter, chocolate is a favourite. Ice cream is also a local pref-erence but since it's stored outdoors, it has to be warmed in a microwave before it can be eaten. Interestingly, the station gets its water from a well, an improvement over the former inefficient system of melting clean snow, which required large amounts of fuel and time.

of the water, tobogganing along the ice or in cacopho-nous rookeries which are a sight to behold: squawking, gambolling birds, hatching, moulting and caring for their young.

Antarctic Museum at Port Lockroy

8 Each year, tens of thousands of visitors flock to Britain's beautifully restored Bransfield House, the main building of Base A,

built at Port Lockroy during WWII. Not only does it offer the chance to spend up big at the well-stocked souvenir shop and to mail postcards at the busy post office, the museum's old wooden skis, clandestine 1944 radio transmitter and wind-up HMV gramophone are evocative artefacts of the explorers who once lived for years at this wilderness outpost.

VOLODYMYR GOINYK / SHUTTERSTOCK ©

Day & Night

Because the South Pole is at the rotational axis of the earth, the sun and moon do not pass overhead each day. Instead, the sun appears to circle the horizon daily. On the summer solstice (21 December) the sun is at its highest, approximately 23° above the horizon. A spectacular sunset lasts weeks before the sun dips below the horizon on about 22 March. Twilight lingers for another six or seven weeks. Then the darkness sets in, lightened only by the aurora australis, the moon and the stars. During the six-month polar night, the moon is visible for two weeks, then sets for two weeks before rising again and repeat-ing the cycle. Seven weeks of dawn precede sunrise on about 22 September, when winterers rejoice.

CAPITAL	Saint John's
POPULATION	93,600
AREA	442.6 sq km
OFFICIAL LANGUAGE	English

Nelson's Dockyard

Antigua & Barbuda

On Antigua, life is a beach. Its corrugated coasts cradle scores of perfect little strands lapped by beguiling blue water, while the sheltered bays have provided refuge for everyone from Admiral Nelson to pirates and yachties.

If you can tear yourself away from that towel, you'll discover that there's a distinct English accent to this classic Caribbean island with its narrow roads, candy-colored villages and fine historic sights. Antigua's best beaches hem the west coast between Jolly Harbour and Old Road Town. The windswept east is sparsely settled and has only a few beaches.

If life on Antigua is a beach, Barbuda *is* a beach: one smooth, pink-tinged strand hemming the reef-filled waters. There is no such thing as a bad beach in Barbuda. All of them are hypnotic strips of pristine powdery white sand perfect for strolling, swimming, chilling and picnicking. Birds, especially the huffing and puffing frigates, greatly outnumber residents on this perfect Caribbean dream island.

Top Experiences

Nelson's Dockyard

1 Flash back to colonial times at this restored 18th-century naval base. In operation since 1745, Nelson's Dockyard is now Antigua's top sightseeing draw. Once home of the British Royal Navy, it was abandoned in 1889 following a decline in the island's economic and strategic importance. The Dockyard Museum in the brick-and-stone naval officers' residence relates tidbits about the history of the island, the dockyard and life at the forts. Among the many trinkets on display is a telescope once used by Nelson himself.

Shirley Heights Lookout

2 For fabulous views of English Harbour and out to Guadalupe, head up the hill to these 18th-century military fortifications whose ruins are fun to poke around. Some buildings have been restored and house a restaurant-bar whose legendary Sunday barbecue party with live bands has drawn revelers from around the island for three decades.

Frigate Bird Sanctuary

3 Expansive, shallow Codrington Lagoon National Park, which runs along Barbuda's west coast, supports one of the world's largest colonies of frigate birds. More than 5000 of these black-feathered critters nest in sections of the lagoon's scrubby mangroves – with as many as a dozen birds roosting on a single bush. Because of this density, the birds' nesting sites are all

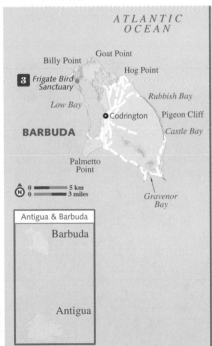

abuzz with squawking, and the sight of all those blood-red inflating throat pouches is mesmerizing. The most popular time to visit is during the mating season, from September to April (December is peak time).

Fig Tree Drive

4 Old Road, a village that juxtaposes a fair amount of poverty with two swanky resorts (Curtain Bluff and Carlisle Bay), marks the start of 5-mile-long (badly potholed) Fig Tree Dr, which winds through rainforest, past big old mango and giant-leaved banana trees (called 'figs' locally) and roadside stands selling fruit, jam and juices.

Rendezvous Bay

5 After a 90-minute walk through the rainforest, you'll have earned bragging rights for making it to one of Antigua's loveliest beaches. Because of its remoteness, it usually delivers footprint-free solitude. The path is not signposted, so either ask for detailed directions locally or sign up with a guide.

Fort James

6 Fort James, a small stronghold at the north side of St John's Harbour, dates back to 1706, but most of what you see today was built in 1739. It still has a few of its 36 cannons, a powder magazine and a fair portion of its walls intact. The site drips with atmosphere: it's moodily run-down and is rarely the scene of crowds. Fort Bay, a narrow beach backed by trees that stretches north from the fort, is popular with islanders but has no facilities.

Getting Around

In season, daily flights link Antigua and Barbuda.

A 90-minute catamaran ride links St John's with Barbuda.

Private minivans travel along Antigua's main roads.

Taxis are plentiful and fares are government-regulated.

MBRAND85 / SHUTTERSTOCK ©

Half Moon Bay

7 Half Moon Bay, in the southeast of the island, is an undeveloped crescent-shaped bay with yet another beautiful white-sand beach lapped by water the color of Blue Curacao. There's usually pretty good bodysurfing along the northern end, while the calmer waters to the south offer decent snorkeling conditions.

Food & Drink

Pepperpot Antigua's national dish is a hearty stew blending meat and vegetables, such as okra, spinach, eggplant, squash and potatoes. It's often served with fungi, which are not mushrooms but cornmeal patties or dumplings.

Black pineapple The local pineapple was first introduced by the Arawaks and is smaller than your garden variety. It's known as 'black' because it's at its sweetest when dark green. It grows primarily on the southwest coast, near Cades Bay.

Rock lobster This hulking crustacean has a succulent tail but no claws and is best served grilled. (And you'll be forgiven if after a few rum punches you're humming a tune by the B-52s while digging in.)

Wadadli Antigua Brewery makes this local brew, a fresh pale lager, with desalinated seawater.

Cavalier & English Harbour The locally produced rums and are best mixed with fruit juice for a refreshing – if potentially lethal – punch.

HEMIS / ALAMY STOCK PHOTO ©

Local Culture

Away from the resorts, Antigua retains its traditional West Indian character, albeit with a strong British stamp. It's manifested in the gingerbread architecture found around the capital, the popularity of steel-pan (steel-band), calypso and reggae music, and in festivities such as Carnival. English traditions also play an important role, as is evident in the national sport of cricket.

Many Barbudans originally come from or have spent time living on their sister island, Antigua, and favor the quieter pace of life on the more isolated Barbuda. In fact, many Barbudans working in tourism are happy with the trickle of tourists that the remote island attracts, and have been reluctant to court the kind of development Antigua has seen.

Approximately 90% of the 86,500 people who live on Antigua are of African descent. There are also small minority populations with British, Portuguese and Lebanese ancestry. The population of Barbuda is approximately 1250, with most people of African descent.

CAPITAL
Buenos Aires

POPULATION
43 million

AREA
2.8 million sq km

OFFICIAL LANGUAGE
Spanish

Iguazú Falls

Argentina

It's apparent why Argentina has long held travelers in awe: tango, gauchos, fútbol, Patagonia, the Andes. The classics alone make a wanderlust cocktail.

Arriving in Buenos Aires is like jumping aboard a moving train. Outside the taxi window, a blurred mosaic of a modern metropolis whizzes by, and then the street life appears – the cafes, the purple jacaranda flowers draped over the sidewalks, and *porteños* (residents of Buenos Aires) in stylish clothing, walking purposefully past early-20th-century stone facades. And it's not just Buenos Aires that's a stunner – Córdoba, Salta, Mendoza and Bariloche each have their unforgettable attractions.

From mighty Iguazú Falls in the subtropical north to the thunderous, crackling advance of the Glaciar Perito Moreno in the south, Argentina is also a vast natural wonderland. It's home to rich wetlands that rival Brazil's Pantanal, deserts dotted with cacti, massive ice fields and arid steppes in Patagonia, cool lichen-clad Valdivian forests, Andean salt flats, a spectacular Lake District, penguins, flamingos, capybaras and more. All are stunning sights and adventures just waiting to be experienced.

Top Experiences

Iguazú Falls

1 The peaceful Río Iguazú, flowing through the jungle between Argentina and Brazil, plunges suddenly over a basalt cliff in a spectacular display of sound and fury that is truly one of the planet's most awe-inspiring sights. Iguazú Falls are a primal experience for the senses: the roar, the spray and the sheer volume of water will live forever in your memory. But it's not just the waterfalls – the jungly national parks that contain them offer a romantic backdrop and fine wildlife-watching opportunities.

Cementerio de la Recoleta

2 A veritable city of the dead, Buenos Aires' top tourist attraction is not to be missed. Lined up along small 'streets' are hundreds of old crypts, each uniquely carved from marble, granite and concrete, and decorated with stained glass, stone angels and religious icons. Small plants and trees grow in fissures, while feral cats slink between tombs, some of which lie in various stages of decay. It's a photogenic wonderland, and if there's a strange beauty in death you'll find it in spades here.

Food Scene

3 Believe the hype: Argentine beef is some of the best in the world. Eat, drink and be merry at one of the country's thousands of *parrillas* (steak restaurants), where a leisurely meal can include waiters pouring malbec and serving up slabs of tasty steaks. But there's so much more in Buenos Aires – closed-door restaurants, pop-up restaurants and molecular gastronomy have all become buzzwords in Argentina's capital city, where you can also find nearly any kind of exotic ethnic cuisine.

Glaciar Perito Moreno

4 As glaciers go, Perito Moreno is one of the most dynamic and accessible on the planet. But what makes it exceptional is its constant advance – up to 2m per day. Its slow but constant motion creates incredible suspense, as building-sized icebergs calve from the face and spectacularly crash into Lago Argentino. You can get very close to the action via an extended network of steel catwalks and platforms. A typical way to cap off the day is with a huge steak dinner back in El Calafate.

SJ TRAVEL PHOTO AND VIDEO / SHUTTERSTOCK ©

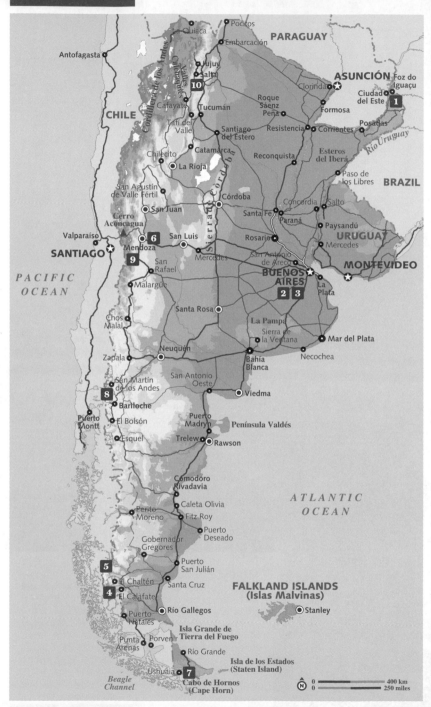

Best in Print

Kiss of the Spider Woman
(Manuel Puig, 1976) Two
prisoners and their developing
relationship in a Buenos Aires
prison; made into the Oscar-
winning 1985 film.

In Patagonia (Bruce Chatwin,
1977) Evocative writing on
Patagonia's history and
mystique.

The Motorcycle Diaries
(Ernesto Che Guevara et al,
1993) Based on the travel
diary of the Argentine-born
revolutionist.

**And the Money Kept Rolling
In (and Out)** (Paul Blustein,
2005) How the IMF helped
bankrupt Argentina.

Food & Drink

Beef Argentines have perfected
grilling beef, instilling a smoky,
salty outer layer to delectable
steaks.

Dulce de leche The world's
best caramel sauce; find it in
most of the country's sweetest
concoctions.

Ice cream Argentina makes
some of the world's best *helado,*
swirled into a miniature peaked
mountain with a spoon stuck in
the side.

Italian food You'll find pizza and
pasta at so many restaurants,
it's a wonder the locals can
consume it all.

Maté Although most first-time
maté drinkers can barely choke
the stuff down, this bitter, grassy
tea is an important social bond-
ing experience.

Wine Exploring Argentina by
the glass will take you from the
malbecs of Mendoza to the tor-
rontés of Cafayate to the syrahs
of San Juan.

Hiking the Fitz Roy Range

5 With rugged
wilderness and shark-
tooth summits, the Fitz
Roy Range is the trekking
capital of Argentina. Experienced mountain climbers
may suffer on its windswept
and tough, world-class
routes, but the beautiful
hiking trails are surprisingly
easy and accessible, and
park rangers help orient
every traveler who comes
into the area. Once on the
trail, the most stunning
views are just a day hike
from town. Not bad for
those who want to reward
their sweat equity with a
craft beer at El Chaltén's
nearby La Cervecería
brewpub.

Wine Tasting Around Mendoza

6 With so much fantastic wine on offer, it's
tempting just to pull up a
bar stool and work your way
through a list – but getting
out there and seeing how
the grapes are grown and
processed is almost as
enjoyable as sampling the
finished product. The best
news is that wine tasting in

When to Go

HIGH SEASON
(Nov–Feb & Jul)
Crowds throng to the
beaches through January.

SHOULDER
(Sep–Oct & Mar–May)
Temperature-wise the best
times to visit Buenos Aires.

LOW SEASON
(Jun, Aug)
Many services close at
beach resorts; mountain
passes can be blocked by
snow.

Argentina isn't just for the
wine snobs – there's a tour
to meet every budget, from
DIY bike tours for back-
packers to tasting-and-
accommodation packages
at exclusive wineries.

Outdoor Adventures

Argentina isn't just for mountaineers: try
kiteboarding in the Andes, paragliding in the
Central Sierras, diving along the Atlantic coast
and fishing for huge trout in the Lake District.

Tango

Watch this steamy national dance at a spectacular
show or catch a casual street performance – both
will wow you with amazing feats of athleticism.

Sports Fanatics

Pato is Argentina's traditional sport, played on horseback and mixing elements from both polo and basketball. It was originally played with a duck (a *'pato'*), but now, thankfully, uses a ball encased in leather handles. Despite its long history and tradition, however, relatively few people follow it.

Today, *fútbol* (soccer) is an integral part of Argentines' lives, and on game day you'll know it by the cheers and yells emanating from shops and cafes. The national team has reached the World Cup final five times and has triumphed twice, in 1978 and 1986. The Argentine team also won Olympic gold twice, at the 2004 and 2008 games.

The most popular teams are Boca Juniors and River Plate (there are around two dozen professional teams in Buenos Aires alone) and the fanatical behavior of the country's *barra brava* (hooligans) rivals that of their European counterparts. Among the best-known *fútbol* players are Diego Maradona, Gabriel Batistuta and, of course, Lionel Messi, who has been voted FIFA's best player of the year five times.

Ushuaia, the End of the Earth

7 Location, location, location. Wedged between the Beagle Channel and the snow-capped Martial Range, this bustling port is the final scrap of civilization seen by Antarctica-bound boats. But more than the end of the earth, Ushuaia is a crossroads for big commerce and adventure. Snow sports brighten the frozen winters and long summer days mean hiking and biking until the wee hours. Happening restaurants, boisterous bars and welcoming B&Bs mean you'll want to tuck in and call this port home for a few days.

Ruta de los Siete Lagos

8 A journey of extraordinary beauty, the Ruta de los Siete Lagos (Seven Lakes Route) is a not-to-be-missed road trip. Your vehicular adventure winds through lush forests, past waterfalls and dramatic mountain scenery, and skirts the various crystal-blue lakes that give it its name. Stop for a picnic and go swimming, fishing and camping. You can also bus it in a couple of hours or bike it in a few days. Experiencing this gorgeous route is a decision you won't regret.

Skiing at Las Leñas

9 Hitting the slopes at Las Leñas isn't just about making the scene, although there is that; this mountain has the most varied terrain, the most days of powder per year and some of the fastest and most modern lift equipment in the country. Splash out for some on-mountain accommodations or choose from a variety of more reasonably priced options just down the road. Whatever you do, if you're a snow bunny and you're here in season, mark this one on your itinerary in big red letters. Outside the ski season Las Leñas is also attempting to attract summer visitors who enjoy week-long packages, offering activities such as mountain biking, horseback riding and hiking.

Colonial Salta

10 Argentina's northwest holds its most venerable colonial settlements, and none is more lovely than Salta. This beautiful city, which was founded in 1582, is set in a fertile valley that acts as a gateway to the impressive Andean cordillera not far beyond. Postcard-pretty churches, a sociable plaza and a wealth of noble buildings give it a laid-back historical ambience that endears it to all who visit. Add in great museums, a lively folkloric music scene, some of the country's most appealing lodging options as well as a fistful of attractions within easy reach: that's one impressive place.

Getting Around

Argentina is a huge country, so flights are good for saving time. Delays happen occasionally, however.

Generally the best way to get around Argentina; buses are fast, frequent, comfortable, reasonably priced and cover the country extensively.

Renting a car is useful (but expensive) for those who want the most travel independence in remote regions such as Patagonia.

A few train lines can be useful for travelers, but generally this is not the most efficient method of transportation.

CAPITAL	Yerevan
POPULATION	3.1 million
AREA	29,743 sq km
OFFICIAL LANGUAGE	Armenian

Musical fountain and National Gallery and History Museum, Yerevan

Armenia

Armenia is a destination where you will be intrigued by history, awed by monuments, amazed by the landscape and charmed by down-to-earth locals.

Few nations have histories as ancient, complex and laced with tragedy as Armenia. And even fewer have a culture that is as rich and resilient.

It's not an easy place to explore – roads are rough, transport is often hard to navigate and those who don't speak Armenian or Russian may find communication difficult – but travelling here is as rewarding as it is revelatory.

The extraordinary collection of medieval monasteries scattered across the country is the number-one attraction, closely followed by a dramatically beautiful landscape that is perfectly suited to hiking and other outdoor activities.

And then there's the unexpected delight of Yerevan – one of Europe's most exuberant and endearing cities. Put together, they offer an enticing and hugely enjoyable travel experience.

Top Experiences

Yerevan

1 Yerevan is a city full of contradictions – top-of-the-range Mercedes sedans share the roads with Ladas so old they should be in museums; old-fashioned teahouses sit next to chic European-style wine bars; and street fashions range from hipster to babushka with many weird and wonderful variations in between. Life here isn't easy, but it's certainly fun. In summer, locals take to the streets every night, congregating around the musical fountain in Republic Sq. In winter, freezing temperatures encourage people into *pandoks* (taverns) around town, where *khoravats* (barbecue meats), *oghee* (fruit vodka) and traditional music are enjoyed with gusto.

Tatev Monastery

2 Perched on the edge of a rocky canyon, the monastery at Tatev has stunning views over to the peaks of Karabakh. The bishops of Syunik built its main church in the 9th century to house important relics. There are faint signs of frescoes, intricate carvings and portraits of the main donors on the northern side. The 11th-century Surp Grigor Church nestles next to it, and there's a miniaturised chapel above the gatehouse.

When to Go

 HIGH SEASON (Mar–Jun & Sep–Nov)

 SHOULDER (Jul–Aug)

 LOW SEASON (Dec–Feb)

Yeghegis Valley

3 The beautiful Yeghegis Valley is surrounded by peaks and is home to picturesque villages with medieval churches. It and the surrounding valleys are well worth exploring. Highlights include Smbataberd fortress, 13th century churches and an 800-year-old Jewish cemetery.

Geghard Monastery

4 Half cathedral, half cave, Geghard is a spooky, dimly lit sanctuary, where voices bounce off walls, sunbeams shoot through the narrow windows and droplets of water ooze through the walls. Ancient *khatchkars* (carved stone crosses) surrounding the church, and crosses carved into the 800-year-old walls, are testament to centuries of pious visitors.

Kasagh Gorge

5 Hike between the spectacularly sited monasteries of Hovhannavank and Saghmosavank in the Kasagh Gorge. Hovhannavank, in the village of Ohanavan, was once an important educational and theological centre where manuscripts were written and illuminated. Saghmosavank (Monastery of Palms) was built on the edge of the Kasagh Gorge and comprises two main church buildings: the Church of Zion and the smaller Church of Karapet; both date from the 13th century. Surrounded by a fortified wall and commanding wonderful views over the Kasagh Gorge and to Mt Aragats, it is the most attractive monastery in the gorge area.

Debed Canyon

6 Nearly every village along the Debed River has a church, a chapel, an old fort and a sprinkling of *khachkars* somewhere nearby. Two World Heritage–listed monasteries, Haghpat and Sanahin, are the main

Getting Around

From Yerevan, there are bus services to many parts of the country as well as to international destinations.

A number of agencies rent out cars in Yerevan. Taxis are cheap and plentiful in Yerevan.

The Yerevan metro is clean, safe and efficient.

KAREN FALJYAN / SHUTTERSTOCK ©

attractions, but there's much more to see. Derelict Soviet-era infrastructure is sadly noticeable along the riverbank, but the scenery is quite idyllic elsewhere.

Noravank Monastery

7 Founded by Bishop Hovhannes in 1105 and sensitively renovated in the 1990s, Noravank (New Monastery) is one of the most spectacular sites in Armenia and should be included on every visitor's itinerary. Around sunset, the reddish hues of the dramatic cliffs surrounding the monastery are accentuated by the setting sun, and the reddish-gold stone of its churches acquires a luminous sheen – it's a totally magnificent sight. Historians say the church is reminiscent of towerlike burial structures created in the early years of Christianity and there's a wonderful carving of Christ flanked by Peter and Paul above the door.

Selim Pass

8 This road over the Vardenis mountain range is the most spectacular driving route in the country. Climbing to an elevation of 2410m, it is covered in heavy snow in winter and so is only open from May to October. Just below its highest point is the Selim Caravanserai, built in 1332 by order of Prince Chesar Orbelian to shelter caravans following the ancient Dvin-Partav trading route. A sturdy basalt building on a windswept plateau, it comprises a three-nave hall, vestibule, domed chapel and rooms where travellers once slept. Destroyed between the 15th and 16th centuries, it was reconstructed in the 1950s and is open to the elements.

8

ALEXEI FATEEV / ALAMY STOCK PHOTO ©

Food & Drink

If there's one word for dining in Armenia, it's *khoravats* (barbecued food). *Ishkhan khoravats* is grilled trout from Lake Sevan. Kebabs are also very common. The signature herb is dill, especially in salads.

Other staples include *dolma* (rice wrapped in vine leaves), soups, vegetable stews and lavash fresh from the oven. *Khash* is a thick winter stew made from animal parts. Starters include cold salads, farmyard-smelling Lori cheese and dips such as *jajik* (yoghurt with cucumbers and fennel). Cured meats include *sujukh* and *yeghchik* (dark, cured spicy sausage) and *basturma* (finely cured ham).

The most popular drink is *soorch* (Armenian coffee), also claimed by Georgians, Greeks and Arabs. The country's national liquor is *konyak* (cognac), which is around 40% alcohol.

If the Shoe Fits

In 2008 an archaeologist exploring a cave in Vayots Dzor, Southern Armenia, found an ancient leather shoe buried under a pile of animal dung. She estimated that the shoe was around 700 years old and dated from the Mongol period. But once the shoe reached the laboratory a new story began to unfold. Testing dated the shoe to around 3500 BC, thus making it the world's oldest leather shoe (300 years older than a shoe found on a frozen mummy in the Alps in 1991).

The shoe is about a women's size 7 (US), designed for the right foot and is made from leather sewn together like a moccasin. It was found stuffed with grass as if its owner wanted to maintain the shape of the shoe. (The whereabouts of the left shoe are unknown.) The shoe is now on display at the History Museum of Armenia.

CAPITALS
Oranjestad (A),
Kralendijk (B),
Willemstad (C)

POPULATION
113,650 (A),
18,900 (B),
149,000 (C)

AREA
180 sq km (A),
294 sq km (B),
444 sq km (C)

OFFICIAL LANGUAGES
Papiamento, Dutch,
English

Eagle Beach

Aruba, Bonaire & Curaçao

The ABCs of the Caribbean, Aruba, Bonaire and Curaçao boast white-sand beaches, world-class diving and an intriguing mix of Dutch culture in the food, language and colonial architecture.

These three tiny islands once formed the Netherlands Antilles and are still independent territories within the Kingdom of the Netherlands, so Dutch culture is very much in evidence.

Aruba is the most touristed island in the southern Caribbean – not surprising given that it has miles of beaches, sociable rum shops, upmarket resorts and a cute main town. Bonaire's appeal is its reef-lined coast and beautiful waters that lure divers from across the globe. Go-go Curaçao balances commerce with Unesco-recognized old Willemstad and hidden beaches along a lush coast. It's a wild mix of urban madness, remote vistas and a lust for life.

Top Experiences

Eagle Beach

1 Frolic on this ribbon of powdery sand northwest of Oranjestad. This is Aruba's best beach and frequently makes the list of the best in the world. Vendors, loungers and shade trees mean you can relax.

Bonaire National Marine Park

2 This Unesco World Heritage marine park covers the entire coast of Bonaire island to a depth of 200ft (60m) and is a diver's paradise with more than 90 named dive sites. The closeness of the reefs and the clarity of the waters make for unparalleled access – you can reach more than half the dive sites from shore.

Willemstad

3 Willemstad is a bit of a holiday black hole: once you get sucked in, you might never leave. There's the Sint Annabaai ship channel, which cleaves the town in two and leads to one of the world's great harbors. Pause while strolling the colonial-era neighborhoods to watch huge freighters pass meters away. Old sailors' districts are being restored, and Pietermaai – a faded area of Dutch traders mansions – is getting edgy new cafes and bars.

When to Go

 HIGH SEASON
(Dec–Apr)

 SHOULDER
(May–Jun & Nov)

 LOW SEASON
(Jul–Oct)

Food & Drink

Funchi Based on cornmeal, it is formed into cakes and fried or used as a coating.

Nasi goreng Indonesian fried rice, thanks to the colonial Dutch.

Curaçao A startling-blue liquor, with an orange flavor.

CAPITAL	
Canberra	
POPULATION	
23.7 million	
AREA	
7.7 million sq km	
OFFICIAL LANGUAGE	
English	

Bondi Baths, Sydney

Australia

Is the grass always greener on the other side of the fence? Peek over the pickets and find out. This vast country is affluent, multicultural and laced with natural splendour.

Most Australians live along the coast, and most of these folks live in cities – 89% of Australians, in fact. It follows that cities here are a lot of fun. Sydney is a glamorous collusion of beaches, boutiques and bars. Melbourne is all arts, alleyways and Aussie Rules football. Brisbane is a subtropical town on the way up; Adelaide has festive grace. Boomtown Perth breathes West Coast optimism; Canberra transcends political agendas. While the tropical northern fron-

tier town of Darwin, and the chilly southern sandstone city of Hobart, couldn't be more different. No matter which city you're wheeling into, you'll never go wanting for an offbeat theatre production, a lofty art-gallery opening or a rockin' live band.

There's a heckuva lot of tarmac across this wide brown land so hire a 4WD and go off-road: Australia's national parks and secluded corners are custom-made for camping trips down the dirt road.

Top Experiences

Great Barrier Reef

1 The Great Barrier Reef – described by Sir David Attenborough as one of the most beautiful places on the planet – is as fragile as it is beautiful. Stretching more than 2000km along the Queensland coastline, it's a complex ecosystem populated with dazzling coral, languid sea turtles, gliding rays, timid reef sharks and tropical fish of every colour and size. Whether you dive on it, snorkel over it or explore it via scenic flight or glass-bottomed boat, this vivid undersea kingdom and its coral-fringed islands is unforgettable.

Sydney Opera House

2 The instantly recognisable Sydney Opera House on Sydney Harbour is Australia's headline act. An exercise in architectural lyricism like no other, Jørn Utzon's building on Bennelong Point more than holds its own amidst the visual feast of the harbour's attention-grabbing bridge, shimmering blue waters and jaunty green ferries. Everyone can experience the magic on offer here – a stunningly sited waterside bar, acclaimed French restaurant, guided tours and star-studded performance schedule make sure of that.

Melbourne

3 Why the queue? Oh, that's just the line to get into the latest 'no bookings' restaurant in Melbourne. The next best restaurant/chef/cafe/barista/food truck may be the talk of the town, but there are things locals would never change: the leafy parks and gardens of the inner city; the crowded trams that whisk creative 'northerners' to sea-breezy southern St Kilda; and the allegiances that living in such a sports-mad city brings. The city's world-renowned street art scene expresses Melbourne's fears, frustrations and joys.

DAVID HANNAH / GETTY IMAGES ©

Uluru-Kata Tjuta National Park

4 No matter how many times you've seen it on postcards, nothing prepares you for the burnished grandeur of Uluru. With its remote desert location, deep cultural significance and dazzling beauty, this is a pilgrimage well worth the many hundreds of kilometres it takes to get there. But Uluru-Kata Tjuta National Park offers much more than the chance to see a big boulder. Along with the equally captivating Kata Tjuta (the Olgas), there are mystical walks, sublime sunsets and ancient desert cultures to encounter.

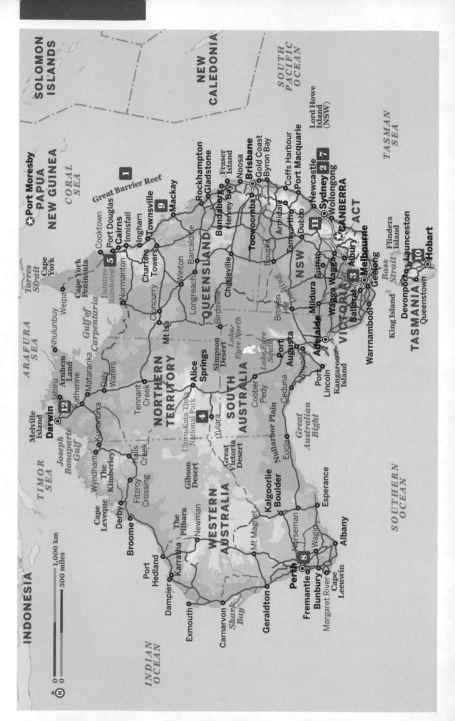

Best on Film

Lantana (director Ray Lawrence; 2001) Mystery for grown-ups: a meditation on love, truth and grief.

Gallipoli (director Peter Weir; 1981) Nationhood in the crucible of WWI.

Mad Max (director George Miller; 1979) Mel Gibson gets angry.

The Hunter (director Daniel Nettheim; 2011) Grumpy Willem Dafoe goes hunting for the last Tasmanian Tiger.

Ten Canoes (directors Rolf de Heer and Peter Djigirr; 2006) The first Australian film scripted entirely in an Aboriginal language.

Food & Drink

Australia varies so much in climate that at any time of the year there's an enormous array of produce on offer. In summer, kitchen bowls overflow with fresh fruit. Seafood is always freshest close to the source; on this big island it's plentiful:

Bugs Shovel-nosed lobsters without a lobster's price tag (try the Balmain and Moreton Bay varieties).

Fish You can sample countless wild fish species but even snapper, trevally and whiting taste fabulous barbecued.

Marron A prehistoric-looking freshwater crayfish from Western Australia.

Oysters Connoisseurs prize Sydney rock oysters and Tasmania is known for its Pacific oysters.

Prawns In Australia these are incredible, particularly sweet school prawns or the eastern king (Yamba) prawns.

Daintree Rainforest

5 Lush green rainforest replete with fan palms, prehistoric-looking ferns and twisted mangroves tumbles down towards a brilliant white-sand coastline in the ancient, World Heritage–listed Daintree rainforest. Upon entering the forest, you'll be enveloped by a cacophony of birdsong, frogs croaking and the buzz of insects. Continue exploring the area via wildlife-spotting night tours, mountain treks, interpretive boardwalks, canopy walks, self-guided walking trails, 4WD trips, horse riding, kayaking, croc-spotting cruises, tropical-fruit orchard tours and tastings... Whew! If you're lucky, you might even spot a cassowary.

Native Wildlife

6 Furry, cuddly, or ferocious – you can find all this and more on a wildlife-spotting journey around Australia. Head to Hervey Bay for whale-watching; see nesting sea turtles (and later, hatchlings) on Queensland beaches; and adorable little penguins and fur seals on Victoria's Phillip Island. Queensland, Western Australia and the Northern Territory shelter dinosaur-like crocodiles, and everywhere Australia's birds make themselves

When to Go

HIGH SEASON
(Dec–Feb)
Summertime: local holidays, busy beaches and cricket.

SHOULDER SEASON
(Mar–May & Sep–Nov)
Warm sun, clear skies, shorter queues.

LOW SEASON
(Jun–Aug)
Head for the desert, the tropical north or the snow.

Beach Lovers

The Coastal Studies Unit at the University of Sydney has deemed there to be 10,685 beaches in Australia.

The Great Ocean Road

The Great Ocean Road (B100) is one of Australia's most famous touring routes. It winds past world-class surf breaks and the limestone formations of the Twelve Apostles, through pockets of rainforest and calm seaside towns, and under koala-filled tree canopies.

Aboriginal Storytelling

Aboriginal people traditionally had an oral culture so storytelling was an important way to learn. Stories gave meaning to life and were used to teach the messages of the spirit ancestors.

Although beliefs and cultural practices vary according to region and language groups, there is a common world-view that these ancestors created the land, the sea and all living things. This is often referred to as the Dreaming. Through stories, the knowledge and beliefs are passed on from one generation to another and set out the social mores.

Yabun (www.yabun.org.au) is held every year on Australia Day (26 January) at Victoria Park in Sydney and is a free festival celebrating the survival of Aboriginal cultures.

known (you can't miss the cackle of the kookaburra). In between, you'll discover a panoply of extraordinary animals found nowhere else on earth: koalas, kangaroos, quokkas, wombats and platypuses.

Bondi Beach

7 Definitively Sydney and irresistibly hip, Bondi is one of the world's great beaches. Surfers, models, skate punks and backpackers surf a hedonistic wave through the pubs, bars and restaurants along Campbell Pde, but the beach is a timeless constant. It's the closest ocean beach to the city, has consistently good (though crowded) waves and is great for a rough 'n' tumble swim. Don't miss a jaunt along the Bondi to Coogee Clifftop

Walk, kicking off at the southern end of the beach.

Fremantle

8 Fremantle – Western Australia's major port 22km south of Perth – is a raffish, artsy, student-filled harbour town, defined by a classic cache of Victorian architecture. It's an isolated place – closer to Singapore than Sydney. But like any port, the world washes in on the tide and washes out again, leaving the locals buzzing with global zeitgeist. Funky Fremantle has sea-salty soul to burn: expect craft-beer breweries, live-music rooms, hipster bars, late-night coffee joints, Indian Ocean seafood shacks, buskers, beaches, markets and students on the run from the books.

The Whitsundays

9 You can hop around a whole stack of tropical islands in this seafaring life and never find anywhere with the sheer beauty of the Whitsundays. Travellers of all monetary persuasions launch yachts from party town Airlie Beach and drift between these lush green isles in a slow search for paradise (you'll probably find it in more than one place). Don't miss Whitehaven Beach – one of Australia's best. Wish you were here?

Hobart & MONA

10 Occupying an improbable riverside location a ferry ride from Hobart's harbourfront, the Museum of Old & New Art – aka MONA – is an innovative, world-class institution.

Described by its owner, Hobart philanthropist David Walsh, as a 'subversive adult Disneyland', three levels of astounding under-ground galleries showcase more than 400 challenging and controversial art-works. You might not like everything you see, but a visit here is a sure-fire conversation starter and one of Australia's unique arts experiences.

Blue Mountains

11 With stunning natural beauty, the World Heritage region of the Blue Mountains is an Australian highlight. The slate-coloured haze that gives the mountains their name comes from a fine mist of oil exuded by the huge eucalypts that form a dense canopy across the landscape of deep, often in-accessible valleys and chis-elled sandstone outcrops. The foothills begin 65km inland from Sydney, rising to an 1100m-high sandstone plateau riddled with valleys eroded into the stone.

Kakadu National Park

12 Kakadu is more than a national park. It's also a vibrant, living acknowledgement of the elemental link between the Aboriginal custodians and the country they have nurtured, endured and respected for thousands of generations. Encompass-ing almost 20,000 sq km (about 200km north–south and 100km east–west), it holds within its boundaries a spectacular ecosystem, periodically scorched and flooded, and mind-blowing ancient rock art.

ANDREW WATSON / GETTY IMAGES ©

Getting Around

 Hire a car to travel at your own tempo, explore remote areas and visit regions with no public transport.

 Fast-track your holiday with affordable, frequent, fast flights between major centres.

 Reliable, frequent long-haul bus services around the country. Not always cheaper than flying.

 Trains are slow, expensive and infrequent...but the scenery is great!

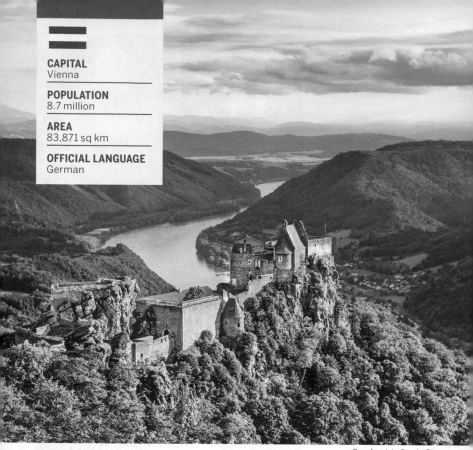

CAPITAL	Vienna
POPULATION	8.7 million
AREA	83,871 sq km
OFFICIAL LANGUAGE	German

Burg Aggstein, Danube River

Austria

No country waltzes so effortlessly between the urban and the outdoors as Austria. One day you're cresting alpine summits, the next you're swanning around imperial Vienna.

Austria might conjure visions of wedding-cake-like baroque churches, dripping with lavish detail, palatial Hapsburg headquarters like Schloss Schönnbrunn, and Gothic crowning glories like the Stephansdom. But the country is more than the sum of its pomp and palaces. A fresh breath of architectural air and a feel of new-found cool is sweeping through the cities, bringing with it a happy marriage of the contemporary and historic.

Outside of the cities, roads meander through deeply carved valleys, railways unzip the Alps to thread along sheer mountain flanks, past glaciers and through flower-freckled meadows, while hikers lace up their boots to reach enticingly off-the-radar corners of the country. In winter, the slopes hum with skiers, while summer beckons white-water rafters and canyoners to glacial rivers and lakes that sparkle like gemstones. Der Berg ruft – the mountain calls!

Top Experiences

Imperial Palaces of Vienna

1 Imagine what you could do with unlimited riches and Austria's top architects at hand for 640 years and you'll have the Vienna of the Habsburgs. The monumentally graceful Hofburg whisks you back to the age of empires; marvel at the treasury's imperial crowns, the equine ballet of the Spanische Hofreitschule and the chandelier-lit apartments fit for Empress Elisabeth. The palace is rivalled in grandeur only by the 1441-room Schloss Schönbrunn, a Unesco World Heritage site, and baroque Schloss Belvedere, both set in exquisite gardens.

Grossglockner Road

2 Hairpin bends: 36. Length: 48km. Average slope gradient: 9%. Highest viewpoint: Edelweiss Spitze (2571m). Grossglockner Road is one of Europe's greatest drives and the showpiece of Hohe Tauern National Park. The scenery unfolds as you climb higher on this serpentine road. And what scenery! Snow-capped mountains, plunging waterfalls and lakes scattered like gemstones are just the build-up to Grossglockner (3798m), Austria's highest peak, and the Pasterze Glacier. Start early and allow enough time, as there's a stop-the-car-and-grab-the-camera view on every corner.

The Wachau

3 When Strauss composed 'The Blue Danube', he surely had the Wachau in mind. Granted Unesco World Heritage status for its harmonious natural and cultural beauty, this romantic stretch of the Danube Valley waltzes you through poetic landscapes of terraced vineyards, forested slopes and apricot orchards. Beyond the highlight attraction of Stift Melk, Dürnstein's Kuenringerburg begs exploration. This

CANADASTOCK / SHUTTERSTOCK ©

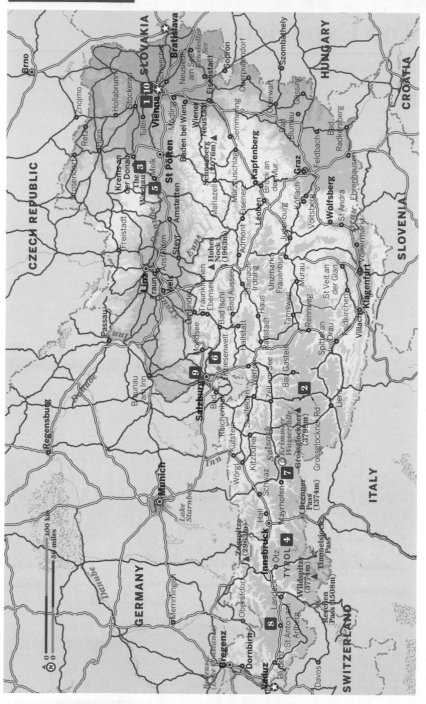

Best on Film

The Third Man (1949) Classic film noir set in Vienna.

The Piano Teacher (2001) Masterpiece directed by Michael Hanecke about a masochistic piano teacher.

Metropolis (1927) Industry and prescient futuristic grunge by director Fritz Lange.

Amour (2012) Michael Hanecke directed and wrote the screenplay of this film about an elderly couple's tested love.

The Dreamed Ones (2016) Ruth Beckermann's literary film homes in on the love of poets as expressed through passionate postal exchanges.

Food & Drink

Graukäse The Zillertal's grey, mouldy, sour-milk cheese is tastier than it sounds, honest!

Käsekrainer A fat cheese-filled sausage, way off the calorie-counting Richter scale. It's a popular wee-hour, beer-mopping snack at Vienna's sausage stands.

Leberknödelsuppe Dig into liver dumpling soup, the starter that gets meals off to a hearty kick all over Austria.

Rindfleischsulz Jellied beef brawn, often drizzled in pumpkin-seed oil vinaigrette.

Schnecken *Escargots* to the French, snails to English speakers, these gastropods are slithering onto many of the top menus in the country.

Waldviertel Mohn Poppy dumplings, desserts, strudels and noodles add a floral addition to menus in the Waldviertel.

ruined hilltop castle is where the troubadour Blondel attempted to rescue Richard the Lionheart from the clutches of Duke Leopold V.

Outdoor Adventure in Tyrol

 4 Anywhere where there's foaming water, a tall mountain or a sheer ravine, there are heart-pumping outdoor escapades in Austria. For a summertime buzz, you can't beat throwing yourself down raging rivers such as the Inn and Sanna in Tyrol, Austria's rafting mecca. Or strap into your harness and be blown away by the alpine scenery, paragliding in the Zillertal. Cyclists use the cable-car network to access the many high-altitude and downhill routes.

Stift Melk

5 Austria's greatest works of art are those wrought for God, some say. Gazing up at the golden glory of Stift Melk, Austria's must-see Benedictine abbey-fortress, you can't help but agree. The twin-

spired monastery church is a baroque tour de force, swirling with prancing angels, gilt flourishes and Johann Michael Rottmayr's ceiling paintings. Such opulence continues in the

When to Go

HIGH SEASON
(Jun–Oct)
Salzburg is busiest in July and August.

SHOULDER
(Apr–May, Sep & Oct)
The weather's changeable, the lakes are chilly and the hiking's excellent.

LOW SEASON
(Nov–Mar)
Many sights are closed; high season for skiing is mid-December to March.

Alpine Flowers

A highlight of the Austrian Alps are its wildflowers, which bring a riot of scent and colour to the high pastures from May to September. The species here are hardy, with long roots to counter strong winds, bright colours to repel some insects and petals that can resist frost and dehydration.

Spring brings crocuses, alpine snowbells and anemones; summer alpine roses and gentians; and autumn thistles, delphiniums and blue aconites. Tempting though it may be to pick them, these flowers really do look lovelier on the slopes and most are protected species.

Men once risked life and limb to pluck edelweiss from the highest crags of the Alps for their sweethearts. The woolly bloom is Austria's national flower, symbolising bravery, love and strength.

Getting Around

Flying within a country the size of Austria is rarely necessary. The main exception is to/from Innsbruck (in the far west of Austria).

Small towns and even small cities often have limited or no car-hire services, so reserve ahead in major cities.

Public transport is excellent for reaching even remote regions, but it takes longer. Most provinces have an integrated transport system offering day passes covering regional zones for both bus and train travel.

The Danube serves as a thoroughfare between Vienna and Lower and Upper Austria. Boat services are generally slow, scenic excursions rather than functional means of transport.

library and marble hall, both embellished with illusionary trompe l'œil tiers by Paul Troger. If you can, stay to see the monarch of monasteries strikingly lit at night.

Eisriesenwelt

6 The twinkling chambers and passageways of Eisriesenwelt are like something out of Narnia under the White Witch. Sculpted drip by drip over millennia, the icy underworld of the limestone Tennengebirge range is billed as the world's largest accessible ice cave. Otherworldly sculptures, shimmering lakes and a cavernous Eispalast (ice palace) appear as you venture deep into the frozen heart of the mountain, carbide lamp in hand. Even in summer, temperatures down here are subzero, so dress warmly.

Krimmler Wasserfälle

7 No doubt you'll hear the thunderous roar of the 380m-high Krimmler Wasserfälle, Europe's highest waterfall, before you see it. You can't help but feel insignificant when confronted with the sheer force and scale of this cataract, which thrashes immense boulders and produces the most photogenic of rainbows. As with all natural wonders, this one looks best from certain angles, namely from the Wasserfallweg (Waterfall Trail). The path zigzags up through moist, misty forest to viewpoints that afford close-ups of the three-tiered falls and a shower in its fine spray.

Skiing in the Alps

8 In a country where three-year-olds can snowplough, 70-year-olds still slalom and the tiniest speck of a village has its own lift system, skiing is more than just a sport – it's a way of life. Why? Just look around you. There's St Anton am Arlberg for off-piste and après-ski, Mayrhofen for freestyle boarding and its epic Harakiri, Kitzbühel for its perfect mix – the scope is limitless

and the terrain fantastic. Cross-country or back-country, downhill or glacier, whatever your ski style, Austria has a piste with your name on it.

Festung Hohensalzburg

9 Work up a sweat on the steep walk or step into the funicular and sway up to Salzburg's glorious fortress, Festung Hohensalzburg, beckoning on a forested peak above the city. As you make your way around Europe's best-preserved fortress, glide through the Golden Hall, with its celestial ceiling capturing the starlit heavens. After all this beauty, you will find yourself cast among a chilling array of medieval torture instruments in the Fortress Museum, and don't miss the 360-degree views from the tower.

MuseumsQuartier

10 Once the imperial stables, now one of the world's biggest exhibition spaces, Vienna's 60,000-sq-metre Museums Quartier contains more art than some small countries possess. Emotive works by Klimt and Schiele hang out in the Leopold Museum, while the basalt MUMOK highlights provocative Viennese Actionists, and the Kunsthalle new media. Progressive boutiques, workshops and cafes take creativity beyond the canvas. On warm days, Viennese gather in the huge courtyard to chat, drink and watch the world go by.

Celebrity City

Salzburg film locations from *The Sound of Music* include the Mirabellgarten of 'Do-Re-Mi' fame and the 'Sixteen Going on Seventeen' pavilion in Hellbrunn Park.

Salzburg Festival

The much-lauded Salzburg Festival (www.salzburger festspiele.at) celebrates classical music from late July to August.

CAPITAL
Baku

POPULATION
9.8 million

AREA
86,600 sq km

OFFICIAL LANGUAGE
Azerbaijani (Azeri)

Flame Towers, Baku

Azerbaijan

Breathtaking natural beauty, hospitable people, quaint rural backwaters and a cosmopolitan capital make Azerbaijan a thrilling, offbeat discovery.

Selling itself as the 'Land of Fire', Azerbaijan (Azərbaycan) is a tangle of contradictions and contrasts. Neither Europe nor Asia, it's a nexus of ancient historical empires, but also a 'new' nation rapidly transforming itself with a super-charged gust of petro-spending.

The cosmopolitan capital, Baku, rings a Unesco-listed ancient core with dazzling 21st-century architecture and sits on the oil-rich Caspian Sea. In the surrounding semi-desert are mud volcanoes and curious fire phenomena. Yet barely three hours' drive away, timeless rural villages, clad in lush orchards and backed by the soaring Great Caucasus mountains are a dramatic contrast.

In most such places, foreigners remain a great rarity, but in return for a degree of linguistic dexterity, you'll find a remark-able seam of hospitality. And a few rural outposts – from village homestays to glitzy ski- and golf-hotels – now have have the odd English speaker to assist travellers.

Top Experiences

When to Go

 HIGH SEASON (Jul–Aug)

 SHOULDER (May–Jun & Sep–Oct)

 LOW SEASON (Nov–Apr)

Baku's 21st Century Architecture

1 Azerbaijan's capital is the architectural love child of Paris and Dubai... albeit with plenty of Soviet genes floating half-hidden in the background. Baku has been rapidly transforming its skyline with some of the world's most audacious and spectacular new architecture. Counterpointed with the city's medieval Unesco-listed Old City core is a trio of 190m skyscrapers shaped like gigantic glass flames that really appear to burn at night once the remarkable light show comes on. The majestic white curves of Zaha Hadid's Heydar Aliyev Cultural Centre form a similarly thrilling spectacle. And along the Caspian Sea waterfront a series of new projects are destined to add an otherworldly mega-hotel.

Baku's Old City

2 Huddled behind a battlement-topped arc of city wall, Baku's Unesco-listed core is a world away from the traffic and bustle of the surrounding oil-boom city. The winding alleys follow a crooked medieval logic, while the stone buildings run the gamut of eras, from the ancient Maiden's Tower to brand-new, pseudo-classical townhouses via a selection of 19th-century homes and austere mini-mosques. Added to the mix are several caravanserais, a 15th-century palace complex and a whole range of carpet shops all gently spiced with cafes and little hotels.

Şəki

3 Snoozing amid green pillows of beautifully forested mountains, Şəki (Sheki) is Azerbaijan's loveliest town, dappled with tiled-roof old houses and topped off with a glittering little khan's palace. Seek out the unforgettable caravanserai-hotel. The whole setting is majestic with lushly wooded hills backed by high snow-dusted peaks.

Quba's Mountain Villages

4 Behind the peaceable country town of Quba, woodland glades and sheep-nibbled hillsides lead up into the foothills of the Great Caucasus. Here, separated by dramatic canyons and wild river valleys, lie a scattering of remote shepherd villages, some speaking their own unique languages. Best known of these is Xınalıq, where stacked, grey-stone houses constitute what, by some definitions, is 'Europe's highest village'. Slightly further afield, Laza has one of the most spectacular backdrops of any Caucasian mountain settlement and its rustic simplicity contrasts dramatically with the Caucasus' most glitzy ski resort, 4km away.

Lahıc

5 Lahıc is a pretty, highland village that's locally famous for its Persian-based dialect and traditional coppersmiths. It can feel just a little touristy at weekends when Bakuvians arrive to get photographed in vaguely preposterous sheepskin costumes. But stay a day or two and listen to the mellifluous mosques as mists swirl around the part-forested crags and you'll find it a delightful starting

Getting Around

Apart from minibuses to Biləsuvar, most intercity bus services start from the main bus station.

All overnight trains give you a sleeping berth. In Baku, the metro links the Old City with a series of suburban stations.

The purple London-style cabs in Baku are good value and use meters.

DINOZZAVER / SHUTTERSTOCK ©

point for hiking and meeting locals who, more than in any other village in Azerbaijan, have a smattering of English.

Qobustan

6 The Unesco-listed Qobustan Petroglyph Reserve protects thousands of stick-figure stone engravings dating back up to 12,000 years. Themes include livestock, wild animals and shamen. They were carved into what were probably caves but over time have crumbled into a craggy chaos of boulders. English-speaking staff offer guided tours to assist you spotting and deciphering the petroglyphs. Even if you have no particular interest in ancient doodles, Qobustan's eerie landscape and the hilltop views of oil-workings in the turquoise- blue Caspian are still fascinating.

Food & Drink

Bread Behind any apartment block, you're likely to see bags of stale bread hanging on trees or hooks. That's because bread is considered holy and shouldn't be binned or placed on the ground. If you drop bread on the ground, it's good form to kiss it as an apology!

Kebabs *Tikə* kebabs consist of skewered meaty chunks, often including a cube of tail fat that locals consider a delicacy.

Çoban (shepherd) salad Chopped tomato, cucumber, raw onion, dill and coriander leaves.

Fish *Sudak* (pike-perch) or *farel* (trout) are sporadically available, tasting best with tangy *alça* (sour-plum) or *narşarab* (pomegranate juice) sauces.

SAIKO3P / SHUTTERSTOCK ©

Ateşgah Fire Temple

The unique Ateşgah Fire Temple is one of Azerbaijan's most remarkable sights. It stands on the site of a natural gas vent that was sacred to Zoroastrians for centuries, though this temple was actually built by 18th-century Indian Shiva devotees. They lived in the surrounding pentagonal caravanserai and performed extreme ascetic practices such as lying on hot coals or carrying unbearably heavy chains. Such eccentric behaviour is depicted by a number of mannequins in the museum section. But the temple's centrepiece is the flaming stone hearth with four stone side flues that also spit dragon breath. At least when the caretaker bothers to turn on the gas. The original natural vent has long been exhausted, so today the flame comes courtesy of Baku's main gas supply.

CAPITAL
Nassau

POPULATION
354,000

AREA
13,880 sq km

OFFICIAL LANGUAGE
English

Elbow Cay Wall

The Bahamas

Scattered like a handful of pirate's gold across 100,000 sq miles of turquoise ocean, the islands of the Bahamas could practically patent the word 'paradise'.

Dotted like dabs of silver and green paint on an artist's palette, the Bahamas are ready-made for exploration. Just ask Christopher Columbus – he bumped against these limestone landscapes in 1492 and changed the course of history. But the adventure didn't end with the *Niña*, the *Pinta* and the *Santa Maria*. From pirates and blockade dodgers to rum smugglers, wily go-getters have converged and caroused on the country's 700 islands and 2400 cays for centuries.

So what's in it for travelers? There's sailing around the Abacos' history-filled Loyalist Cays. Partying 'til dawn at Paradise Island's over-the-top Atlantis resort. Diving the spooky blue holes of Andros. Kayaking the 365 Exuma Cays. Lounging on Eleuthera's pink-sand beaches. Pondering pirates in Nassau. There's a Bahamian island to match almost every water-and-sand-based compulsion, each framed by a backdrop of mesmerizing blue. So paint your own adventure – the palette awaits.

Top Experiences

Andros Reef

1 Just off the east coast of Andros lies the world's third-largest barrier reef, a 140-mile stretch of otherworldly coral forest, psychedelic sponge grottoes and eerie hidden caverns. The reef teems with sea life – schools of parrotfish, spotted moray eels, giant eagle rays, even the odd sea turtle or shark. The island's bizarre blue holes – water-filled vertical caves occurring both inland and off shore – attract advanced divers and National Geographic crews. On the far side of the reef, the bottom drops dizzyingly into a 6000ft abyss known as the Tongue of the Ocean. A free-fall into its depths is often described as the 'dive of a lifetime'.

Pink Sands Beach

2 The wide and stunning length of Pink Sands Beach is Harbour Island's main attraction. The powdery sand shimmers with a pink glow – a result of finely pulverized coral – that's a faint blush by day and a rosy red when fired by the dawn or sunset. It's been called the world's most beautiful beach by a slew of international glossies, and we won't argue.

When to Go

HIGH SEASON
(Dec–Apr)

SHOULDER
(May)

LOW SEASON
(Jun–Nov)

Hidden Coves, the Bahamas

3 With nearly 700 islands spread across 100,000 sq miles of ocean, the Bahamas has enough secluded beaches and tempting hidden coves for a lifetime of exploration. For ethereal rosy-hued sands, hit up Eleuthera and Harbour Island. The 365 Exuma

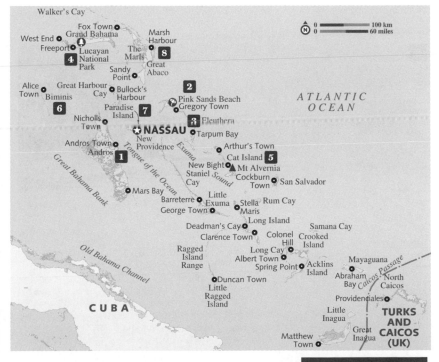

Cays are a wonderland of cerulean waters and uninhabited islets, while Grand Bahama offers luscious sands just a few minutes from bustling downtown Freeport. It's fair to say the Bahamas' ugliest beach would still be a beauty queen in most other places in the world.

Lucayan National Park

4 This 16-hectare (40-acre) park is Grand Bahama's finest treasure. In the north of the park, trails lead onto a limestone plateau riddled with caves that open to the longest underwater cave system in the world. You can walk along the boardwalks that wind through a mangrove swamp and spill out to the beautiful Gold Rock Beach, fringed by soporific dunes.

Mt Alvernia Hermitage

5 The heart of traditional Bahamian culture still beats on Cat Island, one of the islands least touched by tourism. Obeah and bush medicine are still practiced and it has several interesting historic sites, including the Mt Alvernia Hermitage. This blanched-stone church, built by the hermit Father Jerome, has a bell tower that looks like something Merlin might have conjured up in the days of King Arthur. You can enter the small chapel, tiny cloister and a guest cell. It's reached by a rock staircase hewn into the side of the hill. From the top, there's a spiritually reviving 360-degree view. Try to make it at sunrise or sunset.

Getting Around

Interisland flights offer the only quick and convenient way to travel within the Bahamas.

High-speed ferries link Nassau, Andros, the Abacos, Eleuthera and the Exumas. Mail boats and water-taxis are also options.

Driving in traffic-clogged downtown Nassau can be a pain. On the Out Islands, expect potholes.

SOPA_COLLECTION / SHUTTERSTOCK ©

Biminis

6 It's hard to deny the allure of the quiet rhythms and unspoiled views that make the Out Islands the best of the Bahamas for off-the-beaten-path exploring. And for deep-sea fishing, you can't beat the teeny Biminis, Hemingway's old haunt on the edge of the Gulf Stream. It's also tops for diving and snorkeling – check out the bizarrely-symmetrical limestone formation of Bimini Road, said to be the lost city of Atlantis. Nothing else of the 'city' remains, but it's an evocative dive site, often blessed with abundant sea life.

Aquaventure Waterpark

7 Kids and adults alike will hyperventilate at the sight of this astonishing 57-hectare (141-acre) waterpark, an Indiana Jones–style vision of the ruins of the Lost City of Atlantis. The vast park on Paradise Island is centered on a five story Mayan temple, with multiple waterslides shooting guests into a variety of grottoes and caves. If you're not an adrenaline junkie, you can meander along the artificial rapids of a mile-long river ride, swim in various pools, and kayak or snorkel in a peaceful artificial lagoon.

Hope Town, Elbow Cay

8 Postcard-pretty Hope Town welcomes your arrival on Elbow Cay, with its 120ft-high red-and-white lighthouse, set on the eastern slope of a splendid harbor. As you approach the docks, an entrancing collection of immaculate white-and-pastel cottages will come into view. Tiny gardens full of bougainvillea and flowering shrubs spill their blossoms over picket fences and walls, and pedestrians stroll along the two narrow lanes that encircle the village.

Food & Drink

Conch Roasted, cracked (fried), chopped into salads or dipped in dough and fried into fritters, this chewy sea snail is the most ubiquitous food in the Bahamas. Think calamari.

Boil fish A breakfast dish of grouper stewed with lime juice, onions and potatoes. Usually served with johnnycake, a type of flat cornbread.

Spiny Caribbean lobster The Bahamas' native lobster, often served sauteed with onions and pepper.

Souse A thick stew of lamb, sheep's head, pig's trotter or other 'leftover' meats.

Guava duff Boiled pastry filled with sweet guava paste and topped off with rum or cream sauce.

Beer Wash everything down with a cold Kalik or Sands beer.

Rum cocktails Try Goombay Smash or a Bahama Mama.

BLUEORANGE STUDIO / SHUTTERSTOCK ©

Swimming Pigs

Tiny Major Cay, in the Exumas, is a great place for a day of snorkeling and sunning. Don't forget a picnic for yourself and the friendly porcine population to enjoy! Yes, that's right, Major Cay has some famous swimming pigs that like nothing better than a splash, pat and a peanut-butter sandwich.

Al Fatih Grand Mosque, Manama

CAPITAL	Manama
POPULATION	1.4 million
AREA	760 sq km
OFFICIAL LANGUAGE	Arabic

Bahrain

This tiny island state is the smallest of all Arab countries, and is one of the most easygoing of the Gulf states.

Like an oyster, Bahrain has a rough exterior that takes some prising open, but it's always worth the effort. Manama may lack the finesse of other Gulf capitals, but that's key to its appeal. The storied location of ancient Dilmun and the epicentre of the Gulf's pearling past – Bahrain has a history to reflect on with pride. There's even a cheeky claim that it was home to the Garden of Eden.

Nowadays the country has its own Formula 1 grand prix, a growing art and foodie scene frequented by Manama's sizeable expat population, and all the hallmarks of wealth, modern Arabian style. Bahrain's confidence may have been shaken by the uncertain aftermath of the Arab Spring, but its appeal endures, and the lack of visitors means you may have it all to yourself.

Top Experiences

Bahrain National Museum

1 Open the door on ancient Dilmun at Bahrain National Museum in Manama. The museum, housed in a postmodern building with landscaping that brings the water-front up to the windows, showcases archaeological finds from ancient Dilmun. Among these are beautiful agate and carnelian beads along with earthenware burial jars.

Bahrain Fort

2 Take a 16th-century view of the sea from the battlements of Bahrain Fort. This Unesco World Heritage–listed archaeo-logical site was built by the Portuguese in the 16th century as part of a string of defences along the Gulf. The moated fort is particu-larly attractive at night.

Manama Souq

3 This market, in the streets behind Bab Al Bahrain, is the place to go for electronic goods, T-shirts, nuts, spices, sheesha bottles, mango ice cream and a plethora of other Bahraini essentials. Highlights include the Gold Souq, Kingdom of Per-fumes, the Spice Souq and World of Herbs.

Food & Drink

Makbous Rice and spices with meat in a rich sauce.

Rangena Coconut cake.

Khabees Dates in a variety of sizes, colours and states of ripeness.

Alcohol Widely available, with some excellent cocktail bars.

(Map of Bahrain)

THE GULF

Muharraq Island
Muharraq
Karbabad
Al Budaiya
Jiddah Island
Al Janabiya
MANAMA
Sar
Al Hidd
King Fahd Causeway
A'Ali
Tubli Bay
Mina Sulman
Umm al Na'san
Al Jasra
Isa Town
Sitra
Hamad
Riffa
Dar Islands
Awali
Al Zallaq
'Askar
Jebel ad-Dukhan
Ad-Dur
Al Mamtalah
Ar-Rumaythah
Rubud al Sharqiyah
Rubud al Gharbiyah
Hawar Islands
Gulf of Bahrain
Jazirat Hawar
Suwad al Janubiyah
Rabad al Gharbiyah
QATAR

0   10 km
0   5 miles

When to Go

HIGH SEASON (Oct–Mar)

SHOULDER (Apr)

LOW SEASON (May–Sep)

CAPITAL
Dhaka

POPULATION
156 million

AREA
148,460 sq km

OFFICIAL LANGUAGE
Bengali (Bangla)

Bengal tiger, Sundarbans National Park

Bangladesh

Bangladesh is south Asia's greenest jewel – a country criss-crossed with rivers, with a rich culture waiting to be explored by pioneering travellers.

Welcome to river country. Bangladesh is braided together by more than 700 rivers, producing a deliciously lush landscape with more shades of green than you ever imagined. This is one of the world's most densely populated countries, but once you're slowly floating downriver on a small wooden rowboat, it's easy to imagine you have it all to yourself. Whether you're travelling to hectic Dhaka or to see mangrove forests and tigers of the Sundarbans National Park, boats large and small will help you explore Bangladesh's riches.

Bangladesh is somewhere that tourism remains in its infancy. It's easy to get the sensation that you're breaking ground here, even if your pioneering spirit is frequently attended to by being the centre of attention. Bangla culture is famously welcoming. If you enjoy making friends, mixing with locals and travelling without bumping into too many other tourists, then this is probably just the country to explore.

Top Experiences

Tracking Tigers in the Sundarbans

1 The mangrove forests of the Sundarbans National Park are home to the legendary Royal Bengal tiger and boarding a boat in search of them is an undisputed highlight of a trip to Bangladesh. For a true adventure, and to increase your admittedly slim chances of seeing a tiger, book yourself onto a four-day boat tour from Khulna. Even if you don't see one, the birdlife and scenery are real Bangladeshi highlights.

Swamp Safaris in Ratargul

2 Hidden under the canopies of an evergreen tropical forest, the swampy bayous of Ratargul form an enchanting landscape of silent water channels that you can explore by a wooden dinghy boat.

Food & Drink

The food of Bangladesh has much in common with the food of neighbouring India, with a noticeable leaning towards fish. Rice and dhal are the mainstays, served with a variety of fish, vegetable and meat dishes, often flavoured with chilli, masala spice mixes and mustard oil. Biryani (pot-steamed rice with spices and chicken) is a popular lunch in Muslim areas; in Buddhist areas in the southeast, food has a notable Burmese influence, with the use of bamboo shoots, coconut and shrimp paste. Within the country, the divisions of Sylhet and Khulna are known to make the best food.

When to Go

HIGH SEASON
(Oct–Mar)

SHOULDER
(Apr–May)

LOW SEASON
(Jun–Sep)

Rickshaw Art

One of your first, and perhaps strongest, impressions of Bangladesh is likely to be the rainbow colours of a cycle-rickshaw. More than just a cheap and environmentally sound form of transport, the humble rickshaw is a work of art in Bangladesh, and a fleet of rickshaws is the finest art gallery any country could conjure up. Art passing by on wheels needs to be bold and eye-catching, and able to be taken in quickly. Rickshaw artists aim to decorate the vehicles with as much drama and colour as possible, and paint images that are both simple and memorable. This is street art for the ordinary man or woman, and it is unashamedly commercial.

All the dreams of the working man appear on rickshaws. Common themes include idealised rural scenes, wealthy cities crammed with cars, aeroplanes and high-rise buildings, and unsullied natural environments. Images of Bangladeshi and Indian film and pop stars are by far the most popular designs.

ATHIKHOM SAENGCHAI / SHUTTERSTOCK ©

Known to be Bangladesh's largest freshwater swampland, these outlying marshes are a perfect day trip out of Sylhet and can be accessed by a village road that cuts through some amazing tea plantations and forests.

Hiking off the Beaten Track

3 The country's eastern regions of Sylhet and Chittagong contain forested hills and small, rugged mountains. This is no Himalaya, but the landscape offers plenty of opportunity to stretch your legs with a number of worthwhile hikes on offer. There are relatively simple day hikes you can take from places such as Srimangal, visiting tea estates, the Hum Hum waterfalls, and even spotting gibbons in the forests of Lowacherra National Park.

Chittagong Hill Tracts

4 With most of the country being flat as a paddy field, the forested mountains of the Chittagong Hill Tracts dominate the landscape. It's an undoubtedly stunning region, but it also offers a cultural diversity found nowhere else in the country. Around a dozen Adivasi (tribal) groups live here, and more than half the population is Adivasi. Many have closer ties to the people of Myanmar (Burma) than to Bengalis, and visiting their villages to learn about their different ways of life makes a trip out here more than just a chance to gawp at spectacular scenery.

Old Dhaka

5 For some, the assault on the senses is too much to handle, but for others, the unrivalled chaos that is squeezed into the narrow streets of Old Dhaka is the main attraction of a stay in the capital. No matter where you've come from, or what big cities you've visited before, Old Dhaka will knock you for six with its manic streets, its crazy traffic and its nonstop noise and commotion. But the food is fabulous, the historical narrative fascinating and the sheer weight of humanity absolutely unforgettable.

Getting Around

Dirt cheap local buses and comfortable, more expensive coaches are available.

Trains are a safer option than road travel, although the network and tickets are limited.

Cycle-rickshaws or CNGs (auto-rickshaws) are the best way to get between sights in cities and between villages.

Riding the Rocket

6 Steeped in almost 100 years of history, Bangladesh's famous paddle-wheel steamer may not be the fastest thing on the waterways these days, but it gets more and more romantic each passing year. There are four remaining Rockets – all built in the early part of the 20th century – and although you can no longer ride them all the way from Dhaka to Khulna, you can still take long overnight trips on them. Book yourself a cabin to Barisal, put your feet up and watch Bangladesh float by.

Surfing in Cox's Bazar

7 Every Bangladeshi will proudly tell you that Cox's Bazar has the longest natural beach in the world. What they might not reveal is that it's home to the country's nascent surfing scene. The waves that roll in from the Bay of Bengal are suitable for beginners all the way to those looking to catch livelier breaks. At the end of a day at the beach, chill in the evening with a plate of fresh seafood that the area is celebrated for.

Touring Ancient Mosques in Bagerhat

8 With the largest concentration of medieval mosques and mausoleums in all of Bangladesh, sleepy Bagerhat is a splendid open-air museum that documents the heydays of the region's Islamic history. Peppered with graceful domed mosques, this Unesco-protected town with a friendly population is a delight to explore on foot. There's even a crocodile-infested pond here to capture your imagination!

NICOLASDECORTE / SHUTTERSTOCK ©

8

CAPITAL
Bridgetown

POPULATION
285,000

AREA
432 sq km

OFFICIAL LANGUAGE
English

Rockley Beach

Barbados

From surfing the waves to windsurfing the shallows and snorkeling the reefs, you may never dry off. But if you do, this genteel island's verdant interior might lure you for a tropical hike.

Barbados is ringed by azure water and white-sand visions that fuel the fantasies of those stuck in chilly winter climes. While it's justifiably famed for its fantastic beaches, you'll also find smashing nightlife, a Unesco World Heritage–listed capital, a beautiful interior and a proud and welcoming populace.

No matter your budget or style, you'll find a place to stay, especially on the south and west coasts. Elsewhere, however, is where you'll find what makes the island special.

Barbados has lush scenery among rolling hills. Vast plantation homes show the wealth of European settlers, while several botanical gardens exploit the perfect growing conditions. The wild east coast is a legend with surfers; those looking for action will also find windsurfing, hiking, diving and more.

Away from the glitz, Barbados is still a civilized place (with a 98% literacy rate) of classic calypso rhythms, an island-time vibe and world-famous rums.

Top Experiences

Surfing the Soup

1 Like a monster wave breaking, Barbados has crashed onto the world surf scene. Although long the haunt of surf-happy locals, only recently has Barbados' east-side surf break, called the Soup Bowl, gone supernova. Sets travel thousands of miles across the rough Atlantic and form into huge waves that challenge the world's best. From September to December, faces found in surfing magazines stare wistfully out to sea from the very mellow beach village of Bathsheba. A slight calming from January to May brings out the hopefuls.

Rockley Beach

2 The largest beach in the Bridgetown area, Rockley is a picture-perfect crescent of sand. Backed by shade trees, there's moderate surf. The new boardwalk allows you to walk west for more than 3km to Hastings. There are plenty of shops, banks and ATMs along the main road, Hwy 7.

St Nicholas Abbey

3 St Nicholas Abbey is a Jacobean-style mansion that is one of the oldest plantation houses in the Caribbean and a must-see stop on any island itinerary. The grounds include the Great House, various gardens and a very traditional rum distillery.

Oistins Fish Fry

4 Oistins is the place to be come the weekend when the Oistins Fish Fry draws big crowds. This legendary spot for fresh-fish meals attracts roughly 60% locals, 40%

When to Go

 HIGH SEASON (Dec–Apr)

 SHOULDER (May & Nov)

 LOW SEASON (Jun–Oct)

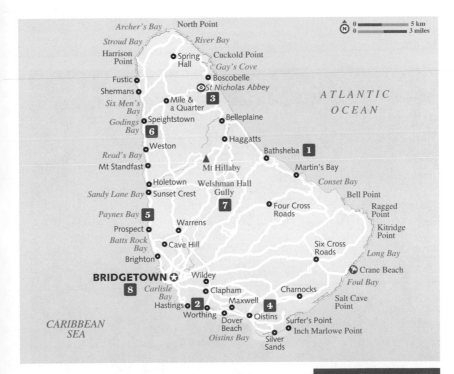

tourists, and there's a joyous electricity in the air on Friday night. It's held in a complex of low-rise modern buildings right on the sand next to the fish market. It features soca, reggae, pop and country music, vendors selling barbecued fish and plenty of rum drinking.

Paynes Bay

5 Fringed by a fine stretch of sand, gently curving Paynes Bay is endlessly popular and its calm waters make it one of the west coast's best spots for swimming and snorkeling (if you're patient enough there's a very good chance of seeing sea turtles). The village itself is little more than a collection of high-end hotels and luxury homes, along with a couple of places to eat and a fish market at the southern end.

Speightstown

6 Easily the most evocative small town on Barbados, Speightstown combines old colonial charms with a vibe that has more rough edges than the endlessly upscale precincts to the south. The settlement was once dubbed 'Little Bristol' as, thanks to its maritime connection to that English town, many of the original settlers originated from there, and it still has a classic nautical vibe.

Welchman Hall Gully

7 Once part of a large estate that covered the area, this National Trust property contains some rare tracts of original Barbados tropical rainforest, although there are also several introduced species present. A trail leads from the car park through a

Getting Around

It's possible to get to virtually any place on the island by public bus. Most buses transit through Bridgetown.

Barbados offers good cycling for the adventurous. It's hilly and roads are narrow, but not usually steep.

Water taxis are not common in Barbados, although there are a couple on the west coast.

narrow canyon lined with diverse tree species and rocks covered in moss, past some wonderful shallow caves draped in vines.

Bridgetown

8 Wandering bustling Bridgetown, with its many sights and old colonial buildings, can easily occupy a day. Nidhe Israel Museum, in a restored 1750 Jewish community center, and the neo-Gothic-style Parliament Buildings are highlights. The entire downtown area and south to the Garrison was named a Unesco World Heritage site in 2012 for its historical significance.

Food & Drink

Bananas Local varieties are green even when ripe (look for them in markets).

Barbadian rum Considered some of the finest in the Caribbean, with Mount Gay being the best-known label.

Conkies A mixture of cornmeal, coconut, pumpkin, sweet potato, raisins and spices, steamed in a plantain leaf.

Cou-cou A creamy cornmeal-and-okra mash.

Cutters Meat or fish sandwiches in a salt-bread roll.

Jug-jug A mixture of cornmeal, green peas and salted meat.

STYVE REINECK / SHUTTERSTOCK ©

Cricket

The national sport, if not national obsession, is cricket. Per capita, Bajans boast more world-class cricket players than any other nation. One of the world's top all-rounders, Bajan native Sir Garfield Sobers, was knighted by Queen Elizabeth II during her 1975 visit to Barbados, while another cricket hero, Sir Frank Worrell, appears on the B$5 bill. In Barbados you can catch an international Test match, a heated local First Division match, or even just a friendly game on the beach or grassy field.

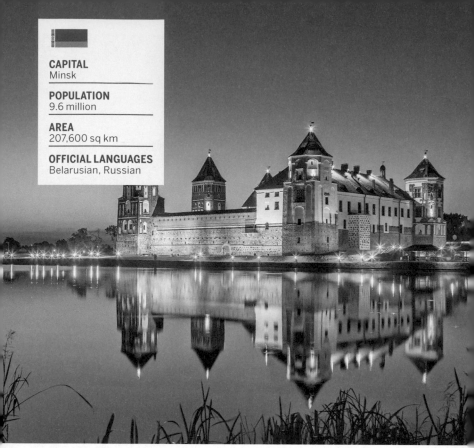

CAPITAL
Minsk

POPULATION
9.6 million

AREA
207,600 sq km

OFFICIAL LANGUAGES
Belarusian, Russian

Mir Castle, Mir

Belarus

Belarus allows the chance to visit a Europe with minimal advertising, no litter or graffiti and a generous people who relish life's simple pleasures.

Eastern Europe's outcast, Belarus lies at the edge of the region and seems determined to avoid integration with the rest of the continent at all costs. Taking its lead from the Soviet Union rather than the European Union, this little-visited dictatorship may seem like a strange choice for travellers, but its isolation lies at the heart of its appeal.

Outside the monumental Stalinist capital of Minsk, Belarus offers a simple yet pleasing landscape of cornflower fields, thick forests and picturesque little villages. The country also has two excellent national parks and is home to Europe's largest mammal, the *zubr* (European bison).

While travellers will always be the subject of curiosity, they'll also be on the receiving end of warm hospitality and a genuine welcome.

Top Experiences

Brest

1 A prosperous and cosmopolitan border town, Brest looks far more to the neighbouring EU than to Minsk. The city's main sight is the Brest Fortress, a moving WWII memorial where Soviet troops held out longer than expected against the Nazi onslaught in the early days of Operation Barbarossa. There are also several good museums, and Belavezhskaya Pushcha National Park is nearby.

Minsk

2 Minsk (Мінск) will almost certainly surprise you. Fashionable cafes, impressive restaurants and crowded nightclubs vie for your attention, while sushi bars and art galleries have taken up residence in a city centre once totally remodelled to the tastes of Stalin. Despite the strong police presence, Minsk is a thoroughly pleasant place.

Mir Castle

3 Rising majestically above the town of Mir, this 16th-century castle overlooks a postcard-perfect lake and resembles something out of Disney. A recent renovation has the place looking lovely, with gorgeous grounds, impressive interiors and a display on the life and times of the Radziwills.

When to Go

 HIGH SEASON
(Jun–Aug)

 SHOULDER
(Apr–May, Sep & Oct)

 LOW SEASON
(Nov–Mar)

Food & Drink

Belavezhskaya A bitter herbal alcoholic drink.

Draniki Potato pancakes, usually served with sour cream.

Kletsky Dumplings stuffed with mushrooms, cheese or potato.

Kvas A mildly alcoholic drink made from black or rye bread.

CAPITAL
Brussels

POPULATION
11.4 million

AREA
30,528 sq km

OFFICIAL LANGUAGES
Dutch, French, German

Bruges canal

Belgium

Belgium's exquisite medieval towns are home to a bounty of Unesco sites, but happening big cities, caves, kayaking, industrial sites and sandy North Sea beaches are just some of the other attractions.

Smack-bang in the middle of Western Europe, this compact multilingual country effortlessly blends the historic with the new; from countless castles, medieval belfries and war memorials to innovative art museums and hip cafes. The historic 'art' cities of Dutch-speaking Flanders seduce visitors with medieval belfries, magical market squares and step-gabled houses overlooking pretty urban canals, all interspersed with superb museums and galleries. Head south and much of French-speaking Wallonia is profoundly rural: impressive caves, castles and bucolic valleys to explore and lots of outdoor fun to be had in the wooded hills.

And with some of the best comfort food on offer, you'll need to pack an empty stomach for gorging on waffles, chocolate, *frites* and piles of steaming mussels, all washed down with the country's famous frothy beer.

Top Experiences

Bruges

1 Laced with canals and full of evocative step-gabled houses, Bruges is the ultimate picture-postcard tourist destination. Of course, that's all too well known and the city is often overrun, but come midweek in February and you may have it largely to yourself. Year-round you can escape the crowds and carriage rides by dipping into some of Bruges' majestic art collections. The Groeningemuseum is hard to beat, offering a potted history of Belgian art, with an outstanding selection of works by the Flemish Primitives.

Brussels' Grand Place

2 Brussels' heart beats in the Grand Place – the most theatrically beautiful medieval square in Europe. It is ringed by gold-trimmed, gabled guildhouses and flanked by the 15th-century Gothic town hall. The cobblestones were laid in the 12th century, when the square was used as a marketplace; the names of the surrounding lanes evoke herbs, cheese and poultry. And indeed the Grand Place still hosts a flower market, as well as Christmas stalls, concerts and – every two years – a dazzlingly colourful 'carpet' of flower petals.

When to Go

 HIGH SEASON (Jul–Aug)

 SHOULDER (May–Jun & Sep)

 LOW SEASON (Oct–Mar)

Antwerp Art & Fashion

3 Fashion-forward Antwerp has it all. Its skyline is still dominated by one of the lowlands' most magnificent stone steeples and its medieval house-museums are stuffed with works by its most famous 17th-century resident, Pieter Paul Rubens. That

said, it's also a dynamic modern city with state-of-the-art museums, vibrant nightlife and an edgy design scene: it's hard to think of anywhere else in the world with so many big-name boutiques, designer consignment shops and brocante dealers packed into a compact city centre.

Flanders Fields

Flanders' fields, once known for potato and hop production, became synonymous with death in the wake of the trench warfare of WWI. The area around Ypres remains dotted with manicured graveyards where white memorial crosses movingly bear silent witness in seemingly endless rows. Museums evoke the context and conditions for everyday soldiers, and the central squares of Diksmuide and Ypres, both rebuilt, are wonders in themselves.

Carnival Capers in Binche

If your neighbours' idea of a good time is to dress up in barrel costumes jingling with little bells, don spooky masks and ostrich-feather hats and then go throwing oranges at passers-by, you might wonder about their sanity. Then again you might just be living in Binche. That's the town whose unique Mardi Gras carnival has long been so indulgent it gave the English language the term 'binge'. Belgium's carnival season stretches way beyond Shrove Tuesday with other unique twists, especially in Stavelot and Aalst.

Getting Around

Buses are useful for accessing rural destinations or places where the train station is out of town.

A car is an easy option for travel at your own pace, though traffic jams on motorways can be frustrating.

The train network is comprehensive with reasonable prices.

RUDY MAREEL / SHUTTERSTOCK ©

3

Castles

6 From French-style *châteaux* to Crusader-era ruins, Belgium is overloaded with spectacular castles. Antwerp and Ghent both retain medieval ones right in their city centres. Ghent's quintessential 12th-century stone castle comes complete with moat, turrets and arrow slits. And Namur, like Huy and Dinant, is dominated by a massive fortress citadel that retained military importance well into the 20th century.

Food & Drink

Chocolate The essential Belgian creations are pralines and creamy *manons*, filled bite-size chocolates.

Gegratineerde witloof/chicons au gratin Endive, commonly wrapped in ham and smothered in cheesy white sauce.

Hot goat (chèvre chaud) Salad topped with warm goats' cheese.

Moules-frites Mussels and chips.

Paling in 't groen/anguilles-au-vert Eel in a bright-green sorrel or spinach sauce.

Stoemp Boiled potatoes mashed together with vegetables and served as a side dish or as a basic meal topped with sausage or ham.

Waffle (wafel/gaufre) Traditionally eaten hot, lightly dusted with icing sugar, but often heaped with cream, fruit or chocolate sauce for tourists. The **gaufre de Liège** has rounder edges and a breadier dough made with a hint of cinnamon.

Waterzooi Cream-based stew made with chicken or fish and vegetables.

Chocolate in Brussels

7 In 1857 Swiss confectioner Jean Neuhaus opened a 'medicinal sweet shop' in Brussels' glorious Galeries St-Hubert – it's still there. But it was in 1912 that Neuhaus' son was credited with creating that most Belgian of morsels, the praline, by filling a chocolate shell with flavoured centres. Belgian chocolates remain world beaters due to the local insistence on 100% cocoa butter, and every town has its selection of chocolatier shops, hushed, hallowed temples where glove-handed assistants patiently load up ballotin boxes with your individual selection.

DANYL / SHUTTERSTOCK©

Belgian Beer

No other country has a brewing tradition as richly diverse as that of Belgium, with beers ranging from pleasant pale lagers to wild, wine-like Flemish reds and lambics. But it's the 'angels and demons' that draw the connoisseurs: these big bold brews often derive from monastery recipes and conjure the diabolical with names like Forbidden Fruit, Judas and Duvel (devil). The most famous of all, six Trappist beers, are still brewed in active abbeys. With alcohol levels coming in at between 7% and 11% alcohol by volume, such brews are designed to be sipped slowly and savoured, certainly not chugged by the pint. For that, you have the standard Belgian lagers, notably Jupiler, Maes and Stella Artois – what you'll get at any *café* (pub/bar) if you just ask for a *pintje/bière* – which perhaps can't rival their German or Czech counterparts, but are deliciously drinkable none the less.

Spotted eagle ray; Glovers Reef

CAPITAL Belmopan	
POPULATION 370,300	
AREA 22,965 sq km	
OFFICIAL LANGUAGE English	

Belize

With one foot in the Central American jungles and the other in the Caribbean Sea, Belize may be small but it's packed with excitement and culture.

Whether you're scuba diving the Blue Hole, zip-lining through the jungle canopy, rappelling down waterfalls or crawling through ancient cave systems, Belize is a genuine adventure.

Belize Barrier Reef is the second largest in the world, and with more than 100 types of coral and some 500 species of tropical fish, it's pure paradise for scuba divers and snorkelers. Inland, a vast (by Belizean standards) network of national parks and wildlife sanctuaries offers a safe haven for wildlife.

Belize is also home to one of the world's most mysterious civilizations – the ancient Maya. Explore excavated tombs and examine intricate hieroglyphs, or descend deep into natural caves to see where the Maya kings performed rituals and made sacrifices to the gods of their underworld. You can appreciate the culture today by staying in village guesthouses and by learning the art of chocolate-making.

Top Experiences

Kayaking Glover's Reef Atoll

1 Lying like a string of white-sand pearls, Glover's Reef Atoll consists of half a dozen small islands surrounded by blue sea as far as the eye can see.

Its unique position, atop a submerged mountain ridge on the edge of the continental shelf, makes it an ideal place for sea kayaking, both between the islands and around the shallow central lagoon. Get a kayak with a clear bottom and you're likely to see spotted eagle rays, southern stingrays, turtles and countless tropical fish swimming beneath as you paddle.

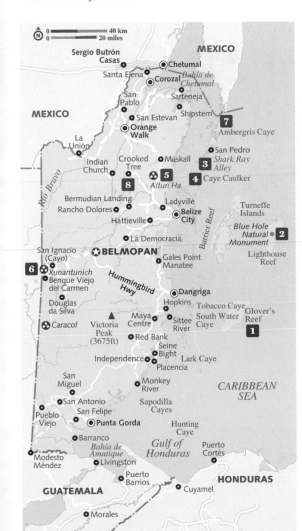

Food & Drink

Alabundiga Garifuna dish of grated green bananas, coconut cream, spices, boiled potato and peppers; served with fried fish fillet (often snapper) and rice.

Rice and beans Stew of coconut milk and red beans cooked together with rice.

Beans and rice Variation on rice and beans where beans in a soupy stew are served separately in a bowl.

Chirmole Maya chicken stew with a chili-chocolate sauce.

Cowfoot soup A glutinous soup featuring an actual cow's foot (or heel).

Gibnut Small native rodent that can occasionally be found as a delicacy on restaurant menus.

Johnnycake Savory biscuit served straight from the oven with butter; usually for breakfast.

When to Go

 HIGH SEASON (Dec–Apr)

 SHOULDER (May & Nov)

 LOW SEASON (Jun–Oct)

The Monkey That Roared

Listen! Up in the sky! It's a jet plane! It's a Harley Davidson! It's a Led Zeppelin! No, it's a howler monkey.

Just how loud is the vociferous simian? The howl of the howler monkey peaks at around 128 decibels, which is louder than a lion's roar, an elephant's trumpet or even a chainsaw. This makes the howler the loudest of all land animals. A hollowed-out bone in the throat gives the 20lb primate the anatomical ability to crank up the volume.

There is one species of howler monkey in Belize – the Yucatan Black Howler, which happens to be the largest of its kind. Even if you do not see a howler monkey on your trip to Belize, you will likely hear one. Its haunting cry carries as far as 5 miles.

CICLOCO / SHUTTERSTOCK ©

Diving the Blue Hole

2 The sheer walls of the Blue Hole Natural Monument drop more than 400ft into the blue ocean. Although it is half filled with silt and natural debris, the depth still creates a perfect circle of startling azure that is visible from above. The wall of the Blue Hole is decorated with a dense forest of stalactites and stalagmites from times past.

A school of reef sharks – as well as plenty of invertebrates and sponges – keeps divers company as they descend into the mysterious ocean depths.

Snorkelling Shark Ray Alley

3 Local fisherfolk used to come to Shark Ray Alley to clean their catch, and their discards would attract hungry nurse sharks and southern stingrays. As a result these predators have long become accustomed to boats, which now bring snorkelers rather than fishers. Shark Ray Alley is the top snorkeling destination in Hol Chan Marine Reserve, a protected part of the Belize Barrier Reef that harbors an amazing diversity of colorful coral and other marine life.

Caye Caulker

4 A brisk breeze is almost always blowing (especially between January and June), creating optimal conditions to cruise across the water on sailboat, windsurfer or kiteboard. The world's second-largest barrier reef is just a few miles offshore, beckoning snorkellers and divers to frolic with the fish. The mangroves teem with life, inviting exploration by kayak. All these adventures await, yet the number-one activity on Caye Caulker is still swinging in a hammock, reading a book and sipping a freshly squeezed fruit juice. Paradise.

Altun Ha

5 You've drunk the beer, now visit the ruins that inspired the Belikin beer-bottle label. The most accessible of Belize's ancient ruins, Altun Ha displays 10 different structures dating from the 6th and 7th centuries, and it was also the site of some of the richest archaeological excavations in Belize, although the artifacts have long since been removed. You'll get your exercise climbing to the tops of the temples to take in the panorama of the surrounding jungle.

Getting Around

There are flights between all major towns. Planes are small, flights are short and fairly affordable.

Most travel is done by bus. All towns from Corozal to Punta Gorda are serviced by private buses; you can usually flag down a bus on the highway.

Caye Caulker and Ambergris are serviced by ferries from Belize City, and there's a boat from Corozal to Ambergris with a possible Sarteneja stop.

Xunantunich

6 Xunantunich isn't Belize's biggest archaeological site, but it's still one of the most impressive, especially for its remarkable hieroglyphics. After taking a hand-cranked ferry across the Mopan River, you'll walk through bird- and butterfly-filled jungle, until you reach a complex of temples and plazas that dates back to the early Classic Maya Period. Once there, you can explore a number of structures and plazas, and even climb to the top of 130ft-high El Castillo for a spectacular 360-degree view.

Ambergris Caye

7 Also known as La Isla Bonita, Ambergris Caye is the ultimate tropical paradise destination (and that's what Madonna thought, too). Spend your days snorkeling the reef, kayaking the lagoon or windsurfing the straits; pamper yourself at a day spa or challenge yourself at a yoga class; ride a bike up the beach or take a nap on your dock. After the sun sets, spend your evenings enjoying the country's most delectable dining and most happening nightlife.

Crooked Tree Wildlife Sanctuary

8 Belize is for the birds. Nowhere is that statement truer than at Crooked Tree, a fishing and farming village centered on a picturesque lagoon. The wetlands attract hundreds of bird species (276 to be exact), including dozens of migrants who stop on their way north or south. Birding is best during the drier months (February to May), when the lagoon dries up and the birds congregate around the remaining puddles. Expert guides will lead you by boat or on foot to spot and identify your feathered friends.

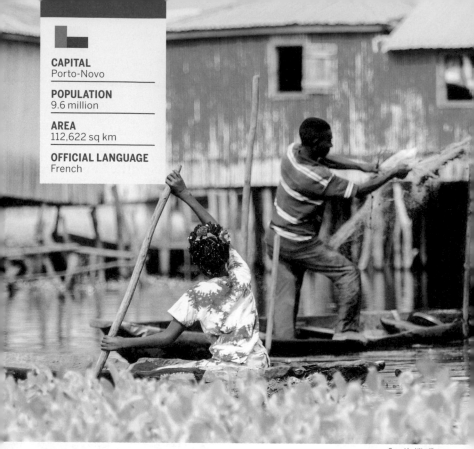

CAPITAL
Porto-Novo

POPULATION
9.6 million

AREA
112,622 sq km

OFFICIAL LANGUAGE
French

Ganvié stilt village

Benin

The birthplace of voodoo and a pivotal platform of the slave trade for nearly three centuries, Benin is steeped in a rich and complex history still very much in evidence across the country.

For culture buffs, Benin will impress with its Afro-Brazilian heritage, voodoo traditions, stilt villages and fascinating Somba culture. The palm-fringed coastline will seduce beach hounds, while the Parc National de la Pendjari is a magnet for wildlife-lovers.

A visit to this small, club-shaped nation could therefore not be complete without exploring the Afro-Brazilian heritage of Ouidah, Abomey and Porto Novo, learning about spirits and fetishes.

But Benin will also wow visitors with its natural beauty, from the beach idyll of the Atlantic coast to the rugged scenery of the north. The Parc National de la Pendjari is one of the best wildlife parks in West Africa. Lions, cheetahs, leopards, elephants and hundreds of other species thrive here.

Top Experiences

Parc National de la Pendjari

1 Set amid the majestic landscape of the Atakora's rugged cliffs and wooded savannah, this 2750-sq-km park is home to the big cats, elephants, baboons, hippos, myriad birds and countless antelopes. The best viewing time is near the end of the dry season, when the animals congregate at waterholes.

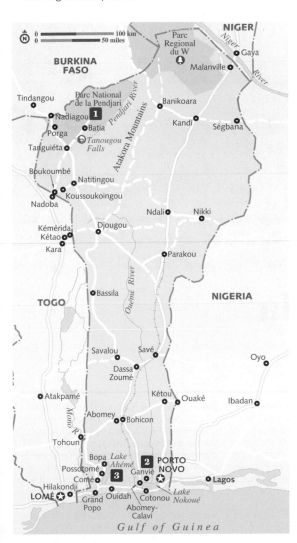

Food & Drink

Fish A highlight. Usually barracuda, dorado or grouper.

La Béninoise The local beer.

Ndole Stew with leaves and nuts.

Pâte Starch staple, often made from millet, corn, plantains, manioc or yams.

Ganvié

2 Ganvié is a fascinating stilt village, where 30,000 Tofinu people live in bamboo huts several kilometres out on Lake Nokoué. Created for the Tofinu people to stay safe from slave hunters, it has become part of their culture and way of life.

Lake Ahémé

3 The fertile shores of Lake Ahémé are a wonderful place to spend a few days, particularly around Possotomé, the area's biggest village. There's good swimming in the lake and various excursions are possible in the area. Learn traditional fishing techniques, meet craftspeople at work or go on a two-hour botanic journey to hear about local plants and their medicinal properties.

Pastel-coloured St George's

Bermuda

Playground of the rich and famous, this little British Overseas Territory in the North Atlantic shines as an island holiday destination with a great mix of luxury life and colonial cool.

Bathed in the balmy turquoise waters of the Sargasso Sea, the string of islands that is Bermuda is ringed by treacherous reefs that make it one of the world's top diving destinations.

With its pastel-colored houses and stately mansions drowning in lush greenery and fragrant frangipani and bougainvillea, their step-like white roofs poised to catch rainwater, Bermuda feels like a genteel chunk of rural England lifted into warmer climes.

But it's much more diverse than that, with British, North American, African, Portuguese and West Indian influences adding to the unique cultural melange.

In spite of its tiny size – just 20 miles by 2 miles – Bermuda's museums and art galleries add touches of urban sophistication and its many forts attract history buffs. Its varied topography makes it ideal for all manner of water sports, hiking, golfing, or just lazing on a picture-perfect pink-sand beach.

Top Experiences

St George's

1 The landing point of the island's first settlers, St George's (the town and the parish) is the historical heart of Bermuda. The 400-year-old town, the oldest permanent English settlement in the New World, was the capital of the island for two hundred years before the action moved to Hamilton. Its narrow grid of streets, lined with centuries-old buildings, was granted Unesco World Heritage Site status due to its historical significance, and is a joy to explore on foot. The parish comprises several islands joined by bridges.

Cooper's Island Nature Reserve

2 Bermudians were granted access to this 77-acre nature reserve made up of woodland, unspoiled beaches, salt marsh and rocky shores when the US Navy pulled out in 1995. Nature trails run through a mixed woodland of remaining Bermuda cedars and olivewoods, mixed with introduced growths of Brazilian pepper and allspice. The seven beaches are tranquil and good for snorkeling, and the salt marsh is a vital habitat for herons, kingfishers and giant land crabs.

When to Go

HIGH SEASON
(May–Oct)

SHOULDER
(Mar, Apr & Nov)

LOW SEASON
(Dec–Feb)

Royal Naval Dockyard

3 When the British were no longer able to use ports in their former American colonies, they chose this site as their 'Gibraltar of the West'. In addition to the superb Bermuda Maritime Museum, Bermuda's largest fortifications comprise a prison, a Victorian victualling yard,

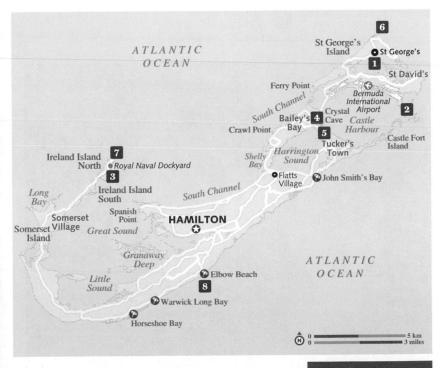

ATLANTIC OCEAN

St George's Island
● St George's
1
6

St David's

Ferry Point
South Channel
Crawl Point
Bailey's **4** Bay
Crystal Cave
Bermuda International Airport
2
Castle Harbour
Castle Fort Island

5
Tucker's Town

Ireland Island North ● Royal Naval Dockyard
7
3

Ireland Island South
Spanish Point
Somerset Village
Somerset Island
Long Bay

South Channel
Shelly Bay
Harrington Sound
● Flatts Village
John Smith's Bay

HAMILTON ✪
Great Sound

Granaway Deep

Little Sound

● Elbow Beach
8

✪ Warwick Long Bay

✪ Horseshoe Bay

ATLANTIC OCEAN

Ⓝ 0 / 0 ⎯ 5 km / 3 miles

barracks-turned-mall, several restaurants, craft markets, artificial beach and snorkel park, and the island's most comprehensive water-sports center.

Crystal Cave & Fantasy Cave

4 The most spectacular of Bermuda's numerous cave systems, Crystal Cave has thousands of crystal-like stalactites hanging above a greenish-blue pond. Despite its enormous size, this huge subterranean cavern wasn't even discovered until 1907 when two boys dropped a rope through a hole in the ground, shimmied down and found themselves inside. Today a series of 82 steps leads 120ft below the surface to a crystal-clear pond that fills the cave floor and state-of-the-art lighting subtly illuminates the delicate straw stalactites and frozen stone waterfalls.

Blue Hole Park & Walsingham Nature Reserve

5 Tom Moore's Jungle, part of this nature reserve that comprises coastal mangroves, native palmetto and cedar woods, caves and swimming grottos, is found behind Tom Moore's Tavern. A path leads to a cave with a deep natural swimming pool inside – a great place to cool down. From here, a woodland trail leads to Blue Hole Park, a former dolphin-show lagoon framed by mangroves; most days, you'll find people jumping off the 12ft to 15ft cliffs there.

Fort St Catherine

6 The most impressive of Bermuda's 91 forts, Fort St Catherine was

Getting Around

Bicycle rental is available, though the terrain is hilly in parts.

Public ferries, which operate daily in the Great Sound and Hamilton Harbour, offer a scenic alternative to the bus.

Bermuda has a good island-wide public bus system that you can use to reach most sights and beaches.

4

originally built on this rocky promontory in 1614 and expanded five times since. A drawbridge leads inside into an air-conditioned museum, featuring dioramas of the site through the centuries and replica Crown Jewels. Head down into the subterranean tunnels to see the gunpowder storage room, shell lift, and armaments room.

National Museum of Bermuda

7 If you only see one museum in Bermuda, make it this one. Taking up the entirety of the Dockyard's 19th-century fortifications, it's divided into two main parts. The vaulted Queen's Exhibition Hall is an atmospheric gallery that showcases the treasures found on 18 key shipwrecks. On the upper grounds, the world's first cast-iron building – the Commissioner's House – features displays on all aspects of Bermuda's history, from slavery to Bermudian participation in WWII.

Food & Drink

Bermudian cuisine is an eclectic mix of dishes with British, Portuguese, African and West Indian influences, with shepherd's pie and fish and chips sitting alongside fried fish sandwiches, Bermudian fish chowder, johnnycakes, jerk chicken, and macaroni and cheese. A traditional Sunday brunch dish is codfish and potatoes. Fresh fish – tuna, wahoo, swordfish – is abundant. Bermuda's typical drinking venues are British-style pubs, though in the city of Hamilton you'll also find wine and cocktail bars.

Elbow Beach

8 Imagine a vast expanse of pristine white sand, cerulean waters and swaying palm trees. Elbow Beach is it, and it's one of Bermuda's loveliest beaches, with nary a clump of seaweed in sight. The beach is flanked by exclusive resorts, but most of it is public territory. Sometimes the waves get choppy and kitesurfers take over.

SOPA COLLECTION / SHUTTERSTOCK ©

Bermuda's Pink-Sand Beaches

Bermuda's fabulous pink-tinged sand is made up of particles of coral, marine invertebrates and various shells, but it takes its distinctive light-pink hue from the bodies of one particular sea creature, a member of the order *foraminifera*. A marine protozoan abundant on Bermudian reefs, *Foraminifers* have hard, tiny shells that wash up on shore after the animal within the shell dies. These pink shell fragments provide the dominant color in what would otherwise be a less-distinctive confetti of bleached white coral and ivory-colored calcium carbonate shells.

CAPITAL
Thimphu

POPULATION
750,000

AREA
38,394 sq km

OFFICIAL LANGUAGE
Dzongkha

Trongsa Dzong, Trongsa

Bhutan

Bhutan is no ordinary place. It is the last great Himalayan kingdom, shrouded in mystery and magic, where a traditional Buddhist culture carefully embraces global developments.

Bhutan could be called the last Shangri La. It has an amazing picture-book landscape, where snow-capped Himalayan peaks rise above shadowy gorges cloaked in primeval forests, and majestic fortress-like *dzongs* and monasteries take prime position.

The Bhutanese pride themselves on a sustainable approach to tourism, and environmental protection goes hand in hand with cultural preservation. For the visitor, this translates into lovely forest hikes and superb birding across a chain of national parks. It's also a deeply Buddhist land, where monks check their smartphones after performing a divination, and where giant protective penises are painted beside the entrance to many houses. Yet Bhutan is not a museum. You will find the Bhutanese well educated, fun loving and well informed about the world around them. It's this blending of the ancient and modern that makes Bhutan endlessly fascinating.

Top Experiences

Taktshang Goemba

1 Bhutan's most famous monastery, Taktshang Goemba is one of its most venerated religious sites. Legend says that Guru Rinpoche flew to this site on the back of a tigress to subdue a local demon; afterwards he meditated here for three months. This beautiful building clings to the sheer cliffs soaring above a whispering pine forest. The steep walk to the monastery is well worthwhile, providing tantalising glimpses of the monastery, views of the Paro valley and splashes of red-blossom rhododendrons.

Thimphu Centenary Farmer's Market

2 Thimphu's bustling weekend Centenary Farmer's Market is the biggest and brightest in the country. The food section is an olfactory overload with dried fish competing with soft cheese, betel nut and dried chilli to assault your nostrils. Curly nakey (fern fronds) and red rice are just some of the exotic offerings. Cross the fast-flowing Wang Chhu on the traditional cantilever footbridge to get to the handicraft and textile stalls where you can barter for 'antiques', rolls of prayer flags or even a human thigh-bone trumpet.

Trongsa Dzong & the Tower of Trongsa Museum

3 Sprawling down a ridge towards an ominous gorge, Trongsa Dzong sits in a central position in Bhutan's geography and in its recent history. Both the first and second kings ruled the country from this strategic position. Inside is

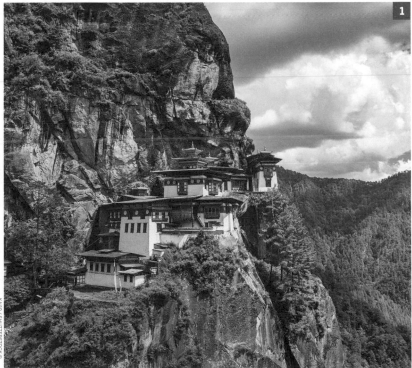

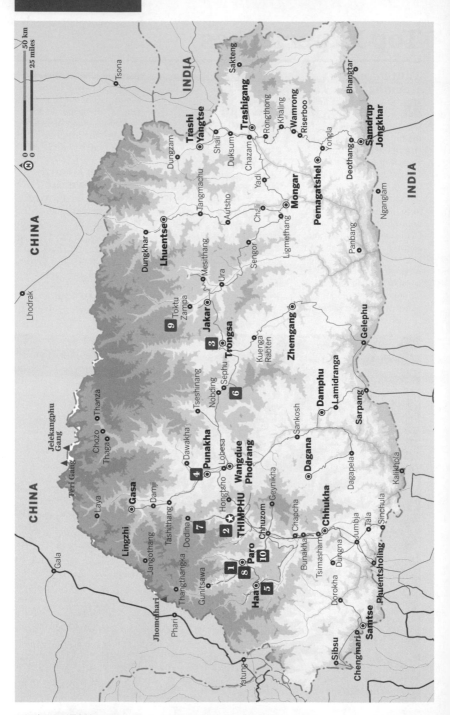

a labyrinth of many levels, narrow corridors and courtyards. Overlooking the *dzong* (Buddhist monastery

Best in Print

The Raven Crown (Michael Aris) Definitive history of Bhutan's monarchy, lavishly illustrated with rare photographs.

The Hero with a Thousand Eyes (Karma Ura) Historical novel based on the life of Shingkhar Lam, a retainer who served in the court of the second, third and fourth kings of Bhutan.

The Circle of Karma (Kunzang Choden) Story of a young woman's journey across Bhutan to find her destiny, revealing the rich detail of everyday life and ritual.

Bhutan: The Land of Serenity (Matthieu Ricard) Superb coffee-table book that sensitively and strikingly reveals Bhutan at its most picturesque.

Food & Drink

Bang chhang A warm beer-like drink made from wheat.

Chilli The Bhutanese love chillies; some dishes consist entirely of chillies, accompanied by chilli-infused condiments.

Chugo Rock-hard, dried yak cheese.

Ema datse Bhutan's national dish; large green (sometimes red) hot chillies, prepared as a vegetable in a cheese sauce.

Nakey Fern fronds.

Momos Small steamed dumplings that may be filled with meat or cheese.

Sud-ja Tibetan-style tea with salt and butter.

and fortress), the Tower of Trongsa Museum is housed in the two-winged watchtower. This excellent museum is dedicated to the history of the *dzong* and the royal Wangchuck dynasty and has exhibits ranging from personal effects of the royals to Buddhist statues.

Punakha Dzong

4 Superbly situated where two rivers converge, Punakha Dzong is the most dramatic and beautiful example of Bhutanese architecture in the country. Visit in spring to see the famous jacaranda trees splash lilac flowers down the whitewashed walls and red-robed monks wandering on a sea of purple petals. The fortress-thick walls are intimidating and are silent one moment, then warmed with the echoes of giggles in another as a horde of young monks head off for a meal.

Haa Valley

5 Just a few hours' drive from Paro, over Bhutan's highest motorable road, this little-visited valley is home to magical cliffside hermitages, ancient temples and charming villages. Accommodation is focused around boutique

When to Go

HIGH SEASON
(Mar–May & Sep–Nov)
Himalayan views are best in October, while rhododendron blooms peak in March and April.

SHOULDER
(Dec–Feb)
Fewer tourists. The weather is still pleasant, though it can be cold in December and January.

LOW SEASON
(Jun–Aug)
Monsoon rains and leeches put an end to most treks.

farmhouses and homestays rather than big group resorts, giving it a more intimate feel. The valley rim is a great place to do some hiking or trekking, either along the Cheli La ridge or up to the Saga La, with its fine views of snow-capped Jhomolhari.

Spirit Catchers

Sometimes in Bhutan you will come across a strange construction of twigs, straw and rainbow-coloured thread woven into a spider-web shape. You may see one near a building or by a roadside, with flower and food offerings. This is a *dzoe* (also known as a *tendo*), a sort of spirit catcher used to exorcise something evil that has been pestering a household. The malevolent spirits are drawn to the *dzoe*. After prayers the *dzoe* is cast away, often on a trail or road, to send away the evil spirits it has trapped.

Getting Around

On tours, most visitors will be moved around by a late-model minibus, 4WD or car.

Some travellers bring their mountain bikes to Bhutan, and several companies can help arrange mountain-biking tours.

Public buses are crowded and rattly, and Bhutan's winding roads make them doubly uncomfortable.

Driving a car in Bhutan is a harrowing experience, with narrow roads and hairpin bends.

Phobjikha Valley

6 Phobjikha is a bowl-shaped glacial valley on the western slopes of the Black Mountains, bordering the Jigme Singye Wangchuck National Park. Because of the large flock of black-necked cranes that winters here, it is one of the most important wildlife preserves in the country. In addition to the cranes there are also muntjacs (barking deer), wild boars, sambars, serows, Himalayan black bears, leopards and red foxes in the surrounding hills. The Nakey Chhu drains the marshy valley, eventually flowing into the lower reaches of the Punak Tsang Chhu. Some people refer to this entire region as Gangte (or Gangtey), after the goemba that sits on a ridge above the valley. Bhutan has the largest proportion of land designated as protected areas in the world, with 65% of its territory covered in forest and mountains, protecting richly varied habitats and an amazing diversity of plants and creatures.

Thimphu Valley

7 Thimphu delights with its museums and cultural attractions, including the Trashi Chhoe Dzong, which celebrates one of the country's most popular tsechus (religious festivals) in autumn. The relatively broad valley surrounding Bhutan's capital is dotted with interesting out-of-town sights. There are several good hikes not far from Thimphu, taking in a handful of perfectly positioned monasteries with excellent views down the valley. And just west of Thimphu's centre, Motithang Takin Preserve is your best bet for spotting Bhutan's extraordinary national animal.

Kyichu Lhakhang

8 Kyichu Lhakhang is one of Bhutan's oldest, most venerated and most beautiful temples and it sits just a short distance from the gateway town of Paro. The oldest temple in this twin-temple complex is believed to have been built in AD 659 by King Songtsen Gampo of Tibet. The outside grounds hum with prayers and spinning prayer wheels, while inside a treasured 7th-century statue of Jowo Sakyamuni sits in the sanctuary. Easy day walks begin in the vicinity of this serene lhakhang (temple).

Bumthang

9 The valleys comprising Bumthang make up the cultural heartland of Bhutan and are ideal for day hikes to monasteries. Bumthang's ancient goembas (monasteries), *dzongs* and temples figured prominently in Bhutan's early development as well as in the foundation of the unique aspects of Bhutanese Buddhism. Witness the imprint of Guru Rinpoche, hoist Pema Lingpa's 25kg chain mail, and stare into the churning waters of Membartsho, where Pema Lingpa uncovered hidden treasures.

Paro Dzong & National Museum

10 Paro's Rinpung Dzong is a hulking example of the fortress-like *dzong* architecture that glowers protectively over the valley and town. Like most *dzongs*, it houses both the monastic body and district government offices. The colourful Paro tsechu is held here in spring; the festival culminates with the unfurling of a thondrol (a huge religious picture) depicting Guru Rinpoche. Above the *dzong* is an old, round watchtower, the Ta Dzong, now converted into the excellent National Museum, which has an informative and eclectic collection.

Trekking

Bhutan offers a wide range of treks, from high-altitude expeditions to relaxing village trails linked by subtropical forest.

Archery

Datse (archery) in Bhutan is entertaining to watch. Narrow misses, competitive banter and singing and dancing accompany the whoosh of arrows.

7

4

CAPITAL La Paz	
POPULATION 11.2 million	
AREA 1.1 million sq km	
OFFICIAL LANGUAGE Spanish, Quechua, Aymará	

Salar de Uyuni

Bolivia

Rough around the edges, superlative in its natural beauty, rugged, vexing, complex and slightly nerve-racking, Bolivia is one of South America's most diverse and perplexing nations.

Bolivia is not for the faint of heart. Whether your tools are crampons and ice-axe for scaling 6000m Andean peaks or a helmet and bravado for jumping into the abyss on a glider, Bolivia's rocks, rivers and ravines will challenge – nay, provoke – you into pushing your own personal limits.

As you travel across this remarkable remote wilderness, you'll marvel at the world's largest salt flat, whimsical rock formations, cacti-encrusted valleys straight out of the Old West, volcanic peaks, technicolor lakes and a sky that seems to stretch forever.

The capital, La Paz, is a mad carnival of honking minivans, street marches and dances, and cavalcades of street vendors. A maze of contradictions, where cobblestones hit concrete, and Gothic spires battle vie with glassine hotels, the city amazes and appalls all who enter.

Top Experiences

Salar de Uyuni

1 Who knew feeling this cold could feel so good? While a three- to four-day jeep tour through the world's largest salt flat will leave your bones chattering, it could quite possibly be the defining experience of your Bolivian adventure. The vastness, austerity and crystalline perfection of the salt flat will inspire you. An early-morning exploration of rock gardens, geyser fields and piping-hot springs along with the camaraderie of three days on the road with your fellow 'Salterians' will create a lasting memory.

Trekking in the Cordillera Real

2 Walk in the path of the Inca along the many trekking routes that weave their way from the Andes into the Amazon Basin, through the remarkable skyward-bound wilderness of the Cordillera Real. These four- to 14-day treks are no small undertaking, but it will be worth every step, every drop of sweat and every blister. Along the way, you'll have the chance to dine with indigenous families, cool off beside cascading waterfalls and connect with Pachamama (Mother Earth) deep within her potent green realm.

Isla del Sol, Lake Titicaca

3 Plopped onto sprawling Lake Titicaca like the cherry on top of an ice-cream sundae, Isla del Sol is considered to be the birthplace of Andean civilization. You can easily spend four

4

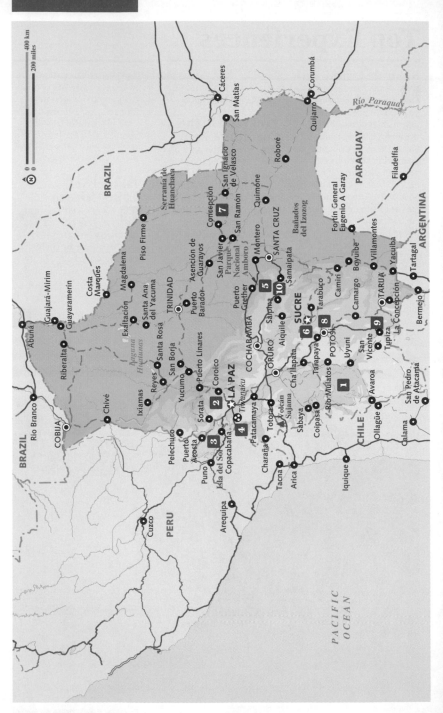

days here, tracking down forgotten Inca roads to small archaeological sites, remote coves and intact indigenous communities. At the end of the day, take in the sunset with a cerveza (beer) from your ridge-top lodge. The lake itself has a magnetism, power and energy unique to this world – no wonder many claim the ancient civilization of Atlantis was found here.

Best on Film

The Devil's Miner (2005) Fascinating documentary on a young boy working in Potosí's silver mine.

Cocalero (2007) A home-spun documentary on Morales' run for the presidency.

Amargo Mar (Bitter Sea; 1984) Highly regarded look at the loss of Bolivia's coastline to Chile.

Food & Drink

Ever had a llama tenderloin? Here's your chance: maybe with a glass of up-and-coming Tarija wine, or artisanal coca or quinoa-based beer. The daily bread varies from the Frisbee-like *mama qonqachi* cheese bread of Cochabamba, as big as your head, to the sourdough-like *maraqueta* hard roll, staple of *paceña* breakfast, to Santa Cruz's mouthwatering *cunapes* (cheese bread balls). Vegetarians can feast on *sonsos*, the yucca-and-cheese pancake of the *camba*, and savor tropical fruit juices such as *maracuya* (passionfruit) and *chirimoya* (custard apple). Fresh Amazon *surubí* tastes like it leapt onto your plate. Yungas coffee and *chuquisaceña* (Sucre) chocolate complete a perfect *postre* (dessert).

Tiwanaku

4 Bolivia's hallmark archaeological site sets your imagination on fire. Despite lacking the power and prestige of other ruins in Latin America – those who have visited Machu Picchu or Tikal will be hard pressed not to strike comparisons – for history buffs this pre-Inca site has a lot to offer. A massive celebration is held on the solstices, and the onsite museum provides a thought-provoking glimpse into life in this religious and astronomical center. An easy day trip from La Paz, Tiwanaku is a good place to start your Andean odyssey.

Parque Nacional & Área de Uso Múltiple Amboró

5 Sandwiched between the old and new roads to Cochabamba is one of Bolivia's most biodiverse, and fortunately most accessible, protected areas – the breathtaking Parque Nacional Amboró. Here the lush, leafy Amazon kisses the thorny, dusty Chaco, and the sweaty lowlands greet the refreshing highlands. The park's range of habitats means that both highland and lowland species are found

here. Mammals include elusive spectacled bears, jaguars, tapirs, peccaries and various monkeys, while more than 800 species of birds have been documented. Stunning scenery, wonderful wildlife and the assistance of professional tour agencies makes this a wilderness just begging to be explored.

When to Go

HIGH SEASON
(May–Sep)
Mostly sunny days but cooler in the altiplano. Be prepared for festival crowds in August.

SHOULDER
(Oct & Nov)
Good for budget hunters.

LOW SEASON
(Dec–Apr)
Summer is the rainy season; it can be miserable in the lowlands.

La Paz Markets

The whirling engine that feeds and fuels a nation, the markets of La Paz are so crazy, so disjointed, so colorful, mad, stinky and remarkable that you'll end up spending at least a few afternoons wandering from stall to stall. There are sections for food, sections for sorcery, sections where you can buy back your stolen camera, sections for pipes and styrofoam – in every shape and form imaginable – and sections packed with fruits, flowers and rotting fish that will push you to olfactory overload.

Getting Around

 Air travel is the quickest and most reliable way to reach out-of-the-way places, and it's reasonably inexpensive.

 Buses are the most popular form of transport; they can be uncomfortable and at times nerve-wracking, but they are cheap and relatively safe.

 Tours are a popular and hassle-free way to get to remote locations like the Salar de Uyuni.

 Trains are around the same price as the buses but much slower. They do however offer heating and air-conditioning.

Sucre

6 Glistening in the Andean sun, the white city of Sucre is the birthplace of the nation and a must-see for any visitor to Bolivia. A glorious ensemble of whitewashed buildings sheltering pretty patios, it's a spruce place that preserves a wealth of colonial architecture. It was declared a Unesco World Heritage site in 1991. Yet it's an eclectic mix of the old and the new, where you can while away your days perusing the historic buildings and museums, and spend your nights enjoying the city's famous nightlife. Visitors to Sucre invariably fall in love with the place.

Jesuit Mission Circuit

7 The seven-town region of *Las Misiones Jesuíticas* hides some of Bolivia's richest cultural and historic accomplishments. Forgotten by the world for more than two centuries, the region and its history captivated the world's imagination when the 1986 Palme d'Or winner

The Mission spectacularly replayed the last days of the Jesuit priests in the region (with Robert de Niro at the helm). Thanks to 25 years of painstaking restoration work, directed by the late architect Hans Roth, the centuries-old mission churches have been restored to their original splendor. To travel through the entire circuit takes five or six days, but for those with an interest in architecture or history, it's a rewarding excursion. If you have less time on your hands, prioritise the two most accessible churches at San José de Chiquitos and Concépcion, which are also conveniently the most representative of the extremes of styles.

Potosí

8 Said to be the highest city in the world, lofty Potosí once sat upon a land laden with silver that funded the Spanish Empire for centuries. Though the mines now lie barren and the city has long been in economic decline, the remnants of the wealthy past

can still be seen through the cracked brickwork of the ornate colonial-era buildings and wonderfully preserved churches. Potosí's most famous museum, the Casa de la Moneda, was once Bolivia's national mint and offers a fascinating insight into the rise and fall of a city that once described itself as 'the envy of kings'.

Tupiza

9 Cut from the pages of a Wild West novel, the canyon country around Tupiza is an awesome place for heading off into the sunset (in a saddle, atop a mountain bike, on foot or in a 4WD). From town you can ramble out into the polychromatic desert wonderlands and canyons, visiting hard-cut mining villages and the town where Butch Cassidy and the Sundance Kid met their end. The pleasant weather and lyrical feel of the town make it a welcome retreat.

Samaipata

10 Cosmopolitan Samaipata manages to retain the air of a relaxing mountain village, despite becoming an increasingly unmissable stop on the Bolivian tourist trail. But it's not just the great-value accommodations and top-class restaurants that bring in the visitors. Samaipata's proximity to the mystical El Fuerte ruins and a series of worthy day trips to nearby areas of outstanding natural beauty mean that many visitors find themselves staying for a lot longer than they planned.

Mountain Biking

With elevation drops of 4000m, Bolivia offers some of the best mountain-bike descents in the world.

Fiesta de La Virgen de Candelaria

This February event is especially big in Copacabana, with music, Aymará dancing, drinking and feasting.

MEZZOTINT / SHUTTERSTOCK ©

9

STEFANO BUTTAFOCO / SHUTTERSTOCK ©

CAPITAL
Sarajevo

POPULATION
3.5 million

AREA
51,129 sq km

OFFICIAL LANGUAGES
Bosnian, Croatian,
Serbian

Pliva River waterfall, Jajce

Bosnia & Hercegovina

Craggily beautiful Bosnia & Hercegovina is most intriguing for its East-meets-West atmosphere born of blended Ottoman and Austro-Hungarian histories.

The Bosnians described their country as a 'heart-shaped land' and looking at a map reveals that such a description is not too wide of the mark geographically. Many international visitors still associate the country with the heartbreaking civil war of the 1990s, and several attractions focus on the horrors of that era. But today, visitors will likely remember the country for its deep, unassuming human warmth, its beautiful mountainscapes and its numerous medieval castle ruins. Apart from modest Neum it lacks beach resorts, but easily compensates with cascading rafting rivers, waterfalls and skiing in its mountainous landscapes.

Major drawcards are the reincarnated historic centres of Sarajevo and Mostar, counterpointing splendid Turkish-era architecture with quirky bars, inviting street-terrace cafes and a vibrant arts scene.

Top Experiences

Stari Most

 World-famous Stari Most (Old Bridge) is Mostar's indisputable visual focus. Its pale stone magnificently throws back the golden glow of sunset or the tasteful night-time floodlighting. The bridge's swooping arch was originally built between 1557 and 1566 on the orders of Suleyman the Magnificent. The current structure is a very convincing 21st-century rebuild following the bridge's 1990s bombardment during the civil war. Numerous well-positioned cafes and restaurants tempt you to sit and savour the splendidly restored scene.

Baščaršija

 Centred on what foreigners nickname Pigeon Sq, Baščaršija is the heart of old Sarajevo. Pad around the fascinating Turkic-era alleyways on soft flagstones that feel like chilled butter underfoot, discovering lively (if tourist-centric) coppersmiths, grand Ottoman mosques, caravanserai-restaurants and lots of inviting little cafes and *ćevapi* serveries.

Jajce Waterfall

 Jajce's impressive 21m-high waterfalls form where the Pliva River tumbles abruptly into the Vrbas river. A new viewing platform has been built opposite the falls' base, accessed from stairs that start between the bus station and petrol station. If you don't want to get sprayed, you can look down on the falls from either lip.

Mehmet Paša Sokolović Bridge

4 The glorious 10-arch Mehmet Paša Sokolović Bridge is Višegrad's main attraction. Built in 1571, the structure was immortalised in Ivo Andrić's Nobel Prize–winning classic *Bridge on the Drina*. Declared a Unesco World Heritage site in 2007, the bridge has been recently restored and is tastefully floodlit at night. It looks especially fine at dusk as the mists rise off the canyon-backed river.

Bjelašnica

5 Bosnia's second Olympic ski field rises above the modest resort of Bjelašnica, around 30km south of Sarajevo. An attraction here is floodlit night skiing and, in summer, the possibilities of exploring the magical mountain villages behind. The most famous is timeless Lukomir. A 360-degree panorama from its knoll-like promontory encompasses the layered stone hamlet, sloping stony sheep pastures behind and a plunging gorge backed by a far horizon of rocky-knobbed peaks.

Tvrdoš Monastery

6 Attractively set amid vines, beehives and orchards, 6km west of Trebinje, delightful Tvrdoš Monastery is best known to outside visitors for its wines – Hercegovina's best, and available for sale from a little shop-kiosk by the driveway gate. For Bosnian Serbs, however, Tvrdoš is of great religious significance as the place where St Basil of Ostrog took his monastic vows. Those with a serious spiritual interest in Serbian Orthodox monasticism might be allowed to venture further into the complex.

Getting Around

Bus stations pre-sell tickets. Between towns it's normally easy enough to wave down any bus en route.

Bosnia & Hercegovina's winding roads are lightly trafficked and a delight for driving if you aren't in a hurry.

Trains are slower and far less frequent than buses but generally slightly cheaper.

DARIO VUKSANOVIC / SHUTTERSTOCK ©

Based around the site of a 4th century Roman church, it became the 16th century seat of the Metropolitan (orthodox archbishop) and today the icon-packed little campanile church is brilliantly painted with interior murals incorporating a few fragmentary remnants of the 1517 originals.

Visočica Hill

7 Visoko was once the capital of medieval Bosnia and the spiritual centre of the controversial Bosnian Church. By the 20th century little of this glory remained and it had become an unremarkable, largely forgotten leather-tanning town. Then came an audacious claim that the partly wooded triangular hill that looms distinctively above Visoko is in fact the world's largest pyramid. Ever since, tourists and new-age mystics have poured in.

Food & Drink

Rich, meaty stews dominate home cooking while *ćevapi* (spicy beef or pork meatballs) is the most common 'fast food'.

Most villages have a *pekara* (bakery) for pastries, bread and often *burek* (meat-filled filo-pastry spirals), also available from specialist outlets called *buregdžinica*.

Vegetarian options are limited.

For dessert, try *tufahije*, baked apple stuffed with walnut paste and topped with whipped cream. Ice creams are divine.

DARIO VUKSANOVIC / SHUTTERSTOCK ©

Međugorje Visions

On 24 June 1981 six local teenagers in Međugorje, Hercegovina, experienced a vision which they believe to have been a manifestation of the Holy Virgin. As a result, this formerly poor winemaking backwater has been utterly transformed into a bustling Catholic pilgrimage centre and continues to grow even though Rome has yet to officially acknowledge the legitimacy of the visions. Apparition Hill (Brdo Ukazanja), where those visions occurred, is around 3km south of Međugorje's central hub, St James Church (pictured above). A white statue of the Virgin Mary marks the site.

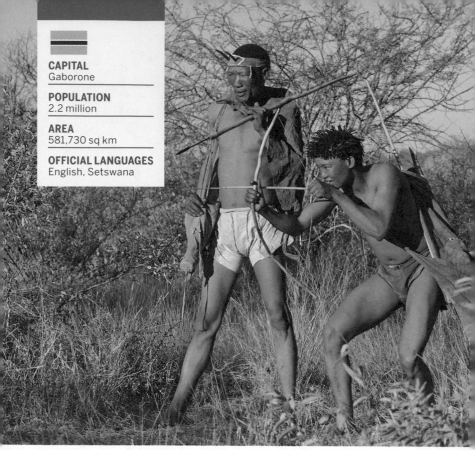

CAPITAL	Gaborone
POPULATION	2.2 million
AREA	581,730 sq km
OFFICIAL LANGUAGES	English, Setswana

San hunters, Central Kalahari Game Reserve

Botswana

Blessed with some of the greatest wildlife spectacles on earth, Botswana is one of the great safari destinations in Africa.

The Okavango Delta – there's nowhere quite like it on earth. This is a place where wild creatures roam and rule, where big cats and much bigger elephants walk free in one of the world's last great wildernesses. The delta is a byword for abundance. And it is also a place of singular and unparalleled beauty where safari possibilities can seem as endless as the waters themselves.

This is contrasted with the magnificent Kalahari Desert – the largest unbroken stretch of sand on the planet – with its salt pans, baobabs, fossil river valleys and wonderful wildlife.

Yet Botswana has turned its back on mass tourism and all the pitfalls it can bring, instead ushering in an era of utterly exclusive safari experiences. These are sumptuous lodges and remote tented camps, sometimes contemporary in style and at other times awash in safari nostalgia. Best of all, they provide a front-row seat for fabulous wildlife spectacles that you may just have all to yourself.

Top Experiences

Okavango Delta Safari

1 Botswana didn't invent the luxury safari, but it may just have perfected it. Nowhere else on earth will you find so many remote and utterly exclusive lodges and tented camps, accessible only by air or boat, where your every dream of the perfect safari comes true. Most are in the Okavango Delta, but you'll also find them in the neighbouring areas of Linyanti, Chobe National Park and the Central Kalahari Game Reserve. Picking favourites is always difficult, but we love Vumbura Plains Camp.

Chobe National Park

2 There are more elephants in Chobe – tens of thousands of them – than anywhere else on arth. And these are big elephants, really big. Then there are the iconic landscapes of Savuti with its elephant-eating lions; or Linyanti, one of the best places on the continent to see the highly endangered African wild dog; or the Chobe Riverfront where most of Africa's charismatic megafauna comes to drink. Put all of this together and it's easy to see why Chobe National Park ranks among the elite of African safari destinations.

Makgadikgadi Pans National Park

3 Part of the world's largest network of salt pans, the endless horizons of Makgadikgadi are one of the Kalahari's least-known treasures. It is here, during the rainy season, that zebras migrate en masse – one of the great wildlife migrations in a continent of many. During the dry season, wildlife draws near to the rejuvenated Boteti River in similarly epic numbers. Meerkats are another highlight. And away across the pans, remote islands of baobabs rise from the salt like evocations of some ancient African oasis.

Central Kalahari Game Reserve

4 There is something about the Kalahari. Perhaps it owes its gravitas to a name that carries more than a whiff of African magic. Or perhaps it is the sheer vastness of this desert, which is Africa's largest protected wilderness area. The presence of black-maned Kalahari lions doesn't hurt, either. Whatever the reason, this is not your average desert. It's home instead to ancient river valleys, light woodland and surprising concentrations of wildlife around its extensive network of salt pans. And then there is the silence of the Kalahari night...

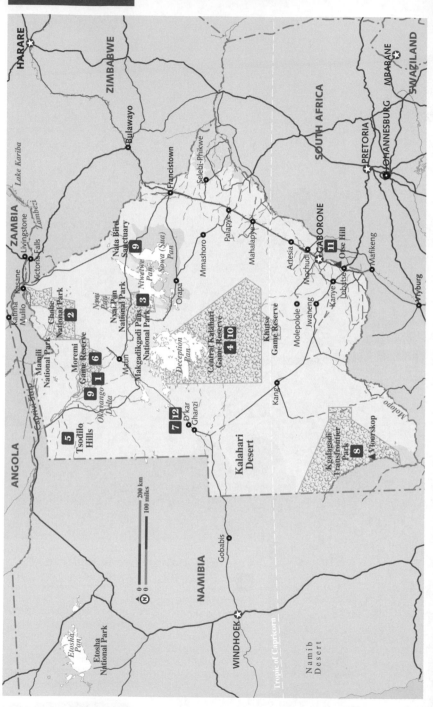

Best in Film

The Gods Must Be Crazy (1984) Cult classic comedy starring Botswana's San.

The Last Lions (2011) Follows a pride of delta lions.

Eye of the Leopard (2006) Coming-of-age story of a young Botswana leopard.

A United Kingdom (2016) Based on the love story of Botswana's first president and his British bride.

Savage Kingdom (2016) Fantastic footage showing the rivalry between predators in the Savuti region.

Best in Print

The No.1 Ladies' Detective Agency (Alexander McCall Smith; 1998) Gentle Botswana detective stories.

The Lost World of the Kalahari (Laurens van der Post; 1958) A 1950s eulogy for San culture.

Cry of the Kalahari (Mark & Delia Owens; 1984) Kalahari wildlife before the tourists arrived.

Twenty Chickens for a Saddle (Robyn Scott; 2008) Heartwarming tale of a Botswana childhood.

Far and Beyon' (Unity Dow; 2000) Fable of modern Botswana.

Rock Art in the Tsodilo Hills

5 The Tsodilo Hills, which became a Unesco World Heritage Site even before the Okavango Delta, is sometimes referred to as the 'Louvre of the Desert'. More than 4000 ancient paintings, many dating back thousands of years, adorn the caves and cliffs of these picturesque mountains, which remain a sacred site for the San people. Expertly rendered in ochre-hued natural pigments, the paintings are at once beautiful and an invaluable chronology of the evolving relationship between human beings and the natural world. And such is their remoteness, you might just have them all to yourself.

Moremi Game Reserve

6 What Chobe is for elephants, Moremi Game Reserve is for just about everything else. Accessible to both self-drive campers and those visitors on fly-in, high-end safaris, Moremi is like a BBC wildlife documentary come to life as a full suite of predators and prey battle for survival. They've got it all out here – big cats in abundance, aquatic antelope, hundreds of bird species and just about every possible species of charismatic African megafauna you can think of.

When to Go

HIGH SEASON
(Jun–Oct)
Warm days and mild nights, but October can be oppressively hot. Extremely cold nights in the Kalahari.

SHOULDER
(Apr, May & Nov)
May nights can be cold, but otherwise a lovely, cheaper time to visit.

LOW SEASON
(Dec–Mar)
Cheaper rates and high availability. Rains can disrupt travel. High season in the Kalahari.

The San People

7 Spending time in the presence of southern Africa's inhabitants of longest standing is one of the most rewarding things to do while in Botswana. Ghanzi, considered by many to be

The Stats

Botswana has one of the lowest population densities on earth: 3.75 people for every square kilometre. The country has a young population, with an average age of 23.2 years.

Mokoro Trips

The Okavango is an astonishing, beautiful, wild place, and there's something special about drifting slowly down its reed-lined channels in a *mokoro* (dugout canoe).

Food & Drink

Local cooking is, for the most part, aimed more at sustenance than exciting tastes. Forming the centre of most Batswana meals nowadays is *mabele* (sorghum) or *bogobe* (porridge made from sorghum), but these staples are rapidly being replaced by imported maize mealies, sometimes known by the Afrikaans name mealiepap, or just plain pap. This provides the base for an array of meat and vegetable sauces such as *seswaa* (shredded goat or lamb), *morogo* (wild spinach) or *leputshe* (wild pumpkin).

For breakfast, you might be able to try *pathata* (like an English muffin) or *megunya*, also known as fat cakes. These are little balls of fried dough that are like doughnuts minus the hole and, depending on your taste, the flavour.

Oh, and don't forget mopane worms. These fat suckers are pulled off mopane trees and fried into little delicacies – they're tasty and a good source of protein. You may be able to buy some from ladies selling them by the bag in the Main Mall in Gaborone or in Francistown.

Botswana's capital of the Kalahari, and the nearby village of D'Kar put you within reach of numerous San-owned craft shops, art centres and camps where you can spend time learning how to forage for bush foods and even hunt as the San have done for thousands of years.

Kgalagadi Transfrontier Park

8 One of the most beautiful expanses of the Kalahari is found in the Kgalagadi Transfrontier Park, which straddles the border between Botswana and South Africa. Some of the desert's most picturesque salt pans and sand dunes provide habitat for desert-adapted wildlife that includes all of the big cats, meerkats, abundant birdlife and old desert favourites such as gemsboks and ostriches. With riverine woodland and some real wilderness stretches, this is one of Botswana's most underrated parks.

Birdwatching

9 Botswana is a birding utopia, with almost 600 species recorded. Species include the delta's famous African skimmers, bee-eaters, Pel's fishing owl, pygmy geese, goshawks, several species of vultures and African fish eagles. In the Okavango Panhandle, a narrow strip of swampland extending about 100km to the Namibian border, the waters spread across the valley to form vast reed beds and papyrus-choked lagoons that offer superb conditions for birdwatching.

Off-Road Driving

10 There's plenty to challenge 4WD enthusiasts who like to get off-road. In many remote places, age-old tracks (in perilous condition after the rains) are the only way to navigate the African wilderness. The Central Kalahari Game Reserve is an off-roader's dream. If you're after solitude, desertscapes and the echo of lions roaring in the night, this enormous heart of the African wilderness could become your favourite. Cross from north to south, with scarcely another vehicle in sight.

Gaborone Game Reserve

11 This reserve was established in 1988 by the Kalahari Conservation Society to give the Gaborone public an opportunity to view Botswana's wildlife in a natural and accessible location. It seems to be working: although the reserve is only 5 sq km, it's the third-busiest in the country and boasts wildebeest, elands, gemsboks, kudus, ostriches and warthogs. The birdlife, which includes kingfishers and hornbills, is particularly plentiful and easy to spot from observation areas.

Kuru Art Project

12 This fabulous art project in D'kar provides opportunities for local artists (14 at last count) to create and sell paintings and other artwork; it's worth spending an hour or two leafing through the various folios of artworks.

JAY BO / SHUTTERSTOCK ©

Getting Around

 Although domestic air services are fairly frequent and reliable, it's not cheap and only a handful of towns are served.

 Buses are cheap and reasonably frequent, but confined to sealed roads between towns.

 Hiring a vehicle is the most practical option.

CAPITAL
Brasilia

POPULATION
205.8 million

AREA
8.5 million sq km

OFFICIAL LANGUAGE
Portuguese

Brazil

One of the world's most captivating places, Brazil is a country of powdery white-sand beaches, verdant rainforests and wild, rhythm-filled metropolises.

Brazil's attractions extend from frozen-in-time colonial towns to otherworldly landscapes of red-rock canyons, thundering waterfalls and coral-fringed tropical islands. Then there's Brazil's biodiversity: its diverse ecosystems boast the greatest collection of plant and animal species found anywhere on earth. Brazil also offers big adventures for travelers – there's horseback riding in the Pantanal, kayaking flooded forests in the Amazon, ascending cliff tops to pano-ramic views, whale-watching off the coast, surfing stellar breaks and snorkeling crystal-clear rivers or coastal reefs.

Carnaval storms through the country's cities and towns with hip-shaking samba and *frevo*, dazzling costumes and parties that last until sun up. *Festas* (festivals) happen throughout the year, and provide a window into Brazil's incredible diversity. And wherever there's music, that carefree lust for life tends to appear.

Top Experiences

Pão de Açúcar, Rio de Janeiro

1 Some say to come around sunset for the best views from this absurd confection of a mountain. But in truth, it doesn't matter when you come; you're unlikely to look at Rio (or your own comparatively lackluster city) in the same way. From here the landscape is pure undulating green hills and golden beaches lapped by blue sea, with rows of skyscrapers sprouting along the shore. The ride up is good fun: all-glass aerial trams that whisk you up to the top. The adventurous can rock-climb their way to the summit.

Amazon Jungle Trips

2 Needless to say, the best reason to visit the Amazon is to get out into the jungle: to ply the winding waterways in a canoe, hike lush leafy trails, and scan the canopy for monkeys, sloths and other creatures. The world's biggest and best known rainforest has outdoor excursions of all sorts, and for all types of travelers: from easy nature hikes to scaling 50m trees, from luxury lodges to makeshift camps in the forest. Whatever your interest, experience, ability or budget, there's a jungle trip in the Amazon waiting to blow your mind.

Salvador

3 The world capital of Afro-Brazil, Salvador is famous for capoeira, Candomblé, Olodum, colonial Portuguese architecture, African street food and one of the oldest lighthouses in the Americas. The city's past, marked by gritty stories of Portuguese seafaring and the heartbreaking history of the African slave trade, is characterized by hardship. But today's lively Bahian capital offers a unique fusion of two vibrant cultures. The festive music and nightlife scene culminates every February when Salvador hosts one of the best Carnavals in Brazil.

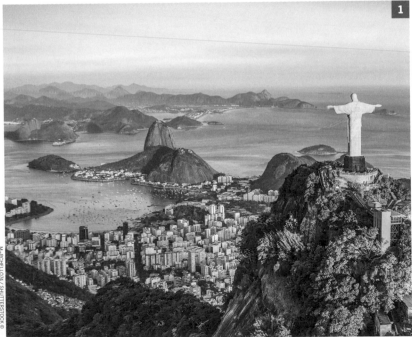

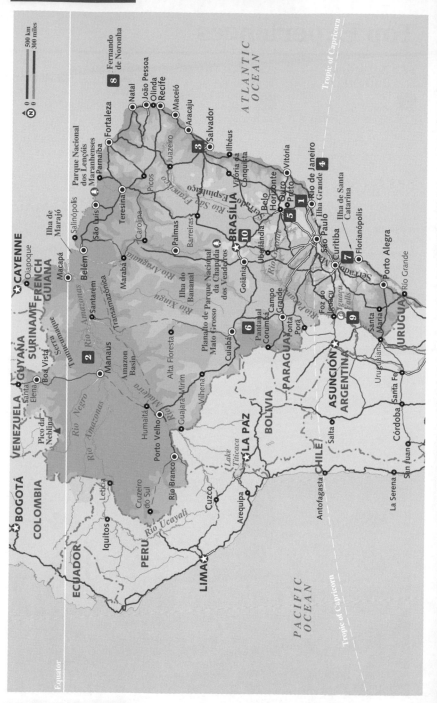

Ilha Grande

4 The fabulous island retreat of Ilha Grande owes its pristine condition to its unusual history. First it was a pirates' lair, then a leper colony and, finally, a penitentiary where political prisoners were held alongside some of Brazil's most violent criminals. All that remains of those days are some half-buried stone foundations, but the island's unsavory reputation kept developers at bay for a long time. Days are spent hiking through lush Atlantic rainforest, snorkeling amid aquamarine seas and basking in crisp waterfalls. With no motor vehicles to spoil the party, this is one clean, green island – a true nature lover's paradise. It's also an easy day's journey from Rio.

Ouro Prêto

5 With more ups and downs than a rollercoaster, Ouro Prêto's 18th-century streets veer precipitously between one baroque wonder and the next. Navigating the vertiginous cobblestone slopes on foot can be exhausting, but you can admire the sculpted masterpieces of Aleijadinho, discover the 18th-century African tribal king turned folk hero Chico-Rei and gaze upon opulent gilded churches. The elaborate Holy Week processions are among the country's most spectacular. From gold town to state capital, revolutionary hotbed to Unesco World Heritage site, this colonial gem has been at the center of the action for more than 300 years.

Best in Film

Tropa de Elite (*Elite Squad*, 2007) An action film of crime and corruption as an elite police squad and drug lords clash. Don't miss the sequel (*The Enemy Within*).

Central do Brasil (*Central Station*, 1998) Walter Salles' moving tale of a homeless boy and an older woman on a road trip across Brazil.

Reaching for the Moon (2013) Tragic love story between an American poet and Brazilian architect, set in 1950s Petrópolis.

Bel Borba Aqui (2012) Colorful documentary of an artist who uses Salvador as his canvas.

Food & Drink

Bolinho de bacalhau Deep-fried codfish balls.

Cachaça High-proof sugarcane alcohol.

Coxinha Pear-shaped cornmeal balls filled with shredded chicken.

Esfiha Triangular pastry filled with meat and spices, spinach or other fillings.

Feijoada Black beans slowly cooked with a great variety of meat seasoned with salt, garlic, onion and oil.

Tapioca A crepe made from manioc flour, filled with chicken, cheese, fruit preserves and more.

When to Go

HIGH SEASON
(Dec–Mar)

Higher prices and minimum stays during Carnaval.

SHOULDER
(Apr & Oct)

The weather is warm and dry along the coast, though it can be chilly in the south.

LOW SEASON
(May–Sep)

Aside from July (school-holidays), you'll find lower prices and mild temperatures in the south.

Capoeira

The only surviving martial art native to the New World, capoeira was invented by Afro-Brazilian slaves about 400 years ago. In its original form, the grappling martial art developed as a means of self-defense against slave owners. Once the fighting art was discovered, it was quickly banned and capoeira went underground. Later the sport was disguised as a kind of dance, allowing them to practice in the open. This is the form that exists today.

Capoeira is accompanied by hand clapping and the plucking of the *berimbau* (a long, single-stringed instrument). Fast tempos dictate the players' exchange of fast, powerful kicks and blows, while slower tempos bring the pace down to a quasi-dance.

Getting Around

Flights are useful for crossing Brazil's immense distances; they can save days of travel; prices are generally high, but airfare promotions are frequent.

Extensive bus services from *comun* (conventional) to *leito* (overnight sleepers) throughout the country, except for the Amazon. For timetables and bus operators, check out Busca Ônibus (www.buscaonibus.com.br).

Boats are a slow, uncomfortable, but brag-worthy transport between towns in the Amazon, with trips measured in days rather than hours. You'll need a hammock, snacks, drinking water and a high tolerance for boredom.

Pantanal

6 Few places on earth can match the wildlife watching experience provided by the Pantanal, a wondrously remote wetland in the heart of Mato Grosso. While Amazon gets the press coverage, the Pantanal is a better place to see wildlife. From cute capybaras to stately storks, the animal life simply abounds and is remarkably easy to see in the open marshy surroundings. There are a million reasons not to miss out on this particular eco-experience, and not least among them is that there is no better place in South America to see the elusive jaguar!

Beers of Blumenau

7 Ubiquitous pale lagers such as Brahma and Skol certainly suffice as beat-the-heat treats throughout the country, but Brazil's best brews come from greater Blumenau. Along with lederhosen and leberkäse (a meat dish), heavy German immigration in the 1800s brought Reinheitsgebot, Germany's beer purity law, and these German-Brazilians aren't too fond of sharing. That means with the exception of the once-micro Eisenbahn, seriously good artisanal suds such as Schornstein Kneipe, Bierland and Das Bier don't fall too far from the tree. You'll need to venture into Santa Catarina's Vale Europeu to quench your thirst.

Fernando de Noronha

8 This archipelago of one 10km-long island and 20 smaller ones, 350km out into the Atlantic from Natal, has everything a tropical getaway should have – jaw-dropping scenery and seascapes, fine beaches, the best diving and snorkeling in the country, good surfing, memorable hikes, plentiful visible wildlife, good accommodations and restaurants – and no crowds, for visitor numbers are restricted by the limited number of plane seats available each day. Visiting Noronha is expensive, but it's worth every centavo if your budget will stretch far enough.

Iguaçu Falls

9 No matter the number of waterfalls you've checked off your bucket list, no matter how many times you have thought to yourself you'd be just fine never seeing another waterfall again, Iguaçu Falls will stomp all over your idea of water trickling over the edge of a cliff. The thunderous roar of 275 falls crashing across the Brazil and Argentina border floors even the most jaded traveler. Occupying an area more than 3km wide and 80m high, she's wider than Victoria, higher than Niagara and more beautiful than both. Loud, angry, unstoppable and impossibly gorgeous, Iguaçu will leave you stunned and slack-jawed at the absolute power of Mother Nature.

Brasília Architecture

10 What the city of the future really needed to back up its claim to be the harbinger of Brazil's 'new dawn' was an architect capable of designing buildings that looked the part. In Oscar Niemeyer Brasília found the right man for the job. The 'crown of thorns' Catedral Metropolitana is a religious masterwork and the interplanetary Teatro Nacional is out of this world! Brasília is a city overloaded with architectural gems designed by a genius inspired by the concept of a better future.

Rock Climbing

Rio de Janeiro is the hub of Brazilian rock climbing, with some 350 documented climbs within an hour's drive of the city.

Reveillon

On 31 December, you can join some 2 million revelers, all dressed in white, on Copacabana Beach, where music concerts and fireworks ring in the New Year.

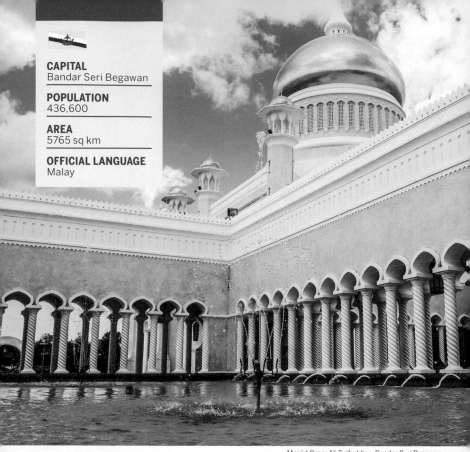

CAPITAL
Bandar Seri Begawan

POPULATION
436,600

AREA
5765 sq km

OFFICIAL LANGUAGE
Malay

Masjid Omar Ali Saifuddien, Bandar Seri Begawan

Brunei

Look beneath the surface of this well-ordered and tightly regulated sultanate and you'll see the underlying warmth of Brunei's people and the wildness of its natural environment.

This quiet *darussalam* (Arabic for 'abode of peace') has the largest oilfields in Southeast Asia, and thanks to the money they've generated, Brunei hasn't turned its rainforests into oil palm plantations. Old-growth greenery abounds, especially in verdant Ulu Temburong National Park.

The citizens of the capital, Bandar Seri Begawan (BSB), are mad for food and shopping (booze is banned). Here magnificent mosques contrast with the charmingly haphazard water village, while the nearby mangrove forest is home to proboscis monkeys and crocs.

This tranquil (sometimes somnolent) nation is the realisation of a particular vision: a strict, socially controlled religious state where happiness is found in pious worship and mass consumption. Visit and judge the results for yourself.

Top Experiences

Kampong Ayer

1 Home to around 30,000 people, Kampong Ayer consists of 42 contiguous stilt villages built along the banks of the Sungai Brunei (Brunei River). Founded at least 1000 years ago, the village is considered the largest stilt settlement in the world. A century ago, half of Brunei's population lived here, and today many Bruneians still prefer the lifestyle of the water village. The village has its own schools, mosques, police stations and fire brigade. To get across the river, just stand somewhere a water taxi can dock and flag one down.

Bandar Seri Begawan

2 Cities built on oil money tend to be flashy places, but with the exception of a palace you usually can't enter, a couple of enormous mosques and one wedding cake of a hotel, Bandar (as the capital is known, or just BSB) is a pretty understated place. Urban life pretty much revolves around malls and culinary delights. BSB does have a few museums and the biggest water village in the world, a little slice of vintage that speaks to the Bruneian love of cosiness and nostalgia.

When to Go

 HIGH SEASON (Jul–Sep)

☼ **SHOULDER** (Mar–Jun)

 LOW SEASON (Oct–Feb)

Omar Ali Saifuddien Mosque

3 Completed in 1958, Masjid Omar Ali Saifuddien is surrounded by an artificial lagoon that serves as a reflecting pool. This being Brunei, the interior is pretty lavish. The floor and walls are made from the finest Italian marble, the chandeliers were

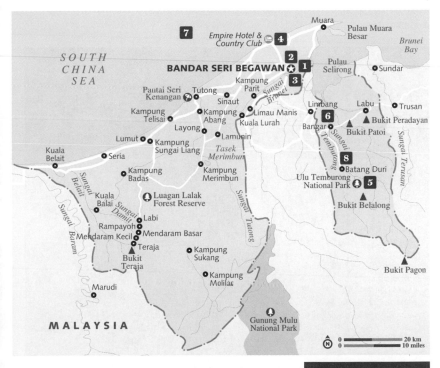

crafted in England and the luxurious carpets were flown in from Saudi Arabia. A 3.5-million-piece glass mosaic overlaying real gold leaf covers the main dome. Come evening, the mosque is basically the happening centre of city life in Bandar; folks come for prayer, then leave to eat or shop, which is sort of Brunei in a nutshell.

Empire Hotel & Country Club

4 Pharaonic in its proportions and opulence, this 522-room extravaganza was commissioned by Prince Jefri as lodging for guests of the royal family and quickly transformed into an upscale resort. Even the cheapest rooms have remote-control everything, hand-woven carpets, gold-plated power points

and enormous bathrooms with marble floors. Online discounts offer substantial savings on the quoted rates.

Ulu Temburong National Park

5 From the sky, Brunei's Temburong District looks like all of Borneo once did: an unbroken carpet of primary rainforest unblemished by roads, buildings or logging gashes. On the ground, most of the sultanate's eastern sliver is off-limits except to researchers, but you can get a taste of the primeval jungle at Ulu Temburong National Park. The only way in is an exciting longboat ride, and once there you can climb into the jungle canopy and have wild fish nibble your feet in a cool stream.

Getting Around

Brunei's limited public bus system is erratic and rather chaotic, at least to the uninitiated.

Brunei has Southeast Asia's cheapest petrol for cars with Brunei number plates. Hiring a car is a good way to explore Brunei's hinterland.

Taxis are a convenient way of exploring BSB – if you can find one.

Bangar

6 Little Bangar, perched on the banks of Sungai Temburong, is the gateway to, and administrative centre of, Temburong District. It can be visited as a day trip from BSB, but you'll get more out of the town's easygoing pace if you stay over and explore the area, which has some fine rainforest. Part of the fun is tearing along mangrove-lined waterways by speedboat on the journey here from BSB.

Diving Reefs & Wrecks

7 Though it's still relatively new, Brunei's burgeoning dive scene has the advantage of having some decent dive operators without the downside of crowds. There are several interesting wrecks – some dating back to WWII – as well as plenty of undamaged reef here. On most of the shipwrecks and all the coral dive sites there is colourful hard and soft coral. Marine life you are likely to see includes cuttlefish, octopus, morays, porcupine fish, giant puffers and sometimes a sea snake or two.

Sumbiling Eco Village

8 If you're looking for Brunei's version of a jungle camp with basic amenities and a chilled-out atmosphere that encourages slipping into a state of relaxed Zen, come to Sumbiling. This ecofriendly rustic camp in a beautiful riverside location offers tasty Iban cuisine and accommodation in bamboo huts or tents.

Food & Drink

Remember that kid in kindergarten who used to eat craft glue? Well, *ambuyat,* Brunei's unofficial national dish, comes pretty darn close. It's a gelatinous porridge-like goo made from the pith of the sago tree, which is ground to a powder and mixed with water, and eaten with a variety of flavourful sauces.

To eat *ambuyat,* you'll be given a special pair of chopsticks called *chandas* that's attached at the top (don't snap them in two!) to make it easier to twirl up the tenacious mucous. Once you've scooped up a bite-sized quantity, dunk it into the sauce. After your *ambuyat* is sufficiently drenched, place the glob of dripping, quivering, translucent mucilage in your mouth and swallow – don't chew, just let it glide down your throat.

Inside the Sultan's Palace

If shaking hands with royalty is your thing, and you happen to be in Brunei for the Hari Raya Aidil Fitri festivities at the end of Ramadan, be sure to call in on the sultan at Istana Nurul Iman, his 1788-room primary residence. In keeping with the local tradition of hosting an open house, during which guests are welcomed into the home and plied with a buffet of curries, dried fruit and cake, for three days the sultan receives members of the public. There is no need for an invitation; simply turn up and join the queue. Wear something modest and reasonably smart.

After the banquet, there is an hour or so of waiting. You'll then be ushered through to shake hands with the sultan (if you are a man) or the queen (if you are a woman), who receive guests in separate rooms. They will greet some 40,000 people a day during the festivities.

Fortress of Veliko Tărnovo

Bulgaria

Soul-stirring mountains rival golden beaches, while cities hum with nightlife and art. Within Bulgaria's beguiling blend of nature and history, unforgettable adventures are guaranteed.

CAPITAL
Sofia

POPULATION
7.2 million

AREA
110,879 sq km

OFFICIAL LANGUAGE
Bulgarian

Whispers of history emanate from Bulgaria's fortresses and ruins. Caves hold traces of Neolithic settlements, the mysterious Thracians left behind dazzling hauls of gold and silver, and the Romans built cities of breathtaking scale, the remnants of which sit nonchalantly in the midst of modern cities such as Varna and Plovdiv. And no visitor to Bulgaria can fail to be impressed by its religious art, from vast gold-domed churches to miniature icon paintings.

Long, sandy beaches and fine weather reel holidaymakers into Black Sea resorts each summer. Seven mountain ranges ripple across the country; glacial lakes sparkle between these snow-dusted peaks, and tangles of forest conceal wolves, bears and lynx. Between trekking among Rodopi villages, thundering across ski fields in Bansko or birdwatching in Pirin National Park, Bulgaria has much to delight lovers of the great outdoors.

Top Experiences

Rila Monastery

 More than 1000 years of uninterrupted spiritual activity have swept through this beautiful monastery, which rises from a valley in the misty Rila Mountains. Credited with safeguarding Bulgarian culture during the dark centuries under Ottoman rule, and a lightning rod for revolution in the 19th century, Rila Monastery remains Bulgaria's most storied spiritual treasure. The monastery grew from a 10th-century hermit's hut; following a fire, the breathtaking mix of elegant archways, soaring domes and apocalyptic frescoes that stands today dates mostly to the 19th century.

Veliko Târnovo

 Bulgaria's long history of warring tsars and epic battles is exceptionally vivid in its former capital, Veliko Târnovo. Topped with a marvellous medieval fortress, this town of Soviet monuments, cobblestoned lanes and barely changed handicraft shops allows for a memorable trip into Bulgaria's past. Home to the second-largest university in Bulgaria, the town also has a simmering nightlife; a creative and multicultural expat community adds to the fun.

Sofia's Aleksander Nevski Memorial Church

 Rising majestically over the rooftops of Sofia, the neo-Byzantine Orthodox church is dedicated to the memory of the 200,000 Russian soldiers who died fighting for Bulgaria's independence

When to Go

☀ **HIGH SEASON** (Jun–Aug)

⛅ **SHOULDER** (Apr, May, Sep & Oct)

❄ **LOW SEASON** (Nov–Mar)

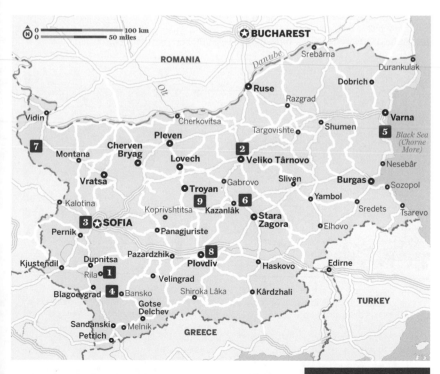

in the Russo-Turkish War (1877–78). An unequalled highlight of the Bulgarian capital, the church took 30 years to construct and was completed in 1912. Its vast, candlelit interior is heavy with incense and decorated with Italian marble, alabaster and fading murals.

Skiing in the Pirin Mountains

4 The Pirin Mountains are truly a land of giants, with more than 100 peaks towering higher than 2000m. Their summer splendour draws hikers to Pirin National Park, but long winters and downy snowfall make Pirin the Balkans' best skiing and snowboarding destination. Nestled at the base of Mt Vihren (2915m), Bansko is Bulgaria's premium winter sports town. Its 75km of pistes, extending to a height of 2600m, have options for all levels.

Black Sea Beaches

5 Whether you're looking for all-day tanning, all-night clubbing, or something a little more relaxing, you're sure to find some patch of sand to your liking along Bulgaria's Black Sea coast. Away from the big, brash package resorts, you'll come across charming seaside towns standing above smaller sandy coves, while the cities of Varna and Burgas both have lengthy, less-crowded urban beaches.

Thracian Tombs

6 The Valley of Thracian Kings, between Shipka and Kazanlâk, is dotted with fine tombs, and more are unearthed every year. But one of the most magnificently preserved examples is the Unesco-listed Thracian Tomb of Sveshtari in Bulgaria's northeast. The tomb dates to 300 BC and

Getting Around

The most reliable transport links between cities are by bus. Seasonal in ski or beach destinations.

Car is the most convenient way to get around, especially for small villages.

Taxis are a good way to reach day-trip destinations; agree on a fare before setting out.

NATALIYA NAZAROVA / SHUTTERSTOCK ©

harbours lovely artwork and reliefs within its three chambers, including 10 elegant female figures. This rare discovery was made in 1982, but tourists are few.

Belogradchik Rocks

7 On the fringe of Bulgaria's Stara Planina mountain range tower these awe-inspiring sandstone pillars, one of Bulgaria's most photogenic geological features. Over an area of 90 sq km, these stone protrusions form a jaw-dropping silhouette: some loom as tall as 200m, and the knottiest turrets have drawn comparison to mythic figures and animals. Nearly blending in with Belogradchik Rocks is the impressive Kaleto Fortress, a Roman and Byzantine-era fortification. Hiking trails weave among the rocks and up to the fortress, allowing wondrous views.

Food & Drink

Banitsa Flaky cheese pasty, often served fresh and hot.

Beer Zagorka, Kamenitza and Shumensko are the most popular nationwide brands.

Kavarma This 'claypot meal', or meat stew, is normally made with either chicken or pork.

Kebabche Thin, grilled pork sausage, a staple of every *mehana* (tavern) in the country.

Shishcheta Shish kebab, consisting of chunks of chicken or pork on wooden skewers with mushrooms and peppers.

Shkembe chorba Traditional tripe soup.

Plovdiv

8 With a charming old town, revitalised artistic quarter and the most exhilarating nightlife outside Sofia, Bulgaria's second city has never looked finer. Ancient buildings nestle right in the centre of this seven-hilled town; a pleasant shopping street flows past its 2nd-century Roman stadium (which still hosts concerts) and a 15th-century mosque in an effortless blend of old and new.

Stara Planina Hiking

9 Hikers have breathtaking choice across the Stara Planina mountain range, rippling for 550km across the length of Bulgaria. Casual strollers can walk through the meadows around Dryanovo or stride to peaceful monasteries such as Sokolski. Meanwhile, dedicated hikers can climb the tallest peak, Mt Botev (2376m). Alternatively, seek out solitude on multiday hikes.

JASMINE_K / SHUTTERSTOCK ©

Yes or No?

One cultural oddity that foreign visitors may find confusing at first is that Bulgarians shake their heads from side to side in a curved, almost wobbly motion to indicate 'yes', and gently jerk their heads up and backwards when they want to say 'no'. To add to the confusion, if Bulgarians know they are addressing a foreigner, they may reverse these gestures in an attempt to be helpful. If you are in any doubt about their real meaning, asking *'Da ili ne?'* ('Yes or no?') will soon set you straight.

Cour Royale, Tiébélé

CAPITAL
Ouagadougou

POPULATION
18.5 million

AREA
274,200 sq km

OFFICIAL LANGUAGE
French

Burkina Faso

Previously called Upper Volta and little noticed in the wider world, Burkina Faso nonetheless ends up being many travellers' favourite West African country.

Burkina should be on everyone's travel list – it may not have many big-ticket attractions, but the warmth of its welcome and the friendliness of the Burkinabé people is unique. Wherever you go you'll be greeted with a memorable *'bonne arrivée'* ('welcome') and a handshake.

There's also the lively cultural scene. The capital, Ouagadougou, and Bobo-Dioulasso, Burkina's two largest and gloriously named cities, are famous for their musical tradi-

tions and beautiful handicrafts. Throw in Fespaco, Africa's premier film festival (held in Ouaga every odd-numbered year), and there's enough to engage your mind and senses for a couple of weeks or so.

Tourism infrastructure is fairly limited, but the true gems of Burkina Faso are in the more remote areas, outside of the cities: the enchanting beauty of the landscapes and the unique culture and genuine hospitality of the Burkinabé.

Top Experiences

Sindou Peaks

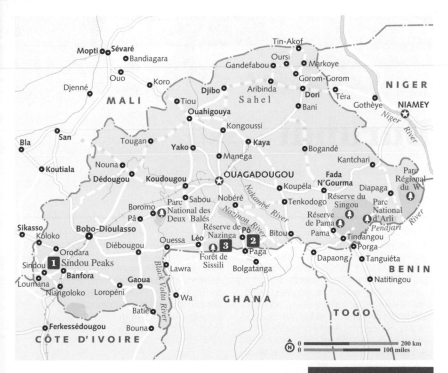

1 Nature's work of art, the otherworldly rock formations of Sindou Peaks are a sight to behold. Cast against the darkening sky of a brewing storm or the lush paddy fields of the plains below, they are one of Burkina's great signature landscapes.

Cour Royale

2 More than 450 people live in Tiébélé's royal court, a large compound of typical *sukhalas* (traditional painted houses). Children live with their grandparents in octagonal huts, couples live in rectangular huts and single people in round ones. Each drawing, whether geometrical or illustrative, has a meaning (such as fertility, afterlife, wisdom etc).

Réserve de Nazinga

3 This reserve is one of Burkina's most loved and accessible wildlife-spotting areas. The multitude of animals – among them antelope, monkeys, caimans and a variety of bird species – attract visitors, but it's the chance to spot elephants that make the park special. The dry season is the best time to see these majestic animals.

When to Go

HIGH SEASON (Jan–Mar)

SHOULDER (Oct–Dec)

LOW SEASON (Apr–Sep)

Food & Drink

Sauces *Arachide* (peanut) or *graine* (hot sauce made with palm nuts) are mainstays.

Aloco Plantain fried with chilli in palm oil.

Dolo Millet beer.

Juice Local juices include *bissap* (hibiscus) and tamarind.

CAPITAL
Bujumbura

POPULATION
10.2 million

AREA
27,830km sq

OFFICIAL LANGUAGES
Kirundi, French

Drummers in Bujumbura

Burundi

Despite troubles Burundians have an irrepressible joie de vivre, and their smiles are as infectious as a rhythm laid down by Les Tambourinaires drummers. However, at this time Burundi is considered unsafe to visit.

Tiny Burundi is an incongruous mix of soaring mountains, languid lakeside communities and a tragic past blighted by ethnic conflict. When civil war broke out in 1993, the economy was destroyed and the tourist industry succumbed to a quick death. The war tragically lasted until 2005, and after it ended the country eventually began to receive a trickle of travellers, particularly to the steamy capital. Bujumbura has a lovely location on the shores of Lake Tanganyika, and just outside the city are some of the finest inland beaches on the continent.

However, the new peace came to a shattering end in 2015 when President Nkurunziza decided to run for what many Burundians believed to be a constitution-breaking third term in office. Violence broke out before the election, and has escalated since.

Snapshot

Parc National de la Rusizi

1 Antelopes and hippos stomp and splash through this national park just outside Bujumbura.

Bujumbura

2 Before the most recent violence, Burundi's sultry capital was known for great nightlife and delicious food. Largely frozen in time due to more than a decade of conflict, there has been very little development in the steamy city, which retains much of its grandiose colonial town planning and a French outlook on life.

Chutes de la Karera

3 The Chutes de la Karera is the collective name for the four beautiful waterfalls near Rutana. The prettiest is the cascade Nyakai I. Upstream is the smallest, Nyakai II. This watercourse is joined by that of Mwaro Falls before creating the tallest waterfall in the area, Karera Falls. The falls are at their best during the wet season.

Source du Nil

4 Burundi's very own pyramid, a memorial marks a small stream in Kasumo at the southernmost source of the Nile.

Food & Drink

Brochettes (kebabs) and *frites* (fries) are a legacy of the Belgian colonial period, but there are also succulent fish from Lake Tanganyika and serious steaks.

When it comes to drink, Burundi is blessed with a national brewery churning out huge bottles of Primus.

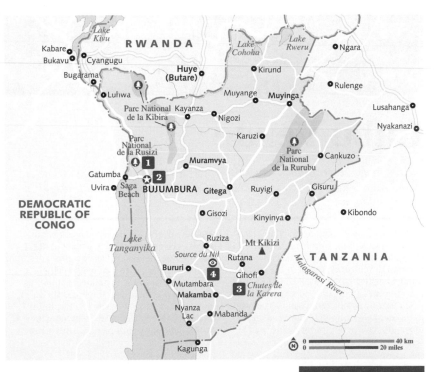

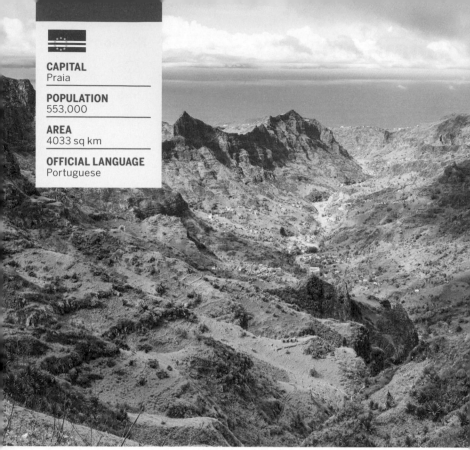

CAPITAL	Praia
POPULATION	553,000
AREA	4033 sq km
OFFICIAL LANGUAGE	Portuguese

Mountainous Serra Malagueta, Santiago

Cabo Verde

Jutting up from the Atlantic, some 500km west of Senegal, this stunning island chain has a captivating blend of mountains, beaches and peaceful seaside villages.

On Santo Antão, craggy peaks hide piercing green valleys of flowers and sugar cane, ideal for epic hikes. São Vicente is home to the cultural capital of the islands, Mindelo, which throbs with bars and music clubs.

On Sal and Maio, undulating windswept dunes merge with indigo-blue seas on unspoilt beaches of powdery white sand.

Meanwhile, far-flung Fogo and Brava in the southwest offer their own enchantments, from surreal volcanic landscapes, to sparkling bays framed by towering peaks. Throw in the constant beat of music that Cabo Verde is famed for and the renowned *morabeza* (Creole for hospitality) of its people and you'll see why many have come – and never left.

Top Experiences

Santo Antão

For many people the main reason for visiting Cabo Verde is the spectacular island of Santo Antão. This dizzyingly vertical isle, ruptured with canyons, gorges and valleys, offers some of the most amazing hiking in West Africa. The second-largest island in the archipelago, it is the only one that puts the verde in Cabo Verde. As you approach from São Vicente by ferry, you wouldn't guess how green it is, as the south side looks barren and harsh. But the northeast of the island, the most populated corner and the most popular with hikers, receives enough regular moisture for forests of pine trees to dominate the hilltops and tropical plants to flourish in the steamy valleys.

Mt Fogo

Cabo Verde's highest peak (2829m/9382ft), the conical, cinder-clad Mt Fogo, rises dramatically out of the floor of an ancient crater known as Chã das Caldeiras. A scenic, cobbled road, punctuated by hamlets with lava-block houses, encircles the island. It's still an active volcano and last erupted from late 2014 to early 2015, yet intrepid farmers continue to grow coffee, grapes and fruit trees on its black slopes.

Sal

If you don't mind the heavy tourist crowds, Sal has a fine restaurant scene, plenty of nightlife and some lovely beaches

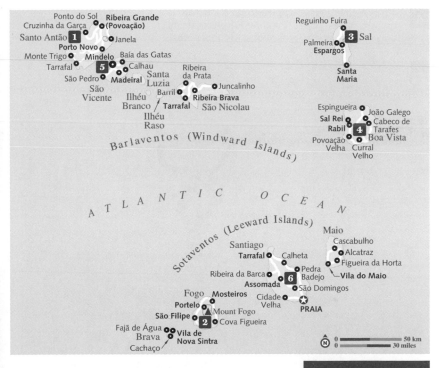

Ponto do Sol · Ribeira Grande (Povoação)
Cruzinha da Garça
Santo Antão 1 · Janela
Porto Novo
Monte Trigo · Mindelo · Baía das Gatas
Tarrafal · Calhau
São Pedro · Madeiral · Santa · Ribeira
São · Luzia · da Prata · Juncalinho
Vicente · Ilhéu · Barril · Ribeira Brava
Branco / Tarrafal · São Nicolau
Ilhéu
Raso

Reguinho Fuira
3 Sal
Palmeira
Espargos
Santa Maria

Espingueira · João Galego
Sal Rei · Cabeço de
Rabil · 4 · Tarafes
Povoação · Boa Vista
Velha · Curral
Velho

Barlaventos (Windward Islands)

ATLANTIC OCEAN

Sotaventos (Leeward Islands)

Maio
Cascabulho
Santiago · Alcatraz
Tarrafal · Calheta · Figueira da Horta
Pedra · Vila do Maio
Ribeira da Barca · 6 · Badejo
Assomada · São Domingos
Fogo · Mosteiros · Cidade
Portelo · Velha · PRAIA
São Filipe · 2 · Mount Fogo
Fajã de Água · Cova Figueira
Brava · Vila de
Cachaço · Nova Sintra

0 — 50 km
0 — 30 miles

where you can unwind and enjoy some water sports. The great attraction is the surreal, lunarlike Pedra do Lume – the crater of an ancient volcano, where seawater is transformed into shimmering salt beds. You can see the old salt extraction machinery, float in the medicinal salt water and have a massage or salt scrub at the small spa. Other points of interest include the fish market in Palmeira, the gorgeous Igrejinha beach at the far eastern end of Santa Maria and the Buracona natural swimming pool (time your visit for noon to see the Blue Eye, a natural light effect in a small underground pool).

Boa Vista

4 With its feathery lines of peachy dunes, stark plains and scanty oases, the island of Boa Vista looks as if a chunk of the Sahara somehow broke off the side of Africa and floated out to the middle of the Atlantic. Though the island offers some fantastic if wind-blown beaches, incredible windsurfing, the pretty little town of Sal Rei and an ever-increasing number of resorts and hotels, it's this desert interior that is the best reason for venturing out here. Be ready for some rough off-roading, as most of Boa Vista's roads are treacherous.

São Vicente

5 Small, stark and undulating, the island of São Vicente would be fairly forgettable were it not for the beautiful Mediterranean town of Mindelo, Cabo Verde's prettiest city and home to one of Africa's

Getting Around

Inter-island flights are generally not expensive.

The only reliable scheduled ferry services in Cabo Verde are between Praia, Brava and Fogo; Praia and Maio; and Mindelo (São Vicente) and Santo Antão.

Known as *colectivos* or *alugue*rs, minibuses provide connections between even relatively small towns on most islands Cabo Verde.

3

most raucous festivals. For a break from the city, Mt Verde (750m), the island's highest peak and only touch of green, is an easy day's hike and offers panoramic views. There are also windy but fine beaches at Baía das Gatas, Calhau and Salamansa. The lovely bay off the latter offers windsurfing and kitesurfing classes – look for the Kitesurf Cabo Verde beach shack.

Santiago

6 Santiago, the largest island of the archipelago and the first to be settled, has a little bit of all the other islands. It has the sandy beaches, the desert plains, the verdant valleys and the mountainous interior as well as the capital, Praia. All this makes it a worthy stop on your Cabo Verdean rambles. The mountain village of Rui Vaz near the town of São Domingos is a picturesque base for hikes into surrounding mountains.

Food & Drink

While Cabo Verdean cuisine may include Portuguese niceties such as imported olives and Alentejo wines, it's built on a firm African base, with *milho* (corn) and *feijão* (beans) the ubiquitous staples. Thanks to the large number of Italian tourists and expats, good pizza and pasta dishes are available in even the most out-of-the-way places.

HENRYK KOTOWSKI / ALAMY STOCK PHOTO ©

Vibrant Festivals

Mindelo, on São Vicente, puts on the sexiest Mardi Gras this side of Río: Creole Carnival, with its colourful street parades. Held 40 days before Easter, it's a sexy, spectacular carnival-type celebration.

For music lovers, the Atlantic Music Expo in Praia, Santiago, always offers a good time, with a line-up of performers from Cabo Verde, Africa, Europe and beyond. There's also a good street market. Held over four days in April, it's followed soon after by the Kriol Jazz Festival.

Apsara dancer

Cambodia

Ascend to the realm of the gods, Angkor Wat. Descend into hell at Tuol Sleng prison. With a history both inspiring and depressing, Cambodia delivers an intoxicating present.

Cambodia is a captivating destination that casts a spell on all those who visit.

Fringed by beautiful beaches and tropical islands, sustained by the mother waters of the Mekong River and cloaked in some of the region's few remaining emerald wildernesses, Cambodia is an adventure as much as a holiday. This is the warm heart of Southeast Asia, with everything the region has to offer packed into one bite-sized chunk.

Despite having the eighth wonder of the world in its backyard, Cambodia's greatest treasure is its people. The Khmers have been to hell and back, but thanks to an unbreakable spirit and infectious optimism they have prevailed with their smiles and spirits largely intact.

CAPITAL
Phnom Penh

POPULATION
16 million

AREA
181,035 sq km

OFFICIAL LANGUAGE
Khmer

Top Experiences

Phnom Penh

1 The Cambodian capital is a chaotic yet charming city that has stepped out of the shadows of the past to embrace a brighter future. Boasting one of the most beguiling riverfronts in the region, Phnom Penh is surprisingly sophisticated thanks to its hip hotels, epicurean eateries and boho bars ready to welcome urban explorers. Experience emotional extremes at the inspiring National Museum and the depressing Tuol Sleng prison, showcasing the best and worst of Cambodian history. Once known as the 'pearl of Asia', Phnom Penh is glistening once more.

Sihanoukville Beaches

2 Despite a reputation for backpacker hedonism, Sihanoukville's real appeal lies in its bustling beaches. It's only a short distance from Sihanoukville's gritty centre to popular Otres Beach, a still mellow and sublime stretch of sand despite the long-looming threat of development. More central, and the town's prettiest beach, is Sokha Beach, its tiny eastern end rarely crowded. The original traveller magnet is Serendipity Beach, which blends right into Occheuteal Beach, popular with locals by day and 24-hour party people by night.

Mondulkiri

3 Eventually the endless rice fields and sugar palms that characterise the Cambodian landscape give way to rolling hills and the wild east of Mondulkiri, home to the hardy Bunong people, who still practise animism and ancestor worship. Wildlife is a big draw here with the opportunity to 'walk with the herd' at Elephant Valley Project or spot doucs or gibbons on a trek through the Seima Protected Forest. Add thunderous waterfalls, a jungle zipline and quad biking to the mix and you have the perfect ingredients for an authentic adventure.

GUOZHONGHUA / SHUTTERSTOCK ©

6

Siem Reap & the Temples of Angkor

4 One of the world's most magnificent sights, the temples of Angkor are even better than the superlatives suggest. Choose from Angkor Wat, the world's largest religious building; Bayon, one of the world's weirdest; or Ta Prohm, where nature runs amok. Siem Reap is the base for exploring the world's grandest collection of temples and is abuzz with a superb selection of restaurants and bars. Beyond the temples lie floating villages on Tonlé Sap lake, adrenalin-inducing activities such as quad biking and microlighting, and cultured pursuits such as cooking classes.

TIMOTHY ALLEN / GETTY IMAGES ©

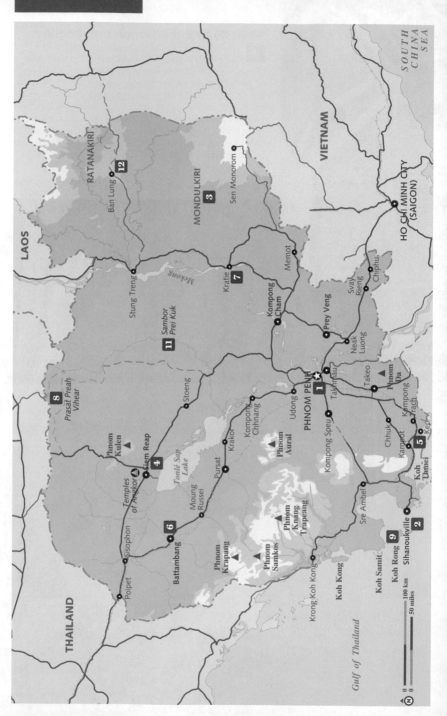

Kampot Province

5 Kampot Province offers atmospheric towns, and attractions as varied as national parks, cave pagodas and tropical beaches. In laid-back Kampot town, choose from backpacker hostels, riverside resorts or boutique hotels to take in the wonderful French architectural legacy, or explore the pretty river by paddle-board or kayak. Sleepier Kep, just down the road, has its famous Crab Market, hiking in Kep National Park and nearby Koh Tonsay (Rabbit Island). Countryside romps include the winding ascent to Bokor Hill Station or exploring the working pepper farms for which Kampot is justly famous.

Battambang

6 This is the real Cambodia, far from the jet-set destinations of Phnom Penh and Siem Reap. Unfurling along the banks of the Sangker River, Battambang is one of the country's best-preserved colonial-era towns. Streets of French shophouses host everything from fair-trade cafes to art galleries. Beyond the town is the Cambodian countryside and a cluster of ancient temples, which, although not exactly Angkor Wat, do, mercifully, lack the crowds. Then there's the 'bamboo train', a unique form of handmade local transport only found here. Battambang in a word? Charming.

Best in Film

The Killing Fields (1984) This definitive film on the Khmer Rouge period in Cambodia tells the story of American journalist Sydney Schanberg and Cambodian photographer Dith Pran during and after the war.

Apocalypse Now (1979) In Francis Ford Coppola's masterpiece, a renegade colonel, played by Marlon Brando, goes AWOL in Cambodia. Martin Sheen plays a young soldier sent to bring him back, and the ensuing encounter makes for a powerful indictment of war.

The Last Reel (2014) Award-winning homegrown Cambodian film about the impact of Cambodia's dark past on the next generation.

Best in Print

Hun Sen's Cambodia (Sebastian Strangio) A no-holds-barred look at contemporary Cambodia and the rule of Prime Minister Hun Sen.

The Gate (François Bizot) Bizot was kidnapped by the Khmer Rouge, and later held by them in the French embassy.

Voices from S-21 (David Chandler) A study of the Khmer Rouge's interrogation and torture centre.

Cambodia's Curse (Joel Brinkley) Pulitzer Prize–winning journalist pulls no punches in his criticism of the government and donors alike.

When to Go

HIGH SEASON
(Nov–Feb)
Cooler and windy, with almost Mediterranean temperatures.

SHOULDER
(Apr & Oct)
Temperatures rise in April; rains taper off in October.

LOW SEASON
(May–Sep)
In May the mercury hits 40°C and visitors melt. The rainy season means emerald-green landscapes.

Kampot Pepper

Before Cambodia's civil war, no Paris restaurant worth its salt would be without pepper from Kampot Province, but the pepper farms were all but destroyed by the Khmer Rouge. Today, Kampot pepper, delicate and aromatic but packing a powerful punch, is making a comeback.

Ziplining with Gibbons

Flight of the Gibbon Angkor, outside Siem Reap, offers a zipline course with 10 lines and the chance to spot some gibbons in the wild.

Snack Foods

Banh chev Rice pancake stuffed with yummy herbs, bean sprouts and a meat or fish staple.

Bobor Rice porridge, like congee in China, popular with dried fish and egg or zip it up with chilli and black pepper.

Chek chien Deep-fried bananas; these are a popular street snack at any time of day.

Nam ben choc Thin rice noodles served with a red chicken curry or a fish-based broth.

Kaun pong tier One of the most popular street snacks in Cambodia – unborn duck foetus.

Loat Small white noodles that almost look like bean sprouts; they taste delicious fried up with beef.

Kratie

7 Gateway to the rare freshwater Irrawaddy dolphins of the Mekong River, Kratie (pronounced kra-*cheh*) is a busy crossroads on the overland route between Phnom Penh and northeastern Cambodia or southern Laos. The supremely mellow riverside town has a certain decaying colonial grandeur and boasts some of the country's best Mekong sunsets. Nearby Koh Trong island is a relaxing place to experience a homestay or explore on two wheels. North of Kratie lies the Mekong Discovery Trail, with adventures and experiences themed around the mother river, including community-based homestays, bicycle rides and boat trips. Beyond the river, Kratie Province is a remote and wild land that sees few outsiders.

Prasat Preah Vihear

8 The mother of all mountain temples, Prasat Preah Vihear stands majestically atop the Dangkrek Mountains, forming a controversial border post between Cambodia and Thailand. The foundation stones of the temple stretch to the edge of the cliff as it falls precipitously away to the plains below, and the views are incredible. The 300-year chronology of its construction also offers an insight into the metamorphosis of carving and sculpture during the Angkorian period. It's all about location, though, and it doesn't get better than this.

The Southern Islands

9 In Cambodia's up-and-coming southern islands, Koh Rong and Koh Rong Sanloem, off the coast of Sihanoukville, fulfil those Southeast Asian paradise fantasies. Koh Rong is party central, with its hippie trippy travel hub of Koh Tuch village; the rest of the island, fringed by silicon sand and clad in dense jungle, is an escape. More mellow and family friendly is Koh Rong Sanloem, with some tropical hideaway resorts and gentle, shallow bays. There are more islands along the coast, including the Koh Sdach archipelago and the large, almost undeveloped Koh Kong.

Khmer Cuisine in Siem Reap

10 Everyone has tried Thai and Vietnamese specialities before they hit the region, but Khmer cuisine, an unexpected epicurean adventure, remains under the culinary radar. *Amok* (baked fish with lemongrass, chilli and coconut) is the national dish, but sumptuous seafood and fresh-fish dishes are plentiful, including Kep crab infused with Kampot pepper. It wouldn't be Asia without street snacks, and Cambodia delivers everything from *mee* (noodles) and *bobo* (congee) to deep-fried tarantulas and roasted crickets, some of which can be sampled on a foodie tour in Siem Reap.

Sambor Prei Kuk

11 Cambodia's most impressive group of pre-Angkorian monuments, Sambor Prei Kuk encompasses more than 100 mainly brick temples huddled in the forest, among them some of the oldest structures in the country. Originally called Isanapura, it served as the capital of Upper Chenla during the reign of the early 7th-century King Isanavarman and continued to serve as an important learning centre during the Angkorian era.

Boeng Yeak Lom

12 At the heart of the protected area of Yeak Lom is a beautiful, emerald-hued crater lake set amid the vivid greens of the towering jungle. It is one of the most peaceful, beautiful locations Cambodia has to offer and the water is extremely clear. Several wooden piers are dotted around the perimeter, making it perfect for swimming. A small Cultural and Environmental Centre has a modest display on ethnic minorities in the province and hires out life jackets for children.

ELIZABETH EDIE / SHUTTERSTOCK ©

Getting Around

 Domestic flights link Phnom Penh and Siem Reap, and Siem Reap and Sihanoukville.

 Boat travel is less common than in the old days of bad roads, but boat trips from Siem Reap to either Battambang or Phnom Penh remain popular.

 Bus is the most popular form of transport for most travellers, connecting all major towns and cities.

 Private car or 4WD is an affordable option for those who value time above money. Motorbikes are an amazing way to travel for experienced riders.

Yaoundé

POPULATION
24.4 million

AREA
475,440 sq km

OFFICIAL LANGUAGES
English, French

Cameroon

Cameroon is Africa's throbbing heart, a crazed, sultry mosaic of active volcanoes, white-sand beaches, thick rainforest and magnificent parched landscapes broken up by the bizarre rock formations of the Sahel.

With both Francophone and Anglophone regions, not to mention some 250 local languages, Cameroon is a vast ethnic and linguistic jigsaw, yet one that enjoys a great deal of stability. The country's rapidly expanding capital, Yaoundé, features a host of art deco, independence-era and 1970s government buildings in various exuberant styles. This is the centre of government and administration, and one of the most attractive sights is people wearing ministry uniforms, with bright tailor-made African fabrics depicting the various departments.

With reasonable road infrastructure, travel is easier here than in many parts of Africa. Still, you'll miss none of those indicators that you're in the middle of this fascinating continent: everyone seems to be carrying something on their heads, *makossa* music sets the rhythm, the street smells of roasting plantains and African bliss is just a piece of grilled fish and a sweating beer away.

170 | CAMEROON

Top Experiences

Village des Artisans

1 South of the attractive Islamic town of Foumban, the Village des Artisans seems to produce more handicrafts than the rest of Cameroon combined. Get ready for some bargaining and banter. Feathered hats and beaded staffs are among the collectable items.

Mt Cameroon

2 This soaring, active volcano is hugely dramatic, and a climb to the summit is a highlight of many visits to the country. Most hikes take two or three days, but it's no stroll in the park. The difficulty stems not only from its height (4095m), but from the fact that you start from near sea level, making a big change in altitude in a relatively short distance.

Limbe

3 Limbe is a charming place, with a fabulous natural position between the rainforest-swathed foothills of Mt Cameroon and the dramatic Atlantic coastline. Popular with tourists, this is a great spot to chill out on the beach for a few days before heading elsewhere.

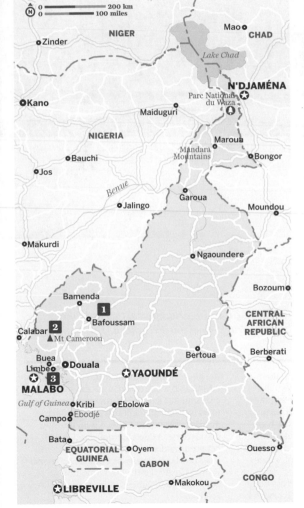

Food & Drink

Beer Drunk at shacks and bars from dawn to dusk.

Fufu Mashed yam, corn, plantain or couscous.

Gambas (prawns) A particular delight.

Ndole A sauce made with bitter leaves similar to spinach and flavoured with smoked fish.

When to Go

 HIGH SEASON (Nov–Feb)

 SHOULDER (Mar & Oct)

 LOW SEASON (Apr–Oct)

CAPITAL	Ottawa
POPULATION	34.6 million
AREA	10 million sq km
OFFICIAL LANGUAGES	English, French

Bow River, Rocky Mountains

Canada

Canada is more than its hulking-mountain, craggy-coast good looks: it also cooks extraordinary meals, rocks cool culture and unfurls wild, moose-spotting road trips.

The globe's second-biggest country has an endless variety of landscapes. Sky-high mountains, glinting glaciers, spectral rainforests and remote beaches are all here, spread across six time zones. It's the backdrop for plenty of awe-inspiring moments – and for a big cast of local characters. That's big as in polar bears, grizzly bears, whales and, everyone's favorite, moose.

Canada is incredibly diverse across its breadth and within its cities. You'll hear it in the music, see it in the arts and taste it in the cuisine. Sip a *café au lait* and tear into a flaky croissant at a sidewalk bistro in Montréal; head to an Asian night market and slurp noodles in Vancouver; join a wild-fiddling Celtic party on Cape Breton Island; kayak between rainforest-cloaked Aboriginal villages on Haida Gwaii; visit the International Fringe Theater Festival in Edmonton or Toronto's world famous International Film Festival.

Top Experiences

Haida Gwaii

1 Once known as the Queen Charlotte Islands, this dagger-shaped archipelago 80km off BC's coast is a magical trip for those who make it. Colossal spruce and cedars cloak the wild, rain-sodden landscape. Bald eagles and bears roam the ancient forest, while sea lions and orcas cruise the waters. But the islands' real soul is the resurgent Haida people, best known for their war-canoe and totem-pole carvings. See the lot at Gwaii Haanas National Park Reserve, which combines lost villages, burial caves and hot springs with some of the continent's best kayaking.

Nahanni National Park Reserve

2 Gorgeous hot springs, haunted gorges and gorging grizzlies fill this remote park near the Yukon border, and you'll have to fly in to reach them. Only about 1000 visitors per year make the trek, half of them paddlers trying to conquer the South Nahanni River. Untamed and spectacular, it churns 500km through the Mackenzie Mountains. Thirty-story waterfalls, towering canyons and legends of giants and lost gold round out the journey north.

Vancouver

3 Vancouver always lands atop the 'best places to live' lists, and who's to argue? Sea-to-sky beauty surrounds the laid-back, cocktail-lovin' metropolis. With skiable mountains on the outskirts, 11 beaches fringing the core and Stanley Park's thick rainforest just blocks from the glass skyscrapers downtown, it's a harmonic convergence of city and nature. It also mixes Hollywood chic (many movies are filmed here) with a freewheeling counterculture (the Marijuana Party political headquarters) and buzzing multicultural communities.

MFFOTO / SHUTTERSTOCK ©

The Rockies

4 The sawtooth, white-topped mountains straddling the British Columbia–Alberta border inspire both awe and action. Four national parks – Banff, Yoho, Kootenay and Jasper – offer countless opportunities to delve into the lush wilderness with ribbons of hiking trails, rushing white water and powdery ski slopes. The train provides another popular way to experience the grandeur: luminous lakes, jumbles of wildflowers and glistening glaciers glide by as the steel cars chug up mountain passes and down river valleys en route to points east or west.

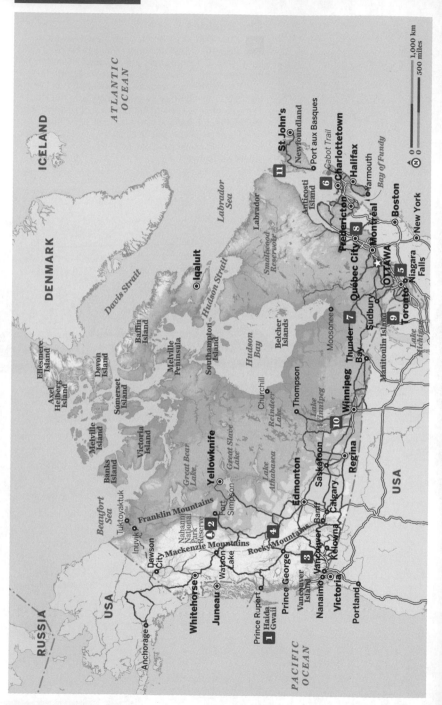

Best for an Adrenaline Rush

Whistler If you want to ski or snowboard Canada's best, Whistler reigns supreme.

Tofino Little Tofino packs big adventure with its Pacific coast surfing, kayaking, hiking and storm watching.

Banff Queen of the Rockies, Banff has it all: skiing, hiking, rafting, horseback riding, mountain biking...phew!

Laurentians The mountain villages speckling the landscape outside Montréal let you ski, luge and rock climb.

Marble Mountain Skiing and snow-kiting in winter, caving and kayaking in summer, and ziplining year-round in Newfoundland.

Fall Foliage

Canada blazes come autumn, which should come as no surprise in a country that's half-covered by forest. Québec's Laurentian Mountains flame especially bright from all the sugar maple trees (which also sauce the nation's pancakes). Cape Breton, Nova Scotia, flares up so beautifully they hold a festival to honor the foliage – it's called Celtic Colours and it's in mid-October. New Brunswick's Fundy Coast and Ontario's Muskoka Lakes area pull in leaf peepers too.

Niagara Falls

5 Crowded? Cheesy? Well, yes. Niagara is short, too – it doesn't even crack the top 500 worldwide for height. But c'mon, when those great muscular bands of water arc over the precipice like liquid glass, roaring into the void below, and when you sail toward it in a mist-shrouded little boat, Niagara Falls impresses big time. In terms of sheer volume, nowhere in North America beats its thundering cascade, with more than one million bathtubs of water plummeting over the edge every second.

Cabot Trail

6 The 300km Cabot Trail winds and climbs over coastal mountains, with heart-stopping sea views at every turn, breaching whales just offshore, moose nibbling roadside and plenty of trails to stop and hike. Be sure to tote your dancing shoes – Celtic and Acadian communities dot the area, and their foot-stompin', crazy-fiddlin' music vibrates through local pubs.

Driving the Trans-Canada Highway

7 Canada's main vein stretches 7800km from St John's, Newfoundland, to Victoria, BC, and takes in the country's greatest hits along the way. Gros Morne National Park, Cape Breton Island, Québec City, Banff National Park and Yoho National Park are part of the path, as are major cities including

When to Go

HIGH SEASON
(Jun–Aug)
Sunshine and warm weather prevail; far northern regions briefly thaw.

SHOULDER
(May & Sep–Oct)
Temperatures are cool but comfortable. Fall foliage areas remain busy.

LOW SEASON
(Nov–Apr)
Places outside the big cities and ski resorts close. Darkness and cold take over.

Scenic Drives

Canada is made for road-tripping. Even if you have just one day, you can take a gobsmacking journey. With more time you can really roll.

Pond Hockey

When it comes to hockey, Canadians play hard and they play well. Grassroots hockey, aka pond hockey, takes place in communities across the country every night on a frozen surface. All you need is a puck, a hockey stick and a few friends to live the dream.

Food & Drink

Beavertails Fried, sugared dough.

Beef Alberta is the nation's beef capital and you'll find Alberta steak at leading restaurants across the country.

Lobster The main dish of the east, boiled in the pot and served with a little butter.

Maktaaq Whale skin cut into small pieces and swallowed whole.

Maple Syrup Québec is the world's largest maple-syrup producer, processing around 6.5 million gallons per year.

Prairie Oysters Bull's testicles prepared in a variety of ways.

Poutine French fries topped with gravy and cheese curds.

Seal Northern speciality, served boiled.

Montréal, Ottawa, Calgary and Vancouver. It takes most road-trippers a good month to drive coast to coast, so what are you waiting for? Fuel up, cue the tunes, and put the pedal to the metal.

Old Québec City

8 Québec's capital is more than 400 years old, and its stone walls, glinting-spired cathedrals and jazz-soaked corner cafes suffuse it with atmosphere, romance, melancholy, eccentricity and intrigue on par with any European city. The best way to soak it up is to walk the Old Town's labyrinth of lanes and get lost amid the street performers and cozy inns, stopping every so often for a *café au lait*,

flaky pastry or heaping plate of *poutine* to refuel.

Manitoulin Island

9 The largest freshwater island in the world and floating right smack in Lake Huron's midst, Manitoulin is a slowpoke place of beaches and summery cottages. Jagged expanses of white quartzite and granite outcroppings edge the shoreline and lead to shimmering vistas. First Nations culture pervades, and the island's eight communities collaborate to offer local foods (wild rice, corn soup) and eco-adventures (canoeing, horseback riding, hiking). Powwows add drumming, dancing and storytelling to the mix.

The Prairies

10 Solitude reigns in Canada's middle ground. Driving through the flatlands of Manitoba and Saskatchewan turns up uninterrupted fields of golden wheat that stretch to the horizon, eventually melting into the sunshine. When the wind blows, the wheat sways like waves on the ocean, punctuated by the occasional grain elevator rising up like a tall ship. Big skies mean big storms that drop like an anvil, visible on the skyline for kilometers. Far-flung towns include arty Winnipeg, boozy Moose Jaw and Mountie-filled Regina, sprinkled between with Ukrainian and Scandinavian villages.

Viking Trail

11 This themed highway, named for the first Europeans that touched shore here, links Newfoundland's west coast to Southern Labrador. The Viking Trail, aka Route 430, connects two World Heritage sites on Newfoundland's Northern Peninsula. Gros Morne National Park, with its fjord-like lakes and geological oddities, rests at its base, while the sublime, 1000-year-old Viking settlement at L'Anse aux Meadows – Leif Eriksson's pad – stares out from the peninsula's tip. The road is an attraction in its own right, holding close to the sea as it heads resolutely north past Port au Choix's ancient burial grounds and the ferry jump-off to big, bad Labrador.

Northern Lights

12 Canada has a lot of middle-of-nowhere, high-latitude places, from the Labrador coast to Arctic villages. They may not seem like much during the day, but at night, drapes of green, yellow, aqua, violet and other polychromatic hues flicker and dance across the sky. Traditionally, some Inuit peoples believed the northern lights (aka the aurora borealis) were the spirits of hunted animals while others feared they were the lanterns of demons chasing lost souls. Seen from September to March, darker skies make the coldest winter months the best for viewing.

Getting Around

An extensive highway system links most towns. Away from the population centers, distances can be deceivingly long and travel times slow.

Outside the Toronto–Montréal corridor, train travel is mostly for scenic journeys.

Public ferry systems operate extensively in British Columbia, Québec and the Maritime provinces.

Regional and national air carriers crisscross the country, taking days off travel time and reaching northern towns inaccessible by road.

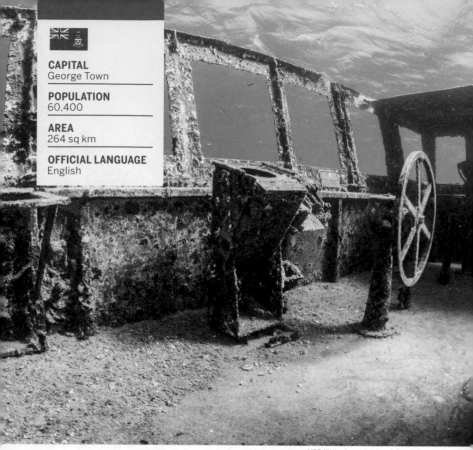

CAPITAL
George Town

POPULATION
60,400

AREA
264 sq km

OFFICIAL LANGUAGE
English

USS *Kittiwake* artificial reef, Grand Cayman

Cayman Islands

Laze on stunning beaches, scuba dive at world-class sites and spot Grand Cayman's brilliant blue iguanas – the Cayman Islands are much more than just a tax haven.

Some two million tourists visit the Cayman Islands each year. Most of them are cruise-ship passengers, who spend a few hours shopping, sunbathing or swimming with stingrays, before pulling out of port. Others hunker down near Seven Mile Beach, enjoying their all-inclusive resort on one of the Caribbean's most beautiful stretches of sand. And a lucky few venture further.

Cayman is a cosmopolitan place – nearly half the population is from somewhere else – but its rich local culture is alive and well, especially in Bodden Town, East End and Cayman Brac. Explore the North Side and the Sister Islands to discover lush forests, diverse bird life, mysterious caves and untrammeled beaches. Under the waves lie underwater walls and accessible shipwrecks.

Dive in. It takes only a small sense of adventure to uncover Cayman's greatest treasures – the hospitality and the fantastic natural phenomena above and below the sea.

Top Experiences

USS Kittiwake

Cayman's top dive site is this 76m US-Navy submarine rescue ship, which was deliberately sunk to create an artificial reef. Ample entries and exits allow divers to swim through and explore the rooms, peek through windows, sit at a table in the mess hall or take a turn at the steering wheel. It lies between 15 and 64 feet below the surface.

Starfish Point

Crystalline waters protect countless red cushion sea stars along this wonderful little stretch of sand. Soaking in a foot of water all along the beach, the starfish are easy to spot from above the surface, so you don't need snorkel gear. Some tours stop here, but otherwise this place feels like a secret spot – known to the starfish and few others.

Little Cayman

The clue is in the name. Little Cayman is tiny indeed, but it abounds with bird life, marine life and glorious natural scenery. With more resident iguanas than humans, this delightful island is the place to head for solitude, tranquility and the odd spot of extraordinary diving.

When to Go

☀ **HIGH SEASON** (Dec–Apr)

⛅ **SHOULDER** (May, Jun & Nov)

☂ **LOW SEASON** (Jul–Oct)

Food & Drink

Conch This large pink mollusk is cooked with onion and spices in a stew, fried as fritters, or sliced raw and served with a lime marinade.

Tortuga rum cake A heavy, moist cake.

Mudslide A creamy cocktail combining Kahlua, Baileys and vodka – invented at Rum Point.

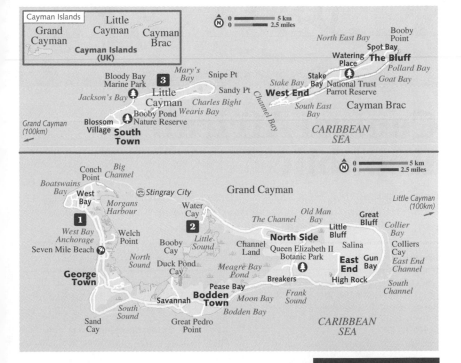

CAPITAL
Bangui

POPULATION
5.5 million

AREA
622,984 sq km

OFFICIAL LANGUAGE
French

Forest elephants, Dzanga-Sangha National Park

Central African Republic

Central African Republic (CAR) is a country with staggering rare natural beauty and some of the world's most amazing wildlife. The country is not currently considered stable or safe enough to travel to.

For centuries CAR has endured rapacity from colonisers and then from its own leaders in collusion with former colonisers. Yet the people of this plundered nation are open and friendly; and their conversations are more full of hope than despair.

It's one of the best places in Africa for encounters with forest elephant and lowland gorillas, and the best place in the world, some say, to see butterflies. It's also one of the most impoverished countries on the continent. CAR is landlocked, its border crossings can be dangerous, and flights are expensive and infrequent.

Snapshot

Dzanga-Sangha National Park

1 This massive forest reserve, in the southwest corner of the Central African Republic, sits at the heart of the newly created Unesco World Heritage–listed Dzanga Trinational reserve. Dzanga-Sangha boasts huge concentrations of elephants, and chimpanzees and gorillas are found in impressive numbers.

Bangui

2 Bangui stretches along the Oubangui River with a row of lush green hills behind it. The French founded it in 1889, and by the 1970s it was known as La Coquette (The Beautiful). The moniker is a little ironic these days, though finally signs of re-birth are far more common than remnants of war.

Chutes de Boali

3 These waterfalls tumble 50m (164ft), which is just a whisker more than Niagara can manage. Although no more than a trickle when its dry, they are dramatic during the rainy season. The water is controlled by a huge Chinese-built dam upriver.

Seasons

 OCT–MAR

 APR–SEP

Food & Drink

Bushmeat May include monkey, boa or antelope.

Bili-bili Sorghum-based alcohol.

Cassava Eaten at virtually every meal.

Forest caterpillars A treat during June.

Piment Hot sauce.

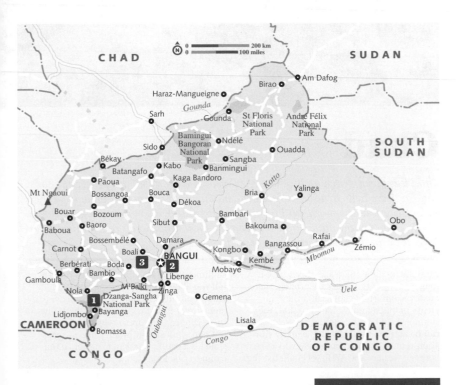

CAPITAL
N'Djaména

POPULATION
11.8 million

AREA
1.3 million sq km

LANGUAGES
French, Arabic

Rock pinnacles, Ennedi desert

Chad

Chad has always been a place where travellers wave goodbye to their comfort zone and say hello to adventure. At the moment terrorism and violence – by Boko Haram in the south, and from conflict spilling over from Libya in the north – has put the dampeners on even the most ambitious travel adventures here. It is simply considered too unsafe to visit.

Even during times of peace, travel here is tough. Many of the roads are broken, there are few comfortable hotels and there is plenty of bureaucracy. Added to that, the summer heat is mind-melting, travel costs can be astronomical and the security situation remains unpredictable. So why even bother, you may ask? Well, we could list the sublime oases lost in the northern deserts, tell you about the stampeding herds of wildlife in the national parks or the deep blue lure of a boat trip on Lake Chad. But these things alone aren't why people come to Chad – put simply, when Chad is accessible it's a country and an experience that can never be forgotten.

Snapshot

Zakouma National Park

 Although poaching and civil war ravaged the area's wildlife the animal population has been steadily increasing and now there are large herds of buffalo, roan antelope and Lelwel's hartebeest – almost 50% of Africa's Kordofan giraffe call the park home too. Notable predators here include cheetah, leopard and spotted hyena. Big herds of elephants and dazzling birds thrive in one of Central Africa's finest national parks.

Ennedi

 Ennedi desert, with its dramatic scenery and rock formations, is perhaps the most spectacular corner of the Sahara. Attractions include prehistoric cave paintings, slot canyons, desert lakes and some unbelievably bizarre rock formations. There are even ancient sea arches, now swimming in sand dunes, formed when Lake Chad stretched out here.

Lake Chad

 Lake Chad was once one of the largest freshwater lakes in the world. Its area can rise to 25,000 sq km at the height of the rains, however, it is slowly drying up, creating problems for fishermen and farmers. A finger of the lake reaches Bol year-round.

Food & Drink

Bili-bili A millet beer; *cochette* is a low-alcohol version.

Brochettes Kebabs.

Jus Fruit drinks with more resemblance to smoothies.

Nachif Minced meat in sauce.

Seasons

☼ JAN–JUN & OCT–DEC

☂ JUL–SEP

CAPITAL
Santiago

POPULATION
17 million

AREA
756,102 sq km

OFFICIAL LANGUAGE
Spanish

Parque Nacional Torres del Paine

Chile

Chile is nature on a colossal scale, but travel here is surprisingly easy if you don't rush it.

Preposterously thin and unreasonably long, Chile stretches from the belly of South America to its foot, reaching from the driest desert on earth to vast southern glacial fields. Diverse landscapes unfurl over a 4300km stretch: parched dunes, fertile valleys, volcanoes, ancient forests, massive glaciers and fjords. There's wonder in every detail and nature on a symphonic scale.

In Chile, adventure is what happens on the way to having an adventure. Pedal the chunky gravel of the Carretera Austral and end up sharing ferries with SUVs and oxcarts, taking a wrong turn and finding heaven in an anonymous orchard.

One thing that stands out is hospitality and the people. Rituals such as the sharing of maté tea and the welcoming attitude of *buena onda* (good vibes) are so integral to the fabric of local life, it's hardly even noticed.

Top Experiences

Parque Nacional Torres del Paine

1 Some rites of passage never lose their appeal, so strap on that heavy pack and hike through howling steppe and winding forests to behold these holiest-of-holy granite mountain spires. Las Torres may be the main attraction of its namesake park, but this vast wilderness has much more to offer. Ice trek the sculpted surface of Glacier Grey, explore the quiet backside of the circuit, kayak the calm Río Serrano or ascend John Gardner Pass for gaping views of the southern ice field.

Moai

2 The strikingly enigmatic *moai* (statues) are the most pervasive image of Easter Island (Rapa Nui). Dotted all around the island, these massive carved figures stand on stone platforms, like colossal puppets on a supernatural stage. They emanate mystical vibes and it is thought that they represent clan ancestors. The biggest question remains: how were these giant statues moved from where they were carved to their platforms? It's a never-ending debate among specialists.

Caleta Condor

3 Sometimes it's about the journey rather than destination; other times the opposite. Caleta Condor, an isolated piece of postcard paradise along a protected stretch of hard-to-reach indigenous coastline, is without question both. Be it by boat, foot or 4WD, preserved Valdivian forest eventually gives way to an impossibly gorgeous bay at the mouth of Río Cholcuaco. The beach, the river and the nearly uninhabited landscape all conspire to be one of Chile's most surprising, inspiring and out-of-place tropical-style nirvanas.

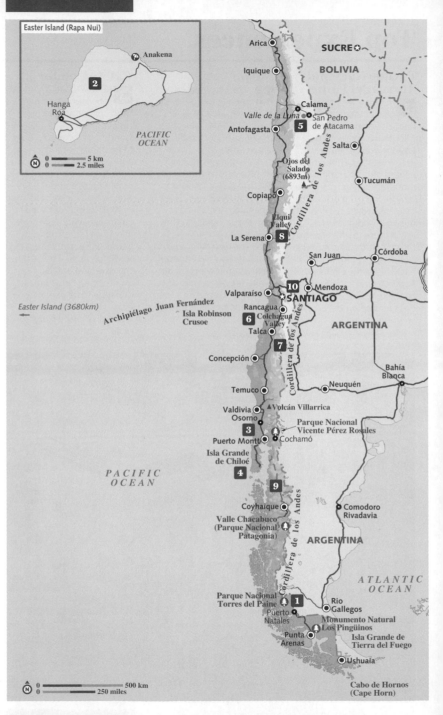

Easter Island (Rapa Nui)

Anakena

2

Hanga
Roa

*PACIFIC
OCEAN*

0 —— 5 km
0 —— 2.5 miles

Arica

SUCRE ◈

BOLIVIA

Iquique

Calama

Valle de la Luna — San Pedro
de Atacama

Antofagasta **5**

Salta

Ojos del
Salado
(6893m)

Copiapó

Elqui
Valley

La Serena **8**

San Juan — Córdoba

Valparaíso — **10** — Mendoza

Rancagua **SANTIAGO**

Easter Island (3680km)

Archipiélago Juan Fernández
Isla Robinson
Crusoe

6 Colchagua
Valley

Talca **7**

ARGENTINA

Concepción

Bahía
Blanca

Temuco — Neuquén

Valdivia — ▲Volcán Villarrica
Osorno

3 Parque Nacional
Vicente Pérez Rosales

Puerto Montt — Cochamó

*Isla Grande
de Chiloé*

4

9

*PACIFIC
OCEAN*

Coyhaique

Valle Chacabuco
(Parque Nacional
Patagonia)

Comodoro
Rivadavia

ARGENTINA

*ATLANTIC
OCEAN*

Parque Nacional
Torres del Paine **1**

Puerto
Natales

Río
Gallegos

Monumento Natural
Los Pingüinos

Punta
Arenas

*Isla Grande de
Tierra del Fuego*

Ushuaia

Cabo de Hornos
(Cape Horn)

0 —— 500 km
0 —— 250 miles

Tucumán

Cordillera de los Andes

Best on Film

Gloria (2013) A fresh and funny portrait of an unconventional 58-year-old woman.

The Maid (2009) A maid questions her lifelong loyalty.

Violeta Went to Heaven (2012) Biopic of rebel songstress Violeta Parra.

Motorcycle Diaries (2004) The road trip that made a revolutionary.

No (2013) Did an ad campaign really take down a dictator?

180° South (2010) Follows a traveler exploring untainted territory.

Food & Drink

Maté A type of tea popular in Patagonia and made from the dried leaves of the yerba maté.

Pisco A grape brandy, is Chile's national alcohol, grown in the dry soil of the north. Pisco sours are a popular start to cocktail hours, and consist of *pisco*, sugar and fresh lemon juice.

Pasteles Find these hearty baked casseroles, a traditional specialty made with *choclo* (corn), *carne* (meat), *jaiva* (crab) or *papas* (potatoes), in small towns and at family tables.

Seafood Chile's long coastline means a bounty of fabulously fresh *pescados* (fish) and *mariscos* (shellfish) used in soups, stews and *ceviche* (marinated raw seafood).

Wine Chile's wine regions are rightfully world-famous; one varietal to try is Carmenere, a rich red that originated in Bordeaux but is now produced only here.

The Churches of Chiloé

4 No matter how many European cathedrals, Buddhist monasteries or Islamic mosques you've seen, the sixteen 17th- and 18th-century wooden churches that make up Chiloé's Unesco World Heritage site will be unlike any previously encountered. Each an architectural marvel marrying European and indigenous design, boasting unorthodox colors and construction, these cathedrals were built by Jesuit missionaries working to convert pagans to the papacy. Their survival mirrors the Chilote people's own uncanny resilience.

Valle de la Luna

5 See the desert don its surrealist cloak as you stand atop a giant sand dune, with the sun slipping below the horizon and multicolored

When to Go

HIGH SEASON
(Nov–Feb)
Patagonia is best (and most expensive) December to February.

SHOULDER
(Sep–Nov & Mar–May)
The best times to visit Santiago; wine country has grape harvests and wine festivals in March.

LOW SEASON
(Jun–Aug)
A good time to visit the North and the best time for ski resorts.

The Flowering Desert

In some years a brief but astonishing transformation takes place in Norte Chico's barren desert. If there has been heavy rainfall, the parched land erupts into a multicolored carpet of wildflowers – turning a would-be backdrop from *Lawrence of Arabia* into something better resembling a meadow scene from *Bambi*.

This exquisite but ephemeral phenomenon is appropriately dubbed the *desierto florido*, or 'flowering desert'. It occurs between late July and September in wetter years when dormant wildflower seeds can be coaxed into sprouting. Many of the flowers are endangered species, most notably the endemic *garra de león* (lion's claw, one of Chile's rarest and most beautiful flowers). Even driving along the Panamericana near Vallenar you may spot clumps of the delicate white or purple *suspiro de campo* (sigh of the field), mauve, purple or white *pata de Guanaco* (Guanaco's hoof) and yellow *corona de fraile* (monk's crown) coloring the roadside.

Llanos de Challe is one of the best places to see this phenomenon, although the region's erratic rainfall patterns make it difficult to predict the best sites in any given year.

Getting Around

Flights are a worthwhile time saver for long distances, with economical regional deals sold in-country.

Bus is the best way to get around Chile: frequent, comfortable and reasonably priced, with service to towns throughout the country.

Renting your own wheels helps to better explore remote regions such as Patagonia.

Trains are limited. A few lines can be useful for travelers in Central Chile.

Navigating southern Chile's jigsaw-puzzle coast by ferry is about more than just getting from A to B – it's an essential part of the travel experience. Chilean Patagonia and Tierra del Fuego are accessed by ferries traveling the intricate maze of islands and fjords with spectacular coastal scenery.

hues bathing the sands, all with a backdrop of distant volcanoes and the rippling Cordillera de la Sal. In Valle de la Luna, the moment the color show kicks in – intense purples, golds, pinks and yellows stretch as far as your eye can see – you'll forget the crowds around you, all squeezing in to catch sundown in the valley.

Wine Tasting in the Colchagua Valley

6 Big round Cabernets and Carmeneres are the signature varietals of the Colchagua Valley, a scorched parcel of earth that has become Chile's premier wine-tasting region. Oenophiles and gastronomes will be entranced by the epicurean delights of the valley's tiny wineries, bistros and posh lodgings. Taste some of South America's richest Cabernet

Sauvignon straight from the barrels at wineries like the posh Lapostolle and the old-fashioned Viu Manent, or make a day of it with a gourmet organic picnic.

Skiing the Andes

7 The Chilean Andes are home to some of the best Southern Hemisphere skiing found throughout this powder-dusted planet. For steep slopes, expansive vistas, hot tub parties and plenty of après-ski revelry, head to top resorts such as the all-in-one Portillo, budget-friendly El Colorado and the ritzy La Parva. Valle Nevado has expanded terrain with more than 7000 skiable acres. At Termas de Chillán you can take an after-ski dip in a hot springs pool.

Elqui Valley

8 Spend a few languid days in the lush Elqui Valley and you'll start

to wax lyrical, or even channel the late Nobel Prize–winning poet Gabriela Mistral who grew up in these parts. Infused by poetry, *pisco*, pretty villages and star-sprinkled night skies, this is a wholesome land of spiritual retreats, ecofriendly inns, hilltop observatories and artisanal distilleries of the potent little grape. Sample food cooked solely by sun rays, get your aura cleaned, feast on herb-infused Andean fusion fare and ride the valley's mystic wave.

The Carretera Austral

9 Find out what adventures await on this 1240km romp through Andean backcountry dotted with parks and pioneer homesteads. The Carretera Austral is every wanderer's dream. The dusty washboard road to nowhere was created in the 1980s under the Pinochet regime, in an attempt to link the country's most isolated residents to the rest of Chile. Now the connection is tenuous. If you have the time, offshoot roads to glaciers, seaside villages and mountain hamlets are worthy detours.

Santiago Dining and Nightlife

10 Santiago's avant-garde restaurants are taking South American fusion to new levels by combining old-school sensibilities with new-school flavors. For culinary forays, explore the pop-deco bistros of Bellavista, the sidewalk charmers in Lastarria and the high-falutin' eateries of Las Condes. Come nighttime, Santiago knows how to rage against the dying of the light, and you'll find raucous beerhalls, decibel-piercing *discotecas*, candlelit poetry houses and just about anything else your inner Bacchus desires along the alleyways of party districts like Bellavista, Bellas Artes and Lastarria.

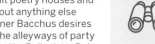

Whale-watching

Whale-watching is increasingly popular in Patagonia. A variety of species can be spotted, including fin, humpback, killer and sperm whales.

The Chilean Miners

While trapped underground, the 33 miners requested wine and cigarettes to help cope with the stress. But their NASA doctor sent nicotine patches instead.

OLGA DANYLENKO / SHUTTERSTOCK ©

2

7

SOREN EGEBERG PHOTOGRAPHY / SHUTTERSTOCK ©

CAPITAL	Běijīng
POPULATION	1.4 billion
AREA	9.6 million sq km
OFFICIAL LANGUAGES	Mandarin, Cantonese

The north gate of the Forbidden City, Běijīng

China

China. The name alone makes you want to get packing. It's going places, so jump aboard, go along for the ride and see where it's headed.

China is vast. Off-the-scale massive. A jumble of wildly differing dialects and climatic and topographical extremes, it's like several different countries rolled into one. Take your pick from the tossed-salad ethnic mix of the southwest, the yak-butter-illuminated temples of Xiàhé, a journey along the dusty Silk Road, spending the night at Everest Base Camp or getting into your glad rags for a night on the Shànghǎi tiles.

These vast geographic and cultural variations, coupled with 1.4 billion food-loving people, mean your taste buds will be tantalised, tested and treated. Wolf down Peking duck in Běijīng, melt over a Chóngqìng hotpot or visit a dim sum trolley down south.

And while its modern face is dazzling, China is seamed with rich antiquity. From the ancient Forbidden City, collapsing sections of the Great Wall, temple-topped mountains and villages that time forgot, to languorous water towns, sublime Buddhist grottoes and ancient forts, you're spoilt for choice.

Top Experiences

Forbidden City

1 Not a city and no longer forbidden, Běijīng's enormous palace is the be-all-and-end-all of dynastic grandeur with its vast halls and splendid gates. No other place in China teems with so much history, legend and good old-fashioned imperial intrigue. You may get totally lost here but you'll always find something to write about on the first postcard you can lay your hands on. The complex also heads the list with one of China's most attractive admission prices and almost endless value-for-money sightseeing.

Great Wall

2 Spotting it from space is both tough and pointless: the only place you can truly put the Great Wall under your feet is in China. Select the Great Wall according to taste: perfectly chiselled, dilapidated, stripped of its bricks, overrun with saplings, coiling splendidly into the hills or returning to dust. The fortification is a fitting symbol of those perennial Chinese traits: diligence, mass people-power, ambitious vision and engineering skill (coupled with a distrust of the neighbours).

Hiking in Jiǔzhàigōu National Park

3 Exploring the forested valleys of Jiǔzhàigōu National Park – past bluer-than-blue lakes and small Tibetan villages, in the shadow of snow-brushed mountains – was always a highlight of any trip to Sìchuān province, but the excellent ecotourism scheme in the Zhārú Valley means travellers can hike and camp their way around this stunning part of southwest China. Bring your sense of adventure and a spare set of camera batteries.

APHOTOSTORYE / SHUTTERSTOCK ©

2

Dūnhuáng

4 Where China starts transforming into a lunar desertscape in the far west, the handsome oasis town of Dūnhuáng is a natural staging post for dusty Silk Road explorers. Mountainous sand dunes swell outside town while Great Wall fragments lie scoured by abrasive desert winds, but it is the magnificent caves at Mògāo that truly dazzle. Mògāo is the cream of China's crop of Buddhist caves, and its statues are ineffably sublime and some of the nation's most priceless cultural treasures.

HELLORF ZCOOL / SHUTTERSTOCK ©

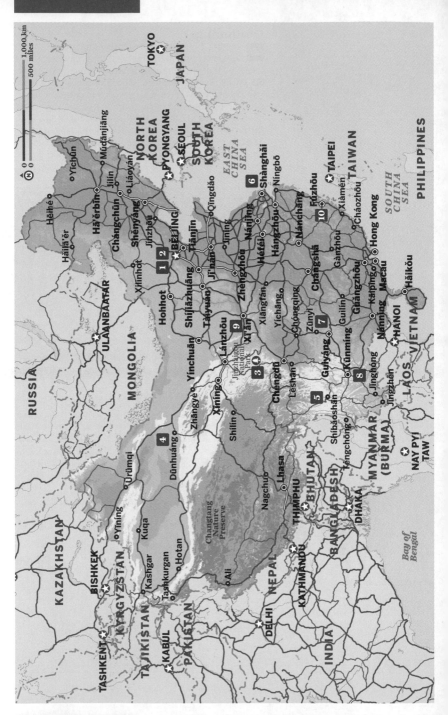

Best on Film

Still Life (Jia Zhangke; 2005) Bleak and hauntingly beautiful portrayal of a family devastated by the construction of the Three Gorges Dam.

Raise the Red Lantern (Zhang Yimou; 1991) Exquisitely fashioned tragedy from the sumptuous palette of the Fifth Generation.

In the Mood for Love (Wong Kar-Wai; 2000) Seductive, stylishly costumed and slow-burning Hong Kong romance.

Best in Print

Country Driving: A Chinese Road Trip (Peter Hessler) Hessler's amusing and insightful journey at the wheel around the highways and byways of China.

Tiger Head, Snake Tails (Jonathan Fenby) Compelling account of contemporary China's myriad challenges and contradictions.

Diary of a Madman & Other Stories (Lu Xun) Astonishing tales from the father of modern Chinese fiction.

Tiger Leaping Gorge

5 Picture snowcapped mountains rising on either side of a gorge so deep that you can be 2km above the river rushing across the rocks far below. Then imagine winding up and down trails that pass through tiny farming villages, where you can rest while enjoying views so glorious they defy superlatives. Cutting through remote northwest Yúnnán for 16km, Tiger Leaping Gorge is a simply unmissable experience. Hikers returning from the gorge invariably give it glowing reviews.

The Bund, Shànghǎi

6 More than just a city, Shànghǎi is the country's neon-lit beacon of change, opportunity and modernity. Its sights set squarely on the not-too-distant future, Shànghǎi offers a taste of all the superlatives China can dare to dream up, from the world's highest observation deck to its fastest commercially operating train. Whether you're just pulling in after an epic 44-hour train trip from Xīnjiāng or it's your first stop, you'll find plenty to indulge in here. Start with the Bund, Shànghǎi's iconic riverfront area.

Fènghuáng

7 Houses perched precariously on stilts, ancestral halls, crumbling temples and gate towers set amid a warren of back alleys full of shops selling mysterious foods and medicines – it's enough on its own to make the

When to Go

HIGH SEASON
(May–Aug)
Prepare for summer downpours and crowds at traveller hot spots.

SHOULDER
(Feb–Apr, Sep & Oct)
Expect warmer days in spring, cooler days in autumn.

LOW SEASON
(Nov–Feb)
Domestic tourism is at a low ebb, but things are busy for Chinese New Year.

Ice & Snow Festival

The arctic temperatures may knock the wind from your lungs, but in January the frost-bitten capital of Hēilóngjiāng province twinkles with an iridescent collection of carved ice sculptures and some of them are truly enormous.

Tibetan Buddhism

Anyone interested in Tibetan Buddhism will find Inner Mongolia easier to reach than Tibet; the province is home to many important and historic Lamaseries, including Dà Zhào in Hohhot, Wǔdāng Lamasery and Guǎngzōng Sì.

Food & Drink

Noodles Noodles range across an exciting spectrum of taste, from the wincingly spicy *dàndan miàn* (spicy noodles) through to the supersalty *zhájiàng miàn* (fried sauce noodles).

Peking duck Once bitten, forever smitten, and only true to form in Běijīng.

Chóngqìng hotpot Sweat like you're in a sauna over China's most volcanic culinary creation.

Xiǎolóngbāo Shànghǎi's bite-sized snack packs a lot of flavour (but watch out for the super heated meat juice).

Dim Sum Head to Hong Kong for the very best in China's bite-size delicacies.

Dumplings Set your compass north and northeast for the best *jiǎozi* (dumplings) – leek, pork, lamb, crabmeat wrapped in an envelope of dough. If you like them crispy, get them *guōtiē* (fried). Shànghǎi's interpretation is *xiǎolóngbāo* – scrummy and steamed.

Sour cabbage fish soup A Sìchuān dish you can find cooked up by chefs across China, which features wholesome fish chunks in a spicy broth.

Hairy crabs A Shànghǎi speciality between October and December. Eaten with soy, ginger and vinegar and downed with warm Shàoxīng wine, the best crabs come from Yangcheng Lake.

ancient town of Fènghuáng an essential stop. Add in the seductive setting on either side of the Tuó River and the chance to stay at an inn right by the water, and you have one of the most evocative towns in the land.

Yuányáng Rice Terraces

8 Hewn out of hills that stretch off into the far distance, the rice terraces of Yuányáng are testimony to the wonderfully intimate relationship the local Hani people have with the sublime landscape they live in. Rising like giant steps, the intricate terraces are a stunning sight at any time of year. But when they are flooded in winter and the sun's rays are dancing off the water at sunrise or sunset, they're absolutely mesmerising and some of the most photogenic spectacles that China has to offer.

Terracotta Warriors

9 Standing silent guard over their emperor for over two millennia, the terracotta warriors are one of the most extraordinary archaeological discoveries ever made. It's not just that there are thousands of the life-sized figures lined up in battle formation; it's the fact that no two of them are alike – each one is animated with a distinct expression. This is an army and one made up entirely of individuals. Either Qin Shi Huang was terrified of the vanquished spirits awaiting him in the afterlife, or as most archaeologists believe, he expected his rule to continue in death as it had in life. Gazing at these skilfully sculpted faces brings the past alive with a unique intensity.

Fújiàn's Tǔlóu Roundhouses

10 Rising up in colonies from the hilly borderlands of Fújiàn and Guǎngdōng, the stupendous *tǔlóu* roundhouses house entire villages, even though occupant numbers are way down these days. The imposing and well-defended bastions of wood and earth – not all circular it must be added – can be most easily found in the Fújiàn counties of Nánjìng and Yǒngdìng. The edifices are remarkable for their ingenuity, but the idyllic rural setting lends an ethereal quality hard to find in modern China. Do the right thing and spend the night in one: this is a vanishing way of life.

ALEXGGS / GETTY IMAGES ©

Getting Around

 China's air network is extensive and growing. Air travel is affordable and excellent for long distances, but delays are common.

 Buses are cheaper and slower than trains but crucial for remote destinations. With the increasing number of intercity highways, journeys are getting quicker.

 China is too large and there are too many restrictions to make travelling by car a viable option.

 Trains are the best way to travel long distance around China in reasonable speed and comfort. They are also adventurous, exciting, fun, practical and efficient, and ticket prices are reasonable to boot.

CAPITAL	Bogotá
POPULATION	47.2 million
AREA	1.1 million sq km
OFFICIAL LANGUAGE	Spanish

Colombia

Soaring Andean summits, unspoiled Caribbean coast, enigmatic Amazon jungle, cryptic archaeological ruins and cobbled colonial communities. Colombia boasts all of South America's allure, and more.

Colombia's equatorial position affords it a true diversity of landscapes. A slight tinkering in altitude takes you from sun-toasted Caribbean sands to coffee-strewn, emerald-green hilltops in the Zona Cafetera. Continue to climb and there's Bogotá, the third-highest capital city in the world. A few thousand meters higher and you find snowcapped peaks, lakes and the eerie, unique vegetation of the páramo.

The Andes give way to Los Llanos, a 550,000-sq-km swath of tropical grasslands shared with Venezuela, often called the Serengeti of South America. Colombia's varied terrain is fertile ground for outdoor adventurers to dive, climb, raft, trek and soar. Providencia's world-class reef spells aquatic heaven for scuba divers, and whale-watchers on the Pacific coast can see humpbacks in the wild.

Top Experiences

Cartagena's Old Town

1 The hands of the clock on the Puerta del Reloj wind back 400 years in an instant as visitors enter the walled old town of Cartagena. Strolling the streets here is to step into the pages of a novel by Gabriel García Márquez. The pastel-toned balconies overflow with bougainvillea and the streets are abuzz with food stalls around magnificent Spanish-built churches, squares and historic mansions. This is a living, working town that just happens to look a lot like it did centuries ago.

Journey to Ciudad Perdida

2 The trip to Ciudad Perdida is one of the continent's most mysterious ancient cities, arguably second only to Machu Picchu. The thrilling jungle walk through some of the country's most majestic tropical scenery has become renowned as one of Colombia's best multiday hikes. Surging rivers pump faster than your pulse can keep pace as you ford them, waist deep, against the otherwise quiet beauty of the Sierra Nevada. Your destination is awe-inspiring – an ancient lost city 'discovered' by graverobbers and gold-digging bandits deep in the mountains, laid out in mysterious, silent terraces – but it's as much about the journey itself.

Caño Cristales

3 Held hostage by guerrillas for two decades, Caño Cristales is once again open for business. One of Colombia's most fascinating natural wonders, this gorgeous river canyon, flanked by the verdant jungle and mountainous terrain that forms the transition to the Colombian Amazon, explodes into an astonishing sea of red for a couple of months between July and November. This unique phenomenon is caused by an eruption of

VARNAK / SHUTTERSTOCK ©

CARIBBEAN SEA

Providencia (Colombia)

San Andrés (Colombia)

NETHERLANDS ANTILLES (NETHERLANDS)

Aruba Curaçao Bonaire

Parque Nacional Natural Tayrona

La Guajira Península **5**

Coro

Santa Marta **2** Riohacha

Barranquilla

Cartagena **1**

Valledupar

Maracaibo

CARACAS

Barquisimeto

Valencia

Lago de Maracaibo

PANAMA **PANAMA CITY**

Sincelejo

Montería

Mérida

VENEZUELA

Cúcuta San Cristóbal

8 Bucaramanga

Barichara

10 Medellín **9** San Gil Parque Nacional Natural El Cocuy

4

Quibdó

Manizales

Puerto Ayacucho

Pereira Zona Cafetera

6 **BOGOTÁ**

Yopal

Buenaventura

Isla Gorgona

Cali

Villavicencio

PACIFIC OCEAN

Neiva

San José Del Guaviare

Popayán

7 San Agustín

3 Parque Nacional Natural Sierra de La Macarena (Caño Cristales)

Pasto Florencia

Mocoa

Ibarra Laguna de la Cocha

QUITO

ECUADOR

BRAZIL

PERU

Machala

Parque Nacional Natural Amacayacu

Río Amazonas

Iquitos

Leticia

Río Yavarí

Trujillo

Best on Film

Todos Tus Muertos (2011) Devastating critique of corruption and apathy in Colombia.

Apaporis (2010) Incisive documentary into indigenous Amazonian life.

Perro Come Perro (2008) Tarantino-esque gangster flick.

Maria Llena Eres de Gracia (2008) Moving tale of teen pregnancy and drug-trafficking.

Soñar No Cuesta Nada (2006) Colombian soldiers find millions of FARC dollars – and keep it.

Rosario Tijeras (2004) Vengeful hit-woman's thrilling tale.

Food & Drink

Don't miss *ajiaco* (an Andean chicken stew with corn, many types of potatoes, avocado, and a local herb known as *guasca*) and *bandeja paisa*, a gut-busting mound of sausage, beans, rice, egg and *arepa* (ground maize flatbread) – Colombia's de facto national dish despite controversy that its prevalence rarely strays from Antioquia.

On the street nationwide you'll find savory *arepas* of all ilk (with cheese, with ham and eggs, with chicken), *mazamorra* (a maize-based beverage), *empanadas* (fried stuffed pastries), and fresh orange juice and fruit salads. Regional options include *llapingachos* (fried potato cakes with meat) and *helado de paila* (ice cream whipped in a copper tin) in Nariño, ceviche on the Caribbean coast, and tamales in Tolima and Huila. There's also plenty for your sweet tooth: *obleas con arequipe* are thin wafers doused in milk caramel; and *cuajada con melao* is fresh cheese with melted jaggery.

kaleidoscopic algae along the riverbed. Trekking between waterfalls and natural swimming pools is a fabulous experience.

Trekking in El Cocuy

4 Parque Nacional Natural (PNN) El Cocuy is one of South America's most coveted stomping grounds – and for good reason. In season (December to February), everything throughout the Sierra Nevada del Cocuy region is characterized by burnt-auburn sunrises that bounce off craggy peaks, and the páramo ecosystem of glacial valleys, mountain plains, high-altitude lakes and rare vegetation. On clear days, entire swaths of Los Llanos can be seen before you from any number of surrounding 5000m-high peak viewpoints.

La Guajira's Dunes & Deserts

5 Reaching this remote desert peninsula may be fun or arduous, depending on how you like to trav-

When to Go

HIGH SEASON
(Dec–Feb)
Sunny skies and warmish days in the Andes.

SHOULDER
(Mar–Sep)
Cartagena shines through April, hard rains begin in May.

LOW SEASON
(Oct–Nov)
Flash floods in the Andean region but excellent hiking and white-sand beaches in the Amazon.

el, but everyone who makes it to South America's most northerly point is blown away by the stunning simplicity of it all. Pink flamin-

The Great Crab Migration

It truly is one of the most extraordinary sights you'll ever see: for a whole week in April the uniquely terrestrial Providencia Black Crab comes down from its habitat in the mountains and makes its way awkwardly towards the sea, where the females lay their eggs and the males then fertilize them, before returning inland shortly afterwards. During this time, the one road that rings this tiny Caribbean island is closed, and life for many becomes very static and even quieter than usual, with islanders only able to move around the island on foot.

A few months later, usually in July, the hatched juvenile crabs, still tiny, crawl out of the sea and head to the mountains. During this second migration the island shuts down again, and the sound of rustling is permanent day and night as the tiny crabs make their way up the hillside in their millions. If you're lucky enough to arrive on Providencia during either of these times, you're in for an unforgettable experience.

Getting Around

Flights are the easiest (but most expensive) way to cover the huge distances between big cities in Colombia. Air travel has become more accessible lately with the advent of budget airlines, and booking in advance can make it a very reasonable way to travel. Nearly all cities have airports, as well as many smaller, more remote towns.

The main way to get around Colombia, buses range from tightly packed *colectivos* (shared minibuses or taxis) to comfortable air-conditioned long-distance buses, and connect nearly every town in the country.

A car is useful for traveling at your own pace, or for visiting regions with minimal public transport. Cars can be hired in major cities, but it's generally not cheap. Driving is on the right.

gos, mangrove swamps, sand-dune beaches and tiny Wayuu settlements dot the vast emptiness of this most magnificent and little-visited corner of Colombia.

The Museums of Bogotá

6 There are few places in the world where you can get a sense of what finding a long-lost buried treasure might be like. Bogotá's Museo del Oro, one of South America's most astonishing museums, will floor you with a sensation of Indiana Jones proportions – and it's merely one of countless museums in the city. Whether you dig portly Boteros, presidential helicopters, cocaine-kingpin firearms, Bolivarian swords, exquisitely tiled bathrooms or broken vases, Bogotá has a museum for you.

Ancient Statues of San Agustín

7 Scattered throughout rolling green hills, the statues of San Agustín are a magnificent window into pre-Columbian culture and one of the most important archaeological sites on the continent. More than 500 of these monuments, carved from volcanic rock and depicting sacred animals and anthropomorphic figures, have been unearthed. Many statues are grouped together in an archaeological park, but many more are in situ, and can be explored on foot or by horseback along trails interspersed with waterfalls and steep canyons.

Whale-Watching on the Pacific Coast

8 There are few sights in nature as impressive as watching a 20-ton whale launch itself through the air against a backdrop of forest-covered mountains. Every year hundreds of humpback whales make a 8000km-plus journey from the Antarctic to give birth and raise young in Colombia's Pacific waters. These spectacular mammals come so close to shore in Ensenada de Utría that you can watch them cavorting in shallow waters from your breakfast table. To get even closer, sign up for a boat tour.

Colonial Barichara

9 There is something immediately transcendent about stepping foot in stunning Barichara, arguably Colombia's most picturesque colonial village: its rust-orange rooftops, symmetrically cobbled streets, whitewashed walls and pot-plant-adorned balconies contrast against a backdrop of postcard-perfect Andean green. Barichara is a slow-paced marvel – its name means 'place of relaxation' in the regional Guane dialect – and finding oneself wandering its streets in a sleepwalker's daze, blindsided by its beauty, wouldn't be unusual.

Exploring Medellín

10 Get a bird's-eye view of life in the real Medellín as you soar in the city's award-winning metrocable system above working-class neighborhoods clinging precariously to steep mountainsides. The maze of haphazard red-brick abodes below is the beating heart of a city where difficult terrain is no obstacle to growth. After dark check out the other end of the spectrum by visiting the chic restaurants, bars and clubs of El Poblado, the center of Medellín's legendary nightlife and popular with the city's well-heeled, fashionable crowd.

Coffee Fincas

Throughout Caldas, Risaralda and Quindío, some of Colombia's best coffee *fincas* (farms) welcome visitors onto their plantations. Learn all about the growing process and the rich culture that has developed around it.

Melodies from the Forest

The *marimba de chonta* is the main musical protagonist in *El Currulao* – the typical dance of Colombia's Pacific coast. Made from the wood of a spiny palm tree, the instrument is traditionally played hanging from the ceiling.

CAPITALS
Moroni (C)
Mamoudzou (M)

POPULATION
752,288 (C),
223,765 (M)

AREA
2235 sq km (C),
374 sq km (M)

OFFICIAL LANGUAGES
Arabic, French (C),
French (M)

Ngoudja, Mayotte

Comoros & Mayotte

*Scattered across the Indian Ocean, the enchanting Comoros islands are the
kind of place you go to drop off the planet for a while.*

The Comoros are so remote even an international fugitive could hide out here. The charming inhabitants come from a legendary stock of Arab traders, Persian sultans, African slaves and Portuguese pirates. Nicknamed 'Cloud Coup-Coup' land because of their crazy politics, the three independent islands have experienced almost 20 coups since gaining independence in 1975. In the last decade, however, the quarrelsome independent islands agreed to put their differences aside and fly under the joint banner of the Union des Comores. The fourth island, Mayotte, is an overseas territory of France, and differs from the other Comorian islands politically in that its people are French citizens governed by French law.

Holidaying in the Comoros isn't for everyone. Everything moves slowly and tourism facilities are far from plush. But if your idea of the perfect holiday is lazy days sipping tea and talking with locals, then the Comoros will be the kind of unpredictable adventure you've been craving.

Top Experiences

Moroni

 Moroni is a timeless place where the air is redolent of the Arabian Nights. Wandering the narrow streets, you'll pass women in colourful wraps chatting on crumbling stone doorsteps, and grave groups of white robed men whiling away the hours with games of dominoes. At sunset Moroni harbour must be one of the most beautiful sights in the Indian Ocean.

Mohéli

 Explore the smallest, wildest and most interesting Comore, Mohéli, with beaches and turquoise seas. It's undeveloped and sparsely populated. There is no question about Mohéli's backwater status: this island hasn't caught up with the 20th century yet, let alone the 21st. But this is a very good thing.

Anjouan

 Called the 'pearl of the Comoros' by its residents, Anjouan is no doubt the most scenic of the Comoros and fulfils any lifelong fantasies of playing Robinson Crusoe on a deserted island. Known by the locals as Ndzouani or Nzwani, this is also the Comorian island that most closely resembles the image most people conjure up when daydreaming of kissing a lover in an exotic far-flung destination.

When to Go

HIGH SEASON
(May–Sep)

SHOULDER
(Oct & Nov)

LOW SEASON
(Dec–Apr)

Food & Drink

Lobster Inexpensive lobster – *langouste à la vanille* is particularly divine.

Tea Drink tea spiced with lemon grass and ginger.

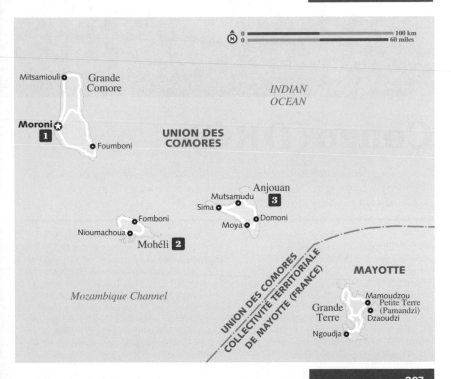

| **CAPITAL** |
| Kinshasa |
| **POPULATION** |
| 81.7 million |
| **AREA** |
| 2.3 million sq km |
| **OFFICIAL LANGUAGE** |
| French |

Congo (DRC)

Compelling conversations with locals; exhilarating interactions in impenetrable forests and beckoning rivers are all on show in the Democratic Republic of the Congo.

Carpeted by huge swathes of rainforest and punctuated by gushing rivers and smoking volcanoes, the Democratic Republic of Congo (DRC, formerly Zaire) is the ultimate African adventure. As much a geographical concept as a fully fledged nation, DRC has suffered a brutal 20th century of colonial exploitation, authoritarian madness and what has been dubbed Africa's first 'world war', which finally ended in 2003 with the rise of the Kabila political dynasty.

While real stability remains many years away, the cautious development of DRC's enormous untapped mineral wealth and the presence of the world's largest UN peacekeeping force have bred optimism among its tormented but resilient population. At the same time, a small but fast-growing tourism industry, centred on the incredible Parc National des Virunga, has seen travellers return to what is easily one of Africa's most thrilling – and challenging – destinations.

Top Experiences

Parc National des Virunga

 Visit the habituated mountain gorillas in the thick forests of Africa's oldest national park or hike to the top of the magnificent Nyiragongo volcano to stare down into a bubbling lava lake below. This is Africa's hauntingly beautiful, beating heart.

Kinshasa

 Shot through with chaos, music and a lust for life, Kinshasa (or Kin, as locals call it) is a city you experience rather than visit. While it shares elements with other African cities, here it's all bigger, faster and louder, and there's no better place for a whirlwind introduction to Congolese life.

Kisangani

 Take the legendary boat trip up the still-wild Congo River to this charmingly remote city. Even though it's the third largest city in DRC, Kisangani is an authentic backwater, and few travellers make it here. Its sandy streets, raucous riverside market and the steamy brown Congo River all produce a languorous air that's infectious.

When to Go

☀ **HIGH SEASON** (Apr–Oct)

⛅ **SHOULDER** (Dec–Mar)

☁ **LOW SEASON** (Jan)

Food & Drink

Congolese cooking is some of Africa's best. Typical dishes include *fufu*, a sticky dough made from cassava flour and *poulet à la moambé*, chicken served in a sauce made from the outer layer of palm nuts. *Pili pili*, an incredibly hot pepper sauce, is served with nearly everything.

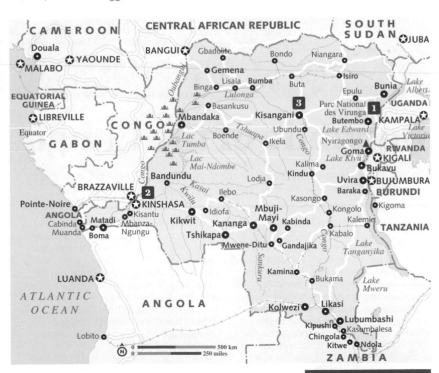

Sangha River

Republic of the Congo

The mighty river which gives the Congo its name snakes through a lush land of untouched jungle, wild animals and difficult history.

A land of steamy jungles hiding gorillas, forest elephants, and chimpanzees, the Republic of the Congo is on the cusp of becoming one of the finest ecotourism destinations in Africa.

Boasting three excellent and little-visited national parks where everything from luxurious safaris to bush camping is possible, the main attraction to this alluring slice of Central Africa is the raw, untrammelled call of nature. However, Congo-Brazzaville (as it's often called to distinguish it from Democratic Republic of Congo, south of the Congo River) also enjoys a pleasantly laid-back capital city in Brazzaville, some decent beaches on its Atlantic coastline and the warm and welcoming Congolese culture. For those ready to heed the call of the wild – and not afraid of adventure – the Congo awaits.

CAPITAL
Brazzaville

POPULATION
4.2 million

AREA
342,000 sq km

OFFICIAL LANGUAGE
French

Top Experiences

Parc National Nouabalé-Ndoki

 A team from *National Geographic* magazine, who visited the fledgling Parc National Nouabalé-Ndoki in the mid-1990s, called this northern corner of Congo the world's 'Last Eden', and they chose their words wisely. So extraordinary is Nouabalé-Ndoki that in 2012 Unesco declared it a World Heritage Site, as a part of the much larger (7500-sq-km) Sangha Trinational Park, which covers both this park and neighbouring Dzanga Ndoki park in CAR and Lobéké park in Cameroon.

Visiting Nouabalé-Ndoki is truly one of those 'once in a lifetime' kind of experiences and is as genuine a slice of raw, wild Africa as you will ever encounter.

Parc National Conkouati-Douli

 Congo's most diverse national park, Parc National Conkouati-Douli, stretches from the Atlantic Ocean through a band of coastal savannah up into jungle-clad mountains. Poaching problems (fed by demand for bushmeat in Pointe-Noire) mean the wildlife-watching has for a long time been somewhat limited, but

When to Go

☼ **HIGH SEASON** (May–Sep)

⛅ **SHOULDER** (Dec–Feb)

☂ **LOW SEASON** (Mar, Apr, Oct & Nov)

recent investment in the park infrastructure and in security means that the elephants, gorillas and buffalo that live here are becoming more common, and more easily seen.

Brazzaville

 With some attractive modernist architecture, a gorgeous riverside

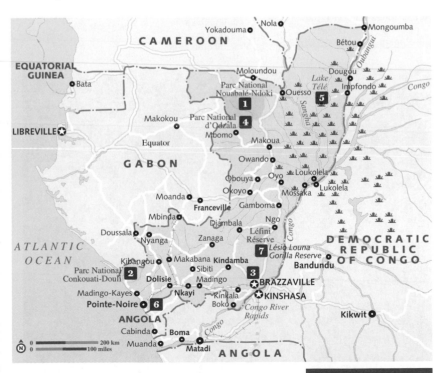

embankment perfect for taking in views of the Congo River and plenty of high-quality eating options, Brazzaville has a lot of charm and character, which makes it a surprisingly pleasant place to while away time between visiting Congo's national parks.

Brazza has always been the junior economic partner to Kinshasa (the DRC's capital) which faces it across the immense river. Brazzaville is by far the more laid-back – and safer – of the two towns.

Parc National d'Odzala

4 The Parc National d'Odzala is easily Congo's most accessible national park and a superb place to visit lowland gorillas and see other Central African megafauna in a virtual wilderness. Unlike the other national parks

in Congo, Odzala has top-notch (and sadly very expensive) camps and services, and this is the closest you'll get to luxury outside Brazzaville or Pointe-Noire.

Lac Télé Reserve

5 In a country like the Congo, getting off the beaten tourist track is not difficult. But for those who really want to immerse themselves in the deepest of jungle adventures, a journey to the perfect circular form of Lac Télé (Lake Télé), hidden away in the unimaginably remote northeast of Congo, is the kind of trip people write books about. It's not just that this lake is surrounded by swamp-forests that remain largely unexplored, nor that there are an estimated 100,000 lowland gorillas inhabiting the area, nor the pygmy groups living an almost completely

Getting Around

Air is the best way to get around if you're in a hurry.

There are bus services across the country's two main roads.

Car and 4WD hire is expensive, but relatively easy.

Trains runs between Brazzaville and Pointe-Noire three times a week .

traditional lifestyle: local lore has it that Lac Télé is also the home of the Mokèlé-mbèmbé, a large semi-aquatic creature that many believers describe as being similar to a Sauropod (a type of long-extinct dinosaur).

Pointe-Noire

6 Congo's second largest city may be rich in oil and SUVs, but otherwise Pointe-Noire is a sprawling and rather unattractive place (even despite its seafront location). Here the shanty towns spread for miles, and in places almost abut the walled mansions of the city's petrochemical classes. Due to the large expat community there's a good choice of international eating options, glitzy hotels and lubricious nightclubs and a few attractive beaches outside the city.

Lésio Louna Gorilla Reserve

7 The Lésio Louna Gorilla Reserve is a very important resource in Congo where orphaned

gorillas are cared for and eventually released back into the wild. Highlights of a visit include seeing the babies in the nursery and watching the adults (who live wild on an island) get fed. You can also swim or

just enjoy the peace and quiet at the lovely Lac Bleu, which makes this a relatively easy excursion into the wild from Brazzaville for those unable to travel to the country's remote national parks.

GUENOV ANDREY / SHUTTERSTOCK ©

Food & Drink

Food is unlikely to be a highlight of your visit to Congo, but if you eat out in Brazzaville or Pointe-Noire you'll have a good choice of local and international cuisines. Northern Congolese are meat eaters (very often bushmeat) while southern Congolese love their fish. Both eat their protein almost exclusively with cassava, though you will sometimes find yams or rice in restaurants. Vegetarians will have a tough time outside Brazzaville and Pointe-Noire.

Travel by Barge

The epic barge ride up the Congo and Oubangui Rivers is the stuff of travel-writing legend. Between June and December, when river levels are high enough, barges run up the Congo and Oubangui River from Brazzaville. The boats used are creaky old multilevel boats that are virtual floating markets. There are hundreds of people packed on board and there's zero privacy or comfort but there is bucketloads of genuine adventure.

Some boats go to Bangui (Central African Republic) and Impfondo, and others veer left at Mossaka taking the even wilder Sangha River to Ouesso. There are more or less weekly departures, but no schedule; boats go when they're full. Ideally the journey between Brazza and Impfondo can be done in five days downstream and nine upstream. Between Bangui and Brazza allow 10 days downstream and two weeks upstream.

To find a boat start your search at the river port in Brazza or Bangui. Take plenty of food and fresh water (although fish and fruit can be bought en route).

| CAPITAL |
| Avarua |
| POPULATION |
| 19,500 |
| AREA |
| 236 sq km |
| OFFICIAL LANGUAGE |
| English |

Tapuaeta'i (One Foot Island), Aitutaki Lagoon

Cook Islands

Fifteen droplets of land cast across 2 million sq km of wild Pacific blue, the Cook Islands are simultaneously remote and accessible, modern and traditional.

With a strong cafe culture, a burgeoning organic and artisan food scene, and a handful of bars and clubs, Rarotonga lives confidently in the 21st century. But beyond the island's tourist buzz and contemporary appearance is a robust culture, firmly anchored by traditional Polynesian values and steeped in oral history.

North of 'Raro', the sublime lagoon of Aitutaki is ringed with tiny deserted islands and is one of the Pacific's most improbably scenic jewels. Venture further and strong Polynesian traditions emerge nearer the surface. Drink home brew at a traditional 'Atiuan *tumunu* (bush-beer drinking club), explore the ancient *makatea* (raised coral cliffs) and taro fields of Mangaia, or swim in the underground cave pools of Mitiaro and Ma'uke. The remote Northern Group is a South Seas idyll experienced by a lucky few.

Top Experiences

Muri Lagoon

With its four *motu* (islets), Muri is the most beautiful section of Rarotonga's encircling lagoon. The blue water is packed with tropical fish, especially around the *motu* (Taakoka, Koromiri, Oneroa and Motutapu), and out towards the reef. Taakoka is volcanic while the others are sand cays. The swimming is wonderful over sparkling white sand. Lagoon cruises and water-sports equipment are available from Muri through Captain Tama's and Koka's Lagoon Cruises. Other attractions include kitesurfing, paddle-boarding and good restaurants.

'Atiu

'Atiu is the Cooks' eco-capital and a haven for naturalists. It also attracts adventurous travellers in search of an island with a more traditional edge.

The *makatea* – the dramatic ring of upthrust rock that's rich in marine fossils and was once the island's exterior reef – is just one of 'Atiu's natural features. The island is also covered with forest and honeycombed with limestone caves. 'Atiu's most famous cave is Anatakitaki, the only known home of the *kopeka* ('Atiuan swiftlet). Te Ana O Rakanui is a burial cave packed with musty old skeletal remains.

When to Go

☼ **HIGH SEASON**
(Jun–Sep)

☼ **SHOULDER**
(Apr, May, Oct & Nov)

☂ **LOW SEASON**
(Dec–Mar)

Aitutaki Lagoon

Aitutaki's stunning lagoon, brimming with marine life and ringed by 15 palm-covered *motu*, is a South Pacific treasure. Maina (Little Girl) offers superb snorkelling and is home to the red-tailed tropicbird, once prized for its crimson feathers. Nearby is the wreck of

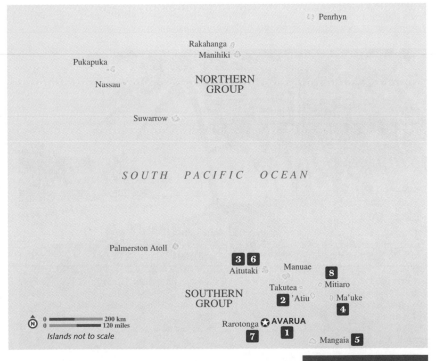

cargo freighter *Alexander*, which ran aground in the 1930s. Tapuaeta'i (One Foot Island) is the best-known *motu*, fringed by white beaches and divided from its neighbour, Tekopua, by a deepwater channel that's teeming with tropical fish.

The Divided Church

4 Ma'uke's Cook Islands Christian Church (CICC) was built by two villages, Areora and Ngatiarua, in 1882. When the outside was completed, there was disagreement about how the inside should be decorated so they built a wall down the middle. The wall has since been removed, though the interior is decorated in markedly different styles. Each village has its own entrance, sits at its own side and takes turns singing the hymns. The minister stands astride the dividing line down the middle of the pulpit. Look for the Chilean coins that are set into the wooden altar. Chilean currency was frequently traded throughout the South Pacific in the 19th century.

Mangaia

5 Mangaia has many spectacular caves, including Te Rua Rere, a huge burial cave that has crystalline stalagmites and stalactites, and some ancient human skeletons. Other caverns worth exploring include the multilevel Tuatini Cave and the long, maze-like Toru a Puru Cave.

Some of the finest old CICCs in the Cooks are on Mangaia. Tamarua CICC is especially beautiful, and still has its original roof beams, woodcarved interiors and sennit-rope binding. The interiors of the Oneroa and Ivirua CICCs were once even

Getting Around

There are several daily flights to Aitutaki, and several weekly flights between Rarotonga and the rest of the Southern Group.

Ships stop off at each island for just a few hours, and only Rarotonga and Penrhyn have decent harbours. At the other islands you go ashore by lighter or barge.

All of the islands are good for cycling.

more impressive, but were sadly mostly removed in the 1980s. For stunning coastal views, take the dirt road to the top of Rangimotia.

Aitutaki's Marae

6 The lagoon may be what draws the tourists here, but Aitutaki's ancient *marae* are also notable for their large stones and cultural significance. Marae Orongo is today in the main village of Arutanga. The main road runs through another large *marae*, and on the inland road between Nikaupara and Tautu are the islands' most magnificent *marae* – including Tokangarangi and Te Poaki O Rae – mostly reclaimed by the jungle.

Diving & Snorkelling off Rarotonga

7 Diving is fantastic around the island, with good visibility and lots of marine life, from sea turtles and tropical fish to reef sharks and eagle rays. There are canyons, caves

and tunnels to explore, and outside the lagoon the island drops off to around 4000m, although most diving is between 3m and 30m. Raro also has several well preserved shipwrecks, including SS *Maitai* off the northern shore. Rarotonga's spectacular lagoon is fantastic for snorkelling and swimming. The water is crystal clear, warm and packed with technicolour fish and coral.

Vai Nauri

8 A real highlight in this region is the deep sparkling-blue Vai Nauri, Mitiaro's natural swimming pool. Local women used to hold gatherings known as *terevai* at Vai Nauri and at nearby Vai Tamaroa, where they met to swim and sing the bawdy songs of their ancestors. With Mitiaro's declining population, the *terevai* tradition is now largely limited to holiday periods.

Food & Drink

Head to Punanga Nui Market for fresh fruit and vegetables, fish and seafood, barbecued snacks, and stalls selling fresh bread and traditional Polynesian food. Foodie treats to discover include delicious fruit smoothies, local coffee, and the stand selling roast pork rolls with apple sauce, and delicious lemon meringue. Don't miss nature's very own electrolyte, a *nu* (young green coconut), chilled and ready to drink. It may also be the drink of choice when you're served lunch on an island tour.

Dance & Music

Cook Islanders love to dance and they're reputed to be the best dancers in Polynesia. Don't be surprised if you're invited to join them at an Island Night. Traditional dance forms include the *karakia* (prayer dance), *pe'e ura pa'u* (drum-beat dance), *ate* (choral song) and *kaparima* (action song). Men stamp, gesture and knock their knees together, while women shake and gyrate their hips in an unmistakeably suggestive manner.

The islanders are also great singers and musicians. The multi-part harmony singing at a Cook Islands' church service is truly beautiful and Polynesian string bands, featuring guitars and ukuleles, often perform at local restaurants and hotels.

CAPITAL
San José

POPULATION
4.8 million

AREA
51,100 sq km

OFFICIAL LANGUAGE
Spanish

Red-eyed tree frog

Costa Rica

All trails lead to waterfalls, misty crater lakes or jungle-fringed, deserted beaches. Explored by horseback, foot or kayak, Costa Rica is a tropical choose-your-own-adventure land.

Rainforest hikes and brisk high-altitude trails, rushing white-water rapids and world-class surfing: Costa Rica offers a dizzying suite of outdoor adventures in every shape and size. National parks allow visitors to glimpse life in the tropical rainforest and cloud forest, simmering volcanoes offer otherworldly vistas, and surf breaks are suited to beginners and experts alike.

Such wildlife abounds in Costa Rica as to seem almost cartoonish: toucans ogle you from treetops and scarlet macaws raucously announce their flight paths. Blue butterflies flit amid orchid-festooned trees, while colorful tropical fish, sharks, rays, dolphins and whales thrive offshore – all as if in a conservationist's dream.

And then there are the people. Costa Ricans, or Ticos as they prefer to call themselves, are proud of their slice of paradise, welcoming guests to sink into the easygoing rhythms of the *pura vida* (pure life).

Top Experiences

Volcán Arenal & Hot Springs

1 While the molten night views are gone, this mighty, perfectly conical giant is still considered active and worthy of a pilgrimage. There are several beautiful trails to explore, especially the magnificent climb to Cerro Chato. At its base, you are just a short drive away from her many hot springs. Some of these springs are free, and any local can point the way. Others are, shall we say, embellished, dressed up, luxuriated – dip your toes into the romantic Eco Termales, for starters.

San José

2 The heart of Tico culture lives in San José, as do university students, intellectuals, artists and politicians. While not the most attractive capital in Central America, it does have some graceful neoclassical and Spanish-colonial architecture, leafy neighborhoods, museums housing pre-Columbian jade and gold, nightlife that goes on until dawn, and some of the most sophisticated restaurants in the country. Street art – of both officially sanctioned and guerrilla varieties – add unexpected pops of color and public discourse to the cityscape. For the

seasoned traveler, Chepe, as it is affectionately known, has its charms.

Poás Region

3 An hour northwest of the capital, Poás is a fairy-tale land of verdant mountains, hydrangea-lined roadsides and the largest and most accessible volcanic crater on the isthmus. Although a 6.2 earthquake rocked the region in 2009, the area's most intriguing attractions endured. The winding drive past strawberry farms and coffee plantations still culminates with the smoking volcano and emerald-green crater lake. And over at La

MICHAL SARAUER / SHUTTERSTOCK ©

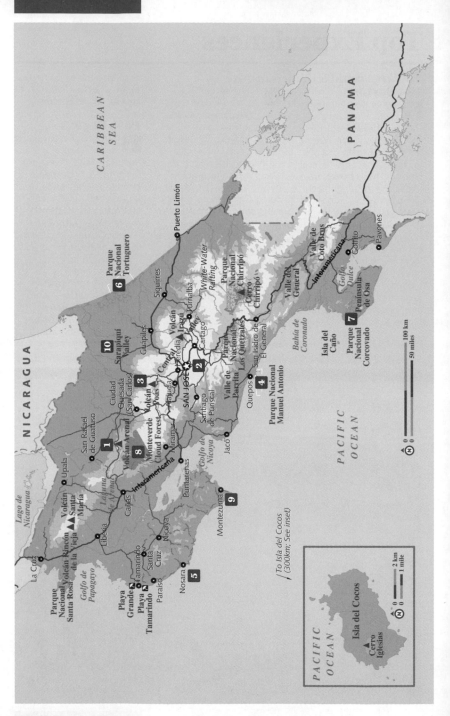

CARIBBEAN SEA

NICARAGUA

PANAMA

PACIFIC OCEAN

Lago de Nicaragua

La Cruz

Upala

San Rafael de Guatuso

Parque Nacional Santa Rosa

Golfo de Papagayo

Volcán Rincón de la Vieja

Volcán Santa María

Libéria

Cañas

1

8

Volcán Arenal

Monteverde Cloud Forest

Laguna de Arenal

Ciudad Quesada (San Carlos)

Volcán Poás

Tilarán

Interamericana

Puntarenas

Golfo de Nicoya

Santa Cruz

Tamarindo

Playa Grande

Playa Tamarindo

Paraíso

Nicoya

Nosara

5

Montezuma

9

Jaco

Sarapiquí Valley

10

Guápiles

Heredia

Alajuela

Central

SAN JOSE

2

3

Santiago de Puriscal

Valle de Parrita

Quepos

Parque Nacional Manuel Antonio

Volcán Irazú

Turrialba

Cartago

Siquirres

White-Water Rafting

Parque Nacional Los Quetzales

San Isidro de El General

4

Puerto Limón

Parque Nacional Tortuguero

6

Parque Nacional Chirripó

Cerro Chirripó

Valle de General

Valle de Coto Brus

Interamericana

Golfo Dulce

Golfito

Pavones

Bahía de Coronado

Isla del Caño

Parque Nacional Corcovado

Península de Osa

7

PACIFIC OCEAN

100 km

50 miles

To Isla del Cocos (300km; See inset)

PACIFIC OCEAN

Isla del Cocos

Cerro Iglesias

2 km

1 mile

Paz Waterfall Gardens, visitors hike to storybook waterfalls and encounter rescued monkeys, tropical birds and wild cats, including three jaguars.

Best on Film

El Regreso (The Return; 2011) Featuring a realistic, contemporary plot, this is the first Tico film to earn international acclaim; Hernán Jiménez wrote, directed, starred in and crowd-funded it.

Agua Fría de Mar (Cold Ocean Water; 2010) Directed by Paz Fábrega, this social commentary unfolds at a paradisiacal Pacific beach; the film won several international awards.

Caribe (Caribbean; 2004) The first Costa Rican film ever to be submitted for Oscar consideration; drama set in Limón.

Food & Drink

In the last few years, locals have started to experiment more with the country's fresh, exotic and plentiful produce. The results have been inspiring and delicious.

Seafood is plentiful, and fish dishes are usually fresh and delicious. While not traditional Tico fare, ceviche (seafood marinated in lemon or lime juice, garlic and seasonings) is on most menus.

Most bars offer the country's most popular *boca* (snack), chifrijo, which derives its name from two main ingredients: *chicharrón* (fried pork) and *frijoles* (beans). Diced tomatoes, spices, rice, tortilla chips and avocado are also thrown in for good measure.

Parque Nacional Manuel Antonio

4 A place of swaying palms and playful monkeys, sparkling blue water and a riot of tropical birds, Parque Nacional Manuel Antonio is the country's smallest (just 19.83 sq km) and most popular national park. It became a protected area in 1972, preserving it from being razed to make room for a coastal development project. It's a truly lovely place; the clearly marked trail system winds through rainforest-backed white-sand beaches and rocky headlands, the wildlife (iguanas, sloths, monkeys) is plentiful, and the views across the bay to the pristine outer islands are gorgeous.

Nosara

5 Nosara is a cocktail of international surf culture, jungled microclimes and yoga bliss, where three stunning beaches are stitched together by a network of swerving, rutted earth roads that meander

When to Go

LOW SEASON
(Aug & Oct)
Rainfall is highest, but this is the best time of year for surfing.

SHOULDER
(May–Jul & Nov)
Roads are muddy, making off-the-beaten-track travel more challenging.

HIGH SEASON
(Dec–Apr)
'Dry' season still sees some rain; beach towns fill with domestic tourists.

over coastal hills. Visitors can stay in the alluring surf enclave of Playa Guiones – where there are some fabulous restaurants and

The Pura Vida

Pura vida – pure life – is more than just a slogan that rolls off the tongues of Ticos (Costa Ricans) and emblazons souvenirs; in the laid-back tone in which it is constantly uttered, the phrase is a bona fide mantra for the Costa Rican way of life. Perhaps the essence of the pure life is something better lived than explained, but hearing *'pura vida'* again and again while traveling across this beautiful country – as a greeting, a stand-in for goodbye, 'cool', and an acknowledgement of thanks – makes it evident that the concept lives deep within the DNA of this country.

The living seems particularly pure when Costa Rica is compared with its Central American neighbors such as Nicaragua and Honduras; there's little poverty, illiteracy or political tumult, the country is crowded with ecological jewels, and the standard of living is high. What's more, Costa Rica has flourished without an army for the past 60 years and is an oasis of calm in a corner of the world that has been continuously degraded by warfare.

Getting Around

Inexpensive domestic flights to/from San José will save you the driving time.

Renting a car allows you to access more remote destinations.

Buses are very reasonably priced, with extensive coverage of the country, though travel can be slow. For door-to-door service between popular destinations, private and shared shuttles can save time.

a drop-dead-gorgeous beach – or in Playa Pelada, which is as romantic as it is rugged and removed. One resident described the area as 'sophisticated jungle living', and who wouldn't want more of that in their life?

Parque Nacional Tortuguero

6 Canoeing the canals of Parque Nacional Tortuguero is a boat-borne safari, where thick jungle meets the water and you can get up close with shy caimans, river turtles, crowned night herons, monkeys and sloths. In the right season, under the cover of darkness, watch the awesome, millennia-old ritual of turtles building nests and laying their eggs on the black-sand beaches. Sandwiched between extravagantly green wetlands and the wild Caribbean Sea, this is among the premier places in Costa Rica to watch wildlife.

Parque Nacional Corcovado

7 Muddy, muggy and intense, the vast, largely untouched rainfor-

est of Parque Nacional Corcovado is anything but a walk in the park. Here travelers with a flexible agenda and a sturdy pair of rubber boots thrust themselves into the unknown and come out the other side with the story of a lifetime. And the further into the jungle you go, the better it gets: the country's best wildlife-watching, most desolate beaches and most vivid adventures lie down Corcovado's seldom-trodden trails.

Bosque Nuboso Monteverde

8 A pristine expanse of virginal forest totaling 105 sq km, Monteverde Cloud Forest owes much of its impressive natural beauty to Quaker settlers, who left the US in the 1950s to protest the Korean War and helped foster conservationist principles with Ticos of the region. But as fascinating as the history is, the real romance of Monteverde is in nature itself: a mysterious Neverland shrouded in mist, dangling with mossy

vines, sprouting with ferns and bromeliads, gushing with creeks, blooming with life and nurturing rivulets of evolution.

Montezuma

9 If you dig artsy-rootsy beach culture, enjoy rubbing shoulders with neo-Rastas and yoga fiends, or have always wanted to spin fire, study Spanish or lounge on sugar-white coves, find your way to Montezuma. Strolling this intoxicating town and rugged coastline, you're never far from the rhythm of the sea. From here you'll also have easy access to the famed Cabo Blanco reserve, and can take the tremendous hike to a triple-tiered waterfall. Oh, and when your stomach growls, the town has some of the best restaurants in the country.

Sarapiquí Valley

10 Sarapiquí rose to fame as a principal port in the nefarious old days of United Fruit dominance, before it meandered into agricultural anonymity, only to be reborn as a paddler's mecca thanks to the frothing serpentine mocha magic of its namesake river. These days it's still a paddling paradise, and it's also dotted with fantastic ecolodges and private forest preserves that will educate you about pre-Columbian life, get you into that steaming, looming, muddy jungle, and bring you up close to local wildlife.

Killing the Snake

The expression *matando la culebra* (meaning 'to be idle', literally 'killing the snake') originates from banana plantations. When foremen would ask what the laborers were doing, the response would be *'¡Matando la culebra!'*

Poison Darts

The eight species of poison-dart frog in Costa Rica are beautiful but have skin secretions of varying toxicity that cause paralysis and death if they get into your bloodstream.

6

8

CAPITAL	Yamoussoukro
POPULATION	23.4 million
AREA	322,463 sq km
OFFICIAL LANGUAGE	French

Azuretti beach, Grand Bassam

Côte d'Ivoire

Côte d'Ivoire is a stunner, shingled with starfish-studded sands, palm-tree forests and roads so orange they resemble strips of bronzing powder.

This is a true tropical paradise, and a country that is striding towards economic progress – it's a nation that is fast modernising its lifestyle and culture, but managing to do so without losing its identity.

In the south, the Parc National de Taï hides secrets, species and nut-cracking chimps under the boughs of its trees, while the peaks and valleys of Man offer a highland climate, fresh air and fantastic hiking opportunities through tropical forests.

The beach resorts of Assinie and Grand Bassam were made for weekend retreats from Abidjan, the capital in all but name, where lagoons wind their way between skyscrapers, and cathedral spires pierce the blue heavens. Several spots on the coast, most notably Assinie and Dagbego, have surf beaches. In Yamoussoukro, the capital's basilica floats on the landscape like a mirage. Sacred crocodiles guard the presidential palace and you can see them being fed in the afternoons.

Top Experiences

Parc National de Taï

1 There are many places in West Africa that could be dubbed one of the region's 'best-kept secrets', but perhaps none so much as this dense rainforest. The park is mostly known for its chimpanzees, who famously use tools in their daily activities, but the general wealth of the flora and fauna inside the park is incredible.

Abidjan

2 Dining on creative Ivoirian dishes, exploring contemporary African art and swaying to the sweet sounds of *coupé-decalé* music in the shadow of the stunning skyline. As you walk around Abidjan's neighbourhoods, local life comes alive and the city's vibrant tropical mood is revealed.

Grand Bassam

3 Arty and bathed in faded glory, beachside Bassam was Côte d'Ivoire's French colonial capital until a yellow-fever epidemic broke out in 1896. Nowadays, weekenders enjoy the relaxed beach vibe.

When to Go

 HIGH SEASON
(Nov–May)

 SHOULDER
(Oct & Jun)

 LOW SEASON
(Jul–Sep)

Food & Drink

Côte d'Ivoire is blessed with a cuisine that's light and flavoursome. *Poisson braisé*, a delicate dish of grilled fish with tomatoes and onions cooked in ginger, is a must-try.

The standard beer brand is Flag, but if you're after a premium lager, ask for a locally brewed Tuborg or a Beaufort.

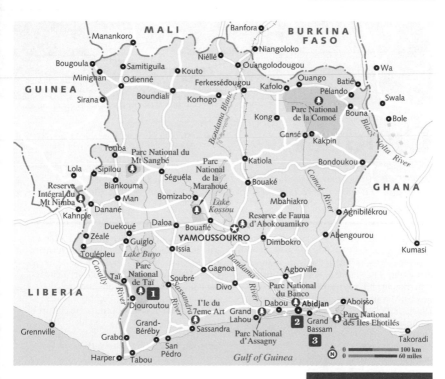

Franciscan monastery, Hvar Island

Croatia

If your Mediterranean fantasies feature balmy days by sapphire waters in the shade of ancient walled towns, Croatia is the place to turn them into reality.

Croatia's extraordinary Adriatic coastline, speckled with 1244 islands and strewn with historic towns, is indisputably its main attraction. The standout is Dubrovnik, its remarkable Old Town ringed by mighty defensive walls. Coastal Split showcases Diocletian's Palace, one of the world's most impressive Roman monuments, where dozens of bars, restaurants and shops thrive amid the old walls. In the heart-shaped peninsula of Istria, Rovinj is a charm-packed fishing port with narrow cobbled streets. The Adriatic isles hold much varied appeal, from glitzy Hvar Town on its name-sake island to the secluded naturist coves of the Pakleni Islands just offshore.

Away from the coast, Zagreb, Croatia's lovely capital, has a booming cafe culture and art scene, while Plitvice Lakes National Park offers a verdant maze of turquoise lakes and cascading waterfalls.

Top Experiences

Dubrovnik

1 Croatia's most popular attraction, the extraordinary walled city of Dubrovnik, is a Unesco World Heritage Site for good reason. Despite being relentlessly shelled in the 1990s during Croatia's Homeland War, its mighty walls, sturdy towers, medieval monasteries, baroque churches, graceful squares and fascinating residential quarters all look magnificent again. For an unrivalled perspective of this Adriatic pearl, take the cable car up to Mt Srđ.

Windsurfing in Bol

2 Bol, on the southern coast of Brač Island, is home to the illustrious Zlatni Rat beach, with its hornlike shape and golden pebbles. The town is a favourite among windsurfers: the channel between the islands of Brač and Hvar provides ideal wind conditions, thanks to the westerly maestral, that typically blows between April and October. The wind picks up slowly in the morning, an excellent time for beginners to hit the water. By early afternoon, the winds are strong – perfect for those looking for a real-deal adrenalin kick.

Hvar

3 Come high summer, there's no better place to dress up and get your groove on than Hvar Town. Gorgeous tanned people descend from their yachts in droves, rubbing shoulders with up-for-it backpackers at après-beach parties as the sun drops below the horizon. While the cashed-up yachtie types keep the town's top-notch restaurants and cocktail bars in business, sun-dazed young revellers do the same for the little dance bars that are the mainstay of the scene.

IHOR PASTERNAK / SHUTTERSTOCK ©

Plitvice Lakes National Park

4 A turquoise ribbon of lakes linked by gushing waterfalls in the forested heart of continental Croatia, Plitvice Lakes National Park is an awe-inspiring sight. There are dozens of lakes – from 4km-long Kozjak to reed-fringed ponds – their startling colours a product of the karstic terrain. Travertine expanses covered with mossy plants divide the lakes, while boardwalks allow you to easily traverse this exquisite watery world.

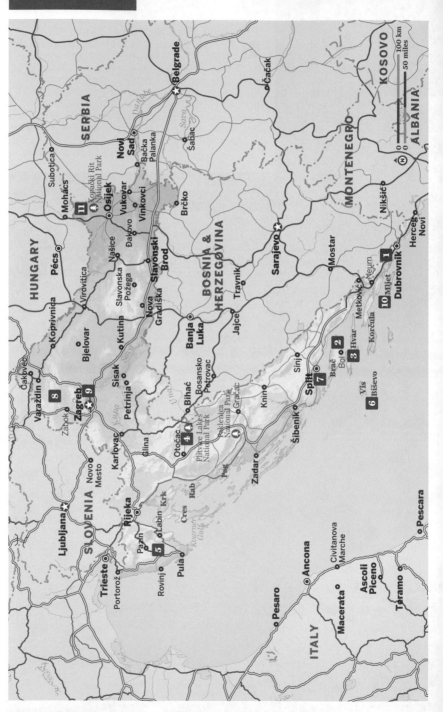

Best on Film

You Only Love Once (*Samo jednom se ljubi;* 1981; Rajko Grlić) Considered one of Croatia's best films, this drama was a Cannes contender.

Cyclops (*Kiklop;* 1982; Antun Vrdoljak) Based on the 1965 namesake novel by Ranko Marinković.

How the War Started on My Island (*Kako je počeo rat na mom otoku;* 1996; Vinko Brešan) An acclaimed black comedy.

Number 55 (*Broj 55;* 2014; Kristijan Milić) The action takes place during Croatia's war of independence.

Best Beaches

Get your kit off or don the latest designer swimsuit on one of the many gorgeous beaches that dot Croatia's coastline and islands.

Zlatni Rat A protrusion of golden pebbles packed with beach bodies and activities galore.

Stiniva A spectacular and secluded cove of white pebbles within a circle of high cliffs.

Dubovica Blue waters dazzle against white pebbles in this isolated spot on the island of Hvar.

Pakleni Islands Pine-shaded beaches for naturists and swimsuit wearers alike.

Wining & Dining in Istria

5 La dolce vita reigns supreme in Istria, Croatia's top foodie destination. The seafood, truffles, wild asparagus and a rare breed of Istrian beef called *boškarin* all stand out, as do myriad regional specialities and award-winning olive oils and wines by small local producers. Slow food is a hit here: you can sample the ritual in upmarket restaurants in seafront towns, in traditional family-run taverns in medieval hilltop villages, and in converted olive mills high up in the hills of the peninsula's verdant interior.

Blue Magic on Biševo

6 Of the numerous caves on the islets surrounding Vis, Biševo's Blue Grotto (Modra Špilja) is the most spectacular. The light show produced by this rare natural phenomenon will amaze you. On a clear morning, the sun's rays penetrate through an underwater hole in this coastal cave, bathing the interior in a mesmerising silvery-blue light. Beneath the iridescent water, rocks glimmer silver and pink, creating an unearthly effect. It's so popular that it's

When to Go

HIGH SEASON
(Jul & Aug)
Peak season brings the best weather. Prices are at their highest and coastal destinations at their busiest.

SHOULDER
(May, Jun & Sep)
The coast is gorgeous, the Adriatic is warm enough for swimming, the crowds are sparser and prices are lower.

LOW SEASON
(Oct–Apr)
Winters in continental Croatia are cold and prices are low.

Diving

Do yourself a favour and pack your mask and snorkel – the clear, warm waters and the abundance of small fish make for lots to see. Serious divers will also find plenty to keep them busy, with numerous wrecks (dating from ancient times to WWII), drop-offs and caves.

Birdwatching

The griffon vulture, with a wingspan of up to 2.6m, has permanent colonies on the islands of Cres, Krk and Prvić. Paklenica National Park is rich in peregrine falcons, goshawks, sparrow hawks, buzzards and owls. Krka National Park is an important winter habitat for migratory marsh birds, as well as eagles. Kopački Rit Nature Park, in eastern Croatia, is an important bird refuge.

Food & Drink

Bazga Homemade elderflower juice is a classic of continental Croatia, fresh and lovely – a singular imbibing joy.

Bermet Intense liqueur made in the town of Samobor, with dried carob and figs, wormwood, orange zest, sage and mustard seeds, all soaked in red wine.

Boškarin Don't skip a taste of Istria's indigenous ox, nearly extinct by the late 20th century but brought back to life recently as a meat delicacy.

Gregada Fish stew made with different types of white fish, potatoes, white wine, garlic and spices.

Komiška pogača Savoury focaccia-like pie from Komiža on Vis island, stuffed with onion, tomatoes and anchovies. If tomatoes are missing, then it's *viška pogača* (from the town of Vis).

Rogačica Among the many *rakija* (grappa) delights Croatia is known for, this Dalmatian liqueur made of carob is perfect if you like your drinks sweet.

often impossible to swim here in summer, but come later in the season for an unmissable experience.

Diocletian's Palace, Split

7 Experience life as it's been lived for thousands of years in Diocletian's Palace, one of the world's most imposing Roman remains. The mazelike streets of this buzzing quarter, the living heart and soul of Split, are chock-full of bars, shops and restaurants. Getting lost in the labyrinth of narrow streets, passageways and courtyards is one of Croatia's most enchanting experiences – and it's small enough for you to find your way out again easily.

Castles in Zagorje

8 The postcard-perfect medieval castles of Zagorje are a prime spot for some time travel. Journey back to 1334 in Trakošćan Castle, although its present-day neo-Gothic exterior is the result of a 19th-century makeover. Learn about Croatian aristocracy in its well-presented museum and wander the 215-acre castle grounds landscaped into a romantic English-style park with exotic trees and an artificial lake. Enter the 16th century via the hilltop castle of Veliki Tabor, worth a visit for its pentagonal towers and turrets, atmospheric interiors, and the bucolic landscapes that surround it.

Zagreb's Coffee Culture

9 Elevated to the status of ritual, having coffee in one of Zagreb's outdoor cafes is a must, involving hours of people-watching, gossiping and soul-searching, unhurried by waiters. To experience the truly European and vibrant cafe culture, grab a table

Getting Around

A surprisingly extensive schedule of domestic flights, especially in summer.

Buses are reasonably priced, with extensive coverage of the country and frequent departures.

Extensive network of car ferries and faster catamarans all along the coast and the islands.

Cars are useful for travelling at your own pace, or for visiting regions with minimal public transport. They can be hired in every city or larger town. Drive on the right.

Trains are less frequent and much slower than buses, with a limited network.

on the cobbled car-free Tkalčićeva, with its endless streetside cafes, or one of the pavement tables on Trg Petra Preradovića or Bogovićeva. Don't miss the Saturday morning *špica*, the coffee-drinking and people-watching ritual in the city centre that forms the peak of Zagreb's weekly social calendar.

Mljet

10 Cloaked in dense pine forests, marvellous Mljet is an island paradise. Legend has it that Odysseus was marooned here for seven years, and it's easy to appreciate why he'd

take his time leaving. The entire western section is a national park, where you'll find two sublime cobalt-coloured lakes, an island monastery and the sleepy little port of Pomena, which is as pretty as a picture. Don't neglect eastern Mljet, home to some tranquil little bays, brilliant beaches and a couple of excellent eateries.

Kopački Rit

11 A flood plain of the Danube and Drava Rivers, Kopački Rit, part of a Unesco Biosphere Reserve, offers breathtaking scenery and some of Europe's best birdwatching. Join a boat

trip and keep your eyes peeled for eagles, black storks, purple herons and woodpeckers – just some of the nearly 300 species recorded here. Explore a flooded forest by canoe, hike the nature trails or saddle up and ride a horse.

IVICA DRUSANY / SHUTTERSTOCK ©

CAPITAL Havana	
POPULATION 11.2 million	
AREA 110,860 sq km	
OFFICIAL LANGUAGE Spanish	

Cuba

Timeworn but magnificent, dilapidated but dignified, fun yet maddeningly frustrating – Cuba is a country of indefinable magic.

Meticulously preserved, Cuba's colonial cities haven't changed much since musket-toting pirates stalked the Caribbean. The atmosphere and architecture is particularly stirring in the Unesco-listed cities – Havana, Trinidad, Cienfuegos and Camagüey – where grandiose squares and cobbled streets tell erstwhile tales of opulence and intrigue.

The attractive arcs of white sand that pepper Cuba's north coast are sublime, but explore beyond Cuba's beaches and you're in a different domain, a land of fecund forests and crocodile-infested swamps and rugged mountains as famous for their revolutionary folklore as for their endemic species.

Across its cities and towns, Cuba hemorrhages music; a dynamic mix of styles with echoes of Africa, flickers of colonial Spain, ghosts of Taíno tribes, and cultural idiosyncrasies imported from Haiti, Jamaica, France and even China. It's an eclecticism that's mirrored in the country's dance, architecture, language, religion, and – most emphatically – its rainbow of people.

Top Experiences

Historic Habana Vieja

1 Only a fool comes to Havana and misses out on the Malecón sea drive, 8km of shabby magnificence that stretches the breadth of the city from Habana Vieja to Miramar and acts as a substitute living room for tens of thousands of cavorting, canoodling, romance-seeking *habaneros*. Traverse it during a storm when giant waves breach the wall, or tackle it at sunset with Benny Moré on your mp3 player, a bottle of Havana Club in your hand and the notion that anything is possible come 10pm.

Diving & Snorkeling in the Caribbean

2 There will be protestations, no doubt, but let's say it anyway: Cuba is home to the best diving in the Caribbean. The reasons are unrivaled water clarity, virgin reefs and sheltered waters that teem with millions of fish. Accessibility for divers varies from the swim-out walls of the Bahía de Cochinos (Bay of Pigs) to the hard-to-reach underwater nirvana of the Jardines de la Reina archipelago. For repeat visitors Punta Francés on Isla de la Juventud – host of an annual underwater photography competition – reigns supreme.

Ciénaga de Zapata's Wildlife

3 One of the few parts of Cuba that has never been truly tamed, the Zapata swamps are as close to pure wilderness as the country gets. This is the home of the endangered Cuban crocodile, various amphibians, the bee hummingbird and over a dozen different plant habitats. It also qualifies as the Caribbean's largest wetlands, protected in numerous ways, most importantly as a Unesco Biosphere Reserve and Ramsar Convention Site. Come here to fish, birdwatch, hike and see nature at its purest.

Labyrinthine Streets of Camagüey

4 Get lost! No, that's not an abrupt put-down; it's a savvy recommendation for any traveler passing through the city of *tinajones* (clay pots), churches and erstwhile pirates – aka Camagüey. A perennial rule-breaker, Camagüey was founded on a street grid that deviated from almost every other Spanish colonial city in Latin America. Here the lanes are as labyrinthine as a Moroccan medina, hiding Catholic churches and triangular plazas, and revealing left-field artistic secrets at every turn.

JULIAN PETERS PHOTOGRAPHY / SHUTTERSTOCK ©

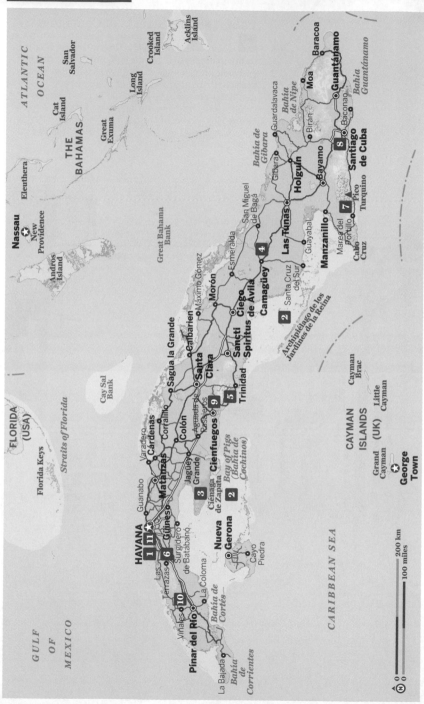

Best in Print

Our Man in Havana (Graham Greene; 1958) Greene pokes fun at both the British Secret Service and Batista's corrupt regime.

Cuba and the Night (Pico Iyer; 1995) Perhaps the most evocative book about Cuba ever written by a foreigner.

Dirty Havana Trilogy (Pedro Juan Gutiérrez; 2002) Dirty, itchy study of life and sex in Havana during the Special Period.

Che Guevara: A Revolutionary Life (Jon Lee Anderson; 1997) Anderson's meticulous research led to the unearthing of Che's remains in Bolivia.

Best on Film

Che: The Argentine (Steven Soderbergh; 2008) First part of the classic biopic focuses on Che's Cuban years.

Before Night Falls (Julian Schnabel; 2000) The life and struggles of Cuban writer Reinaldo Arenas.

Fresa y Chocolate (Tomás Gutiérrez Alea; 1993) Marries the improbable themes of homosexuality and communism.

El Ojo del Canario (Fernando Pérez; 2010) Pérez' atmospheric biopic of José Martí picked up numerous Latin film awards.

Time-Warped Trinidad

5 Soporific Trinidad went to sleep in 1850 and never really woke up. This strange twist of fate is good news for modern travelers who can roam freely through the perfectly preserved mid-19th-century sugar town like voyeurs from another era. Though it's no secret these days, the time-warped streets still have the power to enchant with their grand colonial homestays, easily accessible countryside and exciting live music scene. But this is also a real working town loaded with all the foibles and fun of 21st-century Cuba.

Las Terrazas' Eco-Village

6 Back in 1968, when the fledgling environmental movement was a bolshie protest group for long-haired students in duffel coats, the prophetic Cubans – concerned about the ecological cost of island-wide deforestation – came up with rather a good idea. After saving hectares of denuded forest from an ecological disaster, a group of industrious workers built their own eco-village, Las Terrazas, and set about colonizing it with artists, musicians, coffee growers and the architecturally unique Hotel Moka.

When to Go

HIGH SEASON
(Nov–Mar, Jul & Aug)
Weather is cooler and drier November to March.

SHOULDER
(Apr & Oct)
Look out for special deals outside of peak season.

LOW SEASON
(May, Jun & Sep)
There's a hurricane risk between June and November and higher chance of rain.

Natural Spas

Cuban spas look more like utilitarian hospitals than candlelit pampering houses – not that this detracts from their powers of recuperation. The nation's most popular spas are fed by thermal, mineral-rich water sources and are connected to economical Islazul hotels. They offer a mixture of baths, gymnasiums and assorted therapies.

Exploring Cuba's Caves

Cuba is riddled with caves – more than 20,000 and counting – and cave exploration is available to both casual tourists and professional speleologists. The Gran Caverna de Santo Tomás, near Viñales, is Cuba's largest cavern, with more than 46km of galleries; and the Cueva de los Peces, near Playa Girón, is a flooded cenote (sinkhole) with colorful snorkeling.

Food & Drink

Caibarién This small town in Villa Clara province is Cuba's crab capital.

Baracoa A completely different food universe to the rest of Cuba. Specialties include *cucurucho* (sweet blend of honey, coconut, guava and nuts), *bacán* (tamale with mashed banana, crab and coconut), *teti* (tiny fish indigenous to Toa River), and *lechita* (spicy coconut sauce).

Playa Larga & Zapata Peninsula Crocodiles are farmed and consumed in stews in hotels and *casas particulares* in southern Matanzas province.

Bayamo *Ostiones* (oysters usually served in a tomato sauce) are a staple street-food in Granma's main city.

Oriente *Congrí* – rice and red beans seasoned with cumin, peppers and pork chunks – has its roots in the African-influenced culture of eastern Cuba. In the west, you're more likely to get *moros y cristianos* (with black beans but no pork).

Revolutionary Heritage

7 An improbable escape from a shipwrecked leisure yacht, handsome bearded guerrillas meting out Robin Hood–style justice and a classic David versus Goliath struggle that was won convincingly by the (extreme) underdogs: Cuba's revolutionary war reads like the pages of a – ahem – Steven Soderbergh movie script. Better than watching it on the big screen is the opportunity to visit the revolutionary sites in person. The disembarkation point of the Granma and Fidel's wartime HQ at mountaintop Comandancia de la Plata have changed little in the last half-century.

Folklórico Dance in Santiago de Cuba

8 Ah...there's nothing quite as transcendental as the hypnotic beat of the Santería drums summoning up the spirits of the *orishas* (African deities). But, while most Afro-Cuban religious rites are only for initiates, the drumming and dances of Cuba's folklórico troupes are open to all. Formed in the 1960s to keep the ancient slave culture of Cuba alive, *folklórico* groups enjoy strong government patronage, and their energetic and colorful shows remain spontaneous in Santiago de Cuba, true to their roots and grittily authentic.

Cienfuegos' Classical Architecture

9 There's a certain *je ne sais quoi* about bayside Cienfuegos, Cuba's self-proclaimed 'Pearl of the South'. Through hell, high water and an economically debilitating Special Period, this is a city that has always retained its poise. The elegance is best seen in the

Getting Around

The state-run Víazul bus network links most places of interest to tourists on a regular daily schedule. Local buses are crowded and have no printed schedules.

Rental cars are quite expensive and driving can be a challenge due to the lack of signposts and ambiguous road rules.

Taxis are an option over longer distances if you are traveling in a small group. Rates are approximately CUC$0.50 per kilometer.

Despite its large train network, Cuban trains are slow, unreliable and lacking in comfort. For stoics only!

architecture, a homogenous cityscape laid out in the early 19th century by settlers from France and the US. Dip into the cultural life around the city center and its adjacent garden suburb of Punta Gorda to absorb the Gallic refinement.

Cycling Through the Valle de Viñales

10 With less traffic on the roads than 1940s Britain, Cuba is ideal for cycling and there's no better place to do it than the quintessentially rural Valle de Viñales. The valley offers all the ingredients of a tropi-cal Tour de France: craggy mogotes (flat-topped hills), impossibly green tobacco fields, bucolic *campes-ino* huts and spirit-lifting viewpoints at every gear change. The terrain is relatively flat and, if you can procure a decent bike, your biggest dilemma will be where to stop for your sunset-toasting mojito.

Havana's Food Culture

11 Ever since new privatization laws lifted the lid off Cuba's creative pressure cooker in 2011, a culinary revolution has been in full swing. A country that once offered little more than rice and beans has rediscovered its gastronomic mojo with a profusion of new restaurants experimenting with spices, fusion and – perhaps best of all – a welcome re-evaluation of its own national cuisine. Havana leads the culinary field in number and variety of eating establishments.

CAPITAL	Nicosia (Lefkosia)
POPULATION	1.2 million
AREA	9251 sq km
OFFICIAL LANGUAGES	Greek, Turkish

Old Harbour, Kyrenia

Cyprus

This island country possesses a fractured identity, a passionate people, and a culture, landscape and lifestyle that capture the imagination and produce plenty of surprises.

Cyprus is far more than a lazy beach-time resort; the island is multilayered, like its history, with a compelling culture and landscape, overseen by warm, hospitable people.

First, there are the beaches, from the wild and windswept to the family-friendly and packed. Every conceivable water sport is also on offer, from scuba diving the watery depths to skimming the surface on a kite- or windsurf board. And if you tire of all that blue, just head to the interior where pine-clad mountains, sweeping valleys and densely planted vineyards offer hiking, biking, wine-tasting tours and even winter skiing.

Digging into the island's past has unearthed fascinating relics, including neolithic dwellings, Bronze Age and Phoenician tombs, and exquisite Roman mosaics, while, on the streets, keep your eyes peeled for Venetian walls, Byzantine castles and churches, Roman monasteries and Islamic mosques.

Top Experiences

Kyrenia's Old Harbour

1 With the romantic silhouette of the mountains providing the backdrop, the slow pace of modern life in Northern Cyprus doesn't get any more idyllic than by Kyrenia's Old Harbour. Its charming elevated buildings and well-kept storehouses once stockpiled tonnes of raw carob. Now these edifices proffer chic cafes and restaurants, where you can sit for hours with a Cypriot coffee or experience the nargileh (water pipes) as Turkish gulets (traditional wooden ships) bob sporadically, moored around the harbour's landing and castle.

Pafos Archaeological Site

2 One of the island's most mesmerising archaeological sites is in the southerly resort of Pafos. The ancient city dates back to the late 4th century BC and what you see now is believed to be only a modest part of what remains to be excavated. Highlights include the colourful Roman floor mosaics at the heart of the original complex, first unearthed by a farmer ploughing his field in 1962.

Petra tou Romiou

3 Also known as Aphrodite's Rock & Beach, this is possibly the most famous and mythical beach in Cyprus and it's certainly one of its most unusual and impressive. It's said that waves break over Aphrodite's Rock to form a pillar of foam with an almost human shape. For the best shot to impress your Facebook friends, head to the strategically positioned tourist pavilion at sunset. During

When to Go

HIGH SEASON
(Jun & Aug)

SHOULDER
(Mar–May, Sep & Oct)

LOW SEASON
(Nov–Feb)

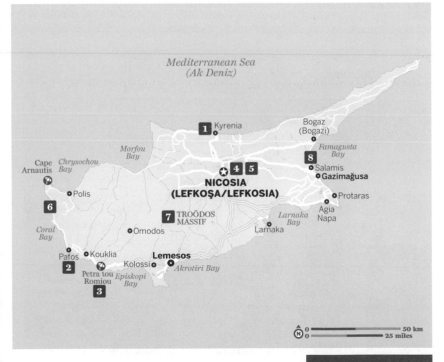

the day, the sea here is delightfully cool and fresh.

Meze in Nicosia

4 Once sampled, never forgotten: meze is a delicious and sociable way to enjoy a wide variety of different foods and flavours. In general you should expect around 30 small dishes, starting with familiar favourites such as hummus, tzatziki, taramasalata and vegetables prepared with lashings of garlic, lemon and olive oil. Next to arrive is the wide range of traditional fish and meat dishes, such as calamari (squid) and *sheftalia* (grilled sausage). It all adds up to a lot of food, so *siga, siga* (slowly, slowly) does it.

North Nicosia's Old City

5 Crossing the Green Line from Nicosia into North Nicosia (Lefkoşa), the Turkish north of the city, is an extraordinary experience. Extending like a tangled web from the Republic's smart Ledra St, old-fashioned shops selling faded jeans and frilly shirts are flanked by kebab kiosks, coffee shops and sweet stalls. Visit the stunning mosque, tranquil hammam and various museums, or just wander the streets, staying until the evening, when the minarets' crescent moons are silhouetted against a backdrop of twinkling stars.

Lara Beach

6 Akamas Heights is an area largely unburdened by development, and access to Lara Beach is via a rough road, backed by desert-like scrubland, tinged with dark ochre and studded with gorse, bushy pines and seasonal wildflowers. This beach is widely considered to be the Repub-

Getting Around

Buses in the South are frequent and run from Monday to Saturday, with limited services on Sunday. Buses in the North are a varied mix of old and newer buses.

In the South, taxis are extensive and available on a 24-hour basis; service taxis are stretch taxis that run on predetermined routes.

Roads are good and well signposted, and traffic moves smoothly. Drive defensively.

ANYAIVANOVA / SHUTTERSTOCK ©

lic's most spectacular and, thankfully, remains relatively untouched by tourism. Cupped by limestone rocks, the sand is soft and powdery and the sea is warm and calm. It's a magical place at sunset. Tread carefully though – this is prime turtle-hatching ground.

Hiking in the Troödos

7 These mountains offer an expanse of flora, fauna and geology across a range of pine forests, waterfalls, rocky crags and babbling brooks. The massif and summit of Mt Olympus, at an altitude of 1952m, provide spectacular views of the southern coastline and a welcome respite from the summer heat, with cool, fresh air you can inhale until your airways sing. Ramblers, campers, flower spotters and birdwatchers alike will be absorbed by the ridges, peaks and valleys that make up the lushest and most diverse hiking and nature trails on the island.

Ancient City of Salamis

8 The once-proud beacon of Hellenic civilisation and culture on the island, Salamis was the most famous and grandiose of the ancient city kingdoms. Since antiquity, with its succession of kings dedicated to expanding the Athenian empire, the city saw great wealth and suffering like no other. Today you can roam the expansive site taking in the ruins of grand statues, porticoes, gymnasiums, pools, baths, courtyards, the agora and even what is left of the formerly prominent temple of Zeus.

Food & Drink

Adana kebab Kebab laced with spicy red pepper.

Dolmades Stuffed vine leaves.

Lahmacun A kind of pizza equivalent, with a crispy, thin base topped with fragrant minced lamb and fresh parsley.

Pide A dough base topped with aromatic meat or fish and cheese and baked in a wood-fired oven.

Pilaf Cracked wheat steamed with fried onions and chicken stock and served with plain yoghurt; generally accompanied by meat and vegetables.

Kandaifi (adaif in Turkish) strands of sugary pastry wound into a roll.

Mahalepi (muhallebi in Turkish) A rice pudding sprinkled with rosewater and pistachios.

Commandaria A famous sweet dessert wine.

KIRILL MAKAROV / SHUTTERSTOCK ©

The Kafeneio & the Teahouse

In South Cyprus' villages, the local *kafeneio* (coffee shop) is the central meeting point. Most will have two such places, distinguished by their political alignment (socialist or nationalist). In the North the village hub is the local teahouse. Both South and North, these cafes are filled with men of all generations, eating haloumi and olives or drinking coffee, tea and (in the South) *zivania* (fermented grape pomace). Many come and go on their way to and from work. Good friends sit in pairs, smoking cigarettes and playing *tavli* (backgammon) in the shade of the vine leaves. Their dice rattle, while moves are counted and strategies are shaped in whispers. And come lunchtime, only the lingering smoke remains, as the men stampede home for their midday meal and siesta, returning in the evening to do it all again.

CAPITAL	Prague
POPULATION	10.6 million
AREA	78,867 sq km
OFFICIAL LANGUAGE	Czech

Charles Bridge, Prague

Czech Republic

Since the fall of communism in 1989, the Czech Republic has evolved into one of Europe's most popular travel destinations.

The Czech Republic's turbulent history has left a legacy of hundreds of castles and chateaux – from grim Gothic ruins clinging to a dizzy pinnacle of rock, to majestic, baroque mansions filled with the finest furniture that Europe's artisans could provide.

Prague is the cradle of Czech culture and one of Europe's most fascinating cities. It offers a medieval core of Gothic architecture that can transport you back 500 years, and an urban centre with an array of cultural offerings, and an emerging foodie scene.

The Czech Republic is a modern, forward-thinking nation riding into the future on the back of the EU and NATO, but areas-such as South Bohemia and Moravia are still rich in folk culture. During the summer festival season, communities from Český Krumlov to Telč to Mikulov don traditional garb, pick up their musical instruments and sing and dance themselves silly, animating ancient traditions in one of the best examples of 'living history' in the Czech Republic.

Top Experiences

Prague

1 Magic, golden, mystical Prague, Queen of Music, City of a Thousand Spires, famed for Kafka, the Velvet Revolution, and the world's finest beers. Unlike battle-scarred Warsaw, Budapest and Berlin, Prague escaped WWII almost unscathed – the city centre is a smorgasbord of stunning architecture, from Gothic, Renaissance and baroque to neoclassical, art nouveau and cubist. There's a maze of medieval lanes to explore, riverside parks for picnics, lively bars and beer gardens, jazz clubs, rock venues, museums and art galleries galore.

Český Krumlov

2 The sleepy, southern Bohemian town of Český Krumlov is arguably the Czech Republic's only other world-class, must-see sight aside from Prague. None other than *National Geographic* has dubbed this former medieval stronghold one of the 'world's greatest places', and once you catch a glimpse of the rocky, rambling Renaissance castle (the second-biggest in the country after Prague's), with its mesmerising multicoloured tower, you'll feel the appeal. Yes, this really is that fairy-tale town the tourist brochures promised.

Karlovy Vary

3 Karlovy Vary is the oldest of the Bohemian spas, and probably the third most popular tourist city in the Czech Republic. It's also the most beautiful of the 'big three' spas – most of the present buildings date from the late 19th and early 20th centuries, a visual feast of 'neo' styles and art nouveau. The various spa treatments are not for casual drop-in visitors, but you're free to sample the sulphurous spring waters till your teeth float. Many locals attribute any sense of well being to the so-called '13th spring', the local Becherovka herb liqueur.

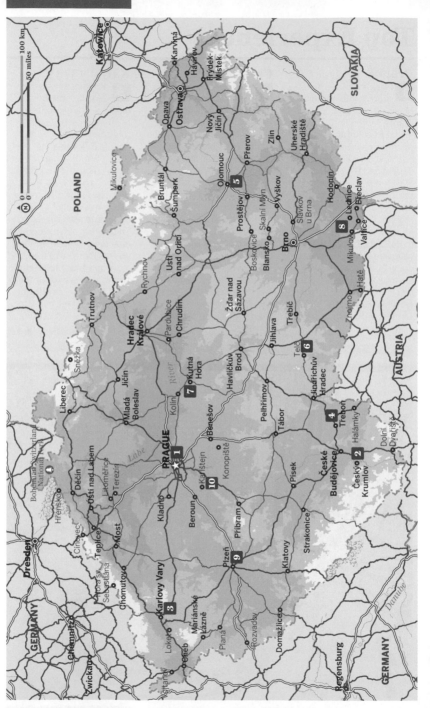

Třeboň

4 Although it lies largely off the tourist trail for overseas visitors, Třeboň has long been a favourite holiday resort for Czech families. And it's not hard to see why – the town is a picturesque maze of baroque and Renaissance buildings clustered around a sleepy chateau, with leafy parkland strung along a waterside setting, and it lies at the centre of a scenic landscape of lakes, woods, canals and wetlands (a Unesco Biosphere Reserve). It's also one of the best places in the country to sample the national dish of fried carp.

Olomouc

5 Olomouc, set in a broad, fertile stretch of the Morava River basin, is one of the Czech Republic's most underrated cities. Legend says it was founded by Julius Caesar. Today it is a youthful, laid-back university town, friendly and cheap, with cobbled streets and the largest trove of historical architecture outside Prague – and hardly a tourist in sight. Despite a somewhat bedraggled, sooty outskirts, its historical centre is certainly northern Moravia's most beautiful town. Don't forget to try

Best on Film

Amadeus (1985) Mozart's love affair with Bohemia gets brilliant treatment.

Kolya (1996) Velvet Revolution-era Prague never looked lovelier.

Loves of a Blonde (1965) Miloš Forman's 'New Wave' classic.

Burning Bush (2013) HBO miniseries on Jan Palach, the Czech student who immolated himself in 1969.

Anthropoid (2016) Big-budget WWII spectacle on the assassination of Nazi leader Reinhard Heydrich.

Food & Drink

Guláš (goulash) A staple of every menu. Cubes of beef or pork are mixed with sliced onions and fried with paprika, then stewed with tomatoes.

Svíčková na smetaně Tender beef, marinated in vinegar, herbs and vegetables, then stewed and served in a sour cream sauce, garnished with lemon and tart cranberries.

Houskové knedlíky Fluffy, light and soft bread dumplings.

Langoše Fried pastry coated with garlic, cheese, butter or jam.

Bramborák Patty made from strips of raw potato and garlic.

Ovocné knedlíky Fruit dumplings.

Beer (pivo) The lifeblood of the Czech Republic; served at cellar temperature with a tall, creamy head.

Slivovice Plum brandy.

When to Go

HIGH SEASON
(Apr–Jun, Sep & Oct)
Prague Spring Festival makes May the capital's most popular month.

SHOULDER
(Jul & Aug)
The midseason has warm, sunny days, ideal for hiking in Moravia.

LOW SEASON
(Nov–Mar)
Hotel rates can drop by 30% or 40% outside holidays.

Czechs' Best Friend

It's sometimes said 'Russians love their children and Czechs love their dogs'. That's not to say Czechs don't love their kids (of course they do), but dogs occupy a special place in the hearts of many people here. Around 40% of Czech families own a dog (one of the highest ownership rates in Europe), and the most popular breeds remain those adorable apartment-sized ones, such as dachshunds, terriers and schnauzers. Among larger breeds, the most sought after are German shepherds, Labradors and golden retrievers.

Czechs routinely bring their dogs along when they go out for dinner, and all but the fanciest restaurants normally allow dogs (on a leash) to accompany their owners.

When it comes to naming their dogs, Czechs seem to have a soft spot for English names. As you wander about and see the dogs romping around, don't be surprised to hear 'Joey' or 'Blackie' or 'Jeffie'. That's simply a local resident calling his or her canine in.

Getting Around

Trains are affordable, with extensive coverage throughout the country and frequent departures.

A car is useful for travelling at your own pace or for visiting regions with minimal public transport. Cars can be hired in every major city. Drive on the right.

Buses are similar to trains in terms of price and travel time. Useful for moving between major cities and destinations where train service is poor.

the cheese, Olomoucký sýr, reputedly the smelliest in the Czech Republic.

Telč

6 Telč is a quiet and pretty town, a good place to relax by the waterside with a book and a glass of wine. The old town, ringed by medieval fish ponds and unspoilt by modern buildings, is a Unesco World Heritage Site with a sprawling, cobble-stoned town square where you can stroll along Gothic arcades and admire elegant Renaissance facades. In the soft light of a summer evening, when the tour groups have gone, it's a peaceful, magical place where photographers and artists find endless inspiration.

Kutná Hora

7 In the 14th century Kutná Hora rivalled Prague as the most important town in Bohemia, growing rich on the veins of silver ore that laced the rocks beneath it. Today it's an attractive town with several fascinating and unusual historical attractions. Get an insight into the life of a medieval miner on a

tour of a former silver mine, or marvel at the ingenuity of the man who created art out of human remains at the grimly fascinating 'bone church' of Sedlec.

Valtice-Lednice

8 The Valtice-Lednice Cultural Landscape comprises 200 sq km of managed woodland, channelled streams, artificial lakes and tree-lined avenues dotted with baroque, neoclassical and neo-Gothic chateaux. Effectively Europe's biggest landscaped garden, it was created over a period of several centuries by the dukes of Liechtenstein, and has been designated a Unesco World Heritage Site. The main attraction is the massive neo-Gothic pile of Lednice Chateau, the summer palace of the aristocratic Leichtenstein family.

Plzeň

9 Plzeň (Pilsen in German) is famed among beer-heads worldwide as the mother lode of all lagers, the fountain of eternal froth – Pilsner lager was invented here

in 1842. It's the home of Pilsner Urquell (Plzeňský prazdroj), the world's first and finest lager beer – 'Urquell' (in German; *prazdroj* in Czech) means 'original source' – and beer drinkers from around the world flock to worship at the Pilsner Urquell brewery. The second-biggest city in Bohemia after Prague, and the EU's choice of 'Cultural Capital' in 2015, Plzeň's other attractions include a pretty town square and historic underground tunnels, while the Techmania Science Centre joins the zoo and puppet museum to make this a kid-friendly destination. The city is close enough to Prague to see the sights in a long day trip, but you'll enjoy the outing much more if you plan to spend the night.

Karlštejn Castle

10 Karlštejn Castle was born of a grand pedigree, starting life in 1348 as a hideaway for the crown jewels and treasury of the Holy Roman Emperor, Charles IV. Perched high on a crag overlooking the Berounka River, this cluster of turrets, sheer walls and looming towers is as immaculately maintained as it is powerfully evocative. The brightest star among the constellation of castles that lie scattered across Bohemia, Karlštejn will fulfil even your wildest expectations as to what a central European fairy-tale castle should look like.

Ice Hockey

It's a toss-up whether football or ice hockey inspires more passion in Prague, but hockey probably wins. Games are fast and furious, and the atmosphere can be electrifying.

Easter

Come Easter, the country celebrates with a mirthful rite of spring: Czech boys swat their favourite girls on the legs with braided willow switches or splash them with water, and the girls respond with gifts of hand-painted eggs.

LAPON PINTA / SHUTTERSTOCK ©

FOTOKON / SHUTTERSTOCK A©

CAPITAL	Copenhagen
POPULATION	5.6 million
AREA	43,094 sq km
OFFICIAL LANGUAGE	Danish

Nyhavn canal, Copenhagen

Denmark

Vikings, Hans Christian Andersen, Danish design, Lego and now New Nordic cuisine – this small country packs a punch.

Denmark is the bridge between Scandinavia and northern Europe. To the rest of Scandinavia, the Danes are fun-loving, frivolous party animals, with relatively liberal, progressive attitudes. Their culture, food, architecture and appetite for conspicuous consumption owe as much, if not more, to their German neighbours to the south as to their former colonies – Sweden, Norway and Iceland – to the north.

Packed with intriguing museums, shops, bars, nightlife and award-winning restaurants, Denmark's capital, Copenhagen, is one of the hippest, most accessible cities in Europe. And while Danish cities such as Odense and Aarhus harbour their own cultural gems, Denmark's other chief appeal lies in its photogenic countryside, sweeping coastline and historic sights such as neolithic burial chambers, the bodies of well-preserved Iron Age people exhumed from their slumber in peat bogs, and atmospheric Viking ruins and treasures from Denmark's conquering sea-going days.

Top Experiences

Copenhagen

1 While this 850-year-old harbour town retains much of its historic good looks (think copper spires, cobbled squares and pastel-coloured gabled abodes), the focus here is on the innovative. Scandinavia's coolest capital is home to a thriving design scene, a futuristic metro system, and clean, green developments. Its streets are awash with effortlessly hip shops, cafes and bars; world-class museums and art collections; brave new architecture; and no fewer than 15 Michelin-starred restaurants.

Legoland

2 Legoland theme park celebrates the 'toy of the century' (as adjudged by *Fortune* magazine in 2000) in the country in which it was invented, also 'the world's happiest nation' (according to a Gallup World Poll). So you've got to believe Legoland will be something special – and it is.

Kronborg Slot

3 Something rotten in the state of Denmark? Not at this fabulous 16th-century castle in Helsingør, made famous as the Elsinore Castle of Shakespeare's Hamlet. Kronborg's

primary function was as a grandiose toll house, wresting taxes for more than 400 years from ships passing through the narrow Øresund between Denmark and Sweden. The fact that Hamlet, Prince of Denmark, was a fictional character hasn't deterred legions of

When to Go

LOW SEASON
(Oct–Apr)

SHOULDER
(May–mid-Jun,
mid-Aug–Sep)

HIGH SEASON
(mid-Jun–
mid-Aug)

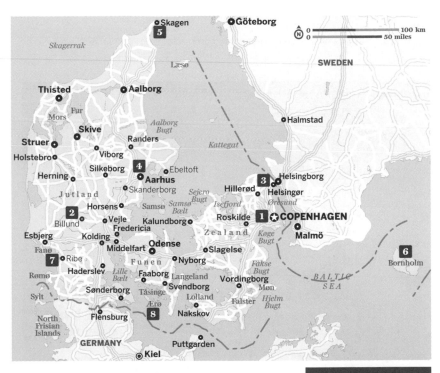

sightseers from visiting the site. It's the venue for summer performances of Shakespeare's plays during the HamletScenen festival.

Aarhus

4 Aarhus, the second-largest city in Denmark, is a terrific place in which to spend a couple of days. It has a superb dining scene, thriving nightlife (much of it catering to the large student population), a waterfront undergoing transformation, picturesque woodland trails and beaches along the city outskirts, as well as one of the country's finest art museums.

Skagen

5 Skagen is an enchanting place, both bracing and beautiful. It lies at Denmark's northern tip and acts as a magnet for much of the population each summer, when the town is full to capacity yet still manages

to charm. In the late 19th century artists flocked here, infatuated with the radiant light's impact on the rugged landscape. Now tourists flock to enjoy the output of the 'Skagen school' artists, soak up that luminous light, devour the plentiful seafood and laze on the fine sandy beaches.

Bornholm

6 Bornholm is a Baltic beauty lying some 200km east of the Danish mainland, located closer to Germany and Sweden than to the rest of Denmark. This magical island holds a special place in the hearts of most Danes, and is beloved for its plentiful sunshine, glorious sandy beaches, endless cycle paths, iconic *rundkirker* (round churches), artistic communities, fish smokehouses and idyllic thatched villages. If that's not enough to lure you, the island is developing

Getting Around

Train trips are reasonably priced, with extensive coverage and frequent departures.

Denmark is perfect for touring by car. Larger towns offer car hire.

Bus All large cities and towns have a local and regional bus system.

a reputation for outstanding restaurants and local edibles.

Ribe

7 Compact, postcard-perfect Ribe is Denmark's oldest town, and it encapsulates the country's golden past in exquisite style, complete with imposing 12th-century cathedral, cobblestone streets, skewed half-timbered houses and lush water meadows. Stay overnight in atmospheric lodgings that exude history (low-beamed rooms in a wonky 1600s inn, or in converted jail cells), and take a free walking tour narrated by the town's nightwatchman – the perfect way to soak up the streetscapes and tall tales of local characters.

Ærø

8 Denmark has been likened to a china plate that's been dropped and smashed into pieces. Each fragment represents an island – and there are 406 of them. The midsized islands, each with their own distinctive character, are the most fun to explore, and south of Funen there's a whole archipelago of them, making it a prime sailing destination. Steeped-in-time Ærø is an idyllic slice of Danish island life: visit for seafaring heritage, rural bike lanes, cobblestoned villages, sandy beaches and postcard-perfect bathing huts.

Food & Drink

New Nordic flavours Sample Nordic produce cooked with groundbreaking creativity at hotspot restaurants such as Copenhagen's Noma, Kadeau or Geranium.

Smørrebrød Rye or white bread topped with anything from beef tartar to egg and shrimp, the open sandwich is Denmark's most famous culinary export.

Sild Smoked, cured, pickled or fried, herring is a local staple, best washed down with generous serves of akvavit (an alcoholic spirit commonly made with potatoes and spiced with caraway).

Kanelsnegle A calorific delight, the 'cinnamon snail' is a sweet, buttery pastry, sometimes laced with chocolate.

Koldskål A cold, sweet buttermilk soup made with vanilla and traditionally served with crunchy biscuits such as *kammerjunkere*.

Beer Carlsberg may dominate, but Denmark's expanding battalion of microbreweries include Mikkeller, Amager Bryghus and Bryghuset Møn.

FRANK BACH / SHUTTERSTOCK ©

Hygge

Befriend a Dane or two and chances are you'll be invited to partake in a little *hygge*. Usually it translates as 'cosy' but in reality, *hygge* (pronounced hoo-guh) means much more than that. Indeed, there really is no equivalent in English. *Hygge* refers to a sense of friendly, warm companionship of a kind fostered when Danes gather together in groups of two or more, although you can actually *hygge* yourself if there is no one else around. The participants don't even have to be friends (indeed, you might only have just met), but if the conversation flows – avoiding potentially divisive topics like politics and the best way to pickle a herring – the bonhomie blossoms and toasts are raised before an open fire (or, at the very least, some candles), you are probably coming close.

CAPITAL
Djibouti

POPULATION
920,000

AREA
23,000 sq km

OFFICIAL LANGUAGES
French, Arabic

Camel caravan heading for Lac Assal

Djibouti

This tiny speck of a country packs a big punch. What it lacks in size, it more than makes up for in beauty.

Few countries in the world, with the possible exception of Iceland, offer such weird landscapes – think salt lakes, extinct volcanoes, sunken plains, limestone chimneys belching out puffs of steam, basaltic plateaus and majestic canyons. Outdoorsy types will enjoy a good mix of land and water activities, including hiking and diving. The Bay of Ghoubbet is one of the most dependable locations in the world for spotting whale sharks.

Barring Djibouti City, the country is refreshingly devoid of large-scale development. It's all about ecotravel, with some sustainable stays in the hinterland that provide a fascinating glimpse into the life of nomadic tribes.

Travelling independently around Djibouti may not come cheap, but despite the high cost of living, you'll surely leave this little corner of Africa with new experiences and wonderful memories.

Top Experiences

Djibouti City

1 Djibouti's capital is evolving at a fast pace, and there's a palpable sense of change in the air. Under the urban bustle, the city remains a down-to-earth place, with jarring cultural and social combinations. Traditionally robed Afar tribesmen, stalwart GIs, and frazzled businessmen with the latest mobile phones stuck to their ear all jostle side by side.

Lac Assal

2 One of the most spectacular natural phenomena in Africa, Lac Assal is encircled by dark, dormant volcanoes and represents the lowest point on the continent. The banks of salt and gypsum surround the lake for more than 10km, and the blinding white contrasts starkly with the black lava fields around it. Truly photogenic.

Goda Mountains

3 The spectacular Goda Mountains offer ample opportunities for hiking. A few Afar villages are scattered around and merit at least a couple of days of your time to soak up their charm. It won't be long before you're smitten by the region's mellow tranquillity and laid-back lifestyle.

When to Go

HIGH SEASON
(Nov–Jan)

SHOULDER
(Feb–Apr & Oct)

LOW SEASON
(May–Sep)

Food & Drink

Djibouti City is *the* place in the Horn of Africa to treat yourself to a fine meal. You'll find excellent seafood, rice, pasta, local meat dishes, such as stuffed kid or lamb, and other treats imported from France.

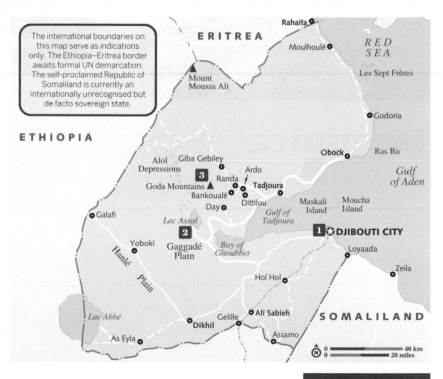

The international boundaries on this map serve as indications only. The Ethiopia–Eritrea border awaits formal UN demarcation. The self-proclaimed Republic of Somaliland is currently an internationally unrecognised but de facto sovereign state.

CAPITAL
Roseau

POPULATION
71,700

AREA
750 sq km

OFFICIAL LANGUAGE
English

Hot spring in Morne Trois Pitons National Park

Dominica

With waterfalls, jungle, sulfur springs, secret swimming holes, rivers, reefs and coastline, this untamed 'nature island' promises the unusual.

Much of volcanic Dominica is blanketed by untamed rainforest that's a verdant backdrop to experiences such as an intense trek to a bubbling lake, soothing your muscles in hot sulfur springs, getting pummeled by a waterfall, snorkeling in a glass of 'champagne', swimming up a narrow gorge – the list goes on.

With its wild coast, thick jungle and hidden coves, Dominica has historically been a popular pirate haunt, so it was only natural that Hollywood came calling when location scouting for the *Pirates of the Caribbean* films. Films two and three were shot in Titou Gorge, Soufriere, the Indian River and Batibou Beach.

In many ways, Dominica is the 'anti-Caribbean' island. It has been spared the mass tourism, in large part because there are very few sandy beaches, no flashy resorts and no direct international flights. The locals are so friendly that they often stop visitors just to wish them a good visit.

Top Experiences

Morne Trois Pitons National Park

 This national park stretches across 17,000 acres of Dominica's mountainous volcanic interior. It's a stunning pastiche of lakes, fumaroles, volcanoes, hot springs and dense tropical forest. Hikes start in the mountain village of Laudat (elevation 1970ft).

Indian River

 The slow and silent boat trip along the shady mangrove-lined Indian River is a memorable experience; you glide past buttressed bwa mang trees whose trunks rise out of the shallows, their roots stretching out laterally along the riverbanks. Enjoy close-up views of egrets, crabs, iguanas, hummingbirds and other creatures.

Boiling Lake

 Dominica's pre-eminent trek, and one of the hardest, is the six hour round-trip to the world's second-largest actively boiling lake (the largest is in New Zealand). Geologists believe the 207ft-wide lake is a flooded fumarole – a crack in the earth that allows hot gases to vent from the molten lava below. The fizzing waters sit inside a deep cauldron and are a spectacular sight. The hike traverses the aptly named Valley of Desolation, whose sulfur rivers, belching steam vents and geysers evoke post-atomic grace. It then follows narrow ridges, snakes up and down mountains and runs along hot streams. Wear sturdy walking shoes and expect to get wet and muddy. The

When to Go

☼ **HIGH SEASON** (Feb–Jun)

⛅ **SHOULDER** (Nov–Jan)

☂ **LOW SEASON** (Jul–Oct)

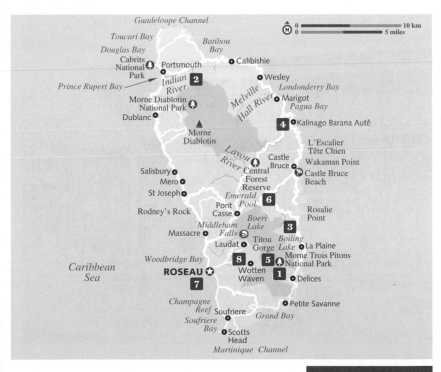

strenuous 6-mile hike to the lake begins at Titou Gorge and requires a guide. Ask for a referral at your accommodation.

Kalinago Barana Autê

4 This recreated traditional village is a good spot to learn about Kalinago history and culture. The 30- to 45-minute tour includes stops at a *karbet*, (men's house), a 10ft-long dugout canoe carved from a single tree, and a waterfall. Tours conclude at a snack bar and gift shop where Kalinago women weave their ornate baskets.

Titou Gorge

5 At the Boiling Lake trailhead, a swimming hole gives way to narrow Titou Gorge, ending at a torrential waterfall. A short, eerily quiet swim through the crystal-clear water is a spooky but memorable experience.

Chaudiere Pool

6 Nicknamed the 'Emerald Pool' of the north, Chaudiere Pool is a refreshing swimming hole at the end of a moderately difficult 45-minute hike through an old plantation. It's deep enough for daredevils to leap off the surrounding rocks into the water. The trailhead is in the village of

Getting Around

Buses are the most economical way of getting around. Private minibuses run between major cities from Monday to Saturday, stopping as needed along the way.

The main island loop road is good. Other roads can be slow going. Drivers need

Bense. There's a sign at the turn-off to the trailhead but the access road is in pretty bad shape, especially after heavy rains, so unless you have a 4WD, you may have to walk. The trail is well marked and takes you to the confluence of two rivers. Cross the river to get to the pool. The round-trip trek takes about 90 minutes and the scenery and deep swimming hole are well worth it. Look out for parrots!

Roseau

7 Roseau (rose-oh) is Dominica's compact, noisy, chaotic but vibrant capital, situated on the coast and the Roseau

Food & Drink

Callaloo A creamy thick soup or stew blending a variety of vegetables (eg dasheen, spinach, kale, onions, carrots, eggplant, garlic, okra) with coconut milk and sometimes crab or ham.

Fresh fruit Dominica grows all sorts of fruit, including bananas, coconuts, papayas, guavas and pineapples, and mangoes so plentiful they litter the roadside in places.

Sea moss Nonalcoholic beverage made from seaweed mixed with sugar and spices and sometimes with evaporated milk. It's sold in supermarkets and at snackettes.

Kubuli Dominica uses the island's natural spring water for its home-grown beer label; you'll see red-and-white signs all over the island with Kubuli's concise slogan – 'The Beer We Drink'.

Macoucherie Rum connoisseurs crave this local concoction. Don't be fooled by the plastic bottles or cheap-looking label, it's an undiscovered gem.

River. Reggae music blares through the narrow streets while people zip around in the daytime, but at night the city all but empties. Roseau's streets are lined with historic stone-and-wood buildings in states ranging from ramshackle to elegant. Roseau is best explored on foot. The most historic section is the French Quarter, south of bustling King George V St.

Wotten Waven

8 Across the valley from Trafalgar, and linked to it by a road across the River Blanc, Wotten Waven is famous for its natural hot sulfur springs. There are mellow options for dipping in waters and then there's Screw's Sulfur Spa, which reflects the lively persona of its Rasta owner.

JAD DAVENPORT / GETTY IMAGES ©

Trafalgar Falls

Your camera will have a love affair with these misty twin waterfalls, whose easy access puts them on the must-see list of just about every visitor to Dominica.

An easy 0.4-mile trail (lots of steps, though) leads to a viewing platform. Water from the upper falls crosses the Titou Gorge before plunging down the sheer 200ft rock face and feeding the hydro-electric plant downhill. The lower falls flow from the Trois Pitons River in the Boiling Lake area.

Following the narrow, rocky trail beyond the platform means negotiating slippery moss-covered boulders, so wear sturdy shoes and watch your step. As a reward, you can cool off in shallow river pools or loll in the warm sulfur springs below the taller fall.

CAPITAL
Santo Domingo

POPULATION
10.6 million

AREA
48,670 sq km

OFFICIAL LANGUAGE
Spanish

Coconut palms on Península de Samaná

Dominican Republic

The Dominican Republic (DR) is one of the Caribbean's most geographically diverse countries, with stunning mountain scenery, desert scrublands, evocative colonial architecture and beaches galore.

Hundreds of miles of coastline define the DR – some of it white-sand beaches shaded by rows of palm trees, other parts lined dramatically with rocky cliffs, wind-swept dunes or serene mangrove lagoons.

Dominicans appreciate their down time and really know how to party, as can be seen at Carnival celebrations held throughout the country and each town's own distinctive fiesta. These events are great windows into the culture, so take the chance to join the fun and elaborate feasts.

Beyond the capital, much of the DR is distinctly rural: driving through the vast fertile interior, you'll see cows and horses grazing alongside the roads and trucks and burros loaded down with produce. Further inland you'll encounter vistas reminiscent of the European Alps, rivers carving their way through lush jungle and stunning waterfalls.

Top Experiences

Santo Domingo's Zona Colonial

1 The past and present coexist rather gracefully in the oldest city in the New World. With its cobblestone streets and beautifully restored mansions, churches and forts, many converted into evocative museums, It's easy to imagine Santo Domingo's landmark quarter as the seat of Spain's 16th-century empire.

Playa Rincón

2 Consistently rated one of the top beaches in the Caribbean by those in the know – people who courageously brave heatstroke and sunburn in a quest for the ideal – Rincón's 3km of pitch-perfect sands is second only to Bahía de Las Águilas in the DR. It's large enough for every daytripper to claim their own piece of real estate without nosy neighbors peeking over the seaweed and driftwood.

Bahía de Las Águilas

3 The remoteness and loneliness of the country's most far-flung and beautiful beach adds savor and spice to the adventure of getting to Bahía de Las Águilas, a stunning 10km-long stretch of postcard-perfect sand nearly hugging Haiti in an extreme corner of the Península de Pedernales. The fact that you have to take a boat that weaves in and out through craggy cliffs and sea-diving pelicans to get here – and that there won't be many tourists here except for you – only adds to its allure.

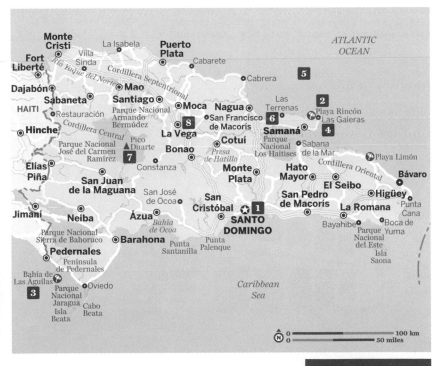

Las Galeras

4 This sleepy fishing village at the far eastern end of the Península de Samaná is an escape from your getaway. Fewer tourists and therefore less development means that the area around Las Galeras includes some of the more scenic locales in all the DR. Swaying palm trees back beaches ready-made for a movie set, and waves crash over hard-to-get-to cliffs.

Whale Watching

5 North Americans and Europeans aren't the only ones who migrate south to the Caribbean in the winter. Every year, thousands of humpback whales congregate off the Península de Samaná to mate and give birth, watched (from a respectful distance) by boatloads of their human fans. Get a front-row seat to this spectacle from mid-

January to mid-March. For an even more intimate experience, week-long live-aboard excursions to the Silver Bank north of Puerto Plata offer the extremely rare opportunity to snorkel alongside these massive mammals.

Las Terrenas Cafe Culture

6 Mellow out in this cosmopolitan beachfront town where French and Italian accents are as common as Dominican. International camaraderie is contagious when every day begins and ends with espresso among baguette-toting foreigners at beachfront open-air cafes and restaurants overlooking the ocean. But the town's relaxed vibe is a marriage between water-sports adventurers swapping tips and the more sedentary set content to admire their exploits from afar while relishing the

Getting Around

Comfortable, frequent bus services run between a network of major cities and towns.

Car is the most convenient option, especially if interested in exploring rural and mountain regions.

Guaguas are small buses or minivans, ubiquitous, least expensive and least comfortable, but often the only public transport available.

SAATON / SHUTTERSTOCK ©

European flare of this former simple fishing village.

Hiking Pico Duarte

7 Hispaniola has some surprisingly rugged terrain in the Central Cordillera, including Pico Duarte, the Caribbean's highest mountain (3087m). You'll need sturdy shoes, warm-weather gear, good stamina and several days, but if you summit when the clouds have dispersed, the views out to both the Atlantic and the Caribbean are more than worth the blisters. Along with the memories of a night huddling around the fire out under the stars, you'll take home a well-earned feeling of accomplishment.

La Vega Carnival

8 Carnival is a huge blowout everywhere in the DR, but especially so in La Vega; the entire city turns out for the parade and every corner and park is transformed into a combination impromptu concert and dance party. Look out for the whips when dancing with costumed devils. Garish, colorful, baroque and elaborately and painstakingly made outfits – capes, demonic masks with bulging eyes and pointed teeth – are worn by marauding groups of revelers.

Food & Drink

La Bandera The most typically Dominican meal consists of white rice, *habichuela* (red beans), stewed meat, salad and fried green plantains, and is usually accompanied by a fresh fruit juice.

Guineos (bananas) Served in a variety of ways, including boiled, stewed and candied, but most commonly boiled and mashed, like mashed potatoes. Prepared the same way, but with plantains, the dish is called *mangú*; with pork rinds mixed in it is called *mofongo*.

Seafood Most commonly a fish fillet served with garlic, in coconut sauce or with a tomato sauce that can be either mild or spicy. Other seafood such as crab, squid, shrimp, octopus, lobster and conch are prepared similarly or in vinegar sauce, a variation on ceviche.

Chivo Goat meat is popular and presented in many ways. Two of the best are *pierna de chivo asada con ron y cilantro* (roast leg of goat with rum and cilantro) and *chivo guisado en salsa de tomate* (goat stewed in tomato sauce).

Locrio The Dominican version of paella with a number of different variations.

8

DANIEL-ALVAREZ / SHUTTERSTOCK ©

A Dominican Passion

Not just the USA's game, *beísbol* (baseball) is an integral part of the Dominican social and cultural landscape. So much so that Dominican ballplayers that have made good in the US are without doubt the most popular and revered figures in the country. More than 400 Dominicans have played in the major leagues (in 2013, nearly 100 out of a total of 856 players were Dominican-born), including stars like David Ortiz, Albert Pujols, Robinson Cano, Sammy Sosa and Juan Marichal, the only Dominican to be inducted into the Hall of Fame.

In winter, the Dominican league's six teams go *cabeza a cabeza* several nights a week – Estadio Quisqueya in Santo Domingo is home field for two longtime rivals – culminating in a championship series at the end of January.

CAPITAL
Quito

POPULATION
15.7 million

AREA
283,561 sq km

OFFICIAL LANGUAGE
Spanish

Iguanas, Galápagos Islands

Ecuador

Picturesque colonial centers, Kichwa villages, Amazonian rainforest and the breathtaking heights of the Andes – Ecuador may be small, but it has a dazzling array of wonders.

The historic centers of Quito and Cuenca are lined with photogenic plazas, 17th-century churches, and beautifully restored mansions. Beyond the cities, the landscape unfolds in all its startling variety. There are Andean villages renowned for their textiles and sprawling markets, Afro-Ecuadorian towns where days end with seafood and sunsets, and remote settlements in the Amazon where shamans still harvest the traditional medicines of their ancestors. The Andes make a fine backdrop for mountain biking, horseback riding or hiking between villages, overnighting at local guesthouses.

Get up close to massive tortoises on the Galápagos Islands or take a tour in the Amazon rainforest for a vastly different wildlife-watching experience. And for a coastal getaway, surf off the Pacific coast or visit tiny settlements like Ayampe and Olón and charming towns on the Galapagos, with great beaches and magnificent sunsets.

Top Experiences

Quito Old Town

1 A Spanish-colonial stunner, Quito's vibrant Centro Histórico is packed with elaborate churches and mournful monasteries (some centuries in the making), people-packed plazas and looming bell towers. H Delve into the past by stepping off the cobblestones and entering beautifully maintained museums, historic mansions and jaw-dropping sanctuaries. Afterwards, have a meal in one of El Centro's old-world restaurants or join the festivities on lively La Ronda street before retiring to one of the many charming guesthouses in the neighborhood.

Galápagos Islands

2 There aren't many places that can beat the Galápagos Islands for close encounters of the pre-historic kind. Rather than scurrying away when approached, the unique lizard species of iguanas found throughout the archipelago go about their slow-moving business with little concern for the clicking cameras. The dark gray or black marine iguanas pile on top of one another like a messy pyramid of cheerleaders basking in the sun, whereas the imposing yellow land iguanas nibble on cactus plants for sustenance.

Vilcabamba

3 The air in Vilcabamba just feels right – not too hot, not too cold; mountain fresh with just a hint of incense on its fleeting skirts – giving this southern highland draw a mystical quality that many travelers find inescapable. Perhaps that's why you'll find more foreigner-owned businesses here than almost anywhere else in Ecuador. And who can blame them? The hiking is great, there's a national park nearby for backwoods adventures on horseback and mountain bike, and the pitch-perfect spa resorts will cater to your every need, whim and desire.

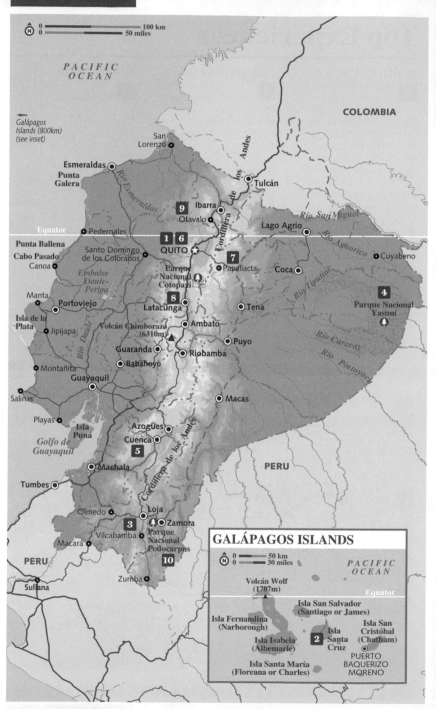

PACIFIC
OCEAN

COLOMBIA

Galápagos
Islands (800km)
(see inset)

San
Lorenzo

Esmeraldas
Punta
Galera

Tulcán

Andes

Río San Miguel

9 Ibarra
Otavalo

Lago Agrio

Río Aguarico

Cuyabeno

Equator Pedernales

1 **6**
QUITO

7
Papallacta

Coca

Punta Ballena
Cabo Pasado
Canoa

Santo Domingo
de los Colorados

Río Tiputini

Embalse
Daule-
Peripa

Parque
Nacional
Cotopaxi

8
Latacunga

Tena

Río Curaray

4
Parque Nacional
Yasuní

Manta

Portoviejo

Isla de la
Plata
Jipijapa

Volcán Chimborazo
(6310m)

Ambato

Puyo

Río Pintoyacu

Guaranda

Riobamba

Babahoyo

Montañita

Guayaquil

Río Daule

Salinas

Macas

Cordillera de los Andes

Playas

Isla Puná

Golfo de
Guayaquil

Azogues

Cuenca

5

Machala

PERU

Tumbes

Olmedo

Loja

Zamora

3
Vilcabamba

Parque
Nacional
Podocarpus

10

Macará

PERU

Zumba

Sullana

GALÁPAGOS ISLANDS

0   50 km
0   30 miles

PACIFIC
OCEAN

Volcán Wolf
(1707m)

Equator

Isla San Salvador
(Santiago or James)

Isla Fernandina
(Narborough)

Isla
Santa
Cruz

2

Isla San
Cristóbal
(Chatham)

Isla Isabela
(Albemarle)

PUERTO
BAQUERIZO
MORENO

Isla Santa María
(Floreana or Charles)

Best on Film

Qué tan lejos (2006) Road movie about two young women on a journey of self-discovery in the Andean highlands.

Entre Marx y una Mujer Desnuda (1996) Portrays a group of young intellectuals in Quito.

Ratas, Ratones, Rateros (1999) Award-winning film about two petty thieves on the run in Quito and Guayaquil.

Food & Drink

Arroz con pollo Rice with small bits of chicken mixed in.

Ceviche Marinated raw seafood.

Churrasco Fried beef, eggs and potatoes, a few veggies, slices of avocado and tomato, and rice.

Corviche A delicious plantain dumpling stuffed with seafood or shrimp.

Cuy Roasted guinea pig.

Empanadas de verde Pasties made from green plantain dough and often stuffed with cheese.

Encebollado A brothy fish and onion soup poured over yuca and served with fried banana chips and popcorn.

Encocado Shrimp or fish cooked in a rich coconut sauce.

Hornado Whole roasted pig.

Llapingachos Fried potato-and-cheese pancakes.

Locro de papa Potato soup served with avocado and cheese.

Maito Fish or chicken grilled in palm leaves.

Pollo a la brasa Roast chicken, often served with fries.

Seco de chivo Goat stew.

Parque Nacional Yasuní

4 This vast tract of protected rainforest contains a simply dazzling biodiversity matched almost nowhere else on earth. Excitement-filled canoe trips through tiny overgrown creeks and hikes across the jungle floor with experienced guides reveal all manner of flowers, plants and creatures, many of which you'll not even have heard of before, let alone seen in real life, while several populations of indigenous peoples continue to resist contact with the outside world here. This natural wonder remains, at present, unspoiled.

Cuenca

5 The fairy-tale colonial center of Cuenca is a Unesco World Heritage Site that's been charming visitors since the 16th century. And while the cobblestone

When to Go

HIGH SEASON
(Jun–Sep)
Warm temperatures and periodic showers on the coast.

SHOULDER SEASON
(Oct & Nov)
Cooler temperatures.

LOW SEASON
(Dec–May)
Cooler, rainier days in the highlands.

streets, polychrome building fronts and remarkably well-preserved cathedral will have you snapping a photo on nearly every

It's a Montecristi!

For well over a century, Ecuador has endured the world mistakenly crediting another country with its most famous export – the panama hat. To any Ecuadorian worth his or her salt, the panama hat is a *sombrero de paja toquilla* (toquilla-straw hat), and to the connoisseur it's a Montecristi, named after the most famous hat-making town of all.

The origin of this misnomer – surely one of the world's greatest – dates to the 1800s, when Spanish entrepreneurs, quick to recognize the unrivaled quality of *sombreros de paja toquilla*, began exporting them via Panama. During the 19th century, workers on the Panama Canal used these light and extremely durable hats to protect themselves from the tropical sun, helping to solidify the association with Panama.

Paja toquilla hats are made from the fibrous fronds of the *toquilla* palm (*Carludovica palmata*), which grows in the arid inland regions of the central Ecuadorian coast, particularly around Montecristi and Jipijapa. A few Asian and several Latin American countries have tried to grow the palm to compete with the Ecuadorian hat trade, but none could duplicate the quality of the fronds grown here.

Getting Around

 Air travel is best for reaching the Galápagos and remote jungle lodges. Good for quick hops to avoid lengthy bus rides.

 Buses go most places you need to go, with frequent departures and rates about $1 to $1.50 per hour of bus travel.

 Inter-island boats are a great way to make a DIY trip around the four main inhabited Galápagos Islands.

 A car is useful for going at your own pace, and the roads are in great shape.

corner, it's the town's laid-back feel, friendly locals and bohemian spirit that will truly fill your heart and soul. Top that off with great nightlife, plenty of museums and galleries, and some of Ecuador's best eateries, and there's no doubt why this is the top highlight of southern Ecuador.

Riding the TelefériQo

6 Proving there's more than one way to summit the Andean peaks, the TelefériQo whisks you up by aerial tram to breathtaking heights (4100m) over Quito. In a city of sublime views, Cruz Loma offers the finest of all – assuming you go on a clear day. Here, Quito spreads out across the Andean valley, with majestic peaks (including Cotopaxi) visible in the distance. At the top, you can extend the adventure by hiking (or taking a horseback ride) to the 4680m summit of Rucu Pichincha.

Papallacta

7 The beautifully maintained public baths just outside the Andean village of Papallacta offer one of Ecuador's best natural highs: move between baths of thermally heated water surrounded by mountains all around, swim in the fantastic pool, enjoy a bracing jump into the icy plunge pool and then get right back into those steaming baths. It's even more magical at night, when you can lie back and watch the stars come out in the giant black sky above.

Quilotoa Loop

8 Adventure begins at 3000m along the popular Quilotoa Loop, a rough travelers' route that takes you through indigenous villages and painters' colonies to a deep-blue crater lake and into the heart of Ecuador's central highlands. The best thing about the loop is that you can custom-build your adventure to fit your

needs. Want to volunteer in a sustainable agriculture project? No problem. Or would you like to hike and bike from village to village on forgotten trails? Yep, they've got that, too.

Otavalo Market

9 Every Saturday the world seems to converge on the bustling indigenous town of Otavalo in the Andes, where a huge market (which goes on in a rather redacted form every other day of the week, too) spreads out from the Plaza de Ponchos throughout the town. The choice is enormous, the quality immensely changeable and the crowds can be a drag, but you'll find some incredible bargains here among the brightly colored rugs, traditional crafts, clothing, striking folk art and quality straw hats.

Parque Nacional Podocarpus

10 Down by the Peruvian border, Parque Nacional Podocarpus is one of the southern highland's least-visited reserves. With elevations ranging from 900m to 3600m, Podocarpus is home to an amazing array of plant and animal life. There are an estimated 3000 plant species here (many of which you will see nowhere else in the world). For bird lovers, an astounding 600 unique types of feathered friends await. Top that off with trails, highland lakes and sweeping views and you have one of Ecuador's most unique off-beat attractions.

Haciendas

The Ecuadorian highlands have some fabulous *haciendas* (historic family ranches that have been refurbished to accept tourists). They usually fall into the top-end price bracket, but the price may include home-cooked meals and activities.

Manco Capac

Inca ruler Huayna Capac had a third son, Manco Capac. He was the last Inca ruler and staged one of the greatest revolts against the Spanish. He was killed by a Spaniard whose life he had saved.

CAPITAL
Cairo

POPULATION
96.7 million

AREA
1 million sq km

OFFICIAL LANGUAGE
Arabic

Feluccas on the Nile River

Egypt

In spite of political, financial and social turmoil, Egyptians remain proud and defiant and are as welcoming as ever to visitors to their land.

With sand-covered tombs, austere pyramids and towering Pharaonic temples, Egypt brings out the explorer in all of us. Visit the Valley of the Kings in Luxor, where Tutankhamun's tomb was unearthed, and see the glittering finds in the Egyptian Museum in Cairo. Hop off a Nile boat to visit Dendara, Edfu or one of the other waterside temples, cross Lake Nasser to see Ramses II's masterpiece at Abu Simbel, or trek into the desert to find the traces of Roman trading outposts.

The coast along the Red Sea has a rugged desert beauty above the waterline and a psychedelic vibrancy below – rewarding to explore on a multiday outing to one of the globe's great dives or on an afternoon's snorkelling jaunt.

Whether you're watching the sun rise between the beautiful shapes of the White Desert or the shimmering horizon from the comfort of a hot spring in Siwa Oasis, Egypt's landscapes are endlessly fascinating.

Top Experiences

Pyramids of Giza

1 Towering over the urban sprawl of Cairo and the desert plains beyond, the Pyramids of Giza and the Sphinx are at the top of every traveller's itinerary. Bring lots of water, an empty memory card and plenty of patience! You'll have to fend off lots of people pushing horse rides and Bedouin headdresses in order to enjoy this ancient funerary complex, but no trip to Egypt is complete without a photo of you in front of the last surviving ancient wonder of the world.

Luxor

2 With the greatest concentration of ancient Egyptian monuments anywhere in Egypt, Luxor rewards time spent here. You can spend days or weeks walking through the columned halls of the great temples on the east bank of the Nile, such as the Ramesseum, or climbing down into the tombs of pharaohs in the Valley of the Kings on the west bank. Watching the sun rise over the Nile or set behind the Theban hills are some of Egypt's unforgettable moments.

Cruising the Nile

3 The Nile is Egypt's lifeline, the artery that runs through the entire country, from south to north. Only by setting adrift on it can you appreciate its importance and its beauty, and more practically, only by boat can you see some archaeological sites as they were meant to be seen. Sailing is the slowest and most relaxing way to go, but even from the deck of a multistorey floating hotel you're likely to glimpse the magic.

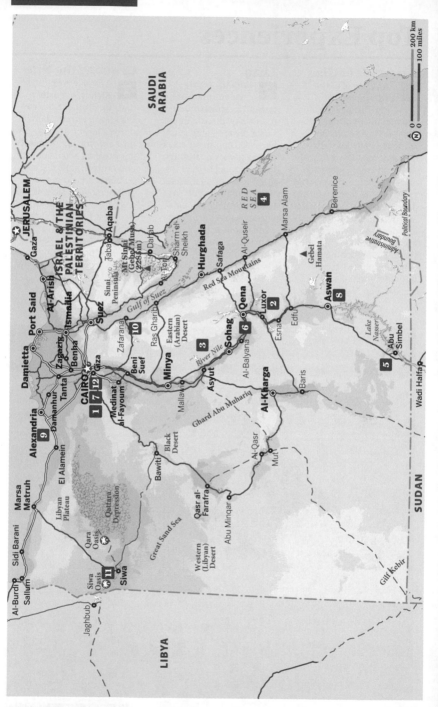

Best on Film

Death on the Nile (1978) Agatha Christie's story about Poirot investigating the murder of a heiress on board a Nile cruiser.

The Yacoubian Building (2006) Blockbuster Egyptian movie adapted from Alaa Al Aswani's novel, portraying the stories of the residents of one block of flats in downtown Cairo.

Ruby Cairo (1992) A wife tracks down her missing husband to a hideaway in Egypt, but the real star of the film is Cairo.

The Spy Who Loved Me (1977) The Pyramids, Karnak and Islamic Cairo all provide glamorous backdrops for the antics of James Bond.

Food & Drink

Shwarma Strips of lamb or chicken sliced from a vertical spit, sizzled on a hot plate with chopped tomatoes and garnish, and then stuffed into shammy bread.

Fiteer The Egyptian pizza has a thin, flaky pastry base, and is topped with salty haloumi cheese and olives, or comes sweet with jam, coconut and raisins.

Mahshi kurumb These rice- and meat-stuffed cabbage leaves are delightful when cooked with plenty of dill and *samna* (clarified butter).

Molokhiyya A slightly slippery but delicious soup made from jute leaves, served with rabbit and garlic.

Hamam mahshi Roast pigeon stuffed with *fireek* (green wheat) and rice.

Mahallabiye A dessert of milk custard with pine nuts and almonds.

Red Sea Diving

4 Egypt's Sinai and Red Sea coastlines are the doorstep to a wonderland that hides below the surface. Whether you're a seasoned diving pro or a first-timer, Egypt's underwater world of coral cliffs, colourful fish and spookily beautiful wrecks is just as staggeringly impressive as the sights above. Bring out your inner Jacques Cousteau by exploring the enigmatic wreck of WWII cargo ship the *Thistlegorm*, a fascinating museum spread across the sea bed.

Abu Simbel

5 Ramses II built Abu Simbel a long way south of Aswan, along his furthest frontier and just beyond the Tropic of Cancer. But these two temples are a marvel of modern engineering as well: in the 1960s they were relocated, block by block, to their current site to protect them from the flooding of Lake Nasser. To appreciate the isolation, spend the night at Abu Simbel, either on a boat on the lake or at Nubian cultural centre and ecolodge Eskaleh.

When to Go

HIGH SEASON
(Oct–Feb)
Egypt's 'winter' is sunny and warm.

SHOULDER
(Mar–May, Sep & Oct)
Warm seas on the Mediterranean.

LOW SEASON
(Jun–Aug)
Scorching summer sun.

Find Your Own Ahwa

The coffeehouse, known as *ahwa* (the Arabic word for coffee is now synonymous with the place in which it's drunk), is one of the great Egyptian social institutions. Traditionally *ahwas* have been all-male preserves, but it's now common to see young, mixed-sex groups of Egyptians in *ahwas*, especially in Cairo and Alexandria.

The *ahwa* is an essential place to unwind, chat and breathe deeply over a *sheesha*. Dusty floors, rickety tables and the clatter of dominoes and *towla* (backgammon) define the traditional ones. But newer, shinier places have expanded the concept, not to mention the array of *sheesha* flavours, which now include everything from mango to bubblegum.

Most *ahwas* are open from 8am to 2am or so, and you can order a lot more than tea and coffee: try *karkadai* (hibiscus, hot or cold), *irfa* (cinnamon), *kamun* (cumin, good for colds), *yansun* (anise) and, in winter, hot, milky *sahlab* (a thick warm drink made with the starch from the orchid tuber, milk and chopped nuts).

Getting Around

Most domestic flights go through Cairo. When using EgyptAir's website, switch your home location to Egypt to get the cheapest domestic fares.

There are frequent buses between Egyptian cities. Buses are comfortable and reliable. Book in advance.

It is not advisable to drive in Cairo, but cars with a driver are readily available and reasonably priced.

Train is the most comfortable option for travelling to Alexandria, Luxor and Aswan.

Abydos & Dendara

6 Time is short and everyone wants to see the Pyramids, Tutankhamun's gold and the Valley of the Kings. But some of the most rewarding moments are to be had away from the crowds in the lesser visited monuments, where you can contemplate the ancients' legacy in peace. Nowhere is this truer than at Abydos, one of the most sacred spots along the Nile, and Dendara, one of the world's best-preserved ancient temples. They're north of Luxor – the opposite direction from the tour buses.

Egyptian Museum

7 The scale of the Egyptian Museum is simply overwhelming. More than a hundred rooms are packed to the rafters with some of the most fascinating treasures excavated in Egypt: glittering gold jewellery, King Tut's socks, and mummies of the greatest pharaohs, plus their favourite pets. On top of it all, very few of the objects are labelled. Don't push yourself to see it all, and do hire a guide for an hour or two to unlock some of the storehouse's secrets.

Aswan

8 Watch the sun set over Aswan, frontier of the ancient Egyptian empire and southernmost outpost for the Romans. It's still the gateway to Nubia, where cultures blend to create a laid-back place that values time to enjoy the view. There is something about the way the river is squeezed between rocks, the proximity of the desert, the lonely burial places of the Aga Khan and of forgotten ancient princes that makes the end of the day more poignant here than anywhere else along the Egyptian Nile.

Alexandria

9 Flaunting the pedigree of Alexander the Great and the powerful queen Cleopatra, Egypt's second-largest city is rich in history, both ancient and modern. Visit the Bibliotheca Alexandrina, the new incarnation of the ancient Great Library, or any number of great small museums around town. Walk the souqs of atmospheric Anfushi, the oldest part of the city, and be sure to feast on fresh seafood with a Mediterranean view.

Monastery of St Anthony

10 It was to the barren mountains and jagged cliffs of the sprawling desert that the first early ascetics came, even then seeking an escape from Egypt's hubbub. The historic Monastery of St Anthony traces its origins to the 4th century AD when monks began to settle at the foot of Gebel al-Galala al-Qibliya, where their spiritual leader, Anthony, lived. Today the monastery is a large complex surrounded by high walls with several churches, a bakery and a lush garden. The 120 monks who live here have dedicated their lives to seeking God in the stillness and isolation of the desert, in a life built completely around prayer.

Siwa Oasis

11 The grandest and most remote of Egypt's Western Desert oases, Siwa on the edge of the Great Sand Sea offers the ultimate oasis experience. This is not only where Alexander the Great came to consult the gods, it is also the perfect place to hang out and relax after travelling along the Nile. Cycle through the palm groves, take a desert tour to the hot and cold water springs and lakes, or slide down a sand dune.

Khan al-Khalili Souq, Cairo

12 The skinny lanes of Khan al-Khalili are basically a medieval-style mall. This agglomeration of shops – many arranged around small courtyards – stock everything from soap powder to semiprecious stones, not to mention toy camels and alabaster pyramids. It's open from early morning to sundown (except Friday morning and Sunday), although many shops are open as long as there are customers. Cairenes have plied their trades here since the *khan* was built in the 14th century, and parts of the market, such as the gold district, are still the first choice for thousands of locals.

Sand Dunes

Egypt has four of the world's five officially identified types of sand dunes, including the *seif* (sword) dunes, so named because they resemble the blades of curved Arab swords.

Cultural Icons

Egypt (or more specifically Cairo) is a powerhouse of film, TV, music and theatre and a great many Egyptian actors and singers are revered cultural icons to Arabic-speakers around the world.

MICHELLE MCMAHON / GETTY IMAGES ©

2

EFESENKO / SHUTTERSTOCK ©

12

CAPITAL	San Salvador
POPULATION	6.4 million
AREA	21,040 sq km
OFFICIAL LANGUAGE	Spanish

Playa El Zonte, La Costa del Bálsamo

El Salvador

Surf's up in El Salvador, Central America's most underrated country, which until recently has been kept off the tourist radar by civil war and bad press.

Visitors who make the effort to visit El Salvador are invariably impressed by just how much this tiny country has to offer: world-class surfing on empty, dark-sand beaches; coffee plantations clinging to the sides of volcanoes; colorful Spanish colonial towns; and sublime national parks. There are few crowds outside the capital, San Salvador, which itself boasts more swagger than its Central American counterparts.

Once only a trickle of headstrong surfers and foreign correspondents passed through its rigorous border posts, but now a new breed of traveler is pushing through in search of an authentic experience in a little-visited land. And they're finding it: the contemporary art scene is vibrant and many villages revolve around creative industries.

Buy a hammock, go diving, hike to a former guerrilla stronghold or swim in the crystal-blue volcanic crater at Lago de Coatepeque. And as for festivals, El Salvador really knows how to get its groove on.

Top Experiences

La Costa del Bálsamo

 La Costa del Bálsamo is surfing paradise, El Sal style. Starting at the tough port city of La Libertad, the coastal highway glides west past tiny two-break, black-sand beaches in the one part of El Salvador that young travelers and ocean lovers gravitate towards without exception.

La Ruta de las Flores

 Traveling La Ruta de las Flores, slowly and purposefully, is like a meander through the story of El Salvador. It's a searingly beautiful series of villages, each with a mix of colonial architecture in indigenous tones. Feast on local food, browse the craft *tiendas* (shops) and track your gourmet coffee from plantation to cup. There's also the Cordillera Apaneca, a volcanic mountain range filled with waterfalls, mountain-bike trails, and pine-forest hikes where white flowers bloom in May.

Tazumal

 The Maya ruins of Tazumal are an unexpected highlight for many travelers. Have them all to yourself, then gaze at the finest architecture in the country at nearby Santa Ana.

When to Go

 LOW SEASON
(May–Aug)

 SHOULDER
(Feb–Apr &
Sep–Nov)

 HIGH SEASON
(Dec & Jan)

Food & Drink

El Salvador's most famous food is by far the *pupusa*, round cornmeal dough stuffed with a combination of cheese, refried beans, wild vegetables such as *ayote* and *mora*, *chicharrón* (pork rinds), or *revuelta* (mixed filling), then grilled. *Curtido*, a mixture of pickled cabbage and vegetables, provides the final topping.

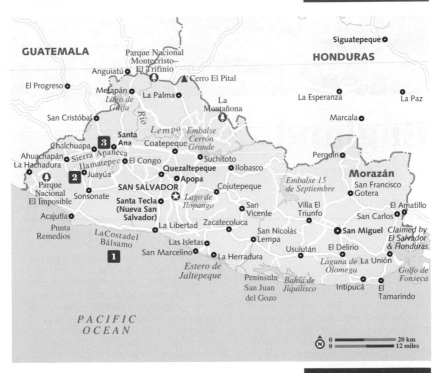

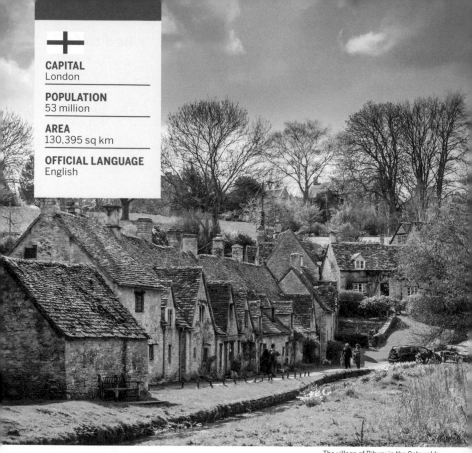

CAPITAL
London

POPULATION
53 million

AREA
130,395 sq km

OFFICIAL LANGUAGE
English

The village of Bibury in the Cotswolds

England

This green land, this sceptred isle, this crucible of empire and pioneer of parliamentary democracy, is the most eccentric, extraordinary and downright intriguing place on Earth.

From the Roman remains of Hadrian's Wall to London's incomparable theatre scene, England is full of astounding variety. In the cities, the streets buzz day and night, filled with tempting shops and restaurants, and some of the finest museums in the world. After dark, cutting-edge clubs, top-class performing arts and formidable live music provide a string of nights to remember. Next day, you're deep in the English countryside or enjoying a classic seaside resort. There really is something for everyone.

Travel here is a breeze, and although the locals may grumble (in fact, it's a national pastime), public transport is very good, and a train ride through the English landscape can be a highlight in itself. Whichever way you get around, in this compact country you're never far from the next town, the next pub, the next national park or the next impressive castle on your hit list of highlights.

Top Experiences

Stonehenge

1 Mysterious and compelling, Stonehenge is England's most iconic ancient site. People have been drawn to this myth-laden ring of boulders for more than 5000 years, and despite countless theories about the site's purpose, we still don't know quite why it was built. Most visitors gaze at the 50-tonne stones from behind the perimeter fence, but with enough planning you can arrange an early-morning or evening tour and gain access to the inner ring itself. In the slanting sunlight, away from the crowds, it's an ethereal place. This is an experience that stays with you.

London

2 You could spend a lifetime exploring London and find that the slippery thing's gone and changed on you. One thing is constant: that great serpent of a river enfolding the city in its sinuous loops, linking London both to the green heart of England and the world. There is no place on Earth that is more multicultural and the narrow streets are steeped in fascinating history, magnificent art, imposing architecture and popular culture. When you add an endless reserve of cool to this mix, it's hard not to conclude that London is one of the world's great cities, if not the greatest.

Hadrian's Wall

3 Hadrian's Wall is one of the country's most revealing and dramatic Roman ruins. Its 2000-year-old, 73-mile-long procession of abandoned forts, garrisons, towers and milecastles marches across the wild and lonely landscape of northern England. This wall was about defence and control, but this edge-of-empire barrier also symbolised the boundary of civilised order – to the north lay the unruly land of the marauding Celts, while to the south was the Roman world of orderly taxpaying, underfloor heating and bathrooms.

2

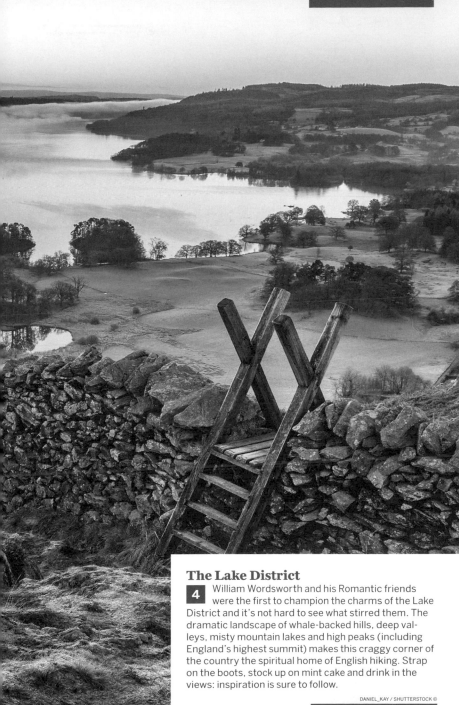

The Lake District

4 William Wordsworth and his Romantic friends were the first to champion the charms of the Lake District and it's not hard to see what stirred them. The dramatic landscape of whale-backed hills, deep valleys, misty mountain lakes and high peaks (including England's highest summit) makes this craggy corner of the country the spiritual home of English hiking. Strap on the boots, stock up on mint cake and drink in the views: inspiration is sure to follow.

DANIEL_KAY / SHUTTERSTOCK ©

Best on Film

Brief Encounter (1945) Classic tale of buttoned-up English love affair.

My Beautiful Laundrette (1985) Touching and comic study of racism and homophobia in Thatcher-era London.

War Horse (2011) Rite-of-passage story of a young man surviving WWI.

Pride (2014) Comic, compassionate depiction of lesbian and gay activists raising money for families hit by the UK Miners' Strike (1984–85).

Suffragette (2015) Compelling account of the pre-WWI fight to secure votes for women.

Best in Print

Notes from a Small Island (Bill Bryson; 1995) It's dated, but this American's fond take on British behaviour is a classic, and is still spot on today.

The English (Jeremy Paxman; 1998) A perceptive take on the national character.

The Rotters Club (Jonathan Coe; 2001) Growing up in the 1970s, amid strikes, IRA bombings and punk rock.

Watching the English (Kate Fox; 2004) A fascinating field guide to the nation's peculiar habits.

A Week in December (Sebastian Faulks; 2009) A state-of-the-nation satire on 2007 London life.

York

 With its Roman and Viking heritage, ancient city walls and maze of cobbled streets, York is a living showcase for the highlights of English history. Join one of the city's many walking tours and plunge into the network of *snickelways* (narrow alleys), each one the focus of a ghost story or historical character. Explore the intricacies of York Minster, the biggest medieval cathedral in all of northern Europe, or admire the exhibits from more recent times at the National Railway Museum, the world's largest collection of historic locomotives.

Oxford

 A visit to Oxford is as close as most of us will get to the brilliant minds and august institutions that have made this city famous across the globe. But you'll catch a glimpse of this rarefied world in the cobbled lanes and ancient quads where cycling students and dusty academics roam. The beautiful college buildings, archaic traditions and stunning architecture have changed little over the centuries, coexisting with a lively, modern, working city.

Bath

 In a nation packed with pretty cities, Bath still stands out as the belle of the ball. Founded by the Romans, who established the spa resort of Aquae Sulis to take advantage of the area's hot springs, Bath hit its stride in the 18th century when the rich industrialist Ralph Allen and architects John Wood the Elder and John

When to Go

HIGH SEASON
(Jun–Aug)
Weather at its best. Accommodation rates are high, particularly in August.

SHOULDER
(Mar–May, Sep & Oct)
March to May sun mixes with sudden rain; September and October can feature balmy 'Indian summers'.

LOW SEASON
(Nov–Feb)
Wet and cold is the norm. Snow can fall, especially up north.

Celtic Language

Despite Anglo-Saxon dominance from around AD 500, the Celtic language was still being spoken in parts of southern England when the Normans invaded in the 11th century.

Wildlife

For a small country, England has a diverse range of plants and animals. Many native species are hidden away, but there are undoubted gems, from lowland woods carpeted in bluebells to stately herds of deer on the high moors.

Food & Drink

Christmas pudding A dome-shaped cake with fruit, nuts and brandy or rum, traditionally eaten at Christmas.

Cornish pasty Savoury pastry, southwest speciality, now available countrywide.

Fish and chips Long-standing favourite, best sampled in coastal towns.

Full English breakfast This usually consists of bacon, sausages, eggs, tomatoes, mushrooms, baked beans and fried bread.

Ploughman's lunch Bread and cheese – pub menu regular, perfect with a pint. Sometimes also includes salad, pickle, pickled onion and dressings.

Roast beef & Yorkshire pudding Traditional Sunday lunch.

Wood the Younger oversaw the city's reinvention as a model of Georgian architecture. Awash with golden stone townhouses, sweeping crescents and Palladian mansions, Bath demands your undivided attention.

The Cotswolds

8 The most wonderful thing about the Cotswolds is that no matter where you go or how lost you get, you'll still end up in an impossibly quaint village of rose-clad cottages and honey-coloured stone. There'll be a charming village green, a pub with sloping floors and fine ales, and a view of the lush green hills. It's easy to leave the crowds behind and find your very own slice of medieval England here – and some of the best boutique hotels in the country.

Cambridge

9 One of England's two great historic university cities, Cambridge highlights include a tour of at least one of the ancient colleges, and time spent marvelling at the intricate vaulting of King's College Chapel. But no trip to Cambridge is complete without an attempt to take a punt (flat-bottomed boat) along the river by the picturesque 'Backs' – the green lawns behind the city's finest colleges. Polish off the day with a pint in one of the many historic pubs. You'll soon wonder how you could have studied anywhere else.

Liverpool Museums

10 After a decade of development, the waterfront is once again the heart of Liverpool. The focal point is Albert Dock, a World Heritage Site of iconic buildings, including a batch of top museums: the Merseyside Maritime Museum and International Slavery Museum ensure the good and bad sides of Liverpool's history are not forgotten, while the Tate Liverpool and the Beatles Story museum celebrate culture and the city's most famous musical sons (still).

Stratford-upon-Avon

11 The pretty town of Stratford-upon-Avon is where William Shakespeare was born and later shuffled off this mortal coil. Today, its tight knot of Tudor streets form a living map of Shakespeare's life. Huge crowds of thespians and theatre lovers come to take in a play. Visit the five historic houses owned by Shakespeare and his relatives, and the school room where he was educated, then take a respectful detour to the old stone church where the Bard was laid to rest.

Peak District

12 Curiously, you won't find many peaks in the Peak District. But you will find blissful miles of tumbling moorland, plunging valleys, eroded gritstone crags, lush farmland and ancient pocket-sized villages. This beautiful landscape attracts a veritable army of outdoor enthusiasts – cyclists, hikers, cavers and rock climbers – while those seeking more relaxing enjoyment can admire the rural market and famous puddings of Bakewell, the Victorian pavilions of spa-town Buxton, and the architectural drama of Chatsworth House – the 'Palace of the Peak'.

Seven Sisters Chalk Cliffs

13 Dover's iconic white cliffs grab the most attention, but the colossal chalky walls of the Seven Sisters are a much more spectacular affair. This 4-mile roller coaster of sheer white rock rollicks along the Sussex shore overlooking the waters of the English Channel, an impressive southern border to the South Downs National Park and most dramatic at the towering headland of Beachy Head. Hikes through the grassy clifftop fields provide wide sea views, breathtaking in every sense.

Getting Around

Travelling by car means you can be independent and flexible, and reach remote places. Downsides for drivers include traffic jams and the high price of fuel.

For long-distance travel around England, trains are fast and comfortable but can be expensive. Good coverage and frequent departures throughout most of the country.

If you're on a tight budget, coaches are nearly always the cheapest way to get around, although they're also the slowest – sometimes by a considerable margin.

England is a compact country, and hiring a bike – for an afternoon, a day, or a week or longer – is a great way to really see the country if you've got time to spare.

Mandrill

CAPITAL	Malabo
POPULATION	1.9 million
AREA	28,051 sq km
OFFICIAL LANGUAGES	Spanish, French

Equatorial Guinea

A country of two distinct halves, Equatorial Guinea is a nation divided not only by the sea but also by oil wealth and its attendant issues.

This is the land of primates with painted faces, soft clouds of butterflies and insects so colourful they belong in the realm of fiction. Yes, Equatorial Guinea has something of a reputation, with a history of failed coups, allegations of corruption, trafficked bushmeat and buckets of oil, but there is plenty to bring you to this country's beautiful black-and-white shores.

The capital, Malabo, boasts fascinating colonial architecture alongside sleek oil company high-rises, yet retains its African flavour with colourful markets and a bustling port. Though the country is currently dripping in oil wealth, many people's taps run dry. Poverty permeates ordinary life, making a trip to Malabo at once hedonistic and heartbreaking.

Beyond Malabo, on Bioko Island, are volcanic views, fishing villages, rain forests full of endangered primates, vibrant birdlife and shores of nesting sea turtles. On the mainland, Rio Muni's white beaches, forest paths and jungle-scapes await.

Top Experiences

Bioko Island

1 Surrounded by beautiful beaches with either black volcanic or white sands, Bioko has rainforests, woodland, savannah and one volcanic peak, Pico Basile (3012m). While the capital, Malabo, can keep you occupied for a few days, marine turtles come ashore to lay their eggs in Ureca, and the dense forest around the Luba Crater is home to the primates for which Equatorial Guinea is so well known.

Isla Corisco

2 For the ultimate getaway with white-sand beaches, warm blue sea and swaying palm trees, look no further than Corisco. And now is the time to go, before the crowds descend. For now, swimming and relaxing on the beach are just about the only pastimes.

Monte Alen National Park

3 Monte Alen is one of Central Africa's best-kept secrets. Covering some 2000 sq km of mountainous rainforest, this national park is home to forest elephants, western lowland gorillas, chimpanzees, buffalo, crocodiles, leopards and quirky creatures such as goliath frogs.

When to Go

HIGH SEASON
(Jun–Aug)

SHOULDER
(Mar–May &
Sep–Nov)

LOW SEASON
(Dec–Feb)

Food & Drink

Equatorial Guinea has a wealth of tropical fruit; vegetables such as cassava, plantains and yams; and a great deal of fish. Most restaurants in Malabo and Bata offer European or Lebanese dishes. A few have African dishes on the menu, such as the local dish of chicken with a creamy peanut sauce, Senegalese *yassa*.

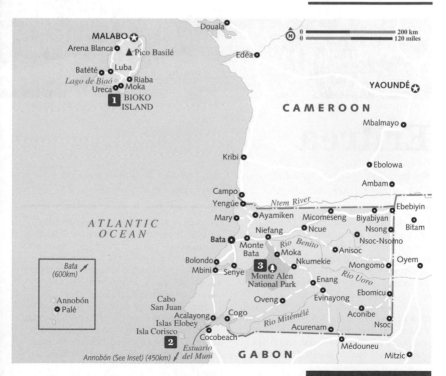

Ruins at Qohaito

Eritrea

Eritrea, a mere sliver on the Horn of Africa, boasts a wealth of culture, history and natural beauty for travellers to experience.

Historically intriguing, culturally compelling and scenically inspiring, Eritrea is one of the most secretive countries in Africa. For those with a hankering for off-the-beaten-track places, it offers challenges and excitement alike, with a unique blend of natural and cultural highlights.

Eritrea wows visitors with its scenery, from the quintessentially Abyssinian landscapes – escarpments, plateaus and soaring peaks – to the deserted and desertified beaches of the Red Sea coast. Culturally,

Eritrea is a melting pot. It might be a tiny country by Africa's standards, but it hosts a kaleidoscopic range of ethnic groups. It also features a superb array of archaeological sites that tell volumes of history. The cherry on top is Asmara, Eritrea's delightful capital and a whimsical art deco city.

Despite the tough political and economic situation and the odd travel restrictions, this country remains one of the most inspiring destinations in Africa, particularly for travellers that want something a little different.

CAPITAL
Asmara

POPULATION
5.8 million

AREA
117,600 sq km

OFFICIAL LANGUAGES
Tigrinya, Arabic, English

Top Experiences

Keren Camel Market

1 From 8am on Monday mornings, a small yard on the Nakfa road comes alive with buyers and sellers haggling over livestock in a lively market. Though the name refers to the obvious highlight – the caravans of camels on the lower level – walk up to the higher terrace for a massive collection of sheep, cows and more.

Qohaito

2 These impressively large city ruins – covering an area of 2.5km by 15km – are testament to its once-great stature. On an old Aksumite trade route, Qohaito's impressive pre-Christian churches on scenic mountain tops and nearby cave paintings offer plenty of opportunity to speculate on Eritrea's mysterious past.

Tank Graveyard

3 Part junkyard, part memorial, the ruins of military vehicles from around the country have been dragged to this open field in the years since heavy fighting ended, and make for poignant reflection on the damage done during decades of fighting.

When to Go

 HIGH SEASON (Oct–Mar)

 SHOULDER (Apr, May & Sep)

 LOW SEASON (Jun–Aug)

Food & Drink

From spicy curries served over *injera* crepes to subtle Italian pasta sauces, there's plenty of good food to be had in Eritrea. Eat well in the capital and don't miss the seafood in Massawa.

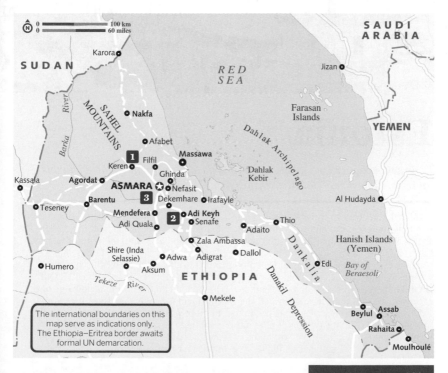

The international boundaries on this map serve as indications only. The Ethiopia–Eritrea border awaits formal UN demarcation.

| CAPITAL |
| Tallinn |
| **POPULATION** |
| 1.3 million |
| **AREA** |
| 45,339 sq km |
| **OFFICIAL LANGUAGE** |
| Estonian |

Rooftops of Tallinn

Estonia

Embracing change with gusto, Estonia is a country of understated charms, an irresistible mix of Baltic earthiness and Nordic flavours.

Estonia doesn't have to struggle to find a point of difference: it's completely unique. It shares a similar geography and history with Latvia and Lithuania, but culturally it's distinct. Its closest ethnic and linguistic buddy is Finland, and although they may love to get naked together in the sauna, 50 years of Soviet rule in Estonia have separated the two. For the last 300 years Estonia's been linked to Russia, but the two states have as much in common as a barn swallow and a bear (their respective national symbols).

With a newfound confidence, singular Estonia has crept from under the Soviet blanket and leapt into the arms of Europe. The love affair is mutual. Europe has fallen head-over-heels for the charms of Tallinn and its Unesco-protected Old Town. Put simply, Tallinn is now one of the continent's most captivating cities. And in overcrowded Europe, Estonia's sparsely populated countryside and extensive swathes of forest provide spiritual sustenance for nature-lovers.

Top Experiences

Tallinn

1 Tallinn has charm by the bucketload, fusing the modern and medieval to come up with a vibrant vibe all of its own. It's an intoxicating mix of ancient church spires, skyscrapers, palaces, appealing eateries, brooding battlements, shopping malls, wooden houses and cafes set on sunny squares – with a few Soviet throwbacks in the mix, for added spice. In addition to this, Tallinn's ever-expanding roster of first-rate restaurants, atmospheric hotels and well-oiled tourist machine make visiting a breeze, no matter which language you speak.

Saaremaa

2 Saaremaa (literally 'island land') is synonymous to Estonians with space, spruce and fresh air – and bottled water, vodka and killer beer. Estonia's largest island (roughly the size of Luxembourg) is still substantially covered in forests of pine, spruce and juniper, while its windmills, lighthouses and tiny villages seem largely unbothered by the passage of time.

Viljandi

3 One of Estonia's most charming towns, Viljandi overlooks a picturesque valley with a tranquil lake at its centre.

When to Go

 HIGH SEASON (May–Sep)

 SHOULDER (Apr, Oct & Nov)

 LOW SEASON (Dec–Mar)

The Knights of the Sword founded a castle here in the 13th century. The town that grew around it is a relaxed kind of place, perfect for time-travelling ambles, with some evocative castle ruins, historic buildings and abundant greenery. Viljandi doubles in size each July for the hugely popular four-day Viljandi Folk Music Festival, which

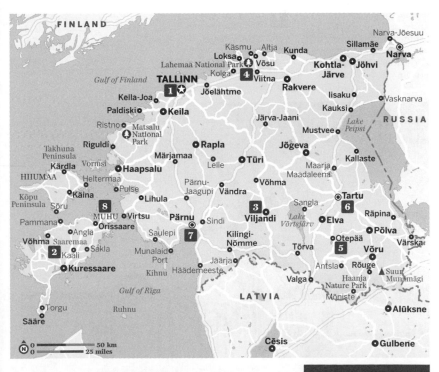

is renowned for its friendly vibe and impressive international line-up.

Lahemaa National Park

4 Estonia's largest *rahvuspark* (national park), the 'Land of Bays' is 725 sq km of unspoiled, rural Estonia, making it the perfect country retreat from the nearby capital. Visitors are well looked after: there are cosy guesthouses, restored manors and an extensive network of forest trails for walkers, cyclists and even neo-knights on horseback.

Otepää

5 The small hilltop town of Otepää is beloved by Estonians for its natural beauty and its many possibilities for hiking, biking and swimming in summer, and cross-country skiing in winter. It's often referred to as Estonia's winter capital, and winter weekends here are busy and loads of fun.

Some have even dubbed the area (tongue firmly in cheek) the 'Estonian Alps' – a reference not to its peaks but to its excellent ski trails.

Tartu

6 Small and provincial, with the tranquil Emajõgi River flowing through it, Tartu is Estonia's premier university town, with students making up nearly a seventh of the population. This injects a boisterous vitality into the leafy, historic setting and grants it a vibrant nightlife for a city of its size. On long summer nights, those students that haven't abandoned the city for the beach can be found on the hill behind the Town Hall, flirting and drinking.

Pärnu

7 Local families, hormone-sozzled youths and German, Swedish and Finnish holiday-makers join together in a collective prayer for sunny

Getting Around

Estonian roads are generally very good and driving is easy.

Touring cyclists will find Estonia mercifully flat.

The national bus network is extensive, linking all the major cities to each other and the smaller towns to their regional hubs.

Major domestic destinations from Tallinn include Rakvere, Tartu, Viljandi and Pärnu.

2

weather while strolling the beaches, sprawling parks and picturesque historic centre of Pärnu (pair-nu). Known as the nation's 'summer capital', Pärnu is quite docile, with leafy streets and expansive parks intermingling with turn-of-the-20th-century villas that reflect the town's fashionable, more decorous past. Older visitors from Finland and the former Soviet Union still visit, seeking rest, rejuvenation and Pärnu's vaunted mud treatments.

Muhu

8 Connected to Saaremaa by a 2.5km causeway, the island of Muhu has the undeserved reputation as the 'doormat' for the bigger island – lots of people passing through on their way from the ferry, but few stopping. In fact, Estonia's third-biggest island offers plenty of excuses to hang around, not least one of the coun-

ANNA GRIGORJEVA / SHUTTERSTOCK ©

Food & Drink

Kama A thick milkshake-like drink made from a powdered mixture of ground peas, rye, barley and wheat with buttermilk.

Kasukas Layered salad of Russian origin containing beetroot, potato, carrots, salted herring, boiled egg and yoghurt.

Rukkileib Rye bread, an Estonian staple.

Sealiha ja kartul Pork and potatoes.

Suitsukala Smoked fish; usually trout or salmon.

Verivorst Blood sausage.

Kiiking

Invented in 1997, *kiiking* is an extreme sport that sees competitors stand on a swing and attempt to complete a 360-degree loop around the top bar, with their feet fastened to the swing base and their hands to the swing arms. The inventor of the sport, Ado Kosk, observed that the longer the swing arms, the more difficult it is to complete a 360-degree loop. Kosk then designed swing arms that can gradually extend, for an increased challenge. In competition, the winner is the person who completes a loop with the longest swing arms – the current record stands at a fraction over 7m! Go to www.kiiking.ee for a more visual idea of the whole thing and to find out where you can see it in action (or even give it a try yourself).

Traditional Ethiopian baskets

CAPITAL	Addis Ababa
POPULATION	102 million
AREA	1.1 million sq km
OFFICIAL LANGUAGE	Amharic

Ethiopia

Ethiopia is like nowhere else on the planet, a beautiful country blessed with a peerless history, fabulous wildlife and some of Africa's most soulful people.

Welcome to Africa's most underrated wildlife destination. It's quite a line-up, from the charismatic Ethiopian wolf, to gelada monkeys and other primates, elephants at Babille, crocodiles in Nechisar, hyenas in Harar, the extravagantly horned walia ibex and some of Africa's best birdwatching.

You can trek more than 3000m above sea level (the Simien and Bale Mountains) or visit the lowest place on the African continent, the Danakil Depression. In between, the country offers lush highlands and stirring deserts, vertiginous canyons and sweeping savannah, vast lakes and high plateaus.

When it comes to human cultures, Ethiopia has an embarrassment of riches. There are the Surmi, Afar, Mursi, Karo, Hamer, Nuer and Anuak, whose ancient customs and traditions have remained almost entirely intact. A highlight of any trip here is witnessing one of the many festivals that are an integral part of the traditional culture, from ceremonies marking rites of passage to Christian celebrations of singular passion.

Top Experiences

Harar

1 By far the most intriguing city in Ethiopia, Harar is a joy to explore. Getting lost in its crooked alleyways is just as fascinating as visiting the many museums, markets and traditional homes packed inside the old city walls. And then there are the hyenas. Two families feed them by hand, and let you do it too, but these large carnivores wander throughout the city and you may just bump into one while walking about at night in one of Ethiopia's most unusual encounters.

Lalibela

2 Nothing prepares you for the first time you see the rock-hewn churches of Lalibela and walk among them for real. Carved entirely out of rock, the still-functioning churches are large, artistically refined and mostly in excellent states of preservation. This is Orthodox Christianity at its most raw and powerful, with the extraordinary architecture adorned with extraordinary paintings and enlivened with the soft chants of white-robed priests and pilgrims.

Bale Mountains

3 The Ethiopian wolf is the rarest canid in the world, but on the 4000m-high Sanetti Plateau in the Bale Mountains you are almost guaranteed to see them. And when you're not watching wolves hunt giant molerats, your eyes will be drawn to the fairy-tale forests draped in 'old man's beard' and the sheer drop of the Harenna Escarpment. Though the mountains are prime trekking territory, there's no need to step out of your car to enjoy them since you can drive right through on the highest all-weather road in Africa.

Simien Mountains

4 With deep canyons and bizarrely jagged mountains sculpting

SARINE ARSLANIAN / SHUTTERSTOCK ©

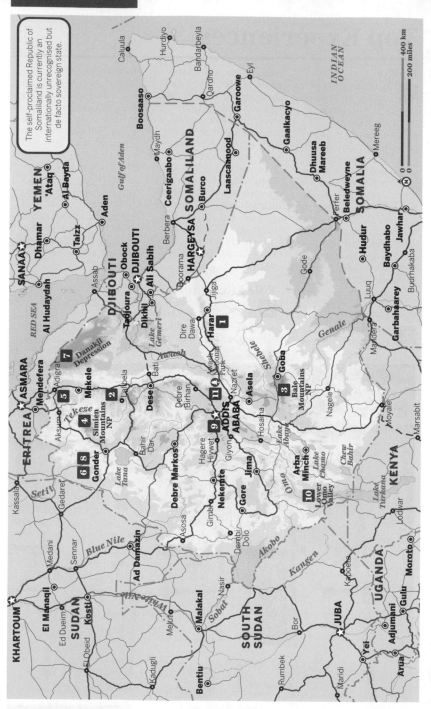

The self-proclaimed Republic of Somaliland is currently an internationally unrecognised but de facto sovereign state.

scenery so awesome that if you saw it in a painting you might question whether it was real, the Simien Moun-

tains are one of the most beautiful mountain ranges in Africa. They offer important protection for some of Ethiopia's endemic wildlife, and sitting amid a troop of tame gelada monkeys is an experience you'll never forget. This is terrific trekking territory, but is also easily accessible by car.

Best on Film

In Search of Myths and Heros (2005) The first in Michael Wood's sumptuously filmed series seeks the truth behind the Sheba legend.

Lost Kingdoms of Africa (2010) Dr Gus Casely-Hayford explores ancient Ethiopian cultures and legends.

The Great Rift: Africa's Wild Heart (2010) A finely crafted portrait of the Rift Valley and its wildlife.

Lamb (2015) The story of a young orphan in rural Ethiopia. It's the first Ethiopian film to make the Cannes festival's official selection.

Food & Drink

Eating Ethiopian-style is a wonderful experience from the sense of community around a shared table to the diverse flavours that make it one of the most varied culinary scenes on the continent. It also means re-thinking many things you might assume about eating. That's because the foundation of almost every meal in Ethiopia is *injera*, a one-of-a-kind pancake of near-universal proportions. At seemingly every turn, plates, bowls and even utensils are replaced by *injera*. Atop its rubbery surface sit delicious multi-coloured mounds of spicy meat stews, tasty vegetable curries and even cubes of raw beef.

Other staples that are ever-present on most menus are the much-heralded *wat* (stew), *kitfo* (mince meat) and *tere sega* (raw meat).

Rock-Hewn Churches of Tigray

5 Hidden like lost treasures in this arid landscape, the ancient rock-hewn churches of Tigray are the stirring mountain counterpoints to Lalibela's more famous city-bound churches. Partially carved and partially constructed, most sit on remote cliffsides requiring long walks (and sometimes steep climbs) and the sense of discovery upon arrival is a big part of their appeal. But they also delight on their artistic and historic merits alone.

When to Go

HIGH SEASON (Jan–Mar) Sunny skies and warm days.

SHOULDER (Oct–Dec) Trekking is great and there are fewer visitors.

LOW SEASON (Apr–Sep) Rainy or scorching hot.

Gonder

6 Gonder preserves a treasure trove of history. The walls of the Royal Enclosure contain a half-dozen medieval palaces

The Ethiopian Handshake

Greeting one another in Ethiopia can be a complicated business. Do you just say hello? Do you offer a hand? Do you kiss the other person on the cheek? Or do you go for the 'fighters salute'? Commonly, as Ethiopians shake hands they also gently knock their shoulders together. This is known as the 'fighters salute' and traditionally was used as a greeting between those who fought the Derg. Today, it's used by almost everyone – male and female – but only in informal situations between friends. You would not use this form of 'handshake' at a business meeting!

There are plenty of other ways to greet people in Ethiopia. Multiple kissing on the cheek is also very common among friends and relatives of either sex. It's also considered polite to kiss babies or young children, even if you've just met them.

And if you do just stick with a boring old handshake then deference can be shown by supporting the right arm (near the elbow) with the left hand during shaking. When Ethiopians enter a room they try and shake hands with everyone (including children). If hands are dirty or wet, limp wrists are offered.

Getting Around

Internal flights are huge time savers. The national carrier has an extensive network and solid safety record. It's usually cheaper to book your flight once in Ethiopia.

Opt for the newer bus companies, which offer better service and more comfortable buses.

Though expensive, we recommend a 4WD with a driver. Having your own car allows you to stop wherever you want and saves time. Shop around and hire through a reputable agency.

and a host of legends; you can easily imagine the grand feasts they held here as you walk among them. Further out are peaceful and atmospheric sites, including Fasiladas' Bath, the Kuskuam complex and Debre Berhan Selassie Church, saved from the marauding Sudanese Dervishes by a swarm of bees.

Danakil Depression

7 The actively volcanic Danakil Depression features a permanent lava lake and a vast field of yellow and orange sulphuric rocks. Just as interesting are the hearty Afar people who eke out a living from the baking, cracked plains. Though there are regular tours into its depths, travel here is not easy (and only possible as part of an organised tour) due to the lack of roads and services, and the highest average temperature of anywhere on Earth. The Danakil Depression may feel inhospitable, but the sense of exploration is very, very real.

Timkat in Gonder

8 Timkat, the feast of Epiphany, celebrates the baptism of Christ with a three-day festival starting on 19 January. Join the procession behind regalia-draped priests as the church *tabots* (replicas of the Ark of the Covenant) are taken to a nearby body of water on the afternoon of the eve of Timkat. Next morning, the *tabots* are paraded back to the church accompanied by much singing and dancing. Easily Ethiopia's most colourful festival and Gonder is the place to experience it.

Addis Ababa

9 Addis Ababa is evolving at a fast pace. The noisy, bustling capital of Ethiopia is blessed with an agreeable climate, with cloudless blue skies for about eight months of the year. It offers plenty of cultural highlights, including the Ethnological Museum and the National Museum. Addis is also famed for its buzzing restaurant scene and nightlife, with lots of

eateries, bars, galleries and clubs. Dive in!

Lower Omo Valley Ethnic Groups

10 The Lower Omo Valley is a remarkable cultural crossroads. From the Mursi people and their lip plates to the Banna with their calabash hats or the body painting Karo, tradition runs deep here. While the commonly held notion that the more than a dozen ethnic groups residing here live completely outside modern society is wrong, walking through the markets and villages or attending one of the many ceremonies really can feel like stepping back in time.

Birdwatching, Awash National Park

11 Easily accessible from Addis Ababa, 756-sq-km Awash National Park is one of Ethiopia's most visited parks. It lies on an important migratory route between the north and the south, bestowing an astonishing amount of birdlife. More than 460 species have been recorded, among them the extremely rare yellow-throated seedeater and sombre rock chat, both found only in and near Awash. Two especially good spots to observe birds are around Filwoha Hot Springs and around the Awash River campsites. An ostrich reintroduction program has recently begun. Among the many raptors are fish eagles, lammergeyer and pygmy falcons.

Want to woo the locals and have some fun streetside? Hone your table-tennis and table-football skills before arriving.

In the past, causes of famine in Ethiopia have had less to do with environmental factors – the country has abundant natural resources – and more to do with economic mismanagement and inequitable and oppressive governments.

MATEJH PHOTOGRAPHY / GETTY IMAGES ©

ANUP SHAH / GETTY IMAGES ©

CAPITAL
Stanley

POPULATION
2,931

AREA
12,173 sq km

OFFICIAL LANGUAGE
English

King penguins at Volunteer Beach

Falkland Islands

Controversially fought over but still staunchly British, the Falkland Islands (Islas Malvinas) sit isolated in the wild Southern Ocean, home to penguins, waterbirds, a few humans and lots of sheep.

Most people associate the Falklands (known as Isla Malvinas in Argentina) with the 1982 war that saw Britain regain control after an invasion by the Argentine military. These days the islands are a popular stopover for cruise ships and intrepid wildlife watchers. Bays, inlets, estuaries and beaches create an attractive and tortuous coastline boasting abundant wildlife. These sea islands attract striated and crested caracaras, cormorants, oystercatchers, snowy sheathbills and a plethora of penguins that share top billing with sea lions, elephant seals, fur seals, five species of dolphin and killer whales.

Stanley, the islands' capital on East Falkland, is an assemblage of brightly painted metal-clad houses and a good place to throw down a few pints and listen to island lore. Elsewhere in 'Camp' – as the rest of the islands are known – you're more likely to bump into a sheep or a penguin than a person.

Top Experiences

Stanley

1 The Falklands' capital is little more than a village, but still holds two-thirds of the total population. Admire the local architecture of recycled shipwrecks, chat with locals at one of the British-style pubs, visit the fascinating Falkland Islands Museum and inspect the poignant war memorials.

Volunteer Beach

2 You don't have to go to Antarctica to see king penguins – Volunteer Beach boasts the northernmost king penguin colonies in the world. Large colonies of gentoo and Magellanic penguins also inhabit the beach, which is named after the *Volunteer,* an American whaling ship which visited nearby Port Louis in 1815.

Sea Lion Island

3 The Falklands' southernmost inhabited island has more wildlife in a smaller area than almost anywhere in the islands. It features all five species of Falklands' penguins, colonies of cormorants, and is a breeding ground for southern elephant seals. The sea lions that give the island its name are far less numerous, however, with fewer than 100 of them.

When to Go

 HIGH SEASON
(Dec–Feb)

 SHOULDER
(Mar, Oct & Nov)

 LOW SEASON
(Apr–Sep)

Food & Drink

Falkland Islands' cuisine is influenced by British food and drink. Fish and chips is a popular staple, as is lamb. Other fish and seafood dishes take advantage of the abundance of fresh fish available.

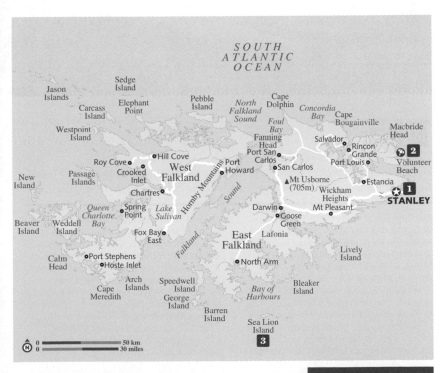

CAPITAL
Suva

POPULATION
915,303

AREA
18,274 sq km

OFFICIAL LANGUAGES
English, Fijian

Tavarua, Mamanucas Islands

Fiji

Set your internal clock to 'Fiji time': exploring the archipelago's exquisite beaches,
undersea marvels, lush interiors and fascinating culture shouldn't be rushed.

Dazzling sands, perfect palm trees and waters so blue they glow – Fiji's beaches look airbrushed. While stunning stretches abound, beaches on the islands of the Mamanucas and Yasawas are the poster-children for paradise.

While it's easy to spend your holiday in, on or under the water, those who take the time to towel off will be rewarded by a wealth of terra firma treats. Fiji offers ample opportunities for hikers, birdwatchers, amblers and forest-fanciers, particularly on the islands of Taveuni and Kadavu, a less-travelled slice of paradise with almost no roads to speak of.

If urban wildlife is your thing, Suva boasts a surprising nightlife scene, while towns like Savusavu entice with rollicking taverns and meet-the-locals haunts. Speaking of locals, you'd be hard-pressed to find a more open and welcoming population. Fijians are famous for their hospitality and warmth, which makes it easy to make friends or immerse yourself in Fijian culture on a village homestay.

Top Experiences

Suva

Steamy Suva offers a multicultural mix of contemporary and colonial Fiji. Gracious old buildings and monuments line a lively waterfront and harbour. Downtown Suva boasts slick, air-conditioned shopping malls and crowded handicraft stalls, both of which are ripe for exploring. Immerse yourself in the colourful chaos of the municipal market, learn about Fiji's wild history at the national museum, and sip cocktails at the beautiful old Grand Pacific Hotel before exploring Suva's diverse restaurant scene.

Navala Village

Nestled in a valley high in the Nausori Highlands, stunning Navala village is the best place in Fiji to witness authentic, age-old indigenous life up close. It's the country's last bastion of traditional architecture: from the chief's home to the outhouses, all of its 200 buildings are constructed using ancient techniques that make use of woven bamboo walls, thatched roofs and ropes made of fibre from the surrounding bush. Visitors are welcomed with a kava ceremony and stuffed full of locally caught,

When to Go

 HIGH SEASON (Jun–Sep & Dec–Jan)

SHOULDER (May & Oct)

LOW SEASON (Nov & Feb–Apr)

picked and harvested food cooked over an open fire.

Sawa-i-Lau Cave

A lone limestone island among the volcanic Yasawas, Sawa-i-Lau hides a mystery within its hollow caverns: carvings, paintings and inscriptions of unknown age and meaning. They're

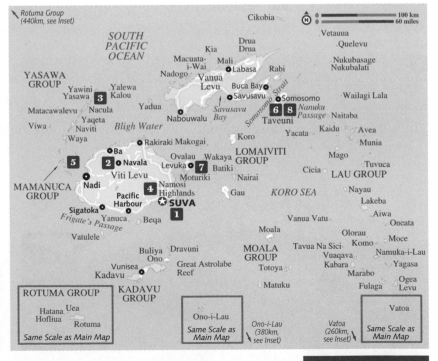

accessible with a torch and a guide (and a shot of courage) by swimming through a short underwater passage from the cave's main chamber. If your breath has already been taken away by the gorgeousness of the grotto, there's more placid paddling to be had in a clear pool beneath the cave's domed ceiling.

Namosi Highlands

4 Geology looms large in the spectacular Namosi Highlands. Sheer canyon walls crowd the Wainikoroiluva River, and the dramatic curtains of rock form the backdrop to Fiji's most scenic river-rafting trip, taken aboard a *bilibili* (bamboo raft). The lower, longer, wider reaches of the palm-fringed waterway are usually covered alongside villagers making their way to or from market on local boats laden with pigs, coconuts, taro and leafy green vegetables.

Surfing at Cloudbreak

5 Fiji is one of the best places in the world to hang ten, with brilliant breaks and tremendous tubes that draw surfers from all over the world. Its most famous breaks are the colossal Cloudbreak and Restaurants, two mighty lefts that are most definitely not for the inexperienced. Dedicated surf resorts dot the archipelago, from the Mamanucas and Yanuca island by Viti Levu, to the further-flung Qamea (in the north) and Kadavu Group (to the south).

Waitavala Water Slide

6 Bruises, bumps and declarations of 'Most fun ever!' are the order of the day at this natural

Getting Around

There are regular flights to many of the outer islands.

Cabs can be an inexpensive option for day trips.

Cheap, often windowless local buses offer a friendly, truly Fijian experience.

Ferries and cargo ships travel between islands.

DON MAMMOSER / SHUTTERSTOCK ©

cascade of rock slides on the island of Taveuni. Start by watching the local kids to get an idea of what you're in for. They make it look easy, tackling the slides standing surfer-style, each turn more outrageously brave/crazy than the last; you, on the other hand, should go down on your bum. Your (doubt-less awkward) attempt will be rewarded by a cool plunge into the pools below.

Levuka Colonial Architecture

7 The Wild West meets the South Seas at Levuka, the country's sleepy one-time colonial capital and Fiji's only Unesco World Heritage Site. You can almost imagine sailors rowdily bursting out from the frayed but colourful timber shopfronts. Back then the structures may have been saloons, but nowadays the buildings, some of which were damaged by Cyclone

Winston in 2016, mainly hold stores of odds and ends. Women from the villages sell *dalo* (taro), and produce on the side of the road, a church rises faded and cracked-white against the sky and the only sounds come from the occasional car chugging through town.

Taveuni Hiking

8 Lush, ridiculously green and humid, Fiji's 'Garden Island' of Taveuni is heaven for hikers, where even the shortest trails lead to rare endemic birdlife, gargantuan trees and bizarre rock formations. About 80% of the island is protected by the Bouma National Park, home to the Lavena Coastal Walk, which takes trekkers on a 5km journey past beautiful beaches and jungle villages and over a suspension bridge to hidden waterfalls. Serious sloggers can head up the steep Des Voeux Peak or to the muddy mountain crater of Lake Tagimaucia.

Food & Drink

Kokoda A raw-fish salad marinated in lime juice, mixed with vegetables and topped with coconut cream.

Lovo Traditional Fijian banquet where food is cooked in an underground oven.

Palusami Corned beef or onions with coconut cream, all wrapped and baked in young taro leaves.

Roti Try the *cepelinai* (potato-dough zeppelin stuffed with meat, mushrooms or cheese).

Thali Set Indian meals with several curries.

Yaqona Also called kava or grog, this mildly narcotic drink is a muddy tea made from a root.

IMAGE SOURCE RF/JUSTIN LEWIS/EYEVWORDS / GETTY IMAGES ©

Village Life

'*Bula*', Fiji's ubiquitous greeting is more than a simple 'hi': it literally translates as 'Life', an apt salutation from a spirited people who seem to live theirs to the fullest. Fijians are genu-inely friendly, and visitors are assured of a warm welcome – often with open arms and song. The best place to experience this hospitality is at one of the villages that dot the countryside: visits usually involve a kava ceremony, and possibly a *meke* (ceremonial dance) or *lovo* (feast from an underground oven), while homestays offer the chance to delve deep into local life.

CAPITAL	Helsinki
POPULATION	5.5 million
AREA	338,145 sq km
OFFICIAL LANGUAGES	Finnish, Swedish

Aurora borealis (Northern Lights), Lapland

Finland

Inspired design, technology and epicurean scenes meet epic stretches of wilderness here in Europe's deep north, where summer's endless light balances winter's eerie frozen magic.

The Finland you encounter will depend on the season of your visit, but whatever the month, there's something pure in the Finnish air and spirit that's vital and exciting. Summer is a time for music festivals, exhibitions, lake cruises, midnight sunshine on convivial beer terraces, idyllic days at remote waterside cottages and lush market produce.

Winter has its own charm as snow blankets the pines and lakes freeze over. The best way to banish those frosty subzero temperatures is to get active and skiing is great through to May. Other pursuits include catching the aurora borealis (Northern Lights), steaming up in a wood-fired sauna and spending a night in a glittering, iridescent ice hotel.

But Finland isn't just vast expanses of pristine wilderness. Vibrant cities stock the southern parts, headlined by the capital, Helsinki, a cutting-edge urban space with world-renowned design and music scenes.

Top Experiences

National Park Hiking, Northern Finland

1 Finland's great swathes of protected forests and fells make it one of Europe's prime hiking destinations. Head to the Karhunkierros near Kuusamo for a striking terrain of hills and sharp ravines, never prettier than in autumn. The Urho Kekkonen National Park in Lapland is one of Europe's great wildernesses; the spectacular gorge of the Kevo Strict Nature Reserve and the fell scenery of Pallas-Yllästunturi National Park are other great northern options. A network of camping huts makes itinerary planning easy and are good spots to meet Finns.

Sledding & Snowmobiling, Lapland

2 Fizzing across Lapland behind a team of huskies under the low winter sun is tough to beat. Short jaunts are great, but overnight safaris give you time to feed and bond with your lovable dogs and try out a wood-fired sauna in the middle of the winter wilderness. It's no fairy-tale ride though; expect to eat some snow before you learn to control your team. If you're more of a cat person, you can enjoy similar trips on a snowmobile or behind reindeer.

Design Shopping, Helsinki

3 Functional, elegant, outrageous or wacky: the choice is yours. The capital's decidedly nonmainstream chic is best explored by browsing the vast variety of design shops that spatter its centre. Whether examining iconic 20th-century Finnish forms in the flagship emporia of brands like

BLUEORANGE STUDIO / SHUTTERSTOCK ©

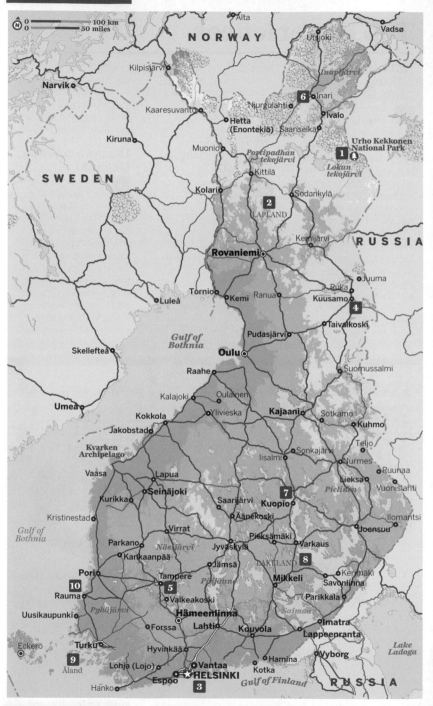

Iittala, Marimekko and Artek, or tracking down the cutting-edge and just plain weird in the bohemian Punavuori district, you're sure to find something you didn't know you needed but just can't do without. And yes, they all deliver.

Bear Watching, Eastern Finland

4 Old Honeypaws, the brown bear (*Ursus arctos*), is the national animal of Finland. Around a thousand of these powerful creatures live in the northeast, coming

and going with impunity across the Finnish–Russian border. Several operators run bear hides close to the frontier, where you can sit a silent night's vigil as bruins snuffle out elk carcasses and carefully hidden chunks of salmon. The best time to see them is between mid-April and August – with a slight gap in July when the bears have mating rather than meals in mind.

Food Markets, Tampere

5 Counters selling local cheeses, rough rye breads, handmade chocolates, Finnish sausages and smoked fish fill each town's indoor *kauppahalli* (covered market). Tampere's – try traditional *mustamakkara* (blood sausage) – is typical, filled with delicious aromas. In summer the *kauppatori* (market square) in each town bursts with straight-from-the-garden vegetables: tiny new potatoes, nutty and sweet, mouthfuls of juicy red strawberries, or peas popped fresh from the pod. Autumn's approach is softened by

Best in Print

Kalevala (Elias Lönnrot) Readable 'national epic' compiled from the songs of bards.

The Year of the Hare (Arto Paasilinna) Offbeat tale of hare-y travels.

Seven Brothers (Aleksis Kivi) Nineteenth-century Finnish classic.

Food & Drink

Smoked fish Head to any market in the country for a huge array.

Lemin särä Majestic mutton roast, cooked on a birch tray.

Ålandspannkaka Semolina pudding with stewed prunes.

Kalakukko Tasty rye loaf stuffed with *muikku* (a small lake fish).

Karjalanpiirakka Rice-filled pastry best with traditional egg butter topping.

Reindeer Staple meat of Lapland that's found right across the region.

When to Go

HIGH SEASON
(Jul)
Attractions and lodgings are open. Numerous festivals across country.

SHOULDER
(Jun & Aug)
Long days with decent temperatures.

LOW SEASON
(Sep–May)
Short, cool or cold days. December to April is busy for winter sports.

piles of peppery chanterelles and glowing Lapland cloudberries, appearing in August like a magician's trick.

Sámi Culture, Inari

6 Finland's indigenous northerners have used technology to

Silence

While the 'silent Finn' concept has been exaggerated over the years, it's true that Finns believe in comfortable silences, so if a conversation dies off naturally there's no need to jump-start it with small talk. Finns quip that they invented text messaging so they didn't have to talk to each other, and sitting in the sauna for 20 minutes with your best friend, saying nothing, is perfectly normal. Finns generally tend to have a quirky, dark, self-deprecating sense of humour and may just be saving their words for a well-timed jibe.

Getting Around

Trains are generally modern and comfortable, with good coverage. Book busy routes in advance.

Car hire is widely available; week or weekend deals booked in advance are much better than sky-high day rates. Automatic transmission is rare.

Buses are around the same price as trains but slower. Cover the whole country. Rarely need booking.

Flights are generally expensive but you can get some good deals on Lapland routes. Multitrip journeys are generally cheaper than one-way flights.

ease the arduous side of reindeer herding while maintaining an intimate knowledge of Lapland's natural world. Their capital, Inari, and the nearby Lemmenjoki National Park are the best places to begin to learn about Sámi culture and traditions, starting at the marvellous Siida museum. Arrange wilderness excursions with Sámi guides, meet reindeer, and browse high-quality handicrafts and music, the sale of which benefits local communities.

Traditional Sauna, Kuopio

7 These days most Finns have saunas at home, but there are still a few of the old public ones left. They smell of old pine, tar shampoo and long tradition, with birch whisks and no-nonsense scrubdowns available as extras. Weathered Finnish faces cool down on the street outside, loins wrapped in a towel and hand wrapped around a cold beer. Helsinki and Tampere are the best places for this, while Kuopio's old-style giant *savusauna* (smoke sauna) takes a day to prepare and offers a more rural experience. It seats 60 and is mixed: you're given towels to wear. Bring a swimsuit for lake dipping – devoted locals and brave tourists do so even when it's covered with ice.

Lakeland

8 The Lakeland seems to have more water than land, so it'd be a crime not to get out on it. You can take three days to paddle the family-friendly Oravareitti (Squirrel Route) or head out into Kolovesi and Linnansaari National Parks to meet freshwater seals. Tired arms? Historic lake boats still ply what were once important transport arteries; head out from any town on short cruises, or make a day of it and head from Savonlinna right up to Kuopio or across Finland's largest lake, Saimaa, to Lappeenranta.

Cycling, Åland Archipelago

9 Charming Åland is best explored by bicycle: you'll appreciate its understated attractions all the more if you've used pedal power to reach them. Bridges and ferries link many of its 6000 islands, and well-signposted routes take you off 'main roads' down winding lanes and forestry tracks. Set aside your bicycle whenever the mood takes you, to pick wild strawberries, wander castle ruins, sunbathe on a slab of red granite, visit a medieval church, quench your thirst at a cider orchard, or climb a lookout tower to gaze at the glittering sea.

Rauma Old Town

10 The largest wooden Old Town in the Nordic countries, Vanha Rauma deserves its Unesco World Heritage status. Its 600 houses might be museum pieces, but they also form a living centre: residents tend their flower boxes and chat to neighbours, while visitors meander in and out of the low-key cafes, shops, museums and artisans' workshops. Rauman giäl, an old sailors' lingo that mixes up a host of languages, is still spoken here, and the town's medieval lace-making heritage is celebrated during Pitsiviikko (Rauma Lace Week).

Nordic Walking

Finland is proud of having invented the burgeoning sport of Nordic Walking. It involves using two hand-held poles while briskly walking, substantially adding to the exercise value of the walk.

Saunas

For centuries the sauna has been a place to meditate, warm up and even give birth, and most Finns still use it at least once a week.

VALERIJAP / GETTY IMAGES ©

10

4

ERIKMANDRE / GETTY IMAGES ©

CAPITAL
Paris

POPULATION
64.4 million

AREA
551,000 sq km

OFFICIAL LANGUAGE
French

Nice, on the Côte d'Azur

France

France lures travellers with its unfalteringly familiar culture, woven around cafe terraces, village-square markets and lace-curtained bistros with their plat du jour chalked on the board.

France seduces with iconic landmarks known the world over and rising stars yet to be discovered. This country's cultural repertoire is staggering – in volume and diversity. And this is where the beauty of la belle France lies: when superstars such as Mademoiselle Eiffel, royal Versailles and the celebrity-ridden French Riviera have been ticked off, there's ample more to thrill.

The terroir (land) of France weaves a varied journey from northern France's cliffs and sand dunes to the piercing blue sea of the French Riviera and Corsica's green oak forests. Outdoor action is what France's lyrical landscape demands – and there's something for everybody. Whether you end up walking barefoot across wave-rippled sand to Mont St-Michel, riding a cable car to glacial panoramas above Chamonix, or cartwheeling down Europe's highest sand dune, France does not disappoint.

Top Experiences

Eiffel Tower

1 No one could imagine Paris today without it. But Gustave Eiffel only constructed this elegant, 320m-tall spire as a temporary exhibit for the 1889 World's Fair. Luckily, the tower's popularity assured its survival. More than seven million people visit the Eiffel Tower annually – and from an evening ascent amid twinkling lights to lunch in one of the restaurants, every visit is unique. Snap a selfie in front of it, ice-skate on the 1st floor in winter or visit it at night. Best up are the special occasions when all 324m of the iconic tower glows a different colour.

Loire Valley

2 If it's aristocratic pomp and architectural splendour you're after, this regal valley is the place to linger. Flowing for more than 1000km into the Atlantic Ocean, the Loire is one of France's last *fleuves sauvages* (wild rivers) and its banks provide a 1000-year snapshot of French high society. The valley is riddled with *châteaux* sporting glittering turrets and ballrooms, lavish cupolas and chapels. If you're a hopeless romantic seeking the perfect fairy-tale castle, head for moat-ringed Azay-le-Rideau, Villandry and its gardens, and less-visited Château de Beauregard.

Dune du Pilat

3 This colossal sand dune, 8km south of Arcachon, stretches from the mouth of the Bassin d'Arcachon southwards for 2.7km. Already Europe's largest, the dune is growing eastwards 1.5m a year – it has swallowed trees, a road junction and even a hotel, so local lore claims. The view from the top – approximately 115m above sea level – is magnificent. To the west you see the sandy shoals at the mouth of the Bassin d'Arcachon, including Cap Ferret and the Banc d'Arguin bird reserve where up to 6000 couples of Sandwich terns nest each spring.

Mont St-Michel

4 The dramatic play of tides on this abbey-island in Normandy is magical and mysterious. Said by Celtic mythology to be a sea tomb to which souls of the dead were sent, Mont St-Michel is rich in legend and history. Walk around it alone or, better still, hook up with a guide in nearby Genêts for a dramatic day hike across the bay.

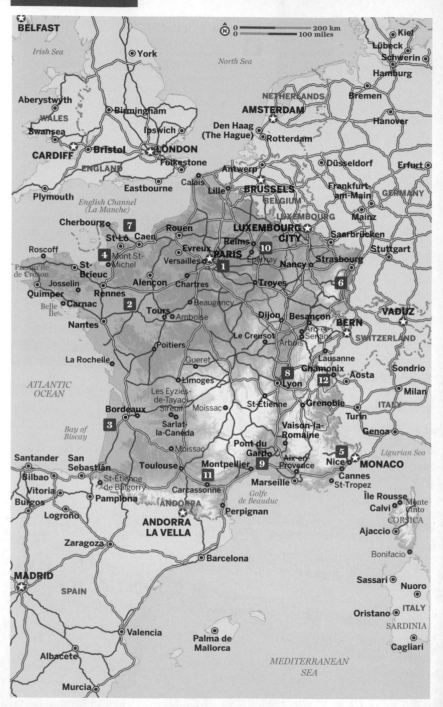

Best in Print

Paris (Edward Rutherford; 2013) Eight centuries of Parisian history.

A Moveable Feast (Ernest Hemingway; 1964) Beautiful evocation of 1920s Paris.

The Hundred Foot Journey (Richard C Morais; 2010) Culinary warfare between two restaurant owners: a boy from Mumbai and a famous chef.

Best on Film

La Môme (La Vie en Rose; 2007) Story of singer Edith Piaf starring French actress Marion Cotillard.

Coco Avant Chanel (2009) Compelling life story of orphan turned fashion designer Coco Chanel, with French actress Audrey Tautou.

Hugo (2011) Martin Scorsese's Oscar-winning children's film pays tribute to Parisian film pioneer Georges Méliès through the adventure of an orphan boy in the 1930s who tends clocks at a Paris train station.

Marseille (2016) Comedy about just that, starring French-Algerian actor and film-maker Kad Merad.

The Three Corniches, Nice

5 It's impossible to drive this dramatic trio of coastal roads, each one higher and with more hairpin bends than the next, without conjuring up cinematic images of Grace Kelly, Hitchcock, the glitz of Riviera high life – all while absorbing views of the sweeping blue sea fringing Europe's most mythical coastline. To make a perfect day out of it, shop for a picnic at the Cours Saleya morning market before leaving Nice.

Alsatian Wine Route

6 It is one of France's most popular drives – and for good reason. Motoring in this far north-east corner of France takes you through a kaleidoscope of lush green vines, perched castles and gentle mist-covered mountains. Drive the Route des Vins d'Alsace in autumn, when vines are heavy with grapes waiting to be harvested and colours are at their vibrant best, stopping at roadside wine cellars, where fruity Alsace vintages can be swirled, tasted and bought.

D-Day Beaches

7 A trip to these peaceful, broad stretches of fine sand and breeze-blown bluffs is one of France's most emotional journeys. On 6 June 1944, beaches here became a cacophony of gunfire and explosions, the bodies of Allied soldiers lying in the sand as their comrades-in-arms charged inland. Just up the hill from Omaha Beach, the long rows of symmetrical gravestones at the Normandy American Cemetery & Memorial bear solemn, silent testimony to the horrible price paid for France's liberation from German occupation.

When to Go

HIGH SEASON
(Jul & Aug)
Book accommodation and restaurant tables well in advance.

SHOULDER
(Apr–Jun & Sep)
Spring brings warm weather, flowers and local produce.

LOW SEASON
(Oct–Mar)
Prices up to 50% lower than high season.

Carnac Megaliths

Pedalling past open fields dotted with the world's greatest concentration of mysterious megaliths gives a poignant reminder of Brittany's ancient human inhabitants.

Provençal Markets

No region is such a market-must. Be it fresh fish by the port in Marseille, strings of pink garlic, melons and cherries or earthy 'black diamond' truffles. Markets in Aix-en-Provence and Antibes are particularly atmospheric.

Food & Drink

Croque monsieur Toasted ham and cheese sandwich; cheesy *croques madames* are egg-topped.

Chestnuts Served piping hot in paper bags on street corners in winter.

Socca Chickpea-flour pancake typical to Nice in the French Riviera.

Pan bagnat Crusty Niçois tuna sandwich dripping in fruity green olive oil.

Flammekueche (tarte flambée in French) Alsatian thin-crust pizza dough topped with sour cream, onions and bacon.

Crêpes Large, round, thin sweet pancakes cooked at street-corner stands while you wait.

Galettes Savoury, naturally gluten-free pancakes, made with buckwheat flour and typically served with *fromage* (cheese) and *jambon* (ham).

Pastilles de Vichy Ubiquitous little sweeties with a history of healing powers.

Beignets au brocciu Corsican deep-fried doughnuts, sweet or savoury, filled with the island's local cream cheese.

Lyonnais Bouchons

8 The red-and-white checked tablecloths, closely packed tables and decades-old bistro decor could be anywhere in France, but it's the local cuisine that makes Lyon's *bouchons* (bistros) unique, plus the quaint culinary customs, such as totting up the bill on the paper tablecloth, or serving wine in a glass bottle wrapped with an elastic band to stop drips, or the 'shut weekends' opening hours. Various piggy parts drive Lyonnais cuisine, but have faith – this French city is said to be the gastronomic capital of France. Dine and decide.

Pont du Gard

9 This Unesco World Heritage Site near Nîmes in southern France is gargantuan: 35 arches straddle the Roman aqueduct's 275m-long upper tier, containing a watercourse that was designed to carry 20,000 cu metres of water per day. View it from afloat a canoe on the River Gard or jig across the top. Oh, and don't forget your swimming gear for some post-Pont daredevil diving and high jumping from the rocks nearby. Flop afterwards on a floating deck a little way downstream.

Champagne

10 Known-brand Champagne houses in the main towns of Reims and Épernay are famed the world over. But – our tip – much of Champagne's finest liquid gold is created by passionate, small-scale *vignerons* (winegrowers) in drop dead-gorgeous villages – rendering the region's scenic driving routes the loveliest way of tasting fine bubbly amid rolling vineyards.

Carcassonne at Dusk

11 That first glimpse of La Cité's sturdy, stone, witch's-hat turrets above Carcassonne in the Languedoc is enough to make your hair stand on end. To properly savour this fairy-tale walled city, linger at dusk after the crowds have left, when the old town belongs to its 100 or so inhabitants and the few visitors staying at the handful of lovely hotels within its ramparts. Don't forget to look back when you leave to view the old city, beautifully illuminated, glowing in the warm night.

Chamonix Action

12 The birthplace of mountaineering and winter playground to the rich, famous and not-so-famous, this iconic ski resort in the French Alps has something for everyone. Snowsport fiends fly down slopes on skies or boards to savour the breathtaking views of Mont Blanc. But there's absolutely no obligation to do so: non-skiers can hop aboard the Aiguille du Midi cable car for the ride of a lifetime above 3800m.

12

ROBERT CAUCINO / SHUTTERSTOCK ©

Getting Around

 Run by the state-owned SNCF, France's rail network is truly first-class, with extensive coverage of the country and frequent departures.

 Away from cities and large towns (where it is hard to park) a car comes into its own. Be aware of France's potentially hazardous 'priority to the right' rule.

 Buses are cheaper and slower than trains. Useful for more remote villages.

 Certain regions – the Loire Valley, Burgundy and the Lubéron in Provence – beg to be explored by two wheels and have dedicated cycling paths, some along canal towpaths or between orchards and vineyards.

The former penal colony on Île Royale, Îles du Salut

CAPITAL	Cayenne
POPULATION	221,500
AREA	91,000 sq km
OFFICIAL LANGUAGES	French, Creole

French Guiana

French Guiana is a tiny country of cleaned-up colonial architecture, eerie prison-camp history and some of the world's most diverse plant and animal life.

It's a strange mix of French law and rainforest humidity where only a few destinations along the coast are easily accessed and travel can be frustratingly difficult as well as expensive.

As a department of France, it's one of South America's wealthiest corners, with funds pouring in to ensure a stable base for the satellite launcher. But not even a European superpower can tame this vast, pristine jungle: you'll find potholes in newly paved roads, and ferns sprouting between bricks, while Amerindians, Maroons and Hmong refugees live traditional lifestyles so far from *la vie Metropole* that it's hard to believe they're connected at all.

Top Experiences

Îles du Salut

1 Cast away to Îles du Salut for sand, palms and a creepy, defunct penal colony. Since the days of Emperor Napoleon III the islands, considered escape-proof, received prisoners from France. Since then, the islands have become a relaxing delight – a place to escape to.

Centre Spatial Guyanais

2 Space junkies will love the free three-hour tours at this space centre. Since 1980 two-thirds of the world's commercial satellites have been launched from French Guiana. Three launchers are also now in service, increasing the number of liftoffs to over a dozen per year; this frequency makes it that much easier to coordinate your visit with a launch

Cacao

3 A slice of Laos in the hills of Guiana, Cacao, about 75km southwest of Cayenne, is a village of clear rivers, vegetable plantations and wooden houses on stilts. The Hmong refugees who left Laos in the 1970s keep their town a safe, peaceful haven, and it's now a favorite weekend day trip among locals from Cayenne.

When to Go

 HIGH SEASON (Jul–Sep)

 SHOULDER (Oct–Dec)

 LOW SEASON (Jan–Jun)

Food & Drink

Gibier Bush meat like capybara, wild boar and agouti is legally hunted and found widely on restaurant menus.

Jamais goûté A delicate freshwater fish that's best steamed in banana leaves.

Ti'punch Literally a 'small punch' made with local rum, lime juice and sugarcane syrup.

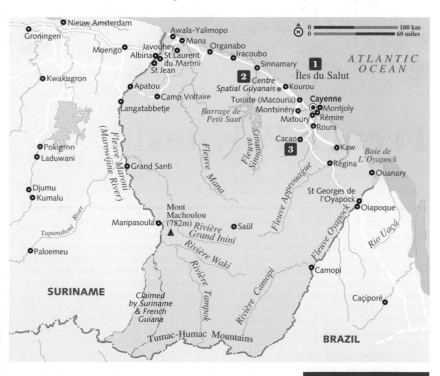

CAPITAL
Pape'ete

POPULATION
280,000

AREA
2.5 million sq km

OFFICIAL LANGUAGES
French, Polynesian

Mo'orea

French Polynesia

Tahiti: Just the word conjures up centuries' worth of images: hibiscus flowers; bronzed dancers in grass skirts; a humid breeze over turquoise sea.

French Polynesia is about as dreamy as reality gets. The slim stretches of white-, pink- and black-sand beaches in French Polynesia are really just pretty springboards into the real draw: the lagoons. Most high islands are surrounded by fringing reef that creates a protected swimming pool of the most intense aqua imaginable. Fish, dolphins, rays, sharks, turtles and more inhabit these clear-water coral gardens that are as wonderful for snorkelling as they are for diving and swimming. Surfers ride glassy wave faces at

reef passes while kitesurfers fly across the water with the trade winds.

Bora Bora's signature of over-the-top indulgence often overshadows what the rest of the country has to offer. Resorts on the 'Pearl of the Pacific' offer private overwater bungalows and spectacular views. But if this isn't your cup of coconut water, don't let that dissuade you from visiting French Polynesia. Small, family-run lodgings offer a closer-to-the-culture experience for considerably less financial output.

Top Experiences

Bora Bora

1 As the plane begins to descend, a magical scene comes into view: a perfect Morse-code ring of *motu* (small islets), mop-topped with palms, separating the indigo of the ocean from the crisp palette of lagoon blues. Bora Bora is a hot favourite for honeymooners. Get in that water via mask, fin and snorkel, on a SUP, with a scuba tank or even just splashing around on a beach.

Mo'orea

2 Mo'orea is a tropical-island cliché brought to life. If you've been dreaming of a holiday-brochure turquoise lagoon, coral beaches, vertical peaks and lush landscapes, you'd be hard-pressed to find better than this gem of an island. Mo'orea has something for everyone. A startling variety of adventure options await: there are mountains to climb, coral gardens to snorkel, scenic areas to quad bike, waves to surf and sloping reefs to dive. But if all you want to do is unwind, a couple of lovely expanses of coral sand beckon.

Cruising the Marquesas

3 Snaggle-toothed volcanic peaks, deep ravines, waterfalls, secret bays and forests that could hold their own in a BBC documentary all await on this iconic boat voyage through the six inhabited islands of the Marquesas archipelago. Part cargo ship, part cruise liner, the Aranui is a huge event at each island and you get to be there for the

When to Go

HIGH SEASON
(Jun–Aug, Dec & Jan)

SHOULDER
(Feb. May & Sep)

LOW SEASON
(Mar, Apr, Oct & Nov)

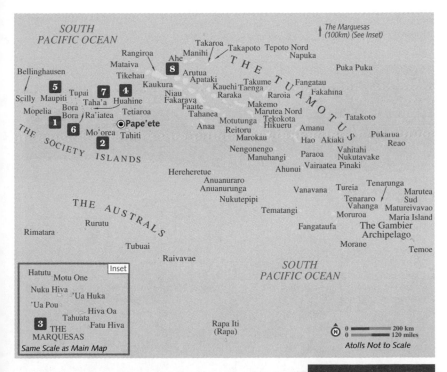

unloading of the supplies. The festive voyage also involves plenty of dance performances, local meals and a guide to explain the extraordinary culture and archaeological remains.

Huahine

4 Boasting some of the best beaches in the country and a snoozy Polynesian charm, Huahine is the perfect spot to recharge the batteries. If you've got energy to burn, there's a slew of activities available, from hiking in the lush interior to snorkelling fabulous coral gardens. Culture buffs will also love Maeva, one of the most extensive complexes of pre-European *marae* (traditional temples) in French Polynesia. Huahine is all about ecotravel, and this is why it's gaining in popularity.

Maupiti

5 Rising out of the lagoon like a mini Bora Bora, Maupiti has as many of the tropical-island-fantasy attributes as its larger neighbour, but only a fraction of the hype. Be ready to say hello to every friendly islander you pass in the village and to explore the magical white sand *motu,* deep blue lagoon and manta ray–filled passes. Don't expect big resorts here – digs are in adorable and intimate family-run hotels and pensions. Rent a kayak, strap on a scuba bottle, hike the mountain or just lounge on the beach in untainted, simple bliss.

Marae Taputapuatea

6 The most important *marae* in French Polynesia – and possibly all of Polynesia – is Marae Taputapuatea on Ra'iatea,

Getting Around

Air is the main way to cover long distances.

There's little public transport, so most people rent cars.

Boats are used to get to more remote locations and between some islands.

Bicycles are best on smaller islands; rentals available.

which has been extensively restored. *Marae* are religious sites built from basalt blocks placed side by side and piled up. In pre-European times, they represented the equivalent of temples, and were places of worship, burial and human sacrifice.

Tahitian Pearl Farms

7 Forget diamonds, black pearls are a Tahitian gal's best friend. They come in silvery white

to black and every colour in between, so it's easy to get seduced by these sea gems' soothing hues. Don't miss visiting a farm (our favourite spots are on Taha'a), where you'll see how the oysters are raised and harvested, and maybe even get to see a technician performing the culturing operation (called a 'graft'). Afterwards, you'll get to drool over lustrous jewellery and hopefully get a great deal on a special souvenir.

Diving & Snorkelling

8 French Polynesia's warm, tropical waters hold some of the greatest varieties of sea life in the South Pacific and you can find most of them in one spot at Tiputa Pass in Rangiroa. Mingle with grey reef sharks, manta rays, dolphins and sharks alongside loads of reef species including stingrays, jacks and clouds of butterfly fish. The lagoon also caters to snorkellers, with some of the clearest waters in the world and healthy coral gardens.

Food & Drink

Modern Tahitian food is a fairly balanced melange of French, Chinese and Polynesian influence; béchamel, soy sauce or coconut milk all have an equal chance of topping your meal.

Open-sea fish (tuna, bonito, wahoo, swordfish and *mahi mahi* – dorado) and lagoon fish (parrotfish, jackfish and squirrelfish) feature prominently in traditional cuisine. *Poisson cru* (raw fish in coconut milk) is the most popular local dish, though fish is also served grilled, fried or poached.

Ma'a Tahiti, traditional Tahitian food, is a heavy mix of starchy taro and *uru* (breadfruit), raw or cooked fish, fatty pork, coconut milk and a few scattered vegetables. On special occasions, the whole lot is neatly prepared and placed in a *hima'a* (cooking pit) where a layer of stones and banana leaves separate the food from the hot coals beneath. The food is covered with more banana leaves then buried so all the flavours and juices can cook and mingle for several hours. The result is a steamy, tender ambrosia of a meal.

MARTIN VALIGURSKY / SHUTTERSTOCK ©

Monoi

What can't *monoi* do? This local concoction, made from coconut oil and *tiare* (fragrant gardenia, and the national flower), is deliciously perfumed with sandalwood, vanilla, coconut or jasmine. It's used liberally as hair oil, ointment, sunscreen and even mosquito repellent. It costs from 400 CFP to 800 CFP a bottle, is great on the skin after a day of sizzling in the sun and makes a great gift (although it does solidify in cooler climates).

CAPITAL
Libreville

POPULATION
1,7 million

AREA
267,667 sq km

OFFICIAL LANGUAGE
French

Forest elephants, Loango National Park

Gabon

With an impressive 11.25% of the country proclaimed as national parkland, Gabon offers a spectacular array of wildlife in its dense rainforests and open savannah to enthral nature enthusiasts.

Alongside the rainforests and savannah, add the superb white-sand beaches, rushing rivers and ethereal landscapes, and you have an Eden-like travel experience in an unexplored part of Africa.

Gabon is the region's most progressive and traveller-friendly destination, although tourism remains extremely DIY. You'll either have to put yourself into the hands of a travel agency, or negotiate the poor roads, infrequent transport options and the almost total lack of reliable infrastructure yourself. Outside the cosmopolitan Libreville and Port-Gentil, the country's largest cities, Gabon is an undiscovered wonderland not to be missed.

Top Experiences

Lambaréné

 Explore this charming, laid-back town made famous by the Nobel prize-winning Albert Schweitzer. Lambaréné – with its glossy lakes, fast-flowing rivers, thick green foliage and in-grained sweetness – feels somehow kind and gentle, as if the profound humanitarian efforts of Schweitzer changed the character of the land. And his legacy is indeed felt everywhere, from the wonderful, still-operational hospital (which Schweitzer founded in 1924 to treat people with leprosy) to the volunteer-staffed lab that researches malaria and other tropical diseases.

The town is divided into three areas spanning the river, quite close to each other. The near bank has the rewarding Schweitzer Hospital Museum; across the bridge is the island with the main markets, the river port, and Le Tribune, from where shared taxis leave; across another bridge is the lively Quartier Isaac.

Mayumba National Park

 Bodysurf the waves while watching humpback whales breach in the distance at Mayumba National Park. Closer to the Republic of the Congo than to Libreville, Mayumba

feels like the edge of the Earth. Some 550 leatherback turtles – in fact 30% of the world's total – lay their eggs here between November and April. Barnacled humpback whales come to mate between June and October, and you'll also see large groups of dolphins, including the rare humpback dolphin.

When to Go

☼ **HIGH SEASON**
(May–Sep)

⛅ **SHOULDER**
(Apr & Oct)

☂ **LOW SEASON**
(Nov–Jan)

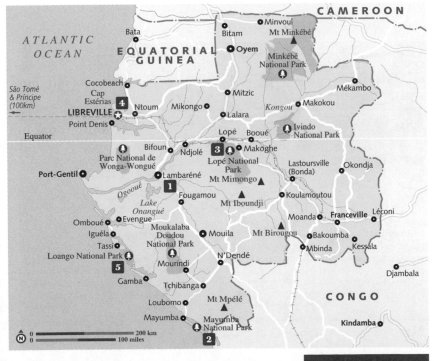

There are elephants and antelopes in the forest. And the land, if you listen to the locals, is hushed by the spirits of ancestors.

Lopé National Park

3 Smack bang on the equator and framed by the beautiful Ogooué River, Lopé National Park, a Unesco World Heritage Site, doesn't disappoint. Undulating hills meet savannah and enclaves of rainforest where elephants, buffaloes, gorillas, chimpanzees and the biggest mandrill troupes in the world can be found. It's estimated there are three elephants per square kilometre, which would make it the highest concentration on the planet. The rare giant forest warbler,

picathartes and seven types of hornbill are some of the more than 400 species of birds.

Libreville

4 The vibrant, muscular heart of Gabon, Libreville is the largest city and home to over a third of Gabon's population. It's also a city awash in oil money: pavements, clean streets, smart restaurants and vast gated villas are the first impressions of the town, but stay a little longer and you'll easily discover Libreville's essentially African heart: crowded street markets and busy residential areas lie further back from the gleaming coastline. Watching a football match at the Omnisport Stadium is unforgettable.

Getting Around

Air is by far the easiest way to move around, but flights aren't cheap or regular.

There's a bus service between Libreville and most major towns. Most buses are old, air-con is an open window and seats are hard.

The Transgabonais Railway line begins at Owendo and runs to Franceville. There are four trains a week in each direction.

Loango National Park

5 Loango is known justifiably as 'Africa's last Eden'. Here, warm streams criss-cross pockets of thick forest and salty savannah, while vast island-dotted lagoons and miles of white-sand beach provide habitat for all manner of creatures. It's perhaps best known for its mythic surfing hippos, but you'll also find the largest concentration and variety of whales and dolphins in the waters, elephants wandering the beaches, western lowland gorillas in the forests and an assortment of rare mammals cavorting in the savannah. If your pockets can take it, Loango is one of the best wildlife-watching destinations on the planet.

Food & Drink

Libreville and Port-Gentil have plenty of restaurants serving mostly European food. Look carefully, though, and you'll find some excellent Gabonese flavours such as sauces *nyemboué* (crushed palm nuts) or *odika* (crushed acacia seeds, known as 'chocolate') with meat and fish dishes. Fish is plentiful on the coast and tropical fruit abounds. The main side dish is cassava (or manioc) formed into sticks.

Bach in Gabon

What does Johann Sebastian Bach circa 1724 have in common with Gabon's Bantu drummers? Until the 1990s, not a lot. But that was before Pierre Akendengué, one of Africa's most celebrated composers, holed up for 100 days in a Paris studio and recorded 'Lambarena', a fabulously energetic track that sets traditional Gabonese drumming and singing to the pure notes of Bach's 'St John Passion'. Akendengué – who has been both 1970s protest singer and cultural advisor to the late Omar Bongo since his first foray into music in the 1940s – recorded the track as a tribute to Dr Albert Schweitzer, founder of the eponymous, world-renowned hospital at Lambaréné. The result is a beautiful, unlikely marriage, like coming across a violin concerto in the middle of the Lopé National Park.

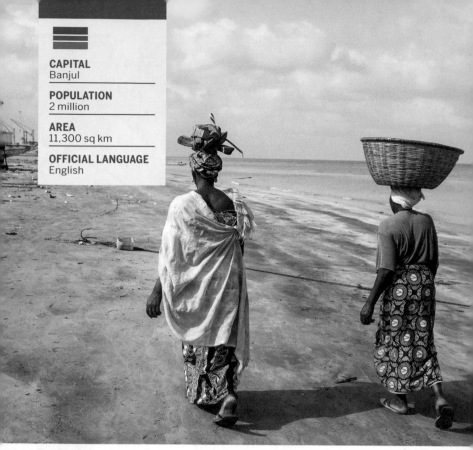

Banjul beach

The Gambia

The smallest country in mainland Africa, The Gambia contains a lot within its compact frame, attracting sun-seekers and birdwatchers and displaying a wealth of natural riches.

CAPITAL
Banjul

POPULATION
2 million

AREA
11,300 sq km

OFFICIAL LANGUAGE
English

The Gambia may be the smallest country on the continent, but its captivating array of attractions belie its tiny size. Surrounded by Senegal, The Gambia has a mere 80km of coastline, but what a magnificent stretch it encompasses: golden beaches backed by swaying palms and sprinkled with scenic lagoons, sleepy fishing villages and biologically rich coastal reserves.

Of course there's more to The Gambia than just sun and surf. Its namesake river is teeming with wildlife, including nearly 600 bird species, plus manatees, hippos, crocodiles and troops of wily colobus monkeys. Boat trips and overnights at forest ecolodges reveal some of the great wonders of the hinterland, from a chimpanzee island reserve to the ruins of a 17th-century British fortress. The greatest treasures, though, are the warm-hearted Gambian people, who more than live up to their homeland's moniker of the 'the smiling coast of Africa'.

Top Experiences

Chimpanzee Rehabilitation Project

1 Comprised of so-called Baboon Island and several smaller islands, this project located in the River Gambia National Park, is one of the most important wildlife sites in The Gambia. Despite the main island's moniker, this place is really the kingdom of chimps – more than 100 of the primates live across it and three other islands in four separate communities. Visitors can see many of the simians during a boat tour around the islands. There's also other wildlife in the area, including hippos, manatees, crocodiles and abundant bird life, not to mention other primates, such as red colobus monkeys, green vervet monkeys and – yes – even baboons.

Bijilo Forest Park

2 This small 51-hectare reserve makes for a lovely escape. A series of well-maintained walking trails (ranging from 900m to 1400m) takes you through lush vegetation, gallery forest, low bush and grass, towards the dunes. You'll likely see green vervet, red colobus and patas monkeys. Monitor lizards will likely come and stare you down, too. Birds are best watched on the coastal side. The more than 100 species that have been counted here include several types of bee-eater, grey hornbill, osprey, Caspian tern, francolin and wood dove. It's worth shelling out the extra money for a guide, who can give a deeper context to the plant and animal life found here.

When to Go

 HIGH SEASON (Nov–Feb)

 SHOULDER (Mar–May & Oct)

 LOW SEASON (Jun–Sep)

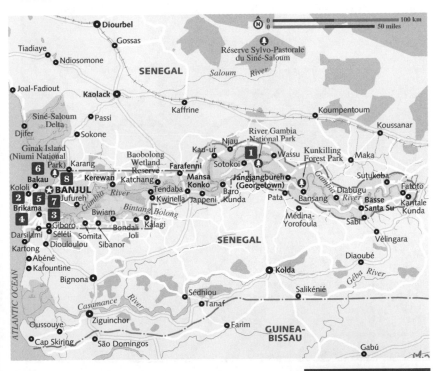

Makasutu Culture Forest

3 Like a snapshot of The Gambia, Makasutu Culture Forest bundles the country's array of landscapes into a dazzling 1000-hectare package. The setting is stunning, comprising palm groves, wetlands, mangroves and savannah plains, all inhabited by plenty of animals, including baboons, monitor lizards and hundreds of bird species.

Tour a mangrove tour by pirogue; take guided walks through a range of habitats, including a palm forest where you can watch palm sap being tapped; visit a crafts centre; and observe demonstrations of traditional dancing.

Sanyang

4 The beautiful beaches of Sanyang, south of Tujering on the coast, are popular with tour groups. That said, the golden sands feel remarkably untouched, and if it is paradise views that you're after, this is a fine place to add to the itinerary.

Abuko Nature Reserve

5 Abuko is rare among African wildlife reserves: it's tiny, it's easy to reach and you don't need a car to go in. With amazing diversity of vegetation and animals, this well-managed reserve is one of the

Getting Around

Regular buses travel along both the south bank and the north bank of the Gambia River.

Driving in The Gambia presents the usual challenges of West African road travel: potholes, nonexistent signage and an abundance of pedestrians, slow-moving vehicles and free-roaming livestock. Always take it slow.

region's best birdwatching haunts (more than 250 bird species have been recorded in its environs). Abuko is located about 11km from the Atlantic Coast and makes an easy day's excursion from most lodgings near the beach.

Kachikally Crocodile Pool

6 One of The Gambia's most popular tourist attractions is a sacred site for locals. As crocodiles represent the power of fertility in The Gambia, women who experience difficulties in conceiving often come here to pray and wash (any child called Kachikally tells of a successful prayer at the pool). The pool and its adjacent nature trail are home to dozens of Nile crocodiles that you can observe basking on the bank. If you dare, many are tame enough to be touched (your guide will point you in their direction).

Wide Open Walls

7 Two huge ibex grazing amid swirling waves, a blue tattooed lion, and a lovestruck blacksmith are just a few of the striking images awaiting visitors who stumble upon the village of Kubuneh. The simple homes of this African settlement have been transformed into a riotous collection of thought-provoking street art, courtesy of a talented group of international artists who have brought a touch of surreal beauty to this corner of West Africa.

Albert Market

8 Since its founding in the mid-19th century, the Albert Market, an area of frenzied buying, bartering and bargaining, has been Banjul's main hub of activity. This cacophony of Banjul life is intoxicating, with its stalls stacked with shimmering fabrics, hair extensions, shoes, household and electrical wares and the myriad colours and flavours of the fruit and vegetable market.

Food & Drink

National dishes include rice with *domoda* (a groundnut sauce) and *benachin* (rice cooked in tomato, fish and vegetable sauce). Fresh seafood is available along the coast, with outstanding grilled ladyfish, barracuda and butterfish. Vegetarians ought to try *niebbe*, spicy red beans that are served with bread on street corners. There are scores of restaurants in the tourist region of the Atlantic coast. Elsewhere, dining options are largely limited to hotels.

The People

With around 115 people per sq km, The Gambia has one of the highest population densities in Africa. The strongest concentration of people is around the urbanised zones of the Atlantic coast. Forty-five per cent of the population is under 14 years old.

The main ethnic groups are the Mandinka (comprising around 34%), the Fula (around 22%) and the Wolof (about 12%). Smaller groups include the Diola – also spelled Jola (11%), the Serer and Manjango. About 96% of the population is Muslim. Christianity is most widespread among the Diola.

CAPITAL	Tbilisi
POPULATION	4.9 million
AREA	69,700 sq km
OFFICIAL LANGUAGE	Georgian

Tbilisi Old Town

Georgia

From its green valleys spread with vineyards to its old churches and watchtowers perched in fantastic mountain scenery, Georgia is one of the most beautiful countries on earth.

Located in the dramatic Caucasus Mountains, Georgia is a marvellous canvas for walkers, horse riders, cyclists, skiers, rafters and travellers of every kind. Equally special are its proud, high-spirited, cultured people: Georgia claims to be the birthplace of wine, and this is a place where guests are considered blessings and hospitality is the very stuff of life.

A deeply complicated history has given Georgia a wonderful heritage of architecture and arts, from cave cities to ancient cathedrals to the inimitable canvases of Pirosmani. Tbilisi, the capital, is still redolent of an age-old Eurasian crossroads. But this is also a country moving forward in the 21st century, with spectacular contemporary buildings, a minimal crime rate and ever-improving facilities for the visitors who are a growing part of its future.

Top Experiences

Tbilisi Old Town

1 Nowhere better blends the romance of Georgia's past with its striving for a new future than Tbilisi's Old Town. Winding lanes lined by rakishly leaning houses lead past tranquil old stone churches to shady squares and glimpses of the ultra-contemporary Peace Bridge spanning the Mtkvari River. Casual cafes and bohemian bars rub shoulders with trendy lounge-clubs, folksy carpet shops, new travellers' hostels and small, quirky hotels. The aeons-old silhouette of Narikala Fortress supervises everything, while Georgia's 21st-century Presidential Palace, with its egg-shaped glass dome, looks on from over the river.

Kazbegi Area

2 Just a couple of hours' drive from Tbilisi, the small town of Kazbegi is the hub of one of the region's most spectacular, yet easily accessed, high-mountain zones. The sight of Tsminda Sameba Church silhouetted on its hilltop against the massive snow-covered cone of Mt Kazbek is Georgia's most iconic image. Numerous walking, horse and mountain-bike routes lead along steep-sided valleys and up to glaciers, waterfalls, mountain passes and isolated villages – just ideal for getting a taste of the high Caucasus.

Davit Gareja

3 Set in remote, arid lands near Georgia's border with Azerbaijan, these much-revered cave monasteries were carved out of a lonely cliff-face long, long ago. They became a cradle

When to Go

 HIGH SEASON (Mar–Jun & Sep–Nov)

 SHOULDER (Jul–Aug)

 LOW SEASON (Dec–Feb)

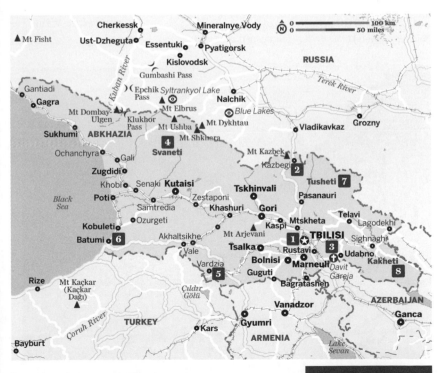

of medieval monastic culture and fresco painting. Saints' tombs, vivid 1000-year-old murals, an otherworldly landscape and the very idea that people voluntarily chose – and still choose – to live in desert caves all combine to make visiting Davit Gareja a startling experience today. Though remote, the site makes an easy day trip from Tbilisi, Telavi or Sighnaghi.

Svaneti

4 The mysterious mountain valleys of Svaneti sit high in the Caucasus, surrounded by spectacular snowy peaks, alpine meadows and thick forests – a paradise for walkers in summer. Long isolated and insulated from the outside world, Svaneti has its own language and a strongly traditional culture, symbolised by the 175 *koshkebi* (ancient stone defensive towers) that stand

picturesquely in its villages, and the 1000-year-old frescoes in its churches. Accessible only by a long road trip until recently, Svaneti also has daily small-plane flights from Tbilisi.

Vardzia

5 The remarkable cave city of Vardzia is a cultural symbol with a special place in Georgian hearts. King Giorgi III built a fortification here in the 12th century, and his daughter, Queen Tamar, established a cave monastery that grew into a holy city housing perhaps 2000 monks, renowned as a spiritual bastion of Georgia and of Christendom's eastern frontier. Its inhabitants lived in rock-hewn dwellings ranging over 13 floors. All together there are more than 400 rooms, 13 churches and 25 wine cellars, and more are still being discovered.

Getting Around

Georgian Airways flies several routes.

Almost every town has a bus or minibus service.

The efficient Tbilisi metro operates from 6am to midnight.

Cycling is becoming popular as a leg of a cross-Asia trip.

Batumi

6 With a backdrop of mist-wrapped hills, Georgia's summer holiday capital has sprouted new hotels and attractions like mushrooms in recent years, but it still owes some of its charm to the belle époque elegance of its original boom time a century ago. Batumi makes a good introduction to Georgia, with its relaxed atmosphere, plentiful accommodation, good restaurants, nightlife and party scene in summer.

Tusheti

7 Tucked away in the Caucasus in Georgia's far northeast corner, Tusheti is an ever more popular summer hiking and horse-trekking area and weekend getaway for lowland Georgians, but remains one of the country's most picturesque, fascinating and pristine high-mountain regions. The single road to Tusheti, over the nerve-jangling 2900m

Abano Pass from Kakheti, is 4WD-only and only passable from about late May to mid-October. The whole area is under environmental protection as the Tusheti Protected Areas (1137 sq km).

Kakheti

8 The eastern region of Kakheti is Georgia's premier wine-producing area. Almost everywhere you go, you'll be invited to

drink a glass of wine and it's easy to find yourself wandering around in a semipermanent mellow haze. Kakheti is also rich in history: here you'll find the incredible monastery complex of Davit Gareja, the picturesque hilltop town of Sighnaghi, and many beautiful churches, castles and mansions around the main town, Telavi.

EFESENKO / SHUTTERSTOCK ©

Food & Drink

Badrijani nigvzit Aubergine slices with walnut-and-garlic paste.

Churchkhela A string of nuts (usually walnuts) coated in an often-pinkish caramel made from grape juice.

Khachapuri Cheese pie.

Khinkali Big spicy dumplings, with a filling of spiced, ground-up meat, or potatoes, mushrooms or sometimes vegetables.

Mtsvadi (ghoris/khbos) Shish kebab (from pork/beef), often just 'barbecue' on English-language menus.

Sulguni A salty cheese, sometimes smoked.

Georgian Voices

Georgian polyphonic singing is a tradition of multi-voice a cappella song that goes back thousands of years. It used to accompany every aspect of daily life, and the songs survive in various genres including *supruli* (songs for the table), *mushuri* (working songs) and *satrpialo* (love songs). It's still alive and well. Mostly male ensembles such as the Rustavi Choir perform in concert halls and at festivals such as Art-Gene, Tushetoba and Shatiloba, but polyphonic song is most electrifying when it happens at less formal gatherings such as around the table at a *supra* (feast), when the proximity, intimacy and volume can be literally spine-tingling. There are varying regional styles but it's typical for some singers to do a bass drone while others sing melodies on top.

CAPITAL
Berlin

POPULATION
81.1 million

AREA
357,672 sq km

OFFICIAL LANGUAGE
German

Berlin cafes

Germany

Prepare for a rollercoaster of feasts, treats and temptations as you take in Germany's soul-stirring scenery, spirit-lifting culture, big-city beauties, romantic palaces and half-timbered towns.

There's something undeniably artistic in the way Germany's scenery unfolds – the corrugated, dune-fringed coasts of the north; the moody forests, romantic river valleys and vast vineyards of the centre, and the off-the-charts splendour of the Alps, carved into rugged glory by glaciers and the elements.

The cities will wow you with a cultural arc from art museums and high-brow opera to naughty cabaret and underground clubs.

And wherever you go, Romanesque, Gothic and baroque classics rub rafters with architectural creations from modern masters.

Few countries have had as much impact on the world as Germany. It is the birthplace of many heavyweights who, each in their own way, have left their mark on human history. You can stand in a Roman amphitheatre, sleep in a medieval castle and walk along remnants of the Berlin Wall – in Germany the past is very much present.

Top Experiences

Berlin

1 Berlin's glamour and grit are bound to mesmerise anyone keen on exploring its vibrant culture, edgy architecture, fabulous food, intense parties and palpable history. Over a quarter century after the Berlin Wall's collapse, the German capital is increasingly grown up without relinquishing its indie spirit and penchant for creative improvisation. There's haute cuisine, all-night parties and world-class art. Visit major historical sites – the Reichstag, Brandenburger Tor and Checkpoint Charlie among them – then feast on a smorgasbord of culture in myriad museums.

Munich

2 If you're looking for Alpine clichés, Munich will hand them to you in one chic and compact package. But the Bavarian capital also has plenty of unexpected trump cards under its often bright-blue skies. Folklore and age-old traditions exist side by side with sleek BMWs, designer boutiques and high-powered industry. It's a sassy, sophisticated and self-confident city with a nonchalant feel. The city's museums showcase everything from artistic masterpieces to technological treasures and Oktoberfest history, while its music and cultural scenes are second only to Berlin's.

Schloss Neuschwanstein

3 Commissioned by Bavaria's most celebrated (and loopiest) 19th-century monarch, King Ludwig II, Schloss Neuschwanstein rises from the forests like a storybook illustration. Inside, the make-believe continues, reflecting Ludwig's obsession with the mythical Teutonic past in a confection that puts even the flashiest oligarch's palazzo in the shade. This sugary folly is said to have inspired Walt's castle at Disney World; now it inspires tourist masses to make the pilgrimage along the Romantic Road, which culminates at its gates.

3

The Black Forest

4 Mist, snow or shine, the deep, dark Black Forest is beautiful. If it's back-to-nature moments you're after, this sylvan slice of southwestern Germany is the place to linger. Every valley reveals new surprises: half-timbered villages looking every inch the fairy-tale fantasy, thunderous waterfalls, cuckoo clocks the size of houses. Breathe in the cold air, drive rollercoaster roads to middle-of-nowhere lakes, have your cake, walk it off on trail after gorgeously wooded trail, then hide away in a heavy-lidded farmhouse. Hear that? Silence. What a wonderful thing.

LEONID ANDRONOV / SHUTTERSTOCK ©

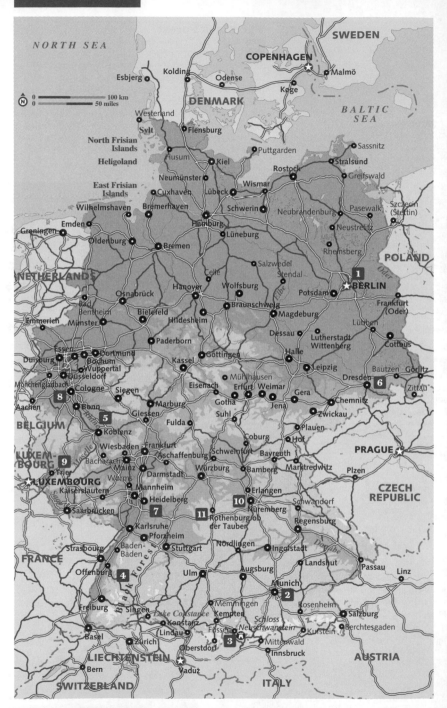

Best in Print

Grimms' Fairy Tales (Jacob & Wilhelm Grimm; 1812) The classic!

The Rise & Fall of the Third Reich (William L Shirer; 1960) 1000 pages of powerful reportage.

Berlin Alexanderplatz (Alfred Döblin; 1929) Berlin in the 1920s.

The Tin Drum (Günter Grass; 1959) WWII seen through the eyes of a boy who refuses to grow up.

The Reader (Bernhard Schlink; 1995) Boy meets girl in WWII, girl gets put on trial for war crimes.

Best in Music

Brandenburg Concertos (JS Bach)

Water Music (Händel)

Beethoven's Nine Symphonies

Brahms' Violin Concerto

Autobahn (Kraftwerk, 1974)

Mutter (Rammstein, 2001)

Nomad Songs (Micatone, 2005)

Sound So (Wir sind Helden, 2007)

Moderat II (Moderat, 2013)

The Romantic Rhine

 As the mighty Rhine flows from Rüdesheim to Koblenz, the landscape's unique face-off between rock and water creates a magical mix of the wild (churning whirlpools, dramatic cliffs), the agricultural (near-vertical vineyards), the medieval (hilltop castles, half-timbered hamlets), the legendary (Loreley) and the modern (in the 19th-century sense: barges, ferries, passenger steamers and trains). From every riverside village, trails take you through vineyards and forests, up to panoramic viewpoints and massive stone fortresses, and back to a romantic evening spent sampling the local wines.

Dresden

 The apocalypse came on a cold February night in 1945. Hours of carpet bombing reduced Germany's 'Florence on the Elbe' to a smouldering pile of bricks and the dead. Dresden's comeback is nothing short of a miracle. Reconstructed architectural jewels pair with stunning art collections that justify the city's place in the pantheon of European cultural capitals. Add to that a contagiously energetic pub quarter, Daniel Libeskind's dramatically redesigned Military History Museum and a tiara of villas and palaces lining up along the river and you've got one enticing package of discovery.

Heidelberg

 The 19th-century romantics found sublime beauty and spiritual inspiration in Germany's oldest university town. Generations of students have attended lectures, sung lustily with beer steins in hand, carved their names into tavern tables and, occasionally, been sent to the student jail. All of this has left its mark on the modern-day city, where age-old traditions endure alongside world-class research, innovative cultural events and a sometimes raucous nightlife scene.

When to Go

HIGH SEASON
(Jul–Aug)
Busy roads and long lines at key sights.

SHOULDER
(Apr–Jun & Sep–Oct)
Sunny, temperate weather ideal for outdoor pursuits.

LOW SEASON
(Nov–Mar)
No queues but shorter hours at key sights.

Picturesque Towns

If you crave beauty along with (relative) serenity, consider a lovely, lesser-known town, such as Quedlinburg, Wismar, Beilstein or Celle.

Alpine Wildlife

Snow hares, marmots and wild goats scamper around the Alps and a rare but wonderful treat for birdwatchers is sighting the golden eagle; Berchtesgaden National Park staff might be able to help you.

Food & Drink

Beer Few things are as deeply ingrained in the German psyche as the love of beer.

Bratwurst Nuremberg's finger-sized links, grilled and served in a bun or with sauerkraut, are top dogs in Germany.

Currywurst Slices of sausage topped with curry powder and ketchup.

Eisbein Salt-cured ham hock with sauerkraut.

Klösse Potato-based dumplings.

Labskaus A Hamburg seafarer mishmash of corned beef, beetroot, potatoes, onions and occasionally herring, topped with a fried egg and served with gherkins.

Mecklenburger Rippenbraten Rolled pork stuffed with lemons, apples, plums and raisins.

Nürnberg Lebkuchen Totally moreish gingerbread made with nuts, fruit peel, honey and spices.

Pinkelwurst Bremen's spicy pork, beef, oat and onion sausage.

Spätzle Noodle-dumpling hybrid, often smothered in cheese or topped with lentils.

Sauere Kuttlen/Nierle/Lüngerl Sour tripe/kidneys/lung simmered in vinegar or wine and spices.

Schwarzwälderkirschtorte The world-famous, off-the-calorie-charts Black Forest gateau.

Quark A yoghurt-like curd cheese, used in everything from potato dips to salad dressings and sauces to cheesecake.

Cologne Cathedral

8 At unexpected moments you see it: Cologne's cathedral, the city's twin-towered icon, looming over an urban vista and the timeless course of the Rhine river. This perfectly formed testament to faith and conviction was started in 1248 and consecrated six centuries later. Climb a tower for views of the surrounding city that are like no others.

Trier

9 There was a time when Trier was the capital of western Europe. OK, that time was 2000 years ago, when emperor Constantine ruled the fading Roman Empire from here. Nowhere has the Roman legacy survived as beautifully and tangibly as in this charming town with its ancient amphitheatre, elaborate thermal baths and famous Porta Nigra city gate. Architectural treasures from later ages include Germany's oldest Gothic church, and Karl Marx' baroque birthplace. Of course it's been a Unesco World Heritage Site since 1986. Today, Germany's oldest city is as unhurried as the Moselle river it sits on, within a grape toss of the country's finest – and steepest – vineyards.

Nuremberg

10 Capital of Franconia, an independent region until 1806, Nuremberg may conjure visions of Nazi rallies and grisly war trials, but there's so much more to this energetic city. Dürer hailed from the Altstadt, his house now a museum. Germany's first railway trundled from here to neighbouring Fürth, leaving a trail of choo-choo heritage. And Germany's toy capital has heaps of things for kids to enjoy. When you're done with sightseeing, the local beer is as dark as the coffee and best employed to chase down Nuremberg's delicious bratwurst. As one of Bavaria's biggest draws it is alive with visitors, especially during the spectacular Christmas market.

Rothenburg ob der Tauber

11 A medieval gem, Rothenburg ob der Tauber (meaning 'above the Tauber River') is top tourist stop along the Romantic

Road. With its web of cobbled lanes, higgledy-piggledy houses and sturdy towered walls, the town is fairy-tale Germany. One might even say it's too cute for its own good, if the deluges of day-trippers are any indication. The trick is

to experience this historic wonderland at its most magical: early or late in the day, when the last coaches have hit the road and you can soak up the romance all by yourself on gentle strolls along moonlit cobbled lanes.

6

Getting Around

 There's an extensive network of long-distance and regional trains with frequent departures; it can be fairly expensive but numerous deals are available.

 German roads are excellent and motoring around the country can be a lot of fun. Useful for travelling at your own pace or for visiting regions with less public transport.

 Buses are cheaper and slower than trains and with a growing long-haul network. Regional bus services fill the gaps in areas not served by rail.

 Flights are only useful for longer distances, eg Hamburg to Munich or Berlin to Munich.

Bushbuk, Mole National Park

CAPITAL	Accra
POPULATION	28 million
AREA	238,533 sq km
OFFICIAL LANGUAGE	English

Ghana

Hailed as West Africa's golden child, Ghana, a historic land boasting a depth of culture and diverse natural attractions, deserves its place in the sun.

One of Africa's great success stories, Ghana is reaping the benefits of a stable democracy in the form of fast-paced development. And it shows: the country is suffused with the most incredible energy.

With its welcoming beaches, gorgeous hinterland, rich culture, vibrant cities, diverse wildlife, easy transport and affable inhabitants, it's no wonder Ghana is sometimes labelled 'Africa for beginners'.

It's easy to come here for a week or a month, but no trip can be complete without a visit to Ghana's coastal forts, poignant reminders of a page of history that defined our modern world. Most of the forts were built during the 17th century by European powers vying for commercial dominance of the Gold Coast and the Gulf of Guinea.

Travel north and you'll feel like you've arrived in a different country, with a different religion, geography and cultural practices. The beauty is that this diversity exists so harmoniously, a joy to experience and a wonder to behold in uncertain times.

Top Experiences

Cape Coast Castle

 Cape Coast's imposing, whitewashed castle commands the heart of town, overlooking the sea. Once one of the world's most important slave-holding sites, it provides horrifying insight into the workings of the trade. Staff conduct hour-long tours, during which you'll visit the dark, damp dungeons, where slaves waited for two to 12 weeks, while contemplating rumours that only hinted at their fate. A visit to the dungeons contrasts sharply with the Governor's bedroom, blessed with floor-to-ceiling windows and panoramic ocean views.

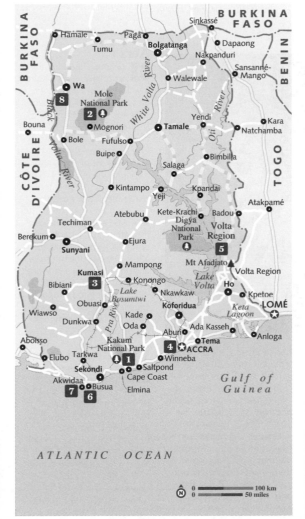

Food & Drink

Fiery sauces and oily soups are the mainstay of Ghanaian cuisine and are usually served with a starchy staple such as rice, *fufu* (cooked and mashed cassava, plantain or yam) or *banku* (fermented maize meal).

Other cuisines, particularly Indian and Chinese, are widely available throughout the country. Accra's ever-evolving dining scene offers everything from top-class sushi to gourmet burgers.

About the most common dish you'll find is groundnut stew, a warming, spicy dish cooked with liquefied groundnut paste, ginger and either fish or meat. Palm-nut soup (fashioned from tomatoes, ginger, garlic and chilli pepper, as well as palm nut) takes its bright colour from palm oil. *Jollof* rice is a spicy dish cooked with tomatoes and onion and usually served with meat. *Red-red* is a bean stew normally served with fried plantain.

When to Go

 HIGH SEASON
(Nov–Mar)

 SHOULDER
(Apr–May &
Sep–Oct)

LOW SEASON
(Jun–Aug)

Music in Ghana

There's no doubt about it: Ghana's got rhythm.

Traditional music doesn't have the popular following that it has in countries such as Burkina. It tends to be reserved for special occasions and is associated with royalty. Contemporary music, on the other hand, is thriving. Highlife, a mellow mix of big-band jazz, Christian hymns, brass band and sailor sonnets, hit Ghana in the 1920s. WWII brought American swing to Ghana's shores, prompting the first complex fusion of Western and African music. Hiplife, a hybrid of rhythmic African lyrics poured over imported American hip-hop beats, has now been ruling Ghana since the early 1990s.

Imported American hip-hop and Nigerian music closely compete for the number two spot after hiplife. Gospel music is also big, as is reggae.

PAUL D SMITH / SHUTTERSTOCK ©

Mole National Park

2 With its swathes of saffron-coloured savannah, Mole National Park offers what must surely be the cheapest safaris in Africa. There are at least 300 species of bird and 94 species of mammal. Sightings of elephants are common from December to April, and you're guaranteed to see other mammals year-round. The park headquarters offers excellent walking and driving safaris. You can arrange for an armed ranger to join you in your own 4WD, but you're not allowed to explore the park unaccompanied. If you tire of elephant spotting, ecotourism venture Mognori Eco Village, on the borders of the park, offers canoe safaris, village tours and the chance to learn about local culture.

Kejetia Market

3 From afar, the Kejetia Market looks like an alien mothership landed in the centre of Kumasi. Closer up, the rusting tin roofs of this huge market (often cited as the largest in West Africa; there are 11,000 stalls and at least four times as many people working here) look like a circular shantytown. Inside, the throbbing Kejetia is quite disorienting but utterly captivating.

Accra

4 Ghana's beating heart probably won't inspire love letters, but you might just grow to like it. The capital's hot, sticky streets are perfumed with sweat, fumes and yesterday's cooking oil. Like balloons waiting to be burst, clouds of dirty humidity linger above stalls selling mangoes, *banku* (fermented maize meal) and rice. The city's tendrils reach out towards the beach, the centre and the west, each one a different Ghanaian experience. The city doesn't have any heavy-hitting sights like Cape Coast or Elmina do but it does have good shopping, excellent nightlife and definitely the best selection of eating options in Ghana.

Volta Region

5 The Volta region has to be Ghana's most underrated gem. The area is covered in lush, fertile farmland flanked by rocks, and mountains offering beautiful vistas. It is prime hiking territory and has great ecotourism ventures.

Don't miss Ghana's tallest waterfalls, the Wli (pronounced 'vlee'), which stand amid an exquisite

Getting Around

There are several daily flights from Accra to Kumasi, Takoradi and Tamale. They tend to be relatively cheap and a huge time saver when travelling north.

A *tro-tro* is generally a minibus that leaves when full. Buses are best for long journeys as they tend to be more comfortable and reliable.

Taxis are the usual form of transport within towns and on some shorter routes between towns.

landscape of rolling hills, forests and bubbling streams. The falls are most impressive from April to October, when you can hear – and feel – the flow of water thundering down.

Busua

6 The small village of Busua, some 30km west of Takoradi, is a magnet for volunteers and backpackers, who love coming here to relax on the beach for a few days. There's a sociable vibe, with a number of chilled out bars and cafes in which to while away the hours; and the village has developed a reputation as a surfing hot spot. There are two excellent surf schools here, both of whom offer lessons for absolute beginners.

Akwidaa & Cape Three Points

7 Akwidaa's unique selling point is its long, pristine, white sandy beach, by far one of the best in

Ghana. From the village, you can hike in the local forests, explore cocoa and rubber plantations, organise canoe trips through mangroves or visit the windswept Cape Three Points, Ghana's southernmost point. In season, you can see turtles on the nearby beaches as well as humpback whales and sperm whales.

Wechiau Hippo Sanctuary

8 This much-hyped hippo sanctuary on the Black Volta River was initiated by local village chiefs in 1999. Hippos can usually be seen from November to March; once the rainy season (April to October) is underway, hippos disappear and the site becomes very hard to reach. Activities include river safaris, birdwatching, village tours and nature walks. Unless you have your own vehicle, you'll need to overnight at the sanctuary.

5

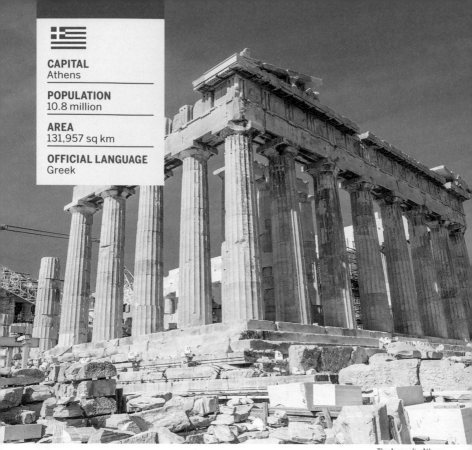

The Acropolis, Athens

Greece

Endless miles of aquamarine coastline, sun-bleached ancient ruins, strong feta and stronger ouzo – the Greek landscape thrills, and the Greek people are passionate about politics, coffee, art and gossiping.

Greece is a magnet for anyone who enjoys the great outdoors. Wander along cobbled, Byzantine footpaths, hike into volcanoes, watch for dolphins and sea turtles, and cycle through lush forests. Discover world-class kitesurfing, diving and rock-climbing locations or simply hop on a boat and set sail into the glittering blue beyond.

Step into the ring where Olympic athletes competed. Gaze at Meteora's monasteries, perched atop towering rock pinnacles.

Contemplate the Oracle's insights from the grandeur of Delphi or take in a starlit drama at an ancient outdoor theatre. Greece balances its past, present and future in a way managed by few other countries. The result is a nation with endless cultural pursuits.

Greeks are passionate and life is lived to the fullest, even at the most difficult of times, and herein lies the secret of how a country, seemingly riddled with challenges, is full of people who remain so in love with life.

CAPITAL
Athens

POPULATION
10.8 million

AREA
131,957 sq km

OFFICIAL LANGUAGE
Greek

Top Experiences

Experiencing the Acropolis

1 There's a reason the Acropolis remains the quintessential landmark of Western civilisation – it is spectacular. Whether experienced during an early morning stroll or from a dinnertime terrace with the Parthenon lit up and glorious, the Acropolis embodies a power and beauty that speak to all generations. Look beyond the Parthenon and you will find more intimate spots like the exquisite Temple of Athena Nike, while the Acropolis Museum cleverly showcases the Acropolis' surviving treasures.

Meteora

2 You're not likely to forget the first moment the magnificent Meteora comes into view – soaring pillars of rock that jut heavenward, and a handful of monasteries at the summit (some dating from the 14th century). The rope ladders that once enabled the monks to reach the top have long been replaced by steps carved into the rock. The geological heart of Meteora is considered the Adhrakhti, or obelisk, a striking column visible from anywhere in Kastraki. Today these spectacular stone towers beckon rock climbers from around the world.

The Zagorohoria

3 After passing through a seemingly endless array of tunnels, the Egnatia Odos highway brings you into rugged Epiros, home of the Pindos Mountains and the Zagorohoria – an immaculately preserved region of 46 traditional stone-and-slate villages spread along the ridges of Europe's deepest canyon, the Vikos Gorge. Here, the air is clear, fresh and cool, and the views astounding. You can explore the region by hiking or mountain biking, or simply get cosy by the fire in one of the many rustic B&Bs dotting the region.

2

EMI CRISTEA / SHUTTERSTOCK ©

Cutting-Edge Capital

4 Life in Athens is a magnificent mash-up of the ancient and the contemporary. Beneath the majestic facades of venerable landmarks, the city teems with life and creativity. Galleries and clubs hold the exhibitions, performances and installations of the city's booming arts scene. Trendy restaurants and humble tavernas rustle up fine, fine fare. Ubiquitous cafes fill with stylin' locals and moods run from punk rock to haute couture. Discos and bars abound ... and swing deep into the night.

MILAN GONDA / SHUTTERSTOCK ©

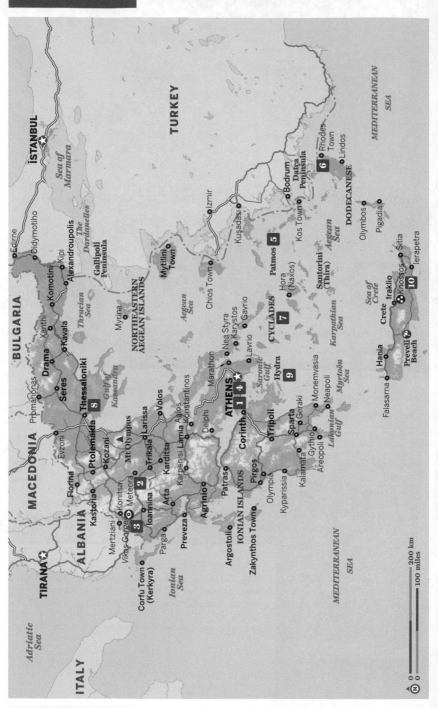

Best in Print

The Odyssey (Homer; 8th century BC) Plagued by Poseidon, Odysseus struggles to return home to Ithaca.

Zorba the Greek (Nikos Kazantzakis; 1946) A spiritual bible to many; one man's unquenchable lust for life.

The Magus (John Fowles; 1966) Creepy mind games set on fictional island Phraxos.

Falling For Icarus: A Journey among the Cretans (Rory MacLean; 2004) A travel writer fulfils his ambition to build his own plane in the land of Icarus.

Colossus of Maroussi (Henry Miller, 1941) A travelogue of prewar Greece and heralded Miller's best work.

Best on Film

300 (2007) Testosterone-fuelled retelling of the Spartans' epic stand against the might of the Persian army in the Battle of Thermopylae, 480 BC.

Mamma Mia (2008) The island of Skopelos shines to the soundtrack of Abba.

Guns of Navarone (1961) Allied soldiers enter Nazi-occupied Greece in this compelling boy's-own thriller.

Shirley Valentine (1989) Classic Greek island romance on Mykonos.

Captain Corelli's Mandolin (2001) Lavish retelling of Louis de Bernières' novel, awash with romance in occupied Greece.

Before Midnight (2013) The third in a trilogy following the relationship of a French-American couple, filmed on the Peloponnese.

Easter Festivities on Patmos

5 While the Greek calendar is chock-full of festivals and holidays, by far the biggest event of the Greek Orthodox church is Easter. And the best place to experience it is on Patmos in the Dodecanese. The island comes to life with fireworks, dancing in the streets, huge outdoor lamb roasts and plenty of ouzo shots. Begin by witnessing the moving, candlelit processions of flower-filled biers through the capital, marking the start of the celebration on Good Friday. By Saturday night you'll be shouting Hristos Anesti (Christ is Risen) and cracking vibrant red-dyed eggs.

Rhodes' Old Town

6 Getting lost in Rhodes' Old Town is a must. Away from the crowds, you will find yourself meandering down twisting, cobbled alleyways with archways above and squares opening up ahead. In these hidden corners your imagination will take off with flights of medieval fancy. Explore the ancient Knights' Quarter, the old Jewish neighbourhood or the Turkish Quarter. Hear traditional live music in tiny tavernas or dine on fresh seafood at atmospheric outdoor restaurants. Wander along the top of the city's walls, with the sea on one side and a bird's-eye view into this living museum.

When to Go

HIGH SEASON
(Easter & May–Aug)
Everything is in full swing and transport is plentiful.

SHOULDER
(Apr & Sep–Oct)
Temperatures are milder, internal flights and ferries have reduced schedules.

LOW SEASON
(Nov–Mar)
Many hotels, sights and restaurants shut, especially on islands.

Cleaner Beaches

With 393 beaches and nine marinas receiving the much coveted Blue Flag in 2014 for cleanliness, Greece now ranks second in a list of 49 countries worldwide.

Old Town of Xanthi

Until recently a place of faded grandeur, Old Xanthi has got a new lease on life. In the evening, the streets are captivating, with lots of atmospheric bars and *mezedopoleia* (cafes serving small plates) spilling out into the little streets.

Food & Drink

Greeks pride themselves on their cuisine and will go out of their way to ensure you are well fed. The tang of homemade tzatziki on gyros and the aroma of souvlaki grilling are just the beginning.

Greeks love eating out, sharing impossibly big meals with family and friends in a drawn out, convivial fashion. Whether you are eating seafood at a seaside table or trying modern Greek fare under the floodlit Acropolis, dining out in Greece is never just about what you eat, but the whole experience.

Greeks traditionally serve fruit rather than sweets after a meal, but there's no shortage of local sweets and cakes. Traditional sweets include baklava, *loukoumadhes* (doughnut balls served with honey and cinnamon), *kataifi* (chopped nuts inside angel-hair pastry), *rizogalo* (rice pudding) and *galaktoboureko* (custard-filled pastry). *Ghlika kutalyu* (syrupy fruit preserves, also known as 'spoon sweets') are served on tiny plates as a welcome offering but are also eaten over yoghurt.

While there is coffee strong enough to stand a spoon in and ouzo that will knock you flat, thankfully Greece also has plenty of tamer options for quenching your thirst.

Island Hopping in the Cyclades

7 From the spirited nightlife and celebrity hideaways of Mykonos and Ios, to the isolated sandy coasts of tiny, far-flung specks like Anafi, hopping through the Cyclades is a Greek experience not to be missed. Peppered with ancient ruins (try Delos), mystical castles (head to Naxos), lush scenery and dramatic coastlines (visit Milos), the islands are spread like Greek jewels across the sea. Speed over the Aegean on catamarans and sway on old-fashioned ferry boats. You won't regret a single saltwater-splashed second of it.

Colourful Thessaloniki

8 Stylish Thessaloniki remains northern Greece's liveliest town, thanks to its universities, cultural scene, arts and nightlife. Explore the old quarter, a neighbourhood full of colourful, winding streets marked by white-plastered houses, lazy cats and Byzantine churches. Taste test your way through the city's *zaharoplasteia* (patisseries) for Ottoman inspired sweets. Drink up with throngs of students at stylish bars and clubs. Tour the galleries of one of the country's most artistically fertile locations and save time for the first-rate museums. Thessaloniki has it all going on.

Hydra

9 Everyone approaches Hydra by sea. There is no airport, there are no cars. As you sail in, you find, simply, a stunningly preserved stone village with white-gold houses filling a natural cove and hugging the edges of surrounding mountains. Then you join the ballet of port life. Sailboats, caïques and mega-yachts fill Hydra's quays and a people-watching potpourri fills the ubiquitous harbourside cafes. Here, a mere hour and a half from Athens, you'll find a great cappuccino, rich naval and architectural history, and the raw seacoast beckoning you for a swim.

Cretan Cuisine

10 Waistlines be damned: Crete is the perfect place to indulge your appetite. The island's Mediterranean diet is known for its health benefits but it's the farm-fresh produce, aromatic herbs, straight-from-the-ocean seafood, soft, tangy cheese and some of the world's best virgin olive oil that make it legendary. Whether it's a bowl of snails, fresh artichokes, mussels or figs, the essence of this rustic cuisine is a balance of flavours. It's hard to beat traditional hand-spun filo, *horta* (wild greens) picked from a backyard garden and red mullet just hauled in.

7

VITMARY / SHUTTERSTOCK ©

Getting Around

 If you're in a hurry, Greece has an extensive domestic air network. Flights are abundant and significantly cut down travel time.

 To most visitors, travelling in Greece means island-hopping via the multitude of ferries that criss-cross the Adriatic and the Aegean.

 Buses are the mainstay of land transport, with a network that reaches out to the smallest villages.

 Car rentals are reasonably priced and found on all but the tiniest islands. They give you the freedom to explore the islands, but you'll need a good dose of bravery and road smarts.

CAPITAL
Nuuk (Godthåb)

POPULATION
57,750

AREA
2.2 million sq km

OFFICIAL LANGUAGES
Greenlandic (East
Inuit), Danish

Ilulissat, Disko Bay

Greenland

Stone Age traditions collide with modern technology to create a complex society where children eat whale blubber while watching satellite TV and hunters learn first-aid skills to qualify as guides.

'When you've seen the world there's always Greenland' goes the old travellers' saying. But why wait till then? Greenland is not a cheap destination, but few places combine such magnificent scenery, such clarity of light and such raw power of nature.

Vast swathes of beautiful, unfenced wilderness give adventurers unique freedom to wander at will, whether on foot, by ski or by dogsled. Splurging on helicopter and boat rides is worth every penny. These whisk you over truly magnificent mountainscapes and glaciers or through some of the planet's most spectacular fjords.

Scattered along the west coast are photogenic little villages as well as the capital, Nuuk (Godthåb). In the south there's an appealing sprinkling of emerald-lawned farms. Allow ample time in each destination to unwind, soak up the midnight sun, witness a glacier calving or to be dazzled by the magic of the aurora borealis.

Top Experiences

Uummannaq

1 The towering red peak that dominates Uummannaq (Heart-shaped Island), lords over the colourful village. Houses cling to the steep shore and wooden steps play snakes and ladders with winding roads. In winter, darkness descends for two months, but spring ushers excellent conditions for dogsledding. Many families still depend on hunting as their main source of income, and a ban on hunting and fishing by snowmobile or motorboat means that the sled and the kayak are still the primary means of transport for hunters. The authenticity of it all hits you with the smell of dogs, drying fish and stretched skins wafting through the air.

Food & Drink

Traditional Greenlandic fare is dominated by meat.

Caribou In September virtually everyone takes time off work to hunt *tuttu* (caribou), which yield superb steaks and very tasty leg-meat, which is rarely sold.

Dovekies North Greenlanders once survived by eating these penguin-like small birds. When stuffed in hollowed-out seal carcasses and left to rot, they form the unappetising *kivioq*.

Seal Cooked by boiling chunks in water for an hour or more. The cooked meat has a deep, chocolate-brown colour. Cuts edged with a centimetre of blubber taste rather like lamb chops.

Whale The best raw *mattak* (whaleskin) comes from beluga or narwhal, taking on a slightly nutty, mushroom-like flavour when cooked.

When to Go

 HIGH SEASON (Apr–Aug)

 SHOULDER (Mar & Sep)

 LOW SEASON (Oct–Feb)

Extreme Skiing

The three-day Arctic Circle Race (www.acr.gl) is one of the toughest ski races in the world. It follows a 160km circular route around the mountains east of Sisimiut, in southwest Greenland, and usually takes place during the first week of April. Two nights are spent camping on the tundra, and dog teams follow skiers for safety reasons.

VADIM PETRAKOV / SHUTTERSTOCK ©

Ilulissat Kangerlua

2 This is why you spent all that money and came to Greenland: the awesome force and beauty of Unesco World Heritage–listed Ilulissat Kangerlua, one of the most active glaciers on the planet. It is one of those places so spectacular that it makes everything else pale in comparison. Just outside Ilulissat town you will be confronted with gargantuan icebergs, some the size of small towns, which lie at the mouth of the fjord. Measuring 5km wide, the glacier annually calves more than 35 cu km of ice – that's about 20 million tonnes per day (enough to supply New York with water for a year) and about a tenth of all icebergs floating in Greenlandic waters.

Qassiarsuk

3 This pretty fjordside village is widely accepted to be the site of Brattahlíð, where Erik the Red (Eiríkur Rauðe) built his farm in the 10th century. An easy-to-miss horseshoe-shaped section of turf is where it is believed the New World's first Christian church was built in AD 1000. Legend has it that Erik the Red's wife Þjóðhildur tried to convert him to Christianity by refusing him sex, until he was baptised. While Erik never relented, he did compromise by allowing a church to be built. A number of Norse ruins, including a longhouse and church, and the re-creation of an Inuit turf hut from the 19th century are also available to visit.

Nanortalik

4 The picture-perfect town of Nanortalik is like a film set of a New England fishing village. It is Greenland's southernmost town, and its name means place of polar bears, referring to the bear population that occasionally pass through. It is worth strolling around the town during different tides and times of the day to enjoy it in a variety of light conditions. Climb the stairs to the curious egg-shaped flagmast rock for a bird's-eye view of the town, or walk out to one of the town's landmarks – a natural stone, which at a particular angle resembles the profile of Artic explorer and national hero Knud Rasmussen.

Dogsleds & Disko

5 Dogsled under the midnight sun on the fabulously named Disko Island, Greenland's largest island. One of the best ways to get around is as the locals do; by dogsled. Greenlandic mushers harness their dogs in a fan formation as opposed to the more complicated and tangle-prone inline formation used by their counterparts in Alaska and Canada. Generally the best season to go dogsledding is March to May, when the

Getting Around

Greenland is well served by air links, while public helicopters offer a unique way of seeing the scenery.

Meet the locals while weaving through magnificent icescapes on the ferries. Ice permitting, summer services link west-coast villages.

Many people still get around by dogsled, and visitors can arrange trips ranging from one day to a two-week expedition. The best season is from March to May.

days are longer and temperatures not so extreme, but summer sledding is available on the island, which remains the only location south of the Arctic Circle where sled dogs are permitted to be kept.

Kayaking the Fjords

6 Greenlandic *qajaq* are the precursors of modern kayaks, so if you don't sea kayak in Greenland, where else would you? One of the best places to get up close to ice-choked fjords is around the village of Tasiilaq, only 100km south of the Arctic Circle. The town is an outdoor adventurer's dream landscape, surrounded by high mountains, green valleys, and water. Lots of water. A paddle from Tasiilaq across the fjord is an easy 4km, while a trip around the fjord is a more challenging 20km to 30km. Paddle up!

Sailing Greenland

7 Sail through south Greenland's most magnificent fjordland scenery from Aappilattoq, a tiny fishing village sitting on a natural inland harbour. Practically inaccessible via land, it offers some of the most spectacular water travel anywhere in the world, including the weekly *Ketil*, sailing between Nanortalik and Aappilattoq from mid-November and April, returning the same day. This unmissable voyage is full of exceptional scenic wonders, but weather and ice conditions mean it is often cancelled. With more time and patience there are yet more fabulous fjords to discover beyond Aappilattoq, though there's always a danger that all access is blocked by pesky floating ice-floes.

5

BMJ / SHUTTERSTOCK ©

CAPITAL
Saint George's

POPULATION
111,219

AREA
340 sq km

OFFICIAL LANGUAGE
English

Grenada

White sand, turquoise sea, palm trees and no crowds make Grenada's beaches truly sublime. And if the mainland's too much fun, island-hop to Carriacou and Petit Martinique.

The most southerly islands in the Windward chain, Grenada and Carriacou (plus little Petit Martinique) are best known for having been invaded by the US in the 1980s and pummeled by Hurricane Ivan in the 2000s. But the storm damage is long gone, the American occupation a distant memory, and today the islands are some of the Caribbean's most appealing.

From palm-backed white sand and translucent water to gray-black dunes and rolling breakers, the beaches are gorgeous. Grenada's corrugated coastline rises up to mist-swathed rainforest laced with hiking trails and swimmable waterfalls. St George's, with its market, forts and postcard-perfect harbor, makes for a picturesque and friendly capital, and is the departure point for ferries. And though cruise ships inject a regular flow of short-stay visitors to Grenada, you'll find all three islands refreshingly quiet and uncrowded.

Top Experiences

Carriacou

1 Enjoy peace, quiet and beautiful beaches on this friendly island. The fact that most people don't realize that there are in fact three islands in the nation of Grenada is a fitting introduction to Carriacou (*carry*-a-cou). You won't find cruise ships, big resorts or souvenir shops – this is Caribbean life the way it was 50 years ago: quiet, friendly and relaxed.

Underwater Sculpture Park

2 This underwater gallery literally lies beneath the surface of the sea, just north of St George's in Molinière Bay. The project was founded by British artist Jason de Caires Taylor and there are now around 80 works in varying condition all slowly becoming encrusted with coral growth. The life-size sculptures include a circle of women clasping hands and a man at a desk. Fish and sponges have also colonized the area making the site a fascinating mix of culture with nature. The park is accessible to both snorkelers and divers and all the dive shops on the island organize visits.

When to Go

 HIGH SEASON (Jan–Apr)

 SHOULDER (May & Dec)

LOW SEASON (Jun–Nov)

Grand Anse

3 Grenada's main resort area is a lovely long sweep of white sand fronted by turquoise water and backed by hills. It has the highest concentration of big hotels, bars, eateries and water sports on the island but its essence has not been totally lost to development. The

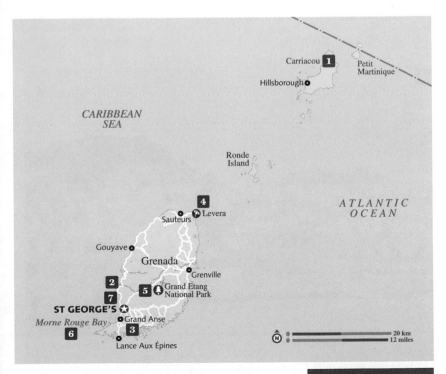

beach here is one of the island's best and is justifiably popular. Unlike some beaches in the Caribbean, it gets a good mix of visitors and locals, who come here to swim, exercise and play sports. It remains the essential Grenadian experience for many. To escape crowds, look for the small access road that spurs off the Grand Anse Rd towards the southern reaches of the bay; it leads to a small parking area and uncrowded sands.

Levera

4 Backed by low, eroding sea cliffs, Levera Beach is a wild, beautiful sweep of sand that gets few visitors. Just offshore is the high, pointed Sugar Loaf Island, while the Grenadine islands dot the horizon to the north. The beach, the mangrove swamp and the nearby pond have been incorporated into Grenada's national-park system and are an important waterfowl habitat and sea-turtle nesting site.

Grand Etang National Park

5 Two and a half miles northeast of Constantine, in eastern Grenada, after the road winds steeply up to an elevation of 1900ft, you enter Grand Etang National Park, a natural wonderland centered around a lovely lake. At the visitor center you can pay your admission, learn a little about the park and get a refreshment. There are many hiking trails within the park, varying in duration and difficulty. Some are well maintained while others are overgrown and require

Getting Around

There are a couple of flights daily between Grenada and Carriacou.

There is a large, fast boat connecting Grenada, Carriacou and Petit Martinique.

Privately run minivans are a great way to get around.

Main roads on Grenada are fairly good and rentals and taxis are available.

DARRYL BROOKS / SHUTTERSTOCK ©

the use of a guide. Within the park you'll find four of Grenada's tallest peaks, the highest of which, bizarrely enough, is the only one without a name.

Morne Rouge Bay

6 Though just down the way from popular Grand Anse Beach, development on this excellent stretch of beach has been modest so it's uncrowded. It's a brilliant example of the snow-white sand and crystal-clear blue water that the Caribbean is known for. It has shade but limited services.

Food & Drink

You'll find a full range of restaurants on the island of Grenada from roadside shacks selling fantastic local dishes to formal waterside dining around St George's and Grand Anse. On Carriacou things are a bit more low key, but there's still plenty of places to dine and the influence of travelers and yachties is evident in the presence of many international flavors. Petit Martinique has just a handful of simple restaurants.

Some essential dishes:

Roti A tasty flat bread wrapped around curried meat and vegetables.

Oil down Beef and salt pork stewed with coconut milk.

Salt fish and bake Seasoned salt fish with onion and veg, and a side of baked or fried bread.

Lambi The local name for conch.

Carib beer Brewed in Grenada and always served ice cold.

Jack Iron rum Ice sinks in this lethal local belly wash.

St George's

7 St George's is one of the most picturesque towns in the Caribbean. It's a fabulous place to explore on foot, from handsome old buildings to the Carenage harbor, with its colorful fishing boats and the bustle of supplies being loaded for other islands. One of the best reasons to wander the atmospheric streets is to discover little shops selling artful goods, unlike those near the cruise-ship docks. Interesting cafes also dot the narrow and busy streets. Visit the island's best-preserved fort, Fort Frederick, and the more than 300-year-old Fort George. You can climb to the top of both to see the cannons and bird's-eye views. Just outside the main Fort George area is a series of dark defensive tunnels to explore.

PHB.CZ (RICHARD SEMIK) / SHUTTERSTOCK ©

Grenada Chocolate

With swathes of the country covered in cocoa plantations, many of which are organic, it's no wonder that Grenada produces some excellent chocolate. The best known producer is the Grenada Chocolate Company (www.grenadachocolate.com), which makes a line of delicious dark chocolate bars that are widely sold.

To get a better idea of how it's made, go on a tour at the Diamond Chocolate Factory, near Victoria. This chocolate-making facility, housed in a former distillery built by French monks, produces the Jouvay brand of chocolate that you'll see on sale around the country. The company is owned as a co-operative by local cocoa growers. Call ahead to book a tour followed by a chance to taste the various products.

La Soufrière volcano

CAPITAL	Basse-Terre
POPULATION	405,700
AREA	1628 sq km
OFFICIAL LANGUAGES	French, Creole

Guadeloupe

Guadeloupe is a fascinating archipelago, with each island offering travelers something different while retaining its rich Franco-Caribbean culture and identity. Guadeloupe's two main islands look like the wings of a butterfly and are joined together by just a couple of bridges and a mangrove swamp.

Grande-Terre, the eastern of the two islands, has a string of beach towns that offer visitors marvelous stretches of sand to laze on and plenty of activities, while mountainous Basse-Terre, the western island, is home to the wonderful Parc National de la Guadeloupe, which is crowned by the spectacular La Soufrière volcano.

As well as the 'mainland' of Guadeloupe, there are a number of small offshore islands including Les Saintes, Marie-Galante and La Désirade, each of which gives visitors its own taste of Guadeloupe's yesteryear. These are some of the most evocative and untouched destinations in the French Antilles, and shouldn't be missed.

Top Experiences

Deshaies

1 The charmingly sleepy spot of Deshaies has just the right balance of traditional fishing village and good eating and drinking options to keep visitors coming here year-round. There's a sweet little beach framed by green hills all around, but as it's a working fishing port, the best beach for swimming and sunbathing is at nearby Grande Anse. Thanks to its sheltered bay, the village is a popular stop with yachties and sailors and has a cosmopolitan air despite its dinky size.

Pigeon Island

2 This long stretch of overlapping beachside towns and villages is a mecca for divers: they come to dive and snorkel at the superb Réserve Cousteau around little Pigeon Island, and to relax on Plage de Malendure's dark-sand beaches. The entire area is backed by steep hills and driving along this stretch of coast is pure pleasure. Plage de Malendure is not the best beach in the area, but it is one of the best in Guadeloupe for activities,

and the competition keeps the prices reasonable.

Terre-de-Haut

3 Lying 10km off Guadeloupe is Terre-de-Haut, the largest of the eight small islands that make up Les Saintes. Since the island was too hilly and

When to Go

HIGH SEASON
(Dec–May)

SHOULDER
(Jun)

LOW SEASON
(Jul–Nov)

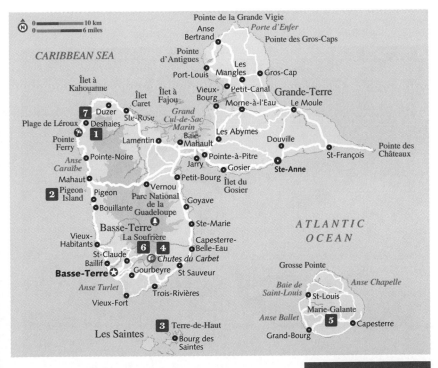

dry for sugar plantations, slavery never took hold here. Consequently, the older islanders still trace their roots to the early seafaring Norman and Breton colonists. Home to most of the island's residents, Bourg des Saintes is a picturesque village with a decidedly Norman accent. Its narrow streets are lined with whitewashed, red-roofed houses with shuttered windows and yards of flowering hibiscus.

Chutes du Carbet

4 Unless it's overcast, the drive up to the Chutes du Carbet lookout gives a view of two magnificent waterfalls plunging down a sheer mountain face. From the lookout you can see the two highest waterfalls from the upper parking lot, where a signboard marks the trailhead

to the falls' base. The well-trodden walk to the second-highest waterfall (110m) takes 20 minutes; it's about a two-hour hike to the highest waterfall (115m).

Marie-Galante

5 Marie-Galante is a delightfully undeveloped island beloved by those who enjoy the quieter pleasures in life and particularly by beach-bums who want to escape the crowds. Compared with the archipelago's other islands, Marie-Galante is relatively flat, its dual limestone plateaus rising only 150m, but even if it doesn't enjoy dramatic landscape, it has knock-out beaches, some fascinating old buildings, and some top-notch eating and sleeping options. There are three settlements on Marie-Galante. Grand-Bourg is the commercial

Getting Around

Air Caraïbes has almost daily flights between Pointe-à-Pitre and Marie-Galante.

Ferries are the principal way to get around between the islands of Guadeloupe.

Guadeloupe has a good public bus system, but for travelers visiting more than one place, a rental car is almost a necessity. Taxis are plentiful but expensive.

and administrative center of the island, while the other two villages, Capesterre on the southeast coast and St-Louis on the northern coast, are both dreamily laid-back fishing ports with good beaches in the vicinity. However, as the island can be crossed in half an hour and nearly everyone hires a car, it makes little difference where you decide to base yourself.

La Soufrière

6 Guadeloupe's active volcano towers above the Parc National de la Guadeloupe. For the adventurous, try the 1¾-hour hike to La Soufrière's sulfurous, moonscape-like summit. In addition to a close-up view of the steaming volcano, the hike offers some fine vistas of the island. A well-beaten trail starts where the road to the volcano ends with a parking lot. The trail travels along a gravel bed and continues steeply up the mountain through a cover of low shrubs and thick ferns. Start early in the morning.

Grande Anse

7 Perhaps Guadeloupe's best beach, with golden sand, huge palms and calm azure waters. This superb beach with no hotel development in sight is just 2km north of Deshaies. This is one of Basse-Terre's longest and prettiest stretches of sand. The entire place is no secret though, and you won't be alone, but it's easy to escape the crowds by walking down the bay. There are a number of beachside restaurants.

OLIVER HOFFMANN / SHUTTERSTOCK ©

Food & Drink

Guadeloupe has some fantastic eating opportunities, from simple beachside grills serving up the catch of the day to gastronomic multicourse blow outs. Fresh lobster, conch, octopus and shrimp are on most menus.

Accras A universally popular hors d'oeuvre in Guadeloupe, *accras* are fried fish, seafood or vegetables fritters in tempura. *Accras de morue* (cod) and *crevettes* (shrimp) are the most common and are both delicious.

Ti-punch Short for *petit punch*, this ubiquitous and strong cocktail is the normal *apéro* (aperitif) in Guadeloupe: a mix of rum, lime and cane syrup, but mainly rum.

Crabes farcis Stuffed crabs are a typical local dish. Normally they're stuffed with a spicy mixture of crabmeat, garlic, shallots and parsley that is then cooked in the shell.

Blaff This is the local term for white fish marinated in lime juice, garlic and peppers and then poached. It's a favorite dish in many of Guadeloupe's restaurants.

What's in a Name

At first glance, the names given to the twin islands that make up Guadeloupe proper are perplexing. The eastern island, which is smaller and flatter, is named Grande-Terre, which means 'big land', while the larger, more mountainous western island is named Basse-Terre, meaning 'flat land'.

The names were not meant to describe the terrain, however, but the winds that blow over them. The trade winds, which come from the northeast, blow *grande* (big) over the flat plains of Grande-Terre but are stopped by the mountains to the west, ending up *basse* (flat) on Basse-Terre.

Talofofo Falls

Guam

Northern Guam is mainly taken up by the US military's Andersen Base but the south is a must-see, with its rural kaleidoscope of historical villages, stunning waterfalls and pristine beaches.

CAPITAL
Hagåtña

POPULATION
163,000

AREA
544 sq km

OFFICIAL LANGUAGES
English, Chamorro

As Micronesia's most populous island, Guam is about as 'cosmopolitan' as it gets, so it cops a lot of attitude from Pacific snobs who reckon it lacks 'real island culture'. Sure, American accents are everywhere (it's an unincorporated US territory and many Guamanian homes fly the US flag) and the Chamorro language isn't spoken quite as widely as it used to be. And if you never stray from Tumon Bay – the island's glitzy duty-free shopping and accommodation hub – then undeniably you may be underwhelmed.

But the island is currently in the throes of retooling itself. There may come a day soon when Chamorro culture (long subsumed by various invasions and occupations) is promoted above all else, with an increased focus on local food and the fascinating stories underlying many of the villages.

Top Experiences

Ritidian Point

1 This national wildlife refuge, at the northernmost tip of Guam, is administered by the Fish and Wildlife Service. The star attraction is the pristine sandy beach. Azure waters, golden beaches, swaying palms – these are the paradisiacal trappings of Ritidian Point. On weekdays the beach is gloriously empty; at weekends, families and picnickers pick up the slack.

War in the Pacific National Historical Park

2 Reflect on Guam's turbulent WWII occupation. A number of former WWII battlefield sites are part of the park's historical holdings. The Asan Beach unit includes Asan Point, a big, peaceful and grassy beach park 1.6km further south, with guns, torpedoes and monuments.

Talofofo Falls

3 This popular swimming and picnic spot is set around a lovely two-tier cascade, with pools beneath each waterfall. At the bottom is a wooden swinging bridge with a splendid view of the falls. There's a 9m drop on the top fall, though it's usually gentle enough to stand beneath.

When to Go

 HIGH SEASON (Jan–May)

 SHOULDER (Jun & Nov–Dec)

 LOW SEASON (Jul–Oct)

Food & Drink

Guam has a fixation with Spam – the Hormel company has even developed a special 'Guam Spam' with a hot-and-spicy flavouring that mimics Tabasco.

The island has the best restaurant scene in Micronesia, featuring a wide range of styles and nationalities. Most of the action is centred in Tumon Bay.

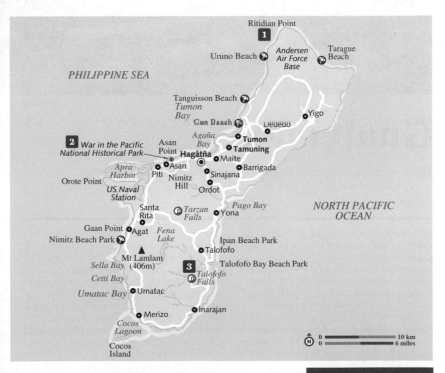

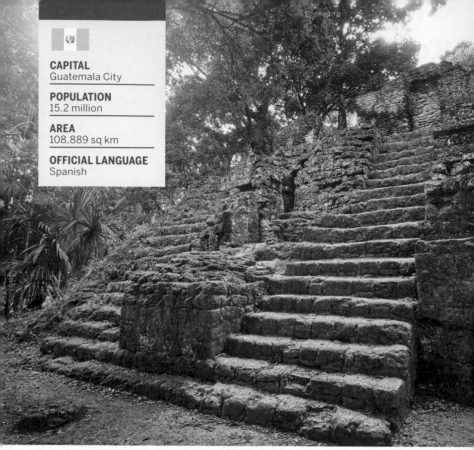

Ancient Maya ruins, Tikal

Guatemala

Mysterious and often challenging, Central America's most diverse country offers landscapes and experiences that have been captivating travelers for centuries.

Guatemala is a magical place. If you're into the Maya, the mountains, the markets, kicking back lakeside or exploring atmospheric pre-Columbian ruins and gorgeous colonial villages, you're bound to be enthralled.

Want to surf in the morning and learn Spanish in the afternoon? No problem. Descend a volcano, grab a shower and hit the sushi bar for dinner? You can do that. Check out a Maya temple and be swinging in a beachside hammock by sunset? Easy.

While many ask whatever happened to the Maya, the simple answer is nothing – they're still here, and some traditions continue to thrive. If you're interested in archaeology, the must-see sites include Tikal, and Guatemala City's superb selection of museums. Living Maya culture can be witnessed in its 'pure' form in towns such as Rabinal and sacred sites such as Laguna Chicabal. And the Maya themselves? Well, they're everywhere.

Top Experiences

Tikal

1 The remarkably restored temples that stand in this partially cleared corner of the jungle astonish for both their monumental size and architectural brilliance – as an early morning arrival at the Gran Plaza proves. Occupied for some 16 centuries, it's an amazing testament to the cultural and artistic heights scaled by this jungle civilization. A highlight is the helicopter-like vantage from towering Temple IV on the west edge of the precinct. Equally compelling is the abundance of wildlife, which can be appreciated as you stroll ancient causeways between ceremonial centers.

Antigua

2 With mammoth volcanic peaks and coffee-covered slopes as a backdrop for the scattered remnants of Spanish occupation, the former capital of Guatemala makes an appealing setting for learning Spanish, and a globally varied population come here to study at such quality institutes as Escuela de Español San José el Viejo. Nowhere else in the country packs in such a great culinary and nightlife scene, along with fabulous souvenir shopping in the markets, a sweet little central plaza replete with bubbling fountain, and picture-postcard vistas around every corner.

Chichicastenango

3 More than just a place to shop, 'Chichi' is a vivid window on indigenous tradition, an ancient crossroads for the area's K'iche' Maya–speaking inhabitants, and a spiritually charged site. At Santo Tomás church in the center of town and the hill of Pascual Abaj on its southern edge, Maya rituals blend with Christian iconography to the point where it's hard to tell where one ends and the other begins. The twice-weekly market is a good place for souvenir hunting, though – particularly if you're after finely woven textiles or carved wooden masks.

MEUNIERD / SHUTTERSTOCK ©

375

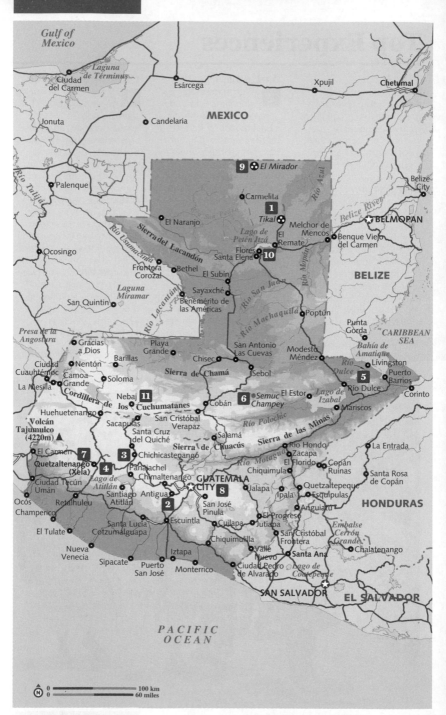

Gulf of
Mexico

Laguna
de Términos
Ciudad
del Carmen

Jonuta

Candelaria

Esárcega

Xpujil

Chetumal

MEXICO

9 ☢ *El Mirador*

Belize
City

Palenque

El Naranjo

Carmelita

1

Río Azul

Belize River

★ **BELMOPAN**

Ocosingo

Sierra del Lacandón

Río Usumacinta

Frontera
Corozal

Bethel

El Naranjo

Lago de
Petén Itzá

El
Remate

Melchor de
Mencos

Santa Elena **10**

Flores

Benque Viejo
del Carmen

San Quintin

Laguna
Miramar

Río Lacantún

El Subín

Sayaxché

Benemérito de
las Américas

Río San Juan

Río Mopán

BELIZE

Presa de la
Angostura

Gracias
a Dios

Playa
Grande

Río Machaquilá

Poptún

Punta
Gorda

*CARIBBEAN
SEA*

Barillas

Chisec

San Antonio
Las Cuevas

Modesto
Méndez

*Bahía de
Amatique*

Ciudad
Cuauhtémoc

Nentón

Camoa
Grande

Soloma

Sierra de Chamá

Sebol

Río
Dulce

Livingston

Puerto
Barrios

La Mesilla

Cordillera de los

Nebaj **11**
Cuchumatanes

Cobán

6 *Semuc
Champey*

El Estor

Lago de
Izabal

Río Dulce **5**

Mariscos

Corinto

Huehuetenango

Sacapulas

San Cristóbal
Verapaz

Río Polochic

**Volcán
Tajumulco
(4220m)** ▲

Santa Cruz
del Quiché

Salamá

Sierra de las Minas

El Carmen **7**

3 Chichicastenango

Sierra de Chuacús

Río Hondo
Zacapa

La Entrada

**Quetzaltenango
(Xela)**

4

Panajachel

El Florido

Copán
Ruinas

Ciudad Tecún
Umán

Santiago
Atitlán

Lago de
Atitlán

Chimaltenango

**GUATEMALA
CITY**

Chiquimula

Quetzaltepeque

Santa Rosa
de Copán

Ocós

Retalhuleu

2

Antigua

8

Jalapa

Ipala

Esquipulas

HONDURAS

Champerico

Santa Lucía
Cotzumalguapa

San José
Pinula

Anguiatú

El Tulate

Nueva
Venecia

Escuintla

Cuilapa

Jutiapa

El Progreso

San Cristóbal
Frontera

*Embalse
Cerrón
Grande*

Sipacate

Iztapa

Puerto
San José

Monterrico

Chiquimulilla

Valle
Nuevo

Ciudad Pedro
de Alvarado

Santa Ana

Lago de
Coatepeque

Chalatenango

SAN SALVADOR ★

EL SALVADOR

*PACIFIC
OCEAN*

Ⓝ 0 ————————— 100 km
0 ————————— 60 miles

Lago de Atitlán

4 Possibly the single worthiest destination in Guatemala, Atitlán elicits poetic outbursts from even the most seasoned traveler. Of volcanic origin, the alternately placid and turbulent lake is ringed by volcanoes and its shores are studded with villages such as Santiago Atitlán, with its thriving indigenous culture, and

Best on Film

Aquí me Quedo (Rodolfo Espinoza; 2010) Subtle political commentary, black comedy and satire abound in this story of a kidnapping, shot in and around Quetzaltenango.

When the Mountains Tremble (Pamela Yates & Newton Thomas Sigel; 1983) Documentary featuring Susan Sarandon and Rigoberta Menchú, telling the story of the civil war.

Capsulas (Verónica Riedel; 2011) A look at greed, corruption and the drug trade from one of Guatemala's few female directors.

Best in Print

The President (Miguel Ángel Asturias; 1946) Nobel Prize–winning Guatemalan author takes some not-too-subtle jabs at the country's long line of dictators.

A Mayan Life (Gaspar Pedro Gonzáles; 1995) The first published novel by a Maya author is an excellent study of rural Guatemalan life.

The Art of Political Murder (Francisco Goldman; 2008) Meticulously researched account of the assassination of Bishop Gerardi.

San Marcos, a haven for seekers who plug into the lake's cosmic energy. Plus there are enough activities – paragliding from Santa Catarina Palopó, kayaking around Santa Cruz La Laguna or hiking the glorious lakeshore trails – to make a longer stay viable.

Río Dulce

5 The Río Dulce (literally, 'sweet river') connects Guatemala's largest lake with the Caribbean coast, and winding along it, through a steep-walled valley, surrounded by lush vegetation, bird calls and the (very occasional) manatee is Guatemala's classic, don't-miss-it boat ride. This is no tourist cruise – the river is a way of life and a means of transportation around here – but you get to stop at a couple of places to visit river-dwelling communities and hot springs, making for a magical, unforgettable experience.

Semuc Champey

6 Guatemala doesn't have all that many freshwater swimming

When to Go

HIGH SEASON
(Dec–Apr & Jun–Jul)
Hotel prices are at their highest during Christmas, New Year and Easter.

SHOULDER
(Oct–Nov)
Rains begin to ease up, but October is peak hurricane season.

LOW SEASON
(May & Aug–Sep)
Prices drop, crowds thin out at archaeological sites, and booking accommodation is rarely necessary.

holes that you'd really want to dive into, but the jungle-shrouded oasis of Semuc Champey is most definitely an exception. Turquoise-colored water

Guatemala's Ancient Ruins

Stretching at its peak from northern El Salvador to the Gulf of Mexico, the Maya empire during its Classic period was arguably pre-Hispanic America's most brilliant civilization. The great ceremonial and cultural centers in Guatemala included Quiriguá, Kaminaljuyú, Tikal, Uaxactún, Río Azul, El Perú, Yaxhá, Dos Pilas and Piedras Negras. Copán in Honduras also gained and lost importance as the empire and its individual kingdoms ebbed and waned.

Visiting a Maya ruin can be a powerful experience, a true step back in time. While some sites are little more than a pile of rubble or some grassy mounds, others (such as Tikal and Copán) have been extensively restored, and the temples, plazas and ballcourts give an excellent insight into what life must have been like in these places.

Getting Around

 If you're accustomed to crazy Latino traffic, driving is a great way to get off the beaten track.

 In areas where there is no bus service pick-up trucks are a common way to get around. Flag one down wherever, climb into the back and hang on.

 'Chicken buses' – recycled US school buses – are cheap, go everywhere, stop for everybody, and have no maximum capacity. Pullman buses run only on major highways and they're the most comfortable choice. Shuttle buses, which can be booked through travel agents and hotels, run between major tourist sights and offer door-to-door service.

cascades down a series of limestone pools, creating an idyllic setting that many call the most beautiful place in the country. You can make it out here on a rushed day tour, but you'd be mad to – Semuc and its surrounds are rural Guatemala at its finest.

Quetzaltenango

7 Quetzaltenango – 'Xela' to most everyone – is a kinder, gentler urban experience than the capital, and its blend of mountain scenery, highlands indigenous life, handsome architecture and urban sophistication attracts outsiders after an authentic slice of city life in Guatemala. Come here to study Spanish at the numerous language institutes, or make it a base for excursions to such excellent high-altitude destinations as Laguna Chicabal, a crater lake and Maya pilgrimage site, or the Fuentes Georginas, a natural hotsprings resort ensconced in a verdant valley.

Guatemala City

8 Vibrant and raw, often confronting and occasionally surprising, the nation's capital is very much a love it or leave it proposition. Many choose the latter – and as fast as they can – but those who hang around and look behind the drab architecture and scruffy edges find a city teeming with life. For culture vultures, fine diners, mall rats, live-music lovers and city people in general, the capital has a buzz that's unmatched in the rest of the country.

El Mirador

9 For true adventurers, the trek to El Mirador is a thrilling chance to explore the origins of Maya history; it is still being uncovered by archaeologists whom you're likely to meet at the site. Among the hundreds of vegetation-shrouded temples is the tallest pyramid in the Maya world, La Danta, which can be climbed for panoramic views of the jungle canopy.

It's at least a six-day hike there and back through the mud and mosquitoes, unless you hop a chopper to the site.

Flores

10 An isle of calm at the threshold of a vast jungle reserve, Flores is both a base for exploring El Petén and a stunning spot to recharge your rambling batteries. Unwinding at the numerous dining and drinking terraces that look across Lago de Petén Ixtá, or cruising in a weathered long boat to even smaller islets, you're likely to find companions for forays to Tikal or more remote places. But the picturesqueness of the town, with its captivating tableau of distant villages, is reason enough to head here.

Nebaj

11 A pocket of indigenous culture in a remote (though easily accessed) alpine setting, Nebaj is little visited, yet it is essential Guatemala. Homeland of the resilient Ixil Maya people, whose language and vivid culture survived the harshest persecutions during the civil war era, it's also a starting point for hikes through the spectacular Cuchumatanes mountain range, with dozens of intensely traditional villages, such as Cocop and Chajul, where community-run lodgings offer locals much-needed extra income and visitors a glimpse into this fascinating corner of the world.

SOFT_LIGHT / SHUTTERSTOCK ©

Scarlet Macaws

To see rare scarlet macaws in the wild, the place to head is La Ruta Guacamaya (the Scarlet Macaw Trail) of El Perú ruins in El Petén.

Maya Rituals

Visitors may be able to observe Maya ceremonies in places such as the Pascual Abaj shrine and the altars on the shore of Laguna Chicabal, but many traditional rites are off-limits to foreigners.

6

2

ALEKSANDAR TODOROVIC / SHUTTER

La Dame de Mali, Fouta Djalon

Guinea

Imagine you're travelling on smooth highways, and then get tempted by a dusty turn-off signed Adventure. Well, that turn-off is Guinea. Little known to most of the world, this is a land of surprising beauty; from the rolling mountain plateau of Fouta Djalon to wide Sahelian lands and thick forests.

Overland drivers have long been drawn here for the challenge of steering their vehicles over rocks and washed-out paths. Nature lovers lose themselves on long hikes past plunging waterfalls, proud hills and tiny villages; or by tracking chimpanzees through sticky rainforest.

But the best thing about Guinea is that almost nobody else bothers to take this turn-off – meaning you'll likely have the country to yourself.

Devastatingly, the country was caught up in the West Africa Ebola outbreak in 2014. The country was officially declared Ebola-free in June 2016, and related travel restrictions were lifted.

CAPITAL
Conakry

POPULATION
11.8 million

AREA
245,857 sq km

OFFICIAL LANGUAGES
French, Malinke,
Pulaar (Fula), Susu

Top Experiences

Îles de Los

 Fancy stretching out on palm-fringed strands, sipping fresh coconut juice? A 30-minute boat ride off Conakry, the Îles de Los are a small huddle of palm-fringed islands that tempt with tropical beach dreams. They have beautifully forested, bird-filled interiors that reward some gentle exploration.

Fouta Djalon

 Green rolling hills, balmy temperatures, forest-filled valleys and gushing waterfalls make the Fouta Djalon region one of West Africa's most enchanting corners. But this undulating, kilometre-high, plateau isn't just pleasing to the eye, it's also superb hiking country, where experienced local guides can take you exploring along a web of trails.

Parc National du Haut Niger

 Covering some 1200 sq km, this national park is one of West Africa's last significant stands of tropical dry forest and one of the most important protected areas in Guinea. The forest, pock marked with areas of tall grassland savannah and run through by the River Niger, has plenty of wildlife, including chimpanzees, duikers, crocodiles and hippos.

When to Go

HIGH SEASON
(Dec–Feb)

SHOULDER
(Mar–Jul)

LOW SEASON
(Aug–Oct)

Food & Drink

You do not come to Guinea for the food. Even in Conakry proper restaurants are a little thin on the ground. Your diet will normally be limited to a lacklustre hotel restaurant meal or a street stall serving *riz gras* (rice fried in oil and tomato paste and served with fried fish or meat).

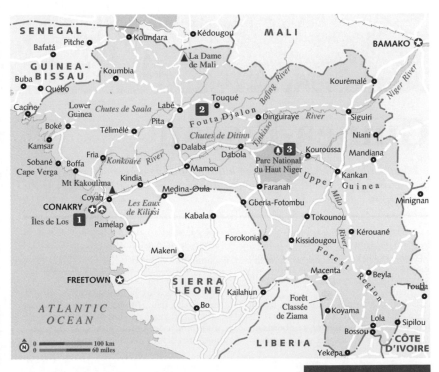

CAPITAL
Bissau

POPULATION
1.7 million

AREA
36,125 sq km

OFFICIAL LANGUAGES
Crioulo, Portuguese,
French, another 20 or
so dialects

Saltwater hippo, Ilha de Orango

Guinea-Bissau

Like a microcosm of Africa, this tiny nation contains multitudes – of landscapes, peoples, cultures and plant and animal life. All of it within reach of the capital, Bissau.

Faded colonial-era houses sag, from tropical decay and the weight of history. Decades of Portuguese colonisation were followed by a long painful liberation struggle and then cycles of civil war and political chaos.

Despite hardships and poverty, Bissau-Guineans persevere. The jokes, like the music, are loud but tender. The bowls of grilled oysters are served with a sauce spicy enough to give a kick, but not so strong as to mask the bitterness.

The jewel in the country's crown is the labyrinth of tropical islands that make up the Arquipélago dos Bijagós. Long white-sand beaches are lapped by waters brimming with fish. Hippos, monkeys, chimps and buffaloes thrive in protected reserves and hundreds of bird species call its vast mangroves and wetlands home.

Top Experiences

Ilha de Orango

1 The heart of Parque Nacional das Ilhas de Orango, Ilha de Orango is the burial site of the Bijagós kings and queens. It's also the site of Anôr Lagoon, where you can spot rare saltwater hippos – considered sacred as they live in both the sea and freshwater.

Parque Nacional de Cantanhez

2 The hardest-to-reach places are often the most beautiful, and so it goes with Parque Nacional de Cantanhez – more than 1000 sq km of the country's last rainforest. With a dense web of giant kapok trees, lianas and palm trees (a total of more than 200 plant species), you'll need to get out on a trail to spot elephants, baboons, buffaloes, colobus monkeys, Africa's western-most troupe of chimpanzees and many species of birds.

Bolama

3 The Portuguese capital of Guinea-Bissau from 1879 to 1943, Bolama's shores are awash with crumbling relics that were abandoned after independence. Tree-lined boulevards are mapped out by lamp posts that no longer shine, and the colonial barracks have been recast as a hospital, now – like much of the island – in a dark and desolate state.

Food & Drink

Seafood is the highlight, including shrimp, oysters and meaty *bica* (sea bream). A national favourite is *chabeu*: deep-fried fish served in a thick palm-oil sauce. Street food includes small pieces of beef, sheep or goat meat skewered and grilled over a fire.

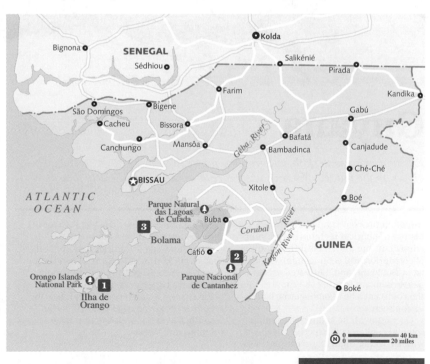

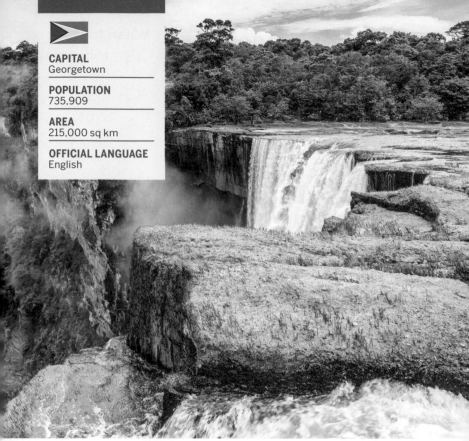

CAPITAL
Georgetown

POPULATION
735,909

AREA
215,000 sq km

OFFICIAL LANGUAGE
English

Kaieteur Falls

Guyana

From towering waterfalls and tropical jungle to caiman-filled rivers, few places on the planet offer raw adventure as authentic as densely forested Guyana.

Although the country has a troubled history of political instability and inter-ethnic tension, underneath the headlines of corruption and economic mismanage-ment is a joyful and motivated mix of people who are turning the country into the continent's best-kept ecotourism desti-nation secret.

Georgetown, the country's crumbling colonial capital, is distinctly Caribbean with a rocking nightlife, great places to

eat and an edgy market. The interior of the country is more Amazonian with its Amerindian communities and unparallel-ed wildlife-viewing opportunities tucked quietly away from the capital's hoopla. From sea turtle nesting grounds along the country's north coast to riding with *vaqueros* (cowboys) at a ranch in the south, Guyana is well worth the mud, bumps and sweat.

Top Experiences

Kaieteur Falls

1 Stand on the ledge of one of the world's highest single-drop fall at Kaieteur Falls. Watching 30,000 gallons of water shooting over a 250m cliff in the middle of a misty, ancient jungle without another tourist in sight is a once-in-a-lifetime experience.

Rupununi Savanna

2 Paddle though thriving populations of giant river otters and black caimans in these Africa-like plains scattered with Amerindian villages, small 'islands' of jungle and an exceptional diversity of wildlife. Rivers full of water lilies cut through plains of golden grasses, while an array of birds fly across the sky.

Shell Beach

3 Take a boat ride through rivers, mangrove swamps and savannahs to Shell Beach, which extends for about 140km toward the Venezuelan border. It's a nesting site for four of Guyana's eight sea turtle species and one of the least developed areas of the entire South American coastline.

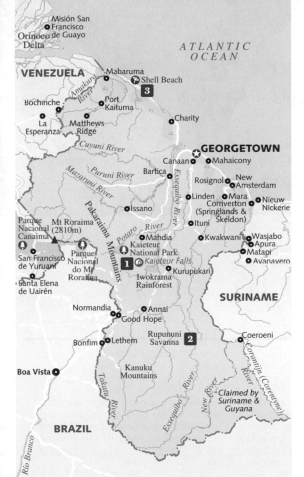

Food & Drink

Some of the best food in Guyana can be had for a few coins in Georgetown.

Bake and saltfish Fried bread and salted cod.

Cow heel soup Caribbean soup made with split peas, vegetables, dumplings and cow heels.

Farine Tasty cassava meal served as an accompaniment.

Pepper pot A savory Amerindian game-and-cassava stew.

When to Go

HIGH SEASON (mid-Nov–mid-Jan)

SHOULDER (mid-Jan–Apr & Sep–mid-Nov)

LOW SEASON (May–Aug)

CAPITAL
Port-au-Prince

POPULATION
10.49 million

AREA
27,750 sq km

OFFICIAL LANGUAGES
Kreyol (Haitian
Creole), French

Haiti

Tranquil beaches, tumbling waterfalls and pine-tree-capped mountains dot the varied and striking landscape, easily rivaling the natural beauty found anywhere else in the Caribbean.

The most common phrase in Haiti might surprise you. It's *'pa gen pwoblem,'* and it translates to 'no have problem.' Haitians use it in a dizzying array of contexts: responding to thank-yous, asserting well-being, filling awkward silences. Despite Haiti's well-documented struggles, exacerbated lately by natural disasters, proud Haitians use the phrase sincerely, conveying an uncanny ability to live in the moment and appreciate what they do have, which is quite a lot.

The world's only successful slave rebellion happened here, and the music, art and culture that came with it make Haiti entirely unique. As those who come to assist Haiti often learn, an encounter with the soul of this fascinating, beautiful country often benefits a traveler far more than one could ever hope to help it.

Top Experiences

Carnival at Jacmel

1 You want shiny sequins and sanitized carnival bling? Plenty of places will serve that up for you. Jacmel's street theater is another game altogether, close to the surreal, where individuals and troupes parade and act in homemade costumes and papier-mâché masks from local artisans. Vodou, sex, death and revolution all play their part, mixed with street music and wild antics, in a parade where both crowd and performers mix as participants. And where else will you see a donkey dressed in sneakers and hat, talking on a cell phone?

Citadelle la Ferrière

2 If ever a country settled on making a statement of intent on winning its independence, Haiti found it in the mighty Citadelle la Ferrière. A giant battleship of a fortress sitting atop a mountain crag, with a Versailles-like ruined palace at its base, it commands its landscape as a proud symbol of the world's first black republic. Epic in concept and execution and largely hidden from the world's gaze, it easily holds its own against the best historical sites the Americas can offer.

When to Go

 HIGH SEASON (Nov–Mar)

 SHOULDER (Apr–Jun)

 LOW SEASON (Aug–Oct)

Parc National la Visite

3 The perfect hike is through Parc National la Visite, from Furcy, high above Port-au-Prince, down to Seguin. The park still has plenty of Haiti's original pine forest, as well as weird broken rock formations, and as the scenery opens up, great views out to the Caribbean Sea. A long day's

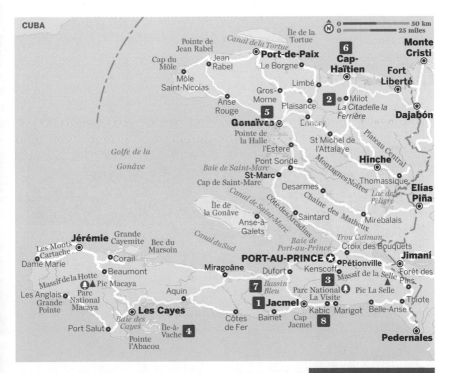

walk on a path shared with local farmers, it's the perfect leg-stretching antidote to the buzz of the big city.

Île-à-Vache

4 The so-called 'Island of Cows,' Île-à-Vache lies about 15km south of Les Cayes. In the 16th century it was a base for the Welsh pirate Henry Morgan as he terrorized Santo Domingo and Colombia. The island today is scattered with rural houses, plantations, mangroves, the odd Arawak burial ground and some great beaches.

Vodou Ceremony

5 If you're thinking zombies and dolls with pins in them, you need to disconnect from Hollywood. Vodou is the wellspring of the Haitian character, a spiritual religion borne of the country's African roots, but which took adopted practices from both the island's original Indian inhabitants and French colonial masters. Attending a Vodou ceremony, with its drums and sung prayers, bright imagery and often-healing nature is the best way to plug yourself in to Haiti's subconscious. People from all over Haiti congregate near Gonaïves to take part in the marathon ceremonies of Souvenance and Soukri – the two biggest Vodou festivals in the country.

Cap-Haïtien

6 Haiti's second city feels a world away from the throng and hustle of Port-au-Prince. During the French colonial era it was the richest city in the Caribbean, and even if that grandeur has long since faded, the city still maintains a relaxed atmosphere, and the old port architec-

Getting Around

Haiti's small size means that flights are short, saving hours on bad roads.

Getting around Haiti by bus and minibus isn't always comfortable, but it's the cheapest way to travel and services run to most places you'll want to get to.

Terrible roads, a lack of road signs, and the perils of wayward pedestrians and traffic are all part of the mix.

6

ROMROODPHOTO / SHUTTERSTOCK ©

ture of high shop fronts and balconies makes it a pleasant place to wander. Most people refer to the city simply as 'Cap,' or 'O'Kap' in the high-lilting local Kreyol accent of its residents. There isn't too much to do in Cap-Haïtien beyond enjoy the atmosphere, but it's an ideal place to base yourself to enjoy the nearby attractions, including the Citadelle la Ferrière and the beaches around Plage Labadie.

Bassin Bleu

7 Bassin Bleu is tucked into the mountains 12km northwest of Jacmel, a series of three cobalt-blue pools linked by waterfalls that make up one of the prettiest swimming holes in Haiti. The three pools are Bassin Clair, Bassin Bleu and Bassin Palmiste. Bassin Clair is the most beautiful of the three, deep into the mountain at the bottom of the waterfall, sheltered and surrounded by smooth rocks draped with maidenhair and creeper ferns. You're sadly less likely to see the nymphs that, according to legend, live in the grottoes, although be

warned that they've been known to grab divers attempting to discover the true depth of the pool.

Kabic

8 About 30 minutes east of Jacmel, just down the street from Cayes Jacmel, this small fishing village turned lush Bohe-mian beach getaway graced the map just a few years ago, attracting artist types with a desire to feel closer to nature and further from the gritty capital. The town is tiny, with just a few hotels and restaurants, bit it's making waves with its azure waters and burgeoning surf school.

TONY WHEELER / GETTY IMAGES ©

Food & Drink

In Haiti you can spend just a few gourdes on *fritay* (fried street food) or dine in posh Pétionville for US$30 a dish. The most typical eatery is a *bar-resto* (a bar-restaurant, less formal than a proper restaurant), with a plateful of goat or chicken with plantains, salad and a beer, all for US$5. Vegetables aren't common, but there's plenty of fresh fruit. Excellent seafood is abundant along the coast.

Voudou Flags

Brightly sparkling Vodou flags are one of Haiti's more unusual and eye-catching forms of art. Used during Vodou services, the *drapo* (flags) are magnificent affairs, made of thousands of beads and sequins sewn onto sacking, which catch the light from every angle. The Bel Air district is the traditional center of Vodou flag production, and it's possible to go direct to the artists themselves, if you're after souvenirs. Artists to look out for are Silva Joseph, a Vodou priest, and Yves Telemaque. There are also a couple of good flag artists in the district of Nazon, such as Ronald Gouin and Georges Valris.

Honduras

With glorious diving around the Bay Islands, ancient Maya ruins, historic colonial towns, Caribbean beaches and steamy mountain jungles, Honduras is waiting to be rediscovered.

<table>
<tr><td>CAPITAL
Tegucigalpa</td></tr>
<tr><td>POPULATION
8.8 million</td></tr>
<tr><td>AREA
112,090 sq km</td></tr>
<tr><td>OFFICIAL LANGUAGE
Spanish</td></tr>
</table>

Honduras, so often hurried through or avoided entirely due to its dangerous image, is actually a vibrant and fascinating place with an enormous amount to offer intrepid travelers. After a decade in which the country spiraled into a whirlwind of terrible violence, Honduras has very definitely begun the journey back from the abyss, and while the challenges ahead are still significant, things haven't looked this positive for years.

Attractions include the Maya ruins of Copán, the pristine diving of the Bay Islands and the majestic scenery of over a dozen national parks. Need another reason to come here? It's also one of the cheapest countries in the region, and you'll be able to do activities for a fraction of the price you'll pay in its neighbors. It's important to take care in the cities, but other than that, Honduras is back open for business and just waiting to be discovered.

Top Experiences

Bay Islands

Spectacular diving and snorkeling draws visitors from around the world to the three Bay Islands – Roatán, Utila and Guanaja – about 50km off the north coast of Honduras. Their reefs are part of the second-largest barrier reef in the world after Australia's Great Barrier Reef.

Copán Ruinas

One of the most important of all Maya civilizations lived, prospered then mysteriously crumbled around the Copán archaeological site, now a Unesco World Heritage Site and a short walk from the charming town of Copán Ruinas. Today you can marvel at intricate stone carvings and epic ancient structures tracing back to an extraordinary Maya empire.

Lago de Yojoa

Search for a quetzal in the cloud forests that rise above the stunningly undisturbed natural world around Lago de Yojoa. Largely undeveloped and ringed by dense tropical forest, this exceptionally scenic lake has world-class birdlife: the latest species count is up to 485 – over half the total in Honduras.

When to Go

☀ **HIGH SEASON**
(Jun–Sep)

☀ **SHOULDER**
(Mar–Apr)

☂ **LOW SEASON**
(Oct–Feb)

Food & Drink

Baleada A traditional Honduran staple made up of a flour tortilla folded in half and filled with refried beans.

Casabe Crispy flat bread

Pan de coco Coconut bread.

Pinchos Grilled meat kebabs.

Tapado Legendary Garifuna fish soup prepared with coconut and spices.

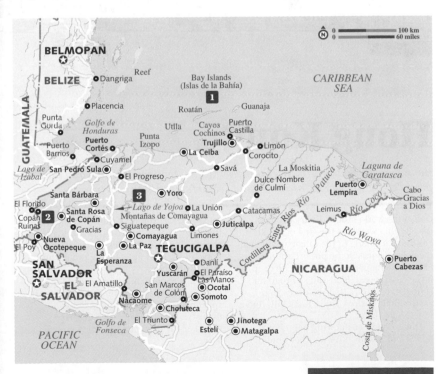

Skyscrapers overlooking Victoria Harbour

CAPITAL
Hong Kong

POPULATION
7.18 million

AREA
1104 sq km

OFFICIAL LANGUAGES
Cantonese, English

Hong Kong

*Hong Kong welcomes with an iconic skyline, a legendary kitchen, and lush,
protected nature where rare birds and colourful traditions thrive.*

One of the world's top culinary capitals,
the city that worships the God of Cookery
has many a demon in the kitchen, whether
the deliciousness in the pot is Cantonese,
Sichuanese, Japanese or French. So deep
is the city's love of food and so broad its
culinary repertoire that whatever your
gastronomic desires, Hong Kong will find a
way to sate them.

Hong Kong's enchanting neighbourhoods and islands offer another kind of
sensory feast. You may find yourself swaying along on a historic double-decker tram,
cheering with the hordes at the city-centre
horse races, or simply gazing out at the
glorious harbour.

Escape the city limits on one of the
world's smoothest transport systems and
spend your day wandering in a Song-
dynasty village, hiking on a deserted
island or kayaking among volcanic sea
arches.

Top Experiences

Star Ferry

1 A floating piece of Hong Kong heritage and a sightseeing bargain, the legendary Star Ferry was founded in 1880 and plies the waters of Victoria Harbour in the service of regular commuters and tourists. At only HK$2.50, the 15-minute ride with views of Hong Kong's iconic skyline must be one of the world's best-value cruises. While the vista is more dramatic when you're Island-bound, the art deco Kowloon pier, resembling a finger pointing over to the Island, is, some think, more charming.

The Peak

2 Rising above the financial heart of Hong Kong, Victoria Peak offers superlative views of the city and the countryside beyond. Ride the hair-raising Peak Tram – Asia's first cable funicular, in operation since 1888 – to the cooler climes at the top, as skyscrapers and apartment blocks recede into the distance. At dusk Victoria Harbour glitters like the Milky Way on a sci-fi movie poster, mysterious and full of promise, as the lights come on.

Mong Kok Markets

3 With its eclectic speciality markets Mong Kok is your best bet for a rewarding shopping crawl. Ladies' Market has a mile-long wardrobe covering everything from 'I Love HK' rugby shirts to granny swimwear. Exotic seeds and gardening tools sit next to buckets of fragrant florals in the flower market. Stalls displaying colourful aquatic life in softly humming, UV-lit tanks line the streets of the goldfish market. There are vertical markets too – a buzzing computer mall, and a multistorey gadget-lovers' heaven.

Man Mo Temple

4 Experience Chinese folk religiosity in Soho. Permanently wreathed in sandalwood

JOSE L VILCHEZ / SHUTTERSTOCK ©

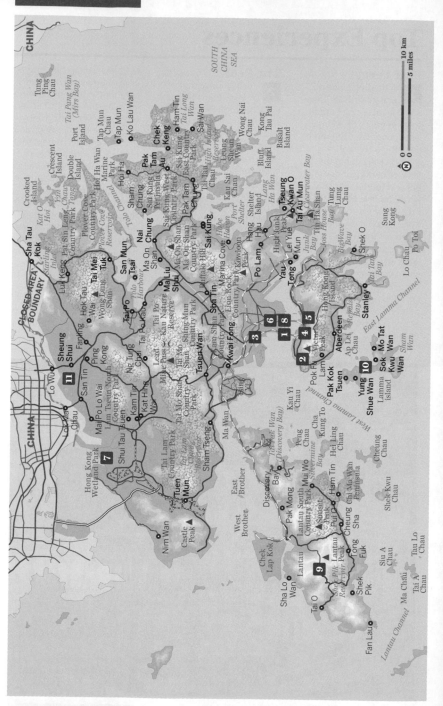

Best on Film

Infernal Affairs (2002) The crime-thriller that inspired Scorsese's *The Departed*.

Election I and II (2005 and 2006) A complex two-part film noir about elections inside a Triad society.

Night and Fog (2010) Auteur Ann Hui's darkly realistic drama on domestic violence and the lives of migrant women.

The Grandmaster (2013) Wong Kar-wai's stylish martial-arts drama about the life of Wing Chun grandmaster Ip Man.

Comrades: Almost a Love Story (1996) Two mainland migrants take a reality check in the maddening city.

Trivisia (2016) Engaging and reflective action crime thriller produced by Johnnie To and Yau Nai-hoi.

Food & Drink

Dim Sum – a Fact of Life
Morning dim sum is a daily ritual for many retirees and a tasty excuse for a family reunion at the weekend.

Tea Break When mid-afternoon comes, *cha chaan tangs* (tea houses) are full of elderly folks debating the morning's meat prices and stock-market fluctuations. They're also boltholes for many a stressed office worker.

Late-Night Sweets After dinner, locals like to head to a dessert shop for sweet soups and other Chinese-style or fusion desserts, such as black sesame soup and durian crepes.

Steamy Winter In winter a hot-pot at a *dai pai dong* (food stall) or a restaurant is a soul-warming, convivial experience. Dip slivers of meat, seafood and vegetables in a vat of steaming broth.

smoke from the hanging incense coils, the famous temple is dedicated to Man (literature) and Mo (war) and the gods who govern them. Formerly a cultural and political focal point for the local Chinese, the temple now commands a following beyond conscientious students and the martially inclined, as locals and tourists come to perform age-old rites and have their fortunes told.

Wan Chai Dining

5 If you were to hurl yourself, eyes closed, into a random neighbourhood and expect to emerge smacking your lips, you'd stand the best chance if you were in Wan Chai. The district is home to a great many restaurants suiting a range of pocket sizes. Regional Chinese cooking, European cuisines, Asian kitchens, East–West fusion, classy, midrange, hole in the wall... just name your craving and head on down to the Wanch; you're certain to find it there.

Temple Street Night Market

6 Beneath the glare of naked bulbs, hundreds of stalls sell a vast array of booty, from sex toys

When to Go

HIGH SEASON
(Oct–early Dec, Chinese New Year)
With moderate temperatures and clear skies, year's end is the best time to visit.

SHOULDER
(Jan–May)
January and February are cloudy and cold but dry; it's warmer from March to May but humid.

LOW SEASON
(Jun–Sep)
Sweltering and humid; beware of typhoons in September.

to Nepalese daggers. You can browse for handy gadgets or quirky souvenirs, and test your bargaining skills. Nearby, fortune-tellers beckon in English from dimly lit tents, and Cantonese opera singers strike a pose. If you're hungry, the many open-air stalls offer snacks or a seafood feast.

'Pantyhose' Milk Tea

Teahouses (*cha chaan tangs*) are perhaps best known for their Hong Kong–style 'pantyhose' milk tea (奶茶; *nai cha*) – a strong brew made from a blend of several types of black tea with crushed egg shells thrown in for silkiness. It's filtered through a fabric that hangs like a stocking, hence the name, and drunk with evaporated milk. 'Pantyhose' milk tea is sometimes mixed with three parts coffee to create the quintessential Hong Kong drink, tea-coffee or *yin yeung*, meaning 'mandarin duck', a symbol of matrimonial harmony.

Getting Around

Relatively fast, buses are an indispensable form of transport to places not reachable by the Mass Transit Railway (MTR) or after midnight.

Hong Kong's MTR system covers most of the city and is the easiest way to get around. Most lines run from 6am to after midnight.

Taxis are cheap compared to Europe and North America. All run on meter.

Trams are slow, but the upper deck offers great views. Runs along the northern strip of Hong Kong Island, from 6am to midnight.

Sure it's touristy, but its mesmerising and impenetrable aura makes everyone – including locals – feel like a welcome visitor.

Hong Kong Wetland Park

7 Surreally nestled under an imposing arc of apartment towers, this 61-hectare ecological park in crowded Tin Shui Wai is a swampy haven of biodiversity. This is urban/nature juxtaposition at its best and, curiously, most harmonious. Precious ecosystems in this far-flung yet easily accessible part of the New Territories provide tranquil habitats for a range of waterfowl and other wildlife. Try to forget the man-made world for a moment and delve into a landscape of mangroves, rivers and fish-filled ponds.

Shopping in Tsim Sha Tsui

8 An afternoon's visit to Tsim Sha Tsui's shopping quarters should yield a few gems. If you're seeking Chinese-style gifts, comb the streets near the southern end of the area for that silk gown, teapot or trinket. If glamour is what floats your boat, join the uber-wealthy mainland tourists for a card-swiping marathon in the mile-long block of luxury malls along Canton Rd. Want something unique? Head over to Granville Rd for that super-sized orange blazer or a micromall nearby for those asymmetrical earrings and thigh-high boots.

Big Buddha

9 A favourite with local day trippers and foreign visitors alike, the world's biggest outdoor seated Buddha lords over the western hills of Lantau Island. Visit this serene giant via the Ngong Ping 360 cable-car. Negotiate the 268 steps to the three-platform altar on which it is seated and check out the three halls along the way. Reward yourself with some monk food at the popular vegetarian restaurant in Po Lin Monastery below. Buddha's Birthday in May is a colourful time to visit this important pilgrimage site.

Exploring Lamma

10 If there were a soundtrack for the island of Lamma, it would be reggae. The island's laid-back vibe attracts herb-growers, musicians and New Age therapists from a rainbow of cultures. Village shops stock prosecco, and island mongrels respond to commands in French. If you hike to the nearest beach, your unlikely compass will be three coal-fired plants against the skyline, looking more trippy than grim. Then, in the glow of the day's final rays, head back for fried calamari and beer by the pier.

Walled Villages of Yuen Long

11 Let Yuen Long's walled villages take you back over half a millennium to a wild and windy time when piracy was rife along the South China coast. Isolated from China's administrative heart, Hong Kong, with its treacherous shores and mountainous terrain, was an excellent hideout for pirates. Its earliest inhabitants built villages with high walls, some guarded by cannons, to protect themselves. Inside these walls today you'll see ancestral halls, courtyards, pagodas, temples and ancient farming implements – vestiges of Hong Kong's pre-colonial history, all carefully restored.

Clockenflap

The highlight in Hong Kong's live-music calendar is the excellent, three-day Clockenflap, featuring local, regional and international acts performing at the West Kowloon promenade.

'Beat the Little Man'

Come March, witness folk sorcery performed by rent-a-curse grannies; rapping curses, they pound cut-outs of clients' enemies with a shoe.

9

7

CAPITAL
Budapest

POPULATION
9.82 million

AREA
93,030 sq km

OFFICIAL LANGUAGE
Hungarian

Széchenyi Baths, Budapest

Hungary

Stunning architecture, vital folk art, thermal spas and Europe's most exciting after-dark capital are Hungary's major drawing cards.

Hungary's vital folk-art tradition is among Europe's richest, from exquisite folk paintings found on the walls and ceilings of the tiny wooden churches of the Bereg region to wonderful embroidery from Hollókő. Traditional music continues to thrive as well, especially at *táncházak* (dance houses) – peasant 'raves' where you'll hear Hungarian folk music and to learn to dance, too.

Architecturally Hungary is a treasure trove, too, with everything from Roman ruins and medieval townhouses to baroque churches, neoclassical public buildings and art nouveau bathhouses and schools. And we're not just talking about its capital, Budapest. Walk through Szeged or Kecskemét, Debrecen or Sopron, and you'll discover an architectural gem at virtually every turn.

Top Experiences

Budapest's Nightlife

1 Budapest can now claim to be the number-one nightlife destination in Europe. Alongside its age-old cafe culture and hallowed music halls, it offers a magical blend of unique drinking holes, fantastic wine, home-grown firewaters and emerging craft beers, all served up with a warm Hungarian welcome and a wonderful sense of fun. Unique are the *romkocsmák* (ruin bars) and *kertek* (gardens) that pop up all over town in the warmer months.

Eger

2 Everyone loves Eger, and it's immediately apparent why. Beautifully preserved baroque architecture gives the town a relaxed, almost Mediterranean feel; it is flanked by two of northern Hungary's most beautiful ranges of hills (Bükk and Mátra), and it is the home of some of Hungary's best wines, including the celebrated Bull's Blood, which can be sampled at cellars in the evocatively named Valley of the Beautiful Women, a mere stroll away from the centre.

Budapest's Thermal Baths

3 With more than 300 thermal hot springs in public use across Hungary, it's not hard to find a place to take the waters. Some of the thermal baths, like the Rudas Baths in Budapest, date back to the 16th century. Increasingly popular are wellness spas and water parks, which draw different crowds.

Szeged

4 The cultural capital of the Great Plain and Hungary's third-largest city, Szeged is filled with eye-popping art nouveau

BRIAN KINNEY / SHUTTERSTOCK ©

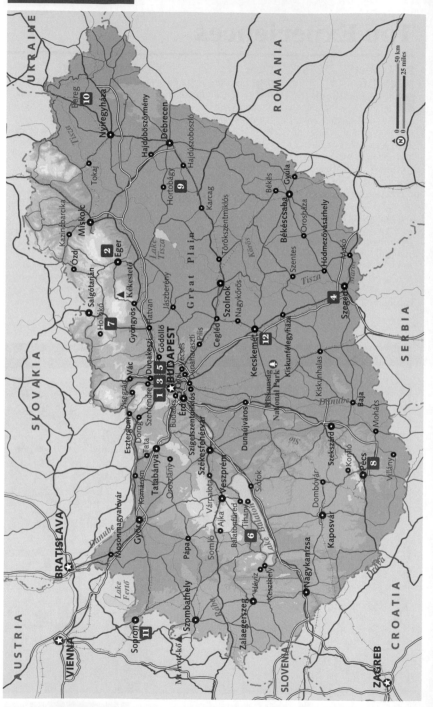

Best on Film

Dollybirds (*Csinibaba;* 1997) Comedy/satire about a contest to cross over the Iron Curtain.

Zimmer Feri (1998) Jokes about German tourists on the Balaton.

Moszkva tér (2001) End-of-communism comedy with kids.

A Kind of America (*Valami Amerika;* 2002) Flimflam film man from the USA.

Children of Glory (*Szabadság, Szerelem;* 2006) The 'blood in the water' water-polo match of 1956.

Food & Drink

Gulyás (goulash) Hungary's signature dish, though here it's more like a soup than a stew and made with beef, onions and tomatoes.

Halászlé Fish soup made from poached freshwater fish, tomatoes, green peppers and paprika.

Lángos Snack of deep-fried dough with various toppings (usually cheese and sour cream).

Pálinka Fruit-flavoured brandy.

Pörkölt Paprika-infused stew; closer to what we would call goulash.

Rétes (strudel) Filled with poppy seeds, cherry preserves or *túró* (curd or cottage cheese).

Savanyúság Literally 'sourness'; anything from mildly sour-sweet cucumbers to almost acidic sauerkraut, eaten with a main course.

Somlói galuska Sponge cake with chocolate and whipped cream.

Unicum A bitter aperitif nicknamed the 'Hungarian national accelerator'.

masterpieces, students, open-air cafes and green spaces, straddling the ever-present Tisza River. Theatre, opera and all types of other classical and popular music performances abound, culminating in the Szeged Open-Air Festival in summer. Szeged is also justly famed for its edibles, including the distinctive fish soup made with local paprika and Pick, Hungary's finest salami.

Budapest's Castle Hill

5 Budapest boasts architectural gems in spades, but the limestone plateau of Castle Hill towering over the Danube River's west bank is the Hungarian capital's most spectacular sight. Enclosed within medieval castle walls, numerous attractions vie for your attention, from the treasures in the Hungarian National Gallery and Castle Museum, to the claustrophobic Hospital in the Rock and the show-stopping view of Parliament across the river in Pest from Fishermen's Bastion.

When to Go

HIGH SEASON
(Jul–Aug)
Summer is warm, sunny and unusually long.

SHOULDER
(Apr–Jun, Sep–Oct)
Holidaymakers have gone home; prices drop.

LOW SEASON
(Nov–Mar)
Prices are rock-bottom; many sights reduce their hours sharply or close altogether.

Lake Balaton's Northern Shore

6 Hungary's 'sea' (and Continental Europe's largest lake) is where people come to sun and swim in

Drinking à la Magyar

Hungarians love their wine and take it seriously. In summer spritzers (or wine coolers) of red or white wine mixed with mineral water are consumed in large quantities; knowing the hierarchy and the art of mixing a spritzer to taste is important and will definitely win you the badge of 'honorary local'. A *kisfröccs* (small spritzer) is 10cL (100mL) of wine and the same amount of mineral water; a *nagyfröccs* (big spritzer) doubles the quantity of wine. A *hosszúlépés* (long step) is 10cL of wine and 20cL (200mL) of water while a *házmester* (janitor) trebles the amount of wine. Any bar in town will serve you these but don't expect one at a *borozó*, a traditional 'wine bar' – usually a dive – serving rotgut.

Stronger libations include the fruit-flavoured brandy called *pálinka* and Unicum, a bitter aperitif nicknamed the 'Hungarian national accelerator'.

Getting Around

 There are no scheduled flights within Hungary; it's small enough to get everywhere by train or bus within the span of a day.

 Buses are cheaper and often faster than trains. Useful for more remote destinations not served by trains.

 A cars is handy for exploring the wilder corners of Hungary.

 Trains are reasonably priced, with extensive coverage of the country.

summertime. The quieter side of Lake Balaton mixes sizzling beaches and oodles of fun on the water with historic waterside towns like Keszthely and Balatonfüred. Tihany, on a peninsula jutting 4km into the lake, is home to a stunning abbey church.

Hollókő

7 It may consist of a mere two streets, but Hollókő is the most beautiful of Hungary's villages. Its 67 whitewashed houses, little changed since their construction in the 17th and 18th centuries, are pure examples of traditional folk architecture and have been on Unesco's World Heritage list since 1987. Most importantly, it is a bastion of traditional Hungarian culture, holding fast to the folk art of the ethnic Palóc people and some of their ancient customs.

Pécs

8 This gem of a city is blessed with rarities: Turkish architecture and early Christian and Roman tombs. Its Mosque Church is the largest Ottoman structure still standing in Hungary, while the Hassan Jakovali Mosque has survived the centuries in excellent condition. Pécs is exceptionally rich in art and museums. What's more, the climate is mild – almost Mediterranean-like – and you can't help noticing all the almond trees in bloom or in fruit here.

Hortobágy National Park

9 Hungarians view the puszta – the Great Plain – romantically, as a region full of hardy shepherds fighting the wind and snow in winter and trying not to go stir-crazy in summer as the notorious délibábak (mirages) rise off the baking soil. It's a nostalgic notion, but the endless plains can be explored in the Hortobágy National Park. You can also watch as Hungarian cowboys ride with five horses in hand in a spectacular show of skill and horsemanship.

Folkloric Northeast

10 Preserved through generations, Hungary's folk-art traditions bring everyday objects to life. Differences in colours and styles easily identify the art's originating region. You'll find exquisite detailed embroidery, pottery, hand-painted or carved wood, dyed Easter eggs and graphic woven cloth right across the country, but the epicentre is in the Bereg region. The culture of the tiny villages of this region in the far northeast of Hungary has much to do with their neighbours to the east, including their brightly dyed Easter eggs.

Sopron

11 Sopron has the most intact medieval centre in Hungary, its cobbled streets lined with one Gothic or colourful early-baroque facade after another. A wander though the backstreets here is like stepping back in time. The icing on the cake is the town's Roman ruins. But architecture aside, the small border city beckons with its many vineyards and cellars in which to sample the local wine.

Kecskemét

12 Lying halfway between the Danube and the Tisza Rivers in the heart of the southern Great Plain, Kecskemét is a city ringed with vineyards and orchards that don't seem to stop at the limits of this 'garden city'. Indeed, Kecskemét's agricultural wealth was used wisely – it was able to redeem all its debts in 1832 – and today it boasts some of the finest architecture of a small city in Hungary.

Along with colourful art nouveau and Secessionist architecture, its fine museums and the region's excellent barackpálinka (apricot brandy) attract. And Kiskunság National Park, the puszta of this part of the plain, is right at the back door.

Sziget Festival

One of the biggest and most popular music festivals in Europe, with half a million revellers at last sighting, the Sziget Festival is held on Budapest's Hajógyár (Óbuda) Island in August.

Museum Night

Hundreds of museums across the country mark the summer solstice in mid-June by reopening their doors at 6pm on a Saturday and not closing them till the wee hours (https://muzej.hu).

11

7

CAPITAL
Reykjavik

POPULATION
330,000

AREA
103,000 sq km

OFFICIAL LANGUAGE
Icelandic

Westfjords

Iceland

Hitting headlines, topping bucket lists, wooing nature lovers and dazzling increasing numbers of visitors – there seems no end to the talents of this breathtaking northern destination.

Iceland is a vast volcanic laboratory where mighty forces shape the earth: geysers gush, mudpots gloop, ice-covered volcanoes rumble and glaciers cut great pathways through the mountains. Add some crisp clean air, an eyeful of the cinematic landscapes, and everyone is transfixed.

Don't for a minute think it's all about the great outdoors. The counterpoint to so much natural beauty is found in Iceland's cultural life, which celebrates a literary legacy that stretches from medieval sagas to contemporary thrillers by way of Nobel Prize winners. Live music is everywhere, as is visual art, handicrafts and locavore cuisine.

Top Experiences

Westfjords

1 Iceland's sweeping spectrum of superlative nature comes to a dramatic climax in the Westfjords – the island's off-the-beaten-path adventure par excellence. Broad, multi-hued beaches flank the southern coast, roaring bird colonies abound, fjordheads tower above and then plunge into the deep, and a network of ruddy roads twists throughout. The region's uppermost peninsula, Hornstrandir, is the final frontier; its sea cliffs are perilous, the Arctic foxes are foxier, and hiking trails amble through pristine patches of wilderness that practically kiss the Arctic Circle.

Jökulsárlón

2 A ghostly procession of luminous-blue icebergs drifts serenely through the 25-sq-km Jökulsárlón lagoon before floating out to sea. This surreal scene (handily, right next to the Ring Road) is a natural film set: in fact, you might have seen it in Batman Begins and the James Bond film Die Another Day. The ice calves come from Breiðamerkurjökull glacier, an offshoot of the mighty Vatnajökull ice cap. Boat trips among the bergs are popular, or you can simply wander the lakeshore, scout for seals and exhaust your camera's memory card.

Driving the Ring Road

3 There's no better way to explore Iceland than to hire a set of wheels and road-trip Rte 1, affectionately known as the Ring Road. This 1330km tarmac trail loops around the island, passing through verdant dales decked with waterfalls, glacier tongues dripping from ice caps like frosting from a cake, desert-like plains of grey outwash sands, and velvety, moss-covered lava fields. It's supremely spectacular – but don't forget to detour. Use the Ring Road as your main artery and follow the veins as they splinter off into the wilderness.

Fimmvörðuháls

4 If you haven't time to complete one of Iceand's multiday treks, the 23km, day-long Fimvörðuháls trek will quench your wanderer's thirst. Start at the shimmering cascades of Skógafoss; hike up into the hinterland to discover a veritable parade of waterfalls; gingerly tiptoe over the steaming remnants of the Eyjafjallajökull eruption; and hike along the stone terraces of a flower-filled kingdom that ends in silent Þórsmörk, a haven for campers, hemmed by a crown of glacial ridges.

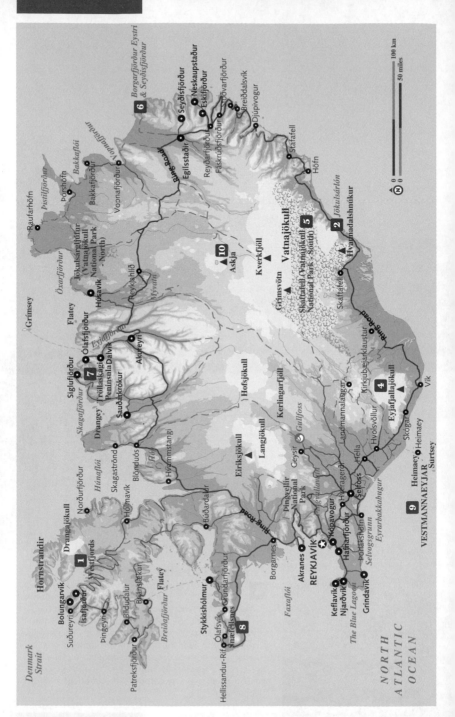

Best on Film

Heima (2007) Follow band Sigur Rós as they perform throughout Iceland.

Rams (*Hrútar*; 2015) Engrossing tale of two estranged brothers and their sheep.

The Homecoming (*Blóðberg*; 2015) Sly modern comedy-drama where a 'perfect' family's life goes topsy-turvy.

Of Horses and Men (2013) A surreal portrait of the intertwining lives of men and horses.

101 Reykjavík (2000) Dark comedy exploring sex, drugs and the life of a loafer in downtown Reykjavík.

Jar City (2006) Carefully crafted detective thriller based on the novel by Arnaldur Indriðason.

Best in Print

The Draining Lake (Arnaldur Indriðason; 2004) One of many engrossing tales from a master of Nordic Noir.

Independent People (Halldór Laxness; 1934–35) Bleak tragi-comedy from the Nobel Laureate.

The Sagas of Icelanders (Jane Smiley et al; 2001) Excellent, readable translations of Iceland's epic, often brutal, tales.

Devil's Island (Einar Kárason; 1983) American culture clashes with rural tradition in postwar Reykjavík.

The Blue Fox (Sjón; 2003) Poetic 19th-century fantasy-adventure tale.

Vatnajökull National Park

5 Europe's largest national park covers nearly 14% of Iceland and safeguards mighty Vatnajökull, the largest ice cap outside the poles (it's three times the size of Luxembourg). Scores of outlet glaciers flow down from its frosty bulk, while underneath it are active volcanoes and mountain peaks. Yes, this is ground zero for those 'fire and ice' clichés. You'll be spellbound by the diversity of landscapes, walking trails and activities inside this park. Given its dimensions, access points are numerous – start at Skaftafell in the south or Ásbyrgi in the north.

Borgarfjörður Eystri & Seyðisfjörður

6 A tale of two east-side fjords. Stunning, art-fuelled Seyðisfjörður garners most of the attention – it's only 27 (sealed) kilometres from the Ring Road, and it welcomes the weekly ferry from Europe into its mountain-lined, waterfall-studded embrace. Beautiful Borgarfjörður Eystri, on the other

When to Go

HIGH SEASON
(Jun–Aug)
Visitors descend en masse, prices peak; prebookings are essential.

SHOULDER
(May & Sep)
Optimal visiting conditions if you prefer fewer crowds and lower prices over cloudless days.

LOW SEASON
(Oct–Apr)
Brief spurts of daylight; long nights with possible Northern Lights viewings.

Getting Into Hot Water

You'll find 'hot-pots' everywhere. Not only are they incredibly relaxing, they're the perfect antidote to a hangover and a great way to meet the locals (this is their social hub, the equivalent of the local pub or town square).

Northern Lights

Northern lights form when solar flares are drawn by the earth's magnetic field towards the North Pole. What results are ethereal veils of green, white, violet or red light, shimmering and dancing like silent fireworks. Look for the lights in clear, dark skies anytime between mid-September and mid-April.

hand, is 70km from the Ring Road, and much of that stretch is bumpy and unsealed. Its selling points are understated: puffins, hidden elves, rugged rhyolite peaks. Both fjords have natural splendour and bumper hiking trails in spades, and we can't help but love 'em equally.

Tröllaskagi Peninsula

7 Touring Tröllaskagi is a joy, especially now that road tunnels link the spectacularly sited townships of Siglufjörður and Ólafsfjörður, once end-of-the-road settlements. The peninsula's dramatic scenery contrasts with the gentle hills that roll through most of northern Iceland. Pit stops with pulling power include

Hofsós' perfect fjord-side swimming pool, Lónkot's plates of fine local produce and Siglufjörður's outstanding herring museum. Plus you'll find glorious panoramas, quality hiking, ski fields (including a growing trade in heliskiing), microbreweries, whale-watching tours, and ferries to offshore islands Grímsey and Hrísey.

Snæfellsnes Peninsula

8 With its cache of wild beaches, bird sanctuaries, horse farms and lava fields, the Snæfellsnes Peninsula is one of Iceland's best escapes – either as a day trip from the capital or as a relaxing long weekend. It's little wonder it's called 'Iceland in miniature' – it even hosts

a national park and glacier-topped stratovolcano. Jules Verne was definitely onto something when he used Snæfellsjökull's icy crown as his magical doorway to the centre of the earth.

Vestmannaeyjar

9 An offshore archipelago of craggy peaks, Vestmannaeyjar is a mere 30-minute ferry ride from the mainland, but feels miles and miles away in sentiment. A boat tour of the scattered islets unveils squawking seabirds, towering cliffs and postcard-worthy vistas of lonely hunting cabins perched atop rocky outcrops. The islands' 4000-plus population is focused on Heimaey, a small town of windswept bungalows with a scar-

Puffins & Whales

Iceland's two biggest wildlife drawcards are its most charismatic creatures: the twee puffin, which flits around like an anxious bumblebee, and the mighty whale, a number of species of which, including the immense blue whale, glide through the frigid blue ringing Iceland's coast. Opportunities to see both abound on land and sea. Whale-watching heartland is Húsavík, and other northern towns and Reykjavík also offer cruises. Colonies of puffins are poised and ready for their close-up at numerous coastal cliffs and offshore isles, including Heimaey, Grímsey, Drangey, Látrabjarg and Borgarfjörður Eystri.

SIMON DANNHAUER / SHUTTERSTOCK ©

ring curl of lava that flows straight through its centre – a poignant reminder of Iceland's volatile landscape.

Askja

10 Accessible for only a few months each year, storied Askja is a mammoth caldera ringed by mountains and enclosing a sapphire-blue lake. To access this glorious, otherworldly place, you'll need a robust 4WD, a few days for hiking, or passage on a super-Jeep tour. Highlands excursions generally incorporate river crossings, impossibly vast lava fields, regal mountain vistas and outlaw hideouts – and possibly a naked soak in geothermal waters. Added bonus: head south from Askja to visit Iceland's freshest lava field at Holuhraun.

Getting Around

 If you're short on time, domestic flights can help you get around efficiently.

 A decent bus network operates from around mid-May to mid-September, shuttling you between major destinations and into the highlands. Outside these months, services are less frequent (even nonexistent).

 Car is the most common way for visitors to get around. Vehicles can be expensive to hire but provide great freedom. Driving into the highlands and on F roads requires 4WDs.

CAPITAL
New Delhi

POPULATION
1.27 billion

AREA
3.3 million sq km

OFFICIAL LANGUAGES
Hindi, English

City Palace, Jaipur

India

A land of remarkable diversity – from ancient traditions and artistic heritage to magnificent landscapes and culinary creations – India will ignite your curiosity, shake your senses and warm your soul.

From the towering icy peaks of the northern mountains to the sun-washed beaches of the southern coast, India's terrain is breathtaking. Exquisite temples rise majestically out of pancake-flat deserts and crumbling fortresses peer over plunging ravines. Aficionados of the great outdoors can scout for big jungle cats on wildlife safaris, paddle in shimmering waters, trek high in the Himalaya, or simply inhale pine-scented air on a meditative forest walk.

Spirituality is the common characteristic painted across the vast and varied canvas that is contemporary India. The multitude of sacred sites and rituals are testament to the country's long and colourful religious history. And then there are its festivals!

India can be challenging, particularly for the first-time visitor. Yet this is part of the India ride – to embrace India's unpredictability is to embrace her soul.

Top Experiences

Taj Mahal

1 Poet Rabindranath Tagore described it as 'a teardrop on the cheek of eternity' and Rudyard Kipling as 'the embodiment of all things pure'. An exquisite tomb that's as much a monument to love as it is to death, the Taj Mahal is arguably the world's most beautiful building. Built by Emperor Shah Jahan in adoration of his third wife, Mumtaz Mahal, this milky-white marble mausoleum is inlaid with calligraphy, precious and semiprecious stones and intricate floral designs representing eternal paradise. It represents the pinnacle of Mughal architecture as well as romance.

Otherworldly Hampi

2 Magnificent, even in ruins, Hampi was once the capital of a powerful Hindu empire. Spread across an emerald-green and terracotta-red landscape, its temples and royal structures combine sublimely with the terrain. Giant rocks balance on slender pedestals near an ancient elephant garage, temples tuck into crevices between boulders, and wicker coracles float by rice paddies near a gargantuan bathtub for a former queen. As the sunset casts a rosy glow over the dreamy landscape, you might just forget what planet you're on.

Ladakh's Moonscapes

3 As you head north, the air grows cooler and you reach historic hill stations, summer escapes that are ringed by snow-capped peaks. In Ladakh, cultural influences came not by coasts but via mountain passes. Tibetan Buddhism thrives, and multilayered monasteries emerge from the steep cliffs as vividly and poetically as the sun rises over Khangchendzonga. Weathered prayer flags flutter in the wind, the soothing sound of monks chanting reverberates in meditation halls, and locals abound with holy offerings, all in the shadow of the mighty Himalaya.

Holy Varanasi

4 Varanasi is a city full of life and death, and one of India's most revered sacred places. Pilgrims flock here to worship, take a holy dip in the Ganges River, or cremate loved ones. Hindus believe the waters of the Ganges cleanse away sins, while dying here is deemed particularly propitious as it offers emancipation from the arduous life-and-death cycle. Varanasi will swiftly sweep you into its dizzying spiritual whirlwind – just take a deep breath and immerse yourself in pondering the meaning of life, death…and beyond.

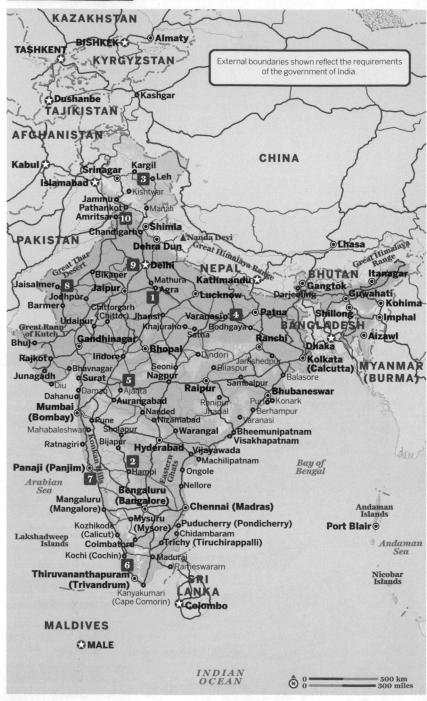

External boundaries shown reflect the requirements of the government of India.

Best in Print

Midnight's Children (1981) Salman Rushdie's allegory about Independence and Partition.

A Fine Balance (1995) Rohinton Mistry's beautifully written, tragic tale set in Mumbai.

White Tiger (2008) Aravind Adiga's Booker-winning novel about class struggle in globalised India.

A Suitable Boy (1993) Vikram Seth's 1300-page novel about romance, heartbreak, family secrets and political intrigue.

The God of Small Things (1997) Arundhati Roy's story of fraternal twins won the Booker Prize.

Henna Designs

Mehndi is the traditional art of painting a woman's hands (and sometimes feet) with intricate henna designs for auspicious ceremonies, such as marriage. If quality henna is used, the design, which is orange-brown, can last up to one month.

In touristy areas, *mehndi-wallahs* are adept at applying henna tattoo 'bands' on the arms, legs and lower back. If you get *mehndi* applied, allow at least a few hours for the design process and required drying time (during drying you can't use your hennaed hands).

It's always wise to request the artist to do a 'test' spot on your arm before proceeding: nowadays some dyes contain chemicals that can cause allergies. (Avoid 'black henna', which is mixed with some chemicals that may be harmful.) If good-quality henna is used, you should not feel any pain during or after the application.

Caves of Ajanta

5 They may have been ascetics, but the 2nd-century-BC monks who created the Ajanta caves certainly had an eye for the dramatic. The 30 rock-cut forest grottoes punctuate the side of a horseshoe-shaped cliff, and originally had individual staircases leading down to the river. The architecture and towering stupas made these caves inspiring places to meditate and live, but the real bling came centuries later, in the form of exquisite carvings and paintings depicting the Buddha's former lives. Renunciation of the worldly life was never so serenely sophisticated.

Backwaters of Kerala

6 It's like heading into a dream, lazily navigating the tropically radiant backwaters of Kerala: what is probably India's most laid-back state has 900km of interconnected rivers, lakes, canals and lagoons lined with the swaying palms of thick coconut groves and picturesque villages. One of the most popular and scenic ways to peruse these parts is by cruising on a teak-and-palm-thatch houseboat. Drift along the waterways – as the sun sinks behind the trees, while snacking on succulent Keralan seafood, later falling

When to Go

HIGH SEASON
(Nov–Mar)
Pleasant weather – warm days, cool nights. Peak tourists. Peak prices.

SHOULDER
(Jul–Oct)
Monsoon rain persists through to September.

LOW SEASON
(Apr–Jun)
May and June are scorching. In June, the monsoon brings draining humidity.

Yoga

Yoga's roots lie in India and you'll find hundreds of schools following different disciplines to suit all levels of skill and commitment. You can practise yoga almost everywhere, from beach resorts to mountain retreats.

India's Bazaars

India's exuberant bazaars offer a treasure trove of goodies, including textiles, woodwork, silver, gemstones and a tremendous mix of village creations. The array of arts and handicrafts is vast and the shopping opportunities are sure to be as inspiring and multifarious as the country itself.

Food & Drink

Chaat Savoury snack, may be seasoned with *chaat masala*.

Gulab jamun Deep-fried balls of dough soaked in rose-flavoured syrup.

Falooda Rose-flavoured drink made with milk, cream, nuts and vermicelli.

Idli South Indian spongy, round, fermented rice cake.

Jalebi Orange-coloured coils of deep-fried batter dunked in sugar syrup; served hot.

Kulfi Flavoured (often with pistachio) firm-textured ice cream.

Lassi Yoghurt-and-iced-water drink.

Pakora Bite-sized vegetable pieces in batter.

Samosa Deep-fried pastry triangles filled with spiced vegetables (sometimes meat).

Puri Puffy fried bread pillows.

Barfi Fudgelike sweet made from milk.

Dhansak Parsi dish; meat, usually chicken or lamb, with curried lentils, pumpkin or gourd, and rice

Vada South Indian doughnut-shaped deep-fried lentil savoury.

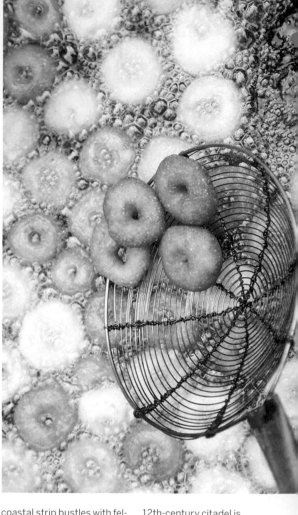

asleep under a twinkling night sky – and forget all about life on land for a while.

Goan Beaches

7 With nodding palms on one side of the sugar-white sands and lapping powder-blue waves on the other, Goa's coastline is lined by beautiful beaches and has an easy-going hedonistic atmosphere that's like nowhere else in India. It's not an undiscovered paradise: this cool coastal strip bustles with fellow travellers, vendors and beach-shack eateries. It's a slice of paradise that appeals to social creatures and fans of creature comforts who like their seafood fresh and their holidays easy.

Jaisalmer's Desert Mirage

8 A gigantic, golden sandcastle that rises like a mirage from the desert of Rajasthan, the 'Land of Kings', Jaisalmer's 12th-century citadel is romantically picturesque. This sandstone fort, with its crenellated ramparts and undulating towers, is a fantastical structure, elegantly blending in with the toffee-gold hues of its desert environs. Inside, a royal palace, atmospheric old havelis (traditional residences), delicately chiselled Jain temples and skinny lanes all conspire to create one of the country's best places to get lost.

Delli

9 India's capital bears the mighty remnants of former empires, from great Mughal tombs to the grandiose British-era mansions. There's so much to see here: the crumbling splendour of Old Delhi – with the Jama Masjid, Red Fort and its havelis, the ancient forts of Tughlabad and Purana Qila, and the wonders of Qutb Minar and Mehrauli Archaeological Park. Then time-travel to modern New Delhi, with its colonial-era parliament buildings and penchant for high tea. Then on to the future: Gurgaon, a satellite city of skyscraping offices and glitzy malls. Add to this the city's many fine eateries, with offerings from street food to Modern Indian, superb museums and amazing shopping, and it's easy to see why Delhi mesmerizes many.

Amritsar's Golden Temple

10 The Golden Temple in Amritsar is the Sikhs' holiest of shrines, and has a magical atmosphere. Seeming to float atop a glistening pool named for the 'nectar of immortality', the temple is truly golden (the lotus-shaped dome is gilded in the real thing). Even when crowded with pilgrims it has a graceful tranquility, with the sounds of *kirtan* (Sikh devotional singing) and birds chirping outside, and the mirror-like sacred pool that surrounds it. The legendary temple is actually just a small part of this huge gurdwara complex, known to Sikhs as Harmandir Sahib..

DMITRY RUKHLENKO / SHUTTERSTOCK ©

Getting Around

 India has a very competitive domestic airline industry, transporting vast numbers of passengers annually.

 Travelling by train is a quintessential Indian experience. Trains offer a smoother ride than buses and are especially recommended for long journeys that include overnight travel. India's rail network is one of the largest and busiest in the world.

 Buses go everywhere; some destinations are served 24 hours but longer routes may have just one or two buses a day.

 Taxis, cycle-rickshaws, autorickshaws, boats and urban trains provide transport around India's cities.

CAPITAL
Jakarta

POPULATION
255 million

AREA
1,904,600 sq km

OFFICIAL LANGUAGE
Bahasa Indonesia

Traditional boat on Gili Meno

Indonesia

Indonesia's numbers astound: more than 17,000 islands, of which 8000 are inhabited, and over 300 languages are spoken across them.

The world's fourth most populous country – 255 million and counting – is a sultry kaleidoscope that runs along the equator for 5000km. From the western tip of Sumatra to the eastern edge of Papua, this nation defies homogenisation. It is a land of so many cultures, peoples, animals, customs, plants, sights, artworks and foods that it is like 100 countries melded into one.

This ever-intriguing, ever-intoxicating land offers some of the last great adventures on earth. Sitting in the open door of a train whizzing across Java, idling away time on a ferry bound for Kalimantan, hanging on to the back of a scooter on Flores, rounding the mystifying corner of an ancient West Timor village or simply trekking through wilderness you're sure no one has seen before – you'll enjoy endless exploration of the infinite diversity of Indonesia's thousands of islands.

Top Experiences

Komodo National Park

1 Indonesia's best-known national park comprises several islands and some of the country's richest waters within its 1817 sq km. Expect hulking mountainous islands blanketed in savannah, laced with trails and patrolled by the world's largest lizard – the Komodo dragon. That's the big draw here, and it's easy to spot them, but there's also big nature beneath the water's surface, where kaleidoscopic bait draw big pelagics like sharks and manta rays in great numbers. Nearby Labuanbajo, on the island of Flores, is the perfect traveller base.

Gili Islands

2 One of Indonesia's greatest joys is hopping on a fast boat from busy Bali and arriving on one of the irresistible Gili Islands. Think sugar-white sand, bathtub-warm, turquoise waters and wonderful beach resorts and bungalows just begging you to extend your stay. Not to mention the coral reefs which are teeming with sharks, rays and turtles. Savour the dining and nightlife on Gili Trawangan, the perfect balance of Gili Air and the pint-sized charms of Gili Meno. Or simply do nothing at all.

Ubud

3 Famous in books and movies, the artistic heart of Bali exudes a compelling spiritual appeal. The streets are lined with galleries where artists, both humble and great, create. Beautiful dance performances showcasing the island's rich culture grace a dozen stages nightly. Museums honour the works of those inspired here over the years, while people walk the rice fields to find the perfect spot to sit in lotus position and ponder life's endless possibilities. Ubud is a state of mind and a beautiful state of being

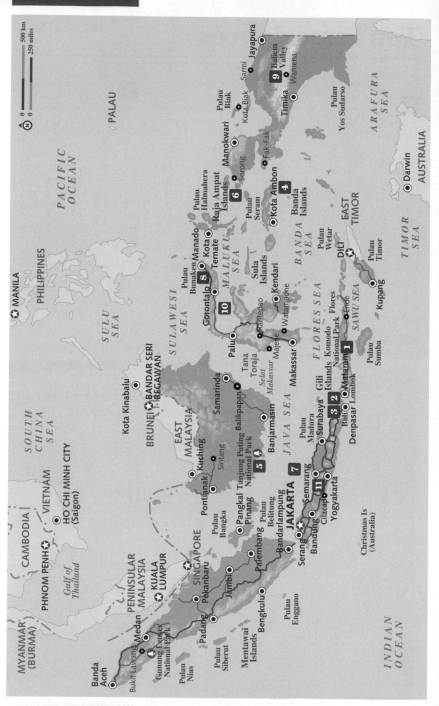

Banda Islands

4 Here is a rich and intoxicating cocktail of history, culture and raw natural beauty. The Banda Islands – a remote archipelago draped in jungle and spice trees, fringed with white sand, surrounded by clear blue seas and pristine reefs – kickstarted colonisation and helped shape the modern world. Fly to the capital – Bandaneira – from Ambon, stroll the wide avenues, admire late-colonial relics, then charter a boat to the outer islands, where village life is warm and easy, and stress peels from your soul by the second

Tanjung Puting National Park

5 *African Queen* meets jungle safari in this ever-popular national park in southern Kalimantan, where you can not only get up close and personal with Asia's largest ape, the orangutan, but also cruise the jungle in high style aboard your own private houseboat. The typically three-day journey takes you on a round trip up the Sungai Sekonyer to Camp Leakey, with stops at several orangutan feeding stations and plenty of impromptu wildlife spotting. Despite its creature

Best in Print

A Brief History of Indonesia (2015) Indonesian expert Tim Hannigan's highly readable and entertaining narrative.

Indonesia Etc (2014) Elizabeth Pisani's brilliant travelogue and exploration of the nation.

This Earth of Mankind (1980) A canvas of Indonesia under Dutch rule by Pramoedya Ananta Toer (1925–2006), one of Indonesia's top writers.

Stranger in the Forest (1988) Eric Hansen was possibly the first nonlocal to walk across Borneo.

Krakatoa – The Day the World Exploded (2003) Simon Winchester melds history, geology and politics, all centred on the 1883 eruption.

Food & Drink

When you eat in Indonesia you savour the essence of the country. The abundance of rice reflects Indonesia's fertile landscape, the spices are reminiscent of a time of trade and invasion, and the fiery chilli echoes the passion of the people. Indonesian cuisine is really one big food swap. Chinese, Portuguese, colonists and traders have all influenced the ingredients that appear at the Indonesian table, and the cuisine has been further shaped over time by the archipelago's diverse landscape, people and culture.

When to Go

HIGH SEASON
(Jul & Aug)
Tourist numbers surge across Indonesia.

SHOULDER
(May, Jun & Sep)
Best weather in Java, Bali and Lombok (dry, not so humid).

LOW SEASON
(Oct–Apr)
Easy to find deals; travel with little advance booking.

Wildlife

From tiny tarsiers to enormous stinking flowers, Indonesia's natural diversity is astounding, and we still don't know the complete story. Great apes, tigers, elephants and monkeys – lots of monkeys – plus one mean lizard (the Komodo dragon) are just some of the more notable critters you may encounter in Indonesia. Here you can find an astonishing 12% of the world's mammal species, and 17% of its bird species.

The diversity is partly a result of evolution occurring in two distinct ecozones, the Australian and Asian, which were later brought together by tectonic migration. This is why you won't find marsupials on the western islands, or tigers in the east.

Scientists continually discover new species such as a fanged frog in Sulawasi in 2015, an owl in Lombok in 2013, and three walking sharks since 2007 in the Malukus. Meanwhile, the 'lost world' of Papua's Foja mountains is a constant source of firsts, including the world's smallest wallaby, recorded in 2010. Unfortunately, the pace of discovery lags far behind the rate of habitat destruction, meaning some of Indonesia's rich biological heritage will pass unrecorded into extinction.

Getting Around

Boats – slow and fast – link the many islands but beware of rogue operators with dodgy safety standards.

Buses of all sizes travel almost everywhere cheaply and slowly.

Rent a small 4WD for US$30 a day, get a car and driver from US$60 a day. Rent a motorbike from 60,000Rp a day.

Ojeks (motorcycle riders) will take pillion passengers for a bargainable price.

Taxis can be found in cities and tourist areas; fairly cheap but only use Bluebird taxis to avoid scams.

comforts, the experience still manages to be authentic adventure travel, and is open to anyone.

Raja Ampat Islands

6 The remote, still-being-discovered Raja Ampat Islands off Papua's northwest tip are a diver's dream. Raja Ampat is home to the greatest diversity of marine life on the planet, from giant manta rays and epaulette sharks that use their fins to 'walk' on the sea floor, to myriad multicoloured nudibranchs ('sea slugs'), fantastic pristine coral, and every size, shape and hue of fish you can imagine. The snorkelling is great too, and the above-water scenery is just as unique and sublime.

Karimunjawa Islands

7 Set 90km off the north coast of Central Java is an archipelago as remote and wild as any in east Indonesia, yet still accessible by ferry and flights from Semarang and Surabaya. The Karimunjawa Islands are a group of 27 coral-fringed beauties, some are uninhabited and off limits to visitors, but most are accessible on day tours from the main island of Karimunjawa, jungled and mountainous, fringed with white-sand beaches and swaying with coconut palms. Magic.

Pulau Bunaken

8 You know those gardens that seem to have hundreds of plant species artistically thriving together in small decorative plots? Now imagine that done with coral in every colour from stark black and white to intense purples. Next cover it all in clear water teeming with iridescent fish, some in thick schools fluttering like sprinkles of sunlight. The water around Pulau Bunaken is more beautiful than you could imagine and yet it gets better: turtles the size of armchairs, reef sharks and, if you're lucky, dolphins and du-gongs that swim casually through the scene.

Baliem Valley

9 Trekking in Papua's Baliem Valley takes you into the world of the Dani, a mountain people whose traditional culture still stands proud despite changes wrought by Indonesian government and Christian missionaries. You'll sleep in their villages of grass-roofed huts, climb narrow jungle trails, traverse panoramic open hillsides, cross raging rivers by wobbly hanging footbridges, and be charmed by the locals' smiles. Tip for those bridges: don't look at the water, but do look where you're putting your feet!

Togoean Islands

10 Almost smack on the equator, the blissful, off-grid Togean Islands are an unadulterated vision of the tropics, with blinding white-sand beaches fringed by coconut palms, a smattering of fishing villages, homestay digs, and world-class snorkelling and diving on majestic coral reefs. Things are so mellow here that there's even a jellyfish lake where the jellies don't sting. You can forget all about news headlines and Facebook updates – internet access and cellular coverage is near zero.

Borobudur

11 The breathtaking Borobudur temple complex is a stunning and poignant epitaph to Java's Buddhist heyday in the 9th century AD. One of the most important Buddhist sites in the world, the temple consists of six square bases topped by three circular ones. Nearly 1500 narrative relief panels on the terraces illustrate Buddhist teachings and tales, while 432 Buddha images sit in chambers on the terraces.

Nyepi

Bali's major Hindu festival celebrates new year with a night of celebrations followed by inactivity – to convince evil spirits that Bali is uninhabited. Held in March or early April.

Beaches

Indonesia has a lot of beaches, from wildly popular beaches on south Bali, to those for hardcore partiers on the Gili Islands, to literally hundreds more where your footprints will be the day's first.

JAN KVITA / SHUTTERSTOCK ©

5

ETHAN DANIELS / SHUTTERSTOCK ©

6

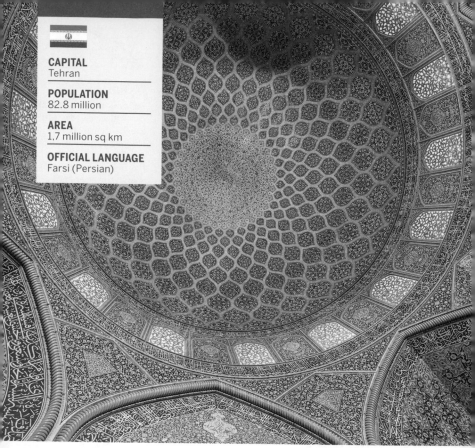

CAPITAL	Tehran
POPULATION	82.8 million
AREA	1,7 million sq km
OFFICIAL LANGUAGE	Farsi (Persian)

Masjed-e Sheikh Lotfollah, Esfahan

Iran

Welcome to what could be the friendliest country on earth. Iran is the jewel in Islam's crown, combining glorious architecture with a warm-hearted welcome.

If you're drawn to places where echoes of ancient civilisations resonate down through the ages, Iran could be your thing. Some of history's biggest names – Cyrus and Darius, Alexander the Great, Genghis Khan – all left their mark here. Walking around the awesome power and beauty of Persepolis, experiencing the remote power of Susa (Shush), and taking in the wonderfully immense Elamite ziggurat at Choqa Zanbil will carry you all the way back to the glory days of Ancient Persia.

Iran is a treasure house for some of the most beautiful architecture on the planet, but its greatest attraction could just be its people. Offers to sit down for tea will be an everyday occurrence, and if you spend any time at all with Iranians you'll find yourself invited often to share a meal in someone's home. Say yes whenever you can, and through it experience Iranian culture first-hand. No matter what you think you know, Iran is a safe country in which to travel and Iranians will go out of their way to look after you.

Top Experiences

Esfahan

1 There are moments in travel that will long stay with you, and your first sight of Esfahan's majestic Naqsh-e Jahan (Imam) Square is one of them. For this square is home to arguably the most majestic collection of buildings in the Islamic world: the perfectly proportioned blue-tiled dome of the Masjed-e Shah, the supremely elegant Masjed-e Sheikh Lotfollah and the indulgent and lavishly decorated Ali Qapu Palace. Robert Byron ranked '...Isfahan among those rarer places, like Athens or Rome, which are the common refreshment of humanity'.

Yazd

2 Few places have adapted to their environment as well as the desert city of Yazd. It's a gem of winding lanes, blue-tiled domes, soaring minarets, covered bazaars, and fine old courtyard homes topped by *badgirs* (windtowers) and watered by ingenious *qanats* (underground water channels). Several of these homes have been restored and converted into marvellously evocative traditional hotels.

Ancient Persepolis

3 The artistic harmony of the monumental staircases, imposing gateways and exquisite reliefs leaves you in little doubt that in its prime Persepolis was at the centre of the known world. Built by kings Darius and Xerxes as the ceremonial capital of the Achaemenid empire, a visit to the World Heritage–listed ruins of the city also testifies to Alexander the Great's merciless destruction of that empire. Don't miss the monolithic tombs at nearby Naqsh-e Rostam.

3

Nomads of the Zagros

4 About two million Iranians from several different ethnic groups still live a nomadic existence, travelling with their goats in spring and autumn in search of pasture. Qashqa'i and Bakhtiyari nomads spend the summer months in the Zagros Mountains, before heading down to the coast for the winter. You can get a taste of nomad life on a day trip from Shiraz, or stay with the Khamseh (and eat their delicious hand-made yoghurt) in the hills above Bavanat.

MARCIN SZYMCZAK / SHUTTERSTOCK ©

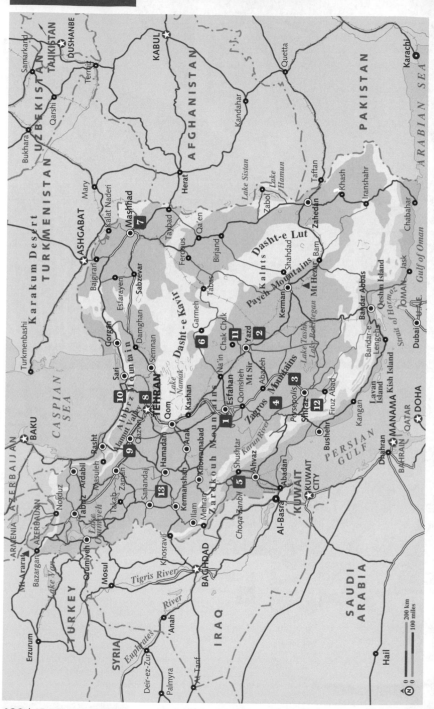

Best on Film

The Salesman (2016) Asghar Farhadi's Oscar-nominated study of modern Iran through a troubled relationship.

Taste of Cherry (1997) Abbas Kairostami looks at the taboo subject of suicide.

The Apple (1998) Samira Makhmalbaf's stunning debut about two adolescent girls locked away by their father.

Taxi (2015) Jafar Panahi's brilliant 'docu-fiction' gives a voice to ordinary Iranians in a Tehran taxi.

A Separation (2012) Asghar Farhadi's Oscar-winning look at a Tehran marriage falling apart.

Best in Music

Googoosh (Googoosh; 2011) Iran's 1970s superstar-in-exile has the most wonderful voice.

Gole Aftabgardoon (The Sunflower; Arian; 2000) Debut album by this hugely popular mixed gender band.

Kherghe Biandaz (O-Hum; 2014) Combines rock music with Persian traditional lyrics and instruments.

Music of Iran (Mohammad Reza Shadjarian & Ensemble Aref; 2012) An excellent introduction to Persian classical music from the World Network label.

Living Fire (The Kâmkârs; 1995) Superstars from Kurdish Iran with hypnotic sounds.

Choqa Zanbil, Susa & Shushtar

5 Even if you don't like ancient ruins, the great bulk, semidesert isolation and fascinating back story make the Choqa Zanbil ziggurat one of the most impressive historical sites in a region full of them. Built by the Elamites in the 13th century BC, it was 'lost' under the sands in the 7th century BC and only rediscovered during a 1935 aerial survey by a British oil company. Now excavated, some of the bricks look as if they came out of the kiln last week.

Desert Oases

6 The welcome is rarely warmer than in the vast, empty silence of Iran's two great deserts. Garmeh is the oasis village of your dreams, with a crumbling castle, swaying date palms and the sound of spring water. It's the sort of place you come for one night and stay four. Nearby Farahzad and tiny Toudeshk Cho, between Esfahan and Na'in, also offer memorable desert-style family homestays; think beds on

When to Go

HIGH SEASON
(Mar–May)
Ideal temperatures in most of Iran with generally mild, clear weather.

SHOULDER
(Jun–Oct)
Warmer weather in June means fewer travellers. September and October temperatures moderate.

LOW SEASON
(Nov–Feb)
Extreme cold, especially in the northeast and west, during winter, but good for skiing.

Persian Carpets

The best-known Iranian cultural export, the Persian carpet, is far more than just a floor covering to an Iranian. A Persian carpet is a display of wealth, an investment, an integral aspect of religious and cultural festivals, and part of everyday life. The oldest surviving carpet is the 'Pazyryk' rug, believed to date from the 5th century BC. Today more than five million Iranians work in the industry.

Zurkhaneh

Unique to Iran, the *zurkhaneh* literally means 'house of strength' and is a mix of sport, theatre and religion. Typically a group of men stand around a circular pit and perform a series of ritualised feats of strength, all to the accompaniment of a leader pounding out a frenetic drumbeat. Most *zurkhaneh* are open to the public and it's usually free to watch.

the floor, basic bathrooms and fresh, delicious home-cooked food.

Mashhad's Haram-e Razavi

7 Iran is an Islamic Republic and while most travellers find Islam is not nearly as all-pervasive as they had expected, the Shiite faith remains an important part of Iranian life. It is at its most obvious in the passionate devotion seen at monuments such as the huge Haram-e Razavi in Mashhad. The main draw there is the Holy Shrine of Imam Reza, the only Shiite imam buried in Iran.

Tehran Art Scene

8 Bustling Tehran can be intimidating but it does have its appeal. Beyond the museums and palaces are a range of hip cafes and contemporary art galleries that provide an entree into a side of life you otherwise only hear about. Sit over coffee for a while and you'll end up in conversation, or wander through the galleries and theatre in and around Park-e Honar Mandan (Artist's Park).

Hiking among the Castles of the Assassins

9 The Alamut Valley offers a tempting invitation to hike, explore and reflect among the fabled Castles of the Assassins. Nestled on widely spread rocky knolls and pinnacles lie the shattered remnants of more than 50 ruined fortresses that were once home to the medieval world's most feared religious cult. Choose a day

hike from Qazvin or more extensive wanderings from Gazor Khan – a full, mule-accompanied crossing to the Caspian hinterland.

Skiing the Alborz Mountains

10 Think Iran and you're unlikely to think skiing, but there are more than 20 ski fields in the country. Most of the action is conveniently concentrated around Tehran. The Dizin and Shemshak resorts are the pick, with steep downhills and plenty of untracked powder to keep skiers of all

levels interested. Chalets and ski passes are inexpensive compared with Western countries, and the slopes are more gender-equal than most of Iran – expect to see exposed female hair.

Zoroastrian Fire Temples

11 Iran may be an Islamic Republic, but its Zoroastrian sites have an otherworldly charm. Chak Chak, out in a deliciously remote location in the Yazd hinterland, has a superb fire temple with a stunning brass door, even more

MARCIN SZYMCZAK / SHUTTERSTOCK ©

that's just the way we like it. Track down Unesco World Heritage–listed Armenian churches. Follow the scenic route through Howraman on your way between Marivan and Paveh. Explore the Aras Valley. Or the Coloured Mountains. Or spend some time getting to know the Kurds around Howraman, the Azeris in the northwest, the Gilan on the Caspian coast, the Arabs of Khuzestan. Put them all together and western Iran is worth building your entire trip around.

Getting Around

An extensive air network of generally reliable domestic flights is a great way to avoid long drives.

You can get almost anywhere by bus. Most buses are comfortable and speed checks have improved safety.

Savaris are shared taxis that are usually quicker than buses but less comfortable.

Trains link most major cities but departures are less frequent.

stunning views, and an air of ritual, ancient and deep. This was the Zoroastrian heartland and remains its most significant pilgrimage site. It's difficult to come here and not imagine yourself in the days before Islam arrived in Iran. There are other fire temples in Kerman and Yazd.

The Poets of Shiraz

12 Iranians like to say that even in the poorest home you'll find two books: a Quran and the poetry of Hafez. It's appropriate for a country whose most celebrated sons are poets, and where almost every person can quote their favourite millennium-old man of words. In Shiraz, the city of nightingales and gardens, the tombs of Hafez and Sa'di draw pilgrims from around the country. Join them as they linger over tea, reciting the works of their heroes.

Scenic Western Iran

13 With the slowdown in overland traveller traffic, surprisingly few make it out west, but

Amadiya

CAPITAL
Baghdad

POPULATION
38.1 million

AREA
437,072 sq km

OFFICIAL LANGUAGES
Arabic, Kurdish

Iraq

Torn between its glorious past and its recent bloody history, Iraq is a country in turmoil. Following the 2003 US-led invasion and the problems that ensued, the country had little time to recover before a wave of violence swept through in June 2014, when jihadist group Isis took control of large swathes of north Iraq. This instability has made the country too dangerous for independent travellers.

Long ago in the fertile valleys between the Tigris and Euphrates Rivers, the great civilisations of the age were born. Modern Iraq was ancient Mesopotamia, from the Greek meaning 'between two rivers', and it was here that human beings first began to cultivate their land, where writing was invented and where the Assyrians, Sumerians and Babylonians all made Iraq the centre of the ancient world.

With the arrival of Islam, Baghdad became one of Islam's greatest capitals, and become a byword for Islam's golden age of learning and sophistication.

Snapshot

Hamilton Road

1 Commissioned in 1928 and named for its builder, the Hamilton Road remains a remarkable feat of engineering through some of the world's most inhospitable terrain. This northeast corner of Iraqi Kurdistan is an unheralded area of beauty marked by waterfalls, snow-capped mountains, deep gorges cut by raging rivers, rolling green hills and lush valleys.

Lake Dukan

2 About 60km northwest of Sulaymaniyah, endless rolling hills encircle the largest artificial lake in Iraq. In the warmer months families from all over the region flock to the banks of the lake to picnic, relax and enjoy time out.

Amadiya

3 The scenic town of Amadiya is an ancient city perched on top of a mountain, 1200m above sea level. Some claim it was the home of the biblical Three Wise Men. It is home to both Muslims and Assyrians, a religious mix noted in the presence of both mosques and churches. Lush valleys and skyscraping mountains encircle the high plateau.

Seasons

 JUL–AUG

 MAY–JUN & SEP–NOV

 DEC–APR

Food & Drink

Masgouf Tigris River fish berbecued on an outdoor grill.

Quzi-sham A biryani-like dish covered in fried pastry.

Tea Usually taken sweet and without milk.

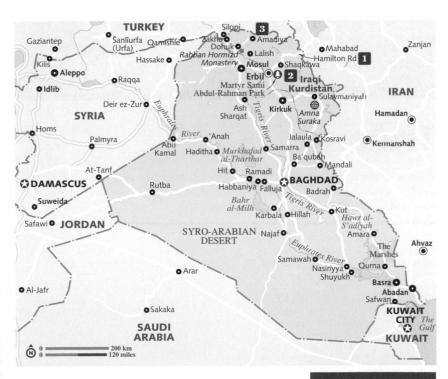

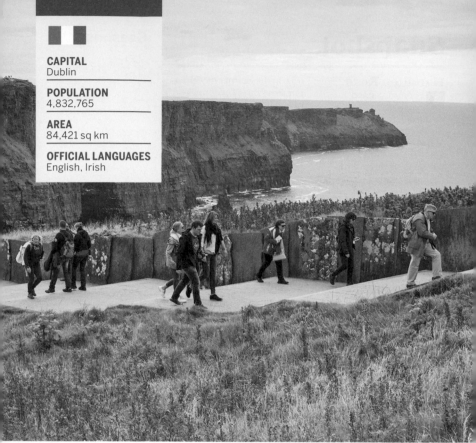

Cliffs of Moher

CAPITAL
Dublin

POPULATION
4,832,765

AREA
84,421 sq km

OFFICIAL LANGUAGES
English, Irish

Ireland

A small country with a big reputation, helped along by a breathtaking ancient landscape and fascinating, friendly people, whose lyrical nature is expressed in the warmth of their welcome.

On the plane and along your travels you might hear it said: *tá fáilte romhat* (taw fall-cha row-at) – 'You're very welcome'. Or, more famously, *céad míle fáilte* – a hundred thousand welcomes. Irish friendliness is a tired cliché, an oversimplification of a character that is infinitely complex, but the Irish are nonetheless warm and welcoming. Wherever you meet them there's a good chance a conversation will begin, pleasantries will be exchanged and, should you be a stranger in town, the offer of a helping hand extended. But, lest you think this is merely an act of unfettered altruism, rest assured that the comfort they seek is actually their own, for the Irish cannot be at ease in the company of those who aren't. A hundred thousand welcomes. It seems excessive, but in Ireland, excess is encouraged, so long as it's practised in moderation.

Top Experiences

Dublin

1 Ireland's capital and largest city by some stretch is the main gateway into the country, and it has enough distractions to keep visitors engaged for at least a few days. From world-class museums and entertainment, superb dining and top-grade hotels, Dublin has all the baubles of a major international metropolis. But the real clinchers are Dubliners themselves, who are friendlier, more easy-going and welcoming than the burghers of virtually any other European capital. And it's the home of Guinness.

Connemara, County Galway

2 A filigreed coast of tiny coves and beaches is the Connemara Peninsula's beautiful border with the wild waters of the Atlantic. Wandering characterful roads bring you from one village to another, each with trad pubs and restaurants serving seafood chowder cooked from recipes that are family secrets. Inland, the scenic drama is even greater. In fantastically desolate valleys, green hills, yellow wildflowers and wild streams reflecting the blue sky provide elemental beauty. Rambles take you far from others, back to a simpler time.

Glendalough, County Wicklow

3 St Kevin knew a thing or two about magical locations. When he chose a remote cave on a glacial lake nestled at the base of a forested valley as his monastic retreat, he inadvertently founded a settlement that would later prove to be one of Ireland's most dynamic universities and, in our time, one of the country's most beautiful ruined sites. The remains of the settlement (including an intact round tower), coupled with the stunning scenery, are unforgettable.

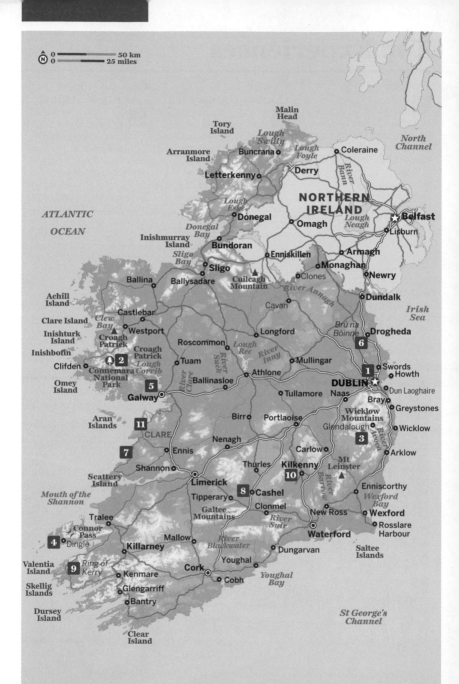

Best in Print

Dubliners (James Joyce, 1914) A collection of short stories still as poignant and relevant today as when they were written.

Room (Emma Donoghue, 2010) A harrowing but beautiful account of a boy and his mother being held prisoner, told from the boy's perspective.

The Secret Scripture (Sebastian Barry, 2008) The story of a 100-year-old patient of a mental hospital who writes her autobiography; now a 2015 film.

The Gathering (Anne Enright, 2007) Powerful account of alcoholism and domestic abuse in an Irish family.

Food & Drink

Potatoes Still a staple of most traditional meals and presented in a variety of forms.

Soda bread The most famous Irish bread is made with bicarbonate of soda and buttermilk. Superbly tasty, it's often on the breakfast menus at B&Bs.

The fry Who can say no to a plate of fried bacon, sausages, black pudding, white pudding, eggs and tomatoes?

Stout While Guinness has become synonymous with stout the world over, there are two other major producers: Murphy's and Beamish & Crawford, both based in Cork city.

Tea The Irish drink more tea, per capita, than any other nation in the world. Taken with milk (and sugar, if you want), preferred blends are very strong.

Whiskey A visit to Ireland reveals a depth of excellence that will make the connoisseur's palate spin while winning over many new friends to what the Irish call *uisce beatha* (water of life).

Dingle, County Kerry

4 Dingle is the name of both the picturesque peninsula jutting into the Atlantic from County Kerry, strewn with ancient ruins, and its delightful main town, the peninsula's beating heart. Fishing boats unload fish and shellfish that couldn't be any fresher if you caught it yourself, many pubs are untouched since their earlier incarnations as old-fashioned shops, artists sell their creations (including beautiful jewellery with Irish designs) at intriguing boutiques, and toe-tapping traditional music sessions take place around roaring pub fires.

Galway City

5 One word to describe Galway City? Craic! Ireland's liveliest city literally hums through the night at music-filled pubs where you can hear three old guys playing spoons and fiddles or a hot, young band. Join the locals as they bounce from place to place, never knowing what fun lies ahead but certain of the possibility. Add in local bounty such as the famous oysters and nearby adventure in the Connemara Peninsula and

When to Go

HIGH SEASON
(Jun–mid-Sep)
Weather at its best; accommodation rates at their highest.

SHOULDER
(Easter–May, mid-Sep–Oct)
Summer crowds and accommodation rates drop off.

LOW SEASON
(Nov–Feb)
Cold and wet weather; fog can reduce visibility.

Gaelic Football & Hurling

Gaelic games are at the core of Irishness and hold a unique place in the heart of the culture. Their resurgence towards the end of the 19th century was entwined with the whole Gaelic revival and the march towards Irish independence, and they are still far and away the most popular sports in Ireland.

Gaelic games are fast, furious and not for the faint-hearted. Challenges are fierce, and contact between players is extremely aggressive. Both Gaelic football and hurling are played by two teams of 15 players whose aim is to get the ball through what resembles a rugby goal, protected by a goalkeeper.

Gaelic football is played with a round, soccer-size ball, and players are allowed to kick it or hand-pass it, like Australian Rules. Hurling, which is considered by far the more beautiful game, is played with a flat stick or bat known as a hurley or *camán*. The small leather ball, called a *sliotar*, is hit or carried on the hurley; handpassing is also allowed. Both games are played over 70 action-filled minutes.

Getting Around

 Dublin operates a bike-share scheme with over 100 stations spread throughout the city.

 An extensive network of public and private buses make them the most cost-effective way to get around; there's service to and from most inhabited areas.

 Car is the most convenient way to explore Ireland's every nook and cranny. Drive on the left.

 A limited train network links Dublin to all major urban centres. Expensive if you're on a budget.

the Aran Islands, and the fun never ends.

Brú na Bóinne, County Meath

6 Looking at once ancient and yet eerily futuristic, Newgrange's immense, round, white stone walls topped by a grass dome is one of the most extraordinary sights you'll ever see. Part of the vast Neolithic necropolis Brú na Bóinne (the Boyne Palace), it contains Ireland's finest Stone Age passage tomb, predating the Pyramids by some six centuries. Most extraordinary of all is the tomb's precise alignment with the sun at the time of the winter solstice.

Clare Coast

7 Bathed in the golden glow of the late afternoon sun, the iconic Cliffs of Moher are but one of the splendours of County Clare. From a boat bobbing below, the towering stone faces have a jaw-dropping dramatic beauty that's enlivened by scores of sea birds, including cute little puffins. Down south in Loop Head, pillars of rock towering above the sea

have abandoned stone cottages whose very existence is inexplicable. All along the coast are cute little villages like trad-session-filled Ennistymon and the surfer mecca of Lahinch.

Rock of Cashel, County Tipperary

8 Soaring up from the green Tipperary pastures, this ancient fortress takes your breath away at first sight. The seat of kings and churchmen who ruled over the region for more than a thousand years, it rivalled Tara as a centre of power in Ireland for 400 years. Entered through the 15th-century Hall of the Vicars Choral, its impervious walls guard an awesome enclosure with a complete round tower, a 13th-century Gothic cathedral and the most magnificent 12th-century Romanesque chapel in Ireland.

Ring of Kerry

9 Driving around the Ring of Kerry is an unforgettable experience in itself, but you don't need to limit yourself to the main route. Along this 179km loop around the

Iveragh Peninsula there are countless opportunities for detours. Near Killorglin, it's a short hop up to the beautiful, little-known Cromane Peninsula. Between Portmagee and Waterville, you can explore the Skellig Ring and the peninsula's interior offers mesmerising mountain views. And that's just for starters. Wherever your travels take you, remember to charge your camera!

Kilkenny City

10 From its regal castle to its soaring cathedral, Kilkenny exudes a permanence and culture that have made it an unmissable stop on journeys to the south and west. Its namesake county boasts scores of artisans and craftspeople and you can browse their wares at Kilkenny's classy shops and boutiques. Chefs eschew Dublin in order to be close to the source of Kilkenny's wonderful produce and you can enjoy the local brewery's brews at scores of delightful pubs.

Traditional Music

11 Western Europe's most vibrant folk music is Irish traditional music, which may have earned fame thanks to the likes of Riverdance, but is best expressed in a more sedate setting, usually an old-fashioned pub. The west of Ireland is particularly musical: from Donegal down to Kerry there are centres of musical excellence, none more so than Doolin in County Clare, the unofficial capital of Irish music. You may not be asked to join in, but there's nothing stopping your foot from tapping and your hands from clapping.

CARL BRUEMMER / GETTY IMAGES ©

Puck Fair

Ireland's oldest, and quirkiest festival: crown a goat king and celebrate for three days. Strange idea, brilliant festival. Killorglin, County Kerry, mid-August.

Walking Ireland

Gentle hills, rocky ridges, wild moorlands, spectacular sea cliffs, remote islands, and the gloriously unpredictable weather – there's something for everyone, from postprandial strolls to challenging 1000m peaks.

PETER UNGER / GETTY IMAGES ©

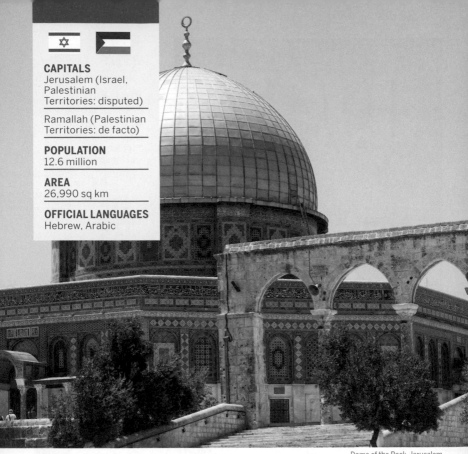

Dome of the Rock, Jerusalem

Israel & the Palestinian Territories

At the intersection of Asia, Europe and Africa – both geographically and culturally – Israel and the Palestinian Territories have been a meeting place of cultures, empires and religions since history began.

CAPITALS
Jerusalem (Israel, Palestinian Territories: disputed)

Ramallah (Palestinian Territories: de facto)

POPULATION
12.6 million

AREA
26,990 sq km

OFFICIAL LANGUAGES
Hebrew, Arabic

Few countries have so much geographic variety packed into such a small space. Distances are short, so you can relax on a Mediterranean beach one day, spend the next floating in the mineral-rich waters of the Dead Sea, and the day after that scuba diving in the Red Sea. Hikers can trek the length of the country on the Israel National Trail, splash through seasonal streams and explore spring-fed oases tucked into the arid bluffs above the Dead Sea.

Explore the 10,000-year-old mud-brick relics of Jericho, twin a visit to Masada, with its dramatic tale of resistance to the mighty legions of Rome, with a tour of Beit She'an, still pulsing with Roman opulence.

Top Experiences

Dome of the Rock

1 The first sight of Jerusalem's Dome of the Rock – its gold top shimmering above a turquoise-hued octagonal base – never fails to take your breath away. Perhaps that's what the unknown architects had in mind more than 1300 years ago when they set to work on this impossibly gorgeous building. The best view, some say, is from the Mount of Olives, but don't miss the chance to see it up close by taking an early-morning walk up to the Temple Mount/Al-Haram ash-Sharif.

The Dead Sea

2 You pass a sign reading 'Sea Level' and then keep driving downhill, eventually catching glimpses of the cobalt-blue waters of the Dead Sea, outlined by snow-white salt deposits, reddish-tan cliffs and tufts of dark-green vegetation. At the oasis of Ein Gedi you can hike through steep canyons to crystal-clear pools and tumbling waterfalls before climbing to the Judean Desert plateau above – or heading down to the seashore for a briny, invigorating dip. To the south around Mt Sodom, outdoor options include adventure cycling along dry riverbeds.

Tel Aviv

3 Brash, forward-looking and unabashedly secular, Tel Aviv is a multicultural swirl of skyscrapers, bike paths, atmospheric cafes, stylish bistros and buff bods tanning on the sand. The 4000 Bauhaus structures of the 'White City' constitute the largest ensemble of Bauhaus buildings in the world, which earned the city recognition as a Unesco World Heritage Site in 2003.

Golan Heights

4 From towering Nimrod Fortress, the 'Galilee Panhandle'

AUDUN BAKKE ANDERSEN / GETTY IMAGES ©

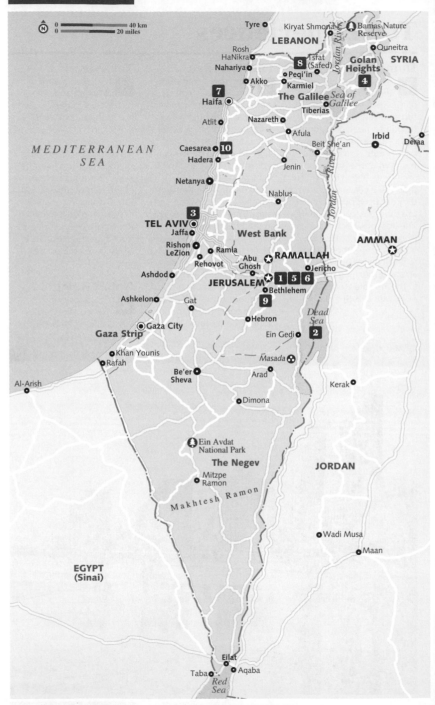

Best on Film

Sallah Shabbati (Ephraim Kishon, 1964) Satire about immigrant life in a 1950s transit camp.

Yossi & Jagger (Eytan Fox, 2002) Secret love between two buff IDF officers.

Zero Motivation (Talya Lavie, 2013) Dark comedy about ditzy, bored female draftees.

Food & Drink

Hummus Made of cooked chickpeas, this beloved paste is made to be dipped or scooped up with fresh pita bread, it's often served with warm *fuul* (fava beans), whole boiled chickpeas or tahina (sesame seed paste).

Felafel Deep-fried balls made of ground chickpeas, best when piping hot and typically served inside a pita or wrapped in a *lafa* (flatbread) along with hummus and/or tahina, tomato, cucumber and pickle slices.

Sabih Deep-fried eggplant, egg, boiled potato, cucumber, tomato, chopped parsley and tahina tucked into a pita.

Shwarma Chicken, turkey or lamb grilled on a giant spit and sliced in layers before being stuffed into a pita – the ultimate non-vegetarian street food.

Labneh (labaneh) A creamy, sour, yoghurt-type cheese, eaten with pita or *lafa,* that's smothered in olive oil and sprinkled with *za'atar* (a blend of local spices that includes hyssop, sumac and sesame).

Shakshuka A spicy Moroccan egg and tomato stew.

Jachnun Rolled-up, buttery dough slow baked in a pot and served with grated tomatoes and *s'chug* hot paste.

spreads out before you like a topographical map. But the looming flanks of Mt Hermon, snow capped well into spring, dwarf even this Crusader-era stronghold. Hikers can take on the alpine peaks of Mt Hermon or follow the cliff-lined wadis of the Banias and Yehudiya Nature Reserves on their way to the Jordan River and the Sea of Galilee. The Golan's basalt soils are ideal for growing grapes, so the local boutique wines are some of the region's finest.

Western Wall

5 For centuries Jews have come to the 2000-year-old western retaining wall of the Temple Mount to pray and to mourn the destruction of the First and Second Temples. The Western Wall's enormous stones, worn smooth by countless caresses, have an almost magnetic power, drawing close the hands and foreheads of the faithful, who come in search of a deep, direct connection with God.

When to Go

HIGH SEASON
(Jul & Aug)
Hotel prices spike and rooms are scarce.

SHOULDER
(Oct, Nov & Mar–Jun)
Spring wildflowers make March and April ideal for hiking.

LOW SEASON
(Dec–Feb)
Chilly in the north but popular time for Eilat and the Dead Sea.

Church of the Holy Sepulchre

6 Built on what St Helena – Constantine the Great's mother – believed to be the site of Jesus's crucifixion and burial, Jerusalem's Church

Jerusalem Syndrome

Each year millions of tourists descend on Jerusalem to walk in the footsteps of the prophets, and a handful come away from the journey thinking they *are* the prophets. This medically recognised ailment, called Jerusalem Syndrome, occurs when visitors become overwhelmed by the metaphysical significance of the Holy City and come to the conclusion that they are biblical characters or that the Apocalypse is near.

Doctors estimate that Jerusalem Syndrome affects between 80 and 100 people per year, and although many have a recorded history of mental illness, about a quarter of recorded cases have no previous psychiatric record. Doctors explain that the syndrome generally lasts a week and when the patient resumes his or her old self, they become extremely embarrassed and prefer not to speak of the incident.

Getting Around

Local buses reach every corner of major cities but if you don't read Hebrew it can be a challenge to figure out the bus routes – just ask locals or any passing bus driver.

All you need is your regular driving licence; an international driving licence is not required.

To Israelis it's a *sherut* (sheh-root) while Palestinians call it a *service* (pronounced ser-vees), but whatever name you use, shared taxis are a useful way to get around. These vehicles, often 13-seat minivans, operate on a fixed route for a fixed price, like a bus except that they don't have pre-set stops.

Israel Railway's famously scenic lines link Tel Aviv with southern Jerusalem, Haifa, Akko and Nahariya. Construction is underway on a high-speed rail link that will cut the travel time between Tel Aviv and Jerusalem to 30 minutes; the planned completion date is 2017.

---

of the Holy Sepulchre is the holiest place in the world for many Christians. In darkened chambers infused with incredible spirituality, a variety of Christian denominations keep alive here some of the oldest traditions of their faith. Visitors are welcome to join the parade of resplendently garbed clergy and simply dressed pilgrims as they shuffle reverently through candle-lit corridors redolent with incense.

Baha'i Gardens

7 Fusing religious symbolism, breathtaking views and meticulous gardening, the 19 terraces of Haifa's Baha'i Gardens present visitors with a sublime expression of humankind's striving for beauty. The gold-domed Shrine of the Bab sits in the middle of the gardens, and tier after tier of geometric flower beds, immaculate lawns, sculptures and fountains cascade down the slopes of Mt Carmel, offering pilgrims and tourists alike a sense of incredible serenity.

Tsfat (Safed)

8 The spirit of the 16th-century rabbis who turned Tsfat into the world's most important centre of Kabbalah (Jewish mysticism) lingers in the alleyways and ancient synagogues of the Synagogue Quarter and in the nearby Artists' Quarter, where intimate galleries offer creative, joyous Judaica (Jewish ritual objects). A Kabbalistic vibe is also palpable in the hillside cemetery, where some of Judaism's greatest sages – the Ari, Yitzhak Luria, Yosef Caro – lie buried.

Old City, Bethlehem

9 For nearly two millennia, pilgrims have been making their way to what Christians believe to be the birthplace of Jesus. Walk the streets around the Church of the Nativity – a Unesco World Heritage Site since 2012 – and Manger Sq and you'll see ancient stone buildings and narrow alleyways that look much as they did centuries ago. But Bethlehem isn't all about the past. The separation wall, which cuts the city off from Jerusalem, has become a vast canvas for street artists, from local Palestinians to British veteran Banksy (whose hotel overlooks the wall).

Caesarea

10 Hugely impressive Roman ruins make it easy to imagine city life here two millennia ago, when crowds in the amphitheatre cheered wildly as slaves fought wild animals and the theatre hosted top musical talent – as it still does today. The remains of Herod's vast port, built to rival Alexandria, have been turned into one of the loveliest spots in Israel for a seaside meal or a cold beer. For a look underneath the harbour's turquoise waters, book an introductory scuba dive.

Cycling in Tel Aviv

Tel Aviv has had remarkable success in convincing city residents to cycle rather than drive and now has some 120km of dedicated bike paths.

Immigration

Since 1948 Israel has absorbed more immigrants than any country on earth, relative to its population. About 900,000 Jews from the former Soviet Union arrived in the 1990s; recent arrivals include thousands of Jews from France.

9

7

Positano, Amalfi Coast

CAPITAL	Rome
POPULATION	59.83 million
AREA	301,230 sq km
OFFICIAL LANGUAGE	Italian

Italy

Italy is an extraordinary feast of heart-thumping, soul-stirring art, food and landscapes rivalled by few and coveted by millions.

Epicentre of the Roman Empire and birthplace of the Renaissance, this sun-kissed virtuoso groans under the weight of its cultural cachet: it's here that you'll stand in the presence of Michelangelo's *David* and Sistine Chapel frescoes, Botticelli's *Birth of Venus* and da Vinci's *The Last Supper*. In fact, Italy has more Unesco World Heritage cultural sites than any other country.

But Italy's fortes extend beyond its galleries, histories and culture – its geography offers extraordinary natural diversity. From the north's icy Alps and glacial lakes to the south's volcanic craters and turquoise grottoes, this is a place for doing as well as seeing.

Italy's word-renowned food springs from superlative ingredients and strictly seasonal produce. So whether you're on a degustation odyssey in Modena, truffle hunting in Piedmont or swilling powerhouse reds in the Valpolicella wine region, prepare to swoon.

Top Experiences

Virtuoso Venice

1 Step through the portals of Basilica di San Marco and try to imagine what it might have been like for a humble medieval labourer glimpsing those glittering gold mosaic domes for the first time. Indeed, one visit is never enough; the basilica's sheer scale, exquisite detailing and ever-shifting light promising endless revelations.

Touring Tuscany

2 From Brunelleschi's Duomo to Masaccio's Cappella Brancacci frescoes, Florence, according to Unesco, contains 'the greatest concentration of universally renowned works of art in the world'. Beyond its blockbuster museums, jewel-box churches and flawless Renaissance streetscapes sprawls an undulating wonderland of regional masterpieces, from the Gothic majesty of Siena, to the Manhattan-esque skyline of medieval San Gimignano, to the vine-laced hills of Italy's most famous wine region, Chianti.

Ghostly Pompeii

3 Frozen in its death throes, the sprawling, time-warped ruins of Pompeii hurtle you 2000 years into the past. Wander through chariot-grooved Roman streets, lavishly frescoed villas and bathhouses, food stores and markets, theatres, even an ancient brothel. Then, in the eerie stillness, your eye on ominous Mt Vesuvius, ponder Pliny the Younger's terrifying account of the town's final hours: 'Darkness came on again, again ashes, thick and heavy. We got up repeatedly to shake these off; otherwise we would have been buried and crushed by the weight'.

Eternal Rome

4 Once *caput mundi* (capital of the world), Rome was legendarily spawned by a wolf-suckled boy, grew to be Western Europe's first superpower, became the spiritual centrepiece of the Christian world and is now the repository of over two millennia of European art and architecture. From the Pantheon and the Colosseum to Michelangelo's Sistine Chapel and countless works by Caravaggio, there's so much to see.

MAPICS / SHUTTERSTOCK ©

Best on Film

La Grande Bellezza (Great Beauty; 2013) Paolo Sorrentino's Fellini-esque tribute to Italy.

La Dolce Vita (Sweet Life; 1960) Federico Fellini capturing Italy's 1950s zeitgeist.

The Leopard (1963) Luchino Visconti's portrayal of the decaying Sicilian nobility.

Ladri di biciclette (Bicycle Thieves; 1948) A moving portrait of post-WWII Italy.

Best in Print

The Italians (Luigi Barzini; 1964) Revealing portrait of the Italian character.

The Leopard (Giuseppe Tomasi di Lampedusa; 1958) Masterpiece about tumultuous 19th-century changes.

Gomorrah (Paolo Saviano; 2006) Unputdownable epic about the Neapolitan Camorra (mafia).

My Brilliant Friend (Elena Ferrante; 2012) Follows the lives of two friends growing up in a neighborhood near Naples in the 1950s.

Amalfi Coast

5 Italy's most celebrated coastline blends superlative beauty and gripping geology: coastal mountains plunge into creamy blue sea in a prime-time vertical scene of precipitous crags, sun-bleached villages and lush forests. Between sea and sky, mountain-top hiking trails deliver Tyrrhenian panoramas fit for a god.

Tackling the Dolomites

6 Scour the globe and you'll find plenty of taller, bigger and more geologically volatile mountains, but few can match the romance of the pink-hued, granite Dolomites. Maybe it's their harsh, jagged summits, the vibrant skirts of spring wildflowers or the rich cache of Ladin legends. Then again, it could just be the magnetic draw of money, style and glamour at Italy's most fabled ski resort, Cortina d'Ampezzo. Whatever the reason, this tiny pocket of northern Italy takes seductiveness to dizzying heights.

Sardinian Shores

7 While perma-tanned celebrities wine, dine and sail along the glossy Costa Smeralda, much of Sardinia remains a wild, raw playground. Explore the is-

When to Go

Cheap Treats

Pizza al taglio 'Pizza by the slice' is the perfect nibble.
Arancini Deep-fried rice balls stuffed with ragù (meat sauce), tomato and vegetables.
Porchetta rolls Warm sliced pork (roasted whole with fennel, garlic and pepper) in a crispy roll.
Pane e panelle Palermo chickpea fritters on a sesame roll.
Gelato The best Italian gelato uses seasonal ingredients and natural colours.

The Caffè Low Down

Caffè latte and cappuccino are considered morning drinks, with espresso and macchiato the preferred post-lunch options. Baristas may offer a glass water, either *liscia* (still) or *frizzante* (sparkling), with your espresso. Coffee with dessert is fine, but ordering one with your main meal is a travesty.

Iconic Cheeses

Parmigiano Reggiano A grainy, nutty cheese high in calcium and relatively low in fat. Produced in the northern provinces of Parma, Reggio Emilia, Modena, Bologna and Mantua, it's made using milk from free-range cows on a prized grass or hay diet.

Gorgonzola Gloriously pungent, this washed-rind, blue-veined cheese is produced in Lombardy and Piedmont. Made using whole cow's milk, it's generally aged three to four months. Varieties include the younger, sweeter *gorgonzola dolce* and the sharper, spicier *gorgonzola piccante* (also known as *stagionato* or *montagna*).

Mozzarella A chewy, silky cheese synonymous with Campania and Puglia and best eaten the day it's made. Top of the range is luscious, porcelain-white DOC *mozzarella di bufala* (buffalo mozzarella), produced using the whole milk of black water buffaloes.

Provolone Its roots in Basilicata, this semi-hard, wax-rind staple is now commonly produced in Lombardy and the Veneto. Like mozzarella, it's made using the *pasta filata* method, which sees the curd heated until it becomes stringy (*filata*).

land's rugged coastal beauty, from the tumbledown boulders of Santa Teresa di Gallura and the wind-chiselled cliffs of the Golfo di Orosei to the windswept beauty of the Costa Verde's dune-backed beaches.

Devouring Emilia Romagna

8 They don't call Bologna 'la grassa' (the fat one) for nothing.

Many of Italy's belt-busting classics call this city home, from mortadella and tortellini to its trademark tagliatelle al ragù. Shop the deli-packed Quadrilatero, and side-trip it to the city of Modena for world-famous aged balsamic vinegar. Just leave room for a trip to Parma, hometown of parmigiano reggiano cheese and the incomparable prosciutto di Parma.

Living Luxe on Lake Como

9 Nestled in the shadow of the Rhaetian Alps, dazzling Lake Como is the most spectacular of the Lombard lakes, its Liberty-style villas home to movie moguls, fashion royalty and Arab sheikhs. Surrounded on all sides by lush greenery, the lake's siren calls include the gardens of Villa Melzi d'Eril, Villa Carlotta and Villa Balbianello, which blush pink with camellias, azaleas and rhododendrons in April and May.

Hiking the Italian Riviera

 For the sinful inhabitants of the Cinque Terre's five sherbert-coloured villages – Monterosso, Vernazza, Corniglia, Manarola and Riomaggiore – penance involved a lengthy and arduous hike up the vertiginous cliffside to the local village sanctuary to appeal for forgiveness. Scale the same trails today, through terraced vineyards and hillsides smothered in macchia (shrubbery). As the heavenly views unfurl, it's hard to think of a more benign punishment.

Savouring Sicily

 'Leave the gun. Take the cannoli.' Even the mobsters in Francis Ford Coppola's The Godfather couldn't resist a Sicilian bite. Sour, spicy and sweet, the flavours of Sicily reflect millennia of cross-cultural influences – Greek, Arab, Spanish and French. Tuck into golden *panelle* (chickpea fritters) in Palermo, fragrant couscous in Trapani and chilli-spiked chocolate in Modica. From Palermo's Mercato di Ballarò to Catania's Pescheria, market stalls burst with local delicacies: just leave room for a slice of sweet Sicilian cassata.

Escaping to Paradiso

 If you're pining for a mind-clearing retreat, wear down your hiking boots on the 724km of marked trails and mule tracks traversing 'Grand Paradise'. Gran Paradiso's pure, pristine spread encompasses 57 glaciers and Alpine pastures awash with wild pansies, gentians and Alpenroses, not to mention a healthy population of Alpine ibex (for whose protection the park was originally established).

Neapolitan Street Life

Nowhere else in Italy are people as conscious of their role in the theatre of everyday life as in Naples. The ancient streets are a stage, cast with boisterous matriarchs, bellowing baristi and tongue-knotted lovers. To savour the flavour, dive into the city's Porta Nolana market, a loud, lavish opera of hawking fruit vendors, wriggling seafood and the irresistible aroma of just-baked *sfogliatelle* (sweetened ricotta pastries).

YULIA GRIGORYEVA / SHUTTERSTOCK ©

Getting Around

Buses are cheaper and slower than trains. Useful for more remote villages not serviced by trains.

A car is handy for travelling at your own pace, or for visiting regions with minimal public transport. Not a good idea for travelling within major urban areas.

Trains are reasonably priced, with extensive coverage and frequent departures. High-speed trains connect major cities.

Street party, Kingston

Jamaica

Jamaica is the Caribbean country that comes with its own soundtrack.
Groove to its singular rhythm as you explore beyond the beaches and resorts.

This tiny island has musical roots that reach back to the folk songs of West Africa and forward to the electronic beats of contemporary dancehall. Simply put, Jamaica is a musical powerhouse, a fact reflected not just in the bass of the omnipresent sound systems, but in the lyricism of the patois language and the gospel sounds from the island's many churches. Music is life in Jamaica, and you'll soon find yourself swaying along with it.

Jamaica is a powerfully beautiful island. It begins with crystalline waters flowing over gardens of coral, lapping onto soft sandy beaches, then rises past red soil and lush banana groves into sheer mountains. Rushing waterfalls seem to erupt out of nowhere. Jamaican culture can be a daunting subject for foreigners to understand, but ultimately it's a matter of appreciating this great green garden of a land and how its cyclical rhythms set the pace of so much island life.

Top Experiences

Climbing Blue Mountain Peak

1 A night hike to reach Jamaica's highest point by sunrise, your path lit by the sparks of myriad fireflies, is an experience unlike any other. As you climb, the vegetation becomes less and less tropical, until you're hiking amid stunted trees draped with old man's beard (lichen) and giant ferns. In the predawn cold at the summit, you wait in rapt silence as the first rays of the sun wash over the densely forested mountain peaks all around you, illuminating the distant coffee plantations and Cuba beyond.

Kingston Nightlife

2 Whether you're attending a nightclub or a street dance, expect a sweaty, lively, no-holds-barred event. Dress up to the nines and follow the locals' lead. At a street dance, two giant speakers are placed facing each other, the street pounding with the bass, while nightclubs provide a similar experience indoors. Expect to be pulled into the melee as the locals will want to see how well you can dance, and bump and grind to some dancehall riddims or slowly skank to the deepest dub.

Negril

3 So you've walked on the snowy sands of Negril's Seven Mile Beach, wandered past the nude sunbathers, seen the sun sink behind the horizon in a fiery ball, plunged into the ocean to scrub your soul and fended off all the hustlers. How about topping off all of those experiences by snorkeling or scuba diving in the cerulean waters that lap against the cliffs, and then rocking out to reggae or dancehall at one of Negril's many music nights?

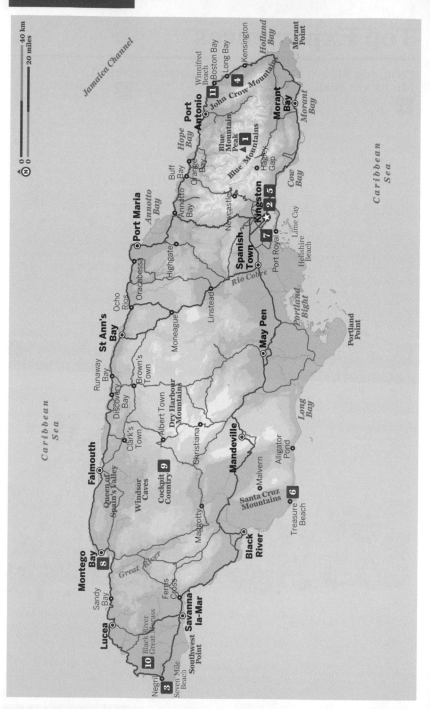

Best in Print

The Book of Night Women
(2009) Gripping tale of a
female-led plantation revolts, by
Marlon James.

The Lunatic (1987) Comic novel
revolving around a village madman and his affair with a tourist,
by Anthony Winkler

Lionheart Gal (1986) A lively
short-story collection that reveals much about patois and the
lives of women.

White Witch of Rose Hall
(1928) Herbert de Lisser's classic Gothic horror, set in colonial
Jamaica.

Food & Drink

Ackee & saltfish The Jamaican
breakfast of champions. Ackee
fruit bears an uncanny resemblance to scrambled eggs when
cooked.

Bread-kind A sort of
catch-all term for starch
accompaniments.

Jerk The island's signature
dish, jerk is a tongue-searing
marinade and spice rub for
meats and fish, and the method
of smoking them slowly over
pimento wood.

Patties Delicious meat pies;
fillings can include spicy beef,
vegetables, fish and shrimp.

Fish tea 'Warm up yuh belly'
with this favorite local cure-all.
Essentially, fish broth.

Rum Jamaica is proud of its
rum. Smooth and dark Appleton
is the most celebrated brand;
Wray & Nephew's white over-
proof rum carries a knockout
blow.

Coffee Blue Mountain coffee is
one of the world's most exotic
and expensive coffees.

Reach Falls

4 On Jamaica's east
coast, past stretches
of jungle and beach that are
completely off the radar of
most tourists, you'll find, up
in the hills, one of Jamaica's
most beautiful waterfalls –
and this is an island with a
lot of beautiful waterfalls.
Hire a guide (you'll need
one, trust us) and clamber
up slippery rocks, over
neon-green moss and into
cool mountain pools of the
freshest spring water. In
some areas you can dive
under watery tunnels and
through blizzards of snowy-
white cascading foam.

Bob Marley Museum, Kingston

5 Marley's creaky
home is crammed
with memorabilia, but the
visitor is drawn to his untouched bedroom, adorned
with objects of spiritual
significance to the artist,
the small kitchen where
he cooked I-tal food, the
hammock in which he lay

When to Go

HIGH SEASON
(Dec–Mar)
Expect sunny, warm days.

SHOULDER SEASON
(Apr & May)
Good time to visit; rates
drop for accommodations.

LOW SEASON
(Jun–Nov)
Sporadic heavy rainfall
across the island, except
the south coast.

to seek inspiration from
the distant mountains,
and the room riddled with
bullet holes, where he and
his wife almost died in an
assassination attempt. The
intimate surrounds and

Experiencing Jamaican Music

It's a surprise to some, but the live music scene in Jamaica is
relatively small. The sound system rules supreme here; many
working musicians head to the resort hotels to earn a crust
playing reggae for tourists, although in recent years the roots
revival has seen more club nights in Kingston featuring live
acts. There are also some excellent reggae festivals, most notably Montego Bay's SumFest every July, and Rebel Salute in St
Ann in January. February is 'Reggae Month' in Jamaica (in part
to honor Bob Marley's birthday on the 6th), when there's lots of
live music to be had, especially in Kingston.

If you want to hear dancehall, there are plenty of clubs,
but the street parties in Kingston are by far the most vibrant.
For the sound systems, the toasting, the street fashion and
the dancing, they're hard to beat. Ask locals, especially those
working in your hotel or guesthouse, where you'll find the best
parties and promoted events. They're on the whole well-run,
community-policed events. Parties run late – don't even think
of arriving before midnight.

Getting Around

Cheap bus travel between towns, but often over-crowded and dangerously driven. More expensive and reliable scheduled coaches also available.

A car is useful for traveling at your own pace, or for visiting regions with minimal public transportation. Drive on the left.

Route taxis run set routes within and between nearby towns and cities. Cheap and convenient.

modest personal effects speak eloquently of Marley's turbulent life.

The Perfect Retreats in Treasure Beach

6 The greatest, most interesting varieties of accommodations in Jamaica can be found in Treasure Beach, on Jamaica's south coast. Here, instead of huge all-inclusive resorts, you'll find quiet, friendly guesthouses; artsy enclaves dreamed up by theater set designers; Rasta retreats favored by budget backpackers; and private villas that are some of the classiest, most elegant luxury residences in the country. Aside from beds and bathrooms, some places offer interesting extras such as cooking classes, rooftop yoga, farm-to-table banquets and movie nights.

Playing Pirates at Port Royal

7 The sleepy fishing village of Port Royal only hints at past glories that made it pirate capital of the Caribbean and 'the wickedest city on Earth.' Stroll in the footsteps of pirate Sir Henry Morgan along the battlements of Fort Charles,

still lined with cannons to repel the invaders; become disorientated inside the Giddy House artillery store, tipped at a jaunty angle; or admire the treasures in the Maritime Museum, rescued from the deep after two-thirds of the town sank beneath the waves in the monstrous 1692 earthquake.

Diving Montego Bay

8 You might find the resorts of Montego Bay to be crowded with people, but wait till you dive in the surrounding waters. They're crowded, yes, although not with human beings – just multicolored fish and swaying sponges. For all the tropical pastels and cool blue hues, this is a subdued seascape, a silent and delicate marine ecosystem that is one of the island's unique natural resources. The best sea walls are to be found at the Point, while more advanced divers should explore the ominous (and gorgeous) Widowmakers Cave.

Cockpit Country

9 The Cockpit Country of the island's interior is some of the most rugged terrain throughout the Caribbean, a series of

jungle-clad round hills intersected by powerfully deep and sheer valleys. The rains gather in these mountains and the water percolates through the rocks, creating a Swiss cheese of sinkholes and caves. Since most of the trails here are badly overgrown, the best way to appreciate the place is to hike the old Barbecue Bottom road along its eastern edge or go caving in the Painted Circuit Cave.

Crocodile-Spotting in Black River Great Morass

10 This is one of our favorite ways of exploring wild Jamaica: setting off by boat in the Black River Great Morass, gliding past spidery mangroves and trees bearded with Spanish moss, whilst white egrets flap overhead. Your tour guide may tell you about the local women who sell bags of spicy 'swimp' (shrimp) on the riverside, and point to a beautiful, grinning American crocodile cruising by.

Boston Bay

11 The best experiences in Jamaica are extremely sensory affairs, but Boston Bay may be the only one that is more defined by smell than sight or sound. Well, smell and taste: Boston Bay is the supposed birthplace of jerk, the spice rub that is Jamaica's most famous contribution to the culinary arts. The turnoff to Boston Bay (itself a lovely beach) is lined with jerk stalls that produce smoked meats that redefine what heat and sweet can do as complementary gastronomic qualities. In plain English: it tastes freaking amazing.

4

Ganja

Ganja (marijuana) has been decriminalized in Jamaica but not legalized: you can't buy it legally, but possession now attracts a fine rather than a criminal record.

Sunday, Day of Rest

Don't plan on getting much done on a Sunday: many sights and restaurants shut for the day.

5

Geisha, Kyoto

Japan

Japan is truly timeless, a place where ancient traditions are fused with modern life as if it were the most natural thing in the world.

The neon-lit streetscapes of Japan's cities look like sci-fi film sets, even though many of them are decades old. Meanwhile, cities like Tokyo and Osaka have been adding new architectural wonders that redefine what buildings – and cities – should look like. There's an indelible buzz to these urban centres, with their vibrant street life, 24-hour drinking and dining scenes, and creative hubs that turn out fashion and pop culture trends consumed the world over.

While on the surface Japan appears exceedingly modern, travelling around it offers numerous opportunities to connect with the country's traditional culture. Spend the night in a ryokan (traditional inn), padding through well-worn wooden halls to the bathhouse. Chant with monks or learn how to whisk bitter *matcha* (powdered green tea) into a froth. From the splendour of a Kyoto geisha dance to the spare beauty of a Zen rock garden, Japan has the power to enthral even the most jaded traveller.

Top Experiences

Onsen

1 Highly volcanic Japan bubbles with onsen (hot springs). The Japanese have turned the simple act of bathing into a folk religion and the country is dotted with temples and shrines to this most relaxing of faiths. Not convinced? Wait until you give it a try (and feel years of stress melt away). There are baths literally everywhere, but Kyūshū and Tōhoku (located in Northern Honshū) are particularly famous for their springs. Two worth-a-detour towns include Kurokawa Onsen and Nyūtō Onsen, both hidden away in the mountains.

Cherry-Blossom Viewing (Hanami)

2 Come spring, countless cherry trees around Japan burst into white and pink flowers. That's the cue for locals to gather in parks and along river banks for sake-fuelled cherry-blossom hanami (viewing parties). More elaborate bacchanals, complete with barbecues and turntables, carry on long past dark for yozakura (night-time cherry blossoms). While the best places to see the blossoms is a hot debate, two favourites include Kyoto's Maruyama-kōen, with its weeping cherry tree, and Tokyo's Yoyogi-kōen, where the grassy lawns become one week-long party scene.

Tokyo's Modern Architecture

3 Tokyo is a city forever reaching into the future, pushing the boundaries of what's possible on densely populated, earthquake-prone land, adding ever taller, sleeker structures. Come see the edgy designer boutiques from Japan's award-winning architects that line the boulevard Omote-sandō; the mega-malls that are redefining the urban landscape; and the world's tallest free-standing tower – Tokyo Sky Tree. Tokyo has long been a source of inspiration for designers around the world; perhaps it will be for you, too.

Kyoto Temples & Gardens

4 Japan's imperial capital for a thousand years, Kyoto is home to more than a thousand temples. Some are monumental: Kinkaku-ji is an exquisite pavilion sheathed entirely in gold leaf. Some are more subtle: the simple beauty of Shōren-in, made of unadorned wood, reveals itself while you sip matcha at the teahouse. Others are more meditative still, particularly Ryōan-ji, with its Zen rock garden. While famous temples draw crowds, the majority see few visitors – meaning there are myriad ways to find moments of peace among tranquil surrounds.

SOMJORK / SHUTTERSTOCK ©

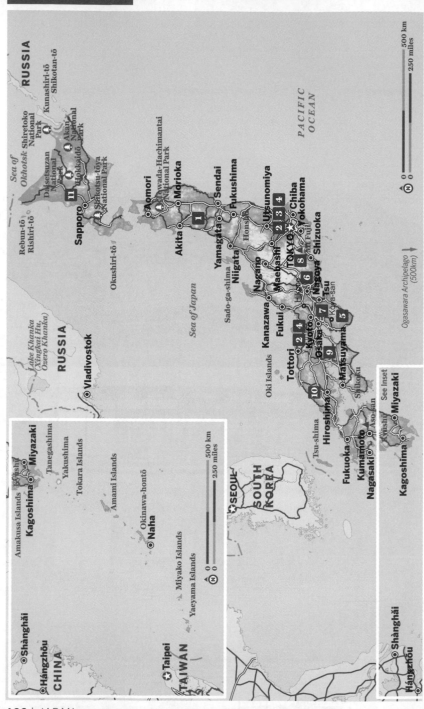

RUSSIA

Sea of Okhotsk

Shiretoko National Park

Kunashiri-tō
Shikotan-tō

Akan National Park

Daisetsuzan National Park

Shikotsu-tōya National Park

HOKKAIDŌ

Rebun-tō
Rishiri-tō

Sapporo

Okushiri-tō

Aomori

Towada-Hachimantai National Park

Morioka

Akita

Yamagata

Sendai

Fukushima

HONSHŪ

Utsunomiya

Chiba

Yokohama

Niigata

Sado-ga-shima

Nagano

Maebashi

Mt Fuji

Shizuoka

Nagoya

Tsu

Kōya-san

Lake Khanka
(Xingkai Hu,
Ozero Khanka)

RUSSIA

Vladivostok

Sea of Japan

Kanazawa

Fukui

Kyōto

Ōsaka

Matsuyama

Oki Islands

Tottori

SHIKOKU

Tsu-shima

Hiroshima

Fukuoka

Kumamoto

Nagasaki

KYŪSHŪ

Aso-san

Miyazaki

See Inset

Kagoshima

SEOUL

SOUTH KOREA

PACIFIC OCEAN

Ogasawara Archipelago
(500km)

500 km
250 miles

0
0

Amakusa Islands

Kōshiki

Miyazaki

Kagoshima

Tanegashima

Yakushima

Tokara Islands

Amami Islands

Okinawa-hontō

Naha

500 km
250 miles

0
0

Miyako Islands

Yaeyama Islands

Shànghǎi

Hángzhōu

CHINA

Taipei

TAIWAN

Kagoshima

Shànghǎi

Hángzhōu

Best on Film

Osaka Elegy (Mizoguchi Kenji; 1936) A modern girl makes her way in Osaka.

Tokyo Story (Ozu Yasujirō; 1953) Portrait of a family in rapidly changing, post-WWII Japan.

Lost in Translation (Sofia Coppola; 2003) Disorienting, captivating Tokyo through the eyes of two Americans.

Adrift in Tokyo (Satoshi Miki; 2008) Two luckless antiheroes on a long walk through the city.

Food & Drink

Okonomiyaki Various forms of batter and cabbage cakes cooked on a griddle.

Sake Most Japanese still consider sake to be the national drink, and it makes the perfect accompaniment to traditional Japanese food.

Shabu-shabu Thin slices of beef and vegetables cooked in a light broth, then dipped in a variety of sauces.

Tonkatsu A deep-fried breaded pork cutlet that is served with a special sauce, usually as part of a set meal (*tonkatsu teishoku*).

Unagi Eel is an expensive and popular delicacy in Japan.

Yakitori Skewers of charcoal-grilled chicken and vegetables.

Oku-no-in at Kōya-san

5 Riding the funicular up to the sacred Buddhist monastic complex of Kōya-san feels, appropriately, like ascending to another world. There are over a hundred temples here, the highlight of which is Oku-no-in, where paths weave their way among towering cryptomeria trees and time-worn stone stupas covered in moss and lichen. Other temples offer a different experience: the chance to spend the night, dine on traditional vegetarian Buddhist cuisine and wake up early for (optional) morning meditation with the resident monks.

Tsumago & Magome

6 Tsumago and Magome are two post towns along the old Nakasendō, one of five foot highways (used by lords and messengers alike) that connected Tokyo and Kyoto during the feudal era. The old path remains, paved with large stones, and it is possible to hike 7.8km between the two towns, through sleepy alpine hamlets and cedar forests, past waterwheels and rice paddies. The towns themselves are a treat too, with narrow lanes and low-slung dark wooden buildings that serve as inns, noodle restaurants and craft shops.

When to Go

HIGH SEASON
(Apr & May, Aug)
Weather in April and May is generally fantastic.

SHOULDER
(Jun & Jul, Sep–Dec)
June and July is rainy season (except Hokkaidō).

LOW SEASON
(Jan–Mar)
Peak ski season, but affordable and uncrowded elsewhere.

Sumo

From the ancient rituals to the thrill of the quick bouts, sumo is a fascinating spectacle. Tournaments take place several times a year (in Tokyo, Nagoya, Osaka and Fukuoka); outside of tournament season you can catch an early morning practice session at one of the stables where wrestlers live and train.

Staying at a Ryokan

Ryokan means 'inn', but the word has come to suggest an inn that is more traditionally Japanese. Most ryokan have tatami (woven reed mat) floors where guests sleep on futons (quilted mattresses) rather than beds. They're usually low-slung buildings with winding corridors of polished wood. In better ones, staff wear kimonos and exquisite meals are served.

Gardens of Japan

Gardening is one of Japan's finest art forms. You'll encounter four major types of gardens during your horticultural explorations.

Funa asobi Meaning 'pleasure boat' and popular in the Heian period, such gardens feature a large pond for boating and were often built around noble mansions. The garden that surrounds Byōdō-in in Uji is a vestige of this style.

Shūyū These 'stroll' gardens are intended to be viewed from a winding path, allowing the design to unfold and reveal itself in stages and from different vantages. A celebrated example is the garden at Ginkaku-ji in Kyoto.

Kanshō Zen rock gardens (also known as *kare-sansui* gardens) are an example of this type of 'contemplative' garden intended to be viewed from one vantage point and designed to aid meditation. Kyoto's Ryōan-ji is perhaps the most famous example.

Kaiyū The 'varied pleasures' garden features many small gardens with one or more teahouses surrounding a central pond. It is meant to be explored on foot and provides the visitor with changing scenes, many with literary allusions. The imperial villa of Katsura Rikyū in Kyoto is the classic example.

Daibutsu (Great Buddha) of Nara

7 Nara's 15m-tall gilt-bronze Buddha statue was first cast in the 8th century, at the dawn of the Japanese empire. It's among the largest gilt-bronze effigies in the world and the temple that houses it, Tōdai-ji, is among the world's largest wooden structures. It's hard, in fact, to describe the Great Buddha without using superlatives; it's simply awesome. It's also just one of many things to see in the pleasing grassy expanse that is Nara-kōen (Nara Park). Nearby Nara National Museum, for example, has fascinating, glittering relics on display.

Mt Fuji

8 Even from a distance Mt Fuji will take your breath away. Close up, the perfectly symmetrical cone of Japan's highest peak is nothing short of awesome. Dawn from the summit? Pure magic. Fuji-san is among Japan's most revered and timeless attractions. Hundreds of thousands of people climb it every year, continuing a centuries-old tradition of pilgrimages up the sacred volcano. Those who'd rather search for picture-perfect views from the less-daunting peaks nearby can follow in the steps of Japan's most famous painters and poets.

Naoshima

Naoshima is one of Japan's great success stories: a rural island on the verge of becoming a ghost town, now a world-class centre for contemporary art. Many of Japan's most lauded architects have contributed structures, including museums, a boutique hotel and even a bathhouse – all designed to enhance the island's natural beauty and complement its existing settlements. The resulting blend of avant-garde and rural Japan is captivating. It has also inspired some Japanese to pursue a slower life outside the big cities, relocating to Naoshima to open cafes and inns.

Hiroshima

Hiroshima today is a forward-thinking city with attractive, leafy boulevards. It's not until you visit the Peace Memorial Museum that the true extent of human tragedy wreaked by the atomic bomb becomes vividly clear. A visit here is a heartbreaking, important history lesson and the park around the museum, much of which was designed by Japan's great modernist Tange Kenzō, offers many opportunities for reflection. But the city's spirit of determination – as well as its food – will ensure that you'll have good memories to take with you when you leave.

Wild Hokkaidō

Hokkaidō is Japan's last frontier, a largely untamed, highly volcanic landscape of massive mountains startlingly pock-marked with crystal-blue caldera lakes and opalescent, sulphur-rich hot springs. Its flora and fauna (of which there is a lot) is more closely related to Sakhalin, part of Russia, to the north, than the rest of Japan to the south. Hikers, cyclists and casual road-trippers are all drawn to the island's big skies, wide-open spaces and dramatic topography. With a new bullet train line connecting Hokkaidō to Tokyo, Japan's northernmost island has never been more accessible.

Getting Around

An extensive network of domestic flights makes air travel a good option for long distances.

Bus is the cheapest way to make long-haul journeys and the only way to get to some mountain and rural destinations.

Rental cars are widely available, roads are great, driving is safe, and a car will give you plenty of freedom.

The best way to get around: trains are fast, efficient, reliable and can get you just about anywhere.

CAPITAL	Amman
POPULATION	9.9 million
AREA	89,342 sq km
OFFICIAL LANGUAGE	Arabic

Wadi Rum

Jordan

A safe haven in a region of conflict, Jordan has delighted visitors for centuries with its World Heritage Sites, friendly towns and inspiring desert landscapes.

Take a ride through Wadi Rum at sunset and it's easy to see why T E Lawrence (Lawrence of Arabia) was so drawn to this land of weathered sandstone and reddened dunes. Jordan has a tradition of welcoming visitors: camel caravans plied the legendary King's Highway transporting frankincense in exchange for spices, and Nabataean tradesmen, Roman legion-naires, Muslim armies and zealous Crusaders all passed through the land, leaving behind impressive monuments.

These monuments, including Roman amphitheatres, crusader castles and Christian mosaics, have fascinated subsequent travellers in search of antiquity and the origins of faith. The tradition of hospitality to visitors remains to this day.

Top Experiences

Petra

1 Ever since the Swiss explorer Jean Louis Burckhardt rediscovered this site in 1812, the ancient Nabataean city of Petra has been drawing the crowds – and with good reason. This is without doubt Jordan's most treasured attraction and when the sun sets over the honeycombed landscape of tombs, carved facades, pillars and sandstone cliffs, its magic is abundantly evident. Allow a couple of days to do the site justice and visit the main monuments at optimum times of the day.

Roman Ruins

2 For so small a country, Jordan punches well above its weight in world-class monuments, with some of the finest Roman ruins outside Rome. In addition to the Citadel and the well-preserved Roman Theatre in Amman, the black basalt ruins of Umm Qais and the extensive amphitheatres and colonnades at Jerash are highlights of the north. Visit Jerash's hippodrome during a chariot race when commentary from a red-plumed centurion will bring this ancient outpost of Rome to life.

Wadi Rum

3 It wasn't just the dramatic vistas of Wadi Rum, with its burnished sandstone cliffs and vivid-coloured dunes, that impressed Lawrence of Arabia as he paced on camelback through the land of the Bedouin. He was also impressed by the stoicism of the people who endured the hardships of desert life. Today, it's possible to get a glimpse of that traditional way of life, with a few more creature comforts, by staying in one of the Bedouin camps scattered across this desert wilderness.

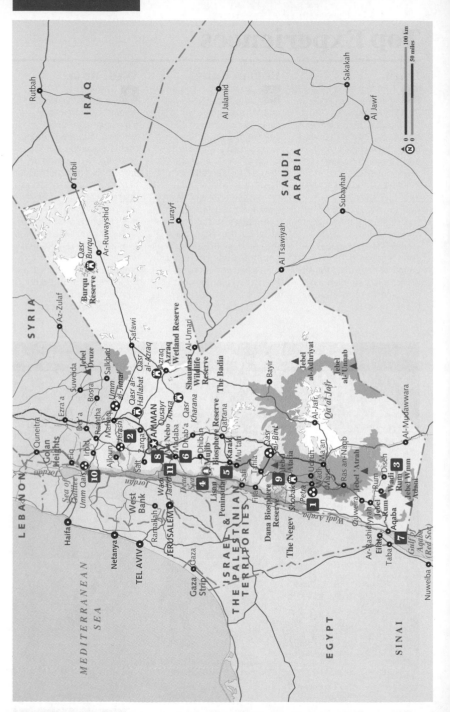

The Dead Sea Experience

4 Floating in the Dead Sea is one of the country's great natural experiences. Floating is the right word for it: with an eye-stingingly high salt content it is virtually impossible to swim in the viscous waters of a sea that is 415m below 'sea level', and equally impossible to sink. The experience is usually accompanied by a mud bath, a bake in the sun and a luxurious, health-giving spa treatment at one of the modern pleasure palaces lined up along the Dead Sea's shores.

Crusader Castles

5 As a frontier in the battle for the soul between Muslim and Christian forces, the Levant is dotted with castles. In Jordan, there are well-preserved examples at Ajloun and Shobak, but Karak Castle, commanding the semi-arid hills above the King's Highway, is the most atmospheric. You don't need to be military-minded to be impressed by the enormous ramparts, but imagination helps to hear the dying howls of those pitched from the parapet by sadistic Renauld de Châtillon.

Madaba's Handmade History

6 For centuries, Madaba, at the head of the ancient King's Highway, has been a crossroads for camel caravans transporting goods, legions of armies pushing the borders of various empires, and Christian pilgrims driven by faith in search of the Promised Land. To this day the town, with its churches, mosques, museums, markets and craft workshops, retains the marks of those cultural exchanges. Perhaps the best evidence of this rich past is Madaba's

Best on Film

Lawrence of Arabia (1962) David Lean's classic.

A Dangerous Man: Lawrence after Arabia (1991) Starring a young Ralph Fiennes.

Indiana Jones and the Last Crusade (1989) Harrison Ford in Petra caper.

Food & Drink

Spring Lamb cooked in a *zerb* (ground oven) will ruin your palate for mutton. Fresh, frothy camel's milk is abundant and giant watermelons ripen in fields alongside the Desert Highway.

Summer The fruit harvest brings pomegranates, pistachios, peaches and limes. During Ramadan, fast with the locals (dawn to dusk) and see how hunger enhances the flavours of traditional evening sweetmeats.

Autumn Pluck dangling figs or grapes from the vine and sample corn drizzled with newly pressed olive oil from local groves. In the Jordan Valley bananas and mangoes ripen in subtropical warmth.

Winter Copper-coloured persimmons ripen for Christmas – a good time to try Bethany's 'Baptism Fish'. It's not carnage on the roads – it's tomatoes. Crates of them fill the fields near Safi.

When to Go

HIGH SEASON
(Mar–May)
Perfect weather with warm days and cool nights.

SHOULDER
(Sep–Feb)
Bitter nights in the desert; rain or snow curtail many activities such as camping.

LOW SEASON
(Jun–Aug)
Temperatures can be stifling.

The Red Sea – A Seventh Wonder

Ever wondered where the Mare Rostrum, or Red Sea, got its name? Some believe it was named after the red sandstone mountain ranges that surround the sea. Others insist it was named after the periodic blooms of algae that tinge the water reddish-brown. But whatever the etymology of the name, the Red Sea is now synonymous with underwater spectacles par excellence – and that's official! In 1989 a panel of scientists and conservationists selected the northern portion of this 1800km-long body of water as one of the Seven Underwater Wonders of the World.

Getting Around

 Limited to intercity buses and buses that serve the needs of local communities, making it hard to reach key destinations without time and patience.

 Hiring a car is recommended, especially for visiting the Dead Sea, Eastern Desert and King's Highway. Driving is on the right.

 Some hotels in Amman, Madaba, Petra and Aqaba organise minibus shuttle services and/or tours to key tourist destinations.

 Many locals get around by shared taxi. Negotiating a half or whole day rate with a taxi driver is a useful alternative to car hire.

collection of mosaics, a heritage continued through the town's unique mosaic school.

Diving the Red Sea

7 It's no secret that the Red Sea is home to some of the most beautiful underwater seascapes in the world. Jordan's Red Sea shoreline along the Gulf of Aqaba is admittedly short, but this comparatively unexploited stretch of water encompasses pristine reefs, crumbling wrecks and kaleidoscopic coral gardens. Snorkelling and diving among damsel fish, turtles and seahorses is a memorable experience easily arranged through dive centres in and around the lively seaside city of Aqaba. Access is both from the beach and by short boat-ride.

Biblical History

8 For many people Jordan is more than just a traveller's destination: it's a place of pilgrimage. Sites resonating with spiritual significance abound in a country delineated by the Jordan Valley. This where John is believed to have baptised Jesus at Bethany-Beyond-the-Jordan, and where, according to the Bible, the towns of Sodom and Gomorrah attracted the wrath of God. It is at Mt Nebo, however, with its view of the Promised Land, that one most senses this is 'hallowed, holy ground'.

The King's Highway

9 It may not be a literal path of kings, but the King's Highway follows some pretty big footsteps. These include those of the Nabataeans (their fabled city of Petra lies at the south end of the King's Highway), the Romans (whose military outpost at Umm ar-Rasas is a Unesco World Heritage Site) and the Crusaders (their Karak and Shobak castles are highlights in their own right). Smaller footsteps include those taken by Salome in her Dance of the Seven Veils at the desolate hilltop of Mukawir.

Desert Flower Displays

10 Carpets of scarlet poppies strewn across the desert, ribbons of oleander in the wadis, the flutter of velvet petals on a black iris along the King's Highway, Jordan is home to beautiful wild flower displays. For the best show, visit the Roman ruins of Umm Qais in the far north of the country on a sunny afternoon in April: armfuls of knee-high daisies and thistles, yellow hollyhocks and pink mallow compete for a sliver of warmth between the fallen masonry.

Wadi Jadid

11 There's nothing new about Wadi Jadid ('New Valley' in Arabic). Lying undisturbed, it typifies all that is constant in rural Jordanian life: grazing sheep, shepherds trotting through thistles astride pot-bellied donkeys, the smell of sage under hot summer sun. In fact the valley would be entirely unremarkable were it not for the clusters of ancient Bronze Age dolmen that dot the terraced hillsides. Heaved into place between 5000 and 3000 BC, these impressive stone monuments are worth the effort it takes to locate them.

Jordanian Hospitality

12 Despite its modest size, Jordan is home to diverse peoples who share a traditional sense of responsibility towards the visitor. It may sound unfashionably romantic to claim that Jordanians are more friendly than most, but it doesn't take long to realise that hospitality is an integral part of the local culture. Whether you're invited for mint tea by Palestinians, bread and salt by Bedouins or pomegranate salads by the Chechens in Amman, your interaction with Jordanian people is sure to be a highlight of your visit.

Distant Heat

As you can't beat August's heat, you may as well join it at Jordan's annual dance in the desert. This all-nighter takes place in Wadi Rum and features top international electronic-dance-music artists.

Walking in Spring

The spring, late March to mid-May, is the best time to visit Jordan's nature reserves. The elusive black iris (Jordan's national flower) blooms and nature lovers can hike through narrow wadis without fear of flash floods.

HILDA WEGES PHOTOGRAPHY / SHUTTERSTOCK ©

ATHIKHOM SAENGCHAI / SHUTTERSTOCK ©

CAPITAL
Astana

POPULATION
18.3 million

AREA
2.7 million sq km

OFFICIAL LANGUAGES
Kazakh, Russian

Chimbulak ski resort, south of Almaty

Kazakhstan

Today Kazakhstan's expanse of Eurasian steppe offers one of the last great undiscovered frontiers of travel with some home comforts and mod cons.

The world's ninth-biggest country is the most economically advanced of the 'stans', thanks to its abundant reserves of oil and most other valuable minerals. This means generally better standards of accommodation, restaurants and transport than elsewhere in Central Asia.

The biggest city, Almaty, is almost reminiscent of Europe with its leafy avenues, chic cafes, glossy shopping centres and hedonistic nightlife. The capital Astana, on the windswept northern steppe, has been transformed into a 21st-century showpiece with a profusion of bold futuristic architecture.

But it's beyond the cities that you'll find the greatest travel adventures, whether hiking in the high mountains and green valleys of the Tian Shan, searching for wildlife on the lake-dotted steppe, enjoying home-spun hospitality in village guesthouses, or jolting across the western deserts to remote underground mosques.

Top Experiences

Almaty

 Central Asia's most cosmopolitan and hedonistic city is a leafy mix of Russian and Central Asian styles. In a couple of days you can visit the Tsarist-era Zenkov Cathedral, view a replica of the famous Scythian-era Golden Man suit, soak in the Arasan Bathhouse and enjoy the region's best cafes, clubs and shops, all fuelled by the country's petrodollar boom. The city is also a gateway to mountain treks and winter sports just south of town and a springboard to Silk Road bus and train routes into China.

Aksu-Zhabagyly Nature Reserve

 This beautiful 1319-sq-km patch of green valleys, rushing rivers, snowcapped peaks and high-level glaciers, abutting the Kyrgyz and Uzbek borders, is the oldest (1926) and one of the most enjoyable and easiest visited of Kazakhstan's nature reserves. The diversity of life in this area where mountains meet steppe is great for botanists, birders and nature lovers in general and the famous, bright-red Greig's tulip is one of over 1300 flowering plants in the reserve. It dots the alpine meadows, and is quite common even in villages, from mid-April to early May.

Astana's Architecture

 Kazakhstan's capital has risen fast from the northern steppe and is already a showpiece for this country in the 21st-century. It is scheduled to go on rising and spreading into a city of over 1 million people

When to Go

☀ **HIGH SEASON** (Apr–Jun, Sep–Oct)

☀ **SHOULDER** (Jul–Aug)

❄ **LOW SEASON** (Nov–Mar)

by 2030. Its skyline grows more fantastical by the year as landmark buildings, many of them by leading international architects, sprout in a variety of Asian, Western, Soviet and wacky futuristic styles. Several spectacular structures are open to visitors and it's hard not be impressed by the very concept of the place.

Turkistan

4 At Turkistan stands Kazakhstan's most important pilgrimage site. The turquoise dome and ornate tilework of the Timurid-era Yasaui Mausoleum is a rare architectural gem in a land ruled by restless nomads. It's also one of the best places to get a sense of Central Asian Sufism and meet local pilgrims as they pray, picnic and tie wishes to trees surrounding the holy shrine.

Mangistau

5 The stony deserts of the Mangistau region stretch 400km east from Aktau to the Uzbekistan border. This labyrinth of dramatic canyons, weirdly eroded, multicoloured rocky outcrops, mysterious underground mosques and ancient necropolises is only beginning to be explored, even by archaeologists. A minor branch of the Silk Road once ran across these wastes, and sacred sites – some with strong Sufic associations – are located where people buried their dead or where holy men dwelt. The underground mosques may have originated as cave hermitages for ascetics who retreated to the deserts. Getting to these places across the otherworldly desertscapes, with only the occasional herd of camels or sheep for company, is part of the fun.

Getting Around

A good network of domestic flights links cities all around Kazakhstan and fares are reasonable.

Trains serve all cities and many smaller places. They're a good way to experience Kazakhstan's terrain, vast size and people.

Taxis offer a much faster alternative to buses and minibuses, which have infrequent departures in increasingly aged vehicles.

6

Altay Mountains

6 In the far eastern corner of Kazakhstan the magnificent Altay Mountains spread across the borders to Russia, China and, 50km away, Mongolia. The hassle of getting to this sparsely populated region is certainly well worth it. Rolling meadows, snow-covered peaks, forested hillsides, glaciers, pristine lakes and rivers, archaeological sites, and rustic villages with Kazakh horsemen riding by make for scenery of epic proportions. Twin-headed Mt Belukha (4506m), on the Kazakh–Russian border, has many mystical associations and Asian legends refer to it as the location of the paradisal realm of Shambhala.

Food & Drink

Beshbarmak Chunks of long-boiled mutton, beef, or perhaps horsemeat, served in a huge bowl atop flat squares of pasta with onions and sometimes potatoes.

Kazy, shuzhuk/shuzhak, karta Types of horsemeat sausage, in horse-intestine casing.

Kuurdak A fatty stew of potatoes, meat and offal from a horse, sheep or cow.

Manty Steamed dumplings.

Baursaki Fried dough balls or triangles, not unlike heavy doughnuts.

Apples Kazakhstan is reckoned to be the original source of apples and wild apple trees still grow in parts of the southeast.

Kymyz Fermented mare's milk; it's mildly alcoholic with a sour, slightly fizzy taste.

VASON / SHUTTERSTOCK ©

Kazakh Music

The national instrument of Kazakhstan is the *dombra,* a small two-stringed lute with an oval box shape. Other instruments include the *kobyz* (a two-stringed fiddle), whose sound is said to have brought Chinggis Khan to tears, and the *sybyzgy* (two flutes strapped together like abbreviated pan pipes).

The most skilled singers or bards are called *akyns,* and undoubtedly the most important form of Kazakh traditional art is the *aitys,* a duel between two *dombra* players who challenge each other in poetic lyrics. You might catch one of these live during Nauryz or other holidays.

CAPITAL
Nairobi

POPULATION
47.7 million

AREA
580,367 sq km

OFFICIAL LANGUAGES
English, Swahili

Blue monkey, Kakamega Forest

Kenya

Vast savannahs peppered with immense herds of wildlife. Snow-capped mountains on the equator. Traditional peoples who bring soul and colour to the earth. Welcome to Kenya.

This is the land of some of Africa's best-known peoples: the Masai Mara, Samburu, Turkana, Swahili, Kikuyu. Drawing near to these cultures, even coming to understand them a little better, could just be a highlight of your visit.

It's also the land of wildebeest and zebras migrating with the great predators of Africa following in their wake, of the red elephants of Tsavo, the Amboseli elephant families in the shadow of Mt Kilimanjaro and the massed millions of pink flamingos stepping daintily through lake shallows.

The survival and abundance of Kenya's wildlife owes everything to one of Africa's most innovative and successful conservation communities. In places like Laikipia and the Masai Mara, private and community conservancies bring tourism together with community development and wildlife conservation. If you want your visit to make a difference, you've come to the right place.

Top Experiences

Wildlife Migration, Masai Mara

1 Its rolling savannah studded with flat-top acacia trees, the Masai Mara, which encompasses both the Masai Mara National Reserve and the private conservancies that surround it, is an iconic East African landscape that's home to some of the highest concentrations of wildlife on the planet. It's fantastic at any time but from July to October, the Mara's plains are flooded with hundreds of thousands of wildebeest on their great migration, along with herds of zebras, elephants and giraffes. Trailing this walking buffet are prides of lions, lurking leopards, solitary cheetahs and packs of hyenas. If you only visit one place in Kenya, make it the Mara.

Elephants of Amboseli National Park

2 There's possibly no better place in the world to watch elephants than Amboseli National Park in the country's south. A big part of the appeal is the setting – Africa's highest mountain, the snow-capped Mt Kilimanjaro, is the backdrop for seemingly every picture you'll take here. Just as significant, Amboseli was spared the worst of Kenya's poaching crisis and these elephants are remarkably tolerant of humans (allowing you to get really close). And their tusks are among the biggest in Kenya.

Wandering Lamu Backstreets

3 Lamu is surely the most evocative destination on the Kenyan coast. With no cars around, the best way to get to know this graceful town is by wandering its backstreets, admiring the grand old Swahili doors, peeking into hidden courtyards bursting with unexpected colours, slipping into an easy chair and sipping on a fruit juice, and accepting

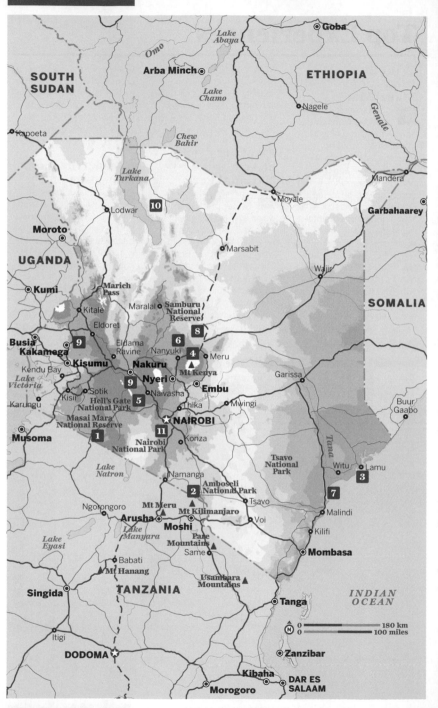

all invitations to stop and shoot the breeze. Do all this and the backstreets of Lamu will become a place you'll dream of forever.

Best in Print

Out of Africa (Karen Blixen, aka Isak Dinesen; 1937) The definitive account of colonial Kenya.

A Primate's Memoir (Robert M Sapolsky; 2002) Funny, poignant account by a young primatologist in Kenya.

No Man's Land (George Monbiot; 1994) The modern struggle of the region's nomadic tribes.

The Flame Trees of Thika (Elspeth Huxley; 1959) A marvellously told colonial memoir.

Petals of Blood (Ngũgĩ wa Thiong'o; 1977) The story of four Kenyans struggling to come to terms with their newly independent country.

The Worlds of a Maasai Warrior: An Autobiography (Tepilit Ole Saitoti; 1988) Extraordinary insight into the Masai world.

Best on Film

The Great Rift (2010) BBC documentary about the Rift Valley.

Echo of the Elephants (1993) Elephants of Amboseli National Park.

Enough is Enough (2004) Critically acclaimed portrayal of the Mau Mau uprising.

Born Free (1966) Lions of legend return to the wild.

Out of Africa (1985) Caused a generation to dream of Africa.

The Constant Gardener (2005) Gripping Hollywood story set in Kenya.

Hiking Mt Kenya

4 Occupying the heart of the country and a special place in the hearts of the Kikuyu people, Mt Kenya, the country's highest peak and the second highest on the continent, is not a mountain to be admired from afar. With four days, some determination and several layers of warm clothing, you could find yourself standing on the frozen summit of Point Lenana, mere minutes from the equator, but a whole world away from the other African experiences.

Hell's Gate National Park

5 It's one thing to watch Africa's megafauna from the safety of your vehicle, quite another to do so on foot or on a bicycle. Hell's Gate National Park – a dramatic volcanic landscape of red cliffs, otherworldly rocky outcrops and deep canyons in Kenya's Rift Valley – may lack predators, but experiencing the African wild at close quarters certainly gives most people a frisson. By placing you in the landscape, Hell's Gate heightens the senses, bringing alive the African wild like no other national park in Kenya.

Laikipia Plateau

6 In the shadow of Mt Kenya, this plateau hosts a network of conservancies and private wildlife reserves – it is both beautiful and one of the

When to Go

HIGH SEASON
(Jun–Oct, Jan & Feb)
Sky-high lodge prices, especially July to October.

SHOULDER
(Nov & Dec)
Prices at most lodges and parks drop from November.

LOW SEASON
(Mar–May)
Long rains mean accommodation is much quieter and prices are low.

Diving & Snorkelling

The Kenyan coast promises some of the best diving and snorkelling in Africa beyond the Red Sea. There are a number of professional dive centres, and in addition to myriad fish species and colourful coral, charismatic marine mammals – including dolphins, sea turtles, whale sharks and humpback whales (August to October) – also frequent these waters.

If you aren't certified to dive, almost every hotel and resort on the coast can arrange an open-water diving course. They're not much cheaper (if at all) than anywhere else in the world – a five-day PADI certification course starts at around US$470. Two tank dives for certified divers go for around US$100, including equipment and transport.

Getting Around

Can Flights can be quite expensive, but also blissfully fast and generally reliable.

Most of Kenya's towns and cities are accessible by local bus, though it's usually necessary to arrange private transport to reach national parks and lodges.

If you're a seasoned driver in African conditions, hiring a sturdy vehicle can also open up relatively inaccessible corners of the country. However, do be aware that Kenyan drivers are some of the most dangerous in the world. Hiring a vehicle with a driver rarely costs a lot more, but paying for the driver's food and accommodation does quickly adds up.

most exciting stories in African conservation. At the forefront of efforts to save endangered species such as lions, African wild dogs, Grevy's zebras and black rhinos, the plateau's ranches offer an enticing combination of high-end lodge accommodation, big horizons and charismatic megafauna. Best of all, this is a more intimate experience than your average national park, with scarcely another vehicle in sight.

Kenyan Beaches

7 Kenya's Indian Ocean coast is one of Africa's prettiest shores. Long stretches of white sand, translucent waters and coves sheltered by palm trees would be sufficient reason for most travellers to visit. But trade winds through the centuries have brought an intriguing mix of African and Arab cultures, resulting in a coastline with attitude: at once laid-back in the finest spirit of hakuna matata, yet bristling with ruins and

the evocative signposts of Swahili culture.

Samburu National Reserve

8 Samburu might not enjoy the fame of other Kenyan parks, but that's just the way we like it. This stunning arid landscape of Kenya's soulful north is given life by the Ewaso Ngiro River, its palm-fringed banks as beautiful as any waterways in inland Kenya. Wildlife, too, is drawn to the river and its hinterland, the rugged terrain swarming with elephants, lions and leopards, but also some signature northern species, among them the blue-legged Somali ostrich and the endangered Grevy's zebra.

Kakamega Forest

9 Paths lace the Kakamega Forest and offer a rare opportunity to ditch the safari 4WD and stretch your legs. This ancient forest is home to an astounding 330 bird species, 400 butterfly species and seven

different primate species. Like all rainforests, though, the trees themselves are the chief attraction here, and in the forest gloom you'll stumble upon the botanical equivalent of beauty and the beast: delicate orchids and parasitic figs that strangle their hosts as they climb towards the light.

The Remote North

10 Amid the deserts and horizonless tracts that characterise so much of Kenya's north, Lake Turkana glitters like a jade and turquoise mirage. Rising from its waters is Teleki, one of the world's most perfectly shaped volcanic cones, while the shores are dotted with dusty and utterly intriguing villages that are home to the beguiling mix of traditional peoples – Turkana, Samburu, Gabbra, El Molo – who call this isolated corner of Africa home. And there are crocodiles here. Lots of them.

Nairobi National Park

11 No other city in the world can boast a national park (home to four of the Big Five) within sight of city skyscrapers. The park may have its detractions – one of Africa's smallest parks, it's almost completely encircled by human settlements – but this is an important refuge for the endangered black rhino (more than 50), all three big cats and abundant birdlife. There's also an elephant orphanage, a nearby breeding centre for the Rothschild's giraffe and numerous opportunities to forget you're in Nairobi at all.

PAUL BANTON / SHUTTERSTOCK ©

Kenya Music Festival

The country's longest-running music festival is held in Nairobi over 10 days during August, and draws worthy international acts along with its predominantly African cast of stars.

Wildlife Spectacular

Following the rains, wildebeest begin arriving in the Masai Mara National Reserve anywhere between mid-June and mid-July and stay until October, with predators following in their wake. It's the greatest wildlife show on earth.

ATHIKHOM SAENGCHAI / SHUTTERSTOCK ©

KBN 111A

1

8

Homes in South Tarawa

Kiribati

A tiny speck of islands in the Pacific, Kiribati still maintains traditional ways. Nothing happens too fast here, so wind down, relax and enjoy living on island time.

The Republic of Kiribati encompasses the Gilbert, Phoenix and Line Islands. Measured by land size, Kiribati is a tiny nation of just over 811 sq km, but its 33 atolls span a huge 3.5 million sq km of the Pacific. Most atolls surround turquoise lagoons and barely rise above the surrounding ocean, so it's rare to be out of the sight and sound of the sea.

Kiribati's recent colonial and WWII history (the islands were occupied by the Japanese in 1942) has had little impact on the outer islands, where the people subsist on coconuts, breadfruit and fish as they have done for centuries. Even on the main island, Tarawa, most locals live in traditional thatched huts. Western influence is increasing, though, in the form of cars, bars and the internet, and inevitably there's an escalating urban drift from the outer islands to Tarawa.

The I-Kiribati, people of the islands, are friendly but laconic – expect a bold 'mauri' (hello) as you pass.

Top Experiences

Outer Gilbert Islands

1 For that castaway feeling, head to the outer Gilbert islands where you can experience traditional I-Kiribati life, and it's rare to find more than a few trucks and some motorbikes. The islands are pristine and packaged Western products are a rarity. People live off fishing and coconuts, and occasionally earn revenue by selling salted clams or copra.

WWII Guns

2 On South Tarawa, Betio retains a sobering collection of eight-inch guns, bunkers and a machine-gun command post left over from WWII. In 1943, 20,000 US marines stormed Betio's beaches and routed the occupying Japanese. There's also a cemetery and a memorial.

Christmas Island

3 Christmas Island is a paradise for visiting sportfishers and one of Kiribati's biggest tourist draws. Fly fishing is the most popular activity, the endless flats of which hold enormous bonefish. Diving is also outstanding, and almost all dives are done in the two coral-rich channels flanking Cook Island, where the reef drops off sharply.

When to Go

☀ **HIGH SEASON** (Dec–Feb, Jun–Aug)

☂ **LOW SEASON** (Mar–May, Sep–Nov)

Food & Drink

Breadfruit Along with the coconut, this is an island staple.

Fish & seafood Local fish dishes are abundant. Most other foods are imported from Australia.

Kaokioki Kiribati's famed local brew is tapped from coconut palms and fermented.

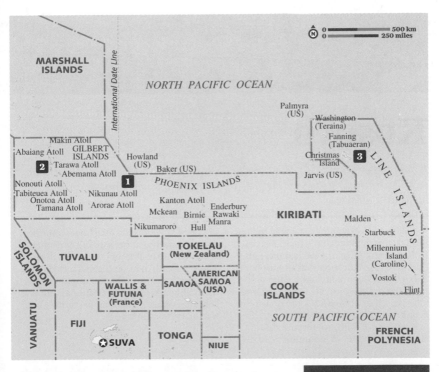

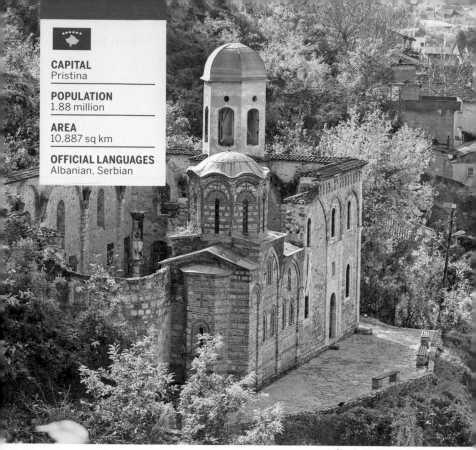

CAPITAL
Pristina

POPULATION
1.88 million

AREA
10,887 sq km

OFFICIAL LANGUAGES
Albanian, Serbian

Church of the Holy Saviour, Prizren

Kosovo

It may be Europe's newest country, but Kosovo's long and dramatic history can be witnessed at every turn in elegant Ottoman towns and little-visited mountain vistas.

While it's perfectly safe to travel here now, this fascinating land at the heart of the Balkans remains one of the last truly off-the-beaten-path destinations in Europe. Barbs of its past are impossible to miss: roads are dotted with memorials to those killed in 1999, while NATO forces still guard Serbian monasteries.

Whether trekking around the stunning landscapes of Rugova Mountains, breathing deep at Peja's Saturday Cheese Market or enjoying the capital's excellent dining and nightlife in Pristina, visitors will be richly rewarded. Kosovo offers welcoming smiles, charming mountain towns, incredible hiking opportunities and 13th-century domed Serbian monasteries – and that's just for starters.

Top Experiences

Prizren's Old Town

1 Prizren's charming old town runs along both sides of the Bistrica river, and is awash with mosques and churches. It's been well restored and is a charming place to wander. Prizren Fortress, high above the city, is a must-see for breathtaking views into the distance.

Bear Sanctuary Pristina

2 In a remote spot beyond the village on Mramor, you can visit brown bears that were rescued from captivity by the charity Four Paws. All the bears here were once kept in tiny cages as restaurant mas-

cots, but when the keeping of bears was outlawed in Kosovo in 2010, Four Paws stepped in to care for these wonderful animals and the excellent living conditions here are heartening indeed.

Visoki Dečani Monastery

3 This ancient monastery is in an incredibly beautiful spot beneath the mountains and surrounded by a forest of pine and chestnut trees. Visitors are very welcome to see the incredible icons in the church, and you'll be hard-pressed to find a more peaceful place anywhere else in the country.

When to Go

☀ **HIGH SEASON** (Jul–Sep)

⛅ **SHOULDER** (May–Jun, Oct–Nov)

❄ **LOW SEASON** (Dec–Apr)

Food & Drink

Byrek Pastry with cheese or meat.

Gjuveç Baked meat and vegetables.

Fli Flaky pastry pie served with honey.

Tavë Meat baked with cheese and egg.

Vranac Red wine from the Rahovec region of Kosovo.

CAPITAL
Kuwait City

POPULATION
2.79 million

AREA
17,818 sq km

OFFICIAL LANGUAGE
Arabic

Kuwait Towers overlooking Kuwait Bay

Kuwait

Long an oasis in the parched desert, Kuwait is now at the vanguard of political change and cultural development in the Gulf of Arabia.

Just as oil rich as other Gulf countries, Kuwait hasn't gone for the glitz and glamour in quite the same way – perhaps it's the years lost to the Iraqi invasion and its aftermath, or maybe it's a conscious decision not to sell its soul to the gods of commercialism. And Kuwait lies just far enough away from those self-same Gulf travel hubs to the south to mean that tourists and expats are fewer here.

The result? A more authentically Arab feel to the country. At the same time, Kuwait remains an oasis in a land of desert plains, and has excellent museums, a fine souq and a corniche of combed beaches and lively restaurants. It all adds up to what could be the Gulf's most intriguing destination.

Top Experiences

Kuwait Towers

1 The Kuwait Towers, with their distinctive blue-green 'sequins', are the instantly recognisable symbols of a nation. The largest of the three rises to a height of 187m and houses a two-level revolving observation deck, gift shop and cafe.

Salmiya Scientific Center

2 Housed in a fine, sail-shaped building on the corniche, the Scientific Center boasts an aquarium that is one of the largest in the Middle East. The unique intertidal display features shoals of black-spotted sweetlips and the ingenious mudskipper. But the most spectacular part of the display is undoubtedly the floor-to-ceiling shark and ray tanks.

Tareq Rajab Museum

3 This exquisite ethnographic museum should not be missed. There are inlaid musical instruments suspended in glass cabinets; Omani silver and Saudi gold jewellery; headdresses, from the humble prayer cap to the Mongol helmet; costumes worn by princesses and by goatherds; Jaipur enamel; and Bahraini pearls.

When to Go

 HIGH SEASON (Nov–Apr)

 SHOULDER (Oct)

 LOW SEASON (May–Sep)

Food & Drink

Baked fish Blended with coriander, turmeric, red pepper and cardamom.

Hamour or pomfret White fish stuffed with parsley, onions and dill.

Gulf prawns Available late autumn and early winter.

Alcohol Not available or permissible.

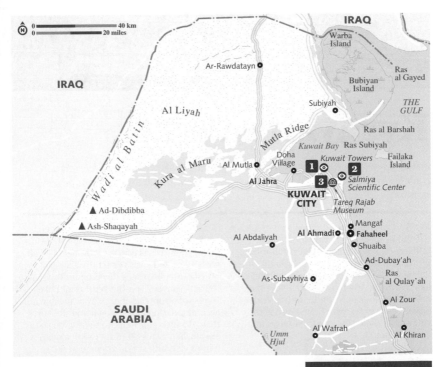

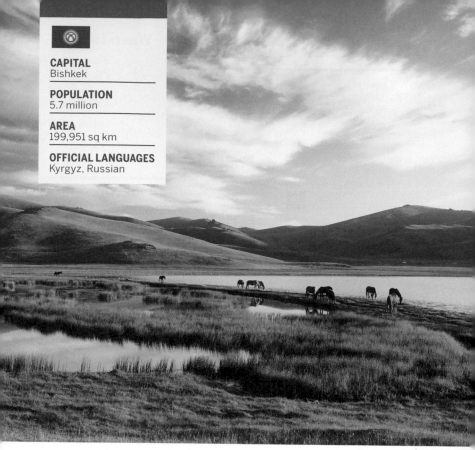

CAPITAL
Bishkek

POPULATION
5.7 million

AREA
199,951 sq km

OFFICIAL LANGUAGES
Kyrgyz, Russian

Song-Köl

Kyrgyzstan

A half-forgotten land of mountain valleys, glittering lakes and felt yurts, Kyrgyzstan is a dream for DIY adventurers, ecotourists and wannabe nomads.

Kyrgyzstan is a nation defined by its natural beauty: joyously unspoilt mountainscapes, stark craggy ridges, and rolling *jailoos* (summer pastures) are brought to life by semi-nomadic, yurt-dwelling shepherd cultures. Add to this a well-developed network of homestays and visa-free travel, and it's easy to see why Kyrgyzstan is the gateway of choice for many travellers in Central Asia.

As can be expected in a country where many attractions are high altitude, the timing of your visit is crucial. Summer is ideal with hikes and roads generally accessible. Midsummer also sees Kazakh and Russian tourists converge on the beaches of Lake Issyk-Köl. From October to May, much rural accommodation closes down and the yurts that add such character to the Alpine vistas are stashed away. So think twice about a winter visit unless you've come to ski.

Top Experiences

Horse Treks

1 Kyrgyzstan is the best place in Central Asia to saddle up and explore the high pastures. Community-based tourism offices throughout the country can organise horse hire by the hour or day. The horses often give the impression they're only a hoof-beat away from reverting to their wild roots and galloping off, but novice riders are seldom given unruly horses if they make their concerns known.

Song-Köl

2 The jewel of central Kyrgyzstan is this high alpine lake, fringed with lush summer pastures

and summer-only Kyrgyz yurt camps. You can trek or drive here but the best option is a horse trek, over-nighting in yurts en route. June to August are the best months to visit Kyrgyzstan's idyllic summer pastures, when you might even catch a horse games festival or a performance by a Kyrgyz bard or eagle hunter. Bring a sleeping bag.

Ala-Archa Canyon

3 In this grand, accessible Y-shaped valley south of Bishkek, you can sit by a waterfall, hike to a glacier or mountaineer up the region's highest peaks. Around 42km from Bishkek, the sealed road ends at the main trailhead known as

the alplager, where a seasonal gaggle of yurts sell kymys (fermented mare's milk). The river divides 300m north of here, where two idyllic Alpine valleys converge. Relatively well-marked trails lead walkers up both branches.

Arslanbob

4 The Babash-Ata Mountains form an impressive wall of snow-sprinkled crags behind the elevated 'oasis' of

When to Go

 HIGH SEASON (Apr–Jun & Oct)

 SHOULDER (Jul–Sep)

 LOW SEASON (Nov–Mar)

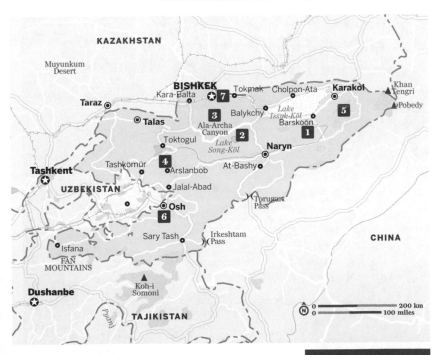

Arslanbob. Ethnically Uzbek and religiously conservative, the very large village sprawls almost invisibly along a network of tree-shaded lanes, and is surrounded by a vast tract of blossoming woodland that constitutes the world's largest walnut grove. The real attractions are hikes, horse-treks, cycle-rides or ski-adventures in the surrounding mountains and forests, but Arslanbob's glorious, garden-homestays are also a great place to unwind.

Altyn-Arashan

5 Probably the most popular destination from the Karakol area is a spartan hot-spring development called Altyn-

Arashan (Golden Spa), set in a postcard-perfect alpine valley at 3000m, with 4260m Pik Palatka looming at its southern end. Much of the area is a botanical research area called the Arashan State Nature Reserve, which is home to about 20 snow leopards and a handful of bears, although the only animals you're likely to see are the horses and sheep belonging to local families. From the springs it's about a five-hour walk on foot to the snout of the Palatka Glacier, wrapped around Pik Palatka.

Osh

6 With a remarkable five-headed crag leaping out of the very

Getting Around

Only a handful of routes employ full-size buses, but minibuses, some timetabled, others departing when full, wait for passengers at most bus stations, as do shared taxis.

Self-drive car rental is a new concept, but there are two agencies in Bishkek and one motorbike agency in Osh.

RADIOKAFKA / SHUTTERSTOCK ©

town centre, Kyrgyzstan's second city certainly has a highly distinctive visual focus. While there's little of architectural merit to show for 3000 years of history, Osh's sprawling bazaar and hospitable citizens provide an atmosphere that is far more archetypically Central Asian than you will find in Bishkek.

Bishkek

7 The green, quiet and laid-back Kyrgyz capital makes a great introduction to the mountain republic. The entire downtown area feels like one big park, with trees sprouting from every crack in the concrete. The Kyrgyz Ala-Too range creates a magnificent backdrop and their glacial melt pours through the city centre in gurgling troughs. The low-rise Soviet-era buildings and the odd Lenin or Frunze statue lend the city a quaint historical time-warp ambience.

Food & Drink

Laghman Mildly spicy, fat noodles generally served in soup.

Hoshan Fried and steamed dumplings; best right off the fire from markets.

Ashlyanfu Cold rice-noodles, jelly, vinegar and eggs.

Bozo Thick, fizzy drink made from boiled fermented millet or other grains.

Boorsok Empty ravioli-sized fried dough-parcels to dunk in drinks or cream.

Kurut Small, very hard balls of tart, dried yoghurt; a favourite snack.

MICHAL KNITL / SHUTTERSTOCK ©

Horse Sports

Horse sports are very popular in Kyrgyzstan and have seen a revival in recent years. The most unforgettable of these is an all-out mounted brawl over a headless goat whose body must be thrown into a circular 'goal'. Known as *kok boru, ulak-tartysh* or *buzkashi*, the Kyrgyz term meaning 'grey wolf' reveals its origins as a hunting exercise. The form played in Kyrgyzstan is essentially a team sport (in contrast to the free-for-all version of Tajikistan), but either way it's a remarkably full-on event at which riders and horses can take an incredible battering.

Other classic horse games include *at chabysh*, a horse race over a distance of 20km to 30km; *jumby atmai,* horseback archery; *tiyin enmei,* where contestants pick up coins off the ground while galloping past; and *udarysh,* horseback wrestling.

CAPITAL
Vientiane

POPULATION
7 million

AREA
236,800 sq km

OFFICIAL LANGUAGE
Lao

Luang Prabang

Laos

A land of lotus eaters amid the bloated development of its neighbours, Laos brings together the best of Southeast Asia in one bite-sized destination.

Adventure seekers can lose themselves in underground river caves, on jungle ziplines or while climbing karsts. Nature enthusiasts can take a walk on the wild side and spot exotic animals such as gibbons or elephants. Culture lovers can explore ancient temples and immerse themselves in Lao spiritual life.

Laos retains many of the traditions that have disappeared in a frenzy of development elsewhere in the region. It's hard to believe somnolent Vientiane is an Asian capital, and there's a timeless quality to rural life, where stilt houses and paddy fields look like they are straight out of a movie set. Magical Luang Prabang bears witness to hundreds of saffron-robed monks gliding through the streets every morning in a call to alms. Intrepid travellers will discover a country untainted by mass tourism and Asia in slow motion – this is Lao People's Democratic Republic (Lao PDR), or 'please don't rush' as the locals like to joke.

496 | LAOS

Top Experiences

Luang Prabang

1 Bordered by the Mekong River and the Nam Khan (Khan River), this timeless city of temples is the stuff of travel legends: rich in royal history, saffron-clad monks, stunning river views, world-class cuisine and some of the best boutique accommodation in the region. Hire a bike and explore the tropical peninsula's backstreets, take a cooking class or just ease back with a restful massage at one of the many affordable spas. Prepare to adjust your timetable and stay a little longer than expected.

Vang Vieng

2 The riverine jewel in Laos' karst country, Vang Vieng sits under soaring cliffs beside the Nam Song (Song River) and is the undisputed adventure capital of Laos. Since the party crowd moved on, tranquillity reigns again with more family-oriented visitors dropping in to soak up such well-organised activities as hot-air ballooning, trekking, caving and climbing. And don't forget the original draw: tubing down the river. Where once there were only budget guesthouses and same-same traveller cafes, now they have been joined by smarter boutique hotels and restaurants serving delicious food.

Si Phan Don

3 Laos' hammock-flopping mecca has been catering to weary travellers for years. While these tropical islands bounded by the waters of the Mekong are best known as a happy haven for catatonic sun worshippers, more active souls are spoilt for choice. Between tubing and cycling through paddy fields, you can grab a kayak, spot rare Irrawaddy dolphins, and then round off your day with a sunset boat trip.

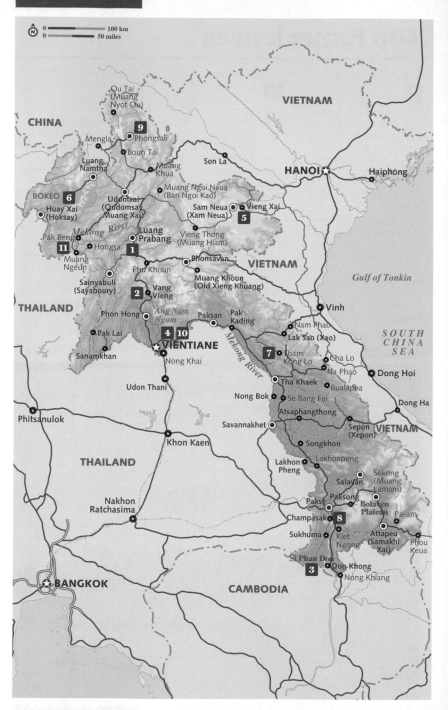

Vientiane

4 Meandering along the banks of the Mekong, Vientiane is surely Southeast Asia's most languid capital. The wide streets are bordered by tamarind trees and the narrow alleys conceal French villas, Chinese shophouses and glittering wats. The city brews a heady mix of street vendors, saffron-clad monks, fine Gallic cuisine, boutique hotels and a healthy vibe that sees visitors slinking off for spa treatments and turning their time to yoga and cycling. It may not have Luang Prabang's looks, but Vientiane has a certain charm all of its own.

Best on Film

The Rocket (2013) The story of a young Lao boy blamed for bringing bad luck to his family. To win back the family's trust he builds a giant firework to enter the annual Rocket Festival.

Bomb Harvest (2007) Powerful documentary about the impact of unexploded ordnance (UXO) on communities in Laos today and the work the Mines Advisory Group (MAG) is doing to clear the legacy of war. For some, the war goes on.

Best in Print

The Coroner's Lunch (Colin Cotterill; 2004) Delve into the delightful world of Dr Siri, full-time national coroner in the 1970s and part-time super sleuth. The first instalment in a 10-part Siri series.

Ant Egg Soup (Natacha Du Pont de Bie; 2004) Subtitled *The Adventures of a Food Tourist in Laos,* the author samples some local delicacies (including some that aren't suitable for a delicate stomach).

One Foot in Laos (Dervla Murphy; 2001) Renowned Irish travel writer explores Laos back in the early days of the 1990s and discovers a country undergoing profound change.

Vieng Xai Caves

5 This is history writ large in stone. An area of outstanding natural beauty, Vieng Xai was home to the Pathet Lao communist leadership during the US bombing campaign of 1964–73. Beyond the breathtaking beauty of the natural caves, it is the superb audio tour that really brings the experience alive. When the bombers buzz overhead to a soundtrack of Jimi Hendrix you'll find yourself ducking for cover in the Red Prince's lush garden.

Gibbon Experience

6 Whiz high above the forest floor attached to a zipline. These brilliantly engineered cables – some longer than 500m – span forest valleys in the lush Bokeo Nature Reserve (habitat of the black-crested

When to Go

HIGH SEASON
(Nov–Mar)
Pleasant temperatures in much of Laos, though it's cold in the mountains.

SHOULDER
(Jul & Aug)
Wet in most parts of Laos, with high humidity.

LOW SEASON
(Apr–Jun, Sep & Oct)
April and May are hot, with the temperature around 40°C. September and October can be very wet.

Food & Drink

Đạm màhk hung A salad of shredded green papaya mixed with garlic, lime juice, fish sauce, sometimes tomatoes, palm sugar, land crab or dried shrimp and chillies.

Fĕr Rice noodles in a broth with vegetables and meat, with fish sauce, lime juice, dried chillies, mint leaves, basil or hot chilli sauce.

Kòw nĕeo Sticky rice served in a small basket. Take a small amount of rice and, using one hand, work it into a ball before dipping it into the food.

Láhp Spicy salad of minced beef, pork, duck, fish or chicken, mixed with fish sauce, small shallots, mint leaves, lime juice, roasted ground rice and lots and lots of chillies.

Lòw-lów Lao liquor or rice whisky, though officially illegal, is popular in the lowlands. It's usually taken neat and offered as a welcoming gesture.

Getting Around

 Laos has an extensive domestic flight network and this can save considerable time on a short visit.

 Rivers are the lifeblood of Laos, making boat journeys an important element of the transport network.

 Laos has some smart buses operating on major routes out of Vientiane, but venture into remote areas and vehicles are as old as the hills.

 For those with a more flexible budget, a rented car with driver is the smoothest way to cover a lot of ground in a limited amount of time.

gibbon and Asiatic tiger). Some of the proceeds go toward protecting the eponymous endangered primate and guides are former poachers turned rangers. Zip into and bed down in vertiginously high tree houses by night, listening to the call of the wild. The Gibbon Experience is Laos' premier wildlife and adventure playground. More ziplining opportunities await around Vang Vieng and on the Bolaven Plateau.

Tham Kong Lor

7 Imagine your deepest nightmare: the snaggle-toothed mouth of a river cave beneath a towering limestone mountain, the boatman in his rickety longtail taking you into the heart of darkness... Puttering beneath the cathedral-high ceiling of stalactites in this extraordinary 7.5km-long underworld in remote Khammuan Province is an awesome experience. You'll be very glad to see the light at the other end of the tunnel! The village of Ban Kong Lor is now the

most convenient base for visiting the cave, after an explosion of guesthouses and small resorts in the last few years.

Wat Phu Champasak

8 Not as majestic as the temples of Angkor, but just as mysterious, this mountainside Khmer ruin has both the artistry and the setting to impress. Once part of an important city, it now sits forlorn on the side of Phu Pasak. You'll discover something special at each level as you walk up to the summit where the views are vast and the crowds are thin. Other related ruins can be found in the rice paddies and forest down below.

Trekking around Phongsali

9 Laos is famous for its wide range of community-based treks, many of which include a traditional homestay for a night or longer. Trekking is possible all over the country, but northern Laos is one of the most popular

areas, and trekking around Phongsali is considered some of the most authentic in Laos and involves the chance to stay with the colourful Akha people.

Pha That Luang

10 Svelte and golden Pha That Luang is the most important national monument in Laos; a symbol of Buddhist religion and Lao sovereignty. Legend has it that Ashokan missionaries from India erected a tâht (stupa) here to enclose a piece of Buddha's breastbone as early as the 3rd century BC. A high-walled cloister with tiny windows surrounds the stupa and contains various Buddha images, including a serene statue of Jayavarman VII, the great Angkor-era king who converted the state religion of the Khmer empire to Buddhism.

River Trips

11 River trips are a major feature of travel through Laos. One of the most popular connects Luang Prabang and Huay Xai, the gateway to the Golden Triangle, via Pak Beng. From local boats to luxury cruises, there are options to suit every budget, including floating through sleepy Si Phan Don in the far south. Beyond the Mekong, many important feeder rivers such as the Nam Ou and Nam Tha connect places as diverse as Nong Khiaw and Muang Khua (for Phongsali). As well as boat trips, it is also possible to kayak some of these regional rivers in multiday activity trips.

GLEN ALLISON / GETTY IMAGES ©

Bun Pi Mai

Lao new year is the most important holiday of the year. Houses are cleaned, people put on new clothes and Buddha images are washed. There are public holidays on 14, 15 and 16 April.

Rocks

Odd-shaped rocks are venerated across Laos. Even in what appears to be the middle of nowhere, you'll see saffron robes draped over rocks that look vaguely like turtles, fishing baskets or stupas.

9

8

ISARESCHEEWIN / SHUTTERSTOCK ©

CAPITAL
Rīga

POPULATION
1.97 million

AREA
64,589 sq km

OFFICIAL LANGUAGE
Latvian

Blackheads' House, Rīga

Latvia

If you've an appetite for Europe's lesser-known lights, a taste of Latvian life with its full-voiced choirs and art nouveau architecture should stimulate the senses.

A tapestry of sea, lakes and woods, Latvia is best described as a vast unspoilt parkland with just one real city – its cosmopolitan capital, Rīga. The country might be small, but the amount of personal space it provides is enormous. You can always secure a chunk of pristine nature all for yourself, be it for trekking, cycling or dreaming away on a white-sand beach amid pine-covered dunes.

Having been invaded over the decades by every regional power, Latvia has more cultural layers and a less homogenous population than its neighbours. People here fancy themselves to be the least pragmatic and the most artistic of the Baltic lot. They prove the point with myriad festivals and a merry, devil-may-care attitude – well, a subdued Nordic version of it.

Top Experiences

Rīga

 The Gothic spires that dominate Rīga's cityscape might suggest austerity, but it is the flamboyant art nouveau architecture that forms the flesh and the spirit of this vibrant cosmopolitan city, the largest of all three Baltic capitals. Like all northerners, it is quiet and reserved on the outside, but there is some powerful chemistry going on inside its hip bars, modern art centres, and in the kitchens of its cool experimental restaurants.

Cape Kolka

 Enchantingly desolate and hauntingly beautiful, a journey to Cape Kolka (Kolkasrags) feels like a trip to the end of the earth. During Soviet times the entire peninsula was zoned off as a high-security military base, strictly out of bounds to civilians. The region's development was subsequently stunted and today the string of desolate coastal villages has a distinctly anachronistic feel – as though they've been locked away in a time capsule.

Cēsis

 With its stunning medieval castle, cobbled streets, green hills and landscaped garden, Cēsis is simply the cutest little town in the whole of Latvia. There is a lot of history there, too. The place started eight centuries ago as a Livonian Order's stronghold in the land of unruly pagans and saw horrific battles right under (or inside) the castle walls. Although it's an easy day trip from Rīga, Cēsis is definitely worth a longer

When to Go

 HIGH SEASON (Jun-Sep)

SHOULDER (May & Oct)

LOW SEASON (Nov-Apr)

stay, especially since there is the whole of Gauja National Park around it to explore.

Ventas Rumba

4 In a country that is acutely short of verticals but rich on horizontals, landscape features appear to be blatantly two-dimensional – even waterfalls. Spanning 240m, Ventas Rumba is branded Europe's widest waterfall, but as it is hardly taller than a basketball player, it risks being dismissed by vile competitors as a mere rapid if it decides to attend an international waterfall congress. That said, it does look like a cute toy Niagara, when observed from the Kuldīga castle hill. The vaulted arches of the old red-brick bridge make the sight all the more scenic.

Rundāle Palace

5 Built as a grand residence for the Duke of Courland, this magnificent palace is a monument to 18th-century aristocratic ostentatiousness, and rural Latvia's architectural highlight. It was designed by Italian baroque genius Bartolomeo Rastrelli, who is best known for the Winter Palace in St Petersburg. About 40 of the palace's 138 rooms are open to visitors, as are the wonderful formal gardens, inspired by those at Versailles.

Liepāja

6 Liepāja doesn't fit any cliche – a port city of gritty red-brick warehouses, moored torpedo boats and an old prison for the main attraction, it also boasts one of the country's most beautiful beaches, and it has

Getting Around

Buses are much more convenient than trains if you're travelling beyond Rīga's clutch of suburban rail lines.

Driving is on the right-hand side. Headlights must be on at all times. The number of automatic cars in Latvia is limited.

The city's network of commuter rails makes it easy for tourists to reach day-tripping destinations.

3

TRAVELSEWHERE / SHUTTERSTOCK ©

generated a totally disproportionate number of major Latvian musicians. Its rough-around-the-edges vibe (that translates into grungy musical sounds) makes Liepāja somewhat akin to Manchester, but in reality its search for identity is only beginning.

Jūrmala

7 The Baltic's version of the French Riviera, Jūrmala (pronounced yoor-muh-lah) is a long string of townships with Prussian-style villas, each unique in shape and decor. Even during the height of communism, Jūrmala was al-ways a place to 'sea' and be seen. These days, Russian tycoons and their glamorous wives comprise a visible part of the population. Wealthy fashionistas flaunt their couture beachwear while worshipping the sun between spa treatments. On summer weekends, vehicles clog the roads when jetsetters and day-tripping Rīgans flock to the resort town for some serious fun in the sun.

5

NIKONAFT / SHUTTERSTOCK ©

Food & Drink

Alus For such a tiny nation there's definitely no shortage of *alus* (beer) – each major town has its own brew.

Black Balzām The jet-black, 45%-proof concoction comes from a secret recipe of more than a dozen fairy-tale ingredients, including oak bark, wormwood and linden blossoms. Try mixing it with a glass of cola to take the edge off.

Kvass Single-handedly responsible for the decline of Coca Cola at the turn of the 21st century, kvass is a beloved beverage made from fermented rye bread.

Mushrooms Mushroom-picking takes the country by storm during the first showers of autumn.

Smoked fish Dozens of fish shacks dot the Kurzeme coast – look out for the veritable smoke signals rising above the tree line. Grab 'em to go; they make the perfect afternoon snack.

Oh Christmas Tree

Rīga's Blackheads' House was known for its wild parties; it was, after all, a clubhouse for unmarried merchants. On a cold Christmas Eve in 1510, the squad of bachelors, full of holiday spirit (and other spirits, so to speak), hauled a great pine tree up to their clubhouse and smothered it with flowers. At the end of the evening, they burned the tree to the ground in an impressive blaze. From then on, decorating the 'Christmas tree' became an annual tradition, which eventually spread across the globe (as you probably know, the burning part never really caught on).

An octagonal commemorative plaque, inlaid in cobbled Rātslaukums, marks the spot where the original tree stood.

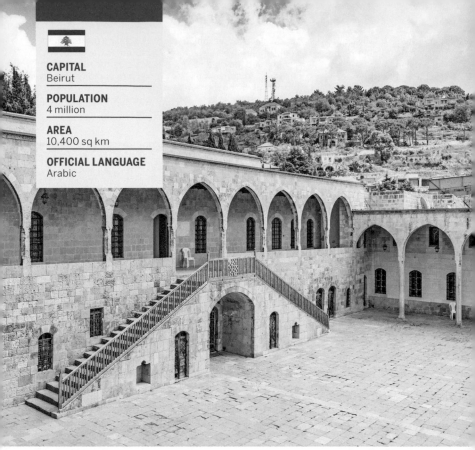

CAPITAL
Beirut

POPULATION
4 million

AREA
10,400 sq km

OFFICIAL LANGUAGE
Arabic

Beiteddine Palace, Beiteddine

Lebanon

Lebanon is one of the most vibrant and most complicated societies on earth, grafted onto one of the Middle East's most beautiful regions.

This diminutive Mediterranean nation is a place where culture, family and religion are all-important, but where sectarian violence can too often erupt – claiming lives and scarring both the landscape and the national psyche. Home to a world-famous national cuisine, a string of sexy beach resorts and the Middle East's most glamorous city (Beirut), this is also a country where the fiery orators and fierce foot soldiers of Hezbollah are based, and

where scores of Palestinian and Syrian refugees currently shelter.

Scarred by decades of civil war, invasions and terrorist attacks, yet blessed with magnificent mountain vistas, majestic ancient ruins and a people who are resilient, indomitable and renowned for their hospitality, Lebanon rewards the traveller with food for thought and a feast for the senses and the stomach. Don't miss it.

Top Experiences

Beirut

1 If you're looking for the real East-meets-West so talked about in the Middle East, you need look no further than Beirut. Fast-paced, fashion-conscious and overwhelmingly friendly, it's not a relaxing city, but its magnificent array of museums, restaurants, bars and clubs make it an essential stop on every Lebanese itinerary. In fact, the country is so small, and day trips to every city and major site so easy, that most travellers tend to base themselves here for their entire visit.

Beiteddine Palace

2 One of the highlights of the Chouf mountains, the early 19th-century Beiteddine Palace was built over a period of 30 years in the early 19th century by Emir Bashir Chehab II, Ottoman-appointed governor of the region. Sitting majestically on a hill surrounded by terraced gardens and orchards, the palace incorporates many traditional forms of Arab architecture. Since it was built in the early 19th century, it has been used for local administration then as the summer residence of Lebanon's first president,

When to Go

 HIGH SEASON (Jun–Aug)

SHOULDER (May–Sep)

 LOW SEASON (Dec–Apr)

damaged during the Israeli invasion and claimed by Druze militia before being restored and returned to the government in 1999.

Byblos

3 A pretty fishing port with an ancient harbour, medieval town centre, Crusader-era castle and atmospheric archaeological site, Byblos (Jbail in Arabic) is a wonderful

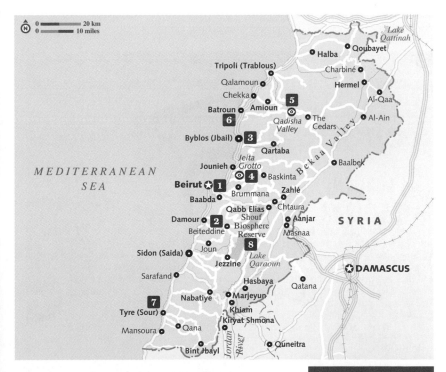

choice for those wanting a night or two out of Beirut, but is also an easy and enjoyable day trip.

Jeita Grotto

 One of the Middle East's greatest natural wonders, the stunning Jeita Grotto cave system extends around 6km into the mountains 18km northeast of Beirut. Discovered in 1836 and opened as a tourist attraction in 1969, the caves were used as an ammunition store during the civil war, despite the fact that their lower strata are flooded each winter because of the rising levels of the Nahr-el-Kalb (or Dog River). The simply extraordinary upper cavern stays open all year and is explored on foot. Accessed via a cable car, the site makes for a spectacular day trip from Beirut.

Qadisha Valley

 The Qadisha Valley, a Unesco World Heritage–listed site, is home to isolated rock-cut monasteries, wildflowers and plenty of wildlife. Red-roofed villages perch atop hills or cling precariously to the mountainsides; the Qadisha River, with its source just below the Cedars ski resort, runs along the valley bottom; and Lebanon's highest peak, Qornet as-Sawda (3090m), soars overhead. With plentiful opportunities for hiking quiet valley trails or scaling isolated mountain landscapes, this is the perfect antidote to the urban mayhem of Beirut.

Batroun

 This small town between Byblos and Tripoli has a semi-somnolent and highly atmospheric old

Getting Around

There are no air services operating within Lebanon, but the country is so small that you don't really need them.

Minibuses travel between Beirut and all of Lebanon's major towns. Large buses run from Beirut to Tripoli.

Most routes around towns and cities are covered by service, or shared, taxis, which are usually elderly Mercedes with red licence plates and a taxi sign on the roof.

JPRICHARD / SHUTTERSTOCK ©

neighbourhood near the water that rewards leisurely exploration. The majority of the town's residents are Christian, and there are many historic churches to visit in the old town's narrow cobbled streets.

Tyre

7 This predominantly Shiite town boasts a proud Phoenician past, wonderful seaside location, Roman ruins and a medieval souq. Home to good beaches and a decent array of hotels, Tyre is a popular holiday destination for Beirutis.

Shouf Biosphere Reserve

8 The largest of Lebanon's three natural protectorates, the Shouf Biosphere Reserve comprises an incredible 5% of Lebanon's total land area, is the largest natural cedar reserve in the country, and has more than 250km of hiking trails. Within it are ancient rock-cut fortress remains as well as six of the country's last remaining cedar forests, some with trees thought to be around 2000 years old. More than 200 species of birds and mammals (including wolves, gazelles and wild boar) inhabit or regularly pass through the area.

ANNA OM / SHUTTERSTOCK ©

Food & Drink

Kibbeh Croquettes of finely ground meat and minced onion, either fried or cooked in broth; a popular vegetarian version features spiced pumpkin.

Labneh Thick yoghurt seasoned with olive oil and garlic.

Moujaddara Lentils cooked with rice and onions.

Sambusas Fried cheese or meat pastries, similar to samosas.

Warak arish Stuffed vine leaves (also known as *wara anaib*).

Fattoush Toasted pitta bread, cos lettuce, cucumbers, tomatoes and sumac.

Tabbouleh Parsley, tomato, spring onion, burghul (cracked wheat) salad and mint.

Kofta Mincemeat with parsley and spices grilled on a skewer.

Sayadieh Fish and rice topped with onion sauce.

Lahma bi-ajeen Spiced ground meat and tomato pizza.

Falafel Deep-fried balls of spiced chickpeas and/or fava beans.

Lebanon's Cedars

The most famous of the world's several species of cedar tree are the cedars of Lebanon, mentioned in the Old Testament, and once covering great swathes of the Mt Lebanon Range.

Jerusalem's original Temple of Solomon was made from this sort of cedar wood, and the ancient Phoenicians, attracted by its fragrance and durability, also used it in their buildings. Unfortunately, a long history of deforestation has meant that today just a few pockets of cedars remain in Lebanon – despite the tree appearing proudly on the nation's flag.

Of these remnants of a once-abundant arboreal past, the best places to view the remaining cedars of Lebanon are either at the Chouf Cedar Reserve, or at the small grove at the Cedars ski resort in the north of the country.

Sehlabathebe National Park

Lesotho

Beautiful, culturally rich, safe, affordable and easily accessible from Durban and Johannesburg, mountainous Lesotho (le-soo-too) is a vastly underrated travel destination.

The contrast with South Africa could not be more striking, with the Basotho people's distinct personality and the altitudinous terrain's topographical extremes. Even a few days in Lesotho's hospitable mountain lodges and trading posts will give you a fresh perspective on Southern Africa.

This is essentially an alpine country, where villagers on horseback in multicoloured balaclavas and blankets greet you around precipitous bends. The hiking and trekking – often on a famed Basotho pony – is world class and the infrastructure of the three stunning national parks continues to improve.

The 1000m-high 'lowlands' offer craft shopping and sights, but don't miss a trip to the southern, central or northeastern highlands, where streams traverse an ancient dinosaur playground. This is genuine adventure travel.

CAPITAL
Maseru

POPULATION
2 million

AREA
30,355 sq km

OFFICIAL LANGUAGES
Sesotho, English

Top Experiences

Malealea Lodge

1 Offering 'Lesotho in a nutshell', Malealea is a deserving poster child for the mountain kingdom. Every sunset, village choirs and bands perform at the mountaintop lodge. Activities are community run and a proportion of tourist revenues and donations goes directly to supporting local projects. The views, meanwhile, are stupendous.

Sehlabathebe National Park

2 Lesotho's most undervisited national park is remote, rugged and beautiful. The rolling grasslands, wildflowers and silence provide complete isolation, with only the prolific bird life (including the bearded vulture) and the odd rhebok for company. Hiking (and horse riding from Sani Top or the Drakensbergs) is the main way to explore and angling is possible in the dams and rivers.

Pony Trekking in the Highlands

3 Pony trekking is one of Lesotho's top drawcards. It's done on sure-footed Basotho ponies, the result of crossbreeding between short Javanese horses and European full mounts. Advance booking is recommended and no prior riding experience is necessary. Whatever your experience level, expect to be sore after a day in the saddle.

Maletsunyane Falls

4 Semonkong (Place of Smoke), a one-pony town in the rugged Thaba

When to Go

HIGH SEASON (Nov-Mar)

SHOULDER (Apr-May, Sep, Oct)

LOW SEASON (Jun-Aug)

Putsoa range, gets its name from the nearby Maletsunyane Falls (204m), which are at their loudest in summer. The town is the starting point for many fine hiking and pony-trekking trails, including the two-day ride via the peaks of the Thaba Putsoa to Ketane Falls (122m).

Katse Dam

5 This engineering marvel stores 1950 million cubic metres of water bound for thirsty Gauteng, South Africa's most populated province. The high-altitude, 35.8-sq-km body of blue also generates hydroelectric power for Lesotho. Ringed by steep, green hillsides, the dam is a serene if surreal spot; the usual Basotho names on signposts give way to 'Mohale Tunnel Outlet' and

the like. Even if you're not impressed by engineering feats, the area makes for a relaxing pause.

Ts'ehlanyane National Park

6 This national park protects a beautiful, 5600-hectare patch of rugged wilderness, including one of Lesotho's only stands of indigenous forest, at a high altitude of 2000m to 3000m. This underrated and underused place is about as far away from it all as you can get and is perfect for hiking. In addition to day walks, there's a 39km day hike or pony trek to/from Bokong Nature Reserve, covering some of Lesotho's most dramatic terrain. Maliba also offers community-run tours of the villages bordering Ts'ehlanyane.

Getting Around

Minibus taxis serve the major towns and many smaller spots. Buses (cheaper and slower) and sprinters (faster and more expensive) serve the major towns. There are no classes and service is decidedly no-frills.

You can now access most of Lesotho in a 2WD car, but it is still not possible to do a complete circuit without a 4WD, due to rough gravel roads in the east. It usually works out cheaper to rent a vehicle in South Africa and drive it over the border.

YOLANDAVANNIEKERK / GETTY IMAGES ©

Crafts in Teyateyaneng

7 Teyateyaneng (Place of Quick Sands; usually known simply as 'TY') is the craft centre of Lesotho and is worth a stop to buy tapestries or watch them being made.

Sani Mountain Lodge

8 At 2874m, this lodge atop the Sani Pass stakes a claim to 'highest drinking hole in Southern Africa'. Pub trivia aside, cosy rondavels and excellent meals reward those who make the steep ascent from KwaZulu-Natal. Backpackers doss down the road in modern rooms that hold between two and six people. In winter, the snow is sometimes deep enough for skiing; pony trekking and village visits can be arranged.

Food & Drink

The diet of Basotho people is fairly simple, with many familes keeping livestock and growing greens, corn and wheat.

Joala Traditional sorghum beer – a white flag flying in a village means that it's available.

Mealie pap Bland but filling maize porridge that can be quite satisfying served with a good sauce or stew.

Motoho Fermented sorghum porridge.

Morogo Leafy greens, usually wild spinach, boiled, seasoned and served with pap.

GIL.K / SHUTTERSTOCK ©

Basotho Culture

Traditional Basotho culture is flourishing, and colourful celebrations marking milestones, such as birth, puberty, marriage and death, are a central part of village life. While hiking you may see the *lekolulo*, a flute-like instrument played by herd boys; the *thomo*, a stringed instrument played by women; and the *setolotolo*, a stringed mouth instrument played by men. Cattle hold an important position in daily life, both as sacrificial animals and as symbols of wealth.

The Basotho believe in a Supreme Being and place a great deal of emphasis on *balimo* (ancestors), who act as intermediaries between people and the capricious forces of nature and the spirit world. Evil is a constant danger, caused by *boloi* (witchcraft; witches can be either male or female) and *thkolosi* (small, mischievous beings, similar to the Xhosa's *tokoloshe*). If these forces are bothering you, visit the nearest *ngaka* (a learned man, part sorcerer and part doctor) who can combat them. Basotho are traditionally buried in a sitting position, facing the rising sun and ready to leap up when called.

Doula Market, Monrovia

Liberia

Founded by freed slaves from the USA and emerging from the devastation of civil war, Liberia is a country rich with natural beauty that is getting back on its feet.

Liberia, a lush, green, friendly and vibrant land, offers everything from excellent surf spots and shops selling wares by edgy local designers, to days spent lolling in a comfy hammock on the edge of the rainforest while listening to tropical birds sing. It's home to one of West Africa's best national parks, and still hangs on to a confident Amcrican spirit mixed with West African roots. And despite the ravages of the past,

it is still a fantastic place to travel, full of hope and energy.

After a decade of dusting themselves off and resuming normal life following their brutal civil war, Liberians experienced another deadly conflict in 2014 – the Ebola virus. While the nation is officially Ebola-free per the WHO, it's struggling economically to recover. With travel restrictions lifted, tourism can play a huge role in this.

Top Experiences

Monrovia

1 Monrovia has been everything over the decades – a splendid African capital brimming with elegant stores and faces, a party city monitored by sheriffs wearing second-hand US police uniforms, a war zone marred by bullet holes and a broken-hearted city struggling to climb to its feet after both war and a deadly Ebola outbreak. Walk along Broad St and you'll hear the original beat of locally brewed hip-co and the gentle rhythm of Liberian English. Monrovia has shaken off many of its old epithets and is infused with a new, exciting energy.

Harper

2 Charming Harper feels like the prize at the end of a long treasure hunt. The capital of the once-autonomous Maryland state, this gem is shingled with decaying ruins that hint at its former grandeur.

Robertsport

3 Framed by gold-spun beaches, phosphorescent waves and a thick mane of forest, this pretty capital of Grand Cape Mount has largely retained its simple, paradise-found feel. Now, as you wind your way through the old town, you're greeted by surf lodges and body-boarders.

When to Go

 HIGH SEASON (Oct–Jan)

 SHOULDER (Aug–Sep & Feb)

 LOW SEASON (Mar–Jun)

Food & Drink

Rice and spicy meat sauces or fish stews are popular Liberian dishes. Palm butter with fish and potato greens are two favourites. Other popular dishes include palava sauce (made with plato leaf, dried fish or meat and palm oil) and *jollof* rice (rice and vegetables with meat or fish).

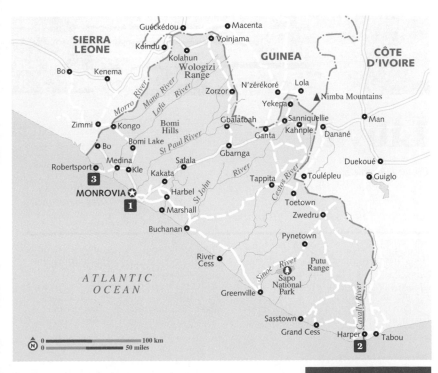

Leptis Magna

CAPITAL
Tripoli

POPULATION
6.54 million

AREA
1.759 million sq km

OFFICIAL LANGUAGE
Arabic

Libya

Libya is a realm of stunning coastlines, dramatic ancient ruins and the majesty of the Sahara. Sadly, the upheaval caused by Libya's revolution in 2011 and 2012 continues; chronic instability and ongoing conflict mean that the whole country remains off-limits to travellers.

Libya is an ancient crossroads of civilisations that bequeathed to the Libyan coast some of the finest Roman and Greek ruins in existence, among them Leptis Magna, Cyrene and Sabratha.

Libya is also home to some of the most beautiful corners of the Sahara Desert, from seas of sand the size of Switzerland (the Ubari Sand Sea) and sheltering palm-fringed lakes, to remote massifs adorned with prehistoric rock art (the Jebel Acacus), labyrinthine caravan towns (Ghadames) and an isolated black-as-black volcano (Wawa al-Namus) in the desert's heart.

Snapshot

Leptis Magna

1 Leptis Magna was once the largest and greatest Roman city in Africa. Because no modern settlement was later built on the site and it was constructed of sturdy limestone, Leptis is that rare ancient site where sufficient traces remain to imagine the city in its heyday.

Tripoli

2 Set on one of North Africa's best natural harbours, Tripoli exudes a distinctive Mediterranean charm infused with a decidedly Arabic-Islamic flavour. Its rich mosaic of historical influences – from Roman ruins and artefacts to the Ottoman-era medina – oozes through the atmospheric whitewashed city.

Ghadames

3 The Unesco World Heritage–listed old city of Ghadames is everything you imagine a desert oasis to be – abundant palm groves, a labyrinthine old town, and an unhurried pace of life unchanged for centuries. Old Ghadames is another world of covered alleyways, whitewashed houses and extensive palm gardens.

Seasons

 FEB–NOV

 DEC–JAN

Food & Drink

Algarra Lamb or seafood cooked in a high-temperature oven in a pottery amphora.

Bourdim Meat slow-cooked in a sand pit.

Fitaat Lentils, mutton and buckwheat pancakes cooked together in a tasty sauce.

Shay Tea, usually served black and with plenty of sugar.

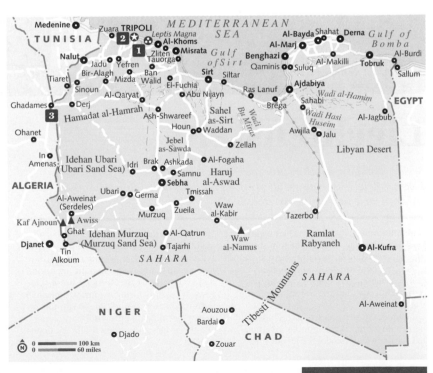

CAPITAL
Vaduz

POPULATION
36,900

AREA
160 sq km

OFFICIAL LANGUAGE
German

Schloss Vaduz

Liechtenstein

Besides the sheer novelty value of visiting one of the world's tiniest countries, Liechtenstein is pure fairytale stuff – embedded deep in the Alps and crowned by whimsically turreted castles.

A mountain principality governed by an iron-willed monarch, Liechtenstein snuggles between Switzerland and Austria. Only 25km long by 12km wide (at its broadest point), Liechtenstein doesn't have an international airport, but the overland journey is worthwhile.

Outdoor enthusiasts are in their element here, with a remarkable number of trails to hike and slopes to ski. Strike out into the Alpine wilderness beyond Vaduz and, suddenly, this landlocked sliver of a micronation no longer seems quite so small.

Come in summer for high-alpine hiking and cycling along the Rhine. Wildflowers bring a burst of spring colour, while golden autumn days are a fine time to sample new wine and game. Downhill and cross-country skiers glide along Malbun's slopes in winter.

Top Experiences

Malbun

1 At the end of the road from Vaduz, the 1600m-high resort town of Malbun feels – in the nicest possible sense – like the edge of the earth. But it's not really as remote as it seems and in high season Malbun is mobbed. However, generally it's perfect for unwinding, especially with the family. The skiing is inexpensive, if not too extensive (23km of pistes), while the hiking is beautiful.

Schloss Vaduz

2 Vaduz Castle looms over the capital from the hill above and, although closed to the public, is worth the climb for the vistas alone. Trails ascend the hill from the end of Egertastrasse. For a rare peek inside the castle grounds, arrive on 15 August, Liechtenstein's National Day, when there are magnificent fireworks and the prince invites all 36,900 Liechtensteiners over to his place for a glass of wine or beer.

Food & Drink

Liechtenstein's cuisine is influenced by its neighbours, Austria to the east and Switzerland to the west.

Beer Liechtenstein breweries produce high-quality lagers, wheat beers and ales.

Wine Tastings are available at many of Liechtenstein's wineries.

Käsknöpfle Tiny cheese-flavoured flour dumplings.

Ribel A semolina dish served with sugar and fruit compote or jam.

Map of Liechtenstein showing: Feldkirch, Sennwald, Hinterschellenberg, Ruggell, Schellenberg, Tisis, Mauren, Haag, Eschen, Bendern, Schaanwald, Nendeln, AUSTRIA, Planken, Three Sisters (Drei Schwestern), Buchs, Schaan, Fürstensteig, Rhine, VADUZ, Gaflei, Silum, Sevelen, Triesenberg, Väluna Valley, Steg, Triesen, Malbun, Trübbach, Balzers, Grauspitz, Sargans, SWITZERLAND. Scale: 0–5 km / 0–2.5 miles.

When to Go

HIGH SEASON (Jul & Aug)

SHOULDER (Apr–Jun, Sep–Oct)

LOW SEASON (Nov–Mar)

Liechtenstein Trivia

Liechtenstein is the only country in the world named after the people who purchased it.

Liechtenstein is the world's largest exporter of false teeth.

In its last military engagement in 1866, none of the country's 80 soldiers were killed. In fact, 81 returned, including a new Italian 'friend'. The army was disbanded soon afterwards.

This is Europe's fourth-smallest nation (only the Vatican, Monaco and San Marino are smaller).

ROSSHELEN / GETTY IMAGES ©

Walsermuseum

3 The star attraction of Triesenberg, this museum recounts the story of the Walsers and contains curious carvings out of twisted tree trunks and branches. The Walsers were a German-speaking 'tribe' from the Valais that emigrated across Europe in the 13th century and settled in many places, including Liechtenstein, where they still speak their own dialect. Ask at the museum about visiting the nearby Walserhaus (Hag 19), a 400-year-old house furnished in 19th-century fashion.

Fürstensteig

4 The country's most famous of its many hiking trails is the Fürstensteig, a rite of passage for nearly every Liechtensteiner. You must be fit and not suffer from vertigo, as in places the path is narrow, reinforced with rope handholds and/or falls away to a sheer drop. Travel light and wear good shoes.

Drei Länder Tour

5 It's easy to pedal across borders of Austria and Switzerland by bike in a day. One of the most scenic and memorable rides is the 59km Drei Länder Tour (Three Countries Tour), which leads from Vaduz to the medieval town of Feldkirch in Austria. The route then heads on to Illspitz and down along the Rhine to Buchs in Switzerland – dominated by its 13th-century castle, Schloss Werdenberg – before heading back to Vaduz.

Burg Gutenberg

6 Balzers' most visible icon is this state-owned, 13th-century hilltop castle, open only for concerts. Restored in the 20th century, the castle cuts a striking figure on the horizon and boasts nice strolls in the vicinity. The area was settled as early as the Neolithic period and Roman elements have been found in its foundations.

Getting Around

A comprehensive bus network traverses the country.

Grab a free orange rental bike at one of the seven stands around the country, or hire an e-bike from one of many locations.

International connections make it easy to travel to Liechtenstein by rail.

Hinterschellenberg

7 The town of Hinterschellenberg briefly entered the stream of world history when about 500 Russian soldiers who had fought on the German side in WWII crossed the border in search of asylum in 1945. They remained for about two-and-a-half years, after which most made for Argentina. A memorial about 100m from the Austrian border marks the event.

Vaduz

8 Vaduz is a postage stamp-sized city with a postcard-perfect backdrop. Crouching at the foot of forested mountains, hugging the banks of the Rhine and crowned by a turreted castle, its location is visually stunning. The centre itself is curiously modern and sterile, with its mix of tax-free luxury-goods stores and cubeshaped concrete buildings. Yet just a few minutes' walk brings you to traces of the quaint village that existed just 50 years ago, as well as quiet vineyards where the Alps seem that bit closer.

Väluna Valley

9 Valuna Valley is Liechtenstein's main cross-country skiing area with 15km of classic and skating track, including a 3km stretch that is illuminated at night. The trail heads start at Steg.

Postmuseum, Vaduz

10 Liechtenstein once made a packet producing souvenir stamps for enthusiasts, but that market has been hit by the rise of email. Here you'll find all national stamps issued since 1912.

WALTER BIBIKOW / GETTY IMAGES ©

CAPITAL
Vilnius

POPULATION
2.9 million

AREA
65,300 sq km

OFFICIAL LANGUAGE
Lithuanian

Gediminas Tower, Vilnius

Lithuania

A land of wood and water, proud, independent Lithuania (Lietuva) is fast being recognised as one of Europe's gems. Southernmost of the Baltic states, it's a pocket-sized republic that's a nature-lover's delight, yet lacks nothing in urban excitement.

Lithuania's foremost attraction is its stunning Baltic coastline, especially the unique sliver of white sand known as Curonian Spit. Lonely coastal wetlands lure migrating birds by the tens of thousands while inland, lush forests watch over burnished lakes.

The capital, Vilnius, is a beguiling artists' enclave, with its timeworn courtyards, cobbled streets and baroque churches animated by the vibrant, optimistic culture of today.

Further afield, remnants of Soviet times – a disused nuclear missile site (now a museum to the Cold War) and a Soviet sculpture park – are reminders of a dark recent past, while the Hill of Crosses and Orvydas stone garden stand testament to the land's enduring faith.

Top Experiences

Vilnius

1 Vilnius, the baroque beauty of the Baltic, is a city of immense allure. It easily tops the country's best-attraction bill, drawing tourists like moths to a flame with an easy, confident charm and a warm, golden glow that makes you wish for long midsummer evenings every day of the year. The capital may be a long way north and east, but it's quintessentially continental, with Europe's largest baroque old town at its heart. Viewed from a hot air balloon, the skyline – pierced by countless Orthodox and Catholic church steeples – looks like a giant bed of nails. Adding to this heady mix is a combination of cobbled alleys, crumbling corners, majestic hilltop views, breakaway states and traditional artists' workshops – all in a city so small you'd sometimes think it was a village.

Hill of Crosses

2 One of Lithuania's most awe-inspiring sights is the legendary Hill of Crosses. The sound of the thousands of crosses – which appear to grow on the hillock – as they tinkle in the breeze is wonderfully eerie. Planted here since at least the 19th century and probably much older, the crosses were bulldozed by the Soviets, but each night people crept past soldiers and barbed wire to plant more, risking their lives or freedom to express their national and spiritual fervour. Some of the crosses are devotional, others are memorials (many for people deported to Siberia) and some are finely carved folk-art masterpieces.

Curonian Spit

3 Breathe the pure air in the fragrant pine forests and high sand dunes of the enchanting Curonian Spit. This magical sliver of land, divided equally between Lithuania and Russia's Kaliningrad region, hosts some of Europe's most precious sand dunes and a menagerie of elk, deer and avian wildlife, with more than half its surface covered by pine forest.

Nemunas Delta

4 The low-lying, marsh-dotted eastern side of the Curonian Lagoon could be the end of the world. Tourism has scarcely touched this remote, rural and isolated landscape, where summer skies offer magnificent views of the spit's white dunes across the lagoon. In winter ice-fishers sit on the frozen lagoon – up to 12km wide in places – waiting for a smelt to bite.

Žemaitija National Park

5 This 200-sq-km park, a magical landscape of lake and forest, is as mysterious as it is beautiful. It's easy to see why it spawns fables of devils, ghosts and buried treasure. The draw here is two-fold. You can swim, boat and bike around at your leisure, as well as pay a visit to one of the country's newest and most bizarre attractions: a museum to the Cold War, housed in what was once a Soviet nuclear missile base.

Druskininkai

6 Nineteenth-century Druskininkai is Lithuania's oldest and most chic spa town. Today it attracts

Getting Around

The national bus network is extensive, linking all the major cities to each other and the smaller towns to their regional hubs.

Lithuanian roads are generally very good and driving is easy.

For common train journeys, such as Vilnius to Kaunas or to Klaipėda, the train is often more comfortable and better value than the bus.

2

GORSH13 / GETTY IMAGES ©

plenty of investment and young, hip and wealthy Lithuanians seeking a quick detox from city life. Tourists also come here, mainly for the many excellent spas. During the days of the USSR, the old and ailing came to this famous health resort in search of miracle cures for all sorts of ailments. While some of these vast dinosaur sanatoriums still remain today, the town is rapidly renovating and restoring much of the charm that was lost during those times.

Aukštaitija National Park

7 In this beloved national park, it's clear where Lithuania's love for nature arose. The natural paradise of deep, whispering forests and blue lakes bewitched this once-pagan country. Around 70% of the park comprises pine, spruce and deciduous forests, inhabited by elk, deer and wild boar. Its highlight is a labyrinth of 126 lakes. White-tailed and golden eagles prey here and storks are plentiful.

FRANZ MARC FREI / GETTY IMAGES ©

Food & Drink

Alus Beer is the most widely drunk alcoholic beverage; pretty good stuff at that.

Blyneliai Pancakes can be served sweet or savoury and eaten at any time during the day; look for *varskečiai*, stuffed with sweet curd.

Cepelinai Parcels of potato dough stuffed with cheese, meat or mushrooms.

Mushrooms Mushroom-picking is especially popular in late August and September, when the forests are studded with dozens of different varieties.

Šaltibarščiai This cold beetroot summer soup is arguably the country's signature dish; served with a plate of boiled potatoes on the side.

Late to the Church

While today Lithuanians are staunchly Roman Catholic, it wasn't always this way. In fact, Lithuania is considered to be the last pagan country in Europe: it wasn't fully baptised into Roman Catholicism until 1413.

There are lots of reasons for this: foremost among them was the Lithuanians' fierce independence, militating against attempts to convert them. The country's relatively recent experience (if you can call the 15th century 'recent') with paganism explains why so much of its religious art, national culture and traditions have pagan roots. However, during the Soviet years, Catholicism was persecuted and hence became a symbol of nationalistic fervour. Churches were seized, closed and turned into 'museums of atheism' or used for other secular purposes by the state. After Independence in 1991, the Catholic Church quickly began the ongoing process of reacquiring church property and reconsecrating places of worship.

These days, around 80% of Lithuanians consider themselves to be Catholics. There are small minorities of other sects and faiths, including Russian Orthodox (4%) and Protestant Christians (2%).

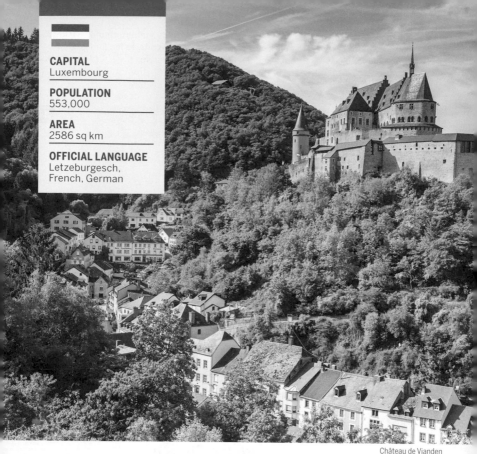

CAPITAL
Luxembourg

POPULATION
553,000

AREA
2586 sq km

OFFICIAL LANGUAGE
Letzeburgesch,
French, German

Château de Vianden

Luxembourg

Fabulously historic yet flush with the shock of the new, this compact,
gentle and decidedly multilingual little country is packed with great, big,
wonderful surprises.

Consistently ranked among the world's top-three nations in both wealth and wine consumption, life in little Luxembourg seems good. But all the lax taxation and bank headquarters conceal an absolutely charming slice of northern Europe.

The capital has a fairy-tale quality to its Unesco-listed historic core, memorably perched along a dramatic cliff top. Beyond, you'll rapidly find yourself in rolling part-forested hills where a string of beguiling villages each form attractive huddles beneath stunning medieval castles. Then there's all the fun of the fizz in Moselle wine country and some loveable walks to take in the pretty micro-gorges of Müllerthal.

All in all, this little country has plenty of surprises. That's some achievement given its wholesale destruction during WWII, a sad history remembered in war museums across the country.

Top Experiences

Chemin de la Corniche

1 This pedestrian promenade in Luxembourg City has been hailed as 'Europe's most beautiful balcony'. It winds along the course of the 17th-century city ramparts, with views across the river towards the hefty fortifications of the Wenzelsmauer (Wenceslas Wall). The rampart-top walk continues along Blvd Victor Thorn to the Dräi Tier (Triple Gate) tower.

Château de Vianden

2 This château's extraordinary outline is the result of an almost-total 20th-century restoration after the original, built from the 11th to 14th centuries, had fallen into complete ruin. Walkways in the bowels of the edifice display different layers of occupation, from Roman onwards. Open to the air, the 'Byzantine Hall' is a marvellous space, while the Gothic polygonal chapel is built around a central well. Plusher halls display fine Flanders tapestries, while photo galleries show the reconstruction process and snaps of famous visitors.

Food & Drink

Judd mat gaardebounen The national dish, smoked pork in a creamy sauce with broad beans and potato chunks.

Liewekniddelen mat sauerkraut Liver meatballs with sauerkraut.

Wine The Moselle Valley produces excellent sparkling wines, Rivaners, Pinot Blancs and Rieslings.

When to Go

HIGH SEASON
(Jul–Aug)

SHOULDER
(May–Jun & Sep)

LOW SEASON
(Oct–Mar)

Royalty

Dutch monarchs wore a second crown as Grand Dukes of Luxembourg from 1815 until 1890. When William III died, his only surviving child became Queen Wilhelmina. However, by Luxembourg's then laws, its crown could not pass to a woman. Thus Adolph of Nassau took over as duke and his descendants rule to this day. Changes to the hereditary rules allowed Marie Adélaïde to become grand duchess, but perceptions of her pro-German stance in WWI meant she was persuaded to abdicate after the war. Thus, remarkably, the Grand Duchy put its royal family up for referendum in 1919. The result was a resounding 'yes' and Marie Adélaïde's younger sister Charlotte took the throne. The current Grand Duke Henri met his wife María Teresa, a Cuban-born commoner, at university in Geneva. Although they live in a castle (the 1911 Château Colmar-Berg), their kids were sent to ordinary schools, and it's quite possible to bump into royals at the shops or cinema. Compared with some royals, the royal family of Luxembourg remain much respected.

CAHIR DAVITT / JOHN WARBURTON-LEE PHOTOGRAPHY LTD / GETTY IMAGES ©

Luxembourg City

3 If you thought that the Grand Duchy's capital was nothing more than banks and EU offices, you'll be delighted at discovering the attractive reality. The Unesco-listed Old Town is one of Europe's most scenic capitals, thanks largely to its unusual setting, draped across the deep gorges of the Alzette and Pétrusse rivers. It's full of weird spaces, tunnels, and surprising nooks to explore. Good museums and a great dining scene makes this a top city to visit. Tuck in to traditional and avant-garde cuisine in the lively restaurants and bars.

Echternach

4 A fine base for hiking in the enchanting woodlands and rocky microcanyons. Echternach, one of Luxembourg's prettiest towns, boasts a strikingly beautiful central square and a long history as a monastery settlement. Its reconstructed 18th-century abbey spreads back from the basilica towards the tree-lined banks of the Sûre. Tucked away just north of the main church, an atmospheric museum occupies the vaulted basement that once formed the famous scriptorium.

Beaufort Castle

5 Across a pretty, part-wooded valley behind the village of Beaufort is a ruinous but very imposing five-storey medieval castle. Once the site of a Roman camp, the sandstone fortress expanded from 12th-century origins but never recovered from WWII bombing during the Battle of the Ardennes. There's no 'interior' or decor but there are many levels to climb and explore. The castle cash desk sells locally made plum and blackcurrant liqueurs.

US Military Cemetery

6 In a beautifully maintained graveyard near Hamm lie over 5000 US WWII dead, including George Patton, the audacious general of the US Third Army who played a large part in Luxembourg's 1944 liberation. It's a humbling sight, with its rows of white crosses (and the odd Star of David).

Getting Around

Luxembourg is served by a comprehensive bus network.

Luxembourg's buses and trains share the same ticketing system. A ticket for all domestic transport costs €2 for up to two hours, and €4 for the whole day.

Moselle Valley

7 The wide Moselle River forms the border with Germany, its steeply rising banks covered with seemingly endless vineyards. All along the scenic riverside from Schengen to Wasserbillig you'll find a succession of villages and wineries. Excellent crémants give Luxembourg the fizz and pop that keeps it buzzing throughout the summer, but the region also produces fruity Rivaners, lush Pinot Blancs and balanced Rieslings, not to mention Pinot Gris, Gewürztraminer and Auxerrois.

Esch-sur-Sûre

8 This tiny, picturesque village wraps around a knoll virtually surrounded by an emerald-green loop of the Sûre river. Topped by a modest 927 AD castle tower, the scene is one of Luxembourg's prettiest, though there's not a great deal to do here except potter about and relax. All the better, many would say. An annual night market, held on a Saturday in July or August, brings the place to vibrant life.

7

HANS GEORG EIBEN / GETTY IMAGES ©

CAPITAL
Macau

POPULATION
597,425

AREA
29.5 sq km

OFFICIAL LANGUAGES
Cantonese,
Portuguese

Ruins of the Church of St Paul

Macau

The last outpost of the Portuguese empire, Macau still has a tangible Mediterranean feel. Nevertheless, Chinese culture shines through in this city state located at the mouth of the Pearl River.

Best known globally as the 'Vegas of China', the Macau Special Administrative Region is indeed a mecca of gambling and glitz. But the city is so much more than that. A Portuguese colony for more than 300 years, it is a city of blended cultures. Ancient Chinese temples sit on streets paved with traditional Portuguese tiles. The sound of Cantonese fills the air on streets with Portuguese names. You can eat Chinese *congee* for breakfast, enjoy a Portuguese lunch of *caldo verde* soup and

bacalhau (cod) fritters, and dine on hybrid Macanese fare such as *minchi* (minced meat cooked with potatoes and onions).

The Macau Peninsula holds the old city centre, where colonial ruins sit next to arty new boutiques. Further south are the conjoined islands of Taipa, Cotai and Coloane. Taipa has gloriously preserved Macanese architecture, Cotai is home to the new megacasinos and Coloane is lined with colonial villages and pretty beaches.

Top Experiences

Ruins of the Church of St Paul

1 Once a Jesuit church in the early 17th century, all that remains of it now are the facade and the stairway. However, with its statues, portals and engravings that effectively make up a sermon in stone, it's one of the greatest monuments to Christianity in Asia.

Taipa Village

2 Dine on Portuguese fare and wander the narrow lanes of this charming old village. An intricate warren of alleys hold traditional Chinese establishments while the broader main roads are punctuated by colonial villas, churches and temples. Avenida da Praia, a tree-lined esplanade, is perfect for a stroll.

Guia Fortress & Guia Chapel

3 Take the cable car to handsome Guia Fort and its gorgeous chapel, a 17th-century colonial complex atop a hill. The highest point on the peninsula affords panoramic views of the city and, when the air is clear, across to the islands and China.

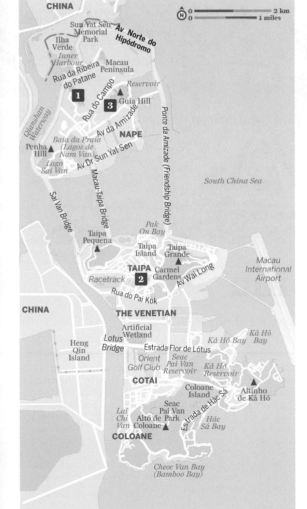

Food & Drink

A famous Macanese speciality is *galinha africana* (African chicken), made with coconut, garlic and chillies. Other popular dishes include *casquinha* (stuffed crab) and *serradura* (a milk pudding). You'll find Portuguese dishes here too, such as *arroz de pato* (rice with duck confit) and *leitão assado no forno* (roasted suckling pig).

When to Go

 HIGH-SEASON (Dec, Feb, Apr-May)

 SHOULDER (Jan, Mar, Oct-Nov)

 LOW SEASON (Jun-Sep)

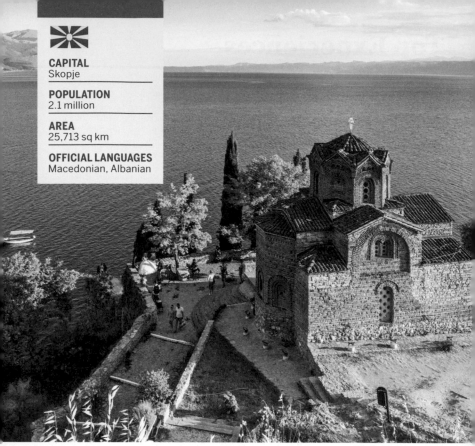

Church of Sveti Jovan, Ohrid

CAPITAL
Skopje

POPULATION
2.1 million

AREA
25,713 sq km

OFFICIAL LANGUAGES
Macedonian, Albanian

Macedonia

Part Balkan, part Mediterranean and rich in Greek, Roman and Ottoman history, Macedonia has a fascinating past and a complex national psyche.

Glittering Lake Ohrid and the historic waterside town of Ohrid itself have etched out a place for Macedonia on the tourist map, but this small nation is far more than just one great lake. Skopje may be the Balkans' most bonkers and unfailingly entertaining capital city, thanks to a government-led building spree of monuments, museums and fountains. What has emerged is an intriguing jigsaw where ancient history and buzzing modernity collide.

The rest of Macedonia is a stomping ground for adventurers. Tourist infrastructure is scant, but locals are unfailingly helpful. Mountains are omnipresent and walking trails blissfully quiet. The national parks of Mavrovo, Galičica and Pelister are also cultivating some excellent cultural and food-tourism initiatives; these gorgeous regions are criminally underexplored. If you want to get off the beaten track in Europe, this is it.

Top Experiences

Church of Sveti Jovan

1 Gaze out over Ohrid from the Church of Sveti Jovan at Kaneo, immaculately set on a bluff above Lake Ohrid. This stunning 13th-century church on a cliff over the lake has pride of place in Macedonia's most important historic town. It is possibly Macedonia's most photographed structure. Peer down into the azure waters and you'll see why medieval monks found spiritual inspiration here. The small church has original frescoes behind the altar.

Skopje

2 Skopje is among Europe's most entertaining and eclectic small capital cities. While a government construction spree has sparked controversy in recent years, Skopje's abundance of statuary, bridges, museums and other structures has visitors' cameras snapping like never before and has defined the ever-changing city. Yet plenty survives from earlier times – Skopje's Ottoman- and Byzantine-era wonders include the 15th-century Kameni Most (Stone Bridge), Čaršija (old Turkish bazaar) and Sveti Spas Church, with its ornate, hand-carved iconostasis. And, with its bars, clubs and galleries, the city has modern culture, too.

Pelister National Park

3 Eat your fill at food-focused village tourism initiatives in this underrated national park,

When to Go

 HIGH SEASON (Jun–Aug)

 SHOULDER (Mar–May, Sep–Nov)

 LOW SEASON (Dec–Feb)

and walk it off the next day. Macedonia's oldest national park, created in 1948, covers 125 sq km of the country's third-highest mountain range, the quartz-filled Baba massif. Eight peaks top 2000m, crowned by Mt Pelister (2601m). Two glacial lakes, known as 'Pelister's Eyes', sit at the top. Summiting both Mt Pelister and the lakes is one of the park's biggest hiking attractions.

Golem Grad

4 Adrift on Lake Prespa, Golem Grad was once the summer playground of Tsar Samuel, but the island is now home to wild tortoises, cormorants and pelicans, and perhaps a few ghosts. A settlement endured here from the 4th century BC to the 6th century AD and during medieval times there was a monastery complex. The ruins, bird life and otherworldly beauty make it well worth exploration.

Tikveš

5 Macedonia's winery heartland, Tikveš, has produced wine since the 4th century BC. Winemaking bacchanalia was suppressed during Ottoman rule, however, and it's only in the past 30 years or so that vines have been replanted in earnest and production ramped up. This region benefits from 300 sun-filled days a year, and has all the hallmarks associated with its major industry: rolling vineyards and dusty agricultural towns, plus lakes, caves, gorges and churches. The region's shining star, Popova Kula Winery hotel and restaurant, makes a wonderful base for appreciating the grapes.

Getting Around

Skopje serves most domestic destinations. Larger buses are new and air-conditioned; *kombi* (minibuses) are usually not.

It's virtually impossible to hire a car with automatic transmission in Macedonia: manual-only here.

Domestic trains are reliable but slow.

Sveti Jovan Bigorski Monastery

6 This revered 1020 Byzantine monastery is located, fittingly, up in the gods along a track of switchbacks off the Debar road, close to Jančе village. Legend attests an icon of Sveti Jovan Bigorski (St John the Baptist) miraculously appeared here; since then the monastery has been rebuilt often – the icon occasionally reappearing too. The complex went into demise during communist rule but has been painstakingly reconstructed and today is as impressive as ever, with some excellent views over Mavrovo's mountains.

Food & Drink

Ajvar Sweet red-pepper sauce; accompanies meats and cheeses.

Bekonegs Not terribly traditional, but you will see this mangled rendition of 'bacon and eggs' on Macedonian breakfast menus.

Rakija Grape-based firewater, useful for toasts (and cleaning cuts and windows!).

Skopsko and Dab lagers Macedonia's favourite brews.

Šopska salata Tomatoes, onions and cucumbers topped with flaky *sirenje* (white cheese).

Uvijač Rolled chicken or pork wrapped in bacon and filled with melted yellow cheese.

Vranec and Temjanika Macedonia's favourite red- and white-wine varietals.

Heraclea Lyncestis

7 Heraclea Lyncestis, 1km south of Bitola, is among Macedonia's best archaeological sites. Founded by Philip II of Macedon, Heraclea became commercially significant before the Romans conquered in 168 BC. In the 4th century Heraclea became an episcopal seat, but it was sacked by Goths and then Slavs. You can see the Roman baths, portico and amphitheatre, and the striking early Christian basilica and episcopal palace ruins, with beautiful, well-preserved floor mosaics. They're unique in depicting endemic trees and animals.

OLLIRG / GETTY IMAGES ©

Lake Ohrid

Lake Ohrid's endemic trout (*Salmo letnica*) is an endangered species and protected from fishing. Locals take the warning quite seriously these days and farm trout to put on their menus instead.

More broadly, the lake's growing popularity as a stop-off on the tourist circuit has become cause for concern among conservation groups. Plans have been drawn up to create a marina, artificial Mediterranean-style beaches and new apartments by draining an important marshland that acts as a natural filter to the lake. A local initiative called Ohrid SOS was set up in 2015 to help challenge the proposals, and the struggle to find a balance between commercial desires and conservation imperatives continues.

Ring-tailed lemur

Madagascar

Lemurs, baobabs, rainforest, desert, hiking and diving: Madagascar is a dream destination for outdoors enthusiasts – half the fun is getting to all these incredible attractions.

Madagascar is unique: 5% of all known animal and plant species can be found here, and here alone. The island's signature animal is the lemur, but there are many more weird and wonderful creatures: the eerie-looking fossa (a catlike predator), colourful and camouflaged chameleons, oddly shaped insects, and humpback whales during the winter months. Trees and plants are just as impressive, be they the distinctively shaped baobabs or the hundreds of orchids.

The remarkable fauna and flora is matched by epic landscapes of an incredible diversity: sandstone canyons, limestone karsts, mountains, fertile hills cascading with terraced rice paddies, forests of every kind and a laterite-rich soil that gave the country its nickname of 'Red Island'. And with 5000km of coastline, the sea is never very far. For those who relish an adventure, this is a one-of-a-kind destination.

CAPITAL
Antananarivo

POPULATION
24.2 million

AREA
587,041 sq km

OFFICIAL LANGUAGES
Malagasy, French

Top Experiences

Parc National d'Isalo

1 It's not just because of its epic desert landscapes – canyons, ravines, gorges, savannah-like plains – that Isalo is so popular. It's also because there is so much to do here: hiking, via ferratas (fixed cable routes), horse riding, mountain biking, 4WD circuits and swimming in natural pools. Let's not forget lemur and birdwatching, nor admiring the technicolour sunsets and exquisite clarity of the night skies.

Nosy Be

2 The 'big island' is a dream destination: you could spend two weeks here and in the surrounding islands and still feel like you haven't had enough. It's not just the world-class diving and snorkelling, the turquoise sea, the exquisitely soft light and arresting views; you can also visit spice plantations, explore kilometres of inland trails, see fabulous wildlife in the marine and nature reserves, feast on an abundance of seafood and sail to small islands nearby.

Tackling the Infamous RN5

3 If you revel in the idea of a road challenge, this is it. It may be a route nationale, but make no mistake, the 240km stretch of the RN5 between Maroantsetra and Soanierana-Ivongo is no road. It is a track, a quagmire, an obstacle course, a river in places, a mountain in others, but not a road. Semantics aside, travellers who complete the journey will have anecdotes to last them a lifetime. Mananara, halfway through the trip, is also one of the few places in Madagascar where you're likely to see an aye-aye.

Tropical Haute Cuisine

4 The freshest of ingredients combined with traditional and colonial culinary influences have produced a divine strand

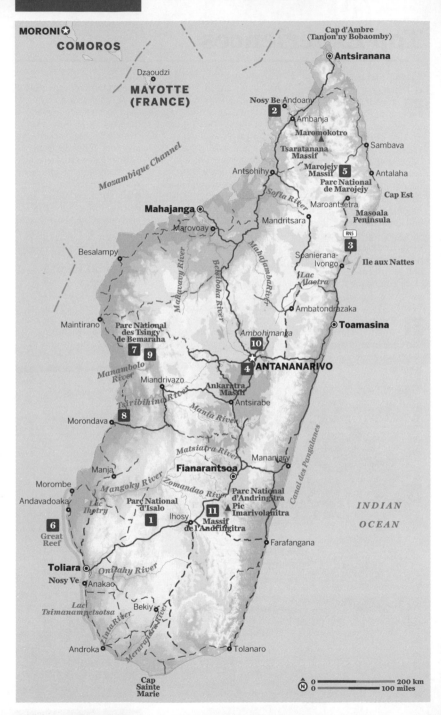

MORONI ✪

COMOROS

Cap d'Ambre
(Tanjon'ny Bobaomby)

◉ **Antsiranana**

Dzaoudzi

**MAYOTTE
(FRANCE)**

Nosy Be · Andoany

2

· Ambanja

Maromokotro ▲

**Tsaratanana
Massif**

· Sambava

Antsohihy ◦

**Marojejy
Massif** **5**

· Antalaha

**Parc National
de Marojejy**

Cap Est

Mozambique Channel

Mahajanga ◉

· Maroantsetra

Sofia River

**Masoala
Peninsula**

Marovoay ◦

Mandritsara ◦

RN5
3

Besalampy ◦

Spanierana-
Ivongo ◦

Ile aux Nattes

Mahavavy River

Betsiboka River

MahajambaRiver

_Lac
Alaotra_

Maintirano ◦

**Parc National
des Tsingy
de Bemaraha**

· Ambatondrazaka

◉ **Toamasina**

7 **9**

Ambohimanga

10

_Manambolo
River_

Miandrivazo ◦

**Ankaratra
Massif**

4 ☆ **ANTANANARIVO**

Tsiribihina River

◦ Antsirabe

8

Manta River

Morondava ◦

Matsiatra River

Mananjary ◦

Fianarantsoa ◉

Canal des Pangalanes

Manja ◦

Mangoky River

Zomandao River

Morombe ◦

**Parc National
d'Andringitra**

Andavadoaka ◦

**Parc National
d'Isalo**

**Pic
Imarivolanitra** ▲

_Lac
Ihotry_

1

Ihosy ◦

11 **Massif
de l'Andringitra**

6

**Great
Reef**

· Farafangana

**INDIAN

OCEAN**

Toliara ◉

Onilahy River

Nosy Ve ◦ · Anakao

_Lac
Tsimanampetsotsa_

Bekily ◦

Linta River

Menarandra River

Mangoky River

Androka ◦

◦ Tolanaro

**Cap
Sainte
Marie**

Ⓝ 0 ————————— 200 km
  0 ————————— 100 miles

of fusion cuisine. The zebu meat rivals beef in succulence and tenderness, spices add piquancy to sauces, and the tropical sun-ripened fruit finds its

Best on Film

Madagascar (2011) A three-part series by the BBC, narrated by Sir David Attenborough, showcasing the island's wildlife.

Madagascar (2005) With a stellar cast of voice-overs, this animation raised Madagascar's profile.

Food & Drink

Rice Often eaten three times a day – in a broth for breakfast, accompanied by a helping of meat and sauce for lunch or dinner.

Condiments Malagasies keep things interesting with an arsenal of condiments, such as *sakay* (a red-hot pepper paste with ginger and garlic), *pimente verde* (a fiery green chilli) and *achards* (hot pickled fruit, such as tomato, lemon, carrot or mango, used as relish).

Rice Water Most Malagasies like to accompany a rice meal with a drink of rice water. Known as *ranovola* or *ranon'apango*, it's made from boiling water in the pot containing the burnt rice residue – definitely an acquired taste.

Zebu These cattle not only provide status and transport, they are also well known for their excellent meat. Zebu beef is prepared in much the same way as European cattle beef – in stews, kebabs (known locally as *masikita*, often tiny in size) and as succulent steak.

way into anything from sorbets to macerated rum. Antananarivo has the best selection of restaurants, but Mad Zebu in Belo-sur-Tsiribihina, La Table d'Alexandre in Nosy Be and Piment Banane in Tamatave are other establishments worth seeking out.

Parc National de Marojejy

5 With its pristine mountainous rainforest, thick root-filled jungle and waterfalls, Marojejy is a primordial place, where the 'angel of the forest' (the endemic silky sifaka) inhabits misty mountains, and spectacular views of the Marojejy Massif open up through the canopy. A superb trail crescendos through the landscape, climaxing with a tough climb to the summit (2132m). Marojejy permits also provide entry to the remote and beautiful Réserve Spéciale d'Anjanaharibe-Sud, where travellers will be rewarded with the wail of the indri.

When to Go

HIGH SEASON
(Jul & Aug)
It's winter – balmy temperatures by day and cool nights (cold in the highlands).

SHOULDER
(Apr–Jun, Sep–Dec)
The best time to go: warm temperatures and fewer visitors.

LOW SEASON
(Jan–Mar)
Rainy season everywhere – many areas inaccessible.

Diving & Snorkelling at Anakao

6 Madagascar boasts the world's fifth-largest coral reef – 450km of fringing, patch and

Famadihana

Famadihana (literally, the 'turning of the bones') is the name given to the traditional exhumations of dead ancestors by the Betsileo and Merina people. *Famadihana* are joyous and intense occasions, which occur in each family roughly every seven years. Amid feasting, drinking, music and dancing, the bodies of the dead are disinterred from the family tomb, wrapped in bamboo mats, and carried and danced around the tomb. The bodies are then re-shrouded and reburied.

Famadihana ceremonies occur in the region around Antsirabe between July and September only. Local tour operators can help you find one and arrange an invitation. If you receive an invite, it's polite to bring a bottle of rum as a gift for the host family, and to ask before taking pictures. Foreigners are generally warmly welcomed, and most people find that the experience, far from being morbid, is moving and fascinating.

Getting Around

Flights can be huge time savers, but they can be expensive and subject to frequent delays and cancellations.

If you can afford it, private vehicle is the best way to explore Madagascar. You'll be able to go anywhere, whenever suits you. The off-road driving can be great fun, too.

They are slow, uncomfortable and not always safe, but *taxi-brousse* (bush taxis) are cheap, go (almost) everywhere and you can't get more local than that.

barrier reefs from Morombe in the north to Itampolo in the south. Work with local communities and marine conservation areas have helped maintain the reef's health despite increasing pressure. Anakao has some of the best infrastructure on the reef, with the added bonus of whale watching in winter. Other spots that will blow you away are the 'cathedrals' at Ifaty and Mangily and the serene village of Ambola.

Parc National des Tsingy de Bemaraha

7 There is nothing else on earth quite like the jagged limestone pinnacles of Parc National des Tsingy de Bemaraha. A Unesco World Heritage Site, the serrated, surreal-looking peaks and boulders are a geological work of art, the result of millennia of water and wind erosion. Just as remarkable is the infrastructure the national park has put in place to explore this natural wonder: via ferratas (fixed-cable routes), rope bridges and ladders, with circuits combining forests,

caves, pirogue trips and even abseiling.

Sunset at Allée des Baobabs

8 Few things say Madagascar more than this small stretch of the RN8 between Morondava and Belo-sur-Tsiribihina. Lined with majestic baobabs, it comes into its own at sunset and sunrise when the trees cast their long shadows on the red sand and the sky lights up with orange and purple hues. In addition to the Allée, you'll find plenty more baobabs across southern and western Madagascar. Some live for up to 1000 years and reach epic proportions: Majunga's sacred baobab measures 21m around its trunk!

Manambolo River

9 Taking a trip down the Manambolo means disconnecting completely from everything: for three days there are no cars, no roads and precious little mobile-phone coverage. It's just you, your guide and the pirogue. It is an experience of utter relaxation, with little more to do

than admire the landscape, gawk at the spectacular gorges, take in local life, sing by the campfire and marvel at the night sky. Make sure you pick a reliable operator.

Ambohimanga

10 This is Madagascar's only cultural site on Unesco's World Heritage list, and with good reason: Ambohimanga was the seat of King Andrianampoinimerina, the Merina sovereign who decided to unify the warring tribes of the island so that his kingdom would have no frontier but the sea. The cultural significance of the site goes beyond history: Ambohimanga is revered as a sacred site by the Malagasy, who come here to invoke royal spirits and request their protection and good fortune.

Massif de l'Andringitra

11 Andringitra (Andrintch) is a majestic central mountain range with two gorgeous valleys on either side, the Namoly and the Tsaranoro (sometimes called the Sahanambo, for the river that runs through it), forming a paradise for walkers and climbers. There are spectacular views in all directions, well-developed hiking trails, excellent accommodation, interesting villages, plus three extraordinary peaks: Pic Boby (Imarivolanitra), at 2658m the second-highest peak in the country; the Tsaranoro Massif, which reaches 1910m, including an 800m vertical column considered to be one of the most challenging climbs in the world; and the great stump of Pic Dondy (2195m). Here's the most amazing part: there are less than 3000 visitors a year! Imagine having Yosemite to yourself and you're not far off the mark.

DENNIS VAN DE WATER / SHUTTERSTOCK ©

Hot Water

Hot water is rare in budget accommodation, hit and miss in midrange places, but reliable in top-end places and the highlands. Central heating is unheard of.

Lychees

Madagascar provides around 70% of Europe's lychees, but fear not, there are plenty left in the country to gorge on. The season runs November to January and lychees are a favourite Christmas food.

DENNISVDW / GETTY IMAGES ©

CAPITAL
Lilongwe

POPULATION
18.6 million

AREA
118,484 sq km

OFFICIAL LANGUAGE
English

Lake Malawi

Malawi

Apart from the legendary Malawian friendliness, what captures you first about this vivid country is its geographical diversity.

Slicing through the landscape in a trough formed by the Great Rift Valley is Africa's third-largest lake: Lake Malawi, a shimmering mass of clear water, its depths swarming with colourful cichlid fish. Whether for diving, snorkelling, kayaking or chilling out on beaches and desert islands, a visit to the lake is a must.

Suspended in the clouds in Malawi's deep south are the dramatic peaks of Mt Mulanje and the mysterious Zomba Plateau, both a hiker's dream, with mist-cowled forests and exotic wildlife. Further north is the otherworldly beauty of the Nyika Plateau, its rolling grasslands resembling the Scottish Highlands.

Malawi was once dismissed as a safari destination, but all that changed with a lion-reintroduction program at Majete Wildlife Reserve, which is now one of a few worthwhile wildlife-watching destinations nationwide.

Top Experiences

Lake Malawi

1 The emerald jewel in Malawi's crown is undoubtedly its interior sea, Lake Malawi. Fringed by golden beaches, the 'calendar lake' – so-called because it measures 365 miles long and 52 miles wide – offers travellers an underwater paradise to swim among brilliantly coloured cichlid fish and desert islands to escape to. The resorts of Chintheche Strip, Nkhata Bay and Cape Maclear also offer a spectrum of great accommodation and activities such as kayaking and windsurfing to ensure you can make the best of it.

Majete Wildlife Reserve

2 Malawi's only Big Five park, this rugged wilderness of hilly miombo (woodland) and savannah hugs the west bank of the Shire River. Since African Parks took over its management in 2003, things have

Food & Drink

The staple diet for most Malawians is *nshima*, a thick, doughy maize porridge that's bland but very filling. It's eaten with the hands and always accompanied by beans or vegetables and a hot relish, and sometimes meat or fish.

Fish is particularly good in Malawi, and *chambo*, the popular breamlike variety, and *kampango*, a lake fish similar to catfish, are both popular.

Traditional beer of the region is made from maize. Malawi's local lager is called Kuche Kuche but most travellers (and many Malawians) prefer the beer produced by Carlsberg at its Blantyre brewery. The most popular brew is Carlsberg 'green' (lager).

When to Go

 HIGH SEASON (May–Oct)

 LOW SEASON (Nov–Apr)

The Boy Who Harnessed the Wind

When the 2001 drought brought famine, and terrible floods decimated his parents' crops, 14-year-old William Kamkwamba was forced from school. While he was educating himself at his old primary school, one book in particular spoke to him; it was about electricity generation through windmills.

A light-bulb moment flashed. Exhausted from his work in the fields every day, William picked around for scrap and painstakingly began his creation: a four-bladed windmill. Soon neighbours were coming to see him to charge their phones on his windmill.

When news of William's invention spread, people from across the globe offered to help him. He was shortly re-enrolled in college and travelling to America to visit wind farms, and he has since been mentoring children on how to create their own independent electricity sources. *The Boy Who Harnessed the Wind* (by William Kamkwamba and Bryan Mealer) is his amazing story, published in 2009.

really been looking up for the once heavily poached reserve. A perimeter fence has been erected, and accommodation and roads have been massively upgraded. With Majete's lion-reintroduction program, the park is now a conservation case study and an exciting destination.

Mt Mulanje

3 A huge hulk of twisted granite rising majestically from the surrounding plains, Mt Mulanje towers over 3000m high. All over the mountain are dense green valleys and rivers that drop from sheer cliffs to form dazzling waterfalls. The locals call it the 'Island in the Sky', and on misty days (and there are many) it's easy to see why: the massif is shrouded in a cotton-wool haze, its highest peaks bursting through the cloud to touch the heavens.

Liwonde National Park

4 With its lodges and safari activities, Liwonde is the closest thing Malawi has to a traditional wildlife park. Dominating the west, the Shire River overflows with hippos and crocodiles and is a favourite stomping ground for the 500-plus elephants. Waterbucks are also common near the water, while beautiful sable and roan antelopes, zebras and elands populate the floodplains. Several black rhinos are protected within a separate enclosure as part of a rhino-breeding program, and there's a rich and colourful array of bird life.

Kaya Mawa

5 Remember Scaramanga's pad in The Man with the Golden Gun? Kaya Mawa, set on an amber-coloured beach lapped by turquoise water, is the ultimate location to live out your inner Bond. Its cliffside chalets, cleverly moulded around the landscape, are so beautiful you'll never want to leave. Imagine plunge pools, the gentle lap of waves and the quiet appearance of a waiter with a bottle of chilled Champagne. Tempted? You should be, for this is one of the finest boutique experiences on the continent.

Getting Around

There are daily flights between Lilongwe and Blantyre, plus scheduled and charter flights on twin-prop planes to Likoma Island and all the major wildlife parks.

The *Ilala* ferry chugs passengers and cargo up and down Lake Malawi once a week.

Bus services operate between Blantyre and Lilongwe, and between Blantyre and Karonga via Lilongwe and Mzuzu. Smaller bus companies service the lakeshore route.

Nkhotakota Wildlife Reserve

6 Comprising 1800 sq km of rough terrain and a couple of navigable roads, this reserve has been undergoing a renaissance. Once poached, abandoned and encroached upon by human settlements, its fortunes have improved thanks to increased funding, two lodges, and management by African Parks, which was halfway through a historic reintroduction of 500 elephants in late 2016. One of the best ways to experience the area is by kayaking down the Bua River, your heart in your mouth as crocs upstream slip soundlessly into the murk to come and take a closer look.

Nyika National Park

7 Malawi's oldest reserve is easily one of the most magical experiences on any trip to the country. Towering over 2000m above sea level, the Nyika Plateau is enigmatic; one moment its rolling grasslands recall the Yorkshire Dales, but then an antelope leaps across your bonnet, you note the nearby mound of steaming elephant dung and you remember you're in Africa (and that Nyika is home to a very large population of leopards!).

Nkhata Bay

8 Nkhata Bay has an almost Caribbean feel, with its fishing boats buzzing across the green bay, market stalls hawking barbecued fish, and reggae filling the languorous afternoons. The friendly fishing town and Rasta haunt makes a wonderful base to spend a few days relaxing. Be careful not to entirely give yourself over to lotus eating, though, for there are loads of activities to enjoy before you hammock flop, be it snorkelling, diving, fish-eagle feeding, kayaking or forest walks.

CHRISTOPHE CERISIER / GETTY IMAGES ©

FISHBALL MEE / SEAFOOD
TUARAN MEE GORENG / CHASAU

CAPITAL
Kuala Lumpur

POPULATION
30,949,962

AREA
329,847 sq km

OFFICIAL LANGUAGE
Bahasa Malaysia

Central Market, Kota Kinabalu

Malaysia

Malaysia offers steamy jungles packed with wildlife, beautiful beaches, idyllic islands, culinary sensations and multiethnic cultures.

Malaysia is like two countries in one, cleaved in half by the South China Sea. While the peninsula flaunts bustling cities, colonial architecture, misty tea plantations and chill-out islands, Malaysian Borneo hosts wild jungles of orangutans, granite peaks and remote tribes, along with some pretty spectacular diving. Throughout is an impressive variety of microcosms ranging from the space-age high-rises of Kuala Lumpur (KL) to the traditional longhouse villages of Sarawak.

If there's one thing that unites all its ethnicities, religions and landscapes, it's food. In Malaysia, the best food is served in the humblest surroundings. The country's seemingly countless vendors serve delicious dishes from mobile carts, stalls and shophouses, many employing recipes handed down from previous generations. You're also spoilt for choice: between the Nonya, Indian, Chinese, Malay and Dayak specialties, plus some impressive Western-style food, travellers will never go hungry here.

Top Experiences

Diving, Pulau Sipadan

1 Sometimes it seems as if the world's most colourful marine life – from the commonplace to utterly alien fish, molluscs and reptiles, creatures that seem to have swum through every slice of the colour wheel – considers the seawall of Sipadan to be prime real estate. They live, play, hunt and eat here, and you, lucky thing, may dance an underwater ballet with them. For any diver, from the amateur to seasoned veterans like Jacques Cousteau, Sipadan is the ultimate underwater adventure.

Chinatown, Kuala Lumpur

2 Plumes of smoke curl upwards from smouldering coils of incense, flower garlands hang like pearls from the necks of Hindu statues and the call to prayer punctuates the honk of traffic. The temples and mosques of the city's Hindus, Muslims and Chinese Buddhists are crammed shoulder-to-shoulder in this atmospheric neighbourhood along the River Klang that epitomises multicultural Malaysia. Don't miss eating at the daytime Madras Lane hawker stalls or savouring the bustle and fun of the night market along Jln Petaling.

Cameron Highlands, Perak

3 Misty mountains, wellies, Tudor-themed architecture, 4WDs, scones, strawberries and tea plantations all converge in this distinctly un–Southeast Asian destination. Activities such as self-guided hiking, nature trekking and agricultural tourism make the Cameron Highlands one of Malaysia's more worthwhile and approachable active destinations. The area also represents a clever escape within a vacation, as the weather in the Cameron Highlands tends to stay mercifully cool year-round.

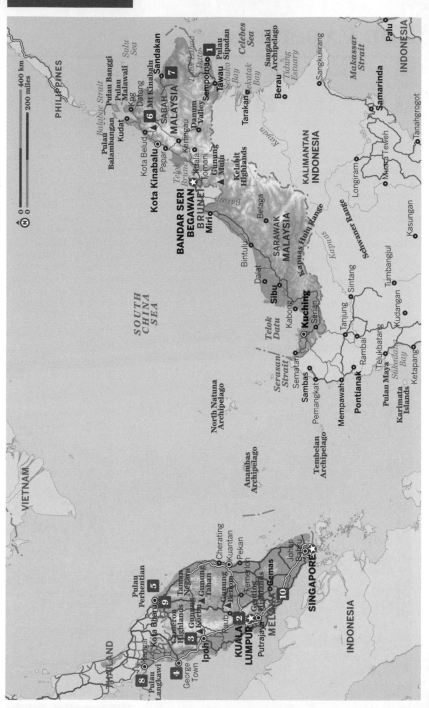

Classic Dishes

Asam laksa Thick rice noodles in a tart, fish- and herb-packed broth; one of Penang's most famous dishes.

Cendol Fine, short strings of green-bean flour dough in coconut milk sweetened with Melaka's famous palm sugar, and topped with shaved ice; the city's signature dessert.

Char kway teow Closely associated with Penang is this dish of silky rice noodles stir-fried with plump prawns, briny cockles, chewy Chinese sausage, crispy sprouts, egg and a hint of chilli.

Hinava Raw fish marinated with lime juice and herbs; a dish associated with Sabah.

Maggi goreng Fried instant noodles; a late-night snack ubiquitous in KL.

Sarawak laksa Thin rice noodles served in a curry broth topped with shrimp, chicken and a shredded omelette.

Top Wildlife-Watching Spots

Taman Negara National Park Malaysia's oldest and most prestigious national park is home to everything from fireflies to elephants.

Royal Belum State Park Home to 10 varieties of hornbill and the majority of Malaysia's big mammals.

Sungai Kinabatangan Spot wild orangutans and pygmy elephants along the banks of Sabah's longest river.

Bako National Park The park's coves and trails are one of the best places to spot proboscis monkeys.

George Town's Colonial District, Penang

4 At one point abandoned by locals and seemingly forgotten by tourists, in the last couple of years George Town has emerged to become one of Southeast Asia's hottest destinations. The 2008 Unesco World Heritage declaration sparked a frenzy of cultural preservation, and the city's charismatic shophouses have been turned into house museums, boutique hotels and chic restaurants. Aggressive drivers aside, it's also one of the best cities in Southeast Asia to explore on foot. And did we mention that George Town is also home to some of Malaysia's best food?

Snorkelling, Pulau Perhentian, Terengganu

5 Though eastern Peninsular Malaysia has several islands offering unparalleled underwater activities, amazing Pulau Perhentian wins flippers-down when it comes to attracting snorkellers. Perhaps it's the water itself: clear and ethereally blue, the seas surrounding Perhentian draw a huge variety of colourful marine life, from sharks and tropical fish to turtles and nesting urchins. Living coral beds lie close to shore, and on most days you won't have to swim much further than the jetty at Long Beach before finding yourself inside a veritable rainbow cloud of fish of all shapes and sizes.

When to Go

HIGH SEASON
(Dec–Feb)
End-of-year school holidays followed by Chinese New Year push up prices.

SHOULDER (Jul–Nov)
The end of Ramadan (Hari Raya) sees increased travel activity.

LOW SEASON
(Mar–Jun)
Enjoy places without the crush of fellow tourists.

Longhouses in Malaysian Borneo

A distinctive feature of indigenous Dayak life in Malaysian Borneo is the longhouse – essentially an entire village under one seemingly interminable roof. Contemporary longhouses fuse age-old forms with highly functional features such as corrugated-iron roofs and satellite dishes. According to long-standing Dayak tradition, anyone who shows up at a longhouse must be welcomed and given accommodation. However, these days turning up at a longhouse unannounced may be an unwelcome imposition on the residents – in short, bad manners. The way to avoid these pitfalls is to hire a locally savvy guide or tour company that can coordinate your visit and make introductions.

Getting Around

 Fly between major destinations in Peninsular Malaysia and Sabah and Sarawak on Malaysian Borneo.

 There are no services connecting Peninsular Malaysia with Malaysian Borneo, but local boats and ferries run to offshore islands.

 There's hardly anywhere you can't get to by bus on Peninsular Malaysia.

 Good idea to hire a car to explore Malaysia's hinterland; avoid using in cities though.

 While trains are comfortable and economical, there are basically only two lines and services are slow.

Mt Kinabalu, Sabah

6 It is the abode of the spirits, the highest mountain in Malaysia, the dominant geographic feature of North Borneo, the bone-shaking rock that has worn out countless challengers. Mt Kinabalu is all of this, and one of the most popular tourism attractions in Borneo. Don't worry; you will still have moments of utter freedom, breathing in the only alpine air in Sabah, and if you're lucky, enjoying a horizon that stretches to the Philippines. Or it will be cloudy. Whatever: the climb is still bloody exhilarating.

Sepilok Orangutan Rehabilitation Centre, Sabah

7 There is no primate quite like the orangutan. These great apes are a stirring combination: brawn and grace; raw power and gentle restraint; stupid amounts of cuteness and even more cuteness. And behind their sparkling eyes, deep reserves of what we can only call wisdom and, sometimes, sadness. All these complicated observations occur at once at the Sepilok Orangutan Rehabilitation Centre, where visitors can see the ginger apes from a (admittedly often crowded) viewing platform, the highlight of many a Sabah trip.

Pulau Langkawi

8 Pulau Langkawi ain't called the Jewel of Kedah for nothin', and its white-sand beaches, isolated resorts, acclaimed diving and pristine jungles live up to the metaphor. Cheap booze (Langkawi is duty-free) and a decent restaurant and bar scene provide just the hint of a party scene, while a glut of kid-friendly activities make it a great destination for families. And best of all, it's not just a holiday island: off-the-beaten-track–type exploration will reveal that Pulau Langkawi has managed to retain its endearing Malay soul.

Markets, Kota Bharu, Kelantan

9 A centre for Malaysian crafts, visitors to Kota Bharu can lose themselves shopping for traditional items such as batik, kain songket (fabric with gold thread), hand-crafted silverware, hand-carved puppets and locally made kites. Both the Central Market and the nearby Bazaar Buluh Kubu are great places to buy spices, brassware and other local goods. For shoppers inclined to roam, the bikeable road from town to Pantai Cahaya Bulan beach is dotted with factories and workshops dedicated to the creation of crafts of all sorts.

Jonker's Walk Night Market, Melaka

10 It starts by the river across from the pink Stadthuys building that glows in the street lights. Dr Ho Eng Hui is doing his nightly street show with a crowd in a circle around him; he makes kung-fu moves to the theme music of Hawaii Five-0. Edge through the crush along Jonker's Walk, which is lined with stalls selling everything from cheap underwear to fresh sugar-cane juice. Haggle, nibble and maybe stop by the Geographer cafe for a cold beer and some people watching.

Thaipusam

Enormous crowds converge at the Batu Caves north of KL for this dramatic Hindu festival involving body piercing. Falls between mid-January and mid-February.

Halal Dining

Practising Muslims can relax in Malaysia, which is a world leader in offering halal food; even fast food outlets sport halal certification. Look for window stickers and on menus to check an outlet's accreditation.

The Maldives

Unrivalled luxury, stunning white-sand beaches and an amazing underwater world make the Maldives an obvious choice for a holiday of a lifetime.

The Maldives is home to perhaps the best beaches in the world; they're on almost every one of the country's nearly 1200 islands and are so consistently perfect that it's hard not to become blasé about them. While some beaches may boast softer granules than others, the basic fact remains: you'll find consistently whiter-than-white powder sand and luminous cyan-blue water like this almost nowhere else on earth. This fact alone is enough to bring over a million people a year to this tiny, remote and otherwise little-known Indian Ocean paradise.

With some of the best diving and snorkelling in the world, the clear waters of the Maldives are a magnet for anyone with an interest in marine life. The richness and variety is astonishing; dazzling coral walls, magnificent caves and schools of brightly coloured tropical fish await you when you get down to the reef. In deeper waters lurk manta rays, turtles, sharks and even the world's largest fish, the whale shark.

Top Experiences

Male

1 The Maldivian capital is definitely the best place to get to know locals and see what makes them tick. The brightly painted houses, crowded markets and convivial teashops where you can chat to regulars and share plates of delicious 'short eats' are just some of the highlights of this unusual capital city – and perfectly complement the resort experience.

Breakfast with the Hammers

2 Hammerhead sharks, definitely one of the weirdest-looking creatures in the sea (and that's saying something), can be seen in abundance in Maldivian

Ihavandhippolhu Atoll
Dhidhdhoo
North Thiladhunmathee Atoll
Kulhuduffushi
South Thiladhunmathee Atoll
Maamakunudhoo Atoll
North Miladhunmadulu Atoll
Funadhoo
South Miladhunmadulu Atoll
Noonu Atoll
Ugoofaaru
Manadhoo
North Maalhosmadulu Atoll
Naifaru
INDIAN OCEAN
Faadhippolhu Atoll
South Maalhosmadulu Atoll
Eydhafushi
Goidhoo Atoll
North Male Atoll
Rasdhoo Atoll **2**
Thulusdhoo
⊛MALE **1** **4**
South Male Atoll
Ari Atoll
Maafushi **6**
5 Mahibadhoo
Felidhoo
Felidhoo Atoll
North Nilandhoo Atoll
Magoodhoo
Mulaku Atoll
South Nilandhoo Atoll
Muli
Kudahuvadhoo
Kolhumadulu Atoll
Veymandhoo
Hadhdhunmathee Atoll
Hithadhoo
INDIAN OCEAN
North Huvadhoo Atoll
Viligili
Thinadhoo
South Huvadhoo Atoll
Foammulah Atoll Fuamulaku
Hithadhoo Addu Atoll
Gan **3**
0   100 km
0   60 miles

Food & Drink

Beer In Male it's all non-alcoholic, even if it doesn't look it. For those gasping for the real thing, you'll need to cross the lagoon to the airport island where alcoholic beer is widely available.

Bis hulavuu A pastry made from eggs, sugar and ghee and served cold.

Coffee Maldivians love their coffee. You can get very good espresso, latte or cappuccino anywhere in Male, as well as at most resorts and guesthouses.

Kavaabu Small deep-fried dough balls with tuna, mashed potato, pepper and lime – a very popular 'short eat'.

Short eats A selection of finger food such as *fihunu mas* (fish pieces with chilli coating), *gulha* (fried dough balls filled with fish and spices), *keemia* (fried fish rolls in batter) and *kuli boakiba* (spicy fish cakes).

When to Go

☀ **HIGH SEASON** (Dec–Feb)

☀ **SHOULDER** (Mar–Apr)

☂ **LOW SEASON** (May–Nov)

Bodu Beru Performance

The cultural highlight of almost any trip to the Maldives is seeing an incredible dance and drum performance known as *bodu beru*, which means 'big drum' in Dhivehi.

These traditional all-male performances are a thrilling experience. Dancers begin with a slow, nonchalant swaying and swinging of the arms, and become more animated as the tempo increases, finishing in a rhythmic frenzy.

There are four to six drummers in an ensemble and the sound has strong African influences. Witnessing it can be a fantastic experience, as the dancing becomes more and more frenetic as the night goes on.

waters – if you know where to look for them. There are few more thrilling experiences than a dawn dive, descending free fall into the deep blue to 30m, before suddenly coming upon a huge school of hungry hammerhead sharks waiting to be fed. The best place to do this is at the world-famous Hammerhead Point (aka Rasdhoo Madivaru) in Rasdhoo Atoll.

3

GEORGETTE DOUWMA / GETTY IMAGES ©

Learn to Dive

3 You simply have to get beneath the water's surface in the Maldives; the corals, tropical fish, sharks, turtles and rays all make up an unforgettably alien world, which is best experienced by diving. All resorts and many guesthouses have diving facilities, and you won't regret deciding to learn here. The Maldives boasts excellent safety standards, modern equipment, passionate and experienced dive staff and – best of all – the water is so warm many people don't even bother diving in a wetsuit. Some top diving sites can be found around Addu Atoll and Ari Atoll.

Take a Seaplane from Male

4 There are few destinations where the mode of transport by which you arrive could be called a highlight, but that's because there are few places in the world where you need seaplanes to reach your hotel. These zippy Twin Otters function like taxis in a country with no roads, and taking off from the water is an unforgettable experience, as is observing the spectacular coral atolls, blue lagoons and tiny desert islands from above.

Swim with a Whale Shark in Ari Atoll

5 The largest fish in the world, the whale shark is prevalent in Maldivian waters, especially in the south of Ari Atoll and during a full moon when the currents between the atolls are at their strongest. Swimming with one of these gentle giants is an incredible experience – they average almost 10m in length – and it's also totally safe, as despite their immense size, whale sharks feed only on plankton.

Maafushi

6 Maafushi is the first inhabited island in the Maldives to become a big traveller centre, with some 30 guesthouses and hotels now operating. It's probably the best place for a cheap beach holiday in the Maldives, with lots of competition and low prices for accommodation, diving, snorkelling and other excursions. There's also a good private beach, which means visitors can swim without offending the local population. What's more, at just a couple of hours away from the international airport, it's also very easy to reach.

Getting Around

Internal flights connect Male to nine regional airstrips at least daily. Chartered seaplanes collect arrivals at Male Airport and fly them direct to their resorts.

Resorts collect guests from Male or regional airstrips by speedboat, a fast and comfortable way to travel. Independent travellers can use the slow but cheap public ferry system to get around.

Most islands are totally car free, with the exception of Male and a few other larger inhabited islands.

Djenné mosque and market

Mali

Like an exquisite sandcastle formed in a harsh desert landscape, Mali is blessed by extraordinary beauty, wonders, talents and knowledge. Yet for now, its landscapes, monuments and stories are off-limits, sealed from tourists by a conflict that is threatening the very culture of Mali.

The heart of the nation is Bamako, where Ngoni and Kora musicians play to dancing crowds from all ethnicities, while in Dogon Country villages still cling to the cliffs as they did in ancient times.

Further west, Fula women strap silver jewellery to their ears and their belongings to donkeys, forming caravans worthy of beauty pageants as they march across the *hamada* (dry, dusty scrubland).

And in the northeast, the writings of ancient African civilisations remain locked in the beautiful libraries of Timbuktu, until a new dawn comes for Mali, and they – and it – can be rediscovered by travellers.

Snapshot

Dogon Country

1 A fairytale of rose-coloured villages, big blue skies, sacred crocodiles and sandstone cliffs make up Mali's Dogon Country. Houses cling to the massive escarpment of the Falaise de Bandiagara. But more than this, Dogon Country is home to a fascinating animist culture with complex traditions and cosmology.

Djenné

2 This Unesco World Heritage-listed old town is one of West Africa's oldest towns. Its incomparable mudbrick mosque is like a mythical apparition. It also provides the backdrop to Djenné's huge, lively and colourful Monday market, which has barely changed since the days when Saharan camel caravans brought salt across the sands to the gates of Djenné.

Timbuktu

3 Few places in the world hold the pursuit of knowledge so dear. Timbuktu fascinates with its ancient libraries, monuments and never-digitised texts on philosophy and astronomy from the ancient world.

Seasons

 OCT–FEB

 MAR–JUN, SEP

 JUL–AUG

Food & Drink

Bissap/djablani Juice brewed from hibiscus petals.

Capitaine Nile Perch A species of freshwater fish.

Castel Malian beer.

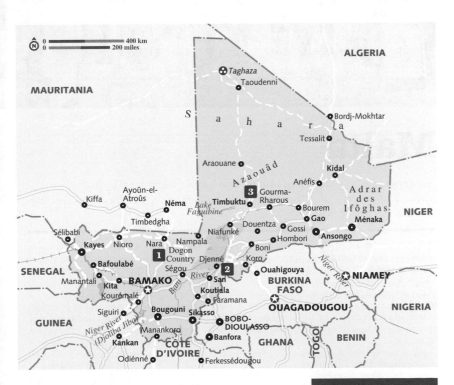

CAPITAL
Valletta

POPULATION
415,200

AREA
316 sq km

OFFICIAL LANGUAGES
Maltese, English

Valetta's old town

Malta

Malta packs glorious variety into its small archipelago. You'll find prehistoric temples, fossil-studded cliffs, hidden coves, thrilling scuba diving and a history of remarkable intensity.

Despite being made up of three tiny islands on the southern edge of Europe, Malta groans under the weight of its rich history and fascinating cultural influences. As a melting pot of Mediterranean culture, Malta merits far deeper exploration than is often given to it by the package crowds whose first priority is hitting the beach.

From ancient stone temples and historic Arabic connections (listen carefully to the local language) to Sicilian-inspired cuisine, Malta will almost certainly surprise you. Valletta and the Three Cities are famed for their grand churches, elegant palaces and honey-coloured limestone fortifications, while nearby Sliema and St Julian are packed with restaurants and bars. And don't forget little Gozo to the northwest – a pretty, rural island where the pace of life is that much slower. It's the perfect chill-out spot with the dramatic Dwejra coastline.

Top Experiences

Valletta

 Malta's capital, named the European Capital of Culture for 2018, is a remarkable city. Only 1km by 600m, with every street leading to the sea, the walled city contains a harmonious ensemble of 16th- and 17th-century townhouses fronted by traditional Maltese balconies – and it's undergoing a renaissance. The last few years have seen Valletta bloom, with new restaurants, renovated buildings, and an emerging nightlife area in its former red-light district Strait St. You'll feel the excitement the moment you walk through the striking contemporary City Gate, designed by Renzo Piano, and see his cutting-edge Parliament Building and Opera House just beyond.

Dwejra

 The thrilling coast line of Dwejra, in Gozo, features beautiful rock formations that have been sculpted by the wind and sea (they're so dramatic they've been used as a location for Game of Thrones). Visit the Inland Sea, a wonderful place to swim and snorkel when the weather is calm. Close to the coast, the great chunk of Fungus Rock rears from the piercing blue Mediterranean.

When to Go

☀ **HIGH SEASON** (Jun–Aug)

⛅ **SHOULDER** (Mar–May, Sep–Oct)

☁ **LOW SEASON** (Nov–Feb)

Vittoriosa's Backstreets

 Vittoriosa is the most fascinating of the Three Cities. This ancient town, perched on its small lip of land, has stunning views and perfectly preserved streets. Still known locally as Birgu (its name before the Great Siege of 1565), Vittoriosa was the

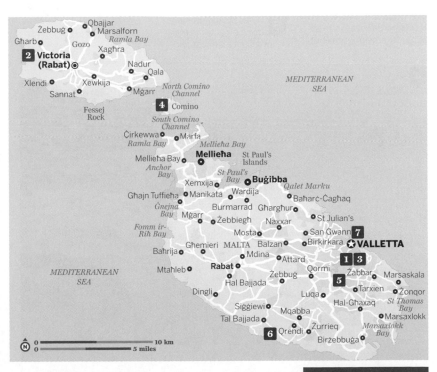

original home of the Knights of Malta. Their headquarters, Fort St Angelo, have been restored, and opened to the public in late 2015. But this town is no museum – it's a living, breathing city with a strong sense of community. You're in luck if your visit is in October: the culmination of BirguFest sees the ancient streets lit solely by candles.

Blue Lagoon

4 The beautiful island of Comino has an eclectic history. It was written of by Ptolemy 1800 years ago, and has been a hermit's hideaway, a cholera isolation zone and a prison camp. But its most extraordinary feature is the otherworldly Blue Lagoon. This serene, limpid sea pool is so blue that it looks like an over-saturated image. It attracts hordes of swimmers in the summer months but even the crowds can't obscure its beauty (still, try to head here in the afternoon, after most people have left).

Hal Saflieni Hypogeum

5 Visiting these ancient underground burial chambers is a unique, mysterious and awe-inspiring experience. Amazingly preserved, the sacred spaces hollowed from the rock are around 5000 years old – painted ochre patterns are still visible decorating the ceilings of some sections. It's a window into an enigmatic ancient world, which leaves a beguiling and perplexing resonance. You'll need to book several months ahead.

Ħaġar Qim & Mnajdra Temples

6 These great prehistoric structures are among Malta's finest and

Getting Around

A floatplane service operates between Valletta and Mġarr Harbour on Gozo, with a flight time of 10 minutes.

Ferries operate between Valletta and Sliema, as well as from near Valletta Waterfront to Cospicua and on to Senglea. Water taxis are also widely used.

Many bus routes on Malta originate from Valletta and radiate to all parts of the island.

PAUL BIRIS / GETTY IMAGES ©

most atmospheric, partly due to their breathtaking location – set high on the edge of coastal cliffs that are carpeted by wildflowers in spring. There are magnificent views out to sea and over to the distant islet of Filfla, marked nature trails around the surrounding countryside, and a fascinating visitor centre to illuminate what is known about the mysterious temple builders.

St John's Co-Cathedral

7 The austere exterior of Valletta's cathedral is no preparation for

the frenzy of baroque gold and lavish decoration in its interior. The floor alone is a carpet of many-coloured marble tombs, on which symbolic pictures are delicately rendered in stone. The chapels, each

pertaining to an auberge, vie to outdo each other in opulence. The outstanding highlight is Caravaggio's Beheading of John the Baptist in the Oratory – the largest work ever produced by the artist.

IAKOV FILIMONOV / SHUTTERSTOCK ©

Food & Drink

Braġioli These 'beef olives' are a thin slice of beef wrapped around a stuffing of breadcrumbs, chopped bacon, hard-boiled egg and parsley, then braised in a red wine sauce.

Fenek The favourite Maltese dish is rabbit – whether fried in olive oil, roasted, stewed, served with spaghetti or baked in a pie.

Ftira Bread baked in a flat disc and traditionally stuffed with a mixture of tomatoes, olives, capers and anchovies.

Ġbejniet Small, hard, white cheese traditionally made from unpasteurised sheep's or goat's milk.

Kinnie The brand name of a local soft drink, flavoured with bitter oranges and aromatic herbs.

Pastizzi Small parcels of flaky pastry filled with ricotta cheese or mushy peas. They're available in most bars or from a *pastizzerija* (usually a hole-in-the-wall takeaway or kiosk).

Malti – A Linguistic Melting Pot

The native language of Malta is Malti (also called Maltese). Some linguists attribute its origins to the Phoenician occupation of Malta in the 1st millennium BC, but most link it to North African Arabic dialects. The language has an Arabic grammar and construction but is formed from a morass of influences, laced with Sicilian, Italian, Spanish, French and English loan-words. Until the 1930s, Italian was the official language of the country, used in the Church and for all administrative matters, even though only the aristocracy could speak it. Malti only became an official language in 1934 (alongside English).

English is taught to schoolchildren from an early age, and almost everyone in Malta speaks it well. Many also speak Italian, helped by the fact that Malta receives Italian TV. French and German are also spoken, though less widely.

Bikini Lagoon, Bikini Atoll

CAPITAL	Majuro
POPULATION	73,376
AREA	181 sq km
OFFICIAL LANGUAGES	English, Marshallese

Marshall Islands

This expanse of slender, flat coral atolls is so surrounded by tropical sea that anywhere at any time you can see, hear, smell and feel salt air and water.

A thousand or so coral islands make up the Republic of the Marshall Islands (RMI). Living on these narrow strips of land between ocean and lagoon, the Marshallese are expert fishers and navigators, having long been reliant on the sea.

Local faces reflect the islands' history. In the late 1700s, after 2000 years of isolation, these Micronesian islands were variously visited, settled, colonised or occupied by British, Russians, Germans, Japanese and Americans (at first by missionaries, later by defence forces). Today, the more developed atolls have a sense of all these influences, with well-stocked stores carrying international groceries, restaurants serving the food of several nations, and basketball courts on many street corners. On the quieter backstreets the Marshallese continue to live in family compounds, surrounded by flowers.

The RMI's charm lies in its outer islands, which still retain the pristine feel of a Pacific paradise.

Top Experiences

Laura

1 If the heady pace of Marshall Island life is getting too much, take a very pleasant drive along the palm-lined road to Laura. Found at the far western end of Majuro Atoll, Laura is famed for its quiet beaches. Pick up a picnic and spend the day lolling on the gorgeous white-sand beach and snorkelling on the shallow reef.

Arno Atoll

2 The Longar area in Arno is famed for its 'love school' where young women were once taught how to perfect their sexual techniques. The waters off Longar Point are known for superb deep-sea fishing, and yellowfin tuna, marlin, mahi-mahi and sailfish abound.

Bikini Atoll

3 Thanks to its ominous nuclear history, Bikini – the site of the first peacetime explosion of the atomic bomb – is one of Micronesia's premier dive spots. A highlight is the USS Saratoga, the world's only diveable aircraft carrier, which still holds racks of bombs. Bikini is a great spot for diving with sharks – spotting a silvertip on the wrecks is not uncommon.

Food & Drink

Coconut Drinking ice-cold coconut juice is a great way to beat the heat.

Coconut crab The largest land-living arthropod in the world is also considered a delicacy.

Pandanus fruit Snack on boiled, sweet pandanus fruit – just watch out for the hairy insides!

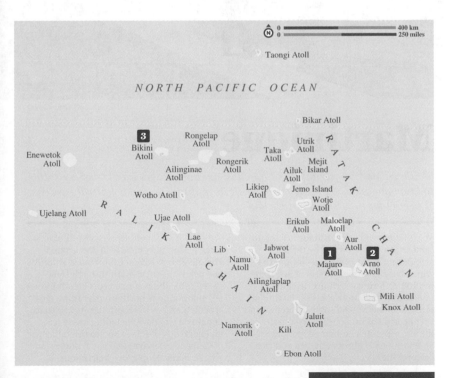

N 0 — 400 km
0 — 250 miles

Taongi Atoll

NORTH PACIFIC OCEAN

Bikar Atoll

Rongelap Atoll

3 Bikini Atoll

Utrik Atoll

Taka Atoll

Enewetok Atoll

Rongerik Atoll

Mejit Island

Ailinginae Atoll

Ailuk Atoll

Likiep Atoll

Jemo Island

Wotho Atoll

Wotje Atoll

Ujelang Atoll

RALIK

Ujae Atoll

Erikub Atoll

Maloelap Atoll

Lae Atoll

Aur Atoll

CHAIN

Lib

Jabwot Atoll

Namu Atoll

1 Majuro Atoll

2 Arno Atoll

CHAIN

Ailinglaplap Atoll

Mili Atoll

Knox Atoll

Namorik Atoll

Kili

Jaluit Atoll

Ebon Atoll

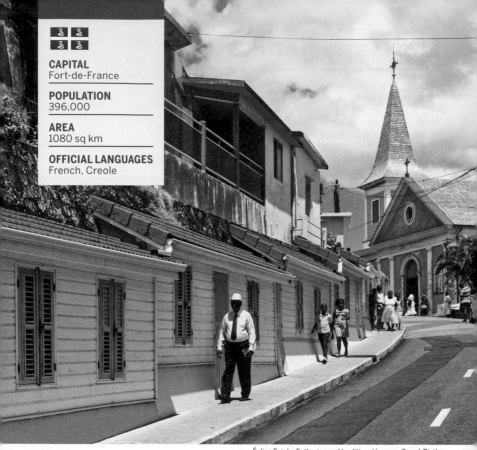

CAPITAL
Fort-de-France

POPULATION
396,000

AREA
1080 sq km

OFFICIAL LANGUAGES
French, Creole

Église Sainte-Catherine and traditional houses, Grand-Rivière

Martinique

Southern Martinique has great beaches, fishing villages and lots of activities to keep you busy, while the north, with its mountains and botanical gardens, is perfect for hikers and nature lovers.

Volcanic in origin, Martinique is a mountainous stunner crowned by the still-smoldering Mont Pelée, the volcano that wiped out the former capital of St-Pierre in 1902. Offering a striking diversity of landscapes and atmospheres, Martinique is a cosmopolitan and sophisticated island that boasts stunning beaches, superb hiking, top-notch culinary experiences, an enormous array of activities and rich cultural life.

While it suffers from overcrowding in some places, particularly in and around Fort-de-France, life becomes more sedate as one heads north or south through some of the island's alluring scenery. The rainforested, mountainous northern part is the most spectacular, but the south has its fair share of natural wonders, including lovely bays and gorgeous beaches. Add to this a dash of Gallic joie de vivre and you'll understand why so many people love Martinique.

Top Experiences

When to Go

HIGH SEASON
(Dec–May)

LOW SEASON
(Jun–Nov)

Grande Anse des Salines

1 Immense, crystalline and glossy, Grande Anse des Salines doesn't disappoint the bevy of swimmers who dabble in its gorgeous depths or the sun worshippers who lie out on the ribbon of golden sand. Des Salines gets its name from Etang des Salines, the large salt pond that backs it; it's about 5km south of Ste-Anne along the D9. There are food vans and snack shops along the beach, but otherwise it's wonderfully undeveloped, a slice of fabulously raw nature.

Route de la Trace

2 The Route de la Trace (known more prosaically on maps as the N3) winds up into the mountains north from Fort-de-France. It's a beautiful drive through a lush rainforest of tall tree ferns, anthurium-covered hillsides and thick clumps of roadside bamboo. The road passes along the eastern flanks of the volcanic mountain peaks of the Pitons du Carbet. Several well-marked hiking trails lead from the Route de la Trace into the rainforest and up to the peaks.

Presqu'île de Caravelle

3 The wonderful Presqu'île de Caravelle is a little-visited peninsula with some gorgeous stretches of beach and a wild, untamed feel. A gently twisting road with spectacular views runs through sugarcane fields to the charming main village of Tartane, and then on to Baie du Galion. On the north side of the peninsula are a

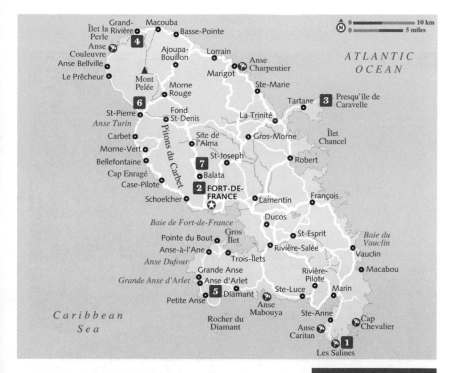

couple of protected beaches, including some spots favored by surfers. With several superb restaurants and hotels, a very atmospheric colonial ruin along with some excellent walking, it's surprising that there's so little tourism here. This is, of course, all the more reason not to miss it.

Grand-Rivière

4 Nestled away at Martinique's most northern point, Grand-Rivière is an isolated and unspoiled fishing village full of 19th-century buildings with a gorgeous position beneath coastal cliffs covered in jungle. Mont Pelée forms a rugged backdrop to the south, while there's a fine view of neighboring Dominica to the north and black-sand beaches on either side. This is Martinique at its wildest and most remote.

Les Anses d'Arlet

5 Les Anses d'Arlet is without a doubt the most charming corner of southern Martinique, retaining as it does an undiscovered feel, some gorgeous scenery and wonderful beaches. The commune of Les Anses d'Arlet contains a string of villages, each named descriptively after its respective anse (cove): Grande Anse, Anse Noire, Anse Dufour and – confusingly – Anse d'Arlet Bourg, the administrative center of Les Anses d'Arlet. The villages are connected by a steep and winding coastal road from where there are superb glimpses down to the waves below.

St-Pierre

6 It's hard to believe that St-Pierre was once the most cosmopolitan city in the Caribbean.

Getting Around

A regular *vedette* (ferry) between Martinique's main resort areas and Fort-de-France provides a nice alternative to dealing with heavy road traffic; it also allows you to avoid the hassles of city parking and is quicker.

Although there are some larger public buses serving the urban area around Fort-de France, most buses elsewhere in Martinique are minivans marked 'TC' (for *taxis collectifs*) on top. Destinations are marked on the vans.

GUIZIOU FRANCK / GETTY IMAGES ©

The one-time capital of Martinique was wiped out in just 10 minutes in 1902 by the towering and still-active Mont Pelée, 7km away. Though a shadow of its former self, St-Pierre is an attractive and interesting place to wander. Packed full of Caribbean charm, it is undoubtedly one of Martinique's loveliest towns, with a tranquil azure bay backed by steamy rainforest on the mountainside behind it. Full of colonial-era buildings, St-Pierre also boasts an attractive dark-gray sand beach and the perfect location for superb sunsets.

Jardin de Balata

7 The excellent Jardin de Balata, a mature botanical garden in a rain-forest setting, is one of Martinique's best attractions and will please anyone with even a passing interest in botany. The hour-long walk around the garden is clearly marked, and a series of tree walks will keep kids interested. There are some fantastic views from here down to the coast. After the garden, the road winds up into the mountains and reaches an elevation of 600m before dropping down to Site de l'Alma, where a river runs through a lush gorge. There are picnic tables and a couple of short trails into the rainforest.

GUIZIOU FRANCK / GETTY IMAGES ©

Food & Drink

Acras A universally popular hors d'oeuvre in Martinique, *acras* are fish, seafood or vegetable tempura. *Acras de morue* (cod) and *crevettes* (shrimp) are the most common and are both delicious.

Ti-punch Short for *petit punch*; this ubiquitous and strong cocktail is the normal *apéro* (aperitif) in Martinique. It's a mix of rum, lime and cane syrup – but mainly rum.

Crabes farcis Stuffed crabs are a common local dish. Normally they're stuffed with a spicy mixture of crabmeat, garlic, shallots and parsley, and cooked in their shells.

Blaff This is the local term for white fish marinated in lime juice, garlic and peppers, then poached. While it's popular across the Caribbean, its true home is Martinique.

Mont Pelée Eruption

At the end of the 19th century, St-Pierre – then the capital of Martinique – was a flourishing port city. It was so cosmopolitan that it was dubbed the 'Little Paris of the West Indies.' Mont Pelée, the island's highest mountain at 1397m, was just a scenic backdrop to the city.

In the spring of 1902, sulfurous steam vents on Mont Pelée began emitting gases, and a crater lake started to fill with boiling water. Authorities dismissed it all as the normal cycle of the volcano, which had experienced harmless periods of activity in the past.

On May 8, 1902, in the most devastating natural disaster in Caribbean history, Mont Pelée exploded into a glowing burst of superheated gas and burning ash. St-Pierre was laid to waste within minutes; of its 30,000 inhabitants, there were just three survivors.

CAPITAL
Nouakchott

POPULATION
4 million

AREA
1,030,700 sq km

OFFICIAL LANGUAGES
Hassaniya (Arabic),
French, Fula, Soninké,
Wolof

Sand dunes, Adrar

Mauritania

Driving through the vast, sun-bleached landscape of Mauritania, you'd be forgiven for expecting to see a post-apocalyptic hot rod from Mad Max: Fury Road on the horizon. Instead, a solitary, turbaned figure tending a herd of goats tells the story of survival amid millennial-old geological forces.

Mauritania, with one of the world's lowest population densities, is almost equally divided between Moors of Arab-Berber descent and black Africans, a striking cultural combination that is part of its appeal.

There's no doubt that Mauritania has some of Africa's grandest scenery. Millions of migratory birds winter along the coast at Parc National du Banc d'Arguin and the expanding capital Nouakchott is where modernity takes root in the desert.

The Adrar region offers up epic sand dunes, eye-popping plateaux and green oases, plus Africa's biggest monolith. The Tagânt has similar features, and both hide ancient (and World Heritage–listed) caravan towns – Chinguetti, Ouadâne and Oualâta. However, inland Mauritania is currently unsafe for travellers.

Snapshot

Parc National du Banc d'Arguin

1 This World Heritage–listed park is an important stopover and breeding ground for birds migrating between Europe and southern Africa, and as a result is one of the best birdwatching sites on the entire continent. It extends 200km north from Cape Timiris and 235km south of Nouâdhibou. The ideal way to approach the birds is by traditional fishing boat.

Réserve Satellite du Cap Blanc

2 This small nature reserve is dedicated to a colony of endangered Mediterranean monk seals. Resembling elephant seals, these grey-skinned animals have been hunted since the 15th century for their valuable skins and oil. The colony here of roughly 150 seals is one of the last on earth (fewer than 500 worldwide).

Port de Pêche

3 The Port de Pêche is Nouakchott's star attraction. Lively and colourful, you'll see hundreds of teams of mostly Wolof and Fula men dragging in heavy fishing nets. Small boys hurry back and forth with trays of fish, which they sort, gut, fillet and lay out on large trestles to dry.

Seasons

 NOV–MAR

 APR–JUN, OCT

 JUL–SEP

Food & Drink

Mafé A groundnut-based stew.

Méchoui Nomads' feast, where an entire lamb is roasted over a fire and stuffed with cooked rice.

Thieboudiene (cheb-u-jin) Fish-and-rice dish served in white and red (tomato sauce) versions.

Zrig Unsweetened curdled goat or camel milk; often accompanies meals served in homes.

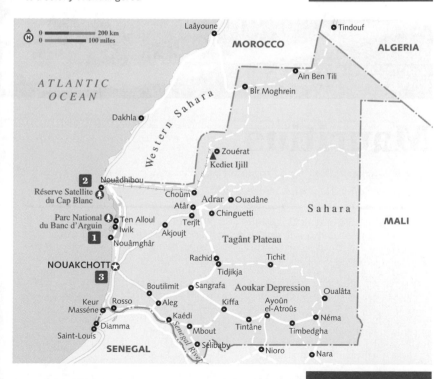

CAPITAL
Port Louis

POPULATION
1.35 million

AREA
2040 sq km

OFFICIAL LANGUAGE
English (though
Creole widely spoken)

Le Morne Peninsula

Mauritius

Mark Twain once wrote, 'Mauritius was made first and then heaven, heaven being copied after Mauritius'. He was right.

Mauritius is rightly famed for its sapphire-blue waters, powder-white beaches and, yes, luxury resorts that provide a front-row seat onto some of the most beautiful views in the Indian Ocean. These are places of the utmost refinement, of impeccable service, of facilities that range from pampering spas, designer rooms and extensive water-sports options to dreamy swimming pools, expansive grounds and world-class restaurants. Your stay will live long in the memory and will have you dreaming of a return.

What to do, what to do? Lie on a beach all day? Or enjoy the wonderful range of activities on offer? Either way, you can't really lose and there's not much you can't do here on the water. The diving and snorkelling is terrific, encircled as Mauritius is by shallow waters, a coral reef, sublime underwater topography and a dramatic ocean drop-off. On land, you'll need to decide between fabulous hiking, horse riding and even championship-standard golf courses. Decisions, decisions...

Top Experiences

West-Coast Diving

 Some of the Indian Ocean's best dives are found off the west coast of Mauritius. The architecture of the underwater rock formations and the substantial schools of fish make the waters off Flic en Flac in particular a world-class dive destination and there are numerous dive schools on hand to take you out, regardless of your level of experience. The best sites are the walls and drop-offs on the edge of the turquoise lagoon, and La Cathédrale, near Flic en Flac, is simply marvellous.

Rodrigues Coastal Walk

 There are few finer trails along the Indian Ocean than the coastal path on east-coast Rodrigues between Graviers and St François. There are no roads on this corner of the island, and you'll find yourself wanting to linger at Trou d'Argent, one of the prettiest beaches anywhere in Mauritius. At the end of the trail (or the beginning, depending on where you decide to start), St François has some fine informal restaurants and the tranquil St François beach.

When to Go

☼ **HIGH SEASON** (Dec–Feb)

☼ **SHOULDER** (Mar–Apr & Oct–Nov)

☼ **LOW SEASON** (May–Sep)

Black River Gorges National Park

 One of the most underrated attractions on Mauritius, Black River Gorges National Park also happens to have the island's most beautiful scenery. Well-maintained and clearly signposted hiking trails weave among forested hills, vertiginous

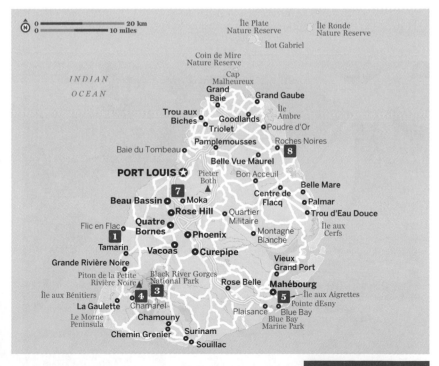

waterfalls and deep gorges where you might see some of the island's signature bird species, while the distinctive white-tailed tropicbird and endangered Mauritian kestrel can sometimes be seen circling high above it all. Even if you don't hike, a good road leads through the park to some of its prettier viewpoints.

Chamarel

4 High in the hills that rise dramatically from the west coast, the mountain village of Chamarel is quietly gathering a reputation as one of Mauritius' best places to eat. Lining the road through town and appearing along the steep climb towards Black River Gorges National Park are all manner of restaurants, from informal family-run places to fine-dining establishments hidden from the outside world.

Île aux Aigrettes

5 Lying offshore from the dramatically beautiful southeastern coast, Île aux Aigrettes is one place where time has moved in reverse. With an ancient ebony forest, and extensive programs to restore wildlife species that were, in the not-too-distant past, in danger of extinction on the mainland, the island can feel like a return to the time before Dutch sailors arrived in 1598.

Rodrigues Isolation

6 Rodrigues is the sort of place where life moves to a different beat. There's so much to do here, from Port Mathurin's busy Saturday market to boat excursions, but we love it just as much for its quiet *chambres d'hôte* (family-run guesthouses), and the nightly *tables d'hôte* (meals

Getting Around

Various private operators offer cruises to offshore islands, or snorkelling and fishing excursions.

Bus travel is cheap and fun and although you won't set any land-speed records, it's generally a fairly easy and reliable way to get around.

Renting a car will allow you to get from most corners of the island to any other in less than 90 minutes.

served at a *chambre d'hôte*) that feature all across the island. La Belle Rodriguaise is one such place: blissfully isolated, it lies beyond the end of the paved road – here you can leave the world and its noise behind.

Eureka Plantation Mansion

7 There are no better excursions to the island's Central Plateau than a trip to Eureka, arguably the finest plantation mansion left on Mauritius. Situated in the cooler climes of Moka, the estate seems to have captured in bricks and mortar all the languid charm of island living. If

you're really taken with the place, you could enjoy a meal at the equally lovely restaurant and then stay the night in the *chambre d'hôte*.

East Coast Beaches

8 It's a Mauritian rule of thumb that if you find a cluster of luxury resorts, you've found a beautiful beach. Mauritius' east coast proves the theory, with

long, stirringly pretty and very often deserted beaches. Our picks are those around Pointe Lafayette, a place sufficiently isolated from the clamour elsewhere on the island to feel like an undiscovered outpost of tropical perfection. The resorts are here, of course, but they're mere blips along this superb and otherwise undisturbed corner of the earth.

Food & Drink

Meat Steaks can be terrific here, especially those from South Africa. Creole sausages are distinctive and are often cooked in a red Creole sauce.

Seafood The mainstay of all the different cuisines on the island. *Crevettes* (prawns) and *ourite* (octopus) are highlights; octopus appears in salads, cooked in saffron, or in a curry. The fish of the day is nearly always a good order.

Street food *Dhal puri* (lentil dhal served in a chapati pancake) and *boulettes* (tiny steamed Chinese dumplings) are fantastic.

Tables d'hôte The eating equivalent of a family-run guesthouse, where diners often eat at a communal table and can enjoy a range of traditional dishes spread over a number of courses. If you don't eat at a *table d'hôte* in Mauritius, you've missed an essential part of its gastronomic culture.

Dead as a Dodo

Illustrations from the logbooks of the first ships to reach Mauritius show hundreds of plump flightless birds running down to the beach to investigate the newcomers. Lacking natural predators, these giant relatives of the pigeon were easy prey for hungry sailors, who named the bird dodo, meaning 'stupid'. It took just 30 years for sailors and their pets and pests to drive the dodo to extinction; the last confirmed sighting was in the 1660s.

In 1865 local schoolteacher George Clark discovered a dodo skeleton in a marshy area on the site of what is now the international airport. The skeleton was reassembled by scientists in Edinburgh, and has formed the basis of all subsequent dodo reconstructions, one of which is on display in the Natural History Museum in Port Louis.

CAPITAL
Mexico City

POPULATION
123 million

AREA
1.9 million sq km

OFFICIAL LANGUAGE
Spanish

Fiesta for Día de la Virgen de Guadalupe, Oaxaca

Mexico

With steaming jungles, smoking, snowcapped volcanoes, cactus-strewn deserts and 10,000km of coast strung with sandy beaches and wildlife-rich lagoons, Mexico is an endless adventure for the senses.

Mexico's pre-Hispanic civilizations built some of the world's great archaeological monuments, and the Spanish colonial era left beautiful towns full of tree-shaded plazas and sculpted stone churches, while modern Mexico has seen a surge of great art. The country has a fascinating history and endless creative verve, from the underground dance clubs and street art of Mexico City to the wonderful handicrafts of the indigenous population.

At the heart of your Mexican experience will be the Mexican people. A super-diverse crew, from Mexico City hipsters to the shy indigenous villagers of Chiapas, they're renowned for their love of color and frequent fiestas, but they're also philosophical folk, to whom timetables are less important than *simpatía* (empathy). You'll rarely find Mexicans less than courteous. They're more often positively charming, and know how to please guests.

Top Experiences

Palenque

1 Gather all your senses and dive head first into the ancient Maya world at exquisite Palenque, where pyramids rise above jungle treetops and furtive monkeys shriek and catapult themselves through dense canopies. Seek out the tomb of the mysterious Red Queen and her sarcophagus, wander the maze-like palace, gazing up at its iconic tower, then scale the stone staircase of the Temple of the Inscriptions, the lavish mausoleum of Pakal (Palenque's mightiest ruler), to survey the sprawling ruins from its summit.

Mexico City

2 The nation's long-standing political capital clearly stands at the forefront of Mexico's cultural scene as well. Remember that this is where many of the country's top muralists left behind their most important works, such as Diego Rivera's cinematic murals in the Palacio Nacional and the social-realism work of José Clemente Orozco in the Palacio de Bellas Artes. Art, music, dance and theater are everywhere – even a gondola ride along the ancient canals of Xochimilco wouldn't be complete without taking in a fervent mariachi ballad.

Oaxaca City

3 This highly individual southern city basks in bright upland light and captivates everyone with its deliciously inventive version of Mexican cuisine, gorgeous handicrafts, frequent colorful fiestas, handsome colonial architecture, booming arts scene and fine mezcals distilled in nearby villages. Within easy reach are the superb ancient Zapotec capital, Monte Albán, dozens of indigenous craft-making villages with busy weekly markets, and the cool, forested hills of the Sierra Norte, perfect for hikers, mountain bikers and horseback riders.

LMSPENCER / SHUTTERSTOCK ©

Pyramids of Teotihuacán

4 Once among Mesoamerica's greatest cities, Teotihuacán lies just an hour out of Mexico City. The immense Pirámide del Sol (Pyramid of the Sun) and Pirámide de la Luna (Pyramid of the Moon) dominate the remains of the metropolis, which even centuries after its collapse in the 8th century AD remained a pilgrimage site for Aztec royalty. Today it's a magnet for those who come to soak up the mystical energies that are believed to converge here.

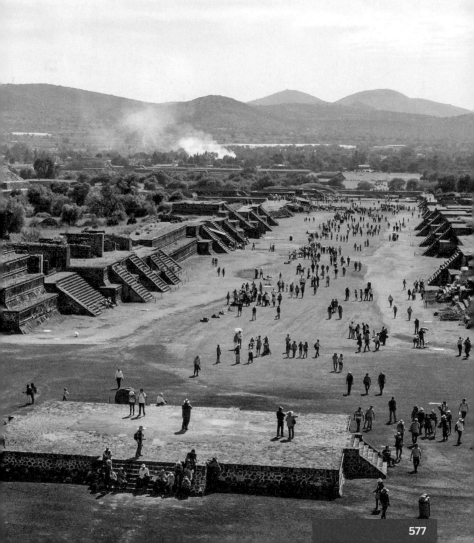

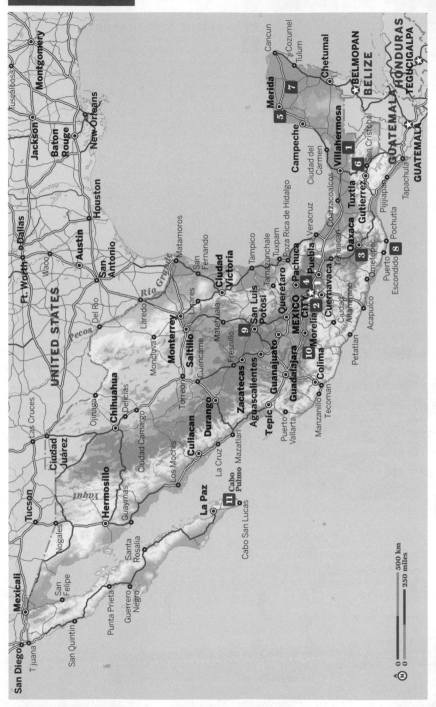

Best on Film

Amores Perros (2000) Gritty groundbreaker that set director Alejandro González Iñárritu and actor Gael García Bernal on the path to stardom.

Y Tu Mamá También (2001) Classic 'growing up' road movie about two privileged Mexico City teenagers.

Heli (2013) Amat Escalante won Cannes' best-director garland for this tale of a young couple caught up in the drugs war.

Food & Drink

Elotes Freshly steamed or grilled corn on the cob, usually coated in mayonnaise and often sprinkled with chili powder.

Enchiladas Lightly fried tortillas filled with chicken, cheese or eggs, covered in a chili sauce.

Quesadillas A tortilla folded in half with a filling of cheese and/or other ingredients.

Tacos The quintessential Mexican dish, made of any cooked meat, fish or vegetable wrapped in a tortilla, with a dash of salsa, onion and cilantro.

Tamales Made with masa mixed with lard, stuffed with stewed meat, fish or vegetables, and steamed in corn husks or banana leaf.

Tequila The Champagne of Mexico.

Mérida

5 The cultural capital of the Yucatán Peninsula, this large but manageable city has a beautifully maintained colonial heart. It's veined with narrow cobbled streets and dotted with sunny plazas, with a wealth of museums and galleries and some of the best food in the region. Just out of town are wildlife reserves, graceful haciendas (estates) and jungle-shrouded cenotes (sinkholes) to swim in. A little further afield, the little-visited Maya sites along the Ruta Puuc allow you to step back in time without the tour groups.

San Cristóbal

6 Saunter the cobblestone streets of hill-ringed San Cristóbal de las Casas, the high-altitude colonial city in the heart of indigenous Chiapas. A heady mix of modern and Maya, with cosmopolitan cafes and traditional culture, it's also a jumping-off point for Chiapas' natural attractions and fascinating Tzotzil and Tzeltal villages. Spend sunny days exploring its churches and bustling markets, or riding a horse through fragrant pine forest, and chilly evenings warmed by the fireplace of a cozy watering hole.

Chichén Itzá

7 There's a reason why this Maya site

When to Go

HIGH SEASON
(Dec–Apr)
The driest months, bringing winter escapees from colder countries.

SHOULDER
(Jul–Aug)
Hot almost everywhere and very wet on the Pacific coast.

LOW SEASON
(May–Jun & Sep–Nov)
May and June see peak temperatures in many areas. September brings heavy rains on the Gulf and Pacific coasts.

was declared one of the new Seven Wonders of the World – it is simply spectacular. From the imposing, monolithic El Castillo pyramid (where the shadow of the plumed serpent god

Great Diversity

One of the top-five most biologically diverse countries on earth, Mexico is home to about 1100 bird species, more than 500 mammals, over 1200 amphibians and reptiles, over 5000 crustaceans, about 2000 butterflies and over 25,000 plants.

Vive Latino

Vive Latino (www.vivelatino.com.mx), a festival held over a weekend in March or April at Mexico City's Foro Sol, is one of the world's major annual *rock en español* (Spanish-language rock) events.

Day of the Dead

Few festivals reveal more about Mexican spirituality than Día de Muertos (Day of the Dead), the remembrance of departed loved ones at the beginning of November.

Today Muertos is a national phenomenon, with people everywhere cleaning graves and decorating them with flowers, holding graveyard vigils, sprinkling the graves with liquor (the dead also like to party!) and building elaborate altars to welcome back their loved ones with their favorite dishes. For the *mestizo* (mixed ancestry) majority, it's a popular folk festival and family occasion.

Sugar skulls, chocolate coffins and toy skeletons are sold in markets everywhere, both as Muertos gifts for children and graveyard decorations; this tradition derives in great measure from the work of artist José Guadalupe Posada (1852–1913), renowned for his satirical figures of a skeletal Death cheerfully engaging in everyday life, working, dancing, courting, drinking and riding horses into battle.

Kukulcán creeps down the staircase during the spring and autumn equinoxes) to the Sacred Cenote and curiously designed El Caracol, the legacy of Mayan astronomers will blow your mind.

Oaxaca Coast

8 Oaxaca's beautiful, little-developed Pacific coast has everything you need for a wonderful time by the ocean. With the near-empty 550km shoreline strung with long golden beaches and lagoons full of wildlife, you can't go wrong. After a few days here you'll be so relaxed you may not be able to leave. Head for the surf mecca and fishing port of Puerto Escondido, the low-key resort of Bahías de Huatulco, or the ultra-laid-back hangouts of Zipolite, San Agustinillo or Mazunte. Soak up the sun, eat good food, imbibe in easygoing beach bars and, when the mood takes you, have a swim, surf or snorkel, or board a boat to sight turtles, dolphins, whales, crocs or birdlife.

Huasteca Potosina, San Luis Potosí

9 Gorgeously green, lush Huasteca Potosina, a subregion of San Luis Potosí (and the wider Huasteca area), offers ruins, fascinating cave visits and wild and wet experiences. You can plunge into, boat to or ogle at a number of stunning waterfalls and rivers. As for color? The turquoises, aquas and greens are as vibrant as any manipulated image. Huastec culture is strong here: don't miss trying a local zacahuil, a massive tamal. The region, too, is home to the surrealist garden Las Pozas, where gigantic Dalí-esque structures 'strut' their quirky stuff.

Volcán Paricutín

10 As volcanoes go, Paricutín is still in its kindergarten years. Blasting out of a Michoacán maize field in 1943, it's one of the youngest volcanoes on Earth and the only one whose life cycle has been fully studied by scientists. Miraculously, Paricutín is also relatively easy to climb. Some rock hop across barren lava fields to bag the peak, others ride horses through hot black sand before dismounting for the final summit scramble. The goal's the same: a chance to stand atop a veritable geological marvel, viewing nature at its rawest and best.

Cabo Pulmo

11 Rediscover the magic of old Baja by visiting the largely undeveloped east coast, discovering world-class diving off Cabo Pulmo, the only coral reef on the west coast of North America and, at 71 sq km, one of the largest and most successful marine protected regions in the world. In this beautiful place you can see expect to see black coral bushes, schools of trigger fish, yellowfin tuna and snapper. Depending on the seasons and currents, you may also spy hammerhead sharks, huge manta rays and whale sharks.

11

LEONARDO GONZALEZ / SHUTTERSTOCK ©

Getting Around

Over 60 cities are served by domestic flights, which are well worth considering for longer inter-city trips. Fares vary widely depending on the airline and how far in advance you pay.

Mexico's efficient, comfortable and reasonably priced bus network is generally the best option for moving around the country. On average you pay about M$1.10 per kilometer on 1st-class buses, covering around 75km per hour. Services are frequent on main routes.

Cars are a convenient option giving maximum independence. Roads are serviceable, with speeds generally slower than north of the border or in Europe.

CAPITAL
Palikir

POPULATION
104,700

AREA
702 sq km

OFFICIAL LANGUAGE
English

Traditional house with stone money in front, Yap Island

Micronesia

The four unique states of Kosrae, Pohnpei, Chuuk and Yap have distinct cultures, traditions and identities as colourful and diverse as the multitudes of coral formations that live in their fringing reefs.

Known collectively as the Federated States of Micronesia (FSM), these four states are otherwise unrelated, and travellers looking to experience a variety of lifestyles are in luck.

Kosrae is a Pacific paradise and arguably FSM's most beautiful island. Its people are true believers, and here everything shuts down on Sunday and full focus is given to vibrant all-singing, all-dancing church ceremonies (with a relaxed island twist).

Pohnpei is home to mysterious ancient ruins and a plethora of lush landforms, and retains a system of chiefs and clan titles.

Chuuk is renowned for its wreck diving, and while it is just coming to terms with international tourism, the uncompromising nature of the Chuukese holds firm.

Yap is a fiercely traditional state. Its people retain their architecture, customs, religions and gigantic stone money – it's an eternally fascinating place.

Top Experiences

Lelu Ruins

1 Lelu Island is where a massive walled city was built between the 13th and 14th centuries for Kosraean royalty. Lelu's ruins are hidden behind thick vegetation but you can still see the dwelling compounds of the high chiefs, two royal burial mounds, a few sacred compounds and numerous large walls, built from huge hexagonal basalt logs.

Nan Madol

2 Comprising 92 artificial islets Nan Madol is built on the tidal flats and reef off the southeastern side of Pohnpei. Wide basalt pillars were quarried on Pohnpei Island and stacked horizontally around the islets as retaining walls; the resultant twisting canals are known as the 'Venice of Micronesia'. On the level surfaces were temples, burial vaults, meeting houses, bathing areas, and pools for turtles, fish and eels.

Yap Island

3 Yap Island's tiny capital, Colonia, wraps around Chamorro Bay, offering sea views most everywhere. Walk to the stone-money bank in the nearby village of Balabat, or visit the Ethnic Art Village, which does a great job of celebrating and preserving indigenous art. Up north, Bechiyal is a friendly beachside village with Yap's oldest *faluw* (men's house).

When to Go

 HIGH SEASON (Dec–Jun)

LOW SEASON (Jul–Nov)

Food & Drink

Pohnpeian dog A traditional feast food, but the casual visitor is unlikely to come across it.

Sakau Local potently narcotic kava drink made from the roots of pepper shrubs.

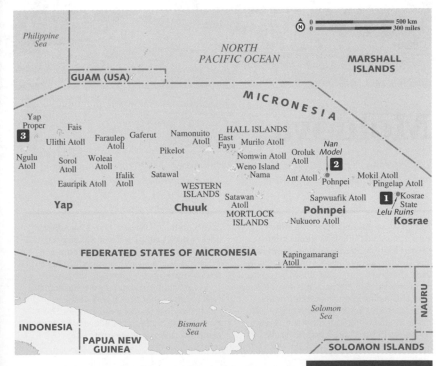

583

CAPITAL
Chişinău

POPULATION
3.5 million (including Transdniestr)

AREA
33,851 sq km

OFFICIAL LANGUAGE
Moldovan

Ciuflea Monastery, Chişinău

Moldova

Travellers are finally waking up to the charms of this little nation wedged between Romania and Ukraine, which is no longer the world's unhappiest place.

Famously so dubbed in a book almost a decade ago, Moldova is increasingly known more for its unspoiled countryside and superb wine tours. As one of Europe's least visited countries, Moldova retains a certain off-the-beaten-track charm. But even that's changing as budget flights from London and other European cities make the lively capital, Chişinău, a popular weekend break. Meanwhile, those looking to plant the flag in a land few others have visited still have their Shangri-La in the form of the breakaway republic of Transdniestr, where the Soviet Union still reigns supreme.

As for Moldova's 'unhappy' reputation? Well it's shed that, too, thank you very much. According to the most recent UN survey on the subject, Moldova is now the world's 55th *happiest* country.

Top Experiences

Chişinău

1 Stroll the tree-lined streets and parks of Moldova's friendly capital. Though razed to the ground by WWII and a terrible 1940 earthquake, Chişinău has arguably never lost its cosmopolitan soul or charm, despite the best efforts of the Soviet authorities who oversaw the rebuilding of the city.

Wineries

2 Designate a driver for tours of Cricova, one of several world-famous wine cellars outside Chişinău. Around 15km north of Chişinău, this is one of Europe's biggest underground wine kingdoms. Some 60km of the 120km-long underground limestone tunnels – dating from the 15th century – are lined wall-to-wall with bottles.

Orheiul Vechi

3 Detox at the fantastic Orheiul Vechi monastery complex. This is unquestionably Moldova's most fantastic and picturesque sight, drawing visitors from around the globe. The complex is carved into a massive limestone cliff in a wild, rocky, remote spot. The Cave Monastery, inside a cliff overlooking the Răut River, was dug by Orthodox monks in the 13th century.

When to Go

 HIGH SEASON (Jun–Aug)

 SHOULDER (Apr–May, Sep & Oct)

 LOW SEASON (Nov–Mar)

Food & Drink

Mămăligă Cornmeal mush with a consistency between porridge and bread that accompanies many dishes.

Brânză Moldova's most common cheese is a slightly salty-sour sheep's milk product.

Wine Look for bottles from quality local wineries such as Cricova, Chateau Vartely and Purcari.

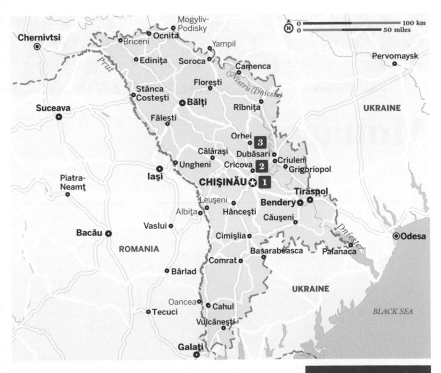

CAPITAL
Monaco

POPULATION
30,581

AREA
2 sq km

OFFICIAL LANGUAGE
French

Port of Monte Carlo

Monaco

Squeezed into just 200 hectares, this principality might be the world's second-smallest country, but what it lacks in size it makes up for in attitude.

A magnet for high-rollers and hedonists since the early 20th century, it's also one of the world's most notorious tax havens (residents pay no income tax). It's also famous for its annual Formula 1 Grand Prix, held every year in May since 1929.

Despite its prodigious wealth, Monaco itself is a long way from the prettiest town on the French Riviera: it's basically an ode to concrete and glass, dominated by high-rise hotels and apartment blocks that rise into the hills like ranks of dominoes, not to mention an utterly bewildering street layout that seems solely designed to confound lowly pedestrians.

It's a rather different story on the rocky outcrop known as Le Rocher, which juts out on the south side of the port and is home to the royal palace, as well as a rather charming little old town that feels a world away from Monte Carlo's skyscrapers and super yachts.

Top Experiences

Changing of the Guard

1 Built as a fortress atop Le Rocher in the 13th century, the Palais Princier de Monaco is the private residence of the Grimaldi Family. It is protected by the blue-helmeted, white-socked Carabiniers du Prince; changing of the guard takes place daily at 11.55am.

Musée Océanographique de Monaco

2 Stuck dramatically to the edge of a cliff since 1910, this world-renowned museum is a stunner. Its centrepiece is its aquarium with a 6m-deep lagoon where sharks and marine predators are separated from colourful tropical fish by a coral reef. Don't miss the sweeping views of Monaco from the rooftop terrace and cafe.

Casino de Monte Carlo

3 Peeping inside Monte Carlo's legendary marble-and-gold casino is a Monaco essential. The building, open to visitors every morning, is Europe's most lavish example of belle-époque architecture. To gamble or watch the poker-faced play, visit after 2pm (when a strict over-18s-only admission rule kicks in).

When to Go

 HIGH SEASON (Jun–Aug)

 SHOULDER (Apr, May, Sep & Oct)

 LOW SEASON (Nov–Mar)

Food & Drink

Eating in Monaco is as diverse as its population. Everything from Monégasque (a variant of Niçois) to Italian, Japanese and gastronomic French cuisine is available, and like most things in the principality, it's rather expensive.

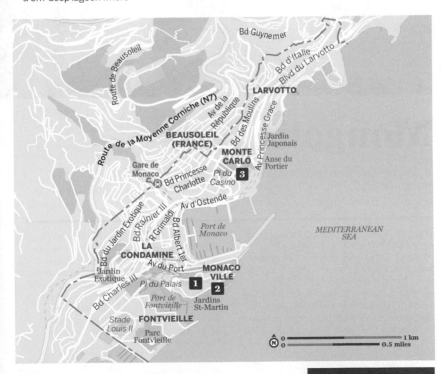

CAPITAL
Ulaanbaatar

POPULATION
3 million

AREA
1.6 million sq km

OFFICIAL LANGUAGE
Khalkha Mongol

Mongolia

Rugged Mongolia is an adventure destination where travellers can see the traditions of the past still practised today by hardy nomads dwelling on the country's vast steppes and deserts.

For most of the 20th century, Mongolia was sealed off from the world; seemingly so distant that the very name of the country became a byword for remoteness and isolation. The 21st century promises the polar opposite as Mongolia has opened up to the world, its citizens are travelling the globe and outsiders are arriving by the planeload for business and travel opportunities. Visas are relatively easy to acquire; a handful of nationals won't even require one.

There are few countries in the world with such a stark difference between the rural and urban populations. While nomadic Mongols live the simple life, their cousins in Ulaanbaatar are lurching headlong into the future. The capital is changing at a dizzying pace and many Mongolians have bought wholeheartedly into the global economy, capitalism and consumerism. By visiting you are contributing to the remarkable developments in this extraordinary land.

Top Experiences

Naadam Festival in Khatgal

1 Mongolians love their naadam. With two or three days of serious wrestling action, awesome horse racing and dazzling archery, who wouldn't? While 'naadam' literally means games, the celebration is much more than that. It's all about fun, getting together with friends and relatives, eating a lot of khuushuur (mutton pancakes) and emptying a bottle or two of vodka. The most traditional festivals happen in small towns such as Khatgal in northern Mongolia, where every member of the community is somehow involved. These village naadams are also ultra-photogenic – the burly wrestlers, sharp-eyed archers and tough jockeys make for quite a spectacle.

Gobi Desert

2 The idea of going to the Gobi for a vacation would probably have Marco Polo turning in his grave. The Venetian traveller, and others like him, dreaded crossing this harsh landscape. Thankfully, travel facilities have improved in the past 800 years, and it's now possible to make a reasonably comfortable visit. There are two-humped camels to ride and dinosaur boneyards to explore. The real highlight is the scenic Khongoryn Els in Gurvan Saikhan National Park – towering sand dunes that whistle when raked by high winds.

Khövsgöl Nuur

3 The natural highlight of Mongolia is Khövsgöl Nuur, a 136km-long lake set on the southernmost fringe of Siberia. For Mongolians the lake is a deeply

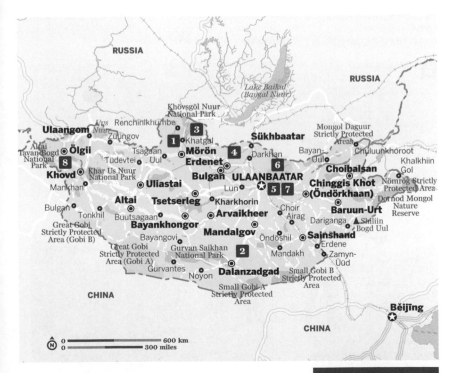

spiritual place, home to powerful nagas (water spirits) and a source of inspiration for shamans who live there. For foreigners Khövsgöl is a place for adventure, with horse riding, fishing, kayaking, trekking and mountain biking a few of the possibilities. Hard-core adventurers can even embark on a 15-day trek around its glorious shoreline.

Amarbayasgalant Khiid

4 The time-worn Buddhist monasteries (*khiid*) that dot the landscape are the most immediate window on Mongolia's spiritual roots. Lamas young and old sit quietly in the pews, carrying on the legacy of a religion brought here from Tibet centuries ago. The laypeople that visit the monasteries pay homage with the spin of a prayer wheel and whispered mantras. As well as a place of pilgrimage, the monasteries are rare slices of tangible history, filled with precious Buddhist icons, sutras and the delicate paintings that grace their ancient walls. Amarbayasgalant Khiid, the country's best-preserved monastery, is dedicated to the great sculptor Zanabazar.

Ulaanbaatar

5 Mongolia is said to be the least-densely populated country on the planet. You would have a hard time believing that if you only visited its capital. The crush of people, cars and development in Ulaanbaatar can be overwhelming and exciting all at once. Beyond the heady nightlife, chic cafes and Hummers, the city has a peaceful side, too. Turn a prayer wheel at Gandan Khiid, saunter across Chinggis Khaan (Sükhbaatar) Sq and

Getting Around

Mongolia relies heavily on air transport. Seats can be difficult to get in summer.

The provincial capitals are accessible by bus and services run daily to most cities. Trains are unnecessary for domestic travel.

Hiring a car and driver is actually cheaper than hiring a car without a driver. A 4WD is essential for most destinations outside the capital.

CHANWIT WHANSEY / SHUTTERSTOCK ©

climb up Zaisan Hill to take a break from this bewildering and ever-changing city.

Hiking at Gorkhi-Terelj National Park

6 With its rugged mountains, serene river valleys and fields of wildflowers, the Mongolian backcountry is begging to be explored on foot. Hiking is a new activity in Mongolia, but with some improvisation, it's certainly possible at places such as Gorkhi-Terelj National Park. Although there are no warming huts and few marked trails, you'll find shelter in gers and encounter locals who are more than willing to show you the way. There are no Sherpas, but a pack horse (or yak) will do nicely. Good maps, a sturdy tent and a sense of adventure will help see you through.

Central Museum of Mongolian Dinosaurs

7 Dinosaurs of all shapes, sizes and appetites once roamed the Gobi Desert. Their fossilised bones and eggs were first uncovered by American explorer Roy Chapman Andrews in the 1920s. Today, you can come face-to-skull with some of the best examples of Mongolian dinosaur fossils in this museum in Ulaanbaatar.

Eagle Hunters of Bayan-Ölgii

8 For centuries, using eagles to catch prey has been a traditional sport among Central Asian nomads. Even Marco Polo mentioned the great raptors kept by Kublai Khaan. The sport is alive and well today, but you'll only find it in a small corner of Mongolia. Travel to Bayan-Ölgii and link up with the Kazakh hunters who capture and train these magnificent birds. The best time to visit is in early October, when you can attend the colourful Eagle Festival in Ölgii city.

2

GALYNA ANDRUSHKO / SHUTTERSTOCK ©

Food & Drink

Buuz Steamed dumplings filled with mutton.

Makh The classic Mongolian dinner staple consists of boiled sheep bits (bones, fat, various organs and the head) with some sliced potato, served in a plastic bucket.

Shölte khool Literally, soup with food – a meal involving hot broth, pasta slivers, boiled mutton and a few potato chunks.

Süütei tsai Milk tea with salt.

Traditional Gers

Of all the different types of domiciles ever conceived, the Mongolian *ger* or *yurt* has to be one of the most useful, versatile and perfectly adapted for the user. Here is a home that one can take apart in less than an hour, move to a different location (with the help of a camel or two) and set up again, all on the same day. *Gers* are not unique to Mongolia; versions can be found across Central Asia, from Xinjiang to Turkmenistan. But while other traditions are fading, use of the *ger* is still common. For travellers, a visit inside a *ger* is central to the Mongolian experience.

Sveti Stefan

Montenegro

Bursting at the seams with majestic mountains, breathtaking beaches and larger-than-life locals, minuscule Montenegro proves once and for all that good things do indeed come in small packages.

It's not even 300km from tip to toe, but Montenegro's coastline crams in some of Europe's most spectacular seaside scenery. Mountains jut sharply from crystal-clear waters in such a way that the word 'looming' is unavoidable. Ancient walled towns cling to the rocks and dip their feet in the water like they're the ones on holiday. In summer, the whole scene is bathed in the scent of wild herbs, conifers and Mediterranean blossoms.

When the beaches fill up with Eastern European sunseekers, intrepid travellers can easily sidestep the hordes by getting off the beaten track in the rugged mountains of Durmitor and Prokletije, or in the many towns and villages where ordinary Montenegrins go about their daily lives. Hike, horse ride, mountain bike or kayak yourself to somewhere obscure and chances are you'll have it all to yourself.

Top Experiences

Kotor

1 Time-travel back to a Europe of moated walled towns with shadowy lanes and stone churches on every square. It may not be as impressive as Dubrovnik's or as shiny as Budva's, but Kotor's Old Town feels much more lived-in and ever so dramatic. The way it seems to grow out of the sheer grey mountains surrounding it adds a thrill of foreboding to the experience – as if they could at any point choose to squeeze the little town in a rocky embrace.

Njegoš Mausoleum

2 Once upon a time there was a Black Mountain. And on top of that mountain there was a tomb guarded by two granite giantesses. And inside the tomb, under a canopy of gold, there rested a great hero, lying in the arms of a giant eagle. This fairy-tale location is the final resting place for the very real 19th-century *vladika* (bishop-prince) Petar II Petrović Njegoš. The simple but affecting structure and monumental statuary do little to distract from the remarkable views over all of Old Montenegro.

Sveti Stefan

3 The postcard-perfect village of Sveti Stefan is a wonder to behold. A fortified island connected to the mainland by a narrow causeway, its photogenic jumble of 15th-century stone villas overlook an impeccable pink-sand beach and tempting turquoise waters. It's a little slice of Mediterranean heaven, with oleanders, pines and olive trees peeking between the terracotta roofs. The island is now owned by a luxurious resort, meaning it's off-limits to all but paying guests. But ogling comes for free.

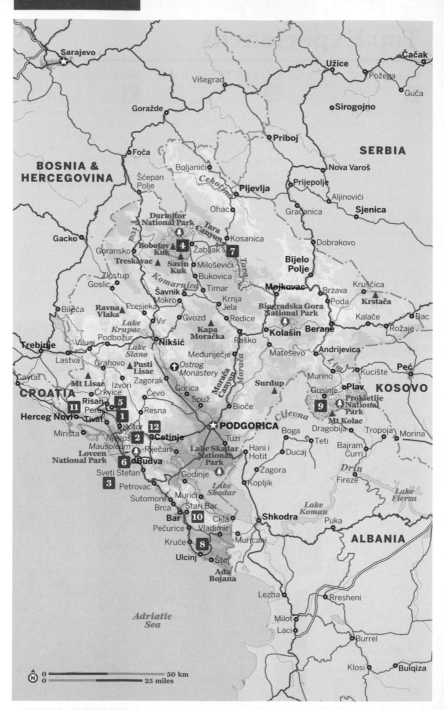

Food & Drink

Loosen your belt and pack pants one size up: you're in for a treat. By default, most of the food is local, fresh and organic, and hence very seasonal. Despite its small size, Montenegro has at least three distinct regional styles: the food of the old Montenegrin heartland, mountain food and coastal cuisine.

Heartland specialities Include *pršut* (smoke-dried ham), *sir* (cheese), and meat stuffed with both, as well as freshwater fish.

Mountain food Traditionally more stodgy and meaty. A traditional method of cooking is *ispod sača*, where meat and vegetables are roasted under a metal lid covered with hot coals.

Coastal cuisine The food most sun-seeking holidaymakers encounter: lots of grilled seafood, garlic, olive oil and Italian-style dishes. Hearty, flavoursome *riblja čorba* (fish soup) is a must-try, as is *lignje na žaru* (grilled squid) – its crispy tentacles coated in garlic and olive oil.

Best in Print

The Son (Andrej Nikolaidis; 2011) Set in Ulcinj over the course of a single night, this novel won a European Union Prize for Literature.

Realm of the Black Mountain (Elizabeth Roberts; 2007) An interesting and detailed dissection of Montenegro's convoluted history.

Montenegro: A Novel (Starling Lawrence; 1997) An entertaining tale of politics, bloodshed and romance set at the dawn of the 20th century.

Black Lamb and Grey Falcon (Rebecca West; 1941) One of the classics of travel literature.

Mountain Eyes, Durmitor National Park

4 Reflecting the beauty of the Durmitor range's imposing grey peaks are 18 glacial lakes, known as *gorske oči* (mountain eyes). The largest and most beautiful is Black Lake; its inky appearance is caused by the surrounding black pines and the peak known as the Bear (Medjed) rearing above it. Black Lake is a breeze to get to and a delight to walk around, but other, more remote lakes await discovery further up along the park's hiking trails.

Perast

5 An oversized village comprised almost entirely of elegant baroque palaces and churches, romantic Perast forms a worthy centrepiece to the entire Bay of Kotor. The positioning is perfect, sitting at the apex of the inner bay, looking straight down the narrow channel leading to the outer section. Catch a boat to Gospa od Škrpjela (Our-Lady-of-the-Rock Island), one of two tiny islands sitting just offshore, where a sky-blue dome covers a church filled with votive offerings left by grateful sailors.

When to Go

HIGH SEASON
(Jul & Aug)
Warmest, driest, busiest and most expensive time.

SHOULDER
(May, Jun, Sep & Oct)
Best time to come, with plenty of sunshine and warm waters.

LOW SEASON
(Nov–Apr)
The ski season kicks in, with peak prices in Kolašin and Žabljak.

Stari Grad, Budva

6 Budva's walled Old Town rises from the Adriatic like a miniature, less frantic Dubrovnik. There's an atmosphere of romance and a typically Mediterranean love of life palpable around every corner. While away the hours exploring the labyrinth of narrow cobbled streets, visiting tiny churches and charming galleries, drinking in alfresco cafe-bars,

Hello Up There

It's not just the mountains that are towering: Montenegrins are among the tallest people in Europe. The average height is 176cm (both genders), but you'll find plenty of folks teetering way above 6ft. With this in mind, it may come as no surprise that gangly world-champion tennis player Novak Djoković (1.88m) is of Montenegrin heritage. The mountain air, mixed gene pool and wholesome food have been cited as reasons for locals' loftiness. Vertically challenged visitors may feel akin to gnomes, while tall women especially will (finally) feel right at home in such statuesque company.

Getting Around

Buses link all major towns and are affordable, reliable and reasonably comfortable.

While you can get to many places by bus, hiring a car will give you freedom to explore some of Montenegro's scenic back roads. Some of these are extremely narrow and cling to the sides of canyons, so it may not suit the inexperienced or faint-hearted.

Trains are cheap but the network is limited and many carriages are old and can get hot. The main line links Bar, Virpazar, Podgorica, Kolašin, Mojkovac and Bijelo Polje, and there's a second line from Podgorica to Danilovgrad and Nikšić.

snacking on pizza and being inspired by the gorgeous sea views from the Citadela. When it's time to relax, there's a beach on either side.

Rafting the Tara River

7 It's hard to get a decent view of the beautiful Tara Canyon – its sheer tree-lined walls, up to 1300m high, tend to get in the way. The effect is most impressive from the water, which goes some way to explaining why rafting is one of the country's most popular tourist activities. You'll hit a few rapids, but outside of April and May it's a relatively gentle experience, gliding over crystalline waters through a landscape untouched by human hands.

Ulcinj

8 There's a special buzz to Ulcinj, Montenegro's southernmost town – an indefinable excitement that's particularly apparent on summer nights, when the beachfront thrums with Eastern-tinged

pop and a constant parade of holidaymakers. Look up: minarets compete with oversized socialist sculpture, and the imposing walls of the Old Town perch high on the cliff. Continuing along the coast, rocky coves give way to the long sandy expanses of Velika Plaža (Big Beach) and the clothing-optional island, Ada Bojana.

Hiking the Prokletije Mountains

9 They're called the 'Accursed Mountains', but for hikers and climbers, this rugged range in Montenegro's far east leans more to the divine than the damned. Snaking across Montenegro, Albania and Kosovo, Prokletije makes up the highest – and arguably hardiest – part of the Dinaric Alps. The prodigious Peaks of the Balkans hiking trail winds 192km through the range, criss-crossing between all three countries with tracks that veer from easy to moderate to once-in-a-lifetime extreme. Whether you tackle the

entire trail or take a brief alpine amble, a Prokletije pilgrimage leaves you feeling on top of the world.

Stari Bar

10 While there's not much to recommend the modern industrial town of Bar, there's a real gem hidden in the hinterland. The ancient city of Stari Bar lies in enigmatic ruins atop a bluff surrounded by gnarled olive trees, many of which are more than a thousand years old. The city itself has been here for around 2800 years but its current state of dilapidation dates from a bombardment in 1878. The whole place is laid bare for you to explore.

Herceg Novi

11 Between the bustling waterfront promenade and the busy highway lies an unassuming Old Town; it's here that the very essence of Herceg Novi hides. Catholic and Orthodox churches abound in equal profusion, cafe-bars set up their tables on sunny squares, and hulking fortresses huddle in silent menace. Order a glass of wine and soak it all in. The town beaches may not be great, but some of Montenegro's very best are only a short boat ride away.

The Museums of Cetinje

12 Cetinje may have been stripped of its capital status by Podgorica, but Montenegro's erstwhile royal city still boasts the country's richest and most important museums. Spanning centuries of history, the four museums – collectively known as the National Museum of Montenegro – include everything from plush palaces to bullet-riddled relics to Montenegro's first ever billiard table (owned by Montenegro's favourite son, Petar II Petrović Njegoš, but of course). Two superb galleries, a magnificent monastery and a host of handsome historic buildings amp up Cetinje's cultural cachet.

Language

You don't have to learn Cyrillic (though it doesn't go astray), but learning the Montenegrin *latinica* alphabet will save you a lot of confusion when reading road signs, menus and the like.

Tivat Airport

Many visitors to the Bay of Kotor traditionally flew into Dubrovnik. But as of 2016 Tivat Airport welcomes direct flights from a number of European cities.

DOMIN_DOMIN / GETTY IMAGES ©

7

2

TATIANA POPOVA / SHUTTERSTOCK ©

CAPITAL
Rabat

POPULATION
33,655,800

AREA
446,550 sq km

OFFICIAL LANGUAGES
Moroccan Arabic
(Darija), Berber
(Amazigh), French

Mausoleum of Moulay Ismail, Meknès

Morocco

Morocco is a gateway to Africa, and a country of dizzying diversity. Here you'll find epic mountain ranges, ancient cities, sweeping deserts – and warm hospitality.

Enjoying Morocco starts with its national pastime – people-watching in a street cafe with a coffee or a mint tea. Use the opportunity to plan your next moves – hiking up North Africa's highest peak, learning to roll couscous, camel trekking in the desert, shopping in the souqs or getting lost in the medina.

From Saharan dunes to the peaks of the High Atlas, Morocco could have been tailor-made for travellers. Lyrical

landscapes carpet this slice of North Africa like the richly coloured and patterned rugs you'll lust after in local co-operatives. It's a storied country, which has, over the centuries, woven its ties to sub-Saharan Africa, Europe and the wider Middle East into a whole cloth. Its mixed Arab and Berber population forms a strong national identity, but an increasingly youthful one, taking the best of its traditions and weaving the pattern anew.

Top Experiences

Djemaa el-Fna Street Theatre

1 Circuses can't compare to the madcap, Unesco-acclaimed *halqa* (street theatre) in Marrakesh's main square. By day, 'La Place' draws crowds with astrologers, snake-charmers, acrobats and dentists with jars of pulled teeth. Around sunset, 100 restaurant stalls kick off the world's most raucous grilling competition. 'I teach Jamie Oliver everything he knows!' brags a chef. 'We're number one ... literally!' jokes the cook at stall number one. After dinner, jam sessions get under way – audience participation is always encouraged, and spare change ensures encores.

Fez Medina

2 The Fez medina is the maze to end all mazes. The only way to experience it is to plunge in head first, and don't be afraid of getting lost – follow the flow of people to take you back to the main thoroughfare, or pay a small boy to show you the way. It's an adventure into a medieval world of hidden squares, enormous studded doors and colourful souqs. The essential footprint of the medina hasn't changed in nearly a millennium. Remember to look up and see intricate plasterwork, magnificent carved cedarwood and curly Arabic calligraphy, while at your feet are jewel-like mosaics.

The High Atlas

3 Zaouiat Ahansal is the Chamonix of the eastern Atlas. Hemmed in by the cracked and fissured summit of Aroudane (3359m), the valley is characterised by kilometres of cliffs, soaring buttresses and dramatic slot canyons. With the arrival of a paved road in 2013, this awesome natural canvas is just beginning to attract attention. For rafters and kayakers the valley is a green jewel where rafts whip between 2.5m-wide limestone walls; for climbers and trekkers the extreme topography and huge routes offer ridiculous views and a thrilling sense of wilderness.

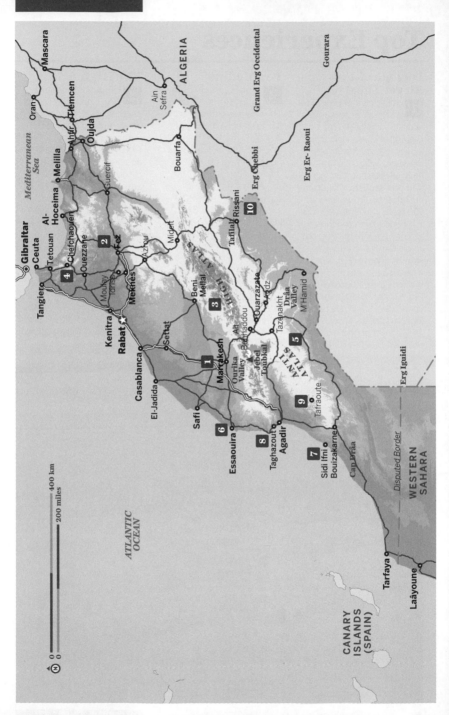

Market Produce

Fragrant Moroccan market produce will leave you with a permanent grudge against those wan, shrivelled items at the supermarket. It's usually harvested by hand when ripe, and bought directly from farmers in the souqs. Follow the crowds to the carts and stalls offering the freshest produce. Just be sure to peel, cook or thoroughly wash produce before you eat it. Seasonal highlights:

Autumn Figs, pomegranates, grapes.

Spring Apricots, cherries, strawberries, peaches.

Summer Watermelon, wild artichokes, tomatoes.

Winter Oranges, mandarins, onions, beets, carrots, potatoes and other root vegetables.

Best in Print

The Sacred Night (Tahar ben Jelloun; 1987) This tale of a Marrakesh girl raised as a boy won France's prestigious Prix Goncourt.

Dreams of Trespass: Tales of a Harem Girlhood (Fatima Mernissi; 1994) The author's memoirs of 1940s Fez blend with other women's stories.

The Polymath (Bensalem Himmich; 2004) A fictionalised retelling of the life of 14th-century scholar Ibn Khaldun.

For Bread Alone (Mohamed Choukri; 1973) A gritty autobiographical novel of growing up in extreme poverty, translated by Paul Bowles.

Welcome to Paradise (Mahi Binebine; 1999) Explores the promise and trauma of migration across the Straits of Gibraltar.

Chefchaouen Medina

4 Steep and cobbled, the Chefchaouen medina tumbles down the mountainside in a shower of red roofs, wrought-iron balconies and geraniums. The blue-washed lanes enchant, making the town a photographer's dream-come-true. With a grand red-hued kasbah lording it over the cafe-packed main square, you could be content for hours just people-watching over a mint tea. Or amble down the riverside walk, stroll to the Spanish mosque on the hill and even venture into the surrounding Talassemtane National Park to explore the Rif Mountains.

Anti Atlas Trekking

5 A sunburned granite range leading to the Sahara, the Anti Atlas remains unexplored compared with the High Atlas. The star attraction for trekkers is the quartz massif of Jebel L'Kest, the 'amethyst mountain', which you can walk to through the lush Ameln Valley. More farming villages and crumbling kasbahs are found around Jebel Aklim, another of the excellent trekking possibilities in this area of blue

When to Go

HIGH SEASON
(Nov–Mar)
Spring and autumn are the most popular times to visit.

SHOULDER
(Apr & Oct)
Accommodation prices and demand jump around Easter.

LOW SEASON
(May–Sep)
Discounts in accommodation and souqs.

Hamams

Visiting a *hamam* (traditional bathhouse) is infinitely preferable to cursing under a cold shower in a cheap hotel. They're busy, social places, where you'll find gallons of hot water, and staff available to scrub you clean. They're also good places to meet the locals and, especially for women, somewhere to escape street hassle.

Every town has at least one *hamam*, often a modern, white-tiled and spacious affair. Often there are separate *hamams* for men and women; others open to either sex at different hours or on alternate days.

Bring your own towels (in a waterproof bag), a plastic mat or something to sit on, and flip-flops (thongs). Some *hamams* sell toiletries; look out for *ghassoul* (clay mixed with herbs, dried roses and lavender), *el-kis* (a coarse glove), black soap made from the resin of olives (which stings if you get it in your eyes) and henna (used by women).

Getting Around

 Buses are cheaper and slower than trains, ranging from modern coaches to rickety local affairs. Useful for destinations not serviced by trains.

 A car is useful for travelling at your own pace, or for visiting regions with minimal public transport. Drive on the right, but beware erratic Moroccan drivers.

 Mercedes 'grands taxis' run set routes between nearby towns and cities. Cheap but cramped.

 Trains are reasonably priced, with good coverage and frequent departures between the major cities, but no lines in the south or along the Mediterranean coast.

skies and Berber shepherds. The landscape has enough variety, from palm-filled gorges to brooding, volcanic Jebel Siroua, to justify multiple treks.

Essaouira

6 Freshened by the endless Atlantic breeze, the old sea walls and gleaming white medina of Essaouira help make one of Morocco's most charming and laid-back destinations. There are swish riads, the freshest seafood unloaded from the small port, and a vibe that seamlessly blends an old visual arts tradition with the active sea sports that the coast here is increasingly known for. As any resident will tell you, Jimi Hendrix was a fan – and you soon will be too.

Sidi Ifni

7 Shhh! Don't tell your travelling friends, but this formerly Spanish seaside town, a camel ride from the Sahara, is every bit as dilapidated, breezy and magical as well-trodden Essaouira. You can walk out along the

sweep of Legzira Plage, or just explore the blue-and-white backstreets of one of southern Morocco's most alluring hang-outs. You might hear Spanish beats blaring from a cafe, and the expats and local cafe crowd are laid-back even by Moroccan standards. The best time to appreciate the art-deco relics – more reminiscent of Cuba than Casa – is sunset, when the Atlantic winds bend the palms and fill the air with a cooling sea mist.

Surfing at Taghazout

8 You can surf all along Morocco's Atlantic coast, but the best place to catch waves is the laid-back fishing village of Taghazout. It's clear what floats the village's board as soon as you arrive: the usual cafes and téléboutiques are joined by surf shops, where locals and incomers wax boards and wax lyrical about the nearby beaches. On the same stretch of coast between Agadir and Essaouira, Tamraght and Sidi Kaouki are also set up for surfing; further

south, Mirleft is Morocco's newest surf destination, with an annual longboard championship.

Tafraoute

9 The Anti Atlas' main town, Tafraoute has a jumble of pink houses and market streets with extraordinary surroundings. The Ameln Valley is dotted with *palmeraies* (palm groves) and Berber villages, and the looming red-granite mountains stage a twice-daily, ochre-and-amber light show. With a relatively undeveloped tourist industry, despite the region's many charms, it's a wonderful base for activities including mountain biking and seeking out prehistoric rock carvings. As if the granite cliffs and oases weren't scenic enough, a Belgian artist applied his paintbrush to some local boulders – with surreal results.

Camel Trekking in the Sahara

10 When you pictured dashing into the sunset on your trusty steed, you probably didn't imagine there'd be quite so much lurching involved. Don't worry: no one is exactly graceful clambering onto a saddled hump. But even if your dromedary leaves you knock-kneed, you'll instinctively find your way to the summit of the dunes at nightfall. Stars have never seemed clearer, and with good reason: at the largest sand sea in Morocco, Erg Chigaga, you're not only off the grid, but several days' camel trek from the nearest street lights.

DARIA PETRICHEVA / 500PX ©

Haggling

Haggling in the souqs is best thought of as a performance rather than a zero-sum game.

Tajine Shopping

Plain terracotta cooking tajines are oven safe, fine for stovetop cooking and cost less than Dh80. Wrap them well against breakages on the trip home.

EKATERINA POKROVSKY / SHUTTERSTOCK ©

CAPITAL
Maputo

POPULATION
25.3 million

AREA
800,000 sq km

OFFICIAL LANGUAGE
Portuguese

Igreja da Misericórdia, Mozambique Island

Mozambique

Mozambique beckons with its coastline and swaying palms, its traditions, its cultures, its vibe and its opportunities for adventure.

This enigmatic southeast African country is well off most travellers' maps, but it has much to offer those who venture here: long, dune-fringed beaches, turquoise waters abounding in shoals of colourful fish, well-preserved corals, remote archipelagos in the north, pounding surf in the south and graceful dhows with billowing sails. Add to this colonial-style architecture, pulsating nightlife, a fascinating cultural mix and vast tracts of bush.

Discovering these attractions is not always easy, but it is unfailingly rewarding. Bring along patience, a tolerance for long bus rides, some travel savvy and a sense of adventure, and jump in for the journey of a lifetime.

Top Experiences

Mozambique Island

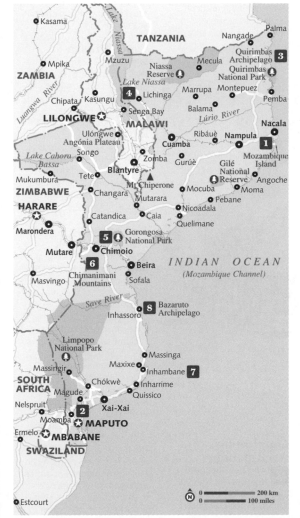

1 Dhows shifting silently through shallow seas, bruised colonial buildings withering elegantly in the tropical heat, and the voices of a church choir competing with the muezzin's call to prayer. You'll encounter all this and more within the crowded confines of Mozambique Island, one of the historical highlights of Africa, a fragrant melange of African, Portuguese, Swahili, French and Goan flavours left to mellow in the iridescent waters of the Indian Ocean for centuries.

Maputo

2 With its waterside setting Mediterranean-style architecture, and wide avenues lined with jacaranda and flame trees, Maputo is easily one of Africa's most attractive capitals. It's also the most developed place in Mozambique, with a wide selection

Food & Drink

Mozambique's cuisine blends African, Indian and Portuguese influences, and is noted for its use of coconut milk and *piri-piri* (chilli pepper).

Staples include *xima or upshwa* (a maize- or cassava-based staple, served with a sauce of beans, vegetables or fish) and *frango grelhado* (grilled chicken), which is cheap and easy to find, and usually served with chips or rice.

Specialities include *matapa* (cassava leaves cooked in a peanut sauce, often with prawns or other additions), *chamusas* (samosas), *caril* (curry) dishes, grilled prawns, lobster and crayfish, *lulas* (calamari) and other seafood.

When to Go

 HIGH SEASON (May–Nov)

 LOW SEASON (Dec–Apr)

Traditional Beliefs

Traditional religions based on animist beliefs are widespread in Mozambique. The spirits of the ancestors are often regarded to have significant powers over the destiny of living people. In connection with these beliefs, there are many sacred sites, such as forests, rivers, lakes and mountains, that play important roles in the lives of local communities.

Closely intertwined with traditional religions is the practice of traditional medicine, which is found throughout the country, sometimes in combination with Western medical treatment. *Curandeiros* (traditional healers) are respected and highly sought after. They are also often relatively well paid, frequently in kind rather than in cash. In some rural areas far from health clinics or a hospital, the *curandeiro* may be the only provider of medical assistance. In addition to *curandeiros*, you may encounter *profetas* (spirit mediums or diviners) and *feticeiros* (witch doctors).

FELIX LIPOV / SHUTTERSTOCK ©

archipelago conceal a multitude of secrets, from the brilliant coral reefs of Medjumbe to the ancient baobab trees of Quilaluia. But none of the 31 islands can equal mysterious Ibo, the archipelago's de facto capital. Haunted by a tumultuous history, and now a bubbling blend of Portuguese, Swahili, Indian and African cultures, Ibo feels as though it fell into a stupor in the 1850s and has yet to awaken.

Lake Niassa

4 The Mozambican shoreline of this lake sees a small but steady stream of adventure travellers who quickly realise they've stumbled upon a wild and wonderful African paradise that few others know about. Within Niassa's deep blue waters are over 500 species of fish, including more than 350 that are unique to the lake.

Gorongosa National Park

5 Although Gorongosa's infrastructure is still being rehabilitated after the ravages of the civil war, and animal populations can't yet compare with those in other Southern African safari destinations, the wildlife here is making a definite comeback: you're likely to see impalas, waterbucks, sable antelope, warthogs, hippos, crocodiles and perhaps even elephants and lions. Another major attraction is the bird life, with over 300 species, including many endemics and near-endemics and abundant waterbirds in the wetlands to the east around the Urema River.

of hotels and restaurants, well-stocked supermarkets, shady pavement cafes and a lively cultural scene.

Quirimbas Archipelago

3 Hidden like pirate treasure off Mozambique's north coast, the islands of the Quirimbas

Getting Around

Flights link Maputo with Inhambane, Vilankulo, Beira, Chimoio, Quelimane, Tete, Nampula, Lichinga and Pemba.

Cycling is a good way to see the real Mozambique, but you'll need plenty of time to cover the long distances, and plenty of pre-planning.

Direct bus services connect major towns at least daily, although vehicle maintenance and driving standards leave much to be desired.

Chimanimani Mountains

6 Silhouetted against the horizon on the Zimbabwean border southwest of Chimoio are the surprisingly green and wooded Chimanimani Mountains, with Mt Binga (2436m), Mozambique's highest peak, rising up on their eastern edge. It's possible to hike throughout the mountains, and climb Mt Binga in two days – most travellers come in their own 4WDs, armed with tents and plenty of supplies.

Inhambane

7 With its serene waterside setting, tree-lined avenues, faded colonial-style architecture and mixture of Arabic, Indian and African influences, Inhambane is one of Mozambique's most charming towns and well worth a visit.

It has a history that reaches back at least a millennium, making it one of the oldest settlements along the coast.

Bazaruto Archipelago

8 This archipelago has clear, turquoise waters filled with colourful fish, and offers diving, snorkelling and birding. It makes a fine upmarket holiday if you're looking for the quintessential Indian Ocean getaway. You'll see dozens of bird species, including fish eagles and pink flamingos. There are also red duikers, bushbucks and, especially on Benguera, Nile crocodiles. Dolphins swim through the clear waters, along with 2000 types of fish, plus loggerhead, leatherback and green turtles. Most intriguing are the elusive dugongs.

8

Fishermen on Inle Lake

Myanmar (Burma)

It's the dawn of a more democratic era in this extraordinary land, where the landscape is scattered with pagodas and the traditional ways of Asia endure.

CAPITAL
Yangon

POPULATION
51.4 million

AREA
261,228 sq miles

OFFICIAL LANGUAGE
Burmese

Myanmar retains the power to surprise and delight even the most jaded of travellers. Be dazzled by the wonder of Shwedagon Paya. Contemplate the 4000 stupas scattered across the plains of Bagan. Stare in disbelief at the Golden Rock at Mt Kyaiktiyo, teetering on the edge of a chasm. These are all important Buddhist sights in a country where pious monks are more revered than rock stars.

In 2015, Myanmar voted in its first democratically elected government in more than half a century. Sanctions have been dropped and swaths of the county, off-limits for years, can now be freely visited.

Thankfully, the pace of change is not overwhelming, leaving the simple pleasures intact. Drift down the Ayeyarwady River in an old river steamer. Stake out a slice of beach on the Bay of Bengal. Trek to minority villages in the Shan Hills. Best of all, you'll encounter locals who are gentle, humorous, engaging, inquisitive and passionate – they want to play a part in the world. Now is the time to make that connection.

Top Experiences

Shwedagon Paya

1 Is there a more stunning monument to religion in Southeast Asia? We don't think so. In fact, the sheer size and mystical aura of Yangon's (Rangoon's) gilded masterpiece may even cause you to question your inner atheist. But it's not all about quiet contemplation: Shwedagon Paya is equal parts religious pilgrimage and amusement park, and your visit may coincide with a noisy ordination ceremony or fortune-telling session. If you're looking for a reason to linger in Yangon before heading elsewhere in the country, this is it.

Inle Lake

2 Almost every visitor to Myanmar makes it to Inle Lake and for good reason: vast and serene, the lake is large enough for everyone to come away with their own, unique experience of life here. If you're counting days, hit the hot spots: the temples, markets and floating gardens. With more time, you can explore the remote corners of the lake, visit the fishing villages around it, or hike in the nearby hills. Whatever you do, the memories of gliding across Inle's placid waters will stay with you forever.

Bagan

3 Despite damage wrought by the 2016 earthquake, the 3000-plus temples scattered across the plains of Bagan remain an awesome sight. Most of the 11th- to 13th-century vintage temples have been renovated, as Bagan is an active religious site and place of pilgrimage. Yes, there are tour buses and crowds at the top sunset-viewing spots, but they can be avoided. Pedal off on a bike and have your own adventure amid the not-so-ruined temples, or float over the incredible scene in a hot-air balloon.

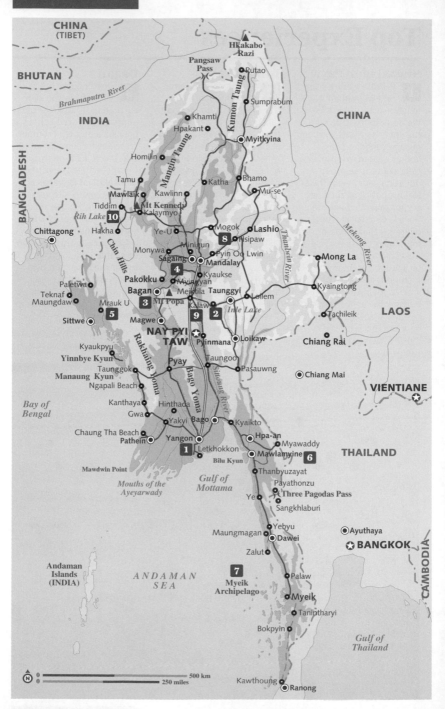

Best in Print

Burma's Spring (Rosalind Russell; 2016) Lively memoir with a broad cast of characters from girl band singers and domestic workers to opposition politicians.

Golden Parasol (Wendy Law-Yone; 2013) An insider's view on key events in modern Myanmar's history; her father, Ed Law-Yone, an influential newspaper editor, was exiled from the country in the 1960s.

River of Lost Footsteps (Thant Myint-U; 2006) Must-read historical review, by the grandson of former UN secretary general U Thant.

Food & Drink

One of the culinary highlights of Burmese food is undoubtedly *athouq* – light, tart and spicy salads made with vegetables, herbs, fruit or meat tossed with lime juice, onions, peanuts, roasted chickpea powder or chillies. Among the most exquisite are *maji·yweq thouq*, made with tender young tamarind leaves, and *shauq·thi dhouq*, made with a type of lemon-like citrus fruit.

A popular finish to Burmese meals, and possibly the most iconic Burmese dish of all, is *leq·p'eq* (often spelled *laphet*), fermented green tea leaves mixed with a combination of sesame seeds, fried peas, fried garlic, peanuts and other crunchy ingredients. A popular variant of the dish is *leq·p'eq thouq*, in which the fermented tea and nuts are combined with slices of tomato and cabbage and a squeeze of lime. The salad is a popular snack, and the caffeine boost supplied by the tea leaves makes the dish a favourite of students who need to stay up late studying.

Sagaing

4 A place of pilgrimage for Myanmar Buddhists, Sagaing is an easy day trip from Mandalay. Its stint as a royal capital may have been brief (just four years) but it established itself and endures as an intellectual centre of gravity for Buddhist traditions. The town is dominated by low hills covered by numerous white and gold stupas – a spectacular sight in themselves. But also take time to visit the cave monastery Tilawkaguru, filled with some of the most impressive preserved cave paintings in the country.

Mrauk U

5 The temples, monasteries, ruined palace and crumbling city walls of the former Rakhine capital of Mrauk U stand as a permanent reminder of what a remarkable place it must have been at its zenith in the 16th century. Back then, wide-eyed Western visitors compared the city to London or Venice. But Mrauk U is no museum piece; its temples are surrounded by working villages and emerald-green rice fields. Best of all, Mrauk U sees no

When to Go

HIGH SEASON
(Dec–Feb)
Rains least and is not so hot. Book well ahead.

SHOULDER
(Mar, Apr, Oct & Nov)
Yangon, Bagan and Mandalay often reach 40°C from March to May.

LOW SEASON
(May–Sep)
The southwest monsoon starts mid-May and peaks from July to September.

Chinlone

Also known as 'cane ball', *chinlone* is a game in which a woven rattan ball about 13cm in diameter is kicked around. It also refers to the ball itself. Informally, any number of players can form a circle and keep the *chinlone* airborne by kicking or heading it soccer-style from player to player; a lack of scoring makes it a favourite pastime with locals of all ages.

In formal play, six players stand in a circle with a circumference of 7m. Each player must keep the ball aloft using a succession of 30 techniques and six surfaces on the foot and leg, allotting five minutes for each part. Each successful kick scores a point, while points are subtracted for using the wrong body part or dropping the ball. The sport was included in the Southeast Asian Games held in Myanmar in December 2013.

A popular variation – and the one used in intramural or international competitions – is played with a volleyball net, using all the same rules as in volleyball except that only the feet and head are permitted to touch the ball.

Getting Around

Fast; reasonably reliable flight schedules, but there have been safety issues with some airlines.

Boat trips offer a chance to interact with locals and pleasant sightseeing, but slow and only cover a few destinations.

Frequent, reliable bus services; speed depends on state of road; overnight trips save on accommodation.

A car provides flexibility but can be expensive; some destinations require a government-approved guide and driver.

Trains offer interaction with locals and countryside views. Can be uncomfortable, slow and suffer long delays.

more than 5000 foreigners a year, so you're likely to have this ruined splendour to yourself.

Mawlamyine

6 A virtual time capsule of the Raj, Mawlamyine has changed little since the colonial era. The former capital of British Burma, Mawlamyine's mix of historic architecture, imposing churches, hill-top temples and a busy harbour remains so timeless that you can still see why writers George Orwell and Rudyard Kipling drew on the city for inspiration. Surrounding Mawlamyine are tropical islands and deep caves, as well as villages where the area's unique Mon culture remains strong, yet visitor numbers remain mysteriously low, allowing all the more space for you.

Myeik Archipelago

7 About 800 barely populated islands with white-sand beaches

sitting in a turquoise sea, some of the best diving in the region, roving sea gypsies and barely a hotel or tourist to be seen. It's hard to believe that a place like the Myeik Archipelago still exists in Southeast Asia. Accessing these gorgeous islands takes time and is not cheap, but those who make the investment will get to live out every beach junkie's fantasy in one of the last unknown areas of Asia.

Hsipaw

8 Attractive, laid-back Hsipaw is ideally placed for quick, easy hikes into fascinating Shan and Palaung villages, as well as more strenuous ones to barely visited hamlets. The surrounding area feels far less discovered than the treks available around Kalaw, or much of Southeast Asia. Hsipaw itself is a historic town with a royal past – it has its very own Shan palace – and an area

known as 'Little Bagan', full of ancient stupas. There's also a great morning market by the Dokhtawady River.

Kalaw

9 With its cooler temperatures, higher elevations and many locals descended from Nepali Gurkha soldiers, Kalaw boasts an almost Himalayan atmosphere. Unsurprisingly, this is one of the best places in Myanmar for upcountry treks, with the authorities relaxed about foreign visitors getting off the beaten track. As you hike through the Danu, Pa-O and Taung Yo villages that dot the forests, fields, trails and roads that link Kalaw with Inle Lake, you'll get a real insight into the lives of the hill peoples who populate the area.

Rih Lake

10 Stranded in splendid isolation on the Myanmar–India border, Rih Lake is small but perfectly formed: a heart-shaped, mystical body of water surrounded by lushly forested hills. As spectacular as the lake is, the rugged journey here through the little-seen mountains, valleys and villages of northern Chin State is also memorable. Only a handful of foreign travellers visit each year, so you are guaranteed attention from the friendly locals. Don't expect much in the way of comfort, or tourist facilities. Instead, revel in being way off the beaten track.

Meditation

Several monasteries run courses on *satipatthana vipassana* (insight-awareness meditation), where foreigners are welcome. Beginners are typically expected to sign up for a 10-day residential course.

Nightlife

Party animals take heed: Myanmar is not big on nightlife. Yangon offers the best range of options, but even here it's still a generally early to bed situation. Elsewhere there are beer stations screening videos and sports TV, and tea-houses for tea and snacks.

FATRICK FOTO / SHUTTERSTOCK ©

SCOTT BIALES / SHUTTERSTOCK ©

CAPITAL	Windhoek
POPULATION	2.4 million
AREA	824,292 sq km
OFFICIAL LANGUAGE	English

Sossusvlei dunes

Namibia

If Namibia is 'Africa for beginners', as is often said, what a wonderful place to start. Few countries in Africa can match Namibia's sheer natural beauty.

There are few more stirring desert realms on the planet, from the sand sea and perfect dead-tree valleys at Sossusvlei to the other-worldliness of sand dunes plunging down to the sea at Sandwich Harbour and the Skeleton Coast. Inland, running through the heart of the country, a spine of mountains creates glorious scenery. With rivers and wetlands in the Caprivi Strip and the endless gold-grass plains of the Kalahari, it's difficult to think of an iconic African landscape that Namibia doesn't possess.

Namibia's human story is every bit as interesting as that written in the rocks, soil and sand of the country. Through their architecture and museums, Lüderitz, Swakopmund and Windhoek tell a complicated story of colonial settlement and oppression, while elsewhere the chance to interact with the many traditional people who call Namibia home will likely provide you with some of your most memorable moments.

Top Experiences

Etosha National Park

1 There are few places in Southern Africa that can compete with the wildlife prospects in extraordinary Etosha National Park. A network of waterholes dispersed among the bush and grasslands surrounding the pan – a blindingly white, flat, saline desert that stretches into the horizon – attracts enormous congregations of animals. A single waterhole can render thousands of sightings over the course of a day, with lions and rhinos the highlights. Etosha is simply one of the best places on the planet for watching wildlife.

Sossusvlei

2 Towering red dunes of incredibly fine sand that feels soft when it trickles through your fingers and changes indelibly with the light, Sossusvlei is an astounding place, especially given that the sands originated in the Kalahari millions of years ago. The Sossusvlei valley is dotted with hulking dunes and interspersed with unearthly dry *vleis* (low, open landscapes). Clambering up the face of these constantly moving giants is a uniquely Namibian experience. You survey the seemingly endless swath of nothingness that surrounds you and it feels as though time itself has slowed.

Fish River Canyon

3 This enormous gash in the surface of the planet in the south of Namibia is an almost implausible landscape. Seen most clearly in the morning, Fish River Canyon is desolate, immense and seemingly carved into the earth by a master builder. The exposed rock and lack of plant life is quite startling and invokes thoughtful reflection and a quiet sense of awe. Its rounded edges and sharp corners create a symphony in stone of gigantic and imposing proportions.

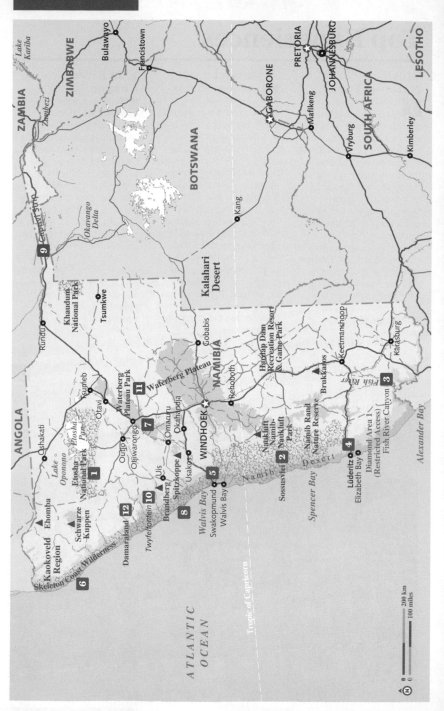

Best Landscapes

Fish River Canyon For once the clichés are true – this really is Africa's equivalent of the Grand Canyon.

Etosha Pan Stand out on the pan and survey an empty saline nothingness that bursts into life after the rains, while just behind is an artist's palette of African savannah.

Northwestern Namibia Some of the region's most incredible landscapes imaginable include the Skeleton Coast and the Kaokoveld with its wide-open vistas and lonely desert roads.

Namib-Naukluft Park Some of the most beautiful sand dunes on the planet and the austerely beautiful Naukluft Mountains.

Spitzkoppe The summit of Namibia's rocky mountain spine that runs for most of the length of the country.

Food & Drink

Traditional Namibian food consists of a few staples, the most common of which is *oshifima*, a dough-like paste made from millet, usually served with a stew of vegetables or meat. Other common dishes include *oshiwambo*, a rather tasty combination of spinach and beef, and *mealie pap*, a basic porridge.

As a foreigner you'll rarely find such dishes on the menu. Most Namibian restaurants in big towns serve a variation on European-style foods alongside an abundance of seafood dishes. Outside these towns you'll rapidly become familiar with fried-food joints.

Namibia is awash with locally brewed lagers. The most popular drop is the light and refreshing Windhoek Lager.

Lüderitz

4 Namibia is a country that defies African stereotypes and this is perhaps nowhere more true than in the historic colonial town of Lüderitz. Straddling the icy South Atlantic and the blazing-hot Namib Desert is this bizarre mini-Deutschland seemingly stuck in a time warp. After walking its streets and sitting down to a plate of sausages and sauerkraut with an authentic weiss beer, you'll survey the German art nouveau architecture, check the map again and shake your head in disbelief.

Swakopmund

5 Easily Namibia's finest urban scene, swanky Swakopmund is a feast of German art nouveau architecture, with its seaside promenades, half-timbered homes and colonial-era buildings. Stuck out on the South Atlantic coast and surrounded by desert, it feels like a movie set.

When to Go

HIGH SEASON
(Jun–Oct)
Accommodation is at a premium; book months in advance.

SHOULDER
(May & Nov)
Good months for cheaper accommodation and higher availability.

LOW SEASON
(Dec–Apr)
Humidity and high temperatures can make days unpleasant.

Let loose on a skydive or horse ride, or sandboard down a 300m-high dune because you are in the

Greetings

The Namibia greeting is practically an art form and goes something like this: *Did you get up well? Yes. Are you fine? Yes. Did you get up well? Yes. Are you fine? Yes.*

This is an example of just the most minimal greeting; in some cases greetings can continue at great length with repeated inquiries about your health, your crops and your family, which will demand great patience if you are in a hurry.

However, it is absolutely essential that you greet everyone you meet, from the most casual encounter to an important first meeting; failing to do so is considered extremely rude. Learn the local words for 'hello' and 'goodbye', and use them unsparingly. Consider broadening your lexicon to include longer and more complex phrases.

If you find yourself tongue-tied, handshakes are another crucial icebreaker. The African handshake consists of three parts: the normal Western handshake, followed by the linking of bent fingers while touching the ends of upward-pointing thumbs, and then a repeat of the conventional handshake.

Getting Around

 An extensive network of local flights operates out of Windhoek's Eros Airport.

 The public-transport network is limited. Public buses serve the main towns, but they won't take you to the country's major sights. Local minibuses depart when full and follow main routes around the country.

 Car is by far the best way to experience Namibia.

adventure capital of the region. 'Swakop' pulls off the backpacker scene and the clinking-wine-glass set equally, so you'll find your niche here.

Skeleton Coast

6 Travel on the Skeleton Coast, a treacherous stretch of shore where many ships have become graveyards, is the stuff of road-journey dreams. It's a murky region with rocky and sandy coastal shallows, where rolling fogs and swirling sandstorms encapsulate its ghostly, isolated and untamed feel. It is among the most remote and inaccessible areas in the vast country of Namibia. And it's here, in this wilderness, that you can put your favourite music on, sit back and let reality meet your imagination.

Okonjima Nature Reserve

7 Namibia has more cheetahs than any other country on earth, but these elegant, graceful speedsters are falling increasingly victim to human-wildlife conflict, often through no fault of their own. In steps AfriCat, with its fine, 200-sq-km Okonjima Nature Reserve dedicated to cheetah and other

wildlife conservation. Track cheetahs, leopards and wild dogs, and learn about this fascinating conservation project at its excellent information centres. With comfortable accommodation, expert guides and a real sense of being out in the wild and supporting a good cause, it will reward you many times over.

Cape Cross

8 It's one of Namibia's most underrated images – a beach in the Cape Cross Seal Reserve backed by Atlantic swell and covered with the oily (and rather odoriferous, it must be said) bodies of more than 100,000 lounging Cape fur seals. In a corner of the world where land-based predators or tusked giants of the dunes get most of the attention, this writhing mass of sea mammals is one of the continent's most memorable wildlife-watching experiences.

Caprivi Strip

9 One of the more curious shapes on the map of Africa, Namibia's Caprivi Strip, otherwise known as Namibia's Zambezi Region, is a narrow finger of land rich in national parks. Poaching

ravaged wildlife populations here in the past, but the animals are making a comeback, and why not? After all, they're just across the border and/or water from Botswana's prolific Okavango Delta and Linyanti wetlands. You're also a stone's throw from both Zambia and Botswana, adding numerous enticing options for your onward journey.

Twyfelfontein

10 When people in the know talk of Southern Africa's fabulous galleries of millennia-old rock art, chances are that they're talking of Unesco World Heritage–listed Twyfelfontein. On the dramatic rocky walls, paintings and engravings tell the story of the region – its wildlife, its people, its climatic ebbs and flows. Tracking these down can feel like stumbling upon hidden treasure, and, taken as a whole, Twyfelfontein evokes a feeling of walking through a priceless library of an otherwise-undocumented period of ancient history.

Waterberg Plateau

11 The rocky spine that runs north–south through the centre of Namibia finds one of its most dramatic expressions in the sandstone Waterberg Plateau. This is one of those landscapes that's as beautiful from afar (it looms 150m straight up from the surrounding barren badlands) as it is intriguing when you venture within. Apart from the scenery, which is wild and wonderful, the Waterberg hosts some of Namibia's most pleasing wildlife possibilities, from black rhinos to sable and roan antelope.

Damaraland

12 Damaraland is Namibia in a rather beautiful nutshell. The landscapes here, turning burnt orange and blood-red with the sinking sun, would be reason enough to visit – this is one beautiful corner of the country, with bouldered mountains, snaking dry valleys, bizarrely photogenic tree shapes – but the wildlife is also a wonderful story. Tracking down the free-roaming black rhinos, desert elephants and desert lions that are such icons of the Namibian wild in such gorgeous surrounds is a wonderful way to spend your time.

Advance Booking

Book your luxury lodge or tented camp, or your self-drive campsite, many months in advance. Ditto for your 4WD rental vehicle.

Return of the Lion

After a difficult few decades, Namibia's lions are making a comeback. Etosha National Park is the main stronghold, with an estimated 450 to 500 lions.

6

12

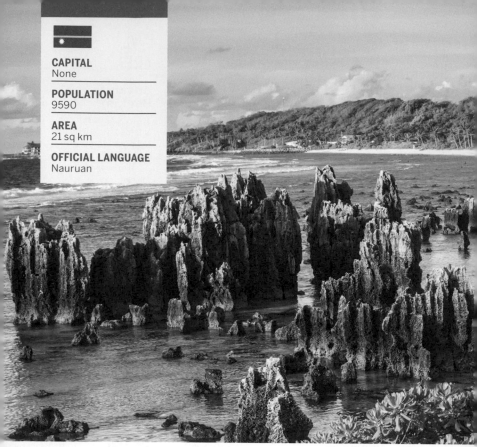

CAPITAL
None

POPULATION
9590

AREA
21 sq km

OFFICIAL LANGUAGE
Nauruan

Limestone pinnacles on Nauru's coast

Nauru

Nauru's beauty can be glimpsed along its coast: seabirds swoop over green cliffs, aqua reigns along wild-ocean vistas and sunsets are spectacular.

While the coast is beautiful – with opportunities to swim and snorkel, or watch a fiery sunset over coconut trees and salt brush – head to the island's interior and you'll find deforestation from phosphate mining and an eerie landscape of limestone pinnacles. The exposed rock reflects the sun's rays and chases away the clouds so there's lots of sunshine but frequent periods of drought.

Meanwhile, the wealth accrued from mining, followed by the poverty once the stores were depleted, have brought the country to near collapse. During the phosphate boom in the 1980s, Nauru was the second-richest country in the world in terms of per capita income; 30 years later the estimated average income is US$2500 per year. Since 2001 Australia's controversial off-shore refugee processing centre has been a major contributor to development on Nauru.

Perhaps tourism, once thought unneeded, could help Nauru get back on its feet. Transport and hospitality services are thin on the ground but smiles are plentiful.

Top Experiences

Command Ridge

 Command Ridge, where the Japanese kept watch in the 1940s, is Nauru's highest point and still holds some rusted WWII guns, including two large rotating six-barrel weapons that once fired 40kg shells. There's also a communications bunker – you can enter if you have a flashlight or lantern and if you look closely you'll see some Japanese writing.

Former Presidents' House

Check out the view from the ruins of the once-splendid former Presidents' House, burned down in 2001 by a local mob who were furious at the government's mismanagement of funds.

Cantilevers

The first shipment of 2000 tonnes of phosphate left Nauru in 1907. By 1908 vast industrial architecture began to be installed. Between the world wars, the first of two huge cantilevers was built on the coast, enabling phosphate to be loaded onto ships more efficiently. After WWII demand for phosphate rose and by the 1960s a second cantilever was in operation.

When to Go

HIGH SEASON (Mar–Oct)

LOW SEASON (Nov–Feb)

Food & Drink

Black noddy bird This bird with the notable strange cry is a local delicacy.

Demangi The island's take on fermented toddy, made from coconut palm sap.

Seafood Catch your own marlin, yellow-fin tuna, barracuda and more with the island's fishers, for a fresh seafood barbecue.

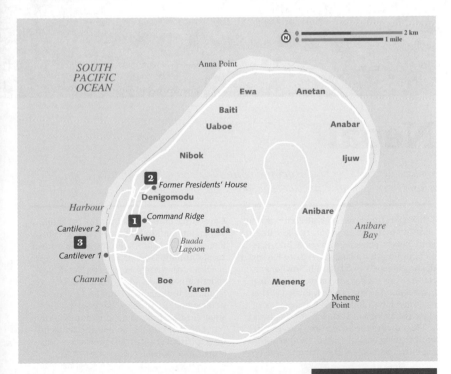

Buddhist monks at Bodhnath monastery

CAPITAL
Kathmandu

POPULATION
29 million

AREA
147,181 sq km

OFFICIAL LANGUAGE
Nepali

Nepal

Wedged between the high Himalaya and the steamy Indian plains, Nepal is a land of snow peaks and Sherpas, yaks and yetis, monasteries and mantras.

The Nepal Himalaya is the ultimate goal for most mountain lovers. Some of the Himalaya's most iconic and accessible hiking is on offer here, with rugged trails to Everest, the Annapurnas and beyond. Nowhere else can you trek for days in incredible mountain scenery, secure in the knowledge that a hot meal, cosy lodge and warm slice of apple pie await you at the end of the day.

Then there's the adrenaline kick of rafting a roaring Nepali river or bungee jumping into a bottomless Himalayan gorge.

Canyoning, climbing, kayaking, paragliding and mountain biking all offer a rush against the backdrop of some of the world's most dramatic landscapes.

Other travellers prefer to see Nepal at a more refined pace, admiring the peaks over a gin and tonic from a Himalayan viewpoint, strolling through the medieval city squares of Kathmandu, Patan and Bhaktapur, and joining Tibetan Buddhist pilgrims on a spiritual stroll around centuries-old stupas and monasteries.

Top Experiences

Old Kathmandu

1 Even after the 2015 earthquake, the historic centre of old Kathmandu remains an open-air architectural museum of magnificent medieval temples, pagodas, pavilions and shrines. Once occupied by Nepal's cloistered royal family and still home to the Kumari, Kathmandu's very own living goddess, Durbar Sq is the gateway to a maze of medieval streets that burst even more vividly to life during spectacular festivals. The hidden backstreet courtyards and temples of the surrounding warren-like old town are wonderful to wander through (just don't get lost!).

Trekking to Everest Base Camp

2 Topping many people's travel bucket list is this two-week-long trek to the base of the world's highest, and most hyped, mountain. Despite some earthquake damage, and only limited views of Mt Everest itself, the surrounding Himalayan peaks are truly awesome, and the half-hour you spend watching the alpenglow ascend beautiful Pumori or Ama Dablam is worth all the altitude headaches you will doubtless suffer. The crowds can be thick in October but the welcome at the Sherpa lodges is as warm as the fresh apple pie that is served.

Trekking the Annapurna Circuit

3 This trek around the 8091m Annapurna massif is Nepal's most popular trek, and it's easy to see why. The lodges are comfortable, there is little earthquake damage, the crossing of the 5416m Thorung La provides a physical challenge and the sense of journey from lowland Nepal to Trans-Himalayan plateau is immensely satisfying. Our best tip is to take your time and explore the spectacular side trips, particularly around Manang. Road construction has

2

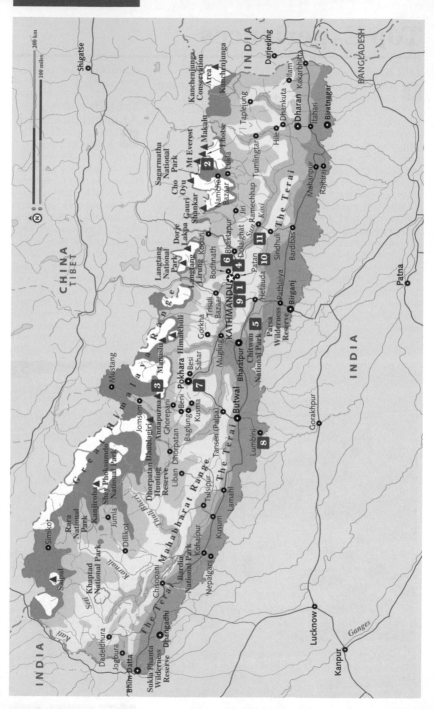

eaten away at the western sections but alternative footpaths continue to avoid the road.

Bhaktapur

4 Of the three former city-states – all Unesco sites – that jostled for power over the Kathmandu Valley, medieval Bhaktapur is the most atmospheric. Despite severe damage in the 2015 quake, its backstreets still burst with temples and pagodas like Nyatapola Temple, Nepal's tallest. Winding lanes lined with red-brick buildings lead onto squares used by locals for drying corn and making pottery – you'll have to pick your way around earthquake damage to explore but the streets are still fabulously evocative. For the full ex-

Best in Print

The Snow Leopard (Peter Matthiessen; 1978) Classic and profound account of a trek to Dolpo.

Arresting God in Kathmandu (Samrat Upadhyay; 2001) Nine short stories from the first Nepali writer to be published in English.

Snake Lake (Jeff Greenwald; 2010) Memoir of family loss set against Nepal's political revolution.

Best on Film

Himalaya (1999; Eric Valli) Stunningly shot in Dolpo; also released as *Caravan*.

Everest (1998; David Breashears) Imax film shot during the disastrous 1997 climbing season.

perience, stay overnight in a guesthouse or attend one of the city's fantastic festivals.

Chitwan National Park

5 In the 'other Nepal', down in the humid plains, Chitwan is one of Asia's best wildlife-viewing spots and the place to don your safari togs and head into the dawn mist in search of rhinos and tigers. There's plenty to keep you busy here: visit local Tharu villages or, for the brave, take a guided walk through the jungle, surrounded by the hoots and roars of the forest.

Bodhnath Stupa

6 The village of Bodhnath is the centre of Nepal's Tibetan community and home to Asia's largest stupa, a spectacular white dome and spire that draws Buddhist pilgrims from hundreds of kilometres away.

When to Go

HIGH SEASON
(Oct–Feb)
Clear skies and warm days make this the peak season.

SHOULDER
(Mar–May)
The second-best time to visit and trek, spring brings warm weather.

LOW SEASON
(Jun–Sep)
The monsoon rains (mostly at night) bring landslides, and clouds often obscure mountain views.

Equally fascinating are the surrounding streets, bustling with monks with shaved heads and maroon

Music in Nepal

The last decade has seen a revival in Nepali music and songs, both folk and 'Nepali modern'. The ever-present Hindi film songs have been partly supplanted by a vibrant local music scene thanks to advances made in FM radio.

In the countryside most villagers supply their own entertainment. Dancing and traditional music enliven festivals and family celebrations, when villages erupt with the energetic sounds of *bansari* (flutes), *madal* (drums) and cymbals, or sway to the moving soulful sounds of devotional singing and the gentle twang of the four-stringed *sarang*. Singing is one important way that girls and boys in the hills can interact and flirt, showing their grace and wit through dances and improvised songs.

Providing a good introduction to Nepali folk music is the group Sur Sudha (www.sursudha.com), Nepal's de facto musical ambassadors, whose evocative recordings will take you back to the region long after you've tasted your last *dal bhat* (lentil soup and rice). Try their *Festivals of Nepal* and *Images of Nepal* recordings.

Getting Around

Flights to/from major centres are efficient, whereas mountain flights to trailheads are highly weather dependent and frequently delayed.

There are plenty of bicycle-rental shops in Kathmandu and Pokhara, and this is a cheap and convenient way of getting around.

Tourist-class buses are comfortable, usually air-conditioned, and relatively safe and reliable. Micro or minibuses are quick but usually overcrowded, and local buses are, without exception, uncomfortable, crowded and slow.

There are no drive-yourself rental cars available in Nepal, but you can easily hire a car or jeep with a driver through a travel agency. Motorcycles can be rented in Kathmandu and Pokhara.

---

robes, and lined with Tibetan monasteries and shops selling prayer wheels and incense. Come at dusk and join the Tibetan pilgrims as they light butter lamps and walk around the stupa on their daily *kora* (ritual circumambulation).

Views from Pokhara

7 Nepal's second-biggest tourist town may lack the historical depth of Kathmandu, but it more than makes up for this with a seductively laid-back vibe and one of the country's most spectacular locations. The dawn views of Machhapuchhare and Annapurna, mirrored in the calm waters of Phewa Tal, or seen from the town's hilltop viewpoints, are simply unforgettable. Take them in on a trek, from the saddle of a mountain bike or, best of all, dangling from a paraglider high above the valley floor, if you dare.

Maya Devi Temple, Lumbini

8 A pilgrimage to the Maya Devi Temple, the birthplace of the Buddha, ranks as one of the subcontinent's great spiritual journeys. You can visit the exact spot where Siddhartha Gautama was born 2500 years ago, rediscovered only a century or so ago, and then tour a multi-national collection of temples. But perhaps the most powerful thing to do is simply find a quiet spot, and a book on Buddhism, and meditate on the nature of existence. Travel experiences don't get much more profound than that.

Swayambhunath

9 The iconic white-washed stupa of Swayambhunath is both a Unesco World Heritage Site and one of Nepal's most sacred Buddhist shrines. The great stupa – painted with iconic, all-seeing Buddha eyes – remains a focal point for Buddhist devotion. Pilgrims wander the shrines, spinning prayer wheels and murmuring mantras, while nearby astrologers read palms, and shopkeepers sell magic amulets and sacred beads. Come at dusk for spectacular views over the city lights of Kathmandu.

Patan

10 Kathmandu's sister city doesn't get the attention it deserves. This is a city of interconnected Buddhist courtyards and hidden temples. Wander the fascinating backstreets, the magnificent central Durbar Sq and the Patan Museum, easily the best museum in the country. Throw in four ancient stupas and the valley's best collection of international restaurants and it's clear you need a couple of trips to take it all in. Best of all, spend the night here and you'll have the backstreets all to yourself.

White-Water Rafting

11 Nepal is one of the world's best rafting and kayaking destinations. Fuelled by water rushing down from Himalayan peaks, rivers such as the Trisuli and Bhote Kosi promise thrilling white water for day trippers. Even better are the longer multi-day adventures – liquid journeys that take you down the Karnali, Tamur and Sun Kosi Rivers through some of Nepal's remotest corners. Companies such as Ultimate Descents everything from roller-coaster white water trips to serene floats through jungle wilderness, with nights spent camping on pristine sand beaches.

Sacred Landscapes

Both Hindus and Buddhists see the land in terms of a sacred landscape. River confluences and sources, mountain lakes and high passes and peaks are all considered sacred.

Holi

During Holi, coloured powder and water are riotously dispensed as a reminder of the cooling monsoon days to come. Foreigners get special attention, so keep your camera protected and wear old clothes. The festival falls in either February or March.

ZZVET / SHUTTERSTOCK ©

3

6

MACIEJ BLEDOWSKI / 500PX ©

CAPITAL
Amsterdam

POPULATION
17 million

AREA
41,543 sq km

OFFICIAL LANGUAGE
Dutch

Canal houses of Amsterdam

The Netherlands

Tradition and innovation intertwine here: artistic masterpieces, windmills, tulips and candlelit cafés coexist with groundbreaking architecture, cutting-edge design and phenomenal nightlife.

Geography plays a key role in the Netherlands' iconic landscapes. More than half the pancake-flat country is below sea level, and 20% has been reclaimed from the sea, making rows of polders (areas of drained land) omnipresent. The flat, fabulously scenic landscapes make cycling in the Netherlands a pleasure (headwinds notwithstanding), and the country is criss-crossed with some 32,000km of cycling paths.

In a country that values socialising and conversation more than drinking, *cafés* (pubs) are places for contemplation and camaraderie. Many *cafés* have outdoor terraces, which are glorious in summer and sometimes covered and heated in winter. Most serve food, from bar snacks to fabulous meals. The most atmospheric is a *bruin café* (brown cafe) – the ultimate place to experience the Dutch state of *gezelligheid* (conviviality, cosiness).

Top Experiences

Canal Ring in Amsterdam

1 The Dutch capital is a watery wonderland. Amsterdam made its fortune in maritime trade, and its Canal Ring was constructed during the city's Golden Age. Stroll alongside the canals and check out the narrow, gabled houses and thousands of houseboats; relax on a canal-side *café* terrace; or, better still, go for a ride. Cruises and boat rentals abound. From boat level you'll see a whole new set of architectural details, such as the ornamentation bedecking the bridges and, come nightfall, glowing lights reflecting in the ripples.

Rotterdam's Architecture

2 Unlike many European cities that emerged from the ashes of WWII with hastily reconstructed city centres, Rotterdam pursued a different path from the start. Its architecture is striking rather than simply functional. The world's best architects compete here for commissions that result in eye-popping, one-of-a-kind designs, such as a 'vertical city', a forest of cube houses, a pencil-shaped tower, a swooping white cable-stayed bridge, a fantastical horseshoe-shaped covered market, and an ethereal 'cloud-like' building housing the city's history museum.

Artistic Masterpieces in the Rijksmuseum

3 The Rijksmuseum in Amsterdam is the Netherlands' premier art trove, splashing Rembrandts, Vermeers and 7500 other masterpieces over 1.5km of galleries. To avoid the biggest crowds, come after 3pm. Or prebook tickets online, which provides fast-track entry. The Golden Age works are the highlight. Feast your eyes on still lifes, gentlemen in ruffled collars and landscapes bathed in pale yellow light. Rembrandt's *The Night Watch* (1642) takes pride of place.

Hoge Veluwe National Park

4 A vast swath of beautiful land that was once private hunting grounds, this national park combines forests, sand dunes, marshes and ponds. It's a bucolic escape from the densely packed cities and you can easily spend a day here just soaking up the natural environment. But the real treat lies at the park's centre. The Kröller-Müller Museum is one of the nation's best with a Van Gogh collection that rivals the namesake museum in Amsterdam. Outside there is a stunning sculpture garden.

Best on Film

Oorlogswinter (2008) A boy's loyalty is tested when he helps the Dutch Resistance shelter a downed British pilot.

Zwartboek (2006) Explores some of the less heroic aspects of the Dutch Resistance in WWII.

The Paradise Suite (2015) A Bulgarian prostitute, a Swedish piano prodigy and a Serbian war criminal cross paths in Amsterdam.

Best in Print

The Diary of Anne Frank (1947) A moving account of a young girl's life hiding from the Nazis.

Amsterdam: A History of the World's Most Liberal City (2013) Russell Shorto, an American transplant, traces the evolution of his adopted city.

In the City of Bikes: The Story of the Amsterdam Cyclist (2013) Pete Jordan explores Amsterdam's evolution into the world's most bike-friendly city.

Cheese-Tasting

5 Names like Gouda and Edam inspire notions of Dutch cheese more immediately than the municipalities that spawned them. In both these towns you can visit traditional cheese markets in season that have taken place on the main squares for centuries. The Netherlands' renowned cheese comes in a vast range of styles and flavours, such as aged cheeses that are crystallised like a fine Parmesan, as well as varieties such as caraway-seed-infused and mustard cheese. Shops stocking huge wheels of cheese span the country.

Amsterdam's Brown Cafés

6 *Gezelligheid* has no English equivalent but is better experienced than defined. It refers to the uniquely Dutch state of conviviality, cosiness, warmth, good humour and sense of togetherness that is a hallmark of the country's famous *bruin cafés* (brown cafes). Named for their aged, tobacco-stained walls from centuries past, these small, snug, history-steeped pubs are filled with good cheer. There are around a thousand in Amsterdam alone, and countless others throughout the country. It takes little time, on even your first visit, to be drawn into their welcoming atmosphere.

When to Go

HIGH SEASON
(Jun–Aug)
Prices peak, so book ahead. Your best odds of balmy weather to enjoy a *café* terrace or a bike ride.

SHOULDER
(Apr–May & Sep–Oct)
There are fewer crowds, but the weather can be wet and cold.

LOW SEASON
(Nov–Mar)
Many sights outside major cities close, and the weather can be chilly and/or snowy.

Hoists & Houses That Tip

Many old canal houses deliberately tip forward. Given the narrowness of staircases, owners needed an easy way to move large goods and furniture to the upper floors. The solution: a hoist built into the gable, to lift objects up and in through the windows. The tilt allowed loading without bumping into the house front. Some properties even have huge hoist-wheels in the attic with a rope and hook that run through the hoist beam.

The forward lean also makes the houses seem larger, which makes it easier to admire the facade and gable – a fortunate coincidence for everyone.

Getting Around

Short- and long-distance bike routes lace the country and you are often pedalling through beautiful areas. All but the smallest train stations have bike-rental shops, as do most towns and all cities.

Buses are used for regional transport rather than for long distances, which are better travelled by train.

Dutch freeways are extensive but prone to congestion, and parking a car can be both a major headache and expensive.

Dutch trains are efficient, fast and comfortable. Trains are frequent and serve domestic destinations at regular intervals

Maastricht

7 Spanish and Roman ruins, sophisticated food and drink, French and Belgian twists in the architecture, a shrugging off of the shackles of Dutch restraint – are we still in the Netherlands? The city where Europe's common currency began has been a meeting place for centuries. The Romans built underground forts here that you can still explore, and every generation since has left its mark. But 2000 years of history, magnificent monuments, mighty ruins, soaring churches and sublime museums aside, where Maastricht really shines is in how it embraces the moment. Few places in the Netherlands have such a dense concentration of cafés and restaurants, filled with people coming together to enjoy every minute of life.

Texel

8 The vast Waddenzee is recognised by Unesco as a World Heritage Site. Its hypnotic tidal mudflats are punctuated by a string of offshore islands, including the largest, Texel. An easy ferry ride from the mainland, Texel offers glorious walks along broad, sandy beaches, near-limitless activities and a stark beauty you can appreciate on land or on a wildlife-spotting boat trip. It has superb places to sleep, eat and drink including a slew of island producers of fruit, cheese, chocolate, ice cream, beer and rare-for-the-Netherlands wine.

Delft

9 The Netherlands has no shortage of evocative old towns that bring the beauty of the Golden Age into the present day. Haarlem, Leiden and Utrecht are some of the more well-known; other historic gems include Enkhuizen and Hoorn. One of the most exquisite (and accessible) of them all is Vermeer's home town, Delft. It's essential to spend an afternoon enjoying the canals, churches and museums, and sitting in a *café* soaking it all in. But Delft is at its most romantic in the evening after the day trippers have left. That's when locals fill the bars and restaurants and the lamplit canals are idyllic for a romantic stroll.

Deventer

10 Deventer surprises. It's at its best on a beautiful August night, when you can wander among the Hanseatic ghosts along the twisting streets searching out the odd detail in the ancient facades. What looks like a crack in the wall is really a tiny passage to the IJssel River. Deventer was already a bustling mercantile port by AD 800, and it maintained its prosperous trading ties for centuries, evidence of which you'll see everywhere in its sumptuously detailed old buildings. Think of it as the Delft of the east.

Cycling

11 Grab a bike and go. You can rent them anywhere and no nation on earth is better suited for cycling. Not only is it as flat as a classic Dutch pancake but there are thousands of kilometres of bike lanes and paths linking virtually every part of the country. You can see *polders* (areas surrounded by dykes where water can be artificially controlled) and creaking traditional windmills (as well as tulips blooming in springtime), and hear cows lowing in expansive green fields before arriving at the next enchanting village. Spin your wheels on the Breda Border Loop, the Ooijpolder Route or Weerribben-Wieden National Park.

SARAH COGHILL / LONELY PLANET ©

Windmills

These national icons were an ingenious development that harnessed nearly constant winds off the North Sea to keep water at bay. First used in the 13th century, windmills pumped water up and over the dykes from land below sea level.

Amstel Gold Race

The biggest Dutch cycling race is the Amstel Gold Race around hilly Limburg. It's 260km in length and features dozens of steep hills. It is considered one of the most demanding races on the professional circuit.

5

SERGEY KOHL / SHUTTERSTOCK ©

7

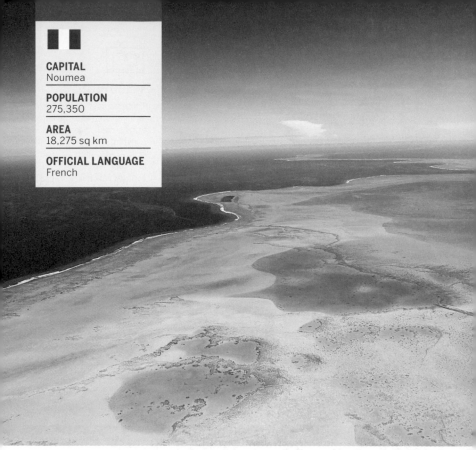

Grand Lagon Nord (north lagoon)

CAPITAL	Noumea
POPULATION	275,350
AREA	18,275 sq km
OFFICIAL LANGUAGE	French

New Caledonia

With its seductive World Heritage–listed lagoons, New Caledonia offers aquamarine hues and white sandy beaches.

It is the South Pacific with a French twist, especially around Noumea, with its warm hospitality, European elegance, gourmet food beneath palm trees, resorts and bungalows. Long gorgeous beaches are backed by cafes and bars, with horizons that display tiny islets. Head out to the Loyalty Islands to experience tribal accommodation and soak up the Kanak culture. Legendary Île des Pins is well worth exploring, and a road trip to the northern coasts of Grande Terre is highly recommended. Be lured into kayaks or microlights, rock climb, sail, dive into a world of corals, canyons, caves and shipwrecks, go whale watching or snorkelling, or relax on the warm sand of a deserted isle.

New Caledonia's dazzling lagoon surrounds it with every hue of blue, green and turquoise. By becoming a World Heritage site, the lagoon has helped bring the people together to celebrate and protect it, from village level through to government.

Top Experiences

La Piscine Naturelle

1 This pool of exquisite turquoise water on Île des Pins is protected from the sea by a narrow waterway. The snorkelling is unbelievable and if you just sit in knee-deep water on the fine white sand, tropical fish will approach you! Highly recommended.

The Far South

2 The far south is adventure central – here you'll find accommodation literally hanging from trees (yep, rock yourself to sleep in a suspended canvas cocoon). Go on a moonlit kayak trip through a forest of drowned kauri trees at the 80-sq-km Parc Provincial de la Rivière Bleue then head to the former convict settlement of Prony. It's one of the more unusual villages in New Caledonia: a mixture of rivers, crumbling stone ruins, historic houses and beach, all on a surprisingly miniature scale.

Ouvéa Lagoon

3 Think 25km of perfect white beach backed with grass, tropical flowers and thick forest inhabited by the protected Ouvéa green parrot. Look out over an exquisite turquoise lagoon that stretches as far as you can see. Add a chain of tiny islets, the Pléiades. Sound unreal? Ouvéa may leave you shaking your head in wonder. The Ouvéa lagoon was one of six marine areas in New Caledonia to be listed as a Unesco World Heritage Site. It's stunning, and there's plenty to do in it, on it and around it.

When to Go

 HIGH SEASON (Sep–Mar)

 SHOULDER (Apr–Aug)

 LOW SEASON (Dec–Mar)

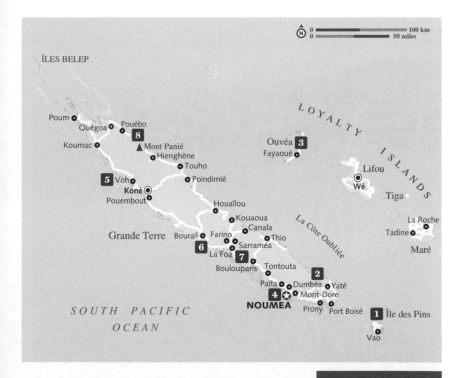

Le Marché, Noumea

4 This colourful multi-hexagonal-shaped market is beside the marina at Port Moselle in Noumea. Fishers unload their catch; trucks offload fruit, vegetables and flowers; and there's fresh-baked bread and cakes, plus delights like terrines and olives. The arts and crafts section includes a central cafe. On Saturday and Sunday live music keeps shoppers entertained. The market is at its busiest early in the morning.

The Heart of Voh

5 This mangove swamp north of Koné on Grande Terre has developed some unusual natural designs. The most intriguing is a perfect heart shape, La Cœur de Voh, which features on the cover of *Earth from Above*, a book of aerial photography by renowned photographer Yann Arthus-Bertrand. It's best seen from the air. Microlight flights also take in the magnificent lagoon, let you look right into a 'blue hole', and fly low enough for you to spot stingrays, turtles and sharks.

La Roche Percée

6 Only a 10-minute drive from Bourail township, La Roche Percée has two famous rock formations: La Roche Percée (pierced rock), a headland with a hole in it that you can walk through, and Le Bonhomme, a stand-up rock off the end of the headland that's shaped like a tubby man. The surf at Plage de la

Getting Around

Very efficient air service to northern Grande Terre, the Loyalty Islands and Île des Pins.

The Betico fast ferry links Noumea to the Loyalty Islands and Île des Pins.

Regular daily bus services on Grande Terre, limited on outer islands.

VINCENT TALBOT / GETTY IMAGES ©

Roche Percée is caused by a break in the fringing reef, so you don't have to go out to the reef to catch a wave. The beaches around here are also known as a nesting spot for sea turtles, and nests are carefully monitored and protected by locals.

Le Parc des Grandes Fougères

7 Lovely 4500-hectare Park of the Great Ferns, in the mountains near La Foa in central Grande Terre, features tropical rainforest with rich and varied flora and fauna. As the name suggests, tree ferns are in abundance, and most examples of New Caledonia's native bird life can be spotted. A number of well signposted hiking tracks range from 45 minutes to six hours, plus there are mountain-bike trails for enthusiasts.

Northeast Coast

8 North of Hienghène is the wildest and most stunning stretch of Grande Terre's coastline. It's covered in tropical vegetation, and waterfalls and streams rush down the mountains to join the sea. You'll discover the captivating three-car ferry across the Ouaïème River, roadside stalls selling fruit and carvings, lots of one-lane bridges, and dogs and chickens wandering out onto the road. The area around Balade is a fascinating historical hot spot. This is where Captain Cook landed and gave New Caledonia its name, and where the French took possession in 1853.

6

DANITA DELIMONT / GETTY IMAGES ©

Food & Drink

Bougna A mixture of yam, sweet potato, taro, vegetables and meat, fish or seafood covered in coconut milk and cooked together in tightly wrapped parcels made from banana leaves.

French dishes French restaurants abound in Noumea and cover a range of styles.

Staple foods Fish, coconut, banana, taro, sweet potato and yam.

Local meats Lobster, coconut crab, dugong and turtle are all traditional food sources. These days the number of turtles and dugongs that can be hunted for food is limited and their killing for commercial purposes is prohibited.

Drinks The preferred alcoholic drinks are *vin* (wine) and *bière* (beer), but you'll also find aperitifs, such as *pastis*, an aniseed-flavoured drink much loved in France.

The Nautilus

Unchanged for more than 100 million years, nautili are living fossils, the only survivors of a family that was common 450 million years ago and also included ammonites (whirled shells like a ram's horn). It's a mystery why most of this group suddenly disappeared 70 million years ago. There are six remaining species of nautili living in the southwest Pacific, one of which, *Nautilus macromphalus,* is found only in New Caledonia.

The nautilus is a mollusc; however, it is the only cephalopod to have an external shell. It moves by water expulsion through a siphon and can vary its buoyancy by changing the levels of gas and air in the individual chambers. It avoids light and warm water, and usually lives on the external slopes of the barrier reef at extraordinary depths of up to 500m.

Kaikoura

CAPITAL
Wellington

POPULATION
4.5 million

AREA
268,838 sq km

OFFICIAL LANGUAGES
English, Māori

New Zealand

As the planet heats up environmentally and politically, it's good to know that New Zealand exists. This green, peaceful and accepting country is the ultimate escape.

New Zealand is bigger than the UK with one-fourteenth the population. Filling in the gaps are the sublime forests, mountains, lakes, beaches and fiords that have made NZ one of the best hiking destinations on earth. Tackle one of nine epic 'Great Walks' or just spend a few hours wandering along a beach, paddling a canoe or mountain biking through some easily accessible wilderness.

See how Māori culture impresses itself on contemporary Kiwi life: across NZ you can hear Māori language, watch Māori TV, join in a *hangi* (Māori feast) or catch a performance with traditional Māori song, dance and usually a blood-curdling *haka* (war dance).

Top Experiences

Wellington

1 One of the coolest little capitals in the world, windy Wellington lives up to the hype by keeping things hip, diverse and rootsy. It's long famed for a vibrant arts-and-music scene, fuelled by excellent espresso and more restaurants per head than New York...but a host of craft-beer bars have now elbowed in on the action. Edgy yet sociable, colourful yet often dressed in black, Wellington is big on the unexpected and unconventional. Erratic weather only adds zest to the experience.

Urban Auckland

2 Held in the embrace of two harbours and built on the remnants of long-extinct volcanoes, Auckland isn't your average metropolis. It's regularly rated one of the world's most liveable cities, and while it's never going to challenge NYC or London in the excitement stakes, it's blessed with good beaches, is flanked by wine regions and has a large enough population to support a thriving dining, drinking and live-music scene. Cultural festivals are celebrated with gusto in this ethnically diverse city, which has the distinction of having the world's largest Pacific Islander population.

Bay of Islands

3 Turquoise waters lapping pretty bays, dolphins frolicking at the bows of boats, pods of orcas gliding gracefully by: chances are these are the kinds of images that drew you to NZ in the first place, and these are exactly the kinds of experiences that the Bay of Islands delivers so well. Whether you're a hardened sea dog or a confirmed landlubber, there are myriad options to tempt you out on the water to explore the 150-odd islands that dot this beautiful bay.

Milford Sound

4 Fingers crossed you'll be lucky enough to see Milford Sound on a clear, sunny day. That's definitely when the world-beating collage of waterfalls, verdant cliffs and peaks, and dark cobalt waters is at its best. More likely, though, is the classic Fiordland combination of mist and drizzle, with the iconic profile of Mitre Peak revealed slowly through shimmering sheets of precipitation. Either way, keep your eyes peeled for seals and dolphins, especially if you're exploring NZ's most famous fjord by kayak.

Best on Film

Lord of the Rings trilogy (Sir Peter Jackson; 2001–03) Hobbits, dragons and magical rings – Tolkien's vision comes to life.

The Hobbit trilogy (Sir Peter Jackson; 2012–14) Hairy feet on the move – more eye-popping Tolkienism.

The Piano (Jane Campion; 1993) A piano and its owners arrive on a mid-19th-century West Coast beach.

Whale Rider (Niki Caro; 2002) Magical tale of family and heritage on the East Coast.

Best in Print

The Luminaries (Eleanor Catton; 2013) Man Booker Prize winner: crime and intrigue on the West Coast goldfields.

Mister Pip (Lloyd Jones; 2007) Tumult on Bougainville, mirroring Dickens' *Great Expectations*.

Live Bodies (Maurice Gee; 1998) Post-WWII loss and redemption in New Zealand.

The 10pm Question (Kate de Goldi; 2009) Twelve-year-old Frankie grapples with life's big anxieties.

Waiheke Island & the Hauraki Gulf

 A yachty's paradise, the island-studded Hauraki Gulf is Auckland's aquatic playground, sheltering its harbour and east-coast bays and providing ample excuse for the City of Sails' pleasure fleet to breeze into action. Despite the busy maritime traffic, the gulf has its own resident pods of whales and dolphins. Rangitoto Island is an icon of the city, its near-perfect volcanic cone providing the backdrop for many a tourist snapshot. Yet it's Waiheke, with its beautiful beaches, acclaimed wineries and upmarket eateries, that is Auckland's most popular island escape.

Geothermal Rotorua

 The first thing you'll notice about Rotorua is the sulphur smell – this geothermal hotspot whiffs like old socks. But as the locals point out, volcanic by-products are what everyone is here to see: gushing geysers, bubbling mud, steaming cracks in the ground, boiling pools of mineral-rich water. Rotorua is unique, a fact exploited by some fairly commercial local businesses. But you don't have to spend a fortune – there are plenty of affordable (and free) volcanic encounters to be had in parks, Māori villages or just along the roadside.

Abel Tasman National Park

 Here's nature at its most seductive: lush green hills fringed with golden sandy coves, slipping gently into warm shallows before meeting a crystal-clear cerulean

Farmers Markets

There are more than 50 farmers markets held around NZ. Most happen on weekends and are upbeat local affairs, where visitors can meet local producers and find fresh regional produce. Check out www.farmersmarkets.org.nz.

The Hongi Greeting

Press forehead and nose together firmly, shake hands, and perhaps offer a greeting such as '*Kia ora*' or '*Tēnā koe*'. Some prefer one press (for two or three seconds, or longer), others prefer two shorter ones (press, release, press).

Tapu

Tapu (spiritual restrictions) and *mana* (power and prestige) are taken seriously in the Māori world. Sit on chairs or seating provided (never on tables), and walk around people, not over them. The *powhiri* (Māori welcoming ceremony) is *tapu*, and mixing food and *tapu* is right up there on the offence-o-meter. Do eat and drink when invited to do so by your hosts. You needn't worry about starvation: an important Māori value is *manaakitanga* (kindness).

Depending on the area, the *powhiri* has gender roles: women *karanga* (call), men *whaikōrero* (orate); women lead the way on to the *marae* (meeting grounds), men sit on the *paepae* (the speakers' bench at the front). In a modern context, the debate around these roles continues.

sea. Abel Tasman National Park is the quintessential postcard paradise, where you can put yourself in the picture assuming an endless number of poses: tramping, kayaking, swimming, sunbathing, or even makin' whoopee in the woods. This sweet-as corner of NZ raises the bar and keeps it there.

Kaikoura

8 First settled by Māori with their taste for seafood, Kaikoura (meaning 'to eat crayfish') is now NZ's best spot for both consuming and communing with marine life. Crayfish is still king, but on fishing tours you can hook into other edible wonders of the deep. Whales, dolphins and seals are definitely off the menu – but it's big business here to take a boat tour or flight to see them. Such tours attract controversy around the globe, but NZ's operators adhere to strict guidelines developed and monitored by the country's Department of Conservation.

The West Coast

9 Hemmed in by the wild Tasman Sea and the Southern Alps, the West Coast is like nowhere else in New Zealand. The far extremities of the coast have a remote, end-of-the-road vibe, from sleepy Karamea butting up against Kahurangi National Park, to the southern end of SH6, gateway to New Zealand's World Heritage areas. In between is an alluring combination of wild coastline, rich wilderness, 'must see' sights like Punakaiki Rocks and Franz Josef and Fox Glaciers, and history in spades.

Central Otago

10 Here's your chance to balance virtue and vice. Take to two wheels to negotiate the easygoing Otago Central Rail Trail, cycling through some of NZ's most starkly beautiful landscapes and the heritage streetscapes of former gold-mining towns. All the while, snack on the summer stone-fruits for which the region is famous. Balance the ledger with well-earned beers at one of the numerous historic pubs. Alternatively, taste your way to viticultural ecstasy in the vineyards of one of the country's most acclaimed wine regions.

Waitomo Caves

 Waitomo is a must-see: an astonishing maze of subterranean caves, canyons and rivers perforating the northern King Country limestone. Black-water rafting is the big lure here (like white-water rafting but through a dark cave), plus glowworm grottoes, underground abseiling and more stalactites and stalagmites than you'll ever see in one place again. Above ground, Waitomo township is a quaint collaboration of businesses: a craft brewery, a cafe, a holiday park and some decent B&Bs. But don't linger in the sunlight – it's party time downstairs!

Queenstown

NICRAM SABOD / SHUTTERSTOCK ©

Queenstown may be world-renowned as the birthplace of bungy jumping, but there's more to NZ's adventure hub than leaping off a bridge attached to a giant rubber band. Against the utterly scenic backdrop of the jagged indigo profile of the Remarkables mountain range, travellers can spend days skiing, hiking or mountain biking, before dining in cosmopolitan restaurants or partying in some of NZ's best bars. Next-day options include hang gliding, kayaking or river rafting, or easing into your NZ holiday with sleepier detours to Arrowtown or Glenorchy.

Getting Around

 Fast-track your holiday with affordable, frequent, fast internal flights.

 Reliable, frequent bus services around the country (usually cheaper than flying).

Travel at your own tempo, explore remote areas and visit regions with no public transport. Hire cars in major towns. Drive on the left.

 Reliable, regular train services (if not fast or cheap) along specific routes on both the North and South islands.

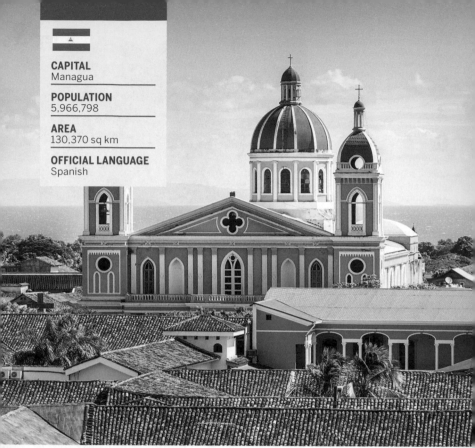

CAPITAL
Managua

POPULATION
5,966,798

AREA
130,370 sq km

OFFICIAL LANGUAGE
Spanish

Catedral de Granada

Nicaragua

Affable Nicaragua embraces travelers with offerings of volcanic landscapes, colonial architecture, sensational beaches and pristine forests that range from breathtaking to downright incredible.

Looking for the ultimate rush? Nicaragua's diverse geography, intense energy and anything-goes attitude is perfect for exhilarating outdoor adventures. Get ready to check a whole gamut of new experiences off your list including surfing down an active volcano, diving into underwater caves, canoeing through alligator-infested wetlands, swimming across sea channels between tiny white-sand islands and landing a 90-plus-kg tarpon beneath a Spanish fortress in the middle of the jungle. And whether it's dipping your toes into the crystalline Caribbean or paddling out to the crashing waves of the pounding Pacific, Nicaragua's beaches always deliver the goods.

Nicaragua's great outdoors are relatively untamed, making this so-called 'land of lakes and volcanoes' a fantastic place for an independent adventure. And no matter how far you go, you'll always find friendly locals willing to share their culture with strangers.

Top Experiences

Granada

1 Granada is a town of immense and palpable magnetism. At the heart of the city's charms are the picture-perfect cobblestone streets, polychromatic colonial homes and churches, and a lilting air that brings the city's spirited past into present-day focus. Most trips here begin and end on foot, and simply dawdling from gallery to restaurant to colonial church can take up the better part of a day. From there, it's off to explore the myriad wild areas, islands, volcanoes and artisan villages nearby.

Little Corn Island

2 With no cars and no noise, just white-sand beaches and secluded coves mixing with the crystal-clear Caribbean, Little Corn Island is the paramount place to take a break from the big city. There is plenty to keep you occupied during the day, including diving with hammerhead sharks or through underground caves, kitesurfing the stiff breeze or scrambling over jungle-covered headlands, and there's just enough to do at night. Add some great food to the mix and it's no surprise that many find it so hard to leave.

Isla de Ometepe

3 Lago de Nicaragua's beloved centerpiece, Isla de Ometepe has it all. Twin volcanoes, lush hillsides cut by walking tracks, archaeological remains, zip lines, monkeys and birdlife, waterfalls, lapping waves at your doorstep, and a laid-back island air that keeps travelers in the now as they kayak, bike and climb their way along. At the heart of the island's charms are the cool hostels, camping areas and peaced-out traveler scenes. Custom-fit your experience from high-end luxury lodges to groovy-groupie hippie huts – Ometepe is big enough for all kinds.

2

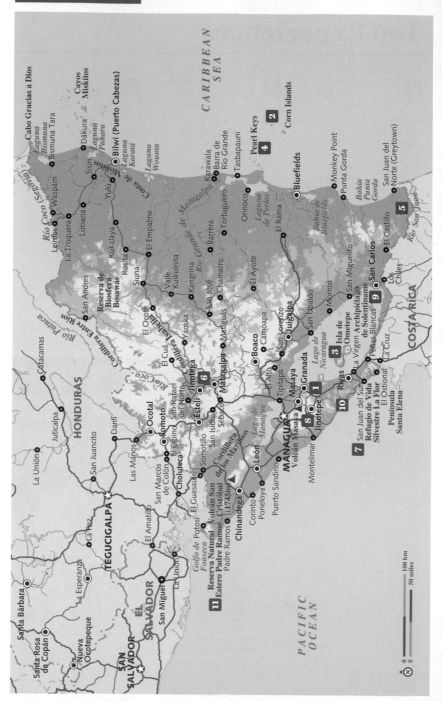

Best for Wildlife

Refugio de Vida Silvestre La Flor Watching thousands of turtles laying their eggs on this beach is one of Latin America's superlative nature experiences.

Refugio Bartola Don rubber boots and head out into the jungle to spot three kinds of monkeys, fluorescent frogs and maybe even a tapir.

Volcán Mombacho Accessible cloud forest with great hiking and birdwatching.

Refugio de Vida Silvestre Los Guatuzos Wetlands with fantastic birdwatching during the day and action-packed crocodile spotting at night.

Islas Solentiname Bring binoculars to spot some of the thousands of migratory birds nesting in this remote archipelago.

Reserva Natural Macizos de Peñas Blancas Clinging to magnificent mountain peaks, this jungle is home to pumas, jaguars and ocelots.

Best in Print

Blood of Brothers (Stephen Kinzer; 1991) Fascinating account of revolution and war.

The Country Beneath My Skin (Gioconda Belli; 2002) Autobiography by revolutionary poet.

Selected Poems of Rubén Darío (translated by Lysander Kemp; 2001) Bilingual anthology of the master poet's best.

The Jaguar Smile (Salman Rushdie; 1987) Accessible insider's look at the Sandinistas during the revolution.

Tycoon's War (Stephen Dando-Collins; 2008) Documents the epic battle between imperialists Vanderbilt and Walker.

Pearl Keys

4 As you approach the dozen tiny islands ringed by snow-white sand and brilliant Caribbean waters that make up the Pearl Keys, you will enter the realms of the ultimate shipwreck fantasy. Fortunately, you'll be marooned with a capable Creole guide who will cook a spectacular seafood meal and source ice-cold beers from a mysterious supply, leaving you more time to swim, snorkel, spot sea turtles, or just lie back in your hammock and take in the idyllic panoramic views.

Río San Juan

5 Once favored by pirates and prospectors as a path to riches, today the Río San Juan is exalted by nature lovers. All along the river, scores of birds nest on branches overhanging its slow surging waters while its lower reaches are dominated by the Reserva Biológica Indio-Maíz, an impenetrable jungle that shelters jaguars and troupes of noisy monkeys. The only human-made attraction along the river's entire length is the grand Spanish fort over the rapids at El Castillo.

When to Go

HIGH SEASON
(Dec–Apr)
Hot, sunny and dry conditions.

SHOULDER
(Nov)
Cool weather and green countryside make for the best trekking.

LOW SEASON
(May–Oct)
The biggest swell on the Pacific side pulls a crowd to the best breaks.

The Writing (Painting) on the Wall

Nothing quite captures Nicaraguans' spirit, creativity and political sentiment like their love for murals. Often strikingly beautiful pieces of art, murals served a practical and political end in the days before the Sandinistas' Literacy Crusade by broadcasting a message to a largely illiterate audience. There are murals in all major cities, but Sandinista strongholds León and Estelí are standouts. The area around the UCA university in Managua has some fine examples, too.

However, some of the best examples have been painted over, often with propaganda from multinational cell-phone networks. Estelí has an NGO teaching mural painting to children and teenagers, and is also home to a new movement of *muralistas*, who use more recognizable graffiti techniques to paint images with a social slant. For a look at murals from around the country, check out the gorgeous *The Murals of Revolutionary Nicaragua* by David Kunzle.

Getting Around

 Domestic flights are moderately priced and the fastest way to get you where you're going; however, they only serve more far-off destinations.

 Nicaragua's old-school buses are slow and uncomfortable but will get you anywhere you want to go for next to nothing. There are more comfortable, but far from luxurious, coach services to some long-distance destinations.

 Renting a car enables travel at your own pace and access to off-the-beaten-track destinations. There is not much traffic on the roads and driving in Nicaragua is fairly stress-free (once you learn how to handle the traffic cops).

Coffee Country

6 A visit to Nicaragua's coffee zone is about more than just sipping plenty of joe; it's about getting out and seeing where it all comes from. Hike among the bushes shaded by ethereal cloud forest around Jinotega and pick ripe cherries alongside your hosts in a community farming cooperative near Matagalpa. And why stop there when you can follow the beans to the roasting plant and then learn to identify flavors in a cupping session. After this, you'll savor your morning cup in a whole new way.

Surfing Near San Juan del Sur

7 Nicaragua sparked into international stardom on the wake of tanned-and-toned surfer dudes and dudettes. And the surfing scene north and south of regional hub San Juan del Sur remains cool, reefed-out, soulful and downright brilliant. The stars of the scene are the long rideable waves that fit the bill for surfers of all abilities, but the relaxed surf camps, beach parties and cool breezes add to the vibe, ensuring a great beach vacation for everybody in your crew (even the boogie boarders).

Refugio de Vida Silvestre La Flor

8 Head to Nicaragua's southern Pacific coast between July and January to witness sea turtles by the thousands come to shore to lay their eggs at Refugio de Vida Silvestre La Flor. There's a decent beach here, as well, but the highlight is a night tour (generally from nearby San Juan del Sur), on which, if you're lucky, you'll see a leatherback or olive ridley mama come to shore to lay her eggs at the end of one of nature's most inspiring and remarkable journeys.

Islas Solentiname

9 The Islas Solentiname are straight out of a fairy tale. You simply must visit in order to experience the magic of this remote jungle-covered archipelago where a community of exceptionally talented artists lives and works among the wild animals that are their inspiration. It's a place where an enlightened priest inspired a village to construct a handsome church alive with the sounds of nature, and shooting stars illuminate the speckled night sky. Even having been there, you still find it hard to believe it's real.

The Remote Beaches of Popoyo

10 It's a bumpy ride from Rivas to the remote beaches of Popoyo, famous for their surf breaks. The reward: huge, rolling waves, laid-back surf lodges, sandy shores strewn with vibrant pink shells, looming rock formations and miles of empty shoreline where you can walk for an hour without seeing another person. New surf lodges and guesthouses are opening left and right in this rapidly developing region, but for the moment, these beaches still feel wild. Bring your board, or a good book.

Reserva Natural Estero Padre Ramos

11 The Reserva Natural Estero Padre Ramos is a vast nature reserve located in the far northwestern corner of Nicaragua. The largest remaining mangrove forest in Central America, the reserve is home to ocelots, alligators and a universe's worth of birds that call the forest home. While this is a wild corner of Nicaragua, basic tourist services will get you into the spider-webbing mangrove forest, to the beaches where sea turtles lay their eggs and good surf dominates, and into local communities.

Language

Take some Spanish classes at the start of your trip. Nicaraguans are outgoing and friendly but few have foreign-language skills.

Window Seat

Always go for a window seat in public transport – the landscapes are absolutely breathtaking.

PAUL KENNEDY / GETTY IMAGES ©

10

MORGAN ARNOLD / GETTY IMAGES ©

6

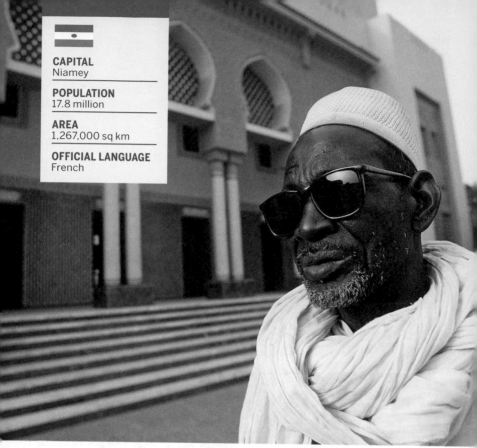

Grand Mosque, Niamey

CAPITAL
Niamey

POPULATION
17.8 million

AREA
1,267,000 sq km

OFFICIAL LANGUAGE
French

Niger

Dominated by two of Africa's most iconic natural features, the Niger River in the southwest and the Sahara in the north, landlocked Niger shares borders with seven countries. At this time, Niger is considered unsafe to visit.

Niger rarely makes waves in the international consciousness, and when it does it's invariably for all the wrong reasons: coups, rebellions and famines. But those who visited this desert republic in the past normally returned with stories of a warm and generous population living in ancient caravan cities at the edge of the Sahara.

In the north, the stark splendour of the Aïr Mountains hides neolithic rock art and stunning oasis towns. Within the expansive dunes of the Ténéré Desert are dinosaur graveyards and deserted medieval settlements, while to the south is the ancient trans-Saharan trade-route town of Agadez and the sultanate of Zinder.

Snapshot

Agadez

1 A spiky summit of a majestic mud mosque overlooking town and the Sahara, Agadez has fallen on decidedly hard times since the Tuareg rebellion reignited. Yet, while the airport no longer sees scheduled flights and many restaurants and hotels are closed due to lack of travellers, the city bustles with local life.

Kouré

2 Kouré is home to West Africa's last remaining giraffe herd, which quietly munches acacia trees and patrols the baking soils around the dusty town.

Ayorou

3 On the River Niger's banks just 24km south of the Malian frontier, this otherwise sleepy town is renowned for its Sunday market. In the livestock section camels, cattle, mules, sheep and goats run riot, under the gaze of their nomadic owners.

Zinder Artisans

4 The work of Zinder's *artisans du cuir* (leatherworkers) is well regarded, and traditional items – such as saddlebags, cushions and tasselled pouches – sit alongside attractive modernities like sandals and briefcases.

Seasons

☀ OCT–JUN

☂ JUL–SEP

Food & Drink

Bière Niger National beer.

Brochettes Kebabs, usually chicken, and beef.

Grilled fish A standard restaurant dish, particularly capitaine, or Nile perch.

Riz sauce Rice with sauce.

Tuareg Thirst-quenching tea.

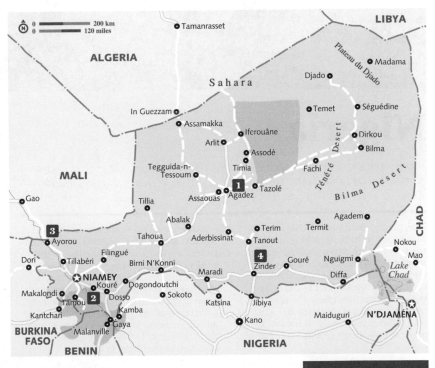

CAPITAL
Abuja

POPULATION
186,053,386

AREA
923,768 sq km

OFFICIAL LANGUAGE
English

Nigeria

Nigeria may well be West Africa's most exciting country, but with the sensory overload of its largest city, Lagos, and reputation as a difficult destination, it's often overlooked by travellers.

Nigeria is a pulsating powerhouse: as the most populous nation on the continent – nearly every fifth African is Nigerian – it dominates the region. Recently, though, the boom has shown a few signs of bust: the economy has been hit by the drop in crude oil prices. But Lagos, the main city, is resurgent: with burgeoning tech industries, posh restaurants and clubs, and an exploding arts scene, this megacity is the face of modern Africa.

Outside Gidi (as Lagosians call their city), you may feel as if you're a lone explorer getting a glimpse of the raw edges of the world, immersing yourself in deep and layered cultures. From Yoruba shrines to the slave ports, from the ancient Muslim cities of the north (currently out of bounds for security reasons) to the river deltas, and among stunning natural environments, there are plenty of wonderful antidotes to a sometimes exhausting journey.

Top Experiences

Lagos

1 Join the gold rush of Nigeria's superconfident boom city. The economic and cultural powerhouse of the country thanks to an influx of oil money, Lagos has an exploding arts and music scene that will keep you engaged far past dawn. If you're headed to Nigeria, you'll have no choice but to jump right in.

Abeokuta

2 Abeokuta is a remarkable place, backed by the huge Olumo Rock. Climb the sacred rock via historic hideouts and shrines, and look out on the picturesque rooftops from a high vantage point. Grand but dishevelled Brazilian and Cuban mansions built by returned slaves sit alongside basic shacks with hand-painted signs, historic mosques and churches, and the rounded mass of the rocks, creating an unforgettable streetscape.

Oshogbo

3 This very special city has been a traditional centre for Yoruba spirituality and, since the 1950s, the birthplace for much contemporary Nigerian art. The best sight is the Osun Sacred Grove, believed to be the dwelling of Osun, the Yoruba fertility goddess. Learn about traditional crafts, browse the impressive galleries and lose yourself on the river bank in the sacred grove.

Benin

4 Starting in the 15th century, Benin City gave rise to one of the first African art forms to be accepted internationally – the

AMYO O ASUNKANMI / SHUTTERSTOCK ©

When to Go

 HIGH SEASON
(Oct–Jan)

 SHOULDER
(Feb-May, Sep)

 LOW SEASON
(Jun–Aug)

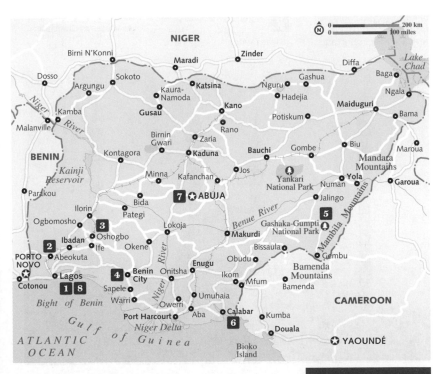

Benin brasses (often given the misnomer bronzes). Today the city is the centre of Nigeria's rubber trade, and a sprawling metropolis. Wander the Brass Casters St, governed by a secret ancient guild, and catch a flavour of the former glory of the marvellous Benin empire.

Gashaka-Gumti National Park

5 Head into the real wilds to explore Gashaka-Gumti National Park, a newly reorganised mountain-meets-savannah place. Nigeria's largest national park is also the most remote and least-explored part of the country. Its 6700-sq-km area contains rolling hills, savannah and montane forest – as wild and spectacular a corner of Africa as you could wish for. It is also one of West Africa's most important primate habitats, and also supports lions, elephants, hippos and buffaloes. The park is open year-round, although access is easiest during the dry season (December to March).

Calabar

6 Tucked into Nigeria's southeastern corner, the capital of Cross River state has a rich history and is well worth a trip. Originally a cluster of Efik settlements, Calabar was once one of Africa's biggest slave ports, and later a major exporter of palm oil. A popular stopover for travellers heading to Cameroon, this tourist-friendly city has a fantastic museum and an excellent primate-conservation centre.

Abuja

7 Nigeria's made-to-measure capital, Abuja was founded during the

Getting Around

Internal flights are a quick way of getting around.

Nigeria's road system is good, but the smooth, sealed roads allow Nigerians to exercise their latent talents as rally drivers and accident rates are high. The only real road rule is survival of the fittest.

Each town has at least one motor park serving as the main transport depot full of minibuses and bush taxis.

boom years of the 1970s. After the divisive Biafran war, the decision was made to move the capital from Lagos to the ethnically neutral centre of the country. Clean, quiet and with a good electricity supply, sometimes Abuja hardly feels like Nigeria at all. It's a good place to catch your breath and do some visa shopping.

Lekki Conservation Centre

8 Run by the Nigerian Conservation Foundation, this centre has a huge tract of wetlands set aside for wildlife viewing. Canopy walkways enable you to see monkeys, crocodiles and various birds; early morning is the best time to visit. There is a conservation centre and a library.

Food & Drink

Nigerians like their food ('chop') hot and starchy. The classic dish is a fiery pepper stew ('soup') with a little meat or fish and starch – usually pounded yam or cassava (*garri*, *eba*, or slightly sour *fufu*). Another popular dish is *jollof* – peppery rice cooked with palm oil and tomato. Cutlery isn't generally used – yam or cassava soaks up the juices of the stew. Eat only with your right hand.

MILA SUPINSKAYA GLASHCHENKO / SHUTTERSTOCK ©

African Beat

In this most musical of countries there's nothing like catching some live music. Here are our favourites.

Bogobiri II Afrobeat, reggae, hip hop – you'll find all sorts of sounds at this Lagos bar. If you're feeling brave take a turn at the awesome open-mike night.

New Afrika Shrine Feel the power of Fela at this Lagos club, where sons Femi and Seun Kuti keep the flame alive.

Jazz Hole This fabulously arty bookshop and record store in Lagos also hosts live music.

Freedom Park An open-air Lagos venue for music festivals and one-off gigs.

Hexagon Great live music with young bands cutting it up in Benin.

CAPITAL
Pyongyang

POPULATION
24.9 million

AREA
120,540 sq km

OFFICIAL LANGUAGE
Korean

Arirang Mass Games, Pyongyang

North Korea

Most people form their opinions of North Korea from news reports and James Bond movies, but there's more to the Democratic People's Republic than military parades and stand-offs with the UN.

Now on its third hereditary ruler, this nominally communist state has defied all expectations and survived a quarter of a century since the collapse of the Soviet empire. This is your chance to visit the world's most isolated nation, where the internet and much of the 21st century remain unknown, and millions live their lives under the rule of an all-encompassing personality cult that affects all aspects of daily life.

Few people even realise that it's possible to visit North Korea, and indeed the compromises required to do so are significant. You'll be accompanied by two state-employed guides at all times and hear a one-sided account of history. Those who can't accept this might be better off staying away – but those who can will be able to undertake a fascinating journey into another, unsettling world.

Top Experiences

Pyongyang

1 Pyongyang's sights divide neatly into two categories: the proliferation of statues, monuments and museums glorifying the Kims; and the far more interesting slices of daily North Korean life to be found in excursions to funfairs, cinemas, parks and on public transport. You can guess which your guides will prefer to show you, and which most tour groups will enjoy more.

Paekdusan

2 One of the most stunning sights on the Korean Peninsula, Paekdusan (Mt Paekdu) straddles the Chinese–Korean border in the far northeastern tip of the DPRK. Apart from it being the highest mountain in the country at 2744m, and an amazing geological phenomenon, it is made all the more magical by its huge mythical importance to the Korean people.

Panmunjom DMZ

3 Feel the full force of Cold War tensions during a visit to Panmunjom in the Demilitarized Zone (DMZ), where an uneasy armistice holds. Seeing the situation from the North, facing off against US troops to the south is a unique chance to witness things from a new perspective.

When to Go

 HIGH SEASON (May, Oct)

 SHOULDER (Jun–Sep)

 LOW SEASON (Nov–Apr)

Food & Drink

While tour groups eat sumptuously by North Korean standards, the standard fare is usually a fairly mediocre diet of kimchi, rice, soups, noodles and fried meat. Vegetarian meals will usually be bland and heavy on rice, egg and cucumber. *Soju* (the local firewater) is also popular; it's rather strong stuff.

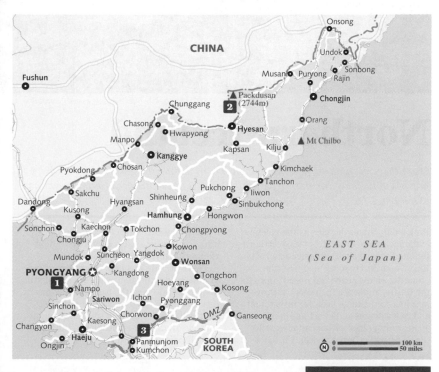

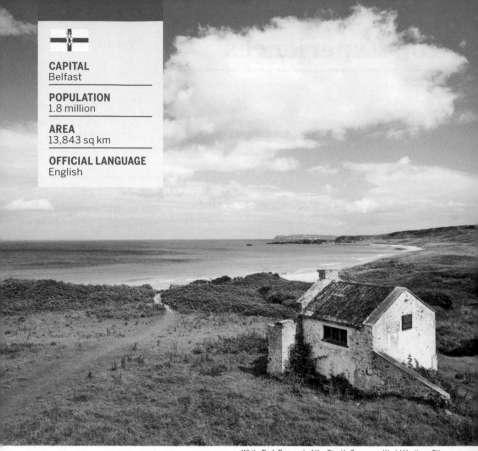

CAPITAL
Belfast

POPULATION
1.8 million

AREA
13,843 sq km

OFFICIAL LANGUAGE
English

White Park Bay, part of the Giant's Causeway World Heritage Site

Northern Ireland

From the breathtaking geological wonders of the north coast to the gritty murals of Belfast, Northern Ireland is full of a dramatic beauty that beckons to the traveller.

Dragged down for decades by the violence and uncertainty of the Troubles, Northern Ireland today is a nation rejuvenated. The 1998 Good Friday Agreement laid the groundwork for peace and raised hopes for the future, and since then this UK province has seen a huge influx of investment and redevelopment. Belfast has become a happening place with a famously wild nightlife, while Derry has come into its own as a cool, artistic city, and the stunning Causeway Coast gets more and more visitors each year.

There are still plenty of reminders of the Troubles – notably the 'peace lines' that still divide Belfast – and the passions that have torn Northern Ireland apart over the decades still run deep. But despite occasional setbacks there is an atmosphere of determined optimism.

Top Experiences

The Wild Coast

1 Northern Ireland's north coast is a scenic extravaganza of sea stacks, pinnacles, cliffs and caves. This mystical landscape's rock formations, ruined castles and wooded glens have made the region an atmospheric backdrop for the TV series *Game of Thrones*, with numerous filming locations here.

Belfast

2 Belfast is in many ways a new city; in recent years it has pulled off a remarkable transformation from bombs-and-bullets pariah to a hip-hotels-and-hedonism party town. The list of attractions includes beautifully restored Victorian architecture, a glittering waterfront lined with modern art, a fantastic foodie scene and music-filled pubs.

Lush Counties

3 County Down's treasures fan out beyond Belfast. Strangford Lough's sparkling waters stretch south, the Mourne Mountains' velvet curves sweep down to the sea near Downpatrick and Lecale, the old stamping grounds of Ireland's patron saint. The lush landscapes and scalloped bays provide a bounty of seasonal ingredients.

When to Go

 HIGH SEASON (Jun–mid-Sep)

 SHOULDER SEASON (Easter–May, mid-Sep–Oct)

 LOW SEASON (Nov–Feb)

Food & Drink

Soda bread, the most famous Irish bread, is made with bicarbonate of soda, to make up for soft Irish flour that traditionally didn't take well to yeast. Combined with buttermilk, it makes a superbly tasty bread, and is often on the breakfast menus at B&Bs.

CAPITAL
Saipan

POPULATION
53,500

AREA
464 sq km

OFFICIAL LANGUAGES
Chamorro, English

Waters off Saipan Island

Northern Mariana Islands

The Northern Marianas can seem like a package-tour nightmare. But show a little curiosity and you'll be rewarded with turquoise waters, white sands, and fine diving and snorkeling.

The Commonwealth of the Northern Mariana Islands (CNMI), located in the northwestern Pacific Ocean, is undergoing massive change as its fiscally challenged capital Saipan painfully comes to terms with the loss of its lucrative Japanese tour market. But travel trends come and go; the charm of the islands endures.

Floating in American accents and convenience stores, the Northern Marianas capital of Saipan is a package-tour favourite. Get beyond the main island and you'll find a less-cluttered version of paradise where turquoise waters and white beaches are livened up by an upsurging Chamorro culture.

Top Experiences

Mañagaha Island

1 Mañagaha is an old patch reef that geological forces lifted above sea level 10,000 years ago. It's now covered with a fringing white-sand beach and has Saipan's best snorkelling. The clear surrounding waters have lots of colorful tropical fish and abundant coral, although much of the near-shore coral shows signs of being trampled on.

The Grotto

2 Among dive heads, Saipan is famous for this unique diving spot, a collapsed limestone cavern with a pool of cobalt-blue seawater filled by three underwater passageways. Sometimes the Grotto is calm and at other times powerful surges of water come whooshing in and out. Once, locals who wanted to swim in the Grotto had to shimmy down a rope, but there are now steep concrete stairs down to the water.

Obyan Beach

3 Obyan Beach is a pretty white-sand beach with calm waters protected by Naftan Point. The expansive beach is good for snorkelling. At the head of the parking area is a large WWII concrete bunker and just inland from a grove of coconut trees are the remains of eight latte stones dating back to 1500 BC.

Food & Drink

The indigenous Chamorro food is a rich mix of Spanish, Filipino and Pacific dishes. The best Chamorro food is generally found at village fiestas.

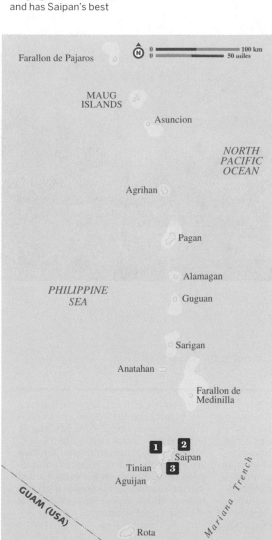

Farallon de Pajaros

0 — 100 km
0 — 50 miles

MAUG ISLANDS

Asuncion

NORTH PACIFIC OCEAN

Agrihan

Pagan

Alamagan

PHILIPPINE SEA

Guguan

Sarigan

Anatahan

Farallon de Medinilla

1 **2** Saipan

Tinian **3**

Aguijan

Mariana Trench

GUAM (USA)

Rota

When to Go

 HIGH SEASON (Dec–Mar)

 SHOULDER (Apr–Sep)

 LOW SEASON (Oct & Nov)

CAPITAL
Oslo

POPULATION
5.2 million

AREA
386,224 sq km

OFFICIAL LANGUAGE
Norwegian

Geirangerfjord

Norway

Norway is a once-in-a-lifetime destination and the essence of its appeal is remarkably simple: this is one of the most beautiful countries on earth.

The drama of Norway's natural world is difficult to overstate. The fjords' fame is wholly merited, but this is also a land of glaciers, grand and glorious, snaking down from icefields that rank among Europe's largest. Elsewhere, the mountainous terrain of Norway's interior resembles the ramparts of so many natural fortresses, and yields to rocky coastal islands that rise improbably from the waters like apparitions. And then, of course, there's the primeval appeal of the Arctic.

In Norway, nature is very much an active pursuit, and Norwegians' passion for exploring their natural world has created one of Europe's most exciting and varied adventure-tourism destinations. Whether you're here in summer when the possibilities seem endless, or in winter for the soul-stirring spectacle of the northern lights, these activities are an exhilarating means of getting close to nature.

Top Experiences

Geirangerfjord

1 The 20km chug along Geirangerfjord, a Unesco World Heritage Site, must rank as the world's loveliest ferry journey. Long-abandoned farmsteads still cling to the fjord's near-sheer cliffs while ice-cold cascades tumble, twist and gush down to emerald-green waters. Take the ferry from Geiranger and enjoy the calm as you leave this small, heaving port or hop aboard at altogether quieter Hellesylt. Prime your camera, grab a top-deck open-air seat and enjoy what's literally the only way to travel Geirangerfjord's secluded reaches.

Lofoten Islands

2 Few visitors forget their first sighting of the Lofoten Islands. The jagged ramparts of this astonishing island chain rise abruptly from the sea in summer greens and yellows or the stark blue and white of winter, their razor-sharp peaks stabbing at a clear, cobalt sky or shrouded mysteriously in swirling mists. Postcard-perfect villages cling to the shoreline while the A-frame racks for drying fish tell of a land and a culture intimately entwined with the sea.

Hurtigruten Coastal Ferry

3 So much more than merely a means of getting around, the iconic Hurtigruten coastal ferry takes you on one of the most spectacular coastal journeys anywhere on earth. On its daily path between Bergen and Kirkenes, it dips into coastal fjords, docks at isolated villages barely accessible by road, draws near to dramatic headlands and crosses the Arctic Circle only to return a few days later. In the process, it showcases the entire length of Norway's most glorious coast.

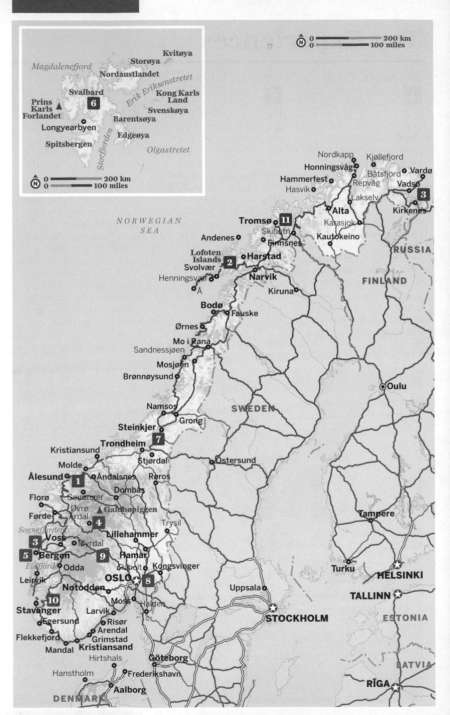

Best in Print

The Almost Nearly Perfect People (Michael Booth; 2014) Entertaining look at modern Scandinavia with Norway at centre stage.

Island Summers: Memories of a Norwegian Childhood (Tilly Culme-Seymour; 2013) Love letter to the Norwegian coast.

The Ice Museum (Joanna Kavenna; 2006) Vividly captures our fascination with the Arctic North.

Fellowship of Ghosts (Paul Watkins; 2004) Solo foot journeys through Norway's high country.

Rowing to Latitude (Jill Fredston; 2002) A journey by rowboat along Norway's coast.

Food & Drink

Reindeer Roast reindeer *(reinsdyrstek)* is something every nonvegetarian visitor should try at least once.

Elk Comes in a variety of forms, including as a steak or burger.

Salmon Don't miss it, grilled *(laks)* or smoked *(røykelaks)*.

Other seafood Common fish include cod *(torsk* or *bacalao*; often dried), boiled or fresh shrimp, herring and Arctic char.

Meatballs Traditional Norwegian meatballs served with mushy peas, mashed potatoes and wild-berry jam is a local, home-cooked favourite.

Wild berries Includes strawberries, blackcurrants, red currants, raspberries, blueberries and the lovely *moltebær* (cloudberries).

Coffee If Norway has a national drink, it's coffee. Most Norwegians drink it black and strong.

Hiking the Jotunheimen

4 The high country of central Norway ranks among Europe's premier summer destinations. Although there are numerous national parks crisscrossed by well-maintained hiking trails, it's Jotunheimen National Park, whose name translates as 'Home of the Giants', that rises above all others. With 60 glaciers and 275 summits over 2000m, Jotunheimen is exceptionally beautiful and home to iconic trails such as Besseggen, Hurrungane and those in the shadow of Galdhøpiggen, Norway's highest peak. Jotunheimen's proximity to the fjords further enhances its appeal.

Bryggen, Bergen

5 Set amid a picturesque and very Norwegian coastal landscape of fjords and mountains, Bergen is one of Europe's most beautiful cities. A celebrated history of seafaring trade has bequeathed to the city the stunning (and Unesco World Heritage–listed) waterfront district of Bryggen, an archaic tangle of wooden buildings. A signpost to a history at once prosperous and tumultuous, the titled and colourful wooden buildings of Bryggen now shelter

When to Go

HIGH SEASON
(mid-Jun–mid-Aug)
Accommodation and transport often booked out in advance.

SHOULDER
(May–mid-Jun & mid-Aug–Sep)
Generally mild, clear weather and fewer crowds.

LOW SEASON
(Oct–Apr)
Can be bitterly cold; many attractions are closed.

Food in a Tube

A Parisian orders a *cafe au lait*, a Londoner kippers. In New York it might be a bagel, in Tokyo rice. Comfort food or culture shock, they're all breakfast, and for Norwegians it comes in a tube.

Cream cheese and *kaviar* (sugar-cured and smoked cod-roe cream) packaged in tubes have been Norwegian favourites for decades. There are two especially popular Norwegian brands: the Trondheim-based Mills, best known for its *kaviar*, and the older Kavli in Bergen. Going strong since 1893 (its first tube food appeared in the 1920s), Kavli now produces bacon, ham, salami, shrimp, tomato, mexicana and jalapeño flavoured cheeses, all packaged in the familiar tubes.

Though both spreads are good alone and are part of a well-rounded Norwegian *frokost* (breakfast), *kaviar* is especially popular coupled with Norvegia cheese or a few slices of boiled egg.

Getting Around

 SAS and Norwegian have an extensive, well-priced domestic network, while Widerøe hops from one small town to the next.

 Ferries, many of which will take cars, connect offshore islands to the mainland.

 Buses go everywhere that trains don't, and services along major routes are fast and efficient.

 Roads are in good condition, but travel times can be slow thanks to winding roads and heavy summer traffic.

 The rail network reaches as far north as Bodø, with an additional branch line connecting Narvik with Sweden further north. Book in advance for considerably cheaper *minipris* tickets.

the artisan boutiques and traditional restaurants for which the city is increasingly famous.

Svalbard

6 The subpolar archipelago of Svalbard is a true place of the heart. Deliciously remote and yet surprisingly accessible, Svalbard is Europe's most evocative slice of the polar north and one of the continent's last great wilderness areas. Shapely peaks, massive icefields (60% of Svalbard is covered by glaciers) and heartbreakingly beautiful fjords provide the backdrop for a rich array of Arctic wildlife (including around one-sixth of the world's polar bears), and for summer and winter activities that get you out amid the ringing silence of the snows.

Kystriksveien Coastal Route

7 The lightly trafficked coastal route through Nordland is an experience of rare and staggering beauty. You may not have time for the full 650km but a sample (preferably from Sandnessjøen to Storvik) is all but mandatory if you're progressing northwards. It's not one to be rushed. The frequent ferry hops offer compulsory, built-in breaks and stunning seascapes, while both inland glaciers and accessible offshore islands – such as Vega, famous for its eider ducks, or Lovund, home to 200,000 puffins – are seductive diversions.

Sami Culture

8 Snowmobiles have ousted sleds and nowadays only a minority of Sami live from their reindeer herds or coastal fishing. But the Sami culture, transcending the frontiers of Norway, Sweden and Finland, lives on and is increasingly accessible to visitors, especially in Kautokeino and Karasjok; in the latter, the Sami Parliament is a masterpiece of traditional design in mellow wood. And Sami identity lies secure in the language and its dialects, traditions such as the joik (a sustained, droned rhythmic poem), and handicrafts such as silversmithing and knife making.

Oslo–Bergen Railway

9 Often cited as one of the world's most beautiful rail journeys, the Oslo–Bergen rail line is an opportunity to sample some of Norway's best scenery. After passing through the forests of southern Norway, it climbs up onto the horizonless beauty of the Hardangervidda Plateau and then continues down through the pretty country around Voss and on into Bergen. En route it passes within touching distance of the fjords and connects (at Myrdal) with the steep branch line down to the fjord country that fans out from Flåm.

Pulpit Rock

10 As lookouts go, Preikestolen (Pulpit Rock) has few peers. Perched atop an almost perfectly sheer cliff that hangs more than 600m above the waters of gorgeous Lysefjord, Pulpit Rock is one of Norway's signature images and most eye-catching sites. It's the sort of place where you'll barely be able to look as travellers dangle far more than seems advisable over the precipice, even as you find yourself drawn inexorably towards the edge. The hike to reach it takes two hours and involves a full-day trip from Stavanger.

Tromsø

11 Tromsø, a cool 400km north of the Arctic Circle, is northern Norway's most significant city with, among other superlatives, the world's northernmost cathedral, brewery and botanical garden. Its busy clubs and pubs – more per capita than in any other Norwegian town – owe much to the university (another northernmost) and its students. In summer, Tromsø's a base for round-the-clock, 24-hour daylight activity. Once the first snows fall, the locals slip on their skis or snowshoes, head out of town and gaze skywards for a glimpse of the northern lights.

Seasons

Norway has two major seasons for activities: summer and winter. Outside these periods, many operators simply shut up shop.

Climate Change

If you're planning on hiking out into the Norwegian wilds, remember that Norway's weather can, even in summer, change rapidly.

TOP: TATYANA VYC / SHUTTERSTOCK ©; BOTTOM: PESK / SHUTTERSTOCK ©

Overlooking Wadi Ghul from Jebel Shams

Oman

Oman is the obvious choice for those seeking out the modern face of Arabia while still wanting to sense its ancient soul.

In Muscat's Grand Mosque, there is a beautiful hand-loomed carpet; it was once the world's largest rug until Abu Dhabi's Grand Mosque, in the United Arab Emirates, pinched the record. This is poignant because Oman doesn't boast many 'firsts' or 'biggests' in a region bent on grandstanding. What it does boast, with its rich heritage and embracing society, is a strong sense of identity, a pride in an ancient, frankincense-trading past and confidence in a highly educated future.

For visitors, this offers a rare chance to engage with the Arab world without the distorting lens of excessive wealth. Oman's low-rise towns retain their traditional charms and Bedouin values remain at the heart of an Omani welcome. With an abundance of natural beauty, from spectacular mountains, wind-blown deserts and a pristine coastline, Oman will delight in more ways than one.

Top Experiences

Jebel Shams

1 Oman's highest mountain, Jebel Shams (3009m), is best known not for its peak but for the view into the spectacularly deep Wadi Ghul lying alongside it; known locally as the Grand Canyon of Arabia, it fissures abruptly between the flat canyon rims, exposing vertical cliffs of 1000m and more. While there is nothing 'to do' exactly at the top, the area makes a wonderful place to take photographs, hike the balcony trail, have a picnic...or buy a carpet. You need only step from your vehicle and you'll find carpet sellers appear from nowhere across the barren landscape clutching piles of striped red-and-black goat-hair rugs.

When to Go

 HIGH SEASON (Nov–Mar)

 SHOULDER (Apr–Jun, Sep & Oct)

 LOW SEASON (Jul–Aug)

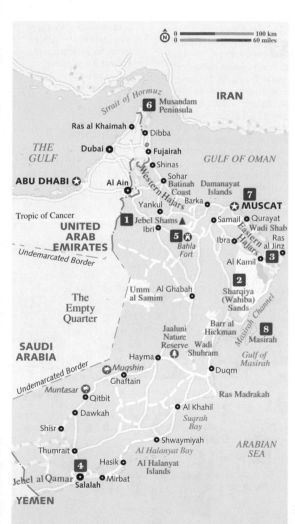

Sharqiya Sands

2 A destination in their own right, or a diversion between Muscat and Sur, these beautiful dunes, still referred to locally as Wahiba Sands, could keep visitors occupied for days. Home to the Bedu, the sands offer visitors a glimpse of a traditional way of life that is fast disappearing as modern conveniences limit the need for a nomadic existence. The sands are a good place to interact with Omani women whose Bedouin lifestyle affords them a more visible social role. Despite their elaborate costumes, they are accomplished drivers, often coming to the rescue of tourists stuck in the sand.

Ras al Jinz

3 Witness the birth drama at Ras al Jinz (Ras al Junayz), the eastern-most point of the Arabian

Peninsula, an important turtle-nesting site for the endangered green turtle. Over 20,000 females return annually to the beach where they hatched in order to lay eggs. Oman has an important role to play in the conservation of this endangered species and takes the responsibility seriously, with strict penalties for harming turtles or their eggs.

Salalah

4 Explore subtropical Salalah, a region famed for gold, frankincense and myrrh. The capital of the Dhofar region is a colourful, subtropical city that owes much of its character to Oman's former territories in East Africa. Flying into Salalah from Muscat, it is hard to imagine that Oman's first and second cities share the same continent. From mid-June to mid-August, monsoon clouds from India bring a constant drizzle to the area and, as a result, the stubble of Salalah's surrounding jebel is transformed into an oasis of misty pastures. Year-round, Salalah's coconut-fringed beaches and plantations of bananas and papayas offer a flavour of Zanzibar in the heart of the Arabian desert.

Bahla Fort

5 After two decades of restoration, be one of the first to visit Bahla Fort, a Unesco World Heritage Site. A remarkable set of battlements is noticeable at every turn in the road, running impressively along the wadi and making Bahla one of the most comprehensive walled cities in the world. These walls extend for several kilometres and are said to have been designed 600 years ago by a woman.

Getting Around

A new bus system is being introduced in Muscat and between cities.

Long-distance shared taxis travel between most major towns. For most places of interest, it's only possible to take an 'engaged' taxi (ie private, not shared).

Musandam Peninsula

6 Separated from the rest of Oman by the east coast of the UAE, and guarding the southern side of the strategically impor-

5

TRABANTOS / SHUTTERSTOCK ©

tant Strait of Hormuz, the Musandam Peninsula is dubbed the 'Norway of Arabia' for its beautiful *khors* (rocky inlets), small villages and dramatic, mountain-hugging roads. Accessible but still isolated in character, this beautiful peninsula with its cultural eccentricities is well worth a visit if you're on an extended tour of Oman, or if you're after a taste of wilderness from Dubai.

Mutrah Souq

7 Bargain for copper pots and gold bangles in Muscat's labyrinthine Mutrah Souq. Many people come to Mutrah Corniche just to visit the souq, which retains the chaotic interest of a traditional Arab market albeit housed under modern timber roofing. Shops selling Omani and Indian artefacts together with a few antiques jostle among

Food & Drink

'Lobster' Local, clawless crayfish.

Harees Steamed wheat and boiled meat.

Shuwa Marinated lamb traditionally cooked in an underground oven.

Halwa Gelatinous sugar or date-syrup confection served at all official functions.

Tap water Safe to drink although most people stick to bottled water.

Alcohol Available at hotels and tourist-oriented restaurants.

Coffee Laced with cardamom and served with dates, it's an essential part of Omani hospitality.

more traditional textile, hardware and jewellery stores.

Masirah

8 Camp on a Masirah beach, with its rocky interior of palm oases and gorgeous rim of sandy coastline for the ultimate

desert island experience. Flamingos, herons and oyster-catchers patrol the coast by day, and armies of ghost crabs march ashore at night. Home to a rare shell, the Eloise, and large turtle-nesting sites, the island is justifiably fabled as a naturalist's paradise.

EQROY / SHUTTERSTOCK ©

Oman's Favourite Sweets

Omanis have a decidedly sweet tooth, which they indulge during important social occasions. It's polite to participate in the communal eating of sweetmeats – using the right hand only, of course.

At official ceremonies, such as event openings and National Day celebrations, *halwa* is offered to guests. Lumps of the sticky, glutinous confection are pinched out of a communal dish between the right finger and thumb, much to the chagrin of those who forgot to bring a hanky. Made of sugar or dates, saffron, cardamom, almonds, nutmeg and rosewater, *halwa* is prepared in huge copper vats heated over a fire and stirred for many hours by men wielding long, wooden pestles.

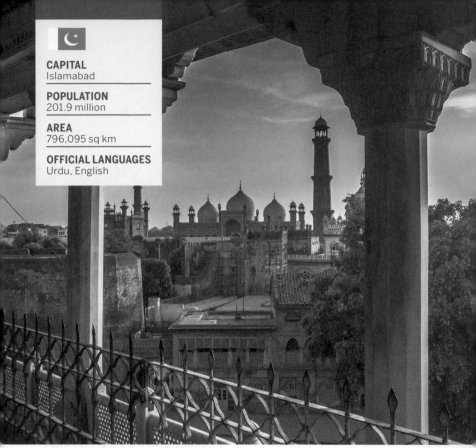

Lahore Grand Mosque from the balcony of Lahore Fort

Pakistan

Pakistan is blessed with abundant natural and historical riches, but plagued by political instability.

CAPITAL
Islamabad

POPULATION
201.9 million

AREA
796,095 sq km

OFFICIAL LANGUAGES
Urdu, English

With armed groups targeting everyone from the government to mountaineers, visitor numbers to Pakistan have slowed to a trickle, which is a shame, as this remains one of Asia's most fascinating destinations. The teeming cities of the south lie on a continuum with the ancient cities of northern India, while the rugged north is a wild frontier that has changed only superficially since Mughal times. In between are scatted ruins and arid deserts, and capping Pakistan to the north is the western spur of the Himalayan mountain range, including K2, the world's second highest mountain.

Pakistan's number one attraction is the Karakoram Highway, stretching north from the Northwest Frontier to Kashgar in China.

Pakistan is a country full of contradictions, where simmering tensions coexist with remarkable friendliness and hospitality, set against an *Arabian Nights* backdrop of desert forts, sultans and djinns.

Top Experiences

Lahore Fort (Shahi Qila)

1 Built, damaged, demolished, rebuilt and restored several times before being given its current form by Emperor Akbar in 1566 (when he made Lahore his capital), the Lahore Fort is the star attraction of the Old City. It has an appealing 'abandoned' atmosphere (unless it's packed with visitors) and is a fabulous place to simply wander around. The fort is entered through the colossal Alamgiri Gate, which was designed to be large enough to allow several elephants to enter at one time. The Shish Mahal (Palace of Mirrors), built in 1631 for the empress and her court, is decorated with glass mirrors set into the stucco interior. Also breathtaking is the Naulakha marble pavilion, lavishly decorated with pietra dura – studded with tiny jewels in intricate floral motifs. There are also three small museums on site.

Multan's Sufi Shrines

2 From the 9th century onward, Multan has been a major Islamic centre and that heritage lives on today. Over the centuries it has attracted more mystics and holy men than perhaps anywhere else on the subcontinent and today is dominated by their awe-inspiring shrines, tombs and mosques. The mausoleum of Sheikh Rukn-i-Alam, with its stunning blue-and-turquoise tiled exterior, is a particular masterpiece. Built entirely of red brick and timber, the structure is not only beautiful but is skilfully executed,

When to Go

 HIGH SEASON (Oct–Feb)

 SHOULDER (Mar–Jun)

 LOW SEASON (Jul–Sep)

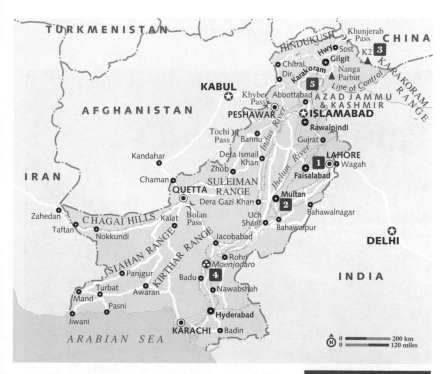

with a brilliant mastery of the squinch (a small arch across the corner of a tower masking the transition from square to dome). It is said that the Tughlaq king Ghiyasud-Din originally built the mausoleum for himself in 1320, but that his son offered it as the saint's resting place out of religious duty.

K2

3 It might be lacking a couple of hundred metres (8611m, compared with Everest's 8850m) and it might not even have a proper name, but K2 must never be underestimated. The world's second-highest peak, standing sentinel over the Pakistan–China border, is treacherous; climbers have around a one-in-four chance of not making it back down alive. As only the most experienced must ever dare to attempt K2, try an alternative adventure. Trek in to Concordia, a glacial confluence surrounded by four of the world's 14 8000m-plus peaks, to admire from a close-yet safe distance.

Moenjodaro

4 Ramble amongst the World Heritage–listed ruins here and experience the traces of what would have been a bustling Indus Valley metropolis in 2500 BC. The 250-hectare complex of excavated assembly halls, baths and houses gives a sense of a complex, sophisticated culture lost to time. The most exposed parts of Moenjodaro City are open to visitors, representing just one-third of the area yet to be excavated. Archaeology buffs will get the most out of it; those with a casual interest may be disappointed given the relative effort needed

Getting Around

Flights connect the major centres, including Islamabad, Karachi and Lahore.

Getting around by bus isn't always terribly comfortable but it's undeniably cheap.

Long-distance train services are often crowded, so sleepers in 1st and air-con class should be booked ahead. Women may book female-only compartments.

3

to get here. The good museum contains relics from the site, including engraved seals, terracotta toys, kitchen utensils, weapons, sculpture, jewellery and other ornaments.

Travelling the Karakoram Highway

5 Humans have been inching along the Indus Valley for millennia, using this Silk Road strand to spread goods and ideologies between East and West. Goodness knows why – it's such difficult terrain to traverse. But traverse it they did

---

Food & Drink

Meat *Gosht* (meat) eaten in Pakistan is usually mutton or chicken, or sometimes beef *(gay ka gosht)*. Seafood and fish *(machlee)* are most common in Karachi, although some restaurants in Lahore and Islamabad offer a commendable selection. Pork is taboo for Muslims.

Roti This unleavened round bread is most often cooked in a tandoor (clay oven) in Pakistan and is usually larger than its Indian equivalent.

Sweets Pakistan has a positively lip-smacking assortment of colourful *mithai* (sweets). Some sweet shops produce their works of art right on the spot – look for *jalebis*, the orange-coloured whorls of deep-fried batter dunked in sticky sugar syrup.

Tea Pakistan is awash with tea *(chai)*, usually 'milky tea' of equal parts water, leaves, sugar and milk brought to a raging boil and often poured from a great height.

and, finally, in 1986 some master-engineering saw it modernised: the 1200km Karakoram Highway was unveiled, linking Islamabad to Kashgar in China via the Karakorams, Himalaya and Hindu Kush ranges. It's a flabbergasting drive. There are potholes, landslides and vertical drops; there are old trucks done up like Christmas squeezing and wheezing along; there are roadblocks and bandits. But it'll be the drive of your life.

KHLONGWANGCHAO / SHUTTERSTOCK ©

Kabbadi

A combination of wrestling, rugby and tag, kabbadi comes from the state of Punjab. Two teams, each of 12 members, are separated by a line in the middle of a 12.5m-by-10m arena. One team sends a 'raider' to the other side; he has to keep uttering the phrase *'kabaddi kabaddi'* and touch as many members of the opposing team as possible without taking a second breath, and must return to his part of the field in the same breath. The defending side must protect themselves and attempt to force the invader to either touch the ground and/or take a second breath. Kabaddi has been famous in the subcontinent for centuries with major 'houses' dominating the scene and competing in national and international competitions.

CAPITAL
Ngerulmud

POPULATION
21,500

AREA
459 sq km

OFFICIAL LANGUAGES
Palauan, English

Palau

You don't have to get wet to enjoy Palau, but it helps. This tiny island nation in the western Pacific Ocean is one of the world's most spectacular diving and snorkelling destinations.

The Republic of Palau is scenically magical. For such a tiny area of land, it packs a big punch. It's hard not to be overwhelmed by its array of natural wonders: this is an archipelago of about 200 largely pristine limestone and volcanic islands, blanketed in emerald forest, surrounded by a turquoise lagoon. Unsurprisingly, diving is the number-one activity here, with world-class dive sites. Divers swear by Palau's exciting seascape, fascinating wrecks and stunning-

ly diverse marine life – it's not dubbed 'the underwater Serengeti' for nothing.

When the underwater wonders have finished working their magic on you, there are other adventure options. Kayaking, snorkelling and off-road driving are fabulous, with the added appeal of fantastic settings. And for history buffs there are plenty of WWII relics scattered in the jungle, as well as a handful of well-organised museums in Koror, Palau's largest town.

Top Experiences

Blue Corner

 Blue Corner is known for its sheer abundance of underwater life and reef configuration – the point juts into the open ocean and then drops to the depths. Divers are dazzled by the variety of fish, including barracudas, jacks, Napoleon wrasses and schooling grey reef sharks.

Rock Islands

 The Rock Islands are like nowhere else on earth. It's no exaggeration to say that these unique island formations scattered across a 32km stretch of turquoise ocean are the reason to come to Palau. From any vantage point, it's a mesmerising fantasy-scape of limestone islets surrounded by crystalline waters.

Peleliu

 The small coral island of Peleliu, in the south of the archipelago, offers a tranquil escape. It's hard to imagine that Peleliu was the site of one the bloodiest WWII battles in the Pacific theatre. Today, the US and Japanese war relics scattered across the island are Peleliu's major attractions.

When to Go

☀ **HIGH SEASON**
(Dec–Mar)

🌂 **SHOULDER**
(Apr, Jul & Aug, Oct & Nov)

☂ **LOW SEASON**
(May & Jun, Sep)

Food & Drink

Palau's cuisine has absorbed influences from Japan, Korea, the Philippines and the USA. You're in luck if you have a seafood fetish – sushi and sashimi are popular, and mangrove crabs and shellfish are common. But the food can be quirky, too: fruit-bat pie is on many menus (they say it tastes like chicken).

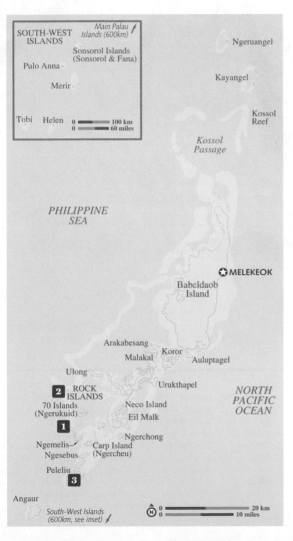

SOUTH-WEST ISLANDS

Main Palau Islands (600km)

Sonsorol Islands (Sonsorol & Fana)

Pulo Anna

Merir

Tobi   Helen

0 ▬▬▬ 100 km
0 ▬▬▬ 60 miles

Ngeruangel

Kayangel

Kossol Reef

Kossol Passage

PHILIPPINE SEA

⭐ MELEKEOK

Babeldaob Island

Arakabesang
Malakal   Koror   Auluptagel

Ulong

Urukthapel

NORTH PACIFIC OCEAN

ROCK ISLANDS
70 Islands (Ngerukuid)

Neco Island
Eil Malk

Ngerchong

Ngemelis
Ngesebus

Carp Island (Ngercheu)

Peleliu

Angaur

South-West Islands (600km, see inset)

Ⓝ 0 ▬▬▬ 20 km
0 ▬▬▬ 10 miles

CAPITAL
Panama City

POPULATION
3.7 million

AREA
75,420 sq km

OFFICIAL LANGUAGE
Spanish

Fiesta de la Pollera, Las Tablas

Panama

From clear turquoise seas to the coffee farms and cloud forests of Chiriquí,
Panama can be as chilled out or as thrilling as you wish.

With a spate of deserted islands, chilled Caribbean vibes on one side and monster Pacific swells on the other, Panama sits poised to deliver the best of beach life. And a whole other world begins at the water's edge. Seize it by scuba diving with whale sharks in the Pacific, snorkeling the rainbow reefs of Bocas del Toro or setting sail in the indigenous territory of Guna Yala, where virgin isles sport nary a footprint. Meanwhile surfers will be psyched to have world-class breaks all to themselves.

Here, wildlife is incidental: a resplendent quetzal on the highland trail, an unruly troupe of screeching howler monkeys outside your cabin or a breaching whale that turns your ferry ride into an adrenaline-filled event. Adventure tourism means zipping through rainforest canopies, swimming alongside sea turtles or trekking to sublime cloud-forest vistas. One small tropical country with two long coasts makes for a pretty big playground.

Top Experiences

Panam City

1 Panam City is high-octane Latin America: think ceviche (marinated seafood), casinos and a stacked skyline. For this sparkling city of nearly a million, transformation is afoot: coastal green space, a biodiversity museum, colonial restoration in Casco Viejo and Central America's first subway system. Sure, the traffic resembles a boa constrictor digesting one megalithic meal, but the city's appeal persists. People are real here and nature is never very far away. Beauty lives in the skewed rhythms, incongruous visions and fiery sunsets.

Panama Canal

2 One of the world's greatest shortcuts, the canal cuts right through the Continental Divide, linking the Atlantic and the Pacific. And it's worth marveling at. Just as stunning as the hulking steel container ships passing through the locks are the legions of creatures watching from the jungle fringes. Two visitors centers offer viewing platforms and museums that lay bare the construction and its expansion. There are also worthwhile boat and kayak trips on the waterway. Or you can book a partial transit and squeeze through the locks yourself.

When to Go

 PEAK HIGH SEASON
(November festivals, Christmas, New Year, Easter)

 HIGH SEASON
(mid-Dec–mid-Apr)

 LOW SEASON
(late Apr-early Dec)

Parque Nacional Coiba

3 Often compared to the Galápagos, this marine park is a veritable lost world of pristine ecosystems and unique fauna. Spy flocks of scarlet macaws, enormous schools of

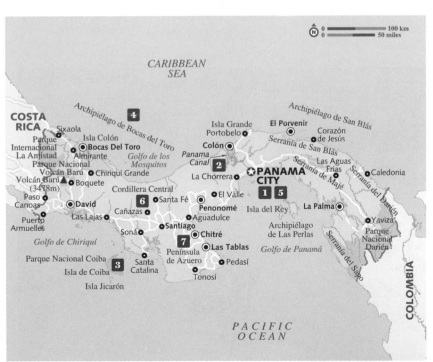

fish, migrating humpback whales with calves, and manta rays scuffing the ocean floor. Scuba divers might glimpse a hammerhead or a whale shark. Most importantly, it's still wild, with few visitors and little infrastructure. Not long ago an infamous prison isolated all on the main island, but now everyone comes here by choice.

Archipiélago de Bocas del Toro

4 No wonder this Caribbean island chain is Panama's number-one vacation spot. 'It's all good,' say the locals. Pedal to the beach on a cruiser bike, hum to improvised calypso on Isla Bastimentos and laze over dinner in a thatched hut on the waterfront. Lodgings range from cheap backpacker digs to stunning jungle lodges and luxury resorts located on outer islands. Surfers hit the breaks, but there's also snorkeling with varied sea life or volunteering opportunities to help nesting sea turtles.

Casco Viejo

5 Don't miss Panama City's historical neighborhood of Casco Viejo, full of crumbling convents and cobblestones. The colonial architecture may hark back to Havana, but this is not a spot where time stands still. It's as much about today's urban mix as the eclectic, easygoing vibe. The Cinta Costera, a recently completed green space, takes walkers and bikers from downtown past Casco Viejo. On sticky evenings artists' booths line the promenade, couples dine under parasols and live music fills the plazas.

Getting Around

Domestic flights depart Panama City's Albrook Airport to destinations throughout the country.

Most cities have a bus terminal with frequent regional departures.

Car rentals are not cheap, but roads are generally in good condition. Some areas, including Panama City and many rural parts of the country, are very poorly signposted.

The Highlands

6 In the tropics, the highlands are the equivalent of a breath of fresh air. Panama's highlands range from lush forest with tiny golden frogs to mist-covered coffee plantations. From Panama City, weekenders take to El Valle and El Copé. Boquete is the classic mountain town, but if you are looking to get off the beaten path, the hamlet of Santa Fé has true mountain tranquility, with local-led horse rides and hikes to waterfalls with swimming holes. Paradise is not lost.

Península de Azuero

7 Sweet landscapes of sculpted hills, lonely beaches and crashing surf feed the growing buzz; this rural peninsula has become today's hot getaway. Yet the strongest impression is one of tradition. Spanish culture has deep roots here, evident in the charm of tiled colonials, country hospitality, religious festivals and elaborate polleras (embroidered lace dresses). Playa Venao has emerged as a major surf destination, while to the west the delightfully untrammeled Sunset Coast has quiet beaches, great surfing and community turtle tours.

GST PRODUCTIONS / SHUTTERSTOCK ©

Food & Drink

Panama's national dish is *sancocho* (chicken-and-vegetable stew). *Ropa vieja* (literally 'old clothes'), a spicy shredded beef combination served over rice, is another common and tasty dish. Rice and beans are a staple in Panama and are usually served with *patacones* (fried green plantains), a small cabbage salad and meat. Seafood is inexpensive and abundant, including *ceviche* (marinated raw seafood).

Fresh tropical juices and coconut water (known as *pipa*) are sold on the street. The national alcoholic drink is made of *seco*, milk and ice. *Seco*, like rum, is distilled from sugarcane, and popular in the countryside. Popular in the central provinces, *vino de palma* is fermented sap extracted from the trunk of a palm tree.

Indigenous Groups

Of the several dozen native tribes that inhabited Panama when the Spanish arrived, only seven now remain. While indigenous culture is much more vibrant and present than in neighboring countries, an inordinately high percentage of the indigenous population lives in poverty. In the *comarcas* (autonomous regions), illiteracy runs between 10% and 30%. Access to health care and education is a serious issue.

Indigenous populations include the Bokotá, who inhabit Bocas del Toro Province, and the Bribrí, found in Costa Rica and in Panama along the Talamanca reserve. Both of these groups maintain their own language and culture, but their numbers and political influence are less than for some of the larger groups.

CAPITAL	Port Moresby
POPULATION	6.8 million
AREA	462,840 sq km
OFFICIAL LANGUAGES	Tok Pisin, English, Hiri Motu

Highland festival, Mt Hagen

Papua New Guinea

Smouldering volcanoes, forest-cloaked mountains and coral reefs set the stage for one of the world's most flamboyant cultures.

Are you up for an adventure? Here in Papua New Guinea you can trek through steaming jungles and ford rushing rivers with expert guides. Your goal may be a remote village, a magnificently plumed bird of paradise or a kangaroo that has elected the life arboreal. Why not test your mettle on a multi-day trek following the steps of Australian diggers along the Kokoda Track, or summit a 4000m-plus Highland peak for a panoramic, coast-to-coast vista.

This is also a world-famous diving destination, with excellent conditions most months of the year. The biodiversity beneath is astounding, with a colourful array of corals and teeming fish life, along with a jaw-dropping collection of wrecks.

One of the best ways to see the country is to stay in a village. By day, be guided to the sights by local guides. By night, watch the sunset, feast on fresh seafood and watch the sky slowly fill with stars while daydreaming about the adventures still ahead.

Top Experiences

Diving & Snorkelling

 PNG ranks among the best of destinations to don a mask and fins, with an irresistible menu of underwater treasures: luminous coral reefs festooned with huge sea fans; warm waters teeming with rainbow-coloured fish; canyons and drop-offs that tumble into the abyss; and a host of eerie WWII wrecks – not to mention the thrill of diving uncrowded sites. A handful of idyllic dive resorts such as Kimbe Bay provide the perfect gateway to your undersea adventure.

Highland Festivals

 Rio's Carnaval has nothing on the magnificent pageantry of a Highland festival. PNG's biggest fests, such as the Mt Hagen and Goroka shows, are pure sensory overload, with massive feather headdresses, rustling grass skirts and evocative face and body paint adorning enormous numbers of participants – over 100 different tribal groups – from all across the Highlands and further afield. Singsing (festival) groups perform traditional songs and dances in this pride-filled extravaganza. The thrill of coming face to face with such uplifting traditional cultures is indescribable – and well worth planning a trip around.

Milne Bay

 At the eastern edge of the mainland, Milne Bay is a landscape of remarkable beauty. You'll find scattered islands, coral reefs, lovely palm-fringed beaches, hidden waterfalls, meandering rivers and

When to Go

HIGH SEASON (May–Oct)

SHOULDER (Apr & Nov)

LOW SEASON (Dec–Mar)

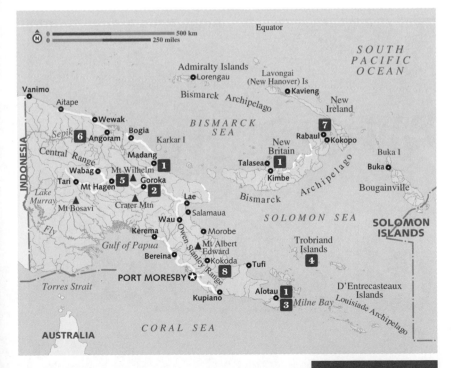

steep-sided, rainforest-covered mountains plunging to the sea. The opportunity for adventure is staggering, with great bird-watching, bushwalking and island- and village-hopping. Alotau is the gateway to it all, and also host of the colourful Canoe Festival, with gyrating singsing groups, string bands and people-packed longboats racing across the waterfront.

Trobriand Islands

4 Anthropologists have long been fascinated with the Trobriand Islands. Here you'll find a remarkably intact Polynesian culture, with unique traditions – based on a strict matrilineal society – and a distinct cosmology. It's well known for its colourfully painted yam houses, wild harvest festival and celebratory cricket matches (complete with singing and dancing). Visitors here are still a rarity, and have a fantastic opportunity to stay in local villages and experience the Trobes firsthand, visiting skull caves and coral megaliths, and taking in the pretty island scenery.

Trekking Mt Wilhelm

5 The craggy ridges of the Bismarck Range culminate in the wind-scoured peak of Mt Wilhelm, the tallest mountain in Oceania. A predawn start has trekkers clambering up its rocky slopes to see the mainland's north and south coasts before the clouds roll in.

Getting Around

Travel between regions is mostly by flight (often via Port Moresby).

Very few roads and expensive rental rates means self driving is not a very useful option.

Taxis are available in the major towns; may not have working meters.

MICKRICK / GETTY IMAGES ©

Sepik River

6 Besieged on all sides by thick jungle and shrouded in mist, the mighty Sepik wanders across northwestern PNG like a lazy brown snake full with food. The river is the region's lifeblood, home to a string of villages rich in artistic tradition, and the cultural treasure chest of the Pacific. Here you can hire a crocodile-headed canoe and thread the seasonal waterways from one village to the next, sleeping in stilt homes and exploring the towering haus tambarans (spirit houses).

Rabaul

7 One of the prettiest towns in the South Pacific was devastated by Mt Tavurvur, which erupted in 1994 and buried much of Rabaul under volcanic ash. Today you can wander the abandoned streets of this once-thriving community, and take in adventures further afield. There are great views to be had, particularly from atop the volcanoes looming over town.

Kokoda Track

8 It's muddy and gruelling, with maddeningly steep uphill scrambles followed by slippery, bone-jarring descents. Treacherous river crossings ensure feet don't stay dry for long, while the humidity wreaks havoc on even the best-prepared trekkers. Why walk the 96km Kokoda Track? To follow in the footsteps of giants, recalling the great men who fought and died on this hellish, mountainous stretch during WWII. As you pass through remote villages and pause beside evocative war memorials you'll find – like the many who've done it before – that the rewards far outweigh the physical challenges.

Food & Drink

Seafood Most coastal resorts, and even some Highlands hotels (where the fresh reef fish are flown in) can put on a great seafood buffet.

Staples The traditional village diet consists largely of starchy vegetables. In the Highlands it will probably be tasty *kaukau* (sweet potato); on the islands, it's taro or yam; and in the Sepik and other swampy areas of PNG, *saksak* (sago) is all the rage. *Rais* (rice) is universally popular.

Meat Pigs are the main source of meat protein, although they are generally saved for feasts. *Kakaruk* (chicken) is also quite popular. A legacy of WWII is the prevalence and popularity of canned meat and fish. Locals often prefer tinned fish *(tinpis)* to fresh fish.

Vegetables Produce available at markets is varied and excellent. You'll see capsicums (bell peppers), tomatoes, peanuts, avocados and spectacular fresh tropical fruit. In the Highlands you can sometimes get strawberries, cauliflower and broccoli.

Unique Wildlife

Australia and New Guinea have the world's only macropods and monotremes. The agile wallaby is found in New Guinea and Australia, but most of New Guinea's macropods are endemic tree kangaroos that are quite distinct from Australia's species of kangaroos and wallabies.

Papua New Guinea is still very much a biological frontier, so it's worth recording carefully any unusual animal you see. In little-visited regions, there's a chance that it will be an undescribed species. There are still hundreds of species – especially frogs, reptiles and insects – waiting to be discovered by Western science.

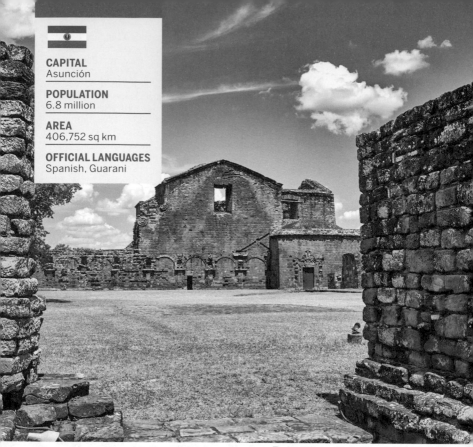

CAPITAL
Asunción

POPULATION
6.8 million

AREA
406,752 sq km

OFFICIAL LANGUAGES
Spanish, Guarani

The Jesuit Mission of La Santísima Trinidad de Paraná

Paraguay

Little-visited and little-known, landlocked Paraguay is a country surrounded by South America's 'big boys', but there's a warm welcome and much to experience here.

Despite its location at the heart of the continent, Paraguay is all too often passed over by travelers who assume that a lack of mega-attractions means there's nothing to see. But it's ideal for those keen to get off the gringo trail for a truly authentic South American experience.

Extraordinary biodiversity makes Paraguay a notable destination for ecotourism, in particular bird-watching, while the Paraguayans themselves are famously laid-back and rightly renowned for their warmth and hospitality. Paraguay is a country of remarkable contrasts: it's rustic and sophisticated; it's extremely poor and obscenely wealthy; it boasts exotic natural reserves and massive human-made dams; it is a place where horses and carts pull up alongside Mercedes-Benz vehicles, artisans' workshops abut glitzy shopping centers, and Jesuit ruins in rural villages lie just a few kilometers from sophisticated colonial towns.

Top Experiences

The Chaco

Although its large-scale deforestation has made international headlines in recent times, the Chaco remains a great place to see wildlife for the time being. This vast plain encompasses the entire western half of Paraguay and stretches into Argentina and Bolivia. It's an animal-lover's paradise, with flocks of waterbirds and birds of prey easily spotted along the roadside.

Laguna Blanca

A pristine, crystal-clear lake, Laguna Blanca is named for its breathtaking sandy beach and lake bed. The surround-

ing cerrado habitat is home to rare birds and mammals such as the maned wolf and the endangered white-winged nightjar, this being one of only three places in the world where the latter species breeds.

Jesuit Missions

Set atop a lush green hill 28km northeast of Encarnación, Trinidad is Paraguay's best-preserved Jesuit *reducción* (settlement). You can hire a Spanish-speaking guide near the gate or hang around until dark for the atmospheric light show, which projects a history of the site onto the walls of the ruins.

When to Go

HIGH SEASON
(Jun–Aug)

SHOULDER
(Apr–May &
Sep–Nov)

LOW SEASON
(Dec–Mar)

Food & Drink

Asado Grilled slabs of beef and pork are the focal point of every social event.

Chipa Cheese bread made with manioc flour.

Chipa guasú Hot maize pudding with cheese and onion.

Tereré Iced yerba maté tea drank constantly.

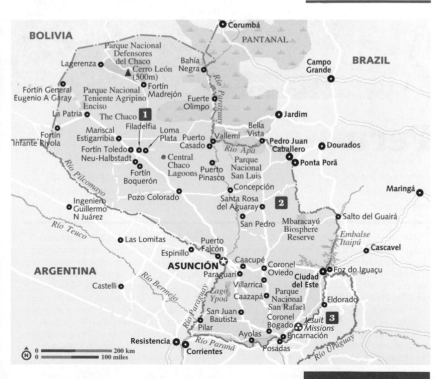

CAPITAL
Lima

POPULATION
30.7 million

AREA
1.3 million sq km

OFFICIAL LANGUAGES
Spanish, Aymara,
Quechua

Floating reed islands, Lake Titicaca

Peru

Peru is as complex as its most intricate and exquisite weavings. Festivals mark ancient rites, the urban vanguard beams innovation and nature brims with splendid diversity.

Visitors pilgrimage to the glorious Inca citadel of Machu Picchu, yet this feted site is just a flash in a 5000-year history of peoples. Explore the dusted remnants of Chan Chan, the largest pre-Columbian ruins in all the Americas. Fly over the puzzling geoglyphs etched into the arid earth at Nazca, or venture into the rugged wilds that hem the stalwart fortress of Kuelap.

Giant sand dunes, chiseled peaks and Pacific breaks a few heartbeats away from the capital's rush-hour traffic: from downtown Lima to smack-dab nowhere, this vast country translates to paradise for the active traveler. All the usual suspects – rafting, paragliding, ziplines and bike trails – are present. Spot scarlet macaws in the Amazon or catch the sunset over the dusty remnants of an ancient civilization. Take this big place in small bites and don't rush. Delays happen. And that's when you realize: in Peru, the adventure usually lies in getting there.

Top Experiences

Machu Picchu

1 A fantastic Inca citadel lost to the world until its rediscovery in the early 20th century, Machu Picchu stands as a ruin among ruins. With its emerald terraces, backed by steep peaks and Andean ridges that echo on the horizon, the sight simply surpasses the imagination. Beautiful it is. This marvel of engineering has withstood six centuries of earthquakes, foreign invasion and howling weather. Discover it for yourself, wander through its stone temples, and scale the dizzying heights of Wayna Picchu.

Floating Reed Islands, Lake Titicaca

2 Less a lake than a highland ocean, the Titicaca area is home to fantastical sights, but none more so than the surreal floating islands crafted entirely of tightly woven totora reeds. Centuries ago, the Uros people constructed the Islas Uros in order to escape more aggressive mainland ethnic groups, such as the Incas. The reeds require near-constant renovation and are also used to build thatched homes, elegant boats and even archways and children's swing sets. See this wonder for yourself

with a homestay visit that includes fishing and learning traditional customs.

Hiking in the Cordillera Blanca

3 The dramatic peaks of the Cordillera Blanca stand sentinel over Huaraz and the surrounding region like an outrageously imposing granite Republican Guard. The range is the highest outside of the Himalayas, and 16 of its ostentatious summits breech 6000m, making it the continent's most challenging collection of summits-in-waiting. Glacial lakes, massive Puya raimondii plants and shards of sky-pointed rock all culminate in Parque

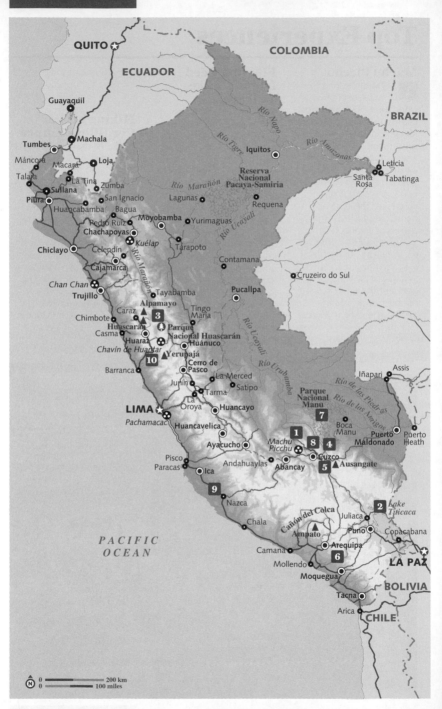

Nacional Huascarán, where the Santa Cruz trek rewards the ambitious with a living museum of razor-sharp peaks.

Inca Trail

4 The continent's most famous pedestrian roadway, the Inca Trail snakes 43km, up stone steps and through thick cloud-forest mists. A true pilgrimage, the four- to five-day trek ends at the famous Intipunku – or Sun Gate – where trekkers get their first glimpse of the extravagant ruins at Machu Picchu. While there are countless ancient roads all over Peru, the Inca Trail, with its mix of majestic views, staggering mountain passes and clusters of ruins, remains the favorite of travellers.

Best in Print

The Last Days of the Inca (Kim MacQuarrie; 2007) The history-making clash between civilizations.

Aunt Julia & the Scriptwriter (Mario Vargas Llosa; 1977) A classic unconventional love story.

Cradle of Gold (Christopher Heaney; 2010) Readable biography of Hiram Bingham, the 'real' Indiana Jones.

Best on Film

La Teta Asustada (The Milk of Sorrow; 2009) Claudia Llosa's feature film examines the life of a girl suffering from a trauma-related affliction.

Undertow (2009) A married fisherman coming to terms with his dead boyfriend's ghost.

Cuzco

5 With ancient cobblestone streets, grandiose baroque churches and the remnants of Inca temples with centuries-old carvings, no city looms larger in Andean history than Cuzco, a city that has been inhabited continuously since pre-Hispanic times. Once the capital of the Inca empire, tourist-thronged Cuzco also serves as the gateway to Machu Picchu. Mystic, commercial and chaotic, this unique city is still a stunner. Where else would you find ornately dressed women walking their llamas on leashes, a museum for magical plants, and the wildest nightlife in the high Andes?

Colonial Arequipa

6 Peru's second-largest metropolis bridges the historical gap between the Inca glories

When to Go

HIGH SEASON
(Jun–Aug)
Dry season in the highlands and eastern rainforest, and the best time for festivals and highland treks.

SHOULDER
(Sep–Nov & Mar–May)
Ideal for less-crowded visits. A good time for rainforest trekking.

LOW SEASON
(Dec–Feb)
Rainy season in the highlands and Amazon; high season for the coast.

Local Cuisine

Peru, once a country where important guests were treated to French meals and Scotch whiskey, is now a place where high-end restaurants spotlight deft interpretations of Andean favorites, including quinoa and *cuy* (guinea pig). The dining scene has blossomed. And tourism outfits have swept in to incorporate a culinary something as part of every tour. In 2000, the country became the site of the first Cordon Bleu academy in Latin America, and in 2009, *Bon Appétit* magazine named Lima the 'next great food city.' In Lima, La Casa de La Gastronomía Peruana is a new museum fully dedicated to celebrating the country's complex culinary heritage. In 2015, Peru won 'best culinary destination' from the World Travel Awards for the third time. Of Peru's 3.1 million annual visitors, 40% do gastronomic tourism.

Foodie fever has infected Peruvians at every level, with even the most humble *chicharrón* (fried pork) vendor hyperattentive to the vagaries of preparation and presentation. No small part of this is due to mediagenic celebrity chef Gastón Acurio, whose culinary skill and business acumen (he owns dozens of restaurants around the globe) have given him rock-star status.

Getting Around

Domestic-flight schedules and prices change frequently. Most big cities are served by modern jets, while smaller towns are served by propeller aircraft.

Buses are the usual form of transportation for most Peruvians and many travelers. Fares are cheap and services are frequent on the major long-distance routes, but buses are of varying quality. Remote rural routes are often served by older, worn-out vehicles.

A car is useful for traveling at your own pace, though cities can be difficult to navigate and secure parking is a must.

The privatized rail system, PeruRail, has daily services between Cuzco and Aguas Calientes, aka Machu Picchu Pueblo, and services between Cuzco and Puno on the shores of Lake Titicaca three times a week.

of Cuzco and the clamorous modernity of Lima. Crowned by some dazzling baroque-mestizo architecture hewn out of the local sillar (white volcanic rock), Arequipa is primarily a Spanish colonial city that hasn't strayed far from its original conception. Its ethereal natural setting, amid snoozing volcanoes and the high pampa, is complemented by a 400-year-old monastery, a huge cathedral and some interesting Peruvian fusion cuisine eloquently showcased in traditional picanterías (spicy restaurants).

Parque Nacional Manu

7 Traverse three climatic zones from rearing Andean mountains to mist-swathed cloud forest of the lower slopes en route to the bowels of the jungle in Parque Nacional Manu, the Amazon's best adventure. Manu has long been Peru's best-protected wilderness, brimming with opportunities to see fabled jungle creatures such as the anaconda, tapir, thousands of feasting macaws festooning clay licks with their colors, and jaguar. In this deep forest, tribespeople live as they have for centuries, with barely any contact with the outside world.

The Sacred Valley

8 Ragtag Andean villages, crumbling Inca military outposts and agricultural terraces used since time immemorial are linked by the Río Urubamba as it curves and widens, coursing through the Sacred Valley. A strategic location between Cuzco and Machu Picchu makes this picturesque destination an ideal base to explore the area's famed markets and ruins. Accommodations range from inviting inns to top resorts, and adventure options include horseback riding, rafting and treks that take you through remote weaving and agricultural villages.

Nazca Lines

9 Made by aliens? Laid out by prehistoric balloonists? Conceived as a giant astronomical chart? No two evaluations of Southern Peru's giant geoglyphs, communally known as the Nazca Lines, are ever the same. The mysteries have been drawing in outsiders since the 1940s when German archaeologist Maria Reiche devoted half her life to studying them. But neither Reiche nor subsequent archaeologists have been able to fully crack the code. The lines remain unfathomed, enigmatic and loaded with historic intrigue, inspiring awe in all who pass.

Chavín de Huántar

10 The Unesco-recognized ruins of Chavín de Huántar were once a righteous ceremonial center. Today, the exceptional feat of engineering, dating between 1200 BC and 800 BC, features striking temple-like structures above ground and a labyrinthine complex of underground corridors, ducts and chambers that invite clambering through. Nearby, the outstanding Museo Nacional de Chavín, home to the lion's share of the intricate and horrifyingly carved tenon heads that once embellished Chavín's walls, helps piece together the enigma.

Semana Santa

The week before Easter Sunday, Holy Week is celebrated with spectacular religious processions almost daily, with Ayacucho recognized for the biggest celebration in Peru, lasting 10 days.

Indigenous Peru

While Peru's social order has been indelibly stamped by Spanish custom, its soul remains squarely indigenous. According to the country's census bureau, Peru is home to 52 different ethnicities, 13 distinct linguistic families and 1786 native communities.

CAPITAL
Manila

POPULATION
102,624,209

AREA
300,000 sq km

OFFICIAL LANGUAGES
Tagalog (Filipino),
English

Jeepney passing rice terraces, Banaue

Philippines

The Philippines is defined by its emerald rice fields, teeming mega-cities, graffiti-splashed jeepneys, smouldering volcanoes, bug-eyed tarsiers, fuzzy water buffalo and smiling, happy-go-lucky people.

The Philippines is a land apart from mainland Southeast Asia – not only geographically, but also spiritually and culturally. The country's overwhelming Catholicism, the result of 350 years of Spanish rule, is its most obvious enigma. Vestiges of the Spanish era include exuberant town fiestas (festivals), unique Spanish-Filipino colonial architecture and centuries-old stone churches.

Malls, fast-food chains and widespread spoken English betray the influence of Spain's colonial successor, the Americans.

Yet despite these outside influences, the country remains very much its own unique entity. The people are, simply, Filipinos – and proud of it. Welcoming, warm and relentlessly upbeat, it is they who captivate and ultimately ensnare visitors.

Top Experiences

Bacuit Archipelago

1 Cruising through the labyrinthine Bacuit Archipelago of northern Palawan, past secluded beaches, pristine lagoons and rocky islets, is an experience not to be missed. Only a short bangka boat ride from the easygoing coastal town of El Nido, Bacuit Bay presents a thrilling mixture of imposing limestone escarpments, palm-tree-lined white-sand beaches and coral reefs. Overnight island-hopping trips in the bay or further north through the Linapacan Strait toward Coron offer an opportunity to bed down in remote fishing villages where the daily catch is grilled for dinner.

Ifugao Rice Terraces

2 It's easy to look at a map of North Luzon and assume the Cordillera is all untamed wilderness. And yes – there's rugged jungle. But what really strikes a visitor to Banaue, Batad and the other towns of Ifugao is how cultivated the mountains are. Even the sheerest cliffs possess little patches of ground that have been tilled into rice paddies. Take all those patches together and you get a veritable blanket of upland-tilled goodness, an unending landscape of hills rounded into rice-producing lumps of emerald.

Southern Negros

3 The 'toe' of boot-shaped Negros offers a little of everything: world-class diving at Apo Island, trekking on Twin Peaks, dolphin- and whale-watching at Bais and perfect beaches pretty much everywhere. As if that weren't enough, wonderfully quirky Siquijor lies just off the coast. It's all within an hour of Dumaguete, an agreeable city in its own right, with lively restaurants and bars plus an airport. No need to worry about advance planning here. Just parachute in and follow your nose. We guarantee it will lead you to somewhere special.

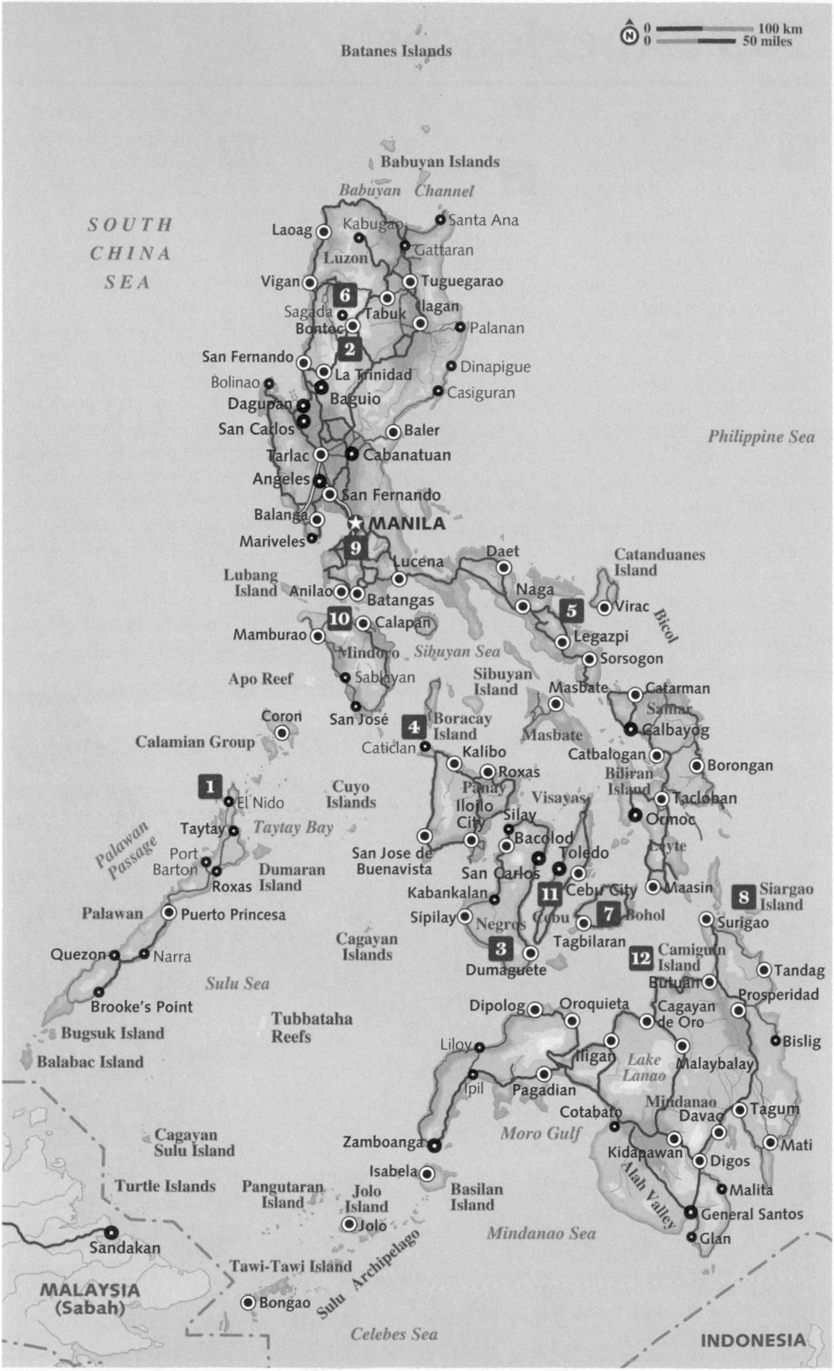
0 100 km
0 50 miles
Batanes Islands
Babuyan Islands
Babuyan Channel
SOUTH CHINA SEA
Laoag
Kabugao
Santa Ana
Gattaran
Luzon
Vigan
Tuguegarao
6
Sagada
Tabuk
Ilagan
Bontoc
Palanan
2
San Fernando
La Trinidad
Dinapigue
Bolinao
Baguio
Casiguran
Dagupan
San Carlos
Baler
Philippine Sea
Tarlac
Cabanatuan
Angeles
San Fernando
Balanga
MANILA
Mariveles
9
Daet
Catanduanes Island
Lubang Island
Lucena
Anilao
Batangas
Naga
5
Virac
10
Calapan
Bicol
Mamburao
Legazpi
Mindoro
Sibuyan Sea
Sorsogon
Apo Reef
Sablayan
Sibuyan Island
Masbate
Catarman
Coron
San José
4
Boracay Island
Samar
Calamian Group
Caticlan
Masbate
Calbayog
Kalibo
Catbalogan
Borongan
1
Cuyo Islands
Roxas
Biliran Island
El Nido
Panay
Visayas
Tacloban
Taytay
Taytay Bay
Iloilo City
Silay
Ormoc
Palawan Passage
Port Barton
Bacolod
Leyte
Dumaran Island
San Jose de Buenavista
Toledo
Roxas
San Carlos
Cebu City
Maasin
Siargao Island
8
Kabankalan
11
Palawan
Puerto Princesa
Sipilay
Negros
Cebu
7
Bohol
Surigao
Tagbilaran
Cagayan Islands
Quezon
Narra
3
12
Camiguin Island
Tandag
Dumaguete
Sulu Sea
Butuan
Brooke's Point
Dipolog
Oroquieta
Prosperidad
Cagayan de Oro
Tubbataha Reefs
Bugsuk Island
Bislig
Liloy
Iligan
Lake Lanao
Malaybalay
Balabac Island
Ipil
Pagadian
Mindanao
Cotabato
Davao
Tagum
Cagayan Sulu Island
Moro Gulf
Zamboanga
Kidapawan
Mati
Digos
Isabela
Turtle Islands
Pangutaran Island
Jolo Island
Basilan Island
Alah Valley
Malita
General Santos
Jolo
Mindanao Sea
Sandakan
Glan
Tawi-Tawi Island
Sulu Archipelago
MALAYSIA (Sabah)
Bongao
Celebes Sea
INDONESIA

Boracay

4 It wasn't that long ago that Boracay was a sleepy, almost unknown backwater. Oh, how times have changed. The world has discovered Boracay, elevating the diminutive island into a serious player in the pantheon of Southeast Asian party beaches. Yet for all that's changed, Boracay remains generally mellower than the likes of Kuta Beach or Ko Samui. And solace can still be found, in particular at the southern end of Boracay's signature White Beach, where the spirit of the old Boracay lives on.

Bicol Adventures

5 Southeast Luzon, geographically defined by the Bicol peninsula, is becoming adventure-travel central for the Philippines. Besides boasting some of the best regional cuisine in the islands, Bicol is a top draw for water and adrenaline junkies via the CamSur Watersports Complex, where wakeboarding rules the roost. Daet, in Camarines Norte, is a burgeoning surf and kitesurfing destination. To experience a more laid-back connection to the water, head to the edge of Luzon and snorkel alongside the gentle whale sharks of Donsol – an unforgettable highlight.

Sagada

6 Sagada is the Philippines' cradle of cool, a supremely mellow mountain retreat deep in the heart of the wild and woolly Cordillera mountains of North Luzon. It has all the elements of a backpacker Shangri La: awesome hikes, eerie caves, hanging coffins, strong coffee, earthy bakeries, and cosy and incredibly cheap accommodation. Fuel up on granola and head out in search of adventure, or chill out in a fireplace-warmed cafe all day reading books or swapping yarns. There are no agendas when you're on Sagada time.

Best in Print

Pacific Rims: Beermen Ballin' in Flip-Flops and the Philippines' Unlikely Love Affair with Basketball (Rafe Bartholomew) As riotous as the title implies.

Playing with Water – Passion and Solitude on a Philippine Island (James Hamilton-Paterson) This timeless account of life on a remote islet sheds much light on Philippine culture.

The Tesseract (Alex Garland) A thrilling romp through Manila's dark side by the author of the cult backpacker hit, *The Beach*.

Food & Drink

Kain na tayo – 'let's eat'. It's the Filipino invitation to eat, and if you travel in the Philippines you will hear it over and over and over again. The phrase reveals two essential aspects of Filipino people: one, that they are hospitable, and two, that they love to, well, eat. A melange of Asian, Latin, American and indigenous cooking, Filipino culinary traditions – hybridised and evolving – reflect the country's unique colonial history and varied geography.

When to Go

HIGH SEASON
(Dec–Apr)
High season is dry season for most of the country.

SHOULDER SEASON
(May & Nov)
Rising May temperatures herald the onset of the wet season.

LOW SEASON
(Jun–Sep)
Accommodation prices drop 30% in resort areas.

Fiestas

Nearly every *barangay* (district) has one. And there's one nearly every day. Fiestas, an integral part of Filipino life and identity, are generally associated with celebrations during the feast of the patron saint. However, like other facets of the culture, some are best understood as the result of syncretism; older rituals and beliefs related to bountiful harvests and abundant seas have been blended into a Catholic architecture, often at the behest of missionaries centuries ago. There are still strictly planting festivities and indigenous, pre-Hispanic traditions. Regardless of the origins, they're jubilant affairs, with entire towns spruced up for loved ones' homecomings.

Getting Around

 Several discount airlines link a vast range of destinations, primarily with Manila and Cebu.

 Bangkas, 'fastcraft', car ferries and large vessels with bunk beds and private cabins link the islands.

 Comfort and reliability runs the gamut, from hobbling skeletons way past their expiration date to long-haul, modern buses with air-con and even wi-fi.

 Tricycles – sidecars bolted to motorcycles – are the Philippine version of a rickshaw. They're everywhere and will transport you several blocks or kilometres.

Bohol Nature & Wildlife

7 While most visitors to Bohol are divers bound for touristy Alona Beach, the real charms of this central Visayan island lie deep in its interior. Perhaps no island in the country is better suited for a half-week romp by motorbike. Perfectly paved roads lead through jungle to peacock-green rivers, chocolatey hills, dramatically placed ziplines and cuddly little tarsiers. The island took a gut-punch with the 2013 earthquake, which toppled many of its centuries-old Spanish churches. Bohol bounced right back though, and is better than ever.

Siargao

8 A chilled-out vibe and friendly breaks for both experts and novices make this island the Philippines' top surf destination. The legendary Cloud Nine break is the hub but waves abound elsewhere; head to tranquil Burgos in the north for an undeveloped experience or take a surf safari to seldom-visited spots. Nonsurfers also have plenty to do, from island hopping to snorkelling to some of the country's best deep-sea fishing. Or just grab a beer on the Cloud Nine pavilion and watch the pros do their thing.

Manila Culture & Nightlife

9 Contrary to popular belief, there's more to this mega-city than just traffic and noise. Manila's nightlife is second to none. From the bongo-infused hipster hang-outs of Quezon City and Cubao X to Makati's sizzling bars and chichi nightclubs, there's something for everyone. The museums are absolutely world-class, and in contemporary art and design circles, Manila is Asia's rising star. Eternally classy Intramuros oozes history. Even the long-maligned culinary scene is finally emerging, as cutting-edge restaurants open alongside earthy cafes and craft-beer bars.

Puerto Galera

10 Puerto Galera on Mindoro is well known as one of the Philippines' dive meccas. Lesser known is that it's also among the most beautiful places on the planet. Serpentine roads leading out of town afford bird's-eye views of gorgeous bays and little islands offshore, while jungle-clad mountains provide a dramatic interior backdrop. Trek to isolated hill-tribe villages by day, then return to base and enjoy a sumptuous five-course Italian meal by night. It's the perfect 'wow' setting for the must-attend Malasimbo Music & Arts Festival in February.

Cebu Sand & Sea

11 Cebu is your quintessential beach-lovers' paradise. Around the island, sandy coves and dramatic cliffs abut an unbroken ribbon of turquoise water. Off the west coast, a wall attracts rich marine life and scores of divers to places like Moalboal, where schooling sardines present an unmissable spectacle. Offshore, Malapascua and Mactan islands are dive meccas known for thresher sharks and turtles, respectively, while Bantayan is the place to get catatonic on the sand. At the heart of it all is the fun and frivolous Visayan capital, Cebu City.

Climbing Volcanic Camiguin

12 From the northern coastline of mainland Mindanao, the rough-hewn landscape of volcanic Camiguin is camouflaged by its lush silhouette. To truly grasp this island's inspiring topography, veer into the interior on roadways that carve through dense forests and culminate in rocky pathways that trail further up into the highlands. Made for do-it-yourself adventurers, Camiguin's peaks and valleys offer streams for scrambling, mountains for scaling, canyons for rappelling and pools at the base of thundering waterfalls in which to wash off the day's exertions.

Beaches

Nothing defines the Philippines more than a remote strip of pearly white sand – there's at least one made-to-order beach on each of the country's 7000+ islands.

Basketball

Basketball players rejoice. Nearly every village, no matter how small and remote, has a court. Call 'next' and be ready to compete.

CAPITAL
Adamstown

POPULATION
54

AREA
47 sq km

OFFICIAL LANGUAGE
English

Pitcairn Island

As the smallest territory in the world and one of the most remote destinations on earth, Pitcairn Island feels both claustrophobic and wildly exhilarating.

The Pitcairn Islands – the last British Overseas Territory in the Pacific – comprises four remote islands: Pitcairn Island itself, plus the uninhabited Oeno, Henderson and Ducie. What's rarely mentioned about Pitcairn, between the infamous *Bounty* story and the 2004 sex-trials scandal, is that it's a place of incredible natural beauty. The island's 5 sq km surface is almost entirely sloped and has a varied landscape – from desolate rock cliffs that look over an infinite expanse of sea to lush hillsides bursting with tropical plenty.

The nearest inhabited island to Pitcairn is Mangareva in French Polynesia, 480km or a 36-hour boat ride away. Besides a few hundred cruise-ship passengers per year, the only visitors are a few yachts, occasional groups of boat-chartering birders and a handful of intrepid tourists. The islanders do a busy trade turning out curios for visiting ships, including woven pandanus baskets, models of the *Bounty* and wood carvings. Pots of local honey and Pitcairn Island stamps are other island must-haves.

Top Experiences

Christian's Cave

1 Climb the precipice to Christian's Cave, look over Adamstown and imagine what must have gone through the mutineer's head as he sat there hundreds of years ago. A well-signposted ecotrail leads up to the cave.

Henderson Island

2 Uninhabited Henderson Island, 170km northeast of Pitcairn Island, is the largest island of the Pitcairn group. The island is populated by four species of endemic land birds – the flightless and fearless Henderson rail, the colourful Stephen's lorikeet, the terri-

torial Henderson fruit dove and the Henderson warbler. Because of its pristine condition and rare birdlife, the island was declared a Unesco World Heritage site in 1988. The usual landing spot is North Beach and, during certain tides, there is sometimes a freshwater spring in a cave at the north of the island.

St Paul's Pool

3 Take a cool dip in the electric blue, glass-clear waters of St Paul's Pool, a stunning, cathedral-like rock formation encircling a sea-fed pool with the ocean waves surging in through gaps in the rocks.

When to Go

 HIGH SEASON
(Apr–Oct)

 LOW SEASON
(Nov–Mar)

Food & Drink

Breadfruit Typically eaten unripe and roasted till charred on an open fire; its flavour is somewhere between a potato and a chestnut.

Drink Have a tipple with the locals at Christian's Cafe on Friday nights.

Honey Local Pitcairn honey is said to be the world's purest.

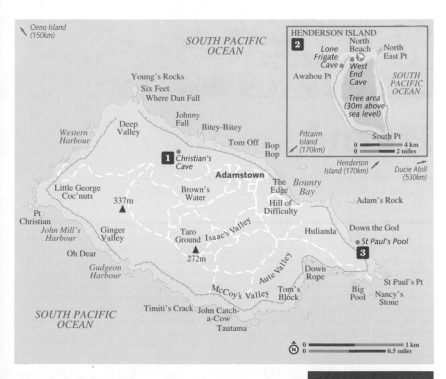

Wawel Castle, Kraków

CAPITAL
Warsaw

POPULATION
38.5 million

AREA
312,685 sq km

OFFICIAL LANGUAGE
Polish

Poland

Chic medieval hot spots like Kraków and Gdańsk vie with energetic Warsaw for your urban attention. Outside the cities, woods, rivers, lakes and hills beckon for some fresh-air fun.

While large swathes of the country are flat, the southern border is lined with a chain of low-lying but lovely mountains that invite days, if not weeks, of splendid solitude. Well-marked hiking paths criss-cross the country, taking you through dense forest, along broad rivers and through mountain passes. Much of the northeast is covered by interlinked lakes and waterways ideal for kayaking and canoeing.

Poland's roots go back to the turn of the first millennium, leaving a thousand years of twists and turns and kings and castles to explore. WWII history buffs are well served. Tragically, Poland found itself in the middle of that epic fight, and monuments and museums dedicated to its battles – and to Poland's remarkable survival – can be seen everywhere.

Top Experiences

Stately Kraków

1 A unique atmosphere drifts through the attractive streets and squares of this former royal capital, with its heady blend of history and harmonious architecture. From the vast Rynek Główny, Europe's largest medieval market square, to the magnificent Wawel Castle on a hill above the Old Town, every part of the city is fascinating. Add to that the former Jewish district of Kazimierz and its scintillating nightlife (and then contrast it with the communist-era concrete structures of Nowa Huta), and it's easy to see why Kraków is an unmissable destination.

Warsaw's Museums & Palaces

2 Poland's capital has an extravagantly dramatic history, and its best museums reflect that complex past. The city's darkest hour in the revolt against Nazi rule is powerfully retold at the Warsaw Rising Museum; while Poland's long Jewish presence is related with energy at the Museum of the History of Polish Jews. Beautiful music can be heard at the Chopin Museum, and the Neon Museum presents a riot of communist-era colour. For stately charm, head to Wilanów Palace, or Łazienki Park's lovely Palace on the Water.

Gdańsk

3 Colossal red-brick churches peer down on slender merchants' townhouses, wedged ornately between palaces that line wide, ancient thoroughfares and crooked medieval lanes. A cosmopolitan residue of art and artefact left behind by a rich maritime and trading past packs whole museums, and tourists from around the world compete with amber stalls and street performers for cobblestone space. This is Gdańsk, a Baltic seaport and Poland's metropolis of the north. It was once part of the Hanseatic League, but now it's in a league of its own.

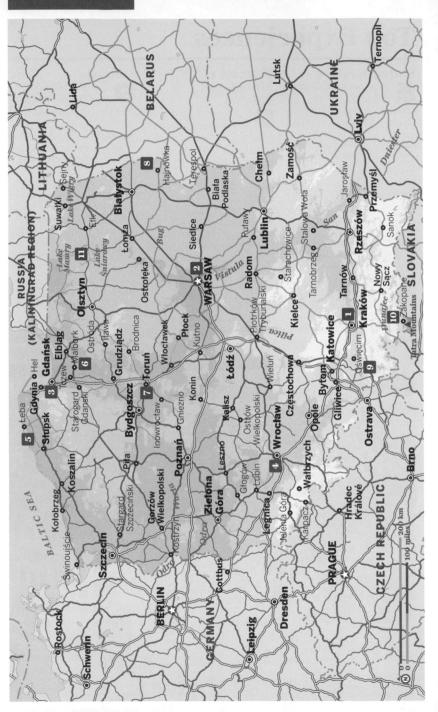

Best on Film

Katyń (Andrzej Wajda; 2007) Moving depiction of a WWII massacre in the Katyń Forest.

Ida (Paweł Pawlikowski; 2013) A young nun-in-waiting discovers her family's hidden history; 2015 Oscar winner.

The Pianist (Roman Polański; 2002) Highly acclaimed film about life in Warsaw's WWII Jewish ghetto.

Best in Print

The Polish Officer (Alan Furst) Gripping spy novel set in Poland on the eve of WWII.

God's Playground: A History of Poland (Norman Davies) Highly readable two-volume set that covers 1000 years of history.

The Painted Bird (Jerzy Kosiński) Page-turner on the travails of an orphan boy on the run during WWII.

Food & Drink

Beer Good, cold and inexpensive.

Bigos A thick sauerkraut and meat stew.

Bread *Chleb* (bread) means more than sustenance to Poles. It's a symbol of good fortune; some older people kiss a piece of bread if they drop it on the ground. Traditional Polish bread is made with rye.

Pierogi Dumplings stuffed with filling.

Soup Hearty examples include *żurek* (sour soup with sausage and hard-boiled egg) and *barszcz* (red beetroot soup).

Vodka Try it plain, or ask for *myśliwska* (juniper-berry flavoured) or *wiśniówka* (with cherries)

Wrocław

 Throughout its turbulent history, this town on the Odra River – the former German city of Breslau – has taken everything invaders could throw at it, and survived. Badly damaged in WWII, it was artfully rebuilt around its beautiful main square, with an intriguing complex of buildings at its centre. Another attraction is the Panorama of Racławice, a vast 19th-century painting hung about the walls of a circular building. Beyond historical gems, however, Wrocław has a vibrant nightlife, with plenty of dining and drinking options throughout the narrow streets of its lively Old Town.

Baltic Beaches

 The season may be brief and the sea one of Europe's nippiest, but if you're looking for a dose of sand, there are few better destinations than the Baltic's cream-white beaches. Many people come for the strands along one of the many coastal resorts, be it hedonistic Darłówko, genteel Świnoujście or the spa town of Kołobrzeg; others opt to flee the masses and head out instead for the shifting dunes of the Słowiński National Park, where the Baltic's constant bluster sculpts mountains of sifted grains.

Malbork Castle

 Medieval monster mother ship of the Teutonic order, Gothic blockbuster Malbork Castle is a mountain of bricks

When to Go

☼
HIGH SEASON
(May–Sep)
Expect sunny skies in June and July, but prepare for rain. Holidays and weekends bring big crowds.

⛅
SHOULDER
(Mar–Apr & Oct)
April and October are cool, with some sunny days. Some attractions may be closed or have shorter hours.

❄
LOW SEASON
(Nov–Feb)
Snow in the mountains brings skiers to the southern resorts. Museums and castles in smaller towns may be closed.

Cycling in the Karkonosze

Slung between Mt Wielki Szyszak (1509m) to the west, and Mt Śnieżka (1602m) to the east, the Karkonosze National Park is not only a treat for hikers. Through its leafy expanse are threaded several mountain-biking trails, covering some 450km, that are easily accessed from the mountain towns of Szklarska Poręba or Karpacz. Pick up a free bike-trail map from the tourist office, hire a bike and head on out through the trees, passing impressively lofty cliffs carved by ice-age glaciers.

Getting Around

 LOT Polish Airlines operates a comprehensive network of domestic routes.

 National Polski Bus service links big cities and can be faster than trains on some routes. Elsewhere, buses are useful for remote towns and villages that aren't serviced by trains.

 Cars are always handy for travelling at your own pace, but Polish highways can be narrow and crowded. Cars can be hired in many towns and cities.

 Polish Rail/PKP Intercity trains offer affordable and fast service between major cities. Slower trains run between cities and towns around the country.

held together by a lake of mortar. It was home to the all-powerful order's grand master and later to visiting Polish monarchs. They have all now left the stage of history, but not even the shells of WWII could dismantle this baby. If you came to Poland to see castles, this is what you came to see; catch it just before dusk when the slanting sunlight burns the bricks kiln-crimson.

Gothic Toruń

7 While many of northern Poland's towns went up in a puff of red-brick dust in WWII's end game, Toruń miraculously escaped intact, leaving today's visitors a magnificently preserved, walled Gothic city by the swirling Vistula. Wander through the Old Town crammed with museums, churches, grand mansions and squares, and when you're all in, perk up with a peppery gingerbread cookie, Toruń's signature snack. Another treat is the city's Copernicus connections – Poland's most illustrious astronomer al-

legedly first saw the light of day in one of Toruń's Gothic townhouses.

Białowieża National Park

8 That bison on the label of a bottle of Żubr beer or Żubrówka vodka starts to make a lot more sense once you've visited this little piece of pristine wood on the Belarus border. The Białowieża National Park holds one of Europe's last vestiges of primeval forest, which you can visit in the company of a guide. Nearby there's a small reserve with another survivor from a bygone era: the once-mighty European bison.

Auschwitz-Birkenau

9 This former extermination camp, established by the German military occupiers in 1941, is a grim reminder of a part of history's greatest genocide, the killing of more than a million people here in the pursuit of Nazi ideology. Now it's a museum and memorial to the victims.

Beyond the infamous 'Arbeit Macht Frei' sign at the entrance to Auschwitz are surviving prison blocks that house exhibitions as shocking as they are informative. Not far away, the former Birkenau camp holds the remnants of the gas chambers used for mass murder. Visiting the complex is an unsettling but deeply moving experience.

Hiking in the Tatras

10 In many ways, the Tatras are the perfect mountain range: awe-inspiring yet approachable, with peaks that even ordinary folks – with a little bit of extra effort – can conquer. That doesn't diminish their impact, especially on a summer day when the clouds part to reveal the mountains' stern rocky visage climbing up over the dwarf pines below. The best approach to the peaks is from the Polish mountain resort of Zakopane.

Great Masurian Lakes

11 Sip a cocktail on the deck of a luxury yacht, take a dip, or don a lifejacket, grab your paddle and slide off into a watery adventure on one of the interconnected lakes that make up this mecca for Polish sailing and water-sports fans. Away from the water, head for one of the region's buzzing resorts, where the slap and jangle of masts competes with the clinking of glasses and the murmur of boat talk. In winter, when the lakes freeze over, cross-country skis replace water skis on the steel-hard surface.

MARK READ / LONELY PLANET ©

8

Jazz in Poland

Jazz has a passionate following in Poland. One of the best festivals is Kraków's Summer Jazz Festival, in July and August.

Landscape Parks

Parki krajobrazowe (landscape parks) play a key role in conservation efforts. As well as their aesthetic contribution, they are often of key historic and cultural value.

10

KAROL MAJEWSKI / GETTY IMAGES ©

CAPITAL
Lisbon

POPULATION
10.8 million

AREA
88,323 sq km

OFFICIAL LANGUAGE
Portuguese

Rooftops of the Alfama, Lisbon

Portugal

Medieval castles, cobblestone villages, captivating cities and golden beaches: the Portugal experience can be many things. History, great food and idyllic scenery are just the beginning...

Celts, Romans, Visigoths, Moors and Christians have all left their mark on this Iberian nation. Here, you can gaze upon 20,000-year-old stone carvings in the Vila Nova de Foz Côa, watch the sunset over mysterious megaliths outside Évora or lose yourself in the elaborate corridors of Unesco World Heritage Sites in Tomar, Belém, Alcobaça or Batalha.

Outside the cities, Portugal's beauty unfolds in all its startling variety. You can go hiking amid the granite peaks of Parque Nacional da Peneda-Gerês or take in the pristine scenery and historic villages of the Beiras. Over 800km of coast offers more places to soak up the splendour. Gaze out over dramatic cliffs, surf stellar breaks or laze peacefully on sandy islands fronting calm blue seas. You'll find dolphin watching in the Sado Estuary, boating and kayaking along the Rio Guadiana, and memorable walks and bike rides all across the country.

Top Experiences

The Alfama

1 Lisbon's Alfama district, with its labyrinthine alleyways, hidden courtyards and curving, shadow-filled lanes, is a magical place in which to lose all sense of direction and delve into the soul of the city. You'll pass breadbox-sized grocers, brilliantly tiled buildings and cosy taverns filled with easygoing chatter, accompanied by the scent of chargrilled sardines and the mournful rhythms of fado drifting in the breeze. Round a bend and catch sight of steeply pitched rooftops leading down to the glittering Tejo, and you'll know you're hooked...

Nightlife in Lisbon

2 Lisbon's dizzying nightlife is a mix of old-school drinking dens, brassy jazz clubs and stylish lounges. The challenge is where to begin. You can start the evening with sunset drinks on a panoramic terrace overlooking the city, then head to Bairro Alto for tapas and early-evening cocktails on people-packed, bar-lined streets. Then head downhill to Cais do Sodré, a former red-light district turned hipster playground, or to Bica for a lively local bar scene. At the end of the night there's always riverside Lux, still one of Portugal's best nightspots.

Porto

3 It would be hard to dream up a more romantic city than Portugal's second largest. Laced with narrow pedestrian laneways, Porto is blessed with baroque churches, epic theatres and sprawling plazas. Its Ribeira district – a Unesco World Heritage Site – is just a short walk across a landmark bridge from centuries-old port wineries in Vila Nova de Gaia, where you can sip the world's best port. And though some walls are crumbling, a sense of renewal – in the form of modern architecture, cosmopolitan restaurants, burgeoning nightlife and a vibrant arts scene – is palpable.

Sintra

4 Less than an hour by train from the capital, Sintra feels like another world. Resembling an illustration from a fairy tale, it is sprinkled with stone-walled taverns and has a whitewashed palace looming over it. Forested hillsides form the backdrop to the village's storybook setting, with imposing castles, mystical gardens, strange mansions and centuries-old monasteries hidden among the woodlands. The fog that sweeps in by night adds another layer of mystery, and cool evenings are best spent fireside in one of Sintra's many charming B&Bs.

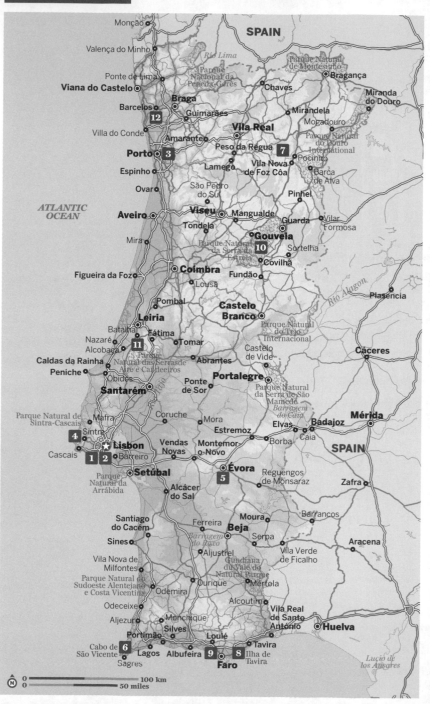

Best on Film

A Lisbon Story (1994) Wim Wenders' love letter to Lisbon.

Letters from Fontainhas (1997–2006) Pedro Costa's arthouse trilogy set in Lisbon.

Capitães de Abril (Captains of April; 2000) Overview of the 1974 Carnation Revolution.

Historic Villages

Portugal is home to many enchanting villages, where a stroll along peaceful cobblestone lanes is like a trip back in time.

Óbidos Medieval architecture, lively festivals and charming guest houses await in this fortified town an hour north of Lisbon.

Mértola Set high above the Rio Guadiana, this remarkably well-preserved Alentejo town is considered an open-air museum.

Monsanto A forlorn village surrounding an age-old, boulder-strewn castle, Monsanto has great walking trails through the rolling countryside nearby.

Miranda do Douro This remote fortress town on the edge of Spain has an imposing 16th-century castle and street signs in the ancient language of Mirandês.

Castelo de Vide Wander the medieval Jewish quarter and take in sweeping views over the surrounding cork and olive groves.

Historic Évora

5 The Queen of the Alentejo and one of Portugal's most beautifully preserved medieval towns, Évora is an enchanting place to spend several days delving into the past. Inside the 14th-century walls, Évora's narrow, winding lanes lead to striking architectural works: an elaborate medieval cathedral and cloisters, Roman ruins and a picturesque town square. Historic and aesthetic virtues aside, Évora is also a lively university town, and its many attractive restaurants serve up excellent, hearty Alentejan cuisine.

Cabo de São Vicente

6 There's something thrilling about standing at Europe's most southwestern edge, a headland of barren cliffs to which Portuguese sailors would bid a nervous farewell as they sailed past, venturing into the unknown during Portugal's golden years of exploration. The windswept cape is redolent of history – if you squint hard (really hard), you'll see the ghost of Vasco da Gama sailing past. These days, a fortress and lighthouse perch on the cape and a new museum beautifully highlights Portugal's maritime-navigation history.

When to Go

HIGH SEASON
(Jul & Aug)
Sweltering temperatures are commonplace.

SHOULDER
(Apr–Jun & Sep–Nov)
Wildflowers and mild days; ideal for hikes and outdoor activities.

LOW SEASON
(Dec–Mar)
Shorter, rainier days; freezing temperatures at higher elevations.

Staying in a Pousada

In 1942 the government started the Pousadas de Portugal (www.pousadas.pt), turning castles, monasteries and palaces into unique, luxurious hotels, roughly divided into rural and historic options; nearly three dozen *pousadas* are spread across the country.

Surfing

Portugal has some of Europe's most curvaceous surf, with 30 to 40 major reefs and beaches. It picks up swells from the north, south and west, giving it remarkable consistency. It also has a wide variety of waves and swell sizes, making it ideal for surfers of all levels.

Snack Foods

Pastel de nata Custard tart, ideally served warm and dusted with cinnamon.

Travesseira A rolled puff pastry filled with almond-and-egg-yolk custard. Find them in Sintra.

Tinned fish Sardines, mackerel and tuna served with bread, olives and other accompaniments are the latest snack craze in Lisbon.

Francesinha Porto's favourite hangover snack is a thick open-faced sandwich covered in melted cheese.

Marzipan In the Algarve, this very sweet almond-infused confection is a local favourite.

Grilled chicken Rotisserie chicken is an art form in Portugal. Spice it up with *piri-piri* (hot sauce).

Bifana A bread roll served with a slice of fried pork inside. You'll find the best ones in the Alentejo.

Sipping the Douro

7 The exquisite Alto Douro wine country is the oldest demarcated wine region on earth. Its steeply terraced hills, stitched together with craggy vines that have produced luscious wines for centuries, loom either side of the Rio Douro. Whether you get here by driving the impossibly scenic back roads, or by train or boat from Porto, take the time to hike, cruise and taste. Countless vintners receive guests for tours, tastings and overnight stays, and if you find one that's still family owned, you may sample something very old and very special.

Ilha de Tavira

8 Ilha de Tavira has the lot for sunseekers, beach bums, nature lovers (and naturists): kilometre after kilometre of golden beach (think sand, sand, sand, as far as the eye can see), a designated nudist area, transport via miniature train, busy restaurants and a campground. To top it off, it's part of the protected Parque Natural da Ria Formosa. Outside the high season, the island feels wonderfully remote and empty, but be warned: during high season (July and August) the hordes descend.

Parque Natural da Ria Formosa

9 This special spot feels like it's in the middle of the wilderness, yet it's right off the Algarvian coast. Enclosing a vast area of *sapais* (marshes), *salinas* (salt pans), creeks and dune islands, the protected lagoon system stretches for an incredible 60km and encompasses 18,000 hectares. And it's all accessible from various towns – have a boat drop you at a deserted beach, or amble along the nature trail among the precious wetland bird life.

Parque Natural da Serra da Estrela

10 Portugal's highest mountains blend rugged scenery, outdoor adventure and vanishing traditional ways. At Torre, the country's highest point (artificially pushed up to 2000m by the addition of a not-so-subtle stone monument!), you can slalom down Portugal's only ski slope. Hikers can choose from a network of high country trails with stupendous vistas. Oh, and did we mention the furry sheepdog puppies that frolic by the roadside? You'll long to take one home.

Alcobaça, Batalha & Tomar

11 These medieval Christian monuments (all Unesco World Heritage Sites) constitute one of Portugal's greatest national treasures. Each has its own magic: the whimsy of Manueline adornments and the haunting roofless shell of the unfinished Capelas Imperfeitas at Batalha's monastery; the great kitchen at Alcobaça's monastery, where a multistorey chimney and fish-stocked river once tended to the appetites of countless monks; and the labyrinthine courtyards and mysterious 16-sided chapel of the Knights Templar at Tomar's Convento de Cristo.

Getting Around

 Buses are cheaper and slower than trains, but useful for more remote villages that aren't serviced by them. Infrequent service on weekends.

 A car is useful for visiting small villages, national parks and other regions with minimal public transport. Drive on the right.

 Trains are extremely affordable, with a decent network between major towns from north to south.

CAPITAL
San Juan

POPULATION
3.5 million

AREA
13,791 sq km

OFFICIAL LANGUAGE
Spanish

Playa Flamenco, Culebra

Puerto Rico

Scented by salty sea breezes, rimmed by sand, colored by swashbuckling history and covered by tropical forests: this sun-washed medley of Spanish and American influences is a pleasure dome for paradise-seekers.

Golden sand, swashbuckling history and wildly diverse terrain make the sun-washed backyard of the United States a place fittingly hyped as the 'Island of Enchantment.' It's the Caribbean's only island where you can catch a wave before breakfast, hike a rainforest after lunch and race to the beat of a high-gloss, cosmopolitan city after dark.

Between blinking casinos and chirping frogs, Puerto Rico is also a land of dynamic contrasts, where the breezy gate of the Caribbean is bedeviled by the hustle of contemporary America. While modern conveniences make it simple for travelers, the condo-lined concrete jungle might seem a bit too close to home. A quick visit for Puerto Rico's beaches, historic forts and craps tables will quicken a visitor's pulse, but the island's singular essence only reveals itself to those who go deeper, exploring the misty crags of the central mountains and crumbling facades of the island's remote corners.

CHAD ZUBER / SHUTTERSTOCK ©

Top Experiences

Evocative Old San Juan

1 Even those limited to a quick visit find it easy to fall under the beguiling spell of the cobblestone streets, pastel-painted colonial buildings and grand fortresses of Old San Juan. From the ramparts of El Morro, the allure of this place is evident in every direction: in the maze of crooked lanes and in the endless sparkle of the Atlantic. By day, lose yourself in historical stories of blood and drama; by night, tap in (and tap along) to the condensed cluster of bars and clubs constituting the neighborhood's nightlife.

Glorious Beaches

2 The rub of sand between your toes, the dazzling shimmer of turquoise water and the rhythmic shush of cresting waves – Puerto Rico's beaches possess all the qualities of a daydream. Take your pick from the golden, crescent-shaped heaven of Culebra's Playa Flamenco (considered among the world's best beaches); the embarrassment of riches on Vieques; the coconut-oil-scented crowds of Playa Isla Verde, San Juan's own little slice of Brazil; the secluded, mangrove-shaded hideaways in the south; or the roaring surf of the west,

culminating in isolated bays like Playa Santa.

Las Cabezas de San Juan Reserva Natural 'El Faro'

3 The diverse ecosystem of the Las Cabezas de San Juan nature reserve is only a day trip from the high-rises of San Juan's urban core and highlights the island's ecological

When to Go

HIGH SEASON
(Dec–Apr & Jul)

SHOULDER
(Oct–Nov & May)

LOW SEASON
(Jun & Aug–Sep)

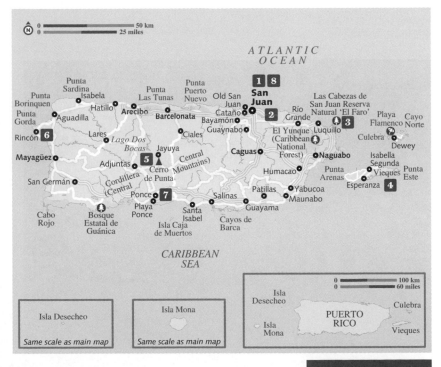

eclecticism at every turn. After an informative trip through the visitors center, travelers begin touring the flora and fauna. The sea grass waves along mangrove forest and coral-protected lagoons, while giant iguanas scuttle from underfoot and crabs scurry along rocky shores. A historic lighthouse with a nature center sports sweeping views of the coastline. At night, there's bioluminescent action.

Bioluminescent Bays

4 Few experiences can inspire the awe of floating on inky waves under a canopy of stars and witnessing one of nature's most tactile magic tricks: the otherworldly sparkle of bioluminescent waters. Kayaking into Puerto Rico's glowing bays and seeing the jewelled flicker of water drip from your hands or illuminate a paddle stroke promises an experience of profound wonder. Or you can just glide along on an electric boat. Best bet: the bay at Vieques.

Coffee in the Central Mountains

5 Puerto Rico's legendary coffee plantations offer caffeine junkies a rare opportunity. In the remote Central Mountains, you can sip a steaming cup of rich, fresh coffee while looking over the hills and valleys where the beans are grown, roasted and brewed. The winding Ruta Panorámica, a white-knuckled scenic route through the peaks, takes travelers past one picturesque plantation after the next and through the village of Jayuya, where haciendas like San Pedro or Pomarrosa offer tasty, and hugely informative coffee breaks.

Getting Around

Exploring Puerto Rico will be more rewarding with your own vehicle, although unnecessary while staying in San Juan: parking is scarce, traffic terrible.

Regular large urban buses run on routes convenient for visitors in San Juan.

Within San Juan, taxis are reasonable. Travel between towns, though, and costs fly up.

3

Surfing at Rincón

6 In winter, the cold weather brings righteous swells to the island's west-coast surfing capital of Rincón, where some of the most consistent, varied and exciting surf locations in the Caribbean can be found. And while the double overheads and excellent tubes attract an international set of would-be pros, beginners can paddle out to tamer breaks nearby. At sunset, crowds of locals and visitors replenish themselves with inexpensive eats and ice-cold beer while they mingle in suave restaurants, in laid-back beach bars and around bonfires on the sand.

Architectural Gems

7 If you tried to savor every single example of colonial grandeur – all the fountains and historic squares, every dignified plantation house and buttressed 19th-century municipal hall – Puerto Rico's architectural gems would

Food & Drink

If you were to draw the Puerto Rican food pyramid, it might only have four elements – rice, beans, plantains and pork. Of these, pork rules the roost; you'll find it fried, grilled, stewed and skewered. But it's the mighty *lechón* (savory, smoky, suckling pig, spit-roasted for up to eight hours) that remains the island's favorite lunch. On the weekends, the roadsides near Guavate abutting the Bosque Estatal de Carite are a virtual parking lot for *lechoneras* (eateries specializing in suckling pig), with locals and visitors feasting alike.

demand a stay of months. But if just one location outside of Old San Juan earns time on your agenda, take a stroll around Ponce and its historic main square. In the west, Puerto Rico's second-oldest city, San Germán, dates to 1511, an age that blows away anything in the continental US.

Salsa

8 Let the scholars debate over whether the origins of salsa are rooted in the clubs of New York or the islands of the Caribbean and just feel it. There's no doubt that it lives on as the essential heartbeat of Puerto Rico (especially at venues in San Juan). You'll hear the basic rhythm of the clavé (percussion instrument; literally 'keystone') driving Puerto Rican pop music and traditional songs. The secret to grooving to its rhythms on the dance floor is handed down from one generation to the next.

Just Relax!

Relax, Puerto Rico is easy. US citizens don't need passports and the currency is the US dollar. Save time to just chill and save plenty of time for the beaches. While there are countless reasons to go exploring, you'll find that road conditions can make endless days in a car stressful. Also, as you do move around, hit the pause button in places like Vieques, which are much more rewarding over several days as opposed to a super-quick day trip from San Juan.

Eat like a local. You can get great international fare or even slum it in familiar fast-food outlets, but why bother? Stands, food trucks and humble open-air cafes dish up the Commonwealth's delicious cuisine, which boasts an enticing medley of Caribbean and Spanish flavors.

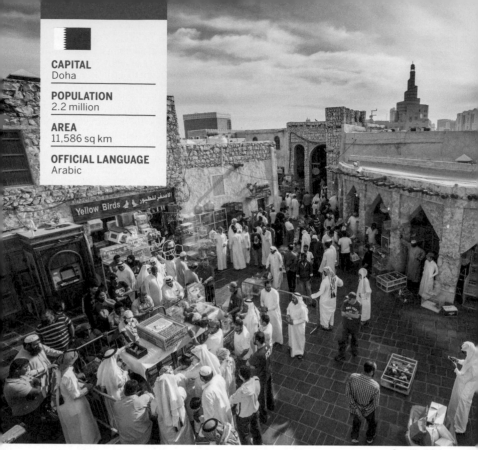

CAPITAL
Doha

POPULATION
2.2 million

AREA
11,586 sq km

OFFICIAL LANGUAGE
Arabic

Yellow Birds الأصفر للطيور

Souq Waqif, Doha

Qatar

Just over a decade ago, we labelled Qatar one of the most boring places on Earth. Now it's fast becoming one of the most exciting.

Doha is a world-class city in the making, with the peerless Museum of Islamic Art, perhaps the finest traditional souq in the Gulf region, and burgeoning arts and culinary scenes.

Qatar is the kind of place where you can learn about the ancient pursuit of falconry or watch camels ridden by remote-controlled robot jockeys race across the desert, admire traditional dhows bobbing on the water alongside one of the world's most spectacular modern skylines, or sample Doha's portfolio of sophisticated restaurants and then watch the sun set over sand dunes that seem to spring from an Arabian fairy tale.

Put simply, Qatar is racing headlong into the future without losing sight of its past – and it's one pretty exciting ride.

Top Experiences

Souq Waqif

1 Reincarnated in the last decade as the social heart of Doha, Souq Waqif is a wonderful place to explore and an undoubted highlight of the city. There has been a souq on this site for centuries, and the entire market area has been cleverly redeveloped to look like a 19th-century souq, with mud-rendered shops, exposed timber beams and some beautifully restored original Qatari buildings. If you want a glimpse of heritage, don't miss the Falcon Souq, afforded its own traditional arcaded building off Souq Waqif.

Al Corniche

2 More than most other Gulf cities, Doha makes full use of its attractive waterfront promenade, helped by the fact that Doha Bay was carefully constructed with landfill to make an attractive crescent. The best views are from the water's edge close to the Museum of Islamic Art, with sit in the foreground and the skyscrapers of West Bay across the

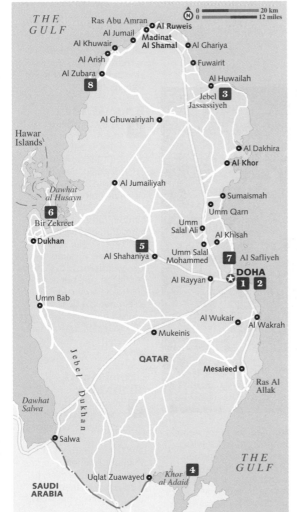

*Map of Qatar showing: THE GULF, Ras Abu Amran, Al Ruweis, Al Jumail, Madinat Al Shamal, Al Khuwair, Al Ghariya, Al Arish, Fuwairit, Al Zubara **8**, Al Huwailah, Jebel Jassassiyeh **3**, Al Ghuwairiyah, Hawar Islands, Al Dakhira, Al Khor, Dawhat al Husayn, Al Jumailiyah, Sumaismah, Umm Qarn, **6** Bir Zekreet, Umm Salal Ali, Al Khisah, Dukhan, **5**, Al Shahaniya, Umm Salal Mohammed, **7** Al Safliyeh, Al Rayyan, DOHA **1 2**, Umm Bab, Al Wukair, Al Wakrah, Mukeinis, Jebel Dukhan, QATAR, Mesaieed, Ras Al Allak, Dawhat Salwa, Salwa, THE GULF, Uqlat Zuawayed, Khor al Adaid **4**, SAUDI ARABIA. Scale: 20 km / 12 miles*

Food & Drink

Alcohol Available only in top-end hotel restaurants and bars.

Coffee Traditionally served pale and spiked with cardamom or dark, strong and sugary.

Tap water Safe to drink, although most people stick to bottled water.

Makbous Rice and spices with chicken, lamb or fish in a rich sauce.

Khabees Dates in a variety of sizes, colours and states of ripeness.

When to Go

HIGH SEASON (Oct–Mar)

LOW SEASON (May–Sep)

Al Jazeera

Al Jazeera has transformed the press in the Arab world. Established in 1996, it differed from all that went before it because it was free from censorship or government control, it offered regional audiences a rare opportunity for debate and independent opinion, and it opened up an alternative perspective on regional issues for the world at large.

Al Jazeera, which means 'The Island' in English, was originally launched as an Arabic news and current-affairs satellite-TV channel, funded with a generous grant from the emir of Qatar. It has been subsidised by the emir on a year-by-year basis since, despite the airing of criticism of his own government.

Al Jazeera has earned its spurs on the frontline of journalism and is today the most widely watched news channel in the Middle East. In November 2006 a 24-hour, seven-day-a-week news channel called Al Jazeera English was launched and it currently broadcasts to more than 260 million households in more than 130 countries.

Jebel Jassassiyeh

3 The petroglyphs of northern Qatar have been seen by very few visitors. This is largely because until very recently their whereabouts was all but a secret. A low-lying rocky outcrop about 60km north of Doha, the unprepossessing Jebel Jassassiyeh is home to a remarkable 900 rock carvings, strewn across 580 sites. While some archaeologists have suggested the carvings could date back to the 3rd century BC, most experts agree that they were created between the 10th and 18th centuries AD.

Khor Al Adaid

4 Without a doubt, the major natural attraction in Qatar is the beautiful 'inland sea' of Khor Al Adaid, near the border with Saudi Arabia. Often described as a sea or a lake, the *khor* is in fact neither: rather it is a creek surrounded by silvery crescents of sand (known as *barchan*). All sand dunes look wonderful in the late-afternoon sun, but those of Khor Al Adaid take on an almost mystical quality under a full moon, when the *sabkha* (salt flats) sparkle in the gaps between the sand.

Camels in Al Shahaniya

5 If you've come to the Middle East hoping to see camels, then there's one place you're guaranteed to find them. At Al Shahaniya camels roam freely around the desert, or you can see them in the famous local camel races.

water. And the best time to come is late afternoon on Friday, when families of all nationalities throng here. Escape the heat by visiting the Museum of Islamic Art while you're nearby. Rising from its own purpose-built island, with an extensive landscape of lawns and ornamental trees – and with the largest collection of Islamic art in the world – this is a fabulous museum.

Getting Around

Once Doha's urban Metro system is complete, there are plans for a rail system that connects most of Qatar's population centres.

The public bus system has air-conditioned services to a number of destinations.

If you're driving around Doha, you'll discover that roundabouts are very common and often redundant in practice. Authorities are strict and heavy on-the-spot fines are handed out freely.

Known as the 'sport of sheikhs', camel races can be seen from a purpose-built stadium, and they involve remote-controlled robot jockeys (!) that weigh 25kg. If you have a car you can drive along the 8km racetrack during the race.

Bir Zekreet

The limestone escarpment of Bir Zekreet is like a geography lesson in desert formations, as the wind has whittled away softer sedimentary rock, exposing pillars and a large mushroom of limestone. The surrounding beaches are full of empty oyster shells, with rich mother-of-pearl interiors, and other assorted bivalves. The shallow waters are quiet and peaceful and see relatively few visitors, making the area a pleasant destination for a day trip.

Katara

Visit an exhibition, enjoy an opera performance, swim at the beach or dine at Katara, an extensive collection of new Qatari-style buildings on the waterfront in Doha. With the superb modern coliseum at its centre, Katara provides a fantastic venue for live entertainment. There is no charge for admission to the grounds, which are home to varied restaurants and a beach.

Al Zubara

Qatar's only Unesco World Heritage Site, Al Zubara occupies an important place in Qatari history, as it was a large commercial and pearling port in the 18th and 19th centuries and is now an important archaeological site.

MATTHEW ASHTON / GETTY IMAGES ©

CAPITAL
Bucharest

POPULATION
21.6 million

AREA
238,391 sq km

OFFICIAL LANGUAGE
Romanian

Carpathian mountain village

Romania

Rugged stone churches and dazzling monasteries dot a pristine landscape of rocky mountains and rolling hills in Romania. Transylvanian towns have stepped out of time, while vibrant Bucharest is all energy.

Transylvania, the land that gave us Dracula, has no shortage of jaw-dropping castles pitched precariously on rocky hilltops, along with fortified churches that date back half a millennium. In medieval towns such as Braşov, Sighişoara and Sibiu, cobbled walkways support chic streetside cafes, while a cacophony of sounds emanating from student bars and clubs echo off the Gothic and baroque facades in lively Cluj-Napoca.

The rocky peaks of Transylvania and Moldavia call out for conquering, and well-marked trails lead to summits from all directions. There are less adventurous but no less rewarding walks in other parts of the country. The vast Danube Delta makes a perfect backdrop for fishing, boating and, especially, birdwatching in spring. In summer, the action moves to the Black Sea coast. Beach resorts fill up with swimmers, divers, sunbathers and partiers.

Top Experiences

Palace of Parliament, Bucharest

1 Depending on your point of view, the Palace of Parliament is either a mind-blowing testament to the waste and folly of dictatorship or an awe-inspiring showcase of Romanian materials and craftsmanship, albeit applied to sinister ends. Most visitors conclude that it's a bit of both. Whatever emotions the former 'House of the People' happens to elicit, the sheer scale of Romania's entry into the 'World's Largest Buildings' competition – on par with the Taj Mahal or the Pentagon – must be seen to be believed.

Bran Castle

2 Perched on a rocky bluff in Transylvania, in a mass of turrets and castellations, Bran Castle overlooks a desolate mountain pass swirling with mist and dense forest. Its spectral exterior is like a composite of every horror film you've ever seen, but don't expect to be scared. Inside, Bran is anything but spooky, with its white walls and geranium-filled courtyard. Legend has it Vlad the Impaler (the inspiration for Count Dracula) was briefly imprisoned here, and you can follow his footsteps through an 'Escheresque' maze of courtyards and hidden passages.

Painted Monasteries of Bucovina

3 Tucked away in the eastern side of the Carpathian mountains,

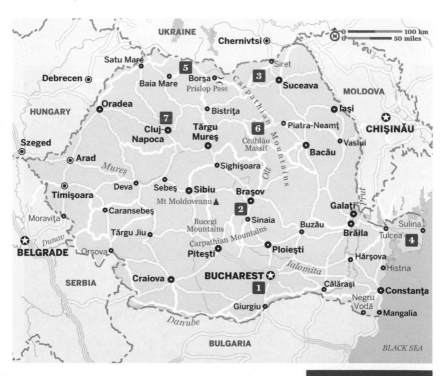

the Unesco-listed painted monasteries of Bucovina proudly show off Romania's unique, Latin-flavoured Orthodox tradition. The churches are at one with their natural surroundings and the dizzying kaleidoscope of colours and intricate details in the frescos bring to life everything from biblical stories to the 15th-century siege of Constantinople. The monasteries are largely the genius of Moldavian prince and national hero Stephen the Great (Ştefan cel Mare), who was later canonised for his works.

Wildlife in the Danube Delta

4 Under the international environmental protection of the Danube Delta Biosphere Reserve Authority, the region has developed into a sanctuary for fish and fowl of all stripes and colours. Birders, in particular, will thrill to the prospect of glimpsing species such as the roller, white-tailed eagle, great white egret and even a bee-eater or two.

Wooden Churches of Maramureş

5 Rising from forested hillsides like dark needles, the eight Unesco-listed wooden churches of Maramureş, in northern Romania, are both austere and beautiful, with roofs of shingle, and weather-beaten, Gothic-style steeples. Inside, you'll discover rich interiors painted with biblical frescos, some of which date back to the 14th century. On Sundays, the villagers don traditional dress for church, and attending one of the services is a special treat.

Getting Around

Flying between cities is a feasible option if time is a primary concern.

A mix of buses, minibuses and 'maxitaxis' form the backbone of the Romanian national transport system.

Roads are generally crowded and in poor condition. The country has only a few stretches of motorway, so most of your travel will be along two-lane highways or secondary roads.

DZIEWUL / SHUTTERSTOCK ©

Trekking in the Carpathians

6 Dense primeval forests leap straight from the pages of a Brothers Grimm story, with bears, wolves, lynx and boar, rugged mountain plateaux, well-marked trails and a network of cabins en route to keep you warm. Trekking is the best way to absorb this vibrant landscape of mountain tops, forests and rolling pastureland. The peaks can be approached from both Transylvania and Moldavia. The Retezat Mountains, with some 80 glacial lakes and peaks towering above 2000m, are a spectacular stretch of the southern Carpathians.

Cluj-Napoca

7 Romania's second-largest city has reawakened from its decades-long slumber and now offers countless bohemian cafes, great restaurants, music festivals, clubs and bars. It's also emerged as the country's contemporary arts hub. The tens of thousands of students here lend a youthful vibe and fuel a vigorous nightlife. With increasing flight links to European cities, the city is welcoming more and more travellers, who usually shoot off to higher-profile burgs like Braşov, Sibiu or Sighişoara, but who come inevitably to regret not allowing enough time for Cluj.

7

MARIA GOLOVIANKO / SHUTTERSTOCK ©

Food & Drink

Ciorbă Sour soup that's a mainstay of the Romanian diet and a powerful hangover remedy.

Covrigi Oven-baked pretzels served warm from windows.

Mămăligă Cornmeal mush that's boiled or fried, sometimes topped with sour cream or cheese.

Sarmale Spiced pork wrapped in cabbage or grape leaves.

Ţuică Romanian moonshine. Home-brewed batches can weigh in at as much as 60% alcohol, and the wallop can be fast and furious. Classic ţuică is usually distilled from plums – purists say only plums – but we've seen other fruits, such as apricots and pears, employed to this nefarious end.

Brain Drain & Gain

In the decade since Romania's accession to the EU in 2007, the country has witnessed profound changes in every sphere. Polls continue to show that about three quarters of Romanians support the EU and their country's membership, but scratch the surface in private conversation and you'll find it's been a mixed bag.

One of the biggest negatives has been the brain drain of talented young Romanians to countries around the EU. The IMF calls Romania the biggest exporter of human resources in the EU, with nearly one in five Romanians living outside the country.

On the positive side of the ledger is a host of benefits and advantages that are hard to quantify, but equally difficult to ignore. Billions of euros in public EU funds have flowed into the country since accession. While the funds have swamped the country's ability to absorb them, Romanians have gained much cleaner air and water, better roads and a much more secure social benefit infrastructure. Romanians are free to travel, study and work where they want. The currency, the leu, has stabilised, and economic prospects are generally good.

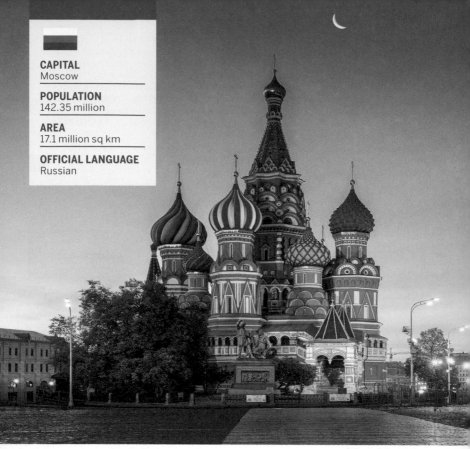

CAPITAL	Moscow
POPULATION	142.35 million
AREA	17.1 million sq km
OFFICIAL LANGUAGE	Russian

St Basil's Cathedral, Moscow

Russia

The world's largest country offers it all, from historic cities and idyllic countryside to artistic riches, epic train rides and vodka-fuelled nightlife.

Whether you're a culture vulture in search of inspiration from great artists and writers or an adventure addict looking for new horizons to conquer, Russia amply delivers. Tread in the footsteps of literary greats, including Tolstoy and Pushkin, on their country estates. Arrange a ski holiday in Krasnaya Polyana, newly spruced up for the 2014 Sochi Winter Olympics, go trekking in the Altai, or even climb an active volcano in Kamchatka – the varied possibilities will make your head spin.

If ancient walled fortresses, glittering palaces and swirly-spired churches are what you're after, focus on European Russia. Here Moscow and St Petersburg are the must-see destinations, twin repositories of eye-boggling national treasures, political energies and contemporary creativity. Within easy reach of these cities are charming historical towns and villages, where the vistas dotted with onion domes and lined with gingerbread cottages measure up to the rural Russia of popular imagination.

Top Experiences

Walking Across Red Square

1 Stepping onto Moscow's Red Square never ceases to inspire: the tall towers and imposing walls of the Kremlin, the playful jumble of patterns and colours adorning St Basil's Cathedral, the majestic red bricks of the State History Museum and the elaborate edifice of GUM, all encircling a vast stretch of cobblestones. Individually they are impressive, but the ensemble is electrifying. Further, it evokes a sense of import to stroll across the place where so much of Russian history has unfolded. Come at night to see the square empty of crowds and the buildings awash with lights.

Banya at Sanduny Baths

2 The quintessential Russian experience is visiting a traditional bathhouse, or *banya*. Forget your modesty, strip down and brave the steam room at the likes of Moscow's Sanduny Baths, the oldest and most luxurious *banya* in the city. As the heat hits, you'll understand why locals wear felt hats to protect their hair. A light thrashing with a bundle of birch branches is part of the fun, as is the invigorating blast that follows the post-steam dive into an icy pool or the douse in a frigid shower – as the locals say, '*S lyogkim parom*!' (Hope your steam was easy!).

The Hermitage

3 Little can prepare most visitors for the scale and quality of the exhibits at the State Hermitage Museum in St Petersburg. Comprising an almost unrivalled history of Western art, the collection includes a staggering number of Rembrandts, Rubens, Picassos and Matisses – the latter two now displayed in new galleries in the General Staff Building. In addition, there are superb antiquities, sculpture and jewellery on display. If that's not enough, then simply content yourself with wandering through the private apartments of the Romanovs, for whom the Winter Palace was home until 1917.

Exploring the Black Sea

4 The serene Black Sea coast has long been a favourite of Russian holidaymakers for its seaside towns, easygoing ambience and magnificent scenery in the nearby Caucasus mountains. The gateway to it all is Sochi, a vibrant city that reinvented itself as a first-rate international resort and host of the 2014 Winter Olympics. The looming peaks of nearby Krasnaya Polyana make a superb destination for ski lovers, while there's great hiking – past waterfalls and up to eagles'-nest heights – in the Agura Valley.

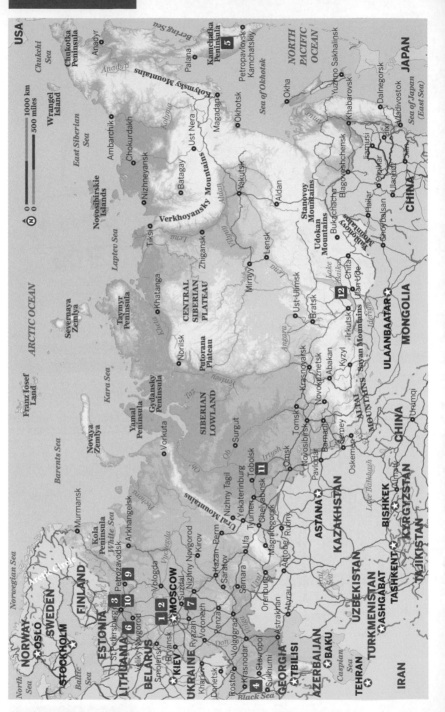

Best on Film

Pussy Riot: A Punk Prayer (2013) Directed by Mike Lerner and Maxim Pozdorovkin, this documentary is about the trial of the Pussy Riot trio.

My Perestroika (2010) Robin Hessman's film focuses on five Russians and the effects on their lives of the past 20 turbulent years.

Winter Journey (2013) Sergei Taramaev and Lubov Lvova direct this art-house feature. It has scooped awards at film festivals abroad but been shunned in Russia because of its gay love theme.

Best in Print

Russia – A Journey to the Heart of a Land and its People (Jonathan Dimbleby; 2008) Also a BBC series, this is a revealing snapshot of a multifaceted country by one of the UK's top broadcasters.

The Last Man in Russia (Oliver Bullough; 2013) Spot-on portrait of modern Russia, told through the tumultuous and tragic life of an Orthodox priest.

Lost Cosmonaut (Daniel Kalder; 2006) and **Strange Telescopes** (2008) Kalder's books explore some of Russia's quirkiest and least-visited locations.

Kamchatka

5 It seems almost trite to describe Kamchatka as majestic. To many Kamchatka is, quite simply, the most beautiful place in the world. It's Yellowstone, Rotorua and Patagonia rolled into one, and it teems with wildlife free to frolic in one of the world's great remaining wildernesses.

Traditionally the domain of well-heeled tourists who could afford helicopter rides to view its trademark volcanoes, geysers and salmon-devouring bears, Kamchatka has finally loosened up a bit for the independent traveller. Now if only they could fix the weather...

Veliky Novgorod's Kremlin

6 In the town that considers itself Russia's birthplace stands one of the country's most impressive and picturesque stone fortresses. Within the kremlin's grounds rise the Byzantine 11th-century Cathedral of St Sophia and a 300-tonne sculpture celebrating 1000 years of Russian history. Climb the Kokui Tower for an overview of the complex, then enter the Novgorod State United Museum to see one of Russia's best collections of iconographic art. A pleasant park and riverside beach also fringe the magnificent brick walls.

When to Go

HIGH SEASON
(Jun–Sep)
Prices can rise, particularly in St Petersburg.

SHOULDER
(May & Oct)
The country is bathed in the fresh greenery or russet shades of the seasons.

LOW SEASON
(Nov–Apr)
Snow falls and temperatures plummet, creating the wintery Russia of the imagination.

Suzdal's Idyll

7 Ding-dong ring the bells of a few dozen churches as you ride your bike through the streets of Suzdal, lined with wooden

Circus

Russian circuses are still like those from childhood stories – prancing horses with acrobats on their backs, snarling lions and tigers, heartstopping high-wire artists and hilarious clowns.

Folk & Native Art

An amazing spectrum of richly decorated folk art has evolved in Russia. Perhaps most popular are the intricately painted, enamelled wood boxes called *palekh*, and *finift*, luminous enamelled metal miniatures from Rostov-Veliky. The most common craft is woodcarving, represented by toys, distaffs and gingerbread moulds in the museums, and in its most clichéd form by the nested *matryoshka* dolls.

Food & Drink

Bliny Pancakes served with *ikra* (caviar) or *tvorog* (cottage cheese).

Kvas A refreshing, beerlike drink.

Pelmeni Dumplings stuffed with meat and eaten with sour cream and vinegar.

Salads A wide variety usually slathered in mayonnaise, including the chopped potato one called Olivier.

Soups Try flavoursome meat *solyanka* or hearty fish *ukha*.

Vodka The quintessential Russian tipple.

Kefir Yoghurt-like sour milk, usually served as a breakfast drink.

Syrniki Cottage-cheese fritters, delicious with jam, sugar and the universal Russian condiment, *smetana* (sour cream).

Zakuski Appetisers such as olives, *bliny* with mushrooms, caviar and salads.

cottages and lush gardens. This is Russia as it would have been, if not for the devastating 20th century – unpretentious, pious and very laid-back. Some of the best religious architecture is scattered around, but you can just as well spend all day lying in the grass and watching the river before repairing to a *banya* for the sweet torture of heat, cold and birch twigs.

Overnight Train Through Siberia

8 One of the pleasures of travelling Russia is to board an overnight train and alight in a different city the following morning. This may be inside a deluxe carriage from St Petersburg, but most likely it's in a four-berth compartment as you travel across Siberia on Russia's 'track of the camel', or perhaps hurtle through a Siberian night in third-class to the snores, silences and groans of more than 50 other travellers.

Kizhi

9 Old buildings made from logs may not usually be synonymous with 'heart-stopping excitement', but Kizhi's collection of wooden masterpieces is enough to spike the blood pressure of those weary of even the most glorious architecture. The first glimpse of the heavenly Transfiguration Church, viewed from the approaching hydrofoil, causes such a ripple that the boat practically bounces: *is it... it is!* Up close, the church is a miracle of design and construct: legend has it that the unnamed builder destroyed his axe upon its completion, correctly assuming that its glory could not be matched.

A Night at the Mariinsky

10 What could be more Russian than a night at the ballet, dressed to the nines, watching *Swan Lake* or *Romeo and Juliet*?

St Petersburg's famed Mariinsky Theatre offers the ultimate in classical ballet or operatic experiences, and now with a contemporary twist as the Mariinsky's long-awaited second stage has finally opened. Also worth a visit is Moscow's Bolshoi Theatre, looking better than ever after a long renovation. Tickets are no longer cheap, but the experience will stay with you forever.

Tobolsk

11 The former capital of Siberia, Tobolsk is today renowned across Russia for its magnificent kremlin. Crowds are rare, though, and if you come on a weekday you're likely to have its grounds almost to yourself. The kremlin is perched high above the old town, a part of Tobolsk where you'll lose track of time as you explore the endless wooden buildings and dramatic churches. Tobolsk is off the main Trans-Siberian route, but its charms are well worth the detour.

Olkhon Island

12 Sacred of the sacred to the shamanist western Buryats, enchanted Olkhon sits halfway up Lake Baikal's western shore. It's obvious why the gods and other beings from the Mongol Geser epic chose to dwell on this eerily moving island, though today you're more likely to see a bunch of backpackers. The island's landscapes are spellbinding and Baikal's waters lap balmiest on its western shore, so it's a great spot for some Siberia-inspired meditation.

Getting Around

Flights can be delayed, often for hours and with no or little explanation.

One of the most pleasant ways of travelling around Russia is by taking a cruise or using scheduled river passenger services.

Long-distance buses tend to complement rather than compete with the rail network.

Trains are generally comfortable and, depending on the class of travel, relatively inexpensive for the distances covered.

CAPITAL
Kigali

POPULATION
12.98 million

AREA
26,338 sq km

OFFICIAL LANGUAGES
Kinyarwanda, English,
French

Gorilla, Volcanoes National Park

Rwanda

While the scars still run deep, Rwanda has done a remarkable job of healing its wounds and turning towards the future with a surprising measure of optimism.

Mention Rwanda to anyone with a small measure of geopolitical conscience, and they'll no doubt recall the horrific genocide that brutalised this country in 1994. But since those dark days a miraculous transformation has been wrought and today the country is one of ethnic unity and relative political stability, and a new-found air of optimism pervades.

Tourism is once again a key contributor to the economy and the industry's brightest star is the chance to track rare mountain gorillas through bamboo forests in the shadow of the Virunga volcanoes. Of course, 'Le Pays des Mille Collines' (the Land of a Thousand Hills) isn't all monkey business: Rwanda is a lush country of endless mountains and stunning scenery. The shores of Lake Kivu conceal some of Africa's best inland beaches, while Parc National Nyungwe Forest protects extensive tracts of montane rainforest.

Top Experiences

When to Go

 HIGH SEASON
(Jun–Sep)

 SHOULDER
(Dec–Feb)

 LOW SEASON
(Mar–May &
Oct–Nov)

Parc National des Volcans

1 Parc National des Volcans, which runs along the border with the Democratic Republic of Congo (DRC) and Uganda, is home to the Rwandan section of the Virungas. Comprising five volcanoes, the Virungas are utterly spellbinding and few would argue that this is not one of the most exciting national parks in Africa. Of all the extraordinary sights and attractions around the Virungas, the one that really draws people here are the mountain gorillas. While most travellers are understandably driven by the desire to have a face-to-face encounter with real gorillas in the mist, rare golden monkeys, a troop of which have been habituated to human contact, can also be visited. There is a variety of rewarding climbing and trekking options in the park, too.

Parc National de Nyungwe

2 Quite simply, Nyungwe Forest National Park is Rwanda's most important area of biodiversity. It has been rated the highest priority for forest conservation in Africa and its protected area covers one of the oldest rainforests on the continent. Despite its huge biodiversity, Nyungwe is little known outside of East Africa and remains overlooked by many tourists. This is a shame as the park offers some superb hiking and the chance to track chimpanzees that have been habituated to human visits.

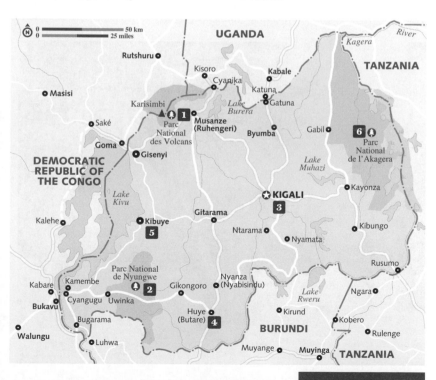

Kigali Genocide Memorial

3 In the span of 100 days, an estimated one million Tutsis and moderate Hutus were systematically butchered by the Interahamwe army. This memorial honours the estimated 250,000 people buried here in mass graves and also has an excellent exhibition that tries to explain how it was that the world watched as the genocide unfolded. This is an intensely powerful and moving memorial for which you should dedicate at least half a day.

National Museum of Rwanda

4 This outstanding museum was given to the city as a gift from Belgium in 1989 to commemorate 25 years of independence. While the building itself is certainly among the most beautiful structures in the city, the museum wins top marks for having one of the best ethnological and archaeological collections in the entire region. The seven exhibition halls contain some very interesting items and everything is unusually well lit and presented.

Kibuye

5 Although it has a stunning location, spread across a series of tongues jutting into Lake Kivu, Kibuye has not caught on as a tourist destination for sun and sand in the same way that Gisenyi has, but for our money – and there are plenty who will disagree – this is the better of the two. True, on this part of the lake good beaches are a lot less

Getting Around

The privately run buses and minibuses are quite organised, with regular, scheduled departures.

Most towns are small enough to negotiate by foot, but in Kigali and Huye (Butare) you'll need to catch a minibus or a taxi to get around. Taxis are plentiful in Kigali although *moto-taxis* are cheaper and faster. Rwanda has a reasonable road system, due mostly to its small size and a large dose of foreign assistance.

SARINE ARSLANIAN / SHUTTERSTOCK ©

common, but the steep hills that fall into the deep green waters and the indented shoreline with a smattering of islands nearby make it extremely picturesque. It's also, even by Rwandan standards, a very clean and green little town where nothing much seems to happen in a hurry.

Parc National de l'Akagera

6 Created in 1934 to protect the lands surrounding the Kagera River, Akagera National Park once protected nearly 10% of Rwanda and was considered to be one of the finest wildlife reserves in the whole of Africa. Sadly, due to the massive numbers of refugees who returned to

Food & Drink

In the rural areas of Rwanda, food is very similar to that in other East African countries. Popular meats include tilapia (Nile perch), goat, chicken and beef *brochettes* (kebabs), though the bulk of most meals are centred on *ugali* (maize meal) and *matoke* (cooked plantains). In the cities, however, Rwanda's French roots are evident in the *plat du jour* (plate of the day), which is usually excellently prepared Continental-inspired cuisine.

Nobody comes to Rwanda to party, but that doesn't mean that your drinking and nightlife options are limited. Indeed, there's plenty of choice in Kigali and Huye (Butare), where there are lots of young people and a burgeoning middle class. Elsewhere things are far quieter, but nearly every hotel in the country has a bar.

Rwanda in the late 1990s, over half of the park was de-gazetted and resettled with new villages. The increased human presence took an incredible toll on what had until recently been semiwil-derness. Human encroach-ment facilitated poaching and environmental deg-radation and Akagera's wildlife was very nearly decimated. However, strict conservation laws, the

reintroduction of lions and black rhinos, the revamping of old camps and the building of new ones has meant that all is not lost and Akagera is quickly recovering. While it's a long road ahead, visiting Akagera is a great way to support Eastern Rwanda's efforts to preserve its fabulous natural heritage.

MICHAEL COOK / ALTA|WORLD PHOTOGRAPHY / GETTY IMAGES ©

Kwita Izina

In traditional Rwandan culture, the birth of a child is a momen-tous event that is celebrated with a tremendous amount of fan-fare. The birth is marked by the presentation of the new infant to the general public, who then proceed to suggest round after round of possible names. After careful consideration, the proud parents select one for their newborn, and celebrate the naming with copious amounts of dining, drinking and dancing.

Gorillas in Rwanda are often awarded the same level of respect and admiration as humans, which is why it's fitting they should be named in a similar manner. Since June 2005, the annual Kwita Izina (Gorilla Naming Ceremony) has been a countrywide event that is increasingly drawing a larger share of the spotlight.

CAPITAL
Apia

POPULATION
199,000

AREA
2831 sq km

OFFICIAL LANGUAGE
Samoan

To Sua Ocean Trench, Upola

Samoa

Serene but spirited, wild yet well-manicured, hushed but birthed by volcanic explosions; stunning Samoa is a paradisaical paradox.

Despite its intense natural beauty – all iridescent seas, jade jungles and crystal waterfalls – this is a humble place, devoid of mega-resorts and flashy attractions, but with welcomes as warm as the island sun.

Geographically and culturally, this small nation is considered the heart of Polynesia. Though the missionaries of the 1800s were enormously influential, the country has nevertheless clung to *Fa'a Samoa*

(the Samoan Way), making it one of the most authentic and traditional of all Pacific societies: in some parts of the islands you're more likely to see someone juggling fire than a house with walls.

Despite its isolation, Samoa offers accessible adventures. From the relative ruckus of Apia to the soul-stirring silence of Savai'i, you'll find a paradise that is safe, sweet and easy to get around.

Top Experiences

To Sua Ocean Trench

1 This outrageously photogenic spot is a Samoan icon. Though the first thing you'll see upon entering the grounds is To Le Sua (a smaller, drier depression), it's To Sua that is the star of the show: more akin to a giant sinkhole than a trench, its sheer, green-draped rock walls plummet 20-odd metres to the almost hallucinatory-blue waters of the magnificent pool below. Swimming access is via a precipitous but sturdy wooden ladder; believe us, it's worth the clamber.

Manono

2 Canines and cars have been banished on Manono, and the only things that might snap you out of a tropical reverie are occasional blasts from stereos and the tour groups that periodically clog the island's main trail. It's obligatory for visitors to do the 1½-hour circumnavigation of the island via the path that wends its way between the ocean and people's houses. They're friendly sorts here; expect to be greeted with a cheery '*malo*' a dozen or so times.

When to Go

 HIGH SEASON (Dec-Jan)

 DRY SEASON (May-Oct)

 LOW SEASON (Nov-Apr)

Dwarf's Cave

3 This intriguing subterranean lava tube leads downwards as if to the centre of the earth. The cave is named after a legendary group of dwarves, who apparently still live in its depths, and leave the occasional footprint. It's said that no one – except maybe the dwarves – has reached the end of it, and

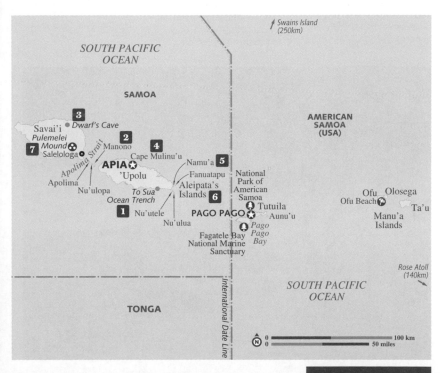

your guides (the village *matai* or local boys) will keep leading you through its prodigious depths, crossed by underground rivers, until you tell them to turn around.

Cape Mulinu'u

4 The country's most western point is not only gorgeously scenic (until Samoa hopped the dateline, it was the last place in the world the sun set each day), but home to many fascinating cultural and archaeological sites. The Fafa O Sauai'i outlook was one of Samoa's most sacred spots in pre-Christian times; there's a great swimming hole here. Nearby is a star mound, Vaatausili Cave and the Vai Sua Toto (the 'Blood Well' – named after the warrior Tupa'ilevaililigi, who threw his enemies' severed heads in here).

Namu'a Island

5 Namu'a is only a short boat ride from Mutiatele, but once you're on this tiny private island, Upolu seems light years away (though it's clearly visible across the strait). It's a perfect place for lounging and languid swims; the more active can do a circumnavigation of the shoreline during low tide, clamber up the steep central peak and snorkel the surrounding reef. *Fale* (beach huts) are open, basic and right on the beach – there's no electricity so everything is lit by oil lamps at night. Meals are mostly local style: simple yet delicious.

Aleipata's Beaches

6 At the southeastern end of Upolu, Aleipata's beaches are among the most spellbindingly beautiful in the world. Check out the undersea

Getting Around

Samoa Air operates charter flights between Upolu and Savai'i.

The ferry from Mulifanua Wharf plies the waters between Upolu and Savai'i. Small boats leave from Cape Fatuosofia for Manono.

Travelling by public bus in Samoa is an experience in itself. The vibrantly painted vehicles (often blasting Samoan pop music) each have their own character.

MARTIN VALIGURSKY / SHUTTERSTOCK ©

magic by walking in off the spectacular white beach at Lalomanu. If you're lucky you might spot a turtle, but beware of strong currents.

Pulemelei Mound

7 Polynesia's largest ancient structure is the intriguing, pyramidal Pulemelei Mound (sometimes called Tia Seu Ancient Mound). Constructed sometime between AD 1100 and 1400, it measures 65m by 60m at its base and rises to a height of more than 12m. Its original purpose continues to baffle experts. It's a stirring place, with views from its stony summit to the ocean and into thick rainforest. The surrounding area is presumably covered in important archaeological finds but, for now, the jungle hides its secrets.

Food & Drink

Umu Traditional Samoan hot-stone ovens are built above ground and used to cook breadfruit, fish, *palusami* and more.

Oka Tender chunks of raw fish are marinated in lime juice, mixed with vegetables and topped with coconut cream.

Palusami Calorie bombs of coconut cream wrapped in young taro leaves and cooked in a stone oven. Find it at the market in Apia.

Koko Samoa-strong coffee-like beverage made with hot water and ground Samoan cacao.

Vailima One of the best beers in the Pacific. A crisp and refreshing lager.

MARK KOLBE / GETTY IMAGES ©

Tattooing

Samoa is the last of the Polynesian nations where traditional tattooing (*tatau*) is still widely practised (albeit against the wishes of some religious leaders). The traditional *pe'a* (male tattoo) covers the man's body from the waist to the knees. Women can elect to receive a *malu* (female tattoo), but their designs cover only the thighs.

The skills and tools of the *tufuga pe'a* (tattoo artist) were traditionally passed down from father to son, and sharpened shark teeth or boar tusks were used to carve the intricate designs into the skin. It was believed that the man being tattooed must not be left alone in case the *aitu* (spirits) took him. In most cases the procedure takes at least a fortnight. Noncompletion would cause shame to the subject and his '*aiga*.

Torre Cesta

San Marino

This landlocked micronation offers spectacular views from its location atop Monte Titano, a dozen kilometres from the Adriatic Coast.

| CAPITAL |
| San Marino |
| POPULATION |
| 33,300 |
| AREA |
| 61 sq km |
| OFFICIAL LANGUAGE |
| Italian |

Of the world's 196 independent countries, San Marino is the fifth smallest and – arguably – the most curious. How it exists at all is something of an enigma. A sole survivor of Italy's once powerful city-state network, it clung on long after the more powerful kingdoms of Genoa and Venice folded. And still it clings, secure in its status as the world's oldest surviving sovereign state and its oldest republic (since AD 301).

Measuring 61 sq km, the country is larger than many outsiders imagine, being made up of nine municipalities each hosting its own settlement. The largest 'town' is Dogana, a place 99.9% of the two million annual visitors skip on their way through to the Città di San Marino, the medieval settlement on the slopes of 750m-high Monte Titano that was added to the Unesco World Heritage list in 2008.

Top Experiences

Torre Cesta

1 Dominating the skyline and offering superb views towards Rimini and the coast, the Cesta castle dates from the 13th century and sits atop Monte Titano. Today you can walk its ramparts and peep into its four-room museum devoted to medieval armaments. The admission price also includes entry to the Castello della Guaita, the older of San Marino's castles, dating from the 11th century.

Piazza della Libertà

2 The neo-Gothic Palazzo Pubblico overlooks Piazza della Libertà, where a half-hourly changing of the guard is held from May to September; it's one of Città di San Marino's summertime highlights.

Quirky Museums

3 Città di San Marino hosts a stash of rather bizarre museums dedicated to vampires, torture, wax dummies and strange facts. The Museo di Stato is San Marino's best museum by far: a well-laid-out state museum, with exhibitions about art, history, furniture and culture. Overtly curious visitors or Trivial Pursuit addicts can brush up on their knowledge at the Museo delle Curiosità, a shrine to throwaway facts.

When to Go

 HIGH SEASON (Jul & Aug)

 SHOULDER (Apr–Jun, Sep & Oct)

 LOW SEASON (Nov–Mar)

Food & Drink

Cheese Tuck into a plate of sliced beef, rocket and *parmigiano*.

Wine Sample a full-bodied Brugneto red or savour a delicate Tessano red, both made from grapes grown on San Marino's steeply terraced vineyards. Other locally produced wines include Biancale, a dry white, and Oro dei Goti, a sweet dessert wine.

CAPITAL
São Tomé (city)

POPULATION
195,000

AREA
1000 sq km

OFFICIAL LANGUAGE
Portuguese

Ilha do Bom Bom

São Tomé & Príncipe

Floating in the Gulf of Guinea, this two-island nation, Africa's second-smallest, blends natural wonders with a gripping history.

Once a vast network of plantations and a centre of global cocoa production, São Tomé & Príncipe (STP) has suffered an economic collapse since independence from Portugal in 1975. In the countryside, squatters inhabit once great mansions; in the capital, historic colonial buildings slowly decay on broken streets. Nevertheless, the country remains amazingly safe and welcoming to visitors, particularly ecotourists, for whom the advancing jungle is a delight.

This is particularly true on tidy and unspoiled Príncipe, an island of just 7000 people. A canopy of green broken by spires of primordial rock, Príncipe is a magnificent Lost World, offering fantastic beaches, jungle exploration, snorkelling, fishing, birdwatching and a handful of interesting accommodation, with minimal tourist pressure. While both islands have their natural rewards, Príncipe should not be missed.

Top Experiences

Baía das Agulhas

1 The spectacular Bay of Spires is not just Príncipe's top attraction, but STP's as well. It's best seen from the water, where the postcard view of the island's world-class skyline slowly unfolds, including phonolite towers named (for obvious reasons) the Father, the Son and the Grandson, along with Table Mountain. You expect to hear the primordial roar of T-Rex at any moment. If you've flown all this way, you do not want to miss this.

Pico de São Tomé

2 Climb the highest peak in the country for an unforgettable jungle adventure. São Tomé's signature climb, this is a two-day adventure through a lush vertical jungle, with an overnight near the summit.

Príncipe

3 Close your eyes. Just imagine: a dramatic landscape of jutting volcanic mountains covered mostly by dense forest; perfect beaches with astonishingly clear water; old plantation estates; and warm greetings from friendly locals at every turn. Príncipe is the perfect place to shift into low gear, but action-seekers won't get bored, as the island also offers excellent hiking and diving options.

Food & Drink

Calulu Traditional stew made with more than 20 different plants and that can take hours to prepare.

Con-con Fish grilled and served with baked breadfruit.

Fish or meat Served with beans, rice or plantains.

Palm wine Freshly gathered from the trees, this is a local favourite.

When to Go

HIGH SEASON (Jun–Sep, Dec–Feb)

LOW SEASON (Mar–May, Oct–Nov)

CAPITAL
Riyadh

POPULATION
28.2 million

AREA
2,2 million sq km

OFFICIAL LANGUAGE
Arabic

Madain Saleh

Saudi Arabia

The birthplace and spiritual home of Islam, Saudi Arabia is as rich in attractions as it is in stirring symbolism. It is also one of the most difficult places on Earth to visit.

For those who do get in, rock-hewn Madain Saleh is Arabia's greatest treasure, with its evocative tombs in a sublime desert setting. Other wonders abound, from the echoes of TE Lawrence along the Hejaz Railway to the mud-brick ruins of Dir'aiyah.

Fascinating Riyadh is a showpiece for modern Saudi Arabia, Jeddah blends ancient and modern and has an enchanting old city made of coral, while the Red Sea coast has world-class diving. With almost 2000 petroglyph, or rock-art sites, Saudi Arabia is one of the richest open-air museums in the world. And for Muslim travellers, Mecca and Medina represent the most sacred destination you can imagine.

There are few places left that can be said to represent the last frontier of tourism. Whether you're an expat or a pilgrim, Saudi Arabia is one of them.

Top Experiences

Madain Saleh

1 The extraordinary Madain Saleh is home to 131 tombs, 45 of which carry inscriptions in late Aramaic script above the entrance. These inscriptions detail the tomb's builders – many constructed by wealthy women. The enigmatic tombs combine of Greco-Roman architecture with Nabataean and Babylonian imagery. Recent excavations have revealed the foundations of unprepossessing houses and a market area for traders and caravans. Qasr Farid is the largest tomb of Madain Saleh and perhaps the most stunning. Carved from a free-standing rock monolith, its location gives it a rare beauty. Try to arrive for sunset, when the enigmatic tomb passes through shades of pink and gold until darkness falls: breathtaking.

Yanbu

2 At first glance, with its port, refineries and petrochemical plants, Yanbu is hardly the Kingdom's most attractive spot. But it's fast becoming the top tourist destination in the country, with its premier scuba-diving locations and pristine white sandy shores, many with resorts and private beaches geared towards families. The industrial section of Yanbu is a good 10km to 15km south of the city centre and has little impact upon the region's gorgeous beaches to the north. The downtown area is small but quaint, with an unhurried atmosphere not found in the larger cities.

When to Go

 HIGH SEASON (Nov–Mar)

 SHOULDER (Jul–Oct)

 LOW SEASON (Apr–Jun)

Jeddah's Old City

3 The country's commercial capital, and a point of convergence for pilgrims and traders for centuries, Jeddah is the most easygoing city in the Kingdom – not to mention its most beguiling. The Al Balad district, the heart of Old Jeddah, is a nostalgic testament to the city's bygone days, with the beautiful coral historic buildings casting some welcome shade over the bustling souqs where shopkeepers hawk their goods.

Dir'aiyah

4 Wander the mud-brick ruins of Dir'aiyah, the birthplace of modern Saudi Arabia. The ancestral home of the Al Saud family in Wadi Hanifa and the birthplace of the Saudi-Wahhabi union, the Turaif district in Dir'aiyah was declared a Unesco World Heritage Site in 2010 and is one of the most evocative places in the Kingdom. Since receiving Unesco recognition, the site has been closed to the public for restoration works, although special permission allows you to enter with a private guide (arranged through any travel agency) and explore the site.

Hejaz Railway

5 The Hejaz Railway cuts across northwestern Arabia with abandoned and evocative stations, substations and garrison forts, many of which remain. The line opened in 1908, stretching over 1000 miles through largely desert terrain; a planned extension to Mecca was never built. During the First World War, TE Lawrence helped to orchestrate the Arab Revolt, harnessing the hostility of the local Bedouin to drive

Getting Around

The buses are comfortable, air-conditioned and clean. The front seats are generally unofficially reserved for 'families' including sole women, and the back half for men.

Despite its impressive public transport system, Saudi Arabia remains a country that glorifies the private car (the shiny 4WD is king). Roads are generally sealed and well maintained. Motorcycles are rare and generally considered a vehicle of the rural poor.

ABALCAZAR / GETTY IMAGES ©

out the Turks. They attacked and sabotaged the railway, which ceased to run after 1918.

Taif

6 Situated 1700m above sea level, Taif can seem like a breath of fresh air in summer, and compared to humid Jeddah it truly is. Its gentle, temperate climate is its biggest attraction. Watch for wild baboons along the mountain roadside on the way into the city from Jeddah. Taif is family friendly, with more than 3000 garden parks scattered throughout the city and outlying areas; in the evening the parks are packed with families spreading out a full supper on blankets. Some bring

sheesha, filling the night air with a sweet, smoky aroma.

Tabuk

7 Tabuk, now a bustling tourist destination, was a strategic stopping place for pre-20th-century hajj pilgrims trekking on foot from Damascus (Syria) to Medina and onward to Mecca. The city's culture was deeply influenced by Egyptian travellers (one of

the largest groups of land-travelling pilgrims) from the west and the Ottomans (who controlled pilgrimage routes for centuries) from the north. Defying the perception that Saudi Arabia is all desert sand and sun, Tabuk also serves as a gateway to a pristine region of white beaches, virtually untouched islands and coral reefs, and snowy mountains in winter.

6

DAVID KIRKLAND / GETTY IMAGES ©

Food & Drink

Fuul Mashed fava beans served with olive oil and often eaten for breakfast.

Baby camel Among the tenderest of Saudi meats, it's a particular specialty of Jeddah and the Hejaz.

Khouzi A Bedouin dish of lamb stuffed with rice, nuts, onions, sultanas, spices, eggs and a whole chicken.

Mezze Truly one of the joys of Arab cooking and similar in conception to Spanish tapas, with infinite possibilities.

Red Sea seafood Fresh and varied and at its best when slow-cooked over coals or baked in the oven; try *samak mashwi* (fish basted in a date puree and barbecued over hot coals).

Shwarma Ubiquitous kebab- or souvlaki-style pita sandwich stuffed with meat.

Literature

Bedouin poetry and storytelling are part of a rich oral tradition with desert and Islamic legends, often in poetic form, at their heart. However, little has been committed to written form and even less translated into English.

Novelists who chronicle the impact of oil money and modernisation on a deeply traditional desert kingdom include Hamza Bogary, Ahmed Abodehman and Abdelrahman Munif; the latter's citizenship was revoked and his books, thinly veiled parables of Saudi Arabia, banned in the Kingdom.

Girls of Riyadh was the first novel by a young Saudi woman, Rajaa Alsanea, describing the intertwining lives of four young Saudi women. The book garnered surprising praise from Arab intellectuals, while eliciting howls of disapproval from Saudi conservatives, scandalised by its frankness.

The Old Man of Storr, Isle of Skye

CAPITAL
Edinburgh

POPULATION
5.3 million

AREA
78,722 sq km

OFFICIAL LANGUAGES
English, Scots,
Scottish Gaelic

Scotland

Despite its small size, Scotland has many treasures crammed into its compact territory – big skies, lonely landscapes, spectacular wildlife, superb seafood and hospitable, down-to-earth people.

Scotland harbours some of the largest areas of wilderness left in western Europe, a wild-life haven where you can see golden eagles soar above the lochs and mountains of the northern Highlands, spot otters tumbling in the kelp along the shores of the Outer Hebrides, and watch whales breach through shoals of mackerel off the coast of Mull.

It's also a land with a rich, multi-layered history, a place where every corner of the landscape is steeped in the past – a deserted croft on an island shore, a moor that was once a battlefield, a cave that sheltered Bonnie Prince Charlie.

A new-found respect for top-quality local produce means that you can feast on fresh seafood mere hours after it was caught, and beef and venison that was raised just a few miles away from your table. Top it all off with a dram of single malt whisky – rich, evocative and complex, it's the true taste of Scotland.

Top Experiences

Skye

1 In a country famous for stunning scenery, the isle of Skye takes top prize. From the craggy peaks of the Cuillins and the bizarre pinnacles of the Old Man of Storr and the Quiraing to the spectacular sea cliffs of Neist Point, there's a photo opportunity at almost every turn. Walkers can share the landscape with red deer and golden eagles, and refuel at the end of the day in convivial pubs and top seafood restaurants.

Loch Lomond

2 Despite being less than an hour's drive from the bustle and sprawl of Glasgow, the bonnie banks and braes of Loch Lomond – immortalised in the words of one of Scotland's best-known songs – comprise one of the most scenic parts of the country. At the heart of Scotland's first national park, the loch begins as a broad, island-peppered lake in the south, its shores clothed in bluebell woods, narrowing in the north to a fjord-like trench ringed by 900m-high mountains.

Edinburgh

3 Scotland's capital may be famous for its festivals, but there's much more to it than that. Edinburgh is a city of many moods: visit out of season to see the Old Town silhouetted against a blue spring sky and a yellow haze of daffodils; or on a chill December morning with the fog snagging the spires of the Royal Mile, rain on the cobblestones and a warm glow beckoning from the window of a pub.

Walking the West Highland Way

4 The best way to really get inside Scotland's landscapes is to walk them. Despite the wind, midges and drizzle, walking here is a pleasure, with numerous short- and long-distance trails, hills and mountains begging to be tramped. Top of the wish list for many

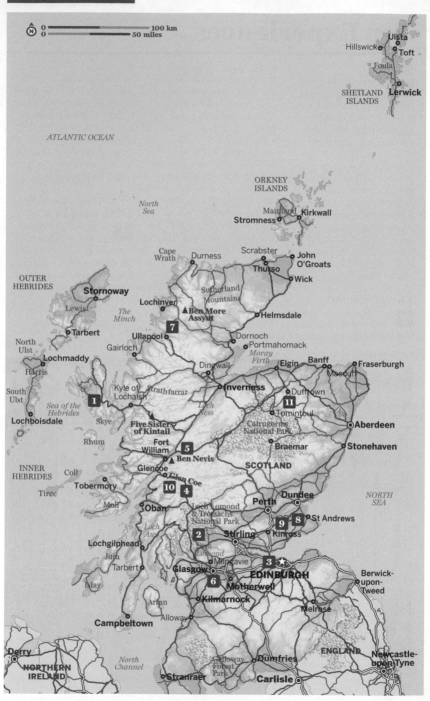

N
0 ——————— 100 km
0 ——————— 50 miles

Hillswick○ ○Ulsta
○Toft
Foula

SHETLAND ●Lerwick
ISLANDS

ATLANTIC OCEAN

ORKNEY
ISLANDS
North   Mainland Kirkwall
Sea   Stromness○

Cape   Scrabster John
Wrath Durness   ○O'Groats
        Thurso
        ○Wick

OUTER
HEBRIDES ●Stornoway
        Lochinver Sutherland
Lewis   Mountains
The   ▲Ben More ○Helmsdale
Minch   Assynt   [7]
●Tarbert Ullapool○   ○Dornoch
North   Gairloch Dingwall Portmahomack
Ulst ●Lochmaddy   Moray
Harris   Firth Elgin Banff ○Fraserburgh
South   Kyle of Strathfarrar   Macduff
Ulst Sea of the Lochalsh ●Inverness ○Dufftown
Hebrides [1]   ○Tomintoul
●Lochboisdale Skye Five Sisters Loch   Cairngorms ●Aberdeen
        of Kintail Ness [11] National Park
Rhum   Fort [5]   Braemar ○Stonehaven
INNER   William ▲Ben Nevis   SCOTLAND
HEBRIDES Coll Glencoe
Tobermory [10] Glen Coe [4]
Tiree Mull ○Oban   Perth Dundee NORTH
        Loch Lomond   SEA
Loch   & Trossachs   [9][8] ○St Andrews
Awe   National Park   Kinross
Lochgilphead○   [2] Stirling
Jura   Loch   Milngavie
Tarbert○   Lomond   [3] ★
Islay   Glasgow○   EDINBURGH Berwick-
        [6] Motherwell   upon-
Arran   ○Kilmarnock   Tweed
Campbeltown Alloway○   Melrose

Derry   North   ENGLAND Newcastle-
NORTHERN Channel   upon-Tyne
IRELAND Galloway Dumfries
        Forest   Carlisle○
        Park
        Stranraer

Best on Film

Whisky Galore! (1949) Classic Ealing comedy about wily islanders outfoxing the government.

Local Hero (1983) Gentle Bill Forsyth comedy-drama sees American oil executive beguiled by the Highland landscape and eccentric locals.

Trainspotting (1996) Danny Boyle's second film (based on the novel by Irvine Welsh) dives into the gritty underbelly of life among Edinburgh drug addicts.

Best Single Malts

Ardbeg (Islay) The 10-year-old from this noble distillery is a byword for excellence. Peaty but well balanced.

Bowmore (Islay) Smoke, peat and salty sea air – a classic Islay malt.

Bruichladdich (Islay) A visitor-friendly distillery with a quirky, innovative approach.

Glendronach (Highland) Sherry casks are used, so the result tastes like Christmas trifle.

Highland Park (Orkney) Full and rounded, with heather, honey, malt and peat.

Isle of Arran (Arran) One of Scotland's newer distilleries, offering a lightish, flavoursome malt.

Macallan (Speyside) The king of Speyside malts, with sherry and bourbon finishes.

Springbank (Campbeltown) Complex flavours – sherry, citrus, pear drops, peat – with a salty tang.

Talisker (Skye) Brooding, heavily peated nose balanced by a satisfying sweetness from this lord of the isles.

The Balvenie (Speyside) Rich and honeyed, this Speysider is liquid gold.

hikers is the 96-mile West Highland Way from Milngavie (near Glasgow) to Fort William, a challenging week-long walk through some of the country's finest scenery, finishing in the shadow of its highest peak, Ben Nevis.

Climbing Ben Nevis

5 The allure of Britain's highest peak is strong – around 100,000 people a year set off up the summit trail, though not all make it to the top. Nevertheless, the highest Munro of them all is within reach of anyone who's reasonably fit. Treat Ben Nevis with respect and your reward (weather permitting) will be a truly magnificent view and a great sense of achievement. Real walking enthusiasts can warm up by hiking the 96-mile West Highland Way first.

When to Go

HIGH SEASON
(Jul–Aug)
Warmest time of year, but often wet.

SHOULDER
(May & Jun–Sep)
Wildflowers bloom in May and June. Statistically, best chance of dry weather, minus midges.

LOW SEASON
(Oct–Apr)
Snow on hills November to March.

Castles

Scotland is home to more than 1000 castles, ranging from meagre 12th-century ruins to magnificent Victorian mansions. They all began with one purpose: to serve as fortified homes for the landowning aristocracy. But as society became more settled and peaceful, defensive features gave way to ostentatious displays of wealth and status.

Norman castles of the 12th century were mainly of the 'motte-and-bailey' type, consisting of earthwork mounds and timber palisades. The first wave of stonebuilt castles emerged in the 13th century, characterised by massive curtain walls up to 3m thick and 30m tall to withstand sieges.

The appearance of the tower house in the 14th century marks the beginning of the development of the castle as a residence. Clan feuds, cattle raiders and wars between Scotland and England meant that local lords built fortified stone towers in which to live.

The arrival of gunpowder and cannons in the 15th century transformed castle design, with features such as gun loops, round towers, bulwarks and bastions making an appearance.

The Scottish Baronial style of castle architecture, characterised by a profusion of pointy turrets, crenellations and stepped gables, had its origins in 16th- and 17th-century castles and reached its apotheosis in the royal residences of Glamis and Balmoral.

Getting Around

Cars are useful for travelling at your own pace, or for visiting regions with minimal public transport. Can be hired in cities and major towns. Drive on the left.

Scotland's train network extends to all major cities and towns, but the railway map has a lot of large, blank areas in the Highlands and the Southern Uplands where you'll need to switch to road transport.

Buses are cheaper and slower than trains, but useful for more remote regions that aren't serviced by rail.

A network of car ferries link the mainland to the islands of western and northern Scotland.

Glasgow

6 Scotland's biggest city lacks Edinburgh's classical beauty, but more than makes up for it with a barrelful of things to do and a warmth and energy that leave every visitor impressed. Edgy and contemporary, it's a great spot to browse art galleries and museums, and to discover the works of local hero Charles Rennie Mackintosh. Add what is perhaps Britain's best pub culture and one of the world's best live-music scenes, and the only thing to do is live it.

Northwest Highlands Coastal Road

7 The Highlands abound in breathtaking views, but the far northwest is truly awe-inspiring. The coastal road between Durness and Kyle of Lochalsh offers jaw-dropping scenes at every turn: the rugged mountains of Assynt, the desolate beauty of Torridon and the remote cliffs of Cape Wrath. These and the nooks of warm Highland hospitality found in classic rural pubs make this an unforgettable corner of the country.

Golf

8 Scotland invented the game of golf and is still revered as its spiritual home by hackers and champions alike. Links courses are the classic experience here – bumpy coastal affairs where the rough is heather and machair and the main enemy is the wind, which can make a disaster of a promising round in an instant. St Andrews, the historic Fife university town, is golf's headquarters, and an alluring destination for anyone who loves the sport.

Perthshire – Big Tree Country

9 Blue-grey lochs shimmer, reflecting the changing moods of the weather; venerable trees, centuries old, tower amid riverside forests; majestic glens scythe their way into remote wildernesses; and salmon leap upriver to the place of their birth.

In Perthshire, the heart of Scotland, picturesque towns bloom with flowers, distilleries emit tempting malty odours and sheep graze in impossibly green meadows. There's a feeling of the bounty of nature that no other place in Scotland can replicate.

Glen Coe

10 Scotland's most famous glen combines those two essential qualities of Highlands landscape: dramatic scenery and deep history. The peacefulness and beauty of this valley today belie the fact that it was the scene of a ruthless 17th-century massacre, when the local MacDonalds were murdered by soldiers of the Campbell clan. Some of the glen's finest walks – to the Lost Valley, for example – follow the routes used by the clanspeople trying to flee their attackers, and where many perished in the snow.

Whisky

11 Scotland's national drink – from the Gaelic *uisge bagh*, meaning 'water of life' – has been distilled here for more than 500 years. More than 100 distilleries are still in operation, producing hundreds of varieties of single malt, with new ones opening every year. Learning to distinguish the smoky, peaty whiskies of Islay from, say, the flowery, sherried malts of Speyside has become a hugely popular pastime. Many distilleries offer guided tours, rounded off with a tasting session, and ticking off the local varieties is a great way to explore the whisky-making regions.

Wildlife

Scotland's wildlife is one of its biggest attractions. Many species that have disappeared from, or are rare in, the rest of Britain survive in Scotland.

Loch Ness

Scotland's largest loch by volume may be most famous for its legendary monster, but it is also one of Scotland's most scenic.

11

GEORGECLERK / GETTY IMAGES ©

10

HELEN HOTSON / SHUTTERSTOCK ©

CAPITAL
Dakar

POPULATION
14.5 million

AREA
196,722 sq km

OFFICIAL LANGUAGE
French

Dakar beach

Senegal

Skimming any holiday brochure about Senegal, you'll sooner or later stumble across the term teranga, meaning 'hospitality'. Senegal takes great pride in being the 'Land of Teranga'.

Though it's one of West Africa's most stable countries, Senegal is far from dull. Perched on the tip of a peninsula, Dakar, the capital, is a dizzying, street-hustler-filled rich introduction to the country: elegance meets chaos, snarling traffic, vibrant markets and glittering nightlife, while nearby Île de Gorée and the beaches of Yoff and N'Gor tap to slow, lazy beats.

In northern Senegal, the enigmatic capital of Saint-Louis, a Unesco World Heritage Site, tempts with colonial architecture and proximity to scenic national parks. Along the Petite Côte and Cap Skirring, wide strips of beaches beckon and the wide deltas of the Casamance invite mesmerising boat journeys amid astounding biodiversity, including hundreds of bird species.

Whether you want to mingle with the trendsetters of urban Africa or be alone with your thoughts and the sounds of nature, you'll find your place in Senegal.

Top Experiences

Dakar

1 At once both intimidating and deeply alluring, Dakar is a fascinating introduction to Senegal, with peaceful islands just offshore. You can spend your days browsing frenetic markets and taking in the sights of bustling downtown, followed by sunset drinks overlooking the crashing waves or enjoying mbalax dance beats long into the night.

Niokolo-Koba National Park

2 This biologically rich national park is home to a spectacular array of flora and fauna, with some 350 bird species and 80 mammal species spread across a vast reserve in southeastern Senegal. Lions, leopards, baboons, hippos and antelope are all found (though not always easily spotted) here. Its terrain encompasses dry savannah, riparian forest and various waterways, including the Gambia River. Sadly, a lack of resources has left the park poorly maintained, so you'll have to anticipate bad access roads and rustic facilities.

The Pink Lake

3 'Lac Rose', also known as Lac Retba, a shallow lagoon surrounded by dunes, is a popular day-trip destination for *dakarois* and tourists alike, all coming to enjoy the calm and catch the lake's magic trick – the vibrant and otherworldly pink hues that sometimes colour its waters. The spectacle is caused by the lake's high salt content, which is 10 times that of ocean water. It's a beautiful sight but can only be enjoyed when the light is right – your best chance is in the dry season, when the sun is high.

When to Go

HIGH SEASON (Nov–Feb)

LOW SEASON (Jul–late Sep)

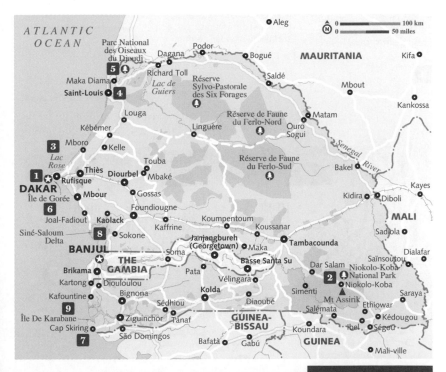

Saint-Louis

4 With its crumbling colonial architecture, horse-drawn carts and peaceful ambience, West Africa's first French settlement has a unique historical charm – so much so that it's been a Unesco World Heritage Site since 2000. The old town centre sits on an island in the Senegal River, but the city sprawls into Sor on the mainland, and onto the Langue de Barbarie, where you'll find the lively fishing community of Guet N'Dar.

Parc National des Oiseaux du Djoudj

5 With almost 300 species of bird, this 160-sq-km park is one of the most important bird sanctuaries in the world. Flamingos, pelicans and waders are most plentiful, and large numbers of migrating birds travel here in November. The lush setting is no less impressive: these vast wetlands comprise lakes, streams, ponds, fords and sandbanks.

Île de Gorée

6 Ruled in succession by the Portuguese, Dutch, English and French, the historical, Unesco-designated Île de Gorée is enveloped by an almost eerie calm. There are no sealed roads and no cars on this island, just narrow alleyways with trailing bougainvilleas and colonial brick buildings with wrought-iron balconies – it's a living, visual masterpiece. But Gorée's calm is not so much romantic as meditative, as the ancient, elegant buildings bear witness to the island's role in the Atlantic slave trade. The island is also home to an active artist community with a sprinkling of small studios.

Getting Around

Groupe Transair flies between Dakar, Ziguinchor and Cap Skirring.

A regular ferry service travels between Dakar and Ziguinchor, and Dakar and Île de Gorée. Senegal's other islands can be visited by pirogue.

The quickest (but uncomfortable) way of getting around the country is by *sept-place* taxi – battered Peugeots that negotiate even the most rugged routes.

4

Cap Skirring

7 The beaches at Cap Skirring are some of the finest in West Africa – and better still, they're usually empty. While there isn't a lot happening here culturally (aside from weekend nights of live music), Cap Skirring makes a fine base for a few days of unwinding. You can also alternate days on the beach with exploring traditional Diola villages to the east, or opt for some of the many activities on offer, including kayaking and mountain biking.

Petite Côte & Siné-Saloum Delta

8 The 150km Petite Côte stretches south from Dakar and is one of Senegal's best beach areas. Where the Siné and Saloum Rivers meet the tidal waters of the Atlantic Ocean, the coast is broken into a stunning area of mangrove swamps, lagoons, forests and sand islands, forming part of the magnificent 180-sq-km Siné-Saloum Delta.

Île De Karabane

9 Elinkine is a busy fishing village and jumping-off point for the peaceful Île de Karabane, a former French trading station (1836–1900). In the island's namesake town, you can still see the Breton-style church, with its dusty pews and crumbling statues, and visit the dilapidated cemetery where settlers and sailors were laid to rest.

Food & Drink

Dakar has a great many restaurants, catering to a wide range of budgets (though prices tend to be higher here than in other parts). Saint-Louis, Saly and Cap Skirring all have a small but vibrant dining scene, but elsewhere, options are sparse, and you'll likely be taking your meals wherever you lodge for the night.

Senegal's national dish is *thiéboudienne* (rice cooked in a thick tomato sauce and served with fried fish and vegetables). Also typical are *poulet yassa* or *poisson yassa* (marinated and grilled chicken or fish) and *mafé* (peanut-based stew).

Local drinks include *bissap*, made from hibiscus flowers, and *bouyi*, made from the fruits of the baobab. The best local beer is Flag.

OKSANA PH / SHUTTERSTOCK ©

Beautiful Beaches

You'll find plenty of reason to linger here, basking on the sandy shorelines of some of West Africa's most pristine beaches.

Île de N'Gor Beach-dotted island with great surfing just offshore from Dakar.

Saly Resorts flanked by the picturesque beaches of Palmarin; long stretches of empty, sparkling sands.

Cap Skirring The coastal jewel of Casamance, with some of Senegal's loveliest beaches.

CAPITAL
Belgrade

POPULATION
7.13 million

AREA
77,474 sq km

OFFICIAL LANGUAGE
Serbian

Republic Square, Belgrade

Serbia

Warm, welcoming and a hell of a lot of fun – everything you never heard about Serbia is true.

Exuding a feisty mix of élan and *inat* (the national trait of rebellious defiance), this country doesn't do 'mild'. Belgrade rivals Berlin as a party destination, the northern town of Novi Sad hosts the epic Exit Festival, and even its hospitality is emphatic – expect to be greeted with *rakija* (fruit brandy) and a hearty three-kiss hello.

While political correctness is about as commonplace as a nonsmoking bar, Serbia is nevertheless a cultural crucible:

the art nouveau town of Subotica revels in its proximity to Hungary, bohemian Niš echoes to the clip-clop of Roma horse carts, and minaret-studded Novi Pazar nudges some of the most sacred sites in Serbian Orthodoxy. In the mountainous Kopaonik, Tara and Zlatibor regions, ancient traditions coexist with après-ski bling. Forget what you think you know: come and say *zdravo* (hello)...or better yet, *živeli* (cheers)!

Top Experiences

Belgrade

 Outspoken, adventurous and audacious, Belgrade is no 'pretty' capital, but its gritty exuberance makes it one of the most happening cities in Europe. While it hurtles towards a brighter future, its chaotic past unfolds before your eyes: socialist blocks are squeezed between art nouveau masterpieces, and remnants of the Habsburg legacy contrast with Ottoman relics. It is here the Sava River meets the Danube, contemplative parkland nudges hectic urban sprawl, and old-world culture gives way to new-world nightlife.

Zlatibor

 Escape reality in the fantastical village of Drvengrad and on a winding, whimsical Šargan 8 train ride. A romantic region of gentle mountains, traditions and hospitality, Zlatibor encompasses the Tara and Šargan mountains in the north and the Murtenica hills bordering Bosnia & Hercegovina. The quirky little village of Mokra Gora is found in Zlatibor's west. The region's name itself serves as poetic introduction; in Serbian, Zlatibor means 'golden pine'.

When to Go

☀ **HIGH SEASON** (Jul & Aug)

⛅ **SHOULDER SEASON** (Apr–Jun, Sep–Nov)

❄ **LOW SEASON** (Dec–Mar)

Exit Festival, Novi Sad

 Home to the epic EXIT Festival, Novi Sad's Petrovaradin Fortress is stormed by tens of thousands of party people each July, here for beats and bacchanalia. The first festival in 2000 lasted 100 days and galvanised

a generation against the Milošević regime, who 'exited' himself just weeks after the event.

Niš

4 Serbia's third-largest metropolis is a lively city of curious contrasts, where Roma in horse-drawn carriages trot alongside new cars, and cocktails are sipped in alleyways. Settled in pre-Roman times, Constantine the Great was born here, as were two other Roman emperors. Niš did it tough during WWII; the Nazis built one of Serbia's most notorious concentration camps here.

Tara National Park

5 Hike, bike or paddle around this scenic slice of Serbia. With 220 sq km of forested slopes, dramatic ravines, jewel-like waterways and rewarding views, Tara (Tapa) is

scenic Serbia at its best. Pressed up against Bosnia & Hercegovina, this western wonderland attracts both adventurers eager for escapism, exploration and fresh-air fun. Watch out for bears!

The Devil's Town

6 Devil's Town, in Serbia's deep south, is a trippy cluster of 202 natural stone pyramids looming eerily over bright red, highly acidic mineral streams. According to local whispers, the towers – which teeter between 2m and 15m in height and are topped with creepy volcanic 'heads' – were formed after guests at an incestuous wedding were petrified by an offended god.

Kalemegdan Citadel

7 Some 115 battles have been fought at this formidable fortress; the

Getting Around

Bus services are extensive, though outside major hubs, sporadic connections may leave you in the lurch for a few hours.

Trains usually not as regular and reliable as buses, and can be murderously slow.

citadel was destroyed more than 40 times throughout the centuries. Fortifications began in Celtic times, and the Romans extended it onto the flood plains during the settlement of 'Singidunum', Belgrade's Roman name. The fort's

bloody history only makes Kalemegdan all the more fascinating.

Fruška Gora National Park

8 Nicknamed 'the jewel of Serbia', Fruška Gora is an 80km stretch of rolling hills in the Vojvodinian district of Srem, where cloistered life has endured since monasteries were built between the 15th and 18th centuries to safeguard Serbian culture and religion from the Turks. Of the 35 original monasteries, 16 remain, and they're open to visitors. Fruška Gora is also famous for its small but select wineries; grapes were first planted here in 3 AD by the Roman Emperor Probus.

Guča Festival

9 Known simply as 'Guča', after the western Serbian village that has hosted it each August since 1961, this four-day annual gathering of brass musicians is hedonism at its most rambunctious: tens of thousands of beer-and-brass-addled visitors dance wild *kola* (fast-paced circle dances) through the streets, gorging on spit-roasted meat and slapping dinar on the sweaty foreheads of the (mostly Roma) *trubači* performers.

ALEKSANDAR KAMASI/ SHUTTERSTOCK ©

Food & Drink

Serbia's cuisine is a riotous fusion of Turkish, Hungarian and Mediterranean influences that zing the palate, fill the stomach and linger on the hips; it's generally fresh and affordable. While grilled meats, *paprika* (capsicum), beans and cabbage are ubiquitous, there can be distinct differences between regional menus, depending on who invaded where and when.

All cities, towns and larger villages have *restorani* (restaurants), *pekare* (bakeries) and *roštilj* (barbecue) joints; *kafane* (taverns) may also serve meals in addition to booze.

Party like a Serbian

Belgrade is Serbia's capital of carousing, with hip bars, decadent nightclubs and bacchanalian barge-clubs *(splavovi)* lending it a raucous reputation to rival Berlin's. Novi Sad and Niš keep the party going in laneway bars, historic pubs and hidden pockets of alternative culture that are well worth seeking out. Outside the big towns, tables get thumped in local *kafane* (taverns) and cafes; there's a good chance you'll be welcomed with *rakija* shots and possibly ear-shattering trumpet *(truba)* serenades.

CAPITAL
Victoria

POPULATION
93,200

AREA
455 sq km

OFFICIAL LANGUAGES
Creole, English,
French

Snorkelling off Mahé

Seychelles

Talcum-powder beaches lapped by topaz waters, lush hills, a sublime laid-back tempo: these dreams of a tropical paradise become reality in the Seychelles.

Mother Nature was very generous with these 115 islands scattered in the Indian Ocean, and has spoiled them rotten. Undeniably, the beaches are the big attraction, and what beaches they are: exquisite ribbons of pearlescent sand lapped by topaz waters and backed by lush hills and big glacis boulders. Diving and snorkelling are the most popular activities in the Seychelles, and rightly so. Healthy reefs, canyon-like terrain, shallow shelves, exciting shipwrecks, impressive granite outcrops and splendid coral gardens give divers and snorkellers access to a variety of environments.

Charge your camera batteries, people – the Seychelles is not dubbed 'The Galápagos of the Indian Ocean' for nothing. Watching sea turtles nesting on Bird Island's sandy beaches or giant Aldabra tortoises roaming freely on Curieuse is one of those once-in-a-lifetime experiences.

Top Experiences

Diving off Mahé's North Coast

1 Anyone who loves the water will adore the Seychelles. Whatever your abilities, you'll experience sensory overload while diving off Mahé's north coast. It offers the greatest variety of the islands, and there is a good balance of healthy reefs, dense marine life and fascinating shipwrecks. Most sites here are suitable for all levels of experience. Avid snorkellers are also catered for, with gin-clear waters and a smattering of healthy coral gardens.

Bird Island

2 If you're into birds, you probably already know that Bird Island is noted for its population of sooty terns, fairy terns and common noddies. You don't even need binoculars, for your feathered friends can easily be approached. The island is also home to giant tortoises. If you're lucky, you may also see hawksbill turtles and green turtles nesting on the beach – an unforgettable experience. You don't need to be super rich to enjoy these natural wonders – Bird Island is one of the most affordable private islands in the country.

When to Go

HIGH SEASON
(Jul, Aug & Dec–Mar)

SHOULDER
(Apr, May, Oct & Nov)

LOW SEASON
(Jun & Sep)

Anse Lazio

3 When it comes to wishing for the archetypal 'idyllic beach', Anse Lazio is at the top of the list. It isn't off the beaten path, true, but there's a reason so many feet beat the path to Praslin's most revered beach, on the northwestern tip of the island. Stretching an almost-uninterrupted

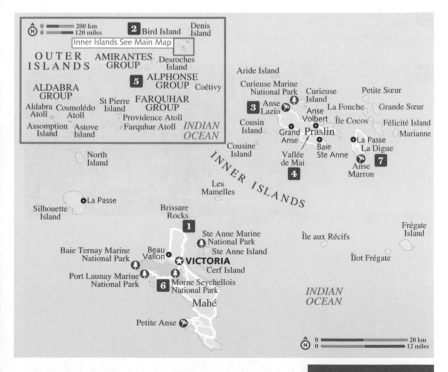

1km of white, soft sand and multihued water good for swimming, this curvaceous bay is fringed with palm and takamaka trees and framed by massive granite boulders (good for snorkelling).

Vallée de Mai

4 If you can tear yourself away from the beach, Vallée de Mai is a paradise of a different kind. Inscribed by Unesco on its World Heritage list, and home to the rare and beautiful coco de mer palms and a host of other endemic plants, Vallée de Mai is all about being immersed in lush tropical forest, serenaded by birdsong, and losing yourself along hiking trails that meander agreeably through verdant mini-wilderness.

Alphonse Island

5 If you want to live out that stranded-on-a-deserted-island fantasy,

you've come to the right place. Alphonse is a coral islet that lies about 400km south of Mahé. This is a great private island resort with a heavy focus on sportfishing. Alphonse offers the finest saltwater fly-fishing on the planet as well as sensational diving and snorkelling a mere 10-minute boat ride away. And there's only one boat: yours. No wonder it's gaining in popularity.

Morne Seychellois National Park

6 Leave your swimsuit in your hotel room and pack your sturdy shoes – you'll want them to explore the various trails running through this splendid national park that covers 20% of the land area of Mahé. It's virtually uninhabited and almost untouched today; you can hike with a guide through

Getting Around

There are excellent flight connections between Mahé and Praslin. Other islands are served on a chartered basis.

There's a fast and reliable boat service between Mahé, Praslin and La Digue. Other islands are not served by passenger boats.

There's a reliable bus network that connects most towns on Mahé and Praslin. Prices are cheap.

ESB PROFESSIONAL / SHUTTERSTOCK ©

dense tropical forest, where endemic plants, birds and insects vie for your attention. And the views over the surrounding craggy summits will be etched in your memory forever. Explore a mysterious part of Mahé you probably didn't think still existed.

Anse Cocos

7 If you're suffering from visions of tropical paradise, here is your medicine. On the east of La Digue, Anse Cocos is the sort of place you'll never want to leave. The

beach here is near perfect, a stereotype come to life with blindingly white sand, casuarina trees and palms arching gracefully to shade beachgoers, shapely boulders forming clandestine coves at either end and startlingly blue waters. Ideal for hours spent lazing on the beach, far from the crowds.

JUSTIN FOULKES / LONELY PLANET ©

Food & Drink

Bat curry Known as *civet de chauve souris*, this is a local delicacy.

Beer Seybrew, the local brand of beer, is sold everywhere. Eku, another locally produced beer, is a bit harder to find.

Fish Fish, fish, fish! And rice. This is the most common combination (*pwason ek diri* in Creole patois) in the Seychelles, served ultra-fresh so it melts in your mouth. You'll devour bourgeois, capitaine, shark, job, parrotfish, caranx, grouper and tuna, among others.

Fruit The Seychelles are dripping with tropical fruits, including mango, banana, breadfruit, papaya, coconut, grapefruit, pineapple and carambole. Mixed with spices, they make wonderful accompaniments, such as the flavourful *chatini* (chutney).

Juice Along with coconut water, freshly squeezed juices are among the most delicious, natural and thirst-quenching drinks you will try in the islands.

Wildlife

Common mammals and reptiles include the fruit bat or flying fox, the gecko, the skink and the tenrec (a hedgehog-like mammal imported from Madagascar). There are also some small snakes, but they are not dangerous.

More noteworthy is the fact that giant tortoises, which feature on the Seychelles coat of arms, are now found only in the Seychelles and the Galápagos Islands, off Ecuador. The French and English wiped out the giant tortoises from all the Seychelles islands except Aldabra, where happily more than 100,000 still survive. Many have been brought to the central islands, where they munch their way around hotel gardens, and there is a free-roaming colony on Curieuse Island.

Almost every island seems to have some rare species of bird: on Frégate, Cousin, Cousine and Aride there are magpie robins; on Cousin, Cousine and Aride you'll find the Seychelles warbler; La Digue and Denis have the *veuve* (paradise flycatcher); and Praslin has the black parrot. The bare-legged scops owl and the Seychelles kestrel live on Mahé, and Bird Island is home to millions of sooty terns.

CAPITAL
Freetown

POPULATION
6 million

AREA
71,740 sq km

OFFICIAL LANGUAGE
English

Bureh Beach, Western Area Rural District

Sierra Leone

For the traveller, Sierra Leone is still West Africa's secret beach destination. Sweet sands rise from the soft waters of the Atlantic, with the backdrop dressed in sun-stained hues, rainforest green and the red, red roads of the north.

In Freetown, colourful stilted houses remember the days when freed slaves from the Caribbean were resettled upon these shores. In the north, the Loma Mountains form the highest point west of Cameroon. Further east national parks and rainforest shelter endangered species like the black-and-white colobus monkey and the elusive pygmy hippo.

The scars of Sierra Leone's civil wars had just healed when the 2014–15 Ebola outbreak knocked the country off its feet once again. Tourism can play an important role in helping its recovery, so join the island-hoppers and adventurers, camp in little-visited rainforests and crack open fresh lobster in the shade of skinny palms and rope-strung hammocks.

Top Experiences

Tiwai Island

 One of the few remaining tracts of ancient rainforest in West Africa, Tiwai Island is Sierra Leone's most popular and accessible nature reserve. The 12 sq km island teems with an astonishing range of flora and fauna, though it's most famous for its primates.

Freetown

 Strung between the mountains and the sea, Sierra Leone's capital is a cheeky, quicksilver city bubbling with energy, colour and charm, against a devastating history of war and Ebola. One minute it's calm, offering up quiet beaches, friendly Krio chat and warm plates of soup and rice. The next it's frenzied and playing dirty, throwing you into the back of a shared taxi and hurtling you up and down its pretty little hills.

Outamba-Kilimi National Park

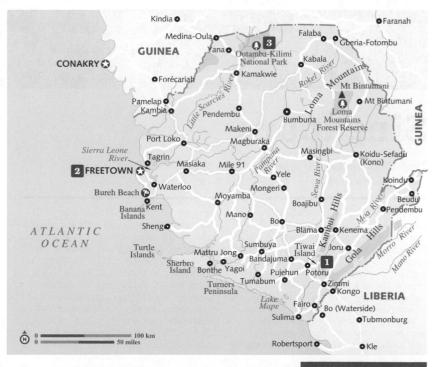 Outamba-Kilimi is a mixture of jungle and savannah, and home to nine species of primate, pygmy hippo, and reputedly, leopard. There are gentle pleasures to be had here, such as searching for elusive forest elephants or gliding down the river listening to the chatter of monkeys and birds in the overhanging trees.

When to Go

 HIGH SEASON (Nov–Feb)

SHOULDER (Mar–May & Oct)

LOW SEASON (Jun–Sep)

Food & Drink

Fry fry Simple sandwiches.

Plasas Sauce of pounded potato or cassava leaves and palm oil.

Poyo Palm wine; light and fruity.

Star Top-selling beer.

Street food Fried chicken, roasted corn, chicken kebabs.

Kindia • Faranah •

Medina-Oula • Falaba • Gberia-Fotombu •

GUINEA Yana • Outamba-Kilimi National Park • Kabala •

CONAKRY • Forécariah • Kamakwie

Rokel River • Loma Mountains • Mt Bintumani

Pamelap • Kambia • Pendembu • Bumbuna • Loma Mountains Forest Reserve • Mt Bintumani

Little Scarcies River • Makeni • **GUINEA**

Port Loko • Magburaka •

Sierra Leone River • Tagrin • Masingbi • Koidu-Sefadu (Kono) •

FREETOWN • Masiaka • Mile 91 • Yele • Koindu •

• Waterloo • Mongeri • Boajibu •

Bureh Beach • Moyamba • Sewa River • Beudu • Pendembu

Banana Islands • Kent • Mano • Boo • Blama • Kenema • Kambui Hills

Sheng • Turtle Islands • Sumbuya • Tiwai Island • Joru • Gola Hills • Morro River

ATLANTIC OCEAN • Mattru Jong • Bandajuma • Pujehun • Potoru • Mano River

Sherbro Island • Bonthe • Yagoi • Tumabum • Zimmi • Kongo • **LIBERIA**

Turners Peninsula • Lake Mape • Fairo • Bo (Waterside) •

Sulima • Tubmonburg •

Robertsport • Kle •

0 — 100 km
0 — 50 miles

Gardens by the Bay

Singapore

Long dismissed as little more than a sterile stopover, Singapore has reinvented itself as one of the world's hot-list destinations.

Asia's perennial geek has finally found its groove. More than just satay and malls, new-school Singapore is all about sci-fi architecture in billion-dollar gardens, contemporary art in converted colonial barracks, and single-origin coffee in heritage shophouses. There's a deepening self-confidence and it's driving everything, from Singapore's striking new hotels to its modern menus.

Singaporeans are obsessed with food – good food – and you'll find it steaming, sizzling and simmering almost everywhere you look. Indeed, food is the greatest unifier across ethnic divides and the country's celebrated hawker centres are a heady mix of Chinese, Malaysian and Indian spices.

The world's aspiring 'City in a Garden' is an unexpected wonderland for fans of all things natural. Catch a city bus and end up in rainforests rustling with monkeys, or wetlands teeming with giant lizards. Or just stay central and escape to the soothing Botanic Gardens. Welcome to the wild side, in an oh-so-Singaporean, user-friendly package.

Top Experiences

Gardens by the Bay

1 Spanning a whopping 101 hectares, Gardens by the Bay is Singapore's hottest horticultural asset. The $1 billion 'super park' is home to almost 400,000 plants, not to mention awe-inspiring contemporary architecture. Two giant conservatories rise beside Marina Bay like futuristic shells, one home to ancient olive trees, the other to a towering, tropical mountain. To the north are the Supertrees; futuristic, botanical giants connected by a commanding Skyway and glowing hypnotically each night.

National Gallery Singapore

2 The breathtaking National Gallery is the newest jewel in the crown of Singapore's art and museum scene. Art-lovers could spend hours wandering the world-class collection of 19th-century and modern Southeast Asian art, while kids are kept busy at the Keppel Centre for Art Education. Some of Singapore's newest, highly acclaimed, restaurants are also tucked within the wings, and the rooftop bar delivers jaw-dropping views.

When to Go

HIGH SEASON
(Dec–Jul)

LOW SEASON
(Aug–Nov)

Singapore Zoo & Night Safari

3 We're calling it: this is possibly the world's best zoo. The open-air enclosures allow for both freedom for the animals to roam and unobstructed visitor views. Singapore Zoo is one of the few places outside of Borneo or Sumatra where you can stand under trees with orangutans a few feet above your head, or where mouse deer and lemurs scamper across

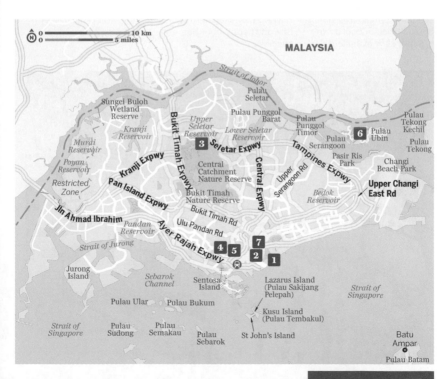

your path. As evening closes in, the Night Safari next door uses open-concept enclosures to get visitors up close and personal with nocturnal creatures such as leopards, free-ranging deer and handsome Malay tigers. You can also check out giant pandas in the newer River Safari located between the zoo and Night Safari.

Botanic Gardens

4 Singapore's Garden of Eden is the perfect antidote to the city's rat-race tendencies. At the tail end of Orchard Rd, it's a sprawling oasis laced with elegant lakes and themed gardens, and no shortage of perfect spots for picnics and people-watching. Stroll through the orchid gardens, looking out for Vanda Miss Joaquim, Singapore's national flower, or cool down in a rare slice of ancient rainforest. The Botanic Gardens are also home to a dedicated Children's Garden, free guided tours and free opera performances at the Shaw Foundation Symphony Stage.

Orchard Road

5 What was once a dusty road lined with spice plantations and orchards is now a 2.5km torrent of magnificent malls, department stores and speciality shops. You'll find every brand imaginable, from emerging local designers to global High St heavyweights and coveted European couture. Indeed, you can shop until you drop, pick yourself up, and continue spending some more. When you've stashed your purchases back at the hotel, duck out to Emerald Hill for Peranakan architecture and happy-hour bar specials.

Getting Around

Buses go everywhere the trains do and more. From 6am till midnight, plus some night buses from the city.

Local subway is the most convenient way to get around between 5.30am and midnight.

Taxis are fairly cheap if you're used to Sydney or London prices. Flag one on the street or at taxi stands. Good luck getting one on rainy days.

Pulau Ubin

6 Singapore's very own rustic island getaway offers a glimpse at the *kampong* (village) life that was a big part of Singapore as recently as the 1960s. By hopping aboard a chugging bumboat from Changi, visitors can explore Pulau Ubin's old-growth mangrove swamps and silent, lotus-peppered lakes; cycle past tin-roof shacks and ramshackle shrines; rampage along a cross-country mountain-bike trail; and end the day by digging into seafood by the sea.

Food & Drink

Carrot cake Squares of radish-flour cake stir-fried with bean sprouts, chilli sauce and salted radish.

Char kway teow Flat rice noodles wok-fried with bean sprouts, cockles, prawns and Chinese sausage in dark soy sauce and chilli sauce.

Hainanese chicken rice Tender poached chicken served on a bed of fragrant rice (cooked in chicken stock) with garlic chilli sauce.

Murtabak Pan-fried pancake stuffed with spiced mince meat (chicken, beef or mutton), garlic, egg and onion.

Nasi padang Steamed white rice served with a choice of meats, vegetables and curries.

Roti prata Fried flatbread typically served with curry.

Tiger beer While not the national drink, Singapore's local brew is a pale lager that goes down a treat.

Little India

7 The most atmospheric of Singapore's historic quarters is as close as it gets to the Singapore of the old chaotic days. Experience it with the masses on the weekends when it gets packed to the gills with Indian workers wanting a slice of home. The five-foot-ways (covered walkways) of colourful shophouses spill over with aromatic spices and Bollywood magazines. Backpackers and coolhunters swill beers at laid-back bars, and insomniacs head to Mustafa Centre to buy iPads at 3am before tucking into *teh tarik* (hot milk tea) and roti prata.

LUCIANO MORTULA / GETTY IMAGES ©

Singlish

While Singapore's official languages are Malay, Mandarin, Tamil and English, its unofficial *lingua franca* is Singlish. Essentially an English dialect mixed with Hokkien, Malay and Tamil, it's spoken in a rapid, staccato fashion, with sentences polished off with innumerable but essentially meaningless exclamatory words – *lah* is the most common, but you'll also hear *mah, lor, meh, leh, hor* and several others.

Other trademarks include a long stress on the last syllable of phrases, while words ending in consonants are often syncopated and vowels distorted. What is Perak Rd to you may well be Pera Roh to your Chinese-speaking taxi driver. Verb tenses? Forget them. Past, present and future are indicated instead by time indicators, so in Singlish it's 'I go tomorrow' or 'I go yesterday'.

Bratislava

Slovakia

Right in the heart of Europe, Slovakia is a land of castles and mountains, occasionally interrupted by concrete sprawl.

More than two decades after Czechoslovakia's break-up, Slovakia has emerged as a self-assured, independent nation. Capital city Bratislava draws the most visitors, thanks to its excellent nightlife, resplendent old town and sheer ease of access from around Europe. Beyond Bratislava are countless gingerbread-style villages, a clear sign that modern Slovakia still reveres its folk traditions.

Slovakia shines brightest for lovers of the outdoors. The High Tatras are heavenly for walking or winter sports, and national parks like Slovenský Raj sparkle with waterfalls. Castles worthy of a Disney princess perch on hills, and quaint churches speckle the less-discovered east around friendly second city Košice. Within a long weekend in this small country, you can hike or ski epic mountains, blink in astonishment at socialist-era oddities and clink glasses in cellar restaurants.

CAPITAL
Bratislava

POPULATION
5.45 million

AREA
49,035 sq km

OFFICIAL LANGUAGE
Slovak

Top Experiences

Bratislava

1 Bratislava doesn't provoke admiring swoons; it intrigues. In the midst of Slovakia's capital, a flying saucer hovers above forest-fringed riverbanks. Its castle presides over a pastel-hued old town, but a concrete jungle looms behind. Despite the march of modernism, Bratislava is green. It banks the Danube River, by the Austrian border, and its hilly parks are threaded with hiking and biking trails. The Male Karpaty (Small Carpathians) roll north, with vineyards in their lowlands. No wonder Bratislava feels like a frenetic mix of wild and urban, classic and contemporary: it became capital of newly independent Slovakia only in 1993. Bratislava preserved spires and squares from its 18th-century heyday, but now socialist-era monuments (and an eyebrow-raising cast of statues) have joined the party. Speaking of which, Bratislava's nightlife is crowd-pleasing whether you prefer beer halls, rooftop cocktails or stag-party mayhem.

Spiš Castle

2 Rising above the village of Spišské Podhradie is Spiš Castle, the former stomping ground of medieval watchmen and Renaissance nobles. This spellbinding ruin is perched on a rocky ridge, surrounded by verdant meadows, and is likely Slovakia's most-photographed sight.

The High Tatras

3 The High Tatras, the tallest range in the Carpathian Mountains,

When to Go

 HIGH SEASON
(Jul & Aug)

 SHOULDER
(Apr, May, Jun & Sep)

 LOW SEASON
(Oct–Mar)

tower over most of Eastern Europe. Some 25 peaks measure above 2500m, but the massif is only 25km wide and 78km long, with pristine snowfields, ultramarine mountain lakes, thundering waterfalls, undulating pine forests and shimmering alpine meadows.

Pastures & Villages

4 Central Slovakia's meadows and forested mountains, speckled with castles, are the ideal backdrop to live out pastoral fantasies. This verdant region is the centre of the shepherding tradition that continues to define Slovak cuisine. Roadside stalls overflow with produce like smoky cheeses, honey, woodland mushrooms and berries. Orava and Bojnice Castles attract the biggest crowds, but village nostalgia also defines attractions like architectural reserve Vlkolínec, Čičmany's geometrically-patterned timber houses and Martin's beautifully restored 19th- and 20th-century houses and *skanzen* (open-air village museums).

Slovenský Raj National Park

5 You don't simply visit Slovenský Raj National Park. It's more accurate to say that you clamber, scramble and get thoroughly drenched in this dynamic landscape of caves, canyons and waterfalls. Hikers in 'Slovak Paradise' climb ladders over gushing cascades, trek to ruined monasteries and shiver within an ice cave – and that's just on day one.

Getting Around

Bus lines run to smaller villages where there is no rail connection.

Roads can be narrow and potholed, and in towns cobblestones and tram tracks can prove dangerous.

For scenery and efficiency, train is an excellent way to travel. Most tourist destinations lie off the main Bratislava–Košice line.

Wooden Churches

6 Seek out iconic, Unesco-listed wooden churches in isolated far-east Slovakia, such as Hervatov or Ladomirová. Travelling east from Bardejov, you come to a crossroads of Western and Eastern Christianity. From the 17th to the 19th centuries, nearly 300 dark-wood, onion-domed churches were erected hereabouts. Of the 40-odd remaining, eight have been recognised by Unesco. A handful celebrate Roman Catholic or Protestant faiths, but most belong to the Eastern rites of Greek Catholicism and Orthodoxy. Typically they honour the Holy Trinity with three domes, three architectural sections and three doors on the icon screen. Richly painted icons and venerated representations of Christ and the saints decorate the iconostases and invariably every inch of the churches' interiors have also been hand-painted. These can be quite a sight, but it's not easy to get inside.

Banská Štiavnica

7 Banská Štiavnica has a glittering history, quite literally. Gold, silver and minerals brought enormous wealth to Slovakia's oldest mining town. Wonderfully intact Gothic and Renaissance buildings date to its 16th-century prime (though miners are believed to have toiled here for centuries before). It grew into the third-largest town in the Kingdom of Hungary. After the 19th century, minerals were depleted, mines closed and townspeople began to leave. But for visitors, Banská Štiavnica's frozen-in-time feel is part of the allure. Medieval castles, burghers' houses and sacred sights all contributed to the historic centre's Unesco listing in 1993, and you can still get a flavour of the old mining days at an open-air museum.

5

CCATBZ / SHUTTERSTOCK ©

Food & Drink

Slovakia isn't renowned for its cuisine and certain stereotypes of stodgy home cooking hold true: menus burst with *bryndzové halušky* (gnocchi with sheep's cheese and bacon), and meat-and-cabbage soups. Nonetheless, the dining scene is cosmopolitan in Bratislava and Košice, with veggie choices sprinkled among upmarket Slovak, Italian and French-inspired restaurants.

There are standout eateries in smaller towns, including Bardejov and Ždiar. High Tatras hike-and-ski hubs focus on carb-heavy fast food.

An Ice-Hockey Obsession

Slovakia's national men's ice-hockey team is usually ranked in the world's top 10 by the International Ice Hockey Federation (IIHF). Not bad, considering the team was only created when Czechoslovakia dissolved in 1993. Local club rivalries are heated, with the most popular teams being HC Slovan in Bratislava (playing in the Kontinental Hockey League since 2012) and HC Košice in Košice. These teams' two stadiums co-hosted the IIHF world championships in 2011. Puck-pushing season is September to May, when games seem to be on TVs everywhere.

CAPITAL	Ljubljana
POPULATION	2.06 million
AREA	20,273 sq km
OFFICIAL LANGUAGE	Slovene

Lake Bohinj, Triglav National Park

Slovenia

An earthly paradise of snow-capped peaks, turquoise-green rivers and Venetian-style coastline, Slovenia enriches its natural treasures with harmonious architecture, charming rustic culture and sophisticated cuisine.

It's a pint-sized place, with a surface area of just more than 20,000 sq km and two million people. But 'good things come in small packages', and never was that old chestnut more appropriate than in describing Slovenia. The country has everything from beaches, snowcapped mountains, hills awash in grape vines and wide plains blanketed in sunflowers to Gothic churches, baroque palaces and art nouveau buildings. Its incredible diversity of climates brings warm Mediterranean breezes up to the foothills of the Alps, where it can still snow in summer.

The capital, Ljubljana, is a culturally rich city that values livability and sustainability over unfettered growth. This sensitivity towards the environment extends to rural and lesser-developed parts of the country as well. With more than half of its total area covered in forest, Slovenia really is one of the 'greenest' countries in the world.

Top Experiences

Ljubljana

 Slovenia's capital city strikes that perfect yet elusive balance between size and quality of life. It's big enough to offer discoveries yet small enough to walk – or better yet, cycle – around at a leisurely pace. And no place in Slovenia waltzes through architecture so adroitly as the capital named 'beloved', from its ancient hilltop castle and splendid art nouveau banks to local boy Jože Plečnik's wondrously decorative pillars, obelisks and orbs found everywhere.

Climbing Mt Triglav

 They say you're not really a Slovene until you climb Mt Triglav and get 'spanked' at the summit. And it's all but stamped in locals' passports once they've made the trek up the country's tallest mountain. The good news for the rest of us is that Triglav is a challenging but accessible peak that just about anyone in decent shape can 'conquer' with an experienced guide. There are several popular approaches, but whichever path you choose, the reward is the same: sheer exhilaration.

When to Go

☀ **HIGH SEASON**
(Jun–Aug)

⛅ **SHOULDER**
(Apr, May, Sep & Oct)

❄ **LOW SEASON**
(Nov–Mar)

Piran

 Venice in Slovenia? That busy merchant empire left its mark up and down the Adriatic coast, and Slovenia was lucky to end up with one of the best-preserved medieval Venetian ports anywhere. It's true that Piran attracts tourist numbers on a massive scale in season, but the

beautiful setting means it's never less than a constant delight. Enjoy fresh fish on the harbour, then wander the narrow streets and end up having drinks and people-watching in a glorious central square.

River Adventures

4 Rarely does a river beckon to be rafted as convincingly as Slovenia's Soča. Maybe it's that piercing sky-blue-bordering-on-green – or is it turquoise? – colour of the water, or the river's refreshing froth and foam as it tumbles down the mountains. Even if you're not the rafting type, you'll soon find yourself strapping on a wetsuit for that exhilarating ride of the summer. Outfitters in Bovec, Bled and Kobarid specialise in guided rafting trips. For gentler floats, try the Krka River.

Ptuj

5 Its name might sound like a cartoon character spitting, but Ptuj is no joke. Rather, it's one of Slovenia's richest historical towns. Everyone since the Romans has left their mark, and the centre is still a maze of red roofs and medieval streets, dotted with churches, towers and museums, as well as street cafes to enjoy the passing scenes. Ptuj is within easy reach of some of the country's best (mostly white) wine-producing regions.

Postojna Cave

6 The cave system at Postojna is Slovenia's biggest subterranean attraction. The entrance might not look like much, but when you get whisked 4km underground on a train and only then start exploring, you start to get a sense of the scale. The caverns are a

Getting Around

Buses are generally efficient and good value but very crowded on Friday afternoons and restricted on Sundays and holidays.

A great way to explore the countryside, with rental firms everywhere including the airport.

Trains are cheaper but usually slower than buses (with the exception of intercity high-speed services).

ROSSHELEN / SHUTTERSTOCK ©

seemingly endless parade of crystal fancies – from frilly chandeliers and dripping spaghetti-like stalactites, to paper-thin sheets and stupendous stalagmites, all laid down over the centuries by the simple dripping of mineral-rich water.

Predjama Castle

7 Slovenia is over-endowed with castles and caves, but one inside the other? Now that's something special. Few fortresses have a setting as grand as this, wedged half-way up a cliff face at the foot of the valley. The location has a story behind it that's equally dramatic: Slovenia's 'Robin Hood', Erazem Lueger, apparently taunted besieging troops here by hurling fresh cherries at them that he collected via a secret passage. He came to a swift and rather embarrassing end, however.

Vipava Valley Wines

8 Slovenia is blessed with the means to produce some of the region's best wines and the Vipava Valley particularly stands out. It enjoys a warm Mediterranean climate freshened by cold winter winds, making it the ideal destination for those wanting to treat their palates. Wineries with some of the best merlots in the world? Check. The best air-dried pršut ham? Yep. Pick up some local fruits and olives and you've got a Slovenian picnic to remember.

Food & Drink

Until recently, except for a few national favourites, you were not likely to encounter many regional specialities on restaurant menus. But all that is changing as Slovenia reclaims (and often redefines and updates) its culinary heritage.

Slovenian cuisine is greatly influenced by its neighbours' cooking styles. From Austria, there's *klobasa* (sausage), *zavitek* or *štrudelj* (strudel) filled with fruit, nuts and/or *skuta* (curd cheese), and *dunajski zrezek* (Wiener schnitzel). The ravioli-like *žlikrofi* (pasta stuffed with potatoes, onion and spiced pork), *njoki* (potato dumplings) and *rižota* (risotto) obviously have Italian origins, and Hungary has contributed *golaž* (goulash), *paprikaš* (piquant chicken or beef 'stew') and *palačinka* ('crepes' filled with jam or nuts and topped with chocolate). From Croatia and the rest of the Balkans come such popular grills as *ćevapčići* (spicy meatballs of beef or pork) and *pljeskavica* (meat patties).

PECOLD / SHUTTERSTOCK ©

Taking the Cure

Slovenia counts upwards of 15 thermal spa resorts, most of them in Štajerska, Dolenjska and Prekmurje. They are excellent places not just for 'taking the cure' but for relaxing and meeting people.

Rogaška Slatina Slovenia's oldest and largest spa town, a veritable 'cure factory' with a fin-de-siècle feel to it.

Dolenjske Toplice Cosy and very wooded resort town with all the mod cons dating back to the 17th century.

Radenci Slightly down-at-the-heel but atmospheric spa town that also boasts Slovenia's premier mineral water.

Terme Olimia Enormous spa complex on the Croatian border with a great fortress looming above it.

CAPITAL
Honiara

POPULATION
635,000

AREA
28,896 sq km

OFFICIAL LANGUAGE
English

Uepi Island in Marovo Lagoon

Solomon Islands

For those seeking an authentic Melanesian experience or an off-the-beaten-track destination, the Solomons are hard to beat.

Forget what travelling the Pacific *used* to be like – around the Solomon Islands it's still that way. These islands are laid-back, welcoming and often surprisingly untouched. From WWII relics scattered in the jungle to leaf-hut villages where traditional culture is alive, there's so much on offer. Then there's the visual appeal, with scenery reminiscent of a Discovery Channel documentary: volcanic islands, croc-infested mangroves, huge lagoons, tropical islets and emerald forests.

Don't expect white-sand beaches and ritzy resorts. With only a smattering of traditional guesthouses and comfortable hideaways, it's tailor-made for ecotourists. For outdoorsy types, lots of action-packed experiences await: climb an extinct volcano, surf uncrowded waves, snorkel pristine reefs or kayak across a lagoon. Beneath the ocean's surface, awesome WWII wrecks and dizzying drop-offs will enthrall divers. The best part is, there'll be no crowds to mar the experience.

Top Experiences

Marovo Lagoon

1 Marovo Lagoon offers plenty of exhilarating dives for both experts and novices. Here's the menu: channels, caves, drop-offs, coral gardens, clouds of technicolour fish and a few wrecks thrown in for good measure. A few iconic sites include Uepi Point, General Store and Lumalihe Passage. With dozens of lovely sites scattered throughout the lagoon, snorkelling is equally impressive. Lodges can organise lagoon tours and snorkelling trips; bring your own gear.

Kolombangara

2 A perfect cone-shaped volcano that rises to 1770m, Kolombangara looms majestically on the horizon, northeast of Ghizo Island. It rises from a 1km-wide coastal plain through flat-topped ridges and increasingly steep escarpments to the rugged crater rim of Mt Veve. For history buffs, there are WWII Japanese relics scattered around the island.

Langa Langa Lagoon

3 Langa Langa Lagoon is indisputably one of Malaita's highlights. Extending from 7km to 32km south of Auki, the lagoon is famous for its artificial islands built of stones and dead corals. It's also a strong centre for traditional activities, especially shell-money making and shipbuilding. One proviso: 'lagoon' is a bit misleading. If it has recently rained, waters may be more chocolate than bright turquoise, and you won't find

When to Go

 HIGH SEASON (Jun–Sep)

 SHOULDER (Apr, May, Oct & Nov)

 LOW SEASON (Dec–Mar)

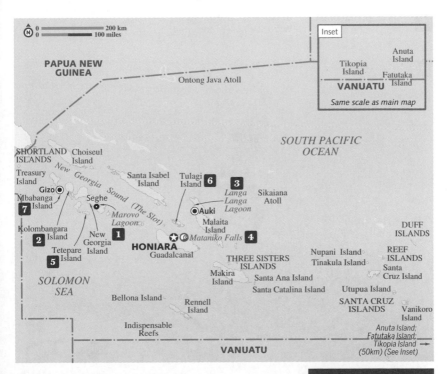

stunning beaches to sun yourself on. People rather come here for the laid-back tempo and the magical setting.

Mataniko Falls

4 One of the star attractions in Honiara's hinterlands is Mataniko Falls, which feature a spectacular thundering of water down a cliff straight into a canyon below. The hike to these waterfalls starts in Lelei village with a steep ascent to a ridge, followed by an easier stretch amid mildly undulating hills. Then you'll tackle a gruelling descent on a muddy path to reach the floor of the little canyon where the Mataniko flows. It's roughly two hours return.

Tetepare Island

5 This large rainforest island is one of the Solomons' conservation jewels. The Tetepare Descendants' Association, which manages the island, welcomes visitors in its rustic yet genuinely eco-friendly leafhouses (no air-con, solar power, shared facilities). What makes this place extra special is the host of environmentally friendly activities available, including snorkelling with dugongs, spotting crocodiles, birdwatching and turtle-tagging. Activities are free (except the ones that involve boat rides), and you'll be accompanied by trained guides. Food is fresh and organic.

Tulagi

6 In the middle of the Florida Islands, Tulagi was the Solomons' former capital; it was also a Japanese base during WWII. It's now a renowned

Getting Around

Solomon Airlines services the country's 20-odd airstrips. Honiara is the main hub.

Outboard-powered dinghies are the most common means of transport in the Solomons. There are a couple of reliable passenger boats from Honiara.

Public minibuses are found only in Honiara. Elsewhere, people pile into open-backed trucks or tractor-drawn trailers.

JAMES MORGAN / GETTY IMAGES ©

playground for divers, with a series of fabulous wrecks lying just offshore. Raiders Hotel, right on the waterfront (no beach), features tip-top rooms and has a professional dive shop that caters mainly to certified divers (no courses are offered). Wreck buffs will need a few days to explore the huge WWII wrecks, including the monster-sized USS Kanawha, the USS Aaron Ward and the Moa.

Mbabanga Island

7 A mere 10-minute boat ride south of Gizo, this island has a brochure-esque appeal, with an expansive lagoon and a string of white-sand beaches.

Food & Drink

Beer The local brand of beer in the Solomon Islands is Solbrew. Smaller places may be BYO.

Central Market The country's bubbling principal food market is in Honiara and has a huge selection of fresh produce, especially fruits and vegetables, which come from outlying villages along the northern coast and from Savo island. A fish market is located at the back.

Restaurants A wide variety of cuisines is available in Honiara's restaurants, from French to Japanese, Chinese and Western foods.

Seafood Fish and seafood, including lobster, is fresh and abundant throughout the islands.

DAVID KIRKLAND / GETTY IMAGES ©

Clan Loyalties

Solomon Islanders' obligations to their clan and village *bigman* (chief) are eternal and enduring, whether they live in the same village all their lives or move to another country. As in most Melanesian cultures, the *wantok* system is observed here. All islanders are born with a set of obligations to their *wantok*, but they're also endowed with privileges that only *wantok* receive. For most Melanesian villagers it's an egalitarian way of sharing the community assets. There's no social security system and very few people are in paid employment, but the clan provides economic support and a strong sense of identity.

Melanesian culture is deeply rooted in ancestor worship, magic and oral traditions. Villagers often refer to their traditional ways, beliefs and land ownership as *kastom*; it's bound up in the Melanesian systems of lore and culture.

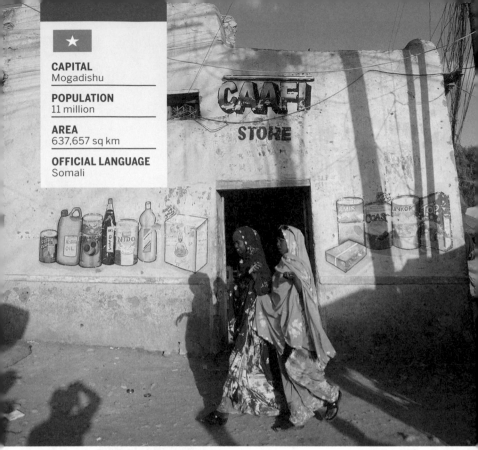

Hargeisa, Somaliland

Somalia & Somaliland

A few decades ago Somalia was a magnet for travellers and, with a bit of luck and a following wind, it could be again. But right now the country is still unsafe for foreigners, with its people, places and infrastructure still recovering from over 25 years of brutal civil war.

Unfortunately, the civil war has over-shadowed Somalia's great natural wonders. There are thousands of miles of pristine beaches along the Gulf of Aden and the Indian Ocean. The islands off Zeila, close to the Djibouti border, are also completely unspoilt and ablaze with technicolour tropical fish. The wild expanses of the Sheekh Mountains (Somaliland) have a rugged beauty and afford stunning views over the coast, as far as Berbera.

Snapshot

Somaliland

 It has a parliament. It has a broadly representative government. It has a capital. It has a flag. It has a currency. It has a university. It has an army. It has multiparty elections. But nobody recognises it. This is Somaliland, the country that does not exist. The self-proclaimed Republic of Somaliland was formed in 1991 after the collapse of unitary Somalia. Although its leaders desperately struggle to gain formal international recognition, it is not recognised as a separate state.

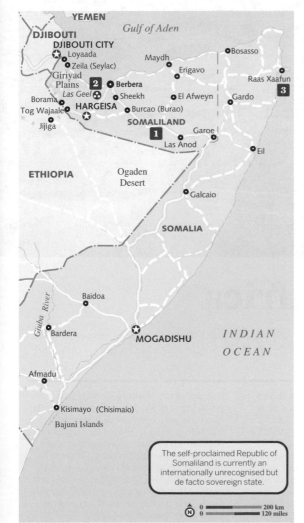

The self-proclaimed Republic of Somaliland is currently an internationally unrecognised but de facto sovereign state.

Seasons

☀ DEC–MAR

⛅ OCT–NOV

☂ APR–SEP

Las Geel

 Las Geel features one of the most impressive collections of ancient rock art on the African continent. Depicting wild animals, decorated cattle and herders, hundreds of magnificent neolithic rock art paintings in perfect condition adorn the walls of several interconnected caves and shelters. Some paintings exceed one metre in length and are exceptionally well preserved.

Raas Xaafun

 At the tip of the Horn of Africa, Raas Xaafun is the easternmost point in the whole of Africa. Once the bustling port of Opone, this ancient bazaar was a trading centre dealing in cinnamon, cloves, spices and incense.

Food & Drink

Goat and camel meat are popular dishes. The standard breakfast throughout the country is fried liver with onions and *loxox*, a flat bread similar to the Ethiopian *injera*, served with honey, sugar and tea. Rice and noodles are also common staples. Tea is the favourite drink.

CAPITALS
Pretoria, Cape Town, Bloemfontein

POPULATION
54 million

AREA
1,219,090 sq km

OFFICIAL LANGUAGES
Zulu, Xhosa, Afrikaans, English, Swati, Tsonga, Southern Sotho, Tswana, Venda, Northern Sotho, Ndebele

Cape Town

South Africa

Black-maned lions framed against Kalahari dunes; powdery beaches lapped by two oceans; star-studded desert skies; jagged, lush mountains – this truly is a country of astounding diversity.

South Africa is one of the best safari destinations, offering the Big Five and more in accessible parks and reserves. But it's not all about big game sightings – wildlife watching here also teaches you to enjoy the little things: a leopard tortoise ambling along the road, a go-away bird chirping its distinctive chant, or an encounter with seals, whales or a great white shark.

To visit South Africa without learning about its tumultuous history is to miss a crucial part of the country's identity. Museum visits, many of which include exhibits on the apartheid era, might not be lighthearted, but will help you to understand the very fabric of South African society and to appreciate how far the country has come. Continue your history lesson with a visit to one of the townships, taking time to chat to locals and to learn that despite a heart-wrenching past, there is great pride here, and an immense sense of promise for the future.

Top Experiences

Cape Town

1 Overlooked by flat-topped Table Mountain, with its cable car, walking trails and abseiling, Cape Town is one of the world's most beautiful cities. Fill your days here visiting beaches and Constantia wine estates, wandering the V&A Waterfront, catching the ferry to Robben Island and, above all, meeting the easygoing Cape locals. In complement to its considerable natural charms, the city is benefiting from ongoing urban renewal, with world-class restaurants, hip food markets and design-savvy arcades opening in once-industrial neighbourhoods such as Woodstock.

Kruger National Park

2 Kruger is one of Africa's great wilderness experiences and the mightiest of the country's national parks – a trip here will sear itself in your mind. Its accessibility, numbers and variety of wildlife, and staggering size and range of activities make Kruger unique and compelling. From wilderness trails and bushwalks to mountain biking and remote 4WD trails, there are myriad opportunities to enjoy both the wild and the wildlife. Kruger is simply one of the best places to see animals – big and small – in the world.

Drakensberg Region

3 Majestic, stunning and mysterious, the mountains and foothills of the World Heritage–listed uKhahlamba-Drakensberg Park are among the country's most awe-inspiring landscapes. Drakensberg means 'Dragon Mountains' in Afrikaans, while the Zulu named the range Quathlamba, meaning 'Battlement of Spears'. The Zulu word is a more accurate description of the sheer escarpment, but the Afrikaans name captures something of the Drakensberg's otherworldly atmosphere. People have lived here for thousands of years,

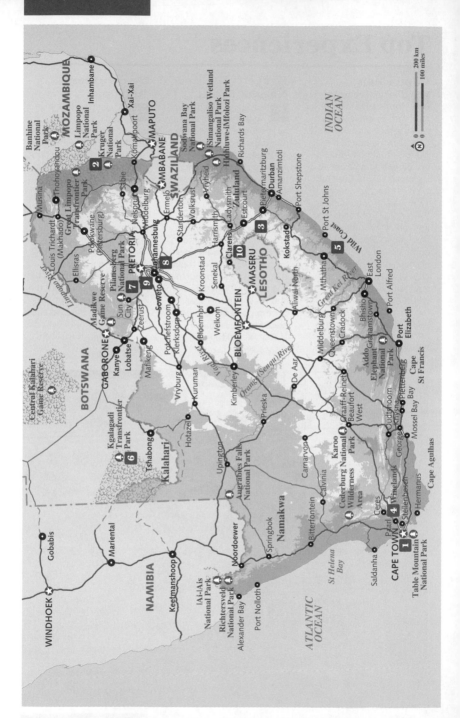

evidenced by the many San rock-art sites. With its Zulu villages, wilderness areas and wildflowers, and good accommodation and eateries, the Drakensberg region is the perfect place for photographers, hikers and adventurous travellers.

Best on Film

Invictus (2009) Covers the historic 1995 Rugby World Cup.

District 9 (2009) Peter Jackson produced this sci-fi gem about giant aliens overrunning Jo'burg.

Mandela: Long Walk to Freedom (2013) Condensed but enjoyable biography, covering Madiba's journey to presidency.

The Bang Bang Club (2010) Based on the true story of four photographers documenting the final days of apartheid.

Best in Print

The Housemaid's Daughter (Barbara Mutch; 2013) Apartheid-era drama set in the Karoo.

Long Walk to Freedom (Nelson Mandela; 1995) Hefty, must-read autobiography of the former president.

Reports Before Daybreak (Brent Meersman; 2011) Moving novel set in 1980s Cape Town.

50 People Who Stuffed Up South Africa (Alexander Parker; 2011) Fast-moving look at history's great villains.

Country of My Skull (Antjie Krog; 1998) A personal account of the Truth and Reconciliation Commission.

Disgrace (JM Coetzee; 1999) Booker Prize–winning novel based in post-apartheid South Africa.

The Winelands

4 Whitewashed Cape Dutch architecture dots an endlessly photogenic landscape of rolling hills and vines in neat rows. The Winelands is the quintessential Cape, where world-class wines are the icing on the proverbial cake. Stellenbosch, Franschhoek and Paarl, the area's holy trinity of wine-tasting towns, host some of the southern hemisphere's oldest, largest and prettiest wine estates. But this is not the only wine region – head to Tulbagh for sparkling wines, the heights of the Cederberg for crisp sauvignon blancs, and Route 62 for robust reds and port.

Wild Coast Walks

5 With its rugged cliffs plunging into the sea, remote sandy beaches, rural Xhosa villages, and history of shipwrecks and stranded sailors, the aptly named Wild Coast is ideally explored on foot. From the

When to Go

HIGH SEASON (Nov–Mar) In popular holiday spots, accommodation prices can rise by 50% or more.

SHOULDER (Apr, May, Sep & Oct) Sunny spring and autumn weather.

LOW SEASON (Jun–Aug) Winter is ideal for wildlife watching.

Great Kei River to Port St Johns, pathways hug the shoreline, cutting through dense vegetation or snaking across denuded hillsides and gorges, and often

Nelson Mandela

Nelson Rolihlahla Mandela, one of the millennium's greatest leaders, was once vilified by South Africa's ruling whites and sentenced to life imprisonment. On his release 27 years later, he called for reconciliation and forgiveness.

Mandela, son of a Xhosa chief, was born on 18 July 1918. After finishing his law degree, he opened South Africa's first black law firm, together with Oliver Tambo. In 1944, along with Tambo and Walter Sisulu, Mandela formed the Youth League of the African National Congress (ANC). During the 1950s, Mandela was at the forefront of the ANC's civil disobedience campaigns. In 1964 Mandela stood trial for sabotage and fomenting revolution. He was sentenced to life imprisonment, and spent the next 18 years in Robben Island prison, before being moved to the mainland. Throughout his incarceration, Mandela refused to compromise his political beliefs.

In 1994, four years after his release, Mandela became the first freely elected president of South Africa. He stepped down in 1997, although he continued to be revered as an elder statesman until his death on 5 December 2013.

Getting Around

Cars are a great option, with affordable rental rates, a good road network and the car-based South African lifestyle.

The Baz Bus backpacker shuttle is a convenient and social option between Cape Town, Durban and Jo'burg/Pretoria.

Tourist class on South Africa's trains is an unsung secret (with sleeper coaches and dining car), linking Jo'burg to Cape Town and the coast.

Several bus lines are useful, covering the country in comfortable vehicles at reasonable rates.

overlook southern right whales and dolphins in the turquoise seas. Power down in rustic accommodation or overnight with families in traditionally designed *rondavels* (round huts with a conical roof).

Kgalagadi Transfrontier Park

6 Kgalagadi covers almost 40,000 sq km of raw Kalahari in the Northern Cape and Botswana, an area roamed by some 2000 predators. But such statistics, albeit impressive, barely scrape the surface of this immense land of sizzling sunsets, velvety night skies and rolling red dunes. The park is one of the world's best places to spot big cats, and you might spy black-maned lions napping under thorn trees, or cheetahs and leopards tracking along the roadside. Best of all, you don't need a 4WD to access the park.

Pilanesberg National Park

7 Sprawling away from Sun City is this underrated park, where the Big Five and day-tripping Jo'burgers roam an extinct volcanic crater. With its tarred roads, Pilanesberg is sometimes dismissed as tame, yet the rhinos lapping at waterholes seem to disagree. To escape the other cars and score an up-close sighting, hit the gravel roads through the bush and stake out a dam. Guided drives and walks are available, as is a range of accommodation, making this a winner for families and those short on time.

Johannesburg

8 With a grisly reputation, the City of Gold is a surprisingly vibey and inspiring place thanks to the regeneration uplifting its inner city. The cultural enclaves of Braamfontein, Newtown, 44 Stanley Avenue and the Maboneng Precinct are dynamic and exciting spots by any city's standards, with galleries, restaurants, bars and boutiques. Take a walking tour to understand the background of this urban transformation and spot Maboneng's public art by international muralists; and try to time your visit to coincide with Braamfontein and Maboneng's weekly markets.

Cradle of Humankind

9 One of the world's most important paleontological zones and a World Heritage Site, the Cradle of Humankind nurses hundreds of square kilometres of beautiful green and brown veld – and an increasing migration of tourists, descended from hominids, who sit with the fossils of their ancestors deep underground, before returning to civilisation at fine restaurants and day spas. There's wilderness to be gawked at, too; only 50km northwest of Jo'burg are free-roaming elands, zebras, giraffes and gazelles.

Clarens

10 The odd international star popping in for a lungful of fresh mountain air gives this well-heeled town celebrity credentials. But with galleries, antiques, classy restaurants, a microbrewery and adventure activities in the surrounding countryside, there's something to appeal to most other visitors too. The laid-back town is perfect for an evening stroll after a day exploring the nearby Golden Gate Highlands National Park. And with plenty of pubs to drop into and bookshops to browse in, Clarens is the best place in the Free State's Eastern Highlands to simply wind down.

Sport

South Africans are sports fanatics, with football (soccer) the most popular spectator sport, followed by rugby and cricket.

Art

Individual works by major 20th-century and contemporary South African artists, including Irma Stern, Pierneef, William Kentridge and Tretchikoff, have fetched over US$1 million at auction.

Boryeong Mud Festival

CAPITAL
Seoul

POPULATION
50,924,172

AREA
99,720 sq km

OFFICIAL LANGUAGE
Korean

South Korea

Split by a fearsome border, the Korean Peninsula offers a dazzling range of experiences, beautiful landscapes and 5000 years of culture and history.

Korea might be known as the Land of the Morning Calm, but dive into its capital, Seoul, and serenity is the last thing you'll feel. You can hardly turn a corner without stumbling across a tourist information booth, a subway station or a taxi in this multifaceted metropolis where meticulously reconstructed palaces rub shoulders with teeming night markets and the latest technological marvel.

South Korea's compact size and superb transport infrastructure mean that tranquillity can be found in easy reach of the urban sprawl. Hike to the summits of craggy mountains enclosed by densely forested national parks. Sail to remote islands, where folk welcome you into their homes. Chill out in serene villages surrounded by rice fields and sleep in rustic *hanok* (traditional wooden houses). South Korea is a dream destination – an engaging, welcoming place where the benefits of a high-tech nation are balanced alongside a reverence for tradition and the ways of old Asia.

Top Experiences

Changdeokgung

1 The 'Palace of Illustrious Virtue' in Seoul was built in the early 15th century as a secondary palace to Gyeongbukgung. These days this Unesco World Heritage–listed property exceeds Gyeongbukgung in beauty and grace, partly because so many of its buildings were actually lived in by members of the royal family well into the 20th century. The most charming section is the Huwon, a 'secret garden' that's a royal horticultural idyll. Book well ahead to snag one of the limited tickets to view this special palace on a moonlight tour held at the full moon from April to June.

Hiking around Jeju-do

2 The frequently dramatic volcanic landscape of Jeju-do, the largest of South Korea's many islands, is best seen on foot. The Jeju Olle Trail is a network of 26 half- to full-day hiking routes that meander around the island's coast, part of the hinterland and three other islands. Spending a day following all or part of a trail is a wonderful way to soak up Jeju's unique charms and beautiful surroundings. The summit of Hallasan, the country's highest peak, is also very achievable and, in good weather, provides spectacular views.

Boryeong Mud Festival

3 Every July, thousands of people converge on the welcoming seaside town of Boryeong and proceed to jump into gigantic vats of mud. Welcome to the Boryeong Mud Festival. The official line is that the local mud has restorative properties, but one look around and it's clear that no one really cares for much except having a slippery, sloshin', messy good time. Mud aside, this foreigner-friendly and high-profile festival also features concerts, raves and fireworks. A tip: don't wear anything you want to keep!

LIM WAI YEN / GETTY IMAGES ©

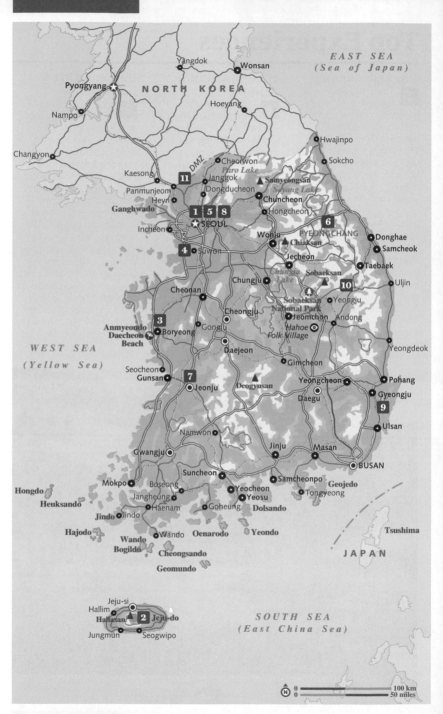

EAST SEA
(Sea of Japan)

NORTH KOREA

Pyongyang

Yangdok   Wonsan

Nampo   Hoeyang

Changyon

Hwajinpo

Sokcho

Kaesong   DMZ   Cheorwon
                                Paro Lake
Panmunjeom   Janggok
Heyri   Dongducheon   Samyeongsan
Ganghwado   Chuncheon
                                   Seyang Lake
1 5 8   Hongcheon

Incheon   SEOUL

                    Wonju   PYEONGCHANG   Donghae
4   Suwon   Chiaksan   Samcheok

                    Jecheon   Taebaek

                Chungju   Sobaeksan   Uljin
Cheonan   Chungju Lake
                Cheongju   Sobaeksan   Yeongju
                            National Park   Andong
Anmyeondo   3   Jeomcheon
Daecheon   Boryeong   Gongju   Hahoe
Beach   Folk Village

WEST SEA   Daejeon
(Yellow Sea)
                            Gimcheon   Yeongdeok
Seocheon
Gunsan   7
          Jeonju   Deogyusan   Yeongcheon   Pohang
                                        Daegu   Gyeongju
                                                        9
                                                   Ulsan
Namwon

Hongdo   Gwangju   Jinju   Masan
Heuksando   BUSAN

          Suncheon   Samcheonpo   Geojedo
Mokpo   Boseong   Tongyeong
Jangheung   Yeocheon
Jindo   Haenam   Yeosu   Dolsando
Hajodo   Jindo   Goheung
                    Wando   Oenarodo   Yeondo   Tsushima
Wando
Bogildo   Cheongsando   JAPAN
          Geomundo

Jeju-si
Hallim   Hallasan   2   Jeju-do   SOUTH SEA
Jungmun   Seogwipo   (East China Sea)

N   0   100 km
          0   50 miles

Best on Film

The Host (2006) Seoul-based classic monster movie that juggles humour, poignancy and heart-stopping action.

Poetry (2010) Lee Chang-dong directs this drama about a woman in her 60s struggling with Alzheimer's disease who enrols in a poetry-writing course.

In Another Country (2012) Hong Sang-soo, director of award-winning *Hahaha*, casts Isabelle Huppert as three different women whose stories intersect in the seaside resort of Mohang.

Food

Flavours Most people think Korean food means *kimchi* and barbecue, which exhibit quintessentially Korean flavours – the ripe tartness of fermented leaves, the delicate marinade of grilled meat. But that's just the starting point. A Korean meal is packed with flavours, unrepentant and full.

Sauces While the basic building blocks of the cuisine are recognisably Asian (garlic, ginger, green onion, black pepper, vinegar and sesame oil), Korean food strikes out on its own in combining them with three essential sauces: *ganjang* (soy sauce), *doenjang* (fermented soybean paste) and *gochujang* (hot red-pepper paste).

Banchan The other distinctive feature is that the main course is always served not only with *bap* (boiled rice), soup and *kimchi*, but also a procession of *banchan* (side dishes). Diners eat a bit from one dish, a bite from another, a little rice, a sip of soup, mixing spicy and mild any way they want.

Suwon's Hwaseong Fortress

4 Built as an act of filial devotion and heavily damaged during the colonisation period of the early 20th century and again in the Korean War, the restoration of this Unesco World Heritage Site began in the 1970s and is now almost finished. A detailed 1801 record of its construction has allowed the 5.52km-long wall and the Hwaseong Haenggung (a palace for the king to stay in during his visits to Suwon) to be rebuilt with great historical accuracy. A walk around the wall takes you through four grand gates.

Cheong-gye-cheon

5 A raised highway was demolished to allow reconstruction of this long-buried stream. The effort has transformed central Seoul, creating a riverside park and walking course that provides a calm respite from the surrounding commercial hubbub. Public art is dotted along the banks of the stream and many events are held here, including a spectacular lantern festival in November, when thousands of giant glowing paper sculptures are floated in the water. There's also a good museum where you can learn about the history of the Cheong-gye-cheon.

When to Go

HIGH SEASON
(Jun–Sep)
July brings sweltering heat and a very heavy rainy season.

SHOULDER
(May & Oct)
The changing seasons see the country bathed in colour.

LOW SEASON
(Nov–Apr)
Snow falls and temperatures plummet.

King Sejong's Gift

Hangeul is a phonetic script: concise, elegant and considered one of the most scientific in the world in rendering sounds. It was developed in 1443, during the reign of Korea's greatest king, Sejong, as a way of increasing literacy – it is much simpler and easier to learn than Chinese characters. But the Confucian elite opposed its wide use, hoping to keep the government exams as difficult as possible so only aristocratic children had the time and money to pass.

Hangeul didn't come into general use until after 1945, and then only in North Korea. South Korea used a Sino-Korean script requiring the mastery of thousands of Chinese characters until the 1990s. Today, though, Chinese characters have mostly disappeared from Korea's public space, to the consternation of Chinese and Japanese travellers who used to be able to read all the street and commercial signs. King Sejong's face, meanwhile, is etched on the ₩10,000 note.

Getting Around

There are dozens of local airports and reasonable fares to several destinations, such as Jeju-do, thanks to competition from budget airlines.

The train network is excellent but not comprehensive, with clean, comfortable and punctual trains. It's worth looking into a KR Pass even for something as straightforward as a return Seoul–Busan train.

A ferry connects the mainland to hundreds of islands.

Driving isn't recommended for first-time visitors: you'll likely spend your time lost, stuck in traffic or taking evasive action. International driving permits required.

Skiing in Pyeongchang County

6 Pyeongchang won the chance to host the Winter Olympics with its third bid. In 2018 the Games will be held at the Alpensia and Yongpyong ski resorts, as well as the Gangneung coastal area. Located near each other, Alpensia and Yongpyong have dozens of runs, including slopes for families and beginners, views of the East Sea (Sea of Japan) on clear days and some spanking-new accommodation and leisure facilities.

Jeonju Hanok Maeul

7 Jeonju's version of a traditional village is impressive even though many of the buildings are new. The slate-roof houses are home to traditional arts – artisan crafted fans, handmade paper and brewed *soju* (local vodka). Foodies will be pleased that the birthplace of *bibimbap* (rice, egg, meat and veggies with chilli sauce) offers the definitive version of this dish. You'll find plenty of traditional guesthouses, where visitors sleep on a *yo* (padded quilt) in an *ondol* (underfloor heating) room. There's even one run by the grandson of King Gojong.

Gwangjang Market

8 During the day this Seoul market is known for its secondhand clothes and fabrics, but it's at night that Gwangjang really comes into its own, when some of the market's alleys fill with vendors selling all manner of street eats. Stewed pigs' trotters and snouts, *gimbap* (rice, veggies and Spam wrapped in rice and rolled in sheets of seaweed) and *bindaettok* (plate-sized crispy pancakes of crushed mung beans and veggies fried on a skillet) are all washed down with copious amounts of *magkeolli* and *soju* (local liquors).

Bulguk-sa

9 It's hard to choose just one standout treasure in and around magnificent Gyeongju, but this Unesco World Heritage cultural site is most likely to take the honour, not least because it contains seven Korean 'national treasures' within its walls. The high point of the so-called golden age of Shilla architecture, this incredibly sophisticated yet wonderfully subtle temple complex, with its internal pagodas, external bridges and gorgeous, undulating scenery, is a monument to the skill of its carpenters, painters, craftspeople and architects.

Templestay at Guin-sa

10 A bell rings and you wake at 3.30am to prepare for a morning meditation session. Breakfast is an austere meal, taken in silence so you can contemplate the ache in your bones from bowing 108 times in front of a Buddha image. Later, you'll have more meditation time to contemplate the surrender of your body and mind in the search for inner peace. A templestay is the perfect antidote to fast-paced modern Korea, and while the country is awash with temples, the impressive fortress-like compound of Guin-sa is among the finest.

The DMZ

11 It's known as the Demilitarized Zone. But this 4km-wide, 250km-long heavily mined and guarded buffer, splitting North from South Korea, is anything but. An enduring Cold War symbol, the DMZ has become a surreal tourist draw, on both sides of the border. The tension is most palpable in the Joint Security Area, the neutral area built after the 1953 Armistice for the holding of peace talks, which can only be visited on an organised tour. Seven observation points along the South Korean side of the DMZ allow visitors to peer into the secretive North.

CHEN WS / SHUTTERSTOCK ©

Holidays

If you are travelling over any of Korea's major holidays, you should book all internal transport well ahead of time.

The Outdoors

Korea's countryside, coastline and islands are a year-round playground with hiking, cycling, diving, surfing, rafting, kayaking and more.

JGREGORYSF / GETTY IMAGES ©

Jia village, near Boma National Park

South Sudan

In July 2011 Africa's largest country, Sudan, split into two and with that South Sudan, the world's newest country, was born. However, until stability is established South Sudan is considered too dangerous for travellers.

The country's birthing process was a violent and bloody one. For decades the people of South Sudan have known little but war as they fought for independence from the north – and sadly it didn't take long for the infant nation to turn on itself, with a civil war erupting between the new government and various rebel groups.

South Sudan is one of the poorest and least-developed nations on the planet, but the very fact that it remains such an unknown is the thing that will likely attract the first visitors here when peace is finally established. Its wealth of tribal groups and national parks packed with vast numbers of large mammals will one day be major drawcards.

Snapshot

Boma National Park

1 This vast wilderness is home to huge quantities of wildlife including migrating herds of over a million antelope. Sadly, Boma is in a particularly volatile part of the country and it hasn't been safe to visit for the last few years. There is not yet any information on how the wildlife is faring during the violence.

Juba

2 The capital is a bustling town with busy markets and the grave of John Garang, the former leader of the South Sudan independence movement.

Tribal People

3 Possibly no other corner of Africa has such a wide diversity of tribal grous, many of whom continue to live a largely traditional lifestyle. There are numerous ethnic groups speaking around 60 languages. The main ethnic groups are the Dinka, who make up around 15% of the population, the Nuer, the Bari and the Azande. Traditional beliefs are widespread and even though Christianity has made inroads it's still very much a minority religion that's often overlaid with traditional beliefs and customs.

Seasons

 DEC & JAN

 FEB & NOV

 MAR–OCT

Food & Drink

Asida Porridge made from sorghum and served with a meaty sauce or vegetables.

White Bull A local beer.

Beans, corn, grains and peanuts Grown during the rainy season, primarily by women.

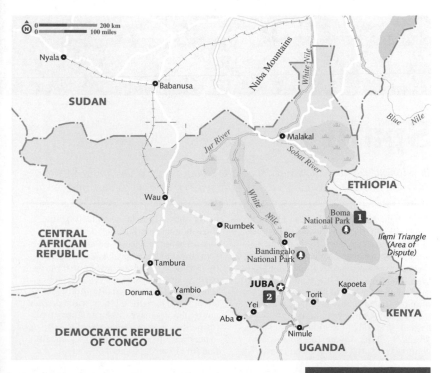

Flamenco performance, Seville

CAPITAL
Madrid

POPULATION
48.6 million

AREA
505,370 sq km

OFFICIAL LANGUAGE
Castilian, Spanish

Spain

Passionate, sophisticated and devoted to living the good life, Spain is both a stereotype come to life and a country more diverse than you ever imagined.

Spanish landscapes stir the soul, from the jagged Pyrenees and wildly beautiful cliffs of the Atlantic northwest to charming Mediterranean coves, while astonishing architecture spans the ages at seemingly every turn. And then there's one of Europe's most celebrated (and varied) gastronomic scenes of seafood, paella, tapas and fine wines.

Poignantly windswept Roman ruins, cathedrals of rare power and incomparable jewels of Islamic architecture speak of a country where the great civilisations of

history have risen, fallen and left behind their indelible mark. Yet for all the talk of Spain's history, this is a country that lives very much in the present and there's a reason 'fiesta' is one of the best-known words in the Spanish language. Perhaps you'll sense it along a crowded after-midnight street when it seems all the world has come out to play. Or maybe when a flamenco performer touches something deep in your soul. Whenever it happens, you'll find yourself nodding in recognition: *this* is Spain..

Top Experiences

Barcelona

1 Home to cutting-edge architecture, world-class dining and pulsating nightlife, Barcelona is one of Europe's most alluring destinations. Days are spent wandering the cobblestone lanes of the Gothic quarter, basking on Mediterranean beaches or marvelling at Gaudí masterpieces. By night, Barcelona is a whirl of vintage cocktail bars, gilded music halls, innovative eateries and dance-loving clubs, with the party extending well into the night. There are also colourful markets, hallowed arenas (such as Camp Nou where FC Barcelona plays) and a calendar packed with traditional Catalan festivals.

Madrid Nightlife

2 Madrid is not the only European city with nightlife, but few can match its intensity and street clamour, which rises to a deafening crescendo as the weekend nears. As Ernest Hemingway said, 'Nobody goes to bed in Madrid until they have killed the night'. There are wall-to-wall bars, small clubs, live venues, cocktail bars and mega-clubs beloved by A-list celebrities all across the city, with unimaginable variety to suit all tastes. But it's in the *barrios* (districts) of Huertas, Malasaña, Chueca and La Latina that you'll really understand what we're talking about.

The Alhambra

3 The palace complex of Granada's Alhambra is close to architectural perfection. It is perhaps the most refined example of Islamic art anywhere, not to mention the most enduring symbol of 800 years of Moorish rule in what was known as Al-Andalus. From afar, the Alhambra's red fortress towers dominate the Granada skyline, set against a backdrop of the Sierra Nevada's snowcapped peaks. Up close, the Alhambra's perfectly proportioned Generalife gardens complement the exquisite detail of the Palacio Nazaríes. Put simply, this is Spain's most beautiful monument.

Seville

4 Nowhere is as quintessentially Spanish as Seville, a city of capricious moods and soulful secrets, which has played a pivotal role in the evolution of flamenco, bull-fighting, baroque art and Mudéjar architecture. Blessed with year-round sunshine and fuelled culturally by a never-ending schedule of ebullient festivals, everything seems more amorous here, a feeling not lost on legions of 19th-century aesthetes, who used the city as a setting in their romantic works of fiction. Head south to the home of Carmen and Don Juan and take up the story.

RUBÉN TOQUERO / 500PX

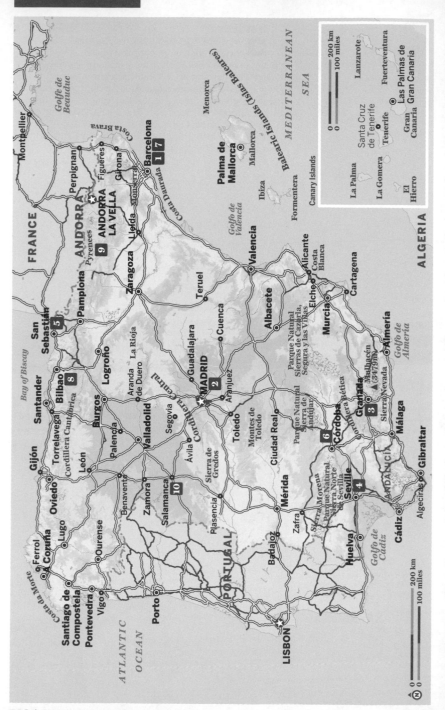

Flamenco Today

Rarely can flamenco have been as popular as it is today, and never so innovative.

Universally acclaimed is José Mercé, from Jerez. Estrella Morente from Granada (Enrique Morente's daughter and internationally best known for being the 'voice' behind the 2006 film *Volver)*, Miguel Poveda from Barcelona and La Tana from Seville are young singers steadily carving out niches in the first rank of performers.

Dance, always the readiest of flamenco arts to cross boundaries, has reached its most adventurous horizons in the person of Joaquín Cortés, born in Córdoba in 1969. Cortés fuses flamenco with contemporary dance, ballet and jazz in spectacular shows with music at rock-concert amplification.

Among guitarists, listen out for Manolo Sanlúcar from Cádiz and Tomatito from Almería, as well as Vicente Amigo from Córdoba and Moraíto Chico from Jerez, who both accompany today's top singers.

Pintxos in San Sebastián

5 Chefs here have turned bar snacks into an art form. Sometimes called 'high cuisine in miniature', *pintxos* (Basque tapas) are piles of flavour mounted on a slice of baguette. As you step into any bar in central San Sebastián, the choice lined up along the counter will leave you gasping. This is Spain's most memorable eating experience. Although the atmosphere is always casual, the serious business of experimenting with taste combinations (a Basque trademark) ensures that it just keeps getting better.

Córdoba's Mezquita

6 A church that became a mosque before reverting back to a church, Córdoba's Mezquita charts the evolution of Western and Islamic architecture over a 1000-year trajectory. Its most innovative features include some early horseshoe arches, an intricate mihrab, and a veritable 'forest' of 856 columns, many of them recycled from Roman ruins. The sheer scale of the Mezquita reflects Córdoba's erstwhile power as the most cultured city in 10th-century Europe. It was also inspiration for even greater buildings to come, most notably in Seville and Granada.

La Sagrada Família

7 The Modernista brainchild of Antoni Gaudí, La Sagrada Família remains a work in progress more than 90 years after its creator's death. Fanciful and profound, inspired by nature and barely restrained by a Gothic style, Barcelona's quirky temple soars skyward with an almost playful majesty. The improbable angles and departures from architectural convention will have you shaking your head in disbelief, but the detail of the decorative flourishes on the Passion Facade, Nativity Facade and

When to Go

HIGH SEASON
(Jun–Aug)
Expect warm, dry and sunny weather; more humid in coastal areas.

SHOULDER
(Mar–May, Sep & Oct)
Mild, clear weather and fewer crowds.

LOW SEASON
(Nov–Feb)
Cold in central Spain; rain in the north and northwest. High season in ski resorts.

La Liga

Spain's La Liga is one of the world's best football leagues, and almost any match is worth attending, if only to experience the Spanish crowd. Spanish football stadiums are extraordinarily one-sided places, with very few travelling fans, but the atmosphere can be electric.

Menú del Día

One great way to cap prices at lunchtime on weekdays is to order the *menú del día*, a full three-course set menu, water, bread and wine. Meal prices start at around €10.

Food & Drink

Cured meats Wafer-thin slices of chorizo, *lomo, salchichón* and *jamón serrano* appear on most Spanish tables.

Jamón ibérico Generally regarded as the elite of Spanish hams – comes from a black-coated pig indigenous to the Iberian Peninsula and a descendant of the wild boar.

Olive oil Spain is the world's largest producer of olive oil.

Paella Traditional Valencian paellas can have almost any ingredients, varying by region and season. The base always includes short-grain rice, garlic, olive oil and saffron.

Tapas These bite-sized morsels range from uncomplicated Spanish staples to pure gastronomic innovation. If you have trouble choosing, ask for '*la especialidad de la casa*' (the house speciality) and it's hard to go wrong.

Sherry The unique wine of Andalucía, sherry is Spain's national dram and is found in almost every bar, *tasca* (tapas bar) and restaurant in the land.

Wine Spain has the largest area of wine cultivation in the world. La Rioja and Ribera del Duero are the best-known wine-growing regions.

elsewhere are worth studying for hours.

Bilbao

8 It only took one building, a shimmering titanium fish called the Museo Guggenheim Bilbao, to turn Bilbao from a byword for industrial decay into a major European art centre. Canadian architect Frank Gehry's inspired use of flowing canopies, towers and flying fins is irresistible. But while it's this most iconic of modern buildings that draws the visitors, it's the hard-working soul of the *Botxo* (Hole), as it's fondly known to its inhabitants, that ends up captivating. And let's face it, there's plenty to be entranced by: riverside promenades, clanky funicular railways, superb *pintxos* bars, an iconic football team, a clutch of quality museums and, yeah OK, a shimmering titanium fish.

Hiking in the Pyrenees

9 Spain is a walker's destination of exceptional variety, but we reckon the Pyrenees in Navarra, Aragón and Catalonia offer the most special hiking country. Aragón's Parque Nacional de Ordesa y

Monte Perdido is one of the high points (pun intended) of the Pyrenees, while its glories are mirrored across the provincial frontier of Parque Nacional d'Aigüestortes i Estany de Sant Maurici in Catalonia. It's tough but rewarding terrain, a world of great rock walls and glacial cirques, accompanied by elusive but soulful Pyrenean wildlife.

Renaissance Salamanca

10 Luminous when floodlit, the elegant central square of Salamanca, the Plaza Mayor, is possibly the most attractive in all of Spain. It is just one of many highlights in a city whose architectural splendour has few peers in the country. Salamanca is home to one of Europe's oldest and most prestigious universities, so student revelry also lights up the nights. It's this combination of grandeur and energy that makes so many people call Salamanca their favourite city in Spain.

Staying in a Beautiful Parador

11 Sleeping like a king has never been easier than in Spain's state-run chain of *paradores* – often palatial, always supremely comfortable former castles, palaces and monasteries. Ranking among Europe's most atmospheric sleeping experiences, many are sited on prime real estate (eg inside the grounds of Granada's Alhambra) and prices are more reasonable than you might think.

Getting Around

 Spain has an extensive network of internal flights, operated by both Spanish airlines and a handful of low-cost international airlines.

 Buses are the workhorses of the Spanish roads, from slick express services to stop-everywhere village-to-village buses.

 A vast network of motorways radiates out from Madrid to all corners of the country, shadowed by smaller but often more picturesque minor roads.

 Spain's rail network is extremely efficient, from slow intercity regional trains to some of the fastest trains on the planet. More routes are added to the network every year.

Nine Arch Bridge, Demodara

Sri Lanka

Endless beaches, timeless ruins, welcoming people, oodles of elephants, rolling surf, cheap prices, fun trains, famous tea and flavourful food describe Sri Lanka.

You might say Sri Lanka has been hiding in plain sight. Years of war and challenges such as tsunamis kept Sri Lanka off many itineraries until recent years, but lying between the more trodden parts of India and Southeast Asia, Sri Lanka is undeniably alluring.

Few places have as many Unesco World Heritage Sites packed into such a small area. Distances are short: see the sacred home of the world's oldest living tree in the morning (Anuradhapura) and stand awestruck by

the sight of hundreds of elephants gathering in the afternoon (Minneriya). Discover a favourite beach, meditate in a 2000-year-old temple, exchange smiles while strolling a mellow village, marvel at birds and wildflowers, and try to keep count of the little dishes that come with your rice and curry.

Sri Lanka is spectacular, it's affordable and it's still often uncrowded. Now is the best time to discover it.

Top Experiences

Travelling by Train to Ella

1 Sometimes there's no way to get a seat on the slow but oh-so-popular train to Ella, but with a prime standing-room-only spot looking out at a rolling carpet of tea, who cares? Outside, the colourful silk saris of Tamil tea pickers stand out in the sea of green; inside, you may get a shy welcome via a smile. At stations, vendors hustle treats, including some amazing corn and chilli fritters sold wrapped in somebody's old homework paper. Munching one of these while the scenery creaks past? Sublime.

Uda Walawe National Park

2 This huge chunk of savannah grassland centred on the Uda Walawe reservoir is the closest Sri Lanka gets to East Africa. There are herds of buffalo (although some of these are domesticated!), sambar deer, crocodiles, masses of birds, and elephants – and we don't just mean a few elephants. We mean hundreds of the big-nosed creatures. In fact, we'd go so far to say that for elephants, Uda Walawe is equal to, or even better than, many of the famous East African national parks.

Ancient Anuradhapura

3 At Anuradhapura, big bits of Sri Lanka's cultural and religious heritage sprawl across 3 sq km. In the centre is one of the world's oldest trees, the Sri Maha Bodhi. That it has been tended uninterrupted by record-keeping guardians for more than two thousand years is enough for shivers down the spine. The surrounding fields of crumbling monasteries and enormous *dagobas* (stupas) attest to the city's role as the seat of power in Sri Lanka for a thousand years. Biking through this heady past is a thrilling experience.

Soaring Sigiriya Rock

4 If it was just the rolling gardens at the base of Sigiriya, they would still be a highlight. Ponds and little man-made rivulets put the water in these water gardens and offer a serene idyll amid the sweltering countryside. But look up and catch your jaw as you ponder this 370m rock that erupts out of the landscape. Etched with art and surmounted by ruins, Sigiriya is an awesome mystery, one that the wonderful museum tries to dissect. The climb to the top is a wearying and worthy endeavour.

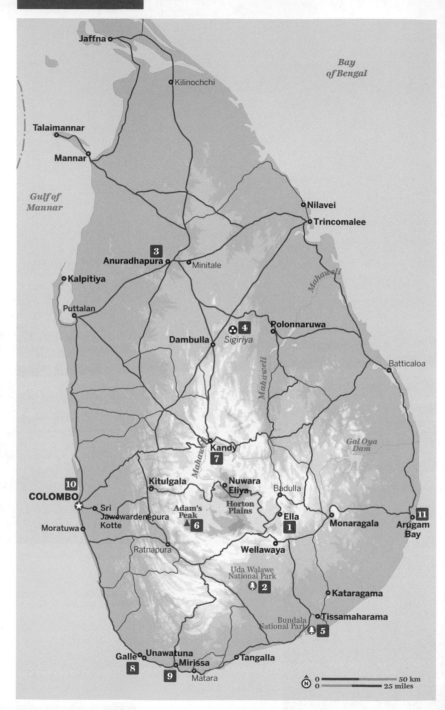

Jaffna

Kilinochchi

Bay
of Bengal

Talaimannar

Mannar

Gulf of
Mannar

3
Anuradhapura

Minitale

Nilavei

Trincomalee

Kalpitiya

Puttalan

Mahaweli

Dambulla

Sigiriya **4**

Polonnaruwa

Batticaloa

Mahaweli

Gal Oya
Dam

Kandy
7

Kitulgala

10
COLOMBO

Nuwara
Eliya

Badulla

Horton
Plains

Ella
1

Monaragala

11
Arugam
Bay

Sri
Jawewardenepura
Kotte

Moratuwa

Adam's
Peak
▲ **6**

Ratnapura

Wellawaya

Uda Walawe
National Park
2

Kataragama

Tissamaharama

Bundala
National Park **5**

Galle
8

Unawatuna

Mirissa
9

Matara

Tangalla

N 0   50 km
   0   25 miles

Best in Print

On Sal Mal Lane (Ru Freeman; 2013) Ruman weaves together the many strands of Sri Lankan society in a beautiful novel set down a Colombo lane.

Running in the Family (Michael Ondaatje; 1982) A comic and reflective memoir of a Colombo family in the 1940s.

Monkfish Moon (Romesh Gunesekera; 1992) Short stories by this Booker Prize–nominated author provide a diverse glimpse of Sri Lanka's ethnic conflict.

Wave (Sonali Deraniyagala; 2013) This searing memoir opens on the morning of 26 December 2004, right before the tsunami kills Deraniyagala's husband, children and parents.

Ayurveda in Paradise

For over 2500 years the inhabitants of the subcontinent have enjoyed the restorative effects of Ayurveda treatments. More than just a way of treating illnesses using natural medicines, Ayurveda is based on the idea of balance in bodily systems and uses herbal treatment, diet and yogic breathing to achieve this.

Today, Ayurveda treatments are a big attraction in Sri Lanka and there are seemingly hundreds of Ayurveda 'hospitals'. Many have qualified Ayurveda doctors, but some are decidedly more dodgy – this is especially true in popular backpacker towns. You should always ask advice from locals about the authenticity of Ayurvedic hospitals in such places as well as asking to see the doctors' qualifications.

The west coast is a particular hot spot for such treatments, and almost all the larger hotels, as well as some cheaper places, have a treatment centre.

Bundala National Park

5 With all the crowds heading to nearby Yala National Park, the Ramsar-recognised Bundala National Park often gets overlooked. But with the park's huge sheets of shimmering waters singing to the sound of birdsong, skipping it is a big mistake. Bundala has a beauty that other parks can only dream of and is one of the finest birding destinations in the country. Oh, and in case herons and egrets aren't glam enough for you, the crocodiles and resident elephant herd will put a smile on your face.

Adam's Peak

6 For over a thousand years, pilgrims have trudged by candlelight up Adam's Peak (Sri Pada) to stand in the footprints of the Buddha, breathe the air where Adam first set foot on earth and see the place where the butterflies go to die. Today tourists join the throngs of local pilgrims and, as you stand in the predawn light atop this perfect pinnacle of rock and watch the sun crawl above

When to Go

HIGH SEASON
(Dec–Mar)
The Hill Country, west- and south-coast beaches are busiest and driest. Wet in the east and north.

SHOULDER
(Apr & Sep–Nov)
April and September offer the best odds for good weather countrywide.

LOW SEASON
(May–Aug)
Monsoon season on the south and west coasts and the Hill Country.

waves of mountains, the sense of magic remains as bewitching as it must have been for Adam himself.

Kandy

7 Kandy is the cultural capital of the island and home to the Temple of the Sacred Tooth Relic,

Kandy Esala Perahera

Sri Lanka's most spectacular and prominent festival is the climax of 10 days and nights of celebrations during the month of Esala. Celebrations feature dancers and other performers.

Beaches

There are long, golden-specked ones, ones with soft white sand, wind- and wave-battered ones, and ones without a footstep for miles. Whichever you choose, the beaches of Sri Lanka really are every bit as gorgeous as you've heard.

Food & Drink

Sambol Condiment made from ingredients pounded with chilli.

Hoppers Bowl-shaped pancakes (also called *appa* or *appam*) made from rice flour, coconut milk and palm toddy. If eggs are added it becomes an egg hopper. *Sambol* is often added for flavouring.

Rice and curry The national dish is a selection of spiced dishes made from vegetables, meat or fish.

Mallung Slightly like a tabbouleh, this salad combines chopped local greens (like kale), shredded coconut and onion.

Pittu Steamed in bamboo, these cylindrical cakes are made from flour and coconut.

Pani pol A small pancake made with a sweet topping of cinnamon and cardamom-infused *jaggery* (a type of sugar).

Lime juice Served with soda water, and salt or sugar.

Toddy An alcoholic drink made from the sap of palm trees, with a sharp taste, a bit like cider.

Tea Sri Lanka is the world's fourth-largest tea-producing nation. Locals drink it with spoonfuls of sugar and hot milk.

said to contain a tooth of the Buddha himself. For the Sinhalese, this is the holiest spot on the island, but for tourists Kandy offers more than just religious satisfaction: there's a pleasing old quarter, a pretty central lake, a clutch of museums and, in the surrounding vicinity, some beautiful botanical gardens. In case you need further blessings from the gods, there's also a series of fascinating ancient temples.

Galle Fort

8 Humans and nature have joined forces in Galle Fort to produce an architectural work of art. The Dutch built the streets and buildings, the Sri Lankans added the colour and style, and then nature got busy covering it in a gentle layer of tropical vegetation, humidity and salty air. The result is an enchanting old town that is home to dozens of art galleries, quirky shops, and boutique cafes and guesthouses plus some splendid hotels. For tourists, it's without doubt the number one urban attraction in the country.

Whale-Watching at Mirissa

9 People once visited the beaches of southern Sri Lanka to laze under palm trees and maybe go and peer at a few little fish on a diving excursion. Then somebody realised that the deep blue was home to more than just schools of workaday fish. It turns out that the waters off Sri Lanka are home to the planet's biggest creature, the blue whale (not to mention the somewhat smaller sperm whale). Now, every morning in season, boats leave Mirissa in search of creatures like no other.

Colonial Legacy in Colombo

10 Yes, the Brits were chased out at independence in 1948, but their legacy lives on. Colombo has wide, tree-shaded streets where you'll see the structures of the empire at its most magnificent. The National Museum building is redolent with empire. Look around a little and you'll find the colonial legacies of the Dutch and Portuguese as well. Just head to restored quarters of Fort and wander, pausing at the hugely popular Old Dutch Hospital.

Surfing at Arugam Bay

11 The heart of Sri Lanka's growing surf scene, the long right break at the southern end of Arugam Bay is considered Sri Lanka's best. From April to September you'll find surfers riding the waves; stragglers catch the random good days as late as November. Throughout the year you can revel in the surfer vibe: there are board-rental and ding-repair joints plus plenty of laid-back cheap hangouts offering a bed on the beach. And if you need solitude, there are fine breaks at nearby Lighthouse Point, Whiskey Point and Okanda.

Getting Around

 Sri Lanka's buses are the country's main mode of transport. They cover most towns, are cheap and are often crowded. Only a few routes have air-con buses. Private buses can offer a bit more comfort than government buses.

 Many travellers use a hired car with a driver for all or part of their trip. This allows maximum flexibility and is the most efficient way to get around. Many drivers are delightful characters and founts of local knowledge.

 The improving railway network serves major towns and can be more comfortable than buses (excepting third-class carriages). Some routes such as Haputale to Ella and Colombo to Galle are renowned for their scenery.

CAPITAL
Basseterre

POPULATION
52,330

AREA
261 sq km (St Kitts
168 sq km; Nevis 93
sq km)

OFFICIAL LANGUAGE
English

Beach on Nevis

St Kitts & Nevis

Near-perfect packages – that's how you might think of St Kitts and Nevis. The two-island nation combines beaches with beauteous mountains, activities to engage your body and rich history to engage your mind.

The local culture here is mellow, friendly and infused with a pulsing soca beat. But if St Kitts and Nevis offer much that's similar, they differ in the details. St Kitts is larger and feels that way, from bustling Basseterre and mighty Brimstone Hill Fortress to the party strip and resorts of Frigate Bay. New roads and tourist development have generated additional verve and excitement.

Across the Narrows, tranquil Nevis is a neater package, anchored by a single volcanic mountain buttressed by a handful of beaches and a tiny colonial capital, Charlestown. Nature walks take you into the verdant upper reaches of the peak. History here centers on the big names of British admiral Horatio Nelson and US founding father Alexander Hamilton.

Top Experiences

Brimstone Hill Fortress

1 St Kitts' historical highlight was made a Unesco World Heritage Site in 1999 for being an exceptionally well-preserved example of 17th- and 18th-century military architecture. Far larger than you'd think, this vast old military stronghold was built by the British with slave labor and offers insight into the violent and tumultuous past of the former Caribbean colonies. After a fire swept through Basseterre in 1867, some of the fort structures were partially dismantled and the stones used to rebuild the capital. In the 1960s major restoration was undertaken, and much of the fortress has been returned to its earlier grandeur. Queen Elizabeth II inaugurated it as a national park during her visit to St Kitts in October 1985.

Charlestown

2 The ferry from St Kitts docks right in charismatic Charlestown, Nevis' toy-town-sized capital whose narrow streets are steeped in colonial history and lined with both brightly painted gingerbread Victorians and Georgian stone buildings. It's well worth strolling up and down the main street with its banks, businesses, tourist office, bars and restaurants. At night the town all but shuts down. The closest beach, lovely Pinney's, is about 1.5 miles north of Charlestown.

Pinney's Beach

3 This 3-mile-long stretch of sand along the west coast of Nevis has decent snorkelling offshore. The northern end is punctuated by the Four Seasons

When to Go

 HIGH SEASON (Dec–Apr)

 SHOULDER (May & Jun)

 LOW SEASON (Jul–Nov)

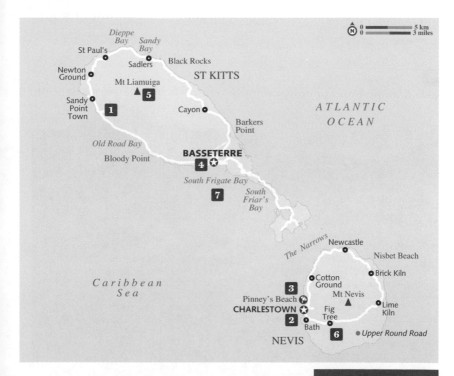

and several beach bars, but quiet patches abound. Sundays are busiest.

Basseterre

4 St Kitts' bustling capital, Basseterre (pronounced 'bass-tear'), has a compact downtown next to the Port Zante cruise-ship terminal, which teems with duty-free shops, souvenir stalls and outdoor bars. If that and cold beer don't do it for you, bone up on island history at the National Museum, then plunge into the charmingly ramshackle maze of narrow streets radiating out from the Circus, a roundabout anchored by a Victorian-style clock tower. On your wanderings, keep an eye out for the occasional architectural gem (Princes St is especially rewarding), then wrap up by joining locals 'liming' (relaxing) on grassy Independence Sq.

Mt Liamuiga

5 Getting to the crater rim of Mt Liamuiga, at 3792ft the country's highest volcanic peak, involves a lung-busting, thigh-burning 2.5-mile trek. The deep crater with its active fumaroles and seasonal lake would make a great Star Wars movie set. The entire trip takes about 4½ to five hours and is tough, tough, tough. Since the trail is not well marked and partly overgrown, it's easy to get disoriented, which is why a guide is recommended.

Botanical Gardens of Nevis

6 It's easy to spend a couple of hours wandering around this enchanting symphony of orchids, palms, water lily ponds, bamboo groves and other global flora interspersed with sculpture,

Getting Around

St Kitts and Nevis are linked by passenger ferry between Basseterre and Charlestown, and by car ferry between Major's Bay and Cades Bay.

Government-licensed private minivans serve communities on an erratic schedule along the main roads.

A local driving permit, available from car-rental agencies, is required for driving in St Kitts & Nevis.

JASON PATRICK ROSS / SHUTTERSTOCK ©

pools, ponds and fountains. In the Rainforest Conservatory parrots patrol the huge tropical plants, waterfalls and Mayan-style sculpture.

Frigate Bay

GARY SHEAFFER - 500PX ©

7 Frigate Bay, some 3 miles southeast of Basseterre, is an isthmus dividing the calm Caribbean side and the surf-lashed Atlantic side, which is dominated by the hulking Marriott. The road leading to the resort – Zenway Blvd – is a restaurant row, but the area's key draw is 'the Strip,' a row of funky beach bars along Frigate Bay South. Swimming is good on both sides, although the Caribbean waters are calmer, of course.

Food & Drink

Stewed saltfish Official national dish; served with spicy plantains, coconut dumplings and seasoned breadfruit.

Pelau Also known as 'cook-up,' this dish is the Kittitian version of paella: a tasty but messy blend of rice, meat, saltfish, vegetables and pigeon peas.

Conch Served curried, marinated or soused (boiled).

Cane Spirit Rothschild More commonly known as CSR, this locally distilled libation is made from pure fermented cane juice and best enjoyed on the rocks mixed with grapefruit-flavored Ting soda.

Brinley Gold Rum Locally blended rum comes in such flavors as vanilla, coffee, mango, coconut and lime. The shop in Port Zante does tastings.

Carib Locally brewed lager.

Two-Island Environment

Both St Kitts and Nevis have grassy coastal areas, a consequence of deforestation for sugar production. Forests tend to be vestiges of the large rainforests that once covered much of the islands, or they are second-growth.

Away from developed areas, the climate allows a huge array of beautiful plants to thrive, especially on Nevis. Flowers such as plumeria, hibiscus and chains-of-love are common along roadsides and in garden landscaping.

Nevis is fairly circular and the entire island benefits from runoff from Mt Nevis. St Kitts' shape resembles a tadpole. The main body is irrigated by water from the mountain ranges. However, this is of little value to the geographically isolated, arid southeast peninsula, which is covered with sparse, desert-like cacti and yucca.

Aside from the vervet monkey, another ubiquitous creature is the mongoose, imported from Jamaica by plantation owners to rid their sugarcane fields of snakes. Both islands provide plenty of avian life for birdwatchers.

Reefs around the two islands face the same threats as elsewhere in the region. On St Kitts, some of the best reefs ring the southeast peninsula.

CAPITAL
Castries

POPULATION
165,595

AREA
616 sq km

OFFICIAL LANGUAGES
English, French Creole

The Pitons

St Lucia

The color wheel is simple on St Lucia: rich green for the tropical land, pure white for the ring of beaches and brilliant blue for the surrounding sea.

Rising like an emerald tooth from the Caribbean Sea, St Lucia definitely grabs your attention. While it fits the image of a glam honeymoon spot, this mountainous island has more to offer than sensuous beaches flanked by sybaritic lodgings.

Blessed by nature, St Lucia has geographic and cultural riches enough to embarrass far bigger nations. Notwithstanding this, it remains a down-to-earth place that wears its breathtaking beauty with nonchalance.

Noted for its oodles of small and luxurious resorts that drip color and flair, it is really two islands in one. Rodney Bay in the north offers lazy days and modern comforts amid a beautiful bay. In the south, Soufrière is at the heart of a gorgeous region of old plantations, hidden beaches and the geologic wonder of the impossibly photogenic Pitons.

JUSTIN FOULKES / LONELY PLANET ©

Top Experiences

Gros Piton

1 If you have time for only one trek during your stay, choose the Gros Piton (2617ft) climb. Starting from the hamlet of Fond Gens Libres, you walk mostly through a thick jungle. Approximately halfway the path goes past a lookout that affords fantastic vistas of Petit Piton and the ocean. The final section is very steep, but the reward is a tremendous view of southern St Lucia and the

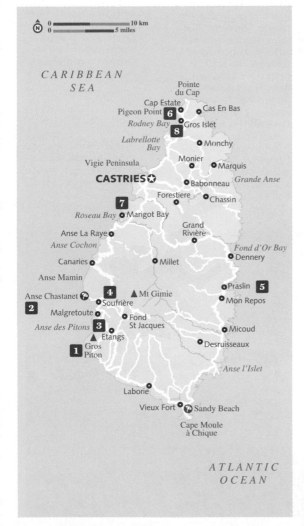

0   10 km
0   5 miles

CARIBBEAN
SEA

Pointe
du Cap

Cap Estate
Pigeon Point **6**   Cas En Bas
Rodney Bay   Gros Islet
8
Labrellotte
Bay   Monchy

Vigie Peninsula   Monier
Marquis
CASTRIES
Babonneau   Grande Anse
Forestiere   Chassin
7
Roseau Bay   Marigot Bay

Grand
Anse La Raye   Rivière
Anse Cochon   Fond d'Or Bay
Canaries   Millet   Dennery
Anse Mamin
Praslin **5**
Anse Chastanet   **4**   Mt Gimie   Mon Repos
2   Soufrière
Malgretoute   Fond
Anse des Pitons **3**   St Jacques   Micoud
Etangs   Desruisseaux
1 Gros
Piton
Anse l'Islet

Laborie
Vieux Fort   Sandy Beach
Cape Moule
à Chique

ATLANTIC
OCEAN

When to Go

 HIGH SEASON (Dec–Mar)

 SHOULDER (Apr–Jun, Nov)

 LOW SEASON (Jul–Oct)

densely forested mountains of the interior.

Anse Chastanet

2 Stretched out in front of the resort of the same name, Anse Chastanet is a fine curving beach. The sheltered bay is protected by high cliffs. The snorkelling just offshore is some of the best on the island; hassle-free access is through the resort, which also offers day passes if you want to use the sun loungers and water-sports facilities.

Sugar Beach

3 The most famous beach on the island, gorgeous Sugar Beach is spectacularly situated between the two Pitons, ensuring phenomenal views both from the sand and in the water. Like most in the area, it was originally a grey-sand beach – the soft white sands are imported from abroad. There are free basic public loungers at the far northern end; alternatively when occupancy is low you can rent one of the resort's more luxurious models.

Soufrière

4 If one town were to be the heart and soul of St Lucia, it would have to be Soufrière. Its attractions include a slew of colonial-era edifices scattered amid brightly painted wooden storefronts and a bustling seafront. The surrounding landscape is little short of breathtaking: the skyscraping towers of rock known as the Pitons stand guard over the town. Jutting from the sea, covered in vegetation and ending in a summit that looks otherworldly, these are St Lucia's iconic landmarks. The area boasts beauty above and below the water as well as historic and natural sights aplenty.

Eastern St Lucia

5 A 30-minute drive from Castries transports you to yet another world, along the Atlantic-battered east coast, where you can experience a St Lucia that's very Creole, laid-back and little visited. While this coast lacks the beaches of the west, it makes up for it with lovely bays backed by spectacular cliffs, a rocky shoreline pounded by thundering surf, and a handful of picturesque fishing towns, including Dennery and Micoud.

Pigeon Island

6 Pigeon Island has a fascinating range of historic sites scattered across the bucolic former 'island.' It is a fun place to explore, with paths winding around the remains of barracks, batteries and garrisons; the partially intact stone buildings create a ghost-town effect. The grounds are well endowed with lofty trees, manicured lawns and fine coastal views. Near the gate is the officers kitchen, dating from 1824, behind which is the officers quarters, which were partially rebuilt in 1993. Across the

Getting Around

Water taxis can be hired to travel to virtually anywhere on the west side of the island.

Buses are frequent between main towns and generally run until around 7pm, except on the busy Castries–Gros Islet corridor where they run until after 10pm.

You can rent a car when you arrive in St Lucia. Nearly all car-rental agencies offer unlimited mileage.

6

grassy area are the ruins of the barracks, originally constructed in 1808, the largest buildings on the site. At the top of Fort Rodney Hill, you'll find the small but well-preserved fortress, a few rusting cannons and cardiac-arresting views.

Marigot Bay

7 Deep, sheltered Marigot Bay is an exquisite example of natural architecture. Sheltered by towering palms and the surrounding hills, the narrow inlet is said to have once hidden the entire British fleet from French pursuers. Yachts play the same trick these days – the bay is a popular place to drop anchor and hide away for a few nights while enjoying nearby beaches.

Rodney Bay & Gros Islet

8 About 10km north of Castries, the vast horseshoe of Rodney Bay boasts the island's most diverse tourist facilities. Within the bay is a large, artificial lagoon and marina, flanked by Rodney Bay Village, a somewhat bland assemblage of bars, restaurants, shops and more. Far more interesting is the fishing village of Gros Islet to the north. Here the historic streets are lined with rum shops and fishing shacks draped with drying nets.

GAVIN HELLIER / ROBERTHARDING / GETTY IMAGES ©

Food & Drink

Seafood Dorado (also known as mahimahi), kingfish, marlin, snapper, lobster, crab and shellfish feature high on the menu.

Meat dishes Chicken and pork dishes are commonly found.

Local specialties Try callaloo soup, *lambi* (conch) and salt fish with green fig (seasoned salt cod and boiled green banana).

Piton The beer of St Lucia; crisp and sweet, it's perfectly light and refreshing.

St Lucian rum The island's sole distillery produces white rums, gold rums and flavored rums.

Wildlife in San Lucia

St Lucia's vegetation ranges from dry and scrubby areas of cacti and hibiscus to lush, jungly valleys with wild orchids, bromeliads, heliconias and lianas.

Under the British colonial administration much of St Lucia's rainforest was targeted for timber harvesting. In many ways the independent St Lucian government has proved a far more effective environmental force, and while only about 10% of the island remains covered in rainforest, most of that has now been set aside as nature reserve. The largest indigenous trees in the rainforest are the gommier, a towering gum tree, and the chatagnier, a huge buttress-trunked tree.

Fauna includes endemic birds, bats, lizards, iguanas, tree frogs, introduced mongooses, rabbitlike agoutis and several snake species, including the fer-de-lance and the boa constrictor.

CAPITAL
Kingstown

POPULATION
109,991

AREA
388 sq km

OFFICIAL LANGUAGE
English

Tobago Cays

St Vincent & the Grenadines

While it's famed for its islands and beaches, this country offers more than just a relax in a hammock. There are volcanoes to climb, refreshing waterfalls to explore and great hiking throughout.

Just the name St Vincent & the Grenadines (SVG) evokes visions of exotic, idyllic island life. Imagine an island chain in the heart of the Caribbean Sea, uncluttered by tourist exploitation, with white-sand beaches on deserted islands, sky-blue water gently lapping the shores and barely a soul around.

While it may sound like a playground for the rich and famous, you don't need your own yacht to enjoy SVG. In fact, cheap ferries make independent exploration of this archipelago nation a breeze and, with so many islands to choose from, there's sure to be one that perfectly meets your needs.

Top Experiences

Tobago Cays

1 With five small islands ringed with coral reefs, the fabled Tobago Cays offer some of the Caribbean's best diving and snorkelling. The islands sit firmly in a national park and are only accessible by boat on a day trip from one of the Grenadines. And what a day trip it can be! The snorkelling is world class and the white-sand beaches look like strips of blinding snow. Underwater, sea turtles and parrot fish are just the start of myriad species you'll see. The coral is gorgeous.

When to Go

HIGH SEASON
(Dec–May)

SHOULDER
(Sep–Nov)

LOW SEASON
(Jun–Aug)

Bequia

2 Bequia (pronounced 'beck-way') is the most perfect island in the whole Grenadines. Stunning beaches dotting the shoreline, accommodations to fit most budgets and a slow pace of life all help to create an environment that is unforgettable. There are fine restaurants, shops that retain their local integrity and enough golden sand and blue water to keep everybody blissful.

Mayreau

3 Blessed with breathtaking beauty yet very little development, the compact palm-covered island of Mayreau is the authentic Grenadines dream. With only a handful of vehicles, no airport and just a smattering of residents, it often feels like the fabled desert isle. Mayreau is a fantastic destination for independent travellers wanting to enjoy some of the Grenadines' best beaches and get a good dose of culture at the same time. There are no resorts and while yachts and bigger ships do dock here, once the sun goes down you'll have the place to yourself.

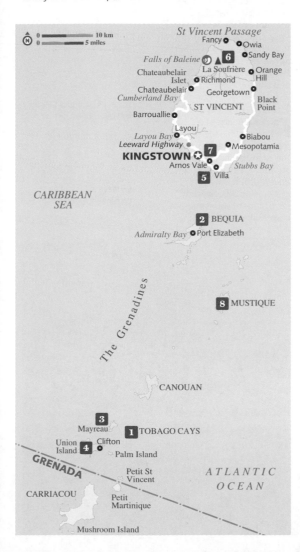

Union Island

4 Union Island feels like an outpost at the bottom of a country – and that's just what it is. Before the introduction of fast boats, its remote location enabled it to become a base for contraband (which historically propped up the economy here) from all over the Caribbean. The small port town of Clifton has an unpretentious charm and a more local feel than some of the towns on the more-visited Grenadine islands. You can easily spend a day wandering its short main street and the surrounding hills. It's an important anchorage for yachts and a transport hub – there are boats to Carriacou in Grenada. It also has decent accommodations, services and just enough nightlife.

Fort Duvernette

5 Perched atop a large volcanic rock offshore from Villa, this eerie fort was constructed to defend the town of Calliaqua and affords fantastic 360-degree views of the southern shoreline. There are 225 steps in the spiral staircase that has been carved into the rock; take care as it can be slippery, with small stones often covering the walkway – bring footwear. At the top, 200ft above sea level, you'll find two batteries of cannons and a picnic area.

La Soufrière

6 St Vincent's La Soufrière volcano dominates the northern part of the island and a hike to its summit is a highlight for adventurous travellers. The crater is an otherworldly environment with shag-carpet-like moss growing

Getting Around

There are airports on all of the main islands except Mayreau.

Buses are a good way to get around St Vincent.

The main islands of SVG are well linked by boats.

Taxis are abundant on St Vincent and Bequia.

4

on the ground and mounds of black rocks all around. There are also some active sulfur outlets. There are two routes to the top. The easiest route, and the one that is officially promoted to visitors, begins from the windward side of the island, where a proper trail leads up from the car park to the summit. It's a moderate 2½-hour hike.

Kingstown

7 Narrow streets, arched stone doorways and covered walkways conjure up a Caribbean of banana boats and colonial rule. Kingstown heaves and swells with a pulsing local community that bustles through its throroughfares and alleyways. Steep hills surround the town, amplify-

---

Food & Drink

Fresh produce St Vincent produces top-quality and delicious fruit and vegetables.

Seafood Lobster, shrimp, conch and fish are all popular and readily available.

Callaloo A spinach-like vegetable used in soups and stews. Many vitamins!

Savory pumpkin soup More squash-like than the American Thanksgiving staple; often like a rich stew.

Saltfish Dried fish that has been cured; delicious when made into fish cakes.

Rotis Curried vegetables, potatoes and meat wrapped in a flour tortilla are a national passion.

Hairoun (pronounced 'high-rone') The light and tasty local lager.

---

ing the sounds of car horns, street vendors and the music filtering through the crowd. The nearby towns of Villa and Indian Bay are where you will find the majority of the island's resorts.

Mustique

8 What can you say about Mustique other than 'Wow!'? First, take an

island that offers stunning beaches and everything else you expect to find in paradise, then add to the mix accommodation that defies description or affordability. With prices that exclude all but the super-rich, film stars and burnt-out musicians, this island is the exclusive playground of the uber-affluent.

SALIM OCTOBER / SHUTTERSTOCK ©

Caribbean Rhythms

Music is the cultural lifeblood of St Vincent. The infectious Caribbean rhythms permeate the air and are inescapable. Musical preference is divided along generational lines. Aging Rastas groove to the mellow jams of the old-school reggae icons. The younger generations are enchanted by the frenetic beats of modern dancehall and imported hip-hop. Everywhere, though, you'll hear the latest Caribbean rhythms of soca, steel pan and whatever latest variation of calypso has caught fire.

Original to SVG is big drum, a music style based on the namesake instrument (usually made from an old rum keg) and having a calypso beat mixed with satirical lyrics performed by a 'chantwell,' a lead female singer. Wild costumes are part of the show.

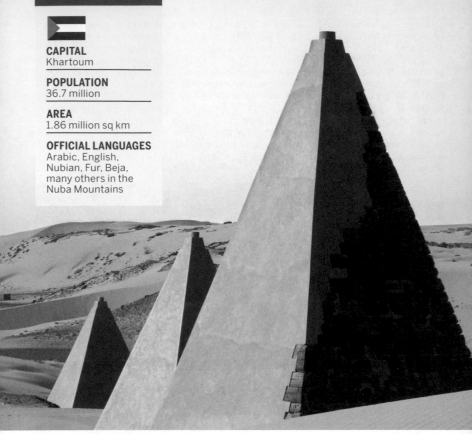

CAPITAL
Khartoum

POPULATION
36.7 million

AREA
1.86 million sq km

OFFICIAL LANGUAGES
Arabic, English,
Nubian, Fur, Beja,
many others in the
Nuba Mountains

Meroe Pyramids

Sudan

There is no country on earth that travellers are as apprehensive to visit as they are pained to leave. The Sudanese are as diverse as they are mysterious, as generous as they are welcoming.

Wake at the break of day under the golden pyramids of godlike kings of old, traverse a searing desert to the place where two Niles become one, and watch a million blood-red fish swarm through gardens of coral. Whichever way you look at it, there's just no denying that among Sudan's sweeping hills of sand lie treasures the rest of the world is only just beginning to discover.

For the few travellers who venture here, Sudan comes as a fantastic surprise.

Visitors invariably agree that the Sudanese are among the friendliest and most hospitable people on earth. And although various ongoing conflicts mean part of this vast nation remains off limits, the northeast is one of the safest places in the world. Whether you rush through on a Cairo–to–Cape Town trip, or spend a slow month soaking up the history and hospitality, visiting Sudan is a memorable experience.

Top Experiences

Meroe Pyramids

1 The one sight that is seen by almost all of Sudan's few visitors are the deeply romantic pyramids of Begrawiya (Meroe). Although they were declared a Unesco World Heritage Site in 2011, these splendid ancient structures have remained so far a hidden treasure. No mass tourism here – you'll probably feel like an explorer wandering among untouched, mysterious ruins.

Kassala

2 Kassala, with its wonderful setting at the foot of the granite peaks of the Taka Mountains, is eas-ily the most exotic corner of northeastern Sudan and a fitting reward for the long journey here. Its huge souq is where half the tribes of northern Sudan seem to meet – expect an ethnic mosaic of colours, smells, noises and experiences. It's also a popular destination for honeymooners.

Khartoum

3 Built where the Blue and White Niles meet, Khartoum defies expectations. It's a boisterous, modern city. As well as an excellent museum, fascinating souqs and fantastic Nile-side views, Khartoum's good facilities, hospitable people

When to Go

 HIGH SEASON (Nov–Feb)

 SHOULDER (Mar–Jun & Oct)

 LOW SEASON (Jul–Sep)

and laid-back vibe mean that most people find it an agree-able destination in itself.

Food & Drink

Fuul Stewed broad beans.

Ta'amiya Meat balls.

Shai saada Black, sometimes spiced, tea (*bi-laban* with milk, *bi-nana* with mint).

Qahwa jebbana Spiced coffee.

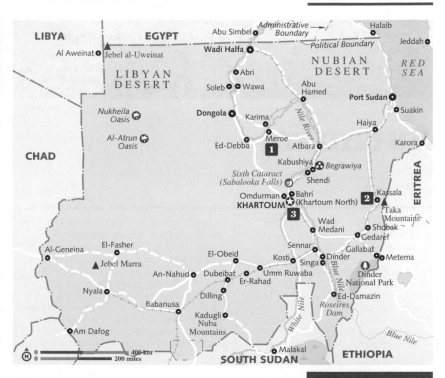

CAPITAL
Paramaribo

POPULATION
585,800

AREA
163,820 sq km

OFFICIAL LANGUAGE
Dutch

Suriname River

Suriname

Suriname is a warm, dense convergence of rivers that thumps with the lively rhythm of ethnic diversity.

From Paramaribo, the country's effervescent Dutch-colonial capital, to the fathomless jungles of the interior, you'll get a genuine welcome to this tiny country – whether from the descendants of escaped African slaves, Dutch and British colonialists, Indian, Indonesian and Chinese indentured laborers or indigenous Amerindians.

Paramaribo is loaded with interesting shopping venues, party-hard night spots and exceptional restaurants, while the untamed jungle, just a few hours away by road or boat, is utterly away from modern development. It's relatively easy to get around this river-heavy, forest-dense country. The mix of languages can make communications interesting, but there is almost always someone around who speaks some English. Don't forget that a meeting of culinary traditions means the food here is as spicy and rich as the country itself.

Top Experiences

Upper Suriname River

 Stay in river lodges on stunning white-sand beaches amid the jungle and get a glimpse into the neighboring Saamaca villages. Swimming and village visits are the main activities, and the more established places put on dance or live music performances at night. A visit to the Maroon Museum in Pikin Slee is a must.

Paramaribo

 This capital of colonial architecture and lively main streets could fill two days of exploring. Southwest along Waterkant from Fort Zeelandia are some of the city's most impressive colonial buildings, mostly merchants' houses. The streets inland from here, particularly Lim-a-Postraat, have many old wooden buildings, some restored, others in picturesque decay.

Raleighvallen

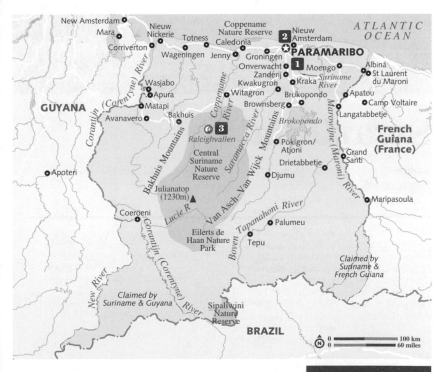 Raleighvallen (Raleigh Falls) is a low, long staircase of cascading water on the upper Coppename River, about two hours upriver from the nearest Maroon (Kwinti people) village. Resident wildlife includes spider monkeys, electric eels and Guiana cock-of-the-rock, a spectacular blood-orange bird.

When to Go

☼ HIGH SEASON (Dec–Mar)

☼ SHOULDER (Apr & Oct–Nov)

☁ LOW SEASON (May–Sep)

Food & Drink

Hagelslag Dutch-style chocolate sprinkles to go on toast for breakfast.

Parbo The local beer is quite good; it's customary to share a *djogo* (1L bottle) among friends.

Pom Creole creation using grated tayer root, shredded chicken, onion and spices baked into a casserole.

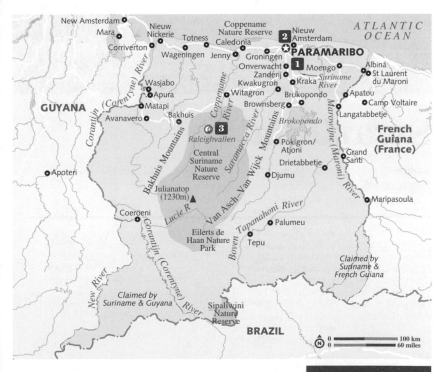

Malolotja Nature Reserve

Swaziland

Ancient traditions are inherent in everyday life in this tiny mountain kingdom, where local festivals provide a rich counterpoint to the activities and wildlife spotting on offer.

In short: big things come in small packages. The intriguing kingdom of Swaziland is diminutive but boasts a huge checklist for any visitor. Adrenaline-boosting activities such as rafting and mountain biking? Tick. Rewarding wildlife-watching? Tick. Lively and colourful local culture, with celebrations and ceremonies still common practice? Tick. Plus there are superb walking trails, stunning mountain and flatland scenery, varied accommodation options and excellent, high-quality handicrafts.

Unlike South Africa, Swaziland has managed to hold on to that slow-down-this-is-Africa feeling, and that's why it's gaining in popularity. Everything remains small and personable, and the atmosphere is remarkably relaxed.

Top Experiences

Mkhaya Game Reserve

1 You're more likely to meet rhinos here than anywhere else in the world, thanks to Mkhaya's rhino protection program. Named after its *mkhaya* (knob-thorn) trees, this private reserve in eastern Swaziland might also be one of Africa's best-value spots. As for the accommodation – where else can you sleep in luxurious semi-open stone-and-thatch cottages in a secluded bush zone? All that, plus a loo with a bush view.

When to Go

 HIGH SEASON (Jun–Oct)

 SHOULDER (May & Nov)

 LOW SEASON (Dec–Apr)

LEGEND
GR Game Reserve
NP National Park
NR Nature Reserve
WS Wildlife Sanctuary

Rafting the Usutu River

2 One of Swaziland's highlights is white-water rafting on the Great Usutu River, shooting the rapids or drifting downriver through stunning gorges. In sections, you'll encounter Grade IV rapids, which aren't for the faint-hearted, although even first-timers with a sense of adventure should handle the day easily. Trips run from the Ezulwini Valley.

Malolotja Nature Reserve

3 The beautiful Malolotja Nature Reserve is a true wilderness area, rugged and for the most part unspoiled. The terrain ranges from mountainous and high-altitude grassland to forest and lower-lying bushveld, all with streams and cut by three rivers, including the Komati River. It's an excellent walking destination, and an ornithologist's paradise, with over 280 species of birds. Wildflowers and rare plants are added attractions; several are found only in this part of Africa.

Bulembu

4 The historic town of Bulembu was built in 1936 for the former Havelock asbestos mine. Following the mine's closure, the 10,000 workers left, and by 2003 Bulembu was a ghost town. Several years ago the town's new investors started a community tourism project, bringing the town back to life – thousands of deserted corrugated-iron houses and many art deco buildings are being renovated. Stunning hikes in the area include the highest mountain in Swaziland, Emlembe Peak (1863m).

Lobamba

5 Lobamba is the heart of Swaziland's Royal Valley. The British-built royal palace, the Embo State Palace, isn't open to visitors, and photos aren't allowed. Swazi kings now live in the Lozitha State House, about 10km from Lobamba. The National Museum has some interesting displays on Swazi culture; the ticket price also allows you to enter the memorial to King Sobhuza II, the most revered of Swazi kings. Next to the museum is the parliament, which is sometimes open to visitors.

Ezulwini & Malkerns Valleys

6 Revel in a royal experience in the regal heartland of Swaziland and splurge on some handicrafts in the Ezulwini and Malkerns Valleys. The pretty valleys begin just outside Mbabane and extend east and south, incorporating the royal domain of Lobamba village. The valleys boast excellent accommodation

Getting Around

There are infrequent (but cheap) domestic buses; most depart in the centre of Mbabane. Generally you'll find minibus taxis are the best domestic public transport; these are plentiful, run almost everywhere and stop often.

Hiring a car will allow you to cover much of the country in a few days. If you have hired your car in South Africa, ensure that you have the written agreement from the rental company to enter Swaziland.

and activities, and have a well-earned reputation for their craft centres and markets.

Mlilwane Wildlife Sanctuary

7 There are many reasons to visit this private reserve – Swaziland's first protected area: it's quiet, easily accessible and really rather beautiful. Its 46 sq km are home to hippos, crocodiles, zebras, blue wildebeest, warthogs and a host of antelope, as well as the Nyonyane Mountain, whose exposed granite peak, known as Execution Rock, reaches 1110m. It's also an outdoor-lover's paradise, with a wide range of activities available.

Sibebe Rock

8 About 8km northeast of Mbabane is Sibebe Rock, a massive granite dome hulking over the surrounding countryside. It's the world's second largest monolith, after Australia's Uluru, but is considerably less visited. Much of the rock is completely sheer, and dangerous if you should

---

Food & Drink

Swaziland isn't a gourmet's paradise, but you won't eat too badly. There's a good range of places to eat in Mbabane and the tourist areas of the Malkerns and Ezulwini Valleys, with international dishes. Portuguese cuisine, including seafood, can often be found. In more remote areas, African staples such as stew and *pap* (also known as mealie meal) are common. In smaller towns, grab some cheap eats on the street.

---

fall, but climbing it is a good adrenaline charge if you're reasonably fit and relish looking down steep rock

faces. Community guides operate guided hikes (E50 per person) – ask at the visitor centre.

FELIX LIPOV / SHUTTERSTOCK ©

Swazi Ceremonies

Colourful ceremonies (and traditional dress, which is still commonly worn) underline the Swazis' proud and unique identity.

The Incwala ceremony is held sometime between late December and early January. It's Swaziland's most sacred ceremony, celebrating the New Year and the first fruits of the harvest in rituals of thanksgiving, prayer, atonement and reverence for the king. As part of the festivities, the king grants his people the right to consume his harvest, and rains are expected to follow the ceremony.

The Umhlanga (Reed Dance) is a great spectacle in August or September, performed by unmarried girls who collect reeds for the repair and maintenance of the royal palace. It is something like a week-long debutante ball for marriageable young Swazi women and is a showcase of potential wives for the king. On the sixth day they perform the reed dance and carry the reeds they have collected to the queen mother. Princesses wear red feathers in their hair.

Buganu Festival is another 'first fruits' festival, taking place in February and celebrating the marula fruit. The women gather the fruit and ferment a brew (known as *buganu;* it packs a punch). Locals – mainly males – gather to drink and celebrate.

CAPITAL
Stockholm

POPULATION
9.9 million

AREA
450,295 sq km

OFFICIAL LANGUAGE
Swedish

The Stockholm archipelago

Sweden

Frozen wastelands, cosy cottages, virgin forest, rocky islands, reindeer herders and Viking lore – Sweden has all that plus impeccable style and to-die-for dining.

To really appreciate this country's charms, you have to leave the city behind. That could mean sailing across an archipelago to visit a lonely island or trekking along a kingly trail through the northern wilderness – or why not try both? Hiking, camping, cycling, skiing, boating, fishing and foraging for mushrooms and berries are all major Swedish pastimes, and it's easy to get in on the action from just about anywhere in the country.

Ancient rune stones poke up out of the grass in parks all over Sweden; huge stone-ship settings and unobtrusive burial mounds are almost as common. Walled medieval cities and seaside fortresses are regular stops on the travellers' circuit. Viking ruins and the stories surrounding them are very much a part of the modern Swedish landscape, and it's easy to feel as if you're walking through history. In fact, you are.

Top Experiences

Stockholm

1 The nation's capital calls itself 'beauty on water', and it certainly doesn't disappoint. Stockholm's many glittering waterways reflect slanted northern light onto spice-hued buildings, and the crooked cobblestone streets of Gamla Stan are magic to wander. Besides its aesthetic virtues, Stockholm also has top-notch museums, first-class dining and all the shopping anyone could ask for. Its clean and efficient public transport, and multilingual locals, make it a cinch to navigate, and at the end of the day you can collapse in a cushy designer hotel.

Norrland Hiking, Abisko

2 Sweden has some absolutely gorgeous hiking trails, most of which are well maintained and supplied with conveniently located mountain huts along the way. The season is relatively short, but it's worth a bit of extra planning to get out into the wilderness: its natural landscape is one of Sweden's best assets. A good place to start your venture is the Norrland village of Abisko, at the top of the Kungsleden long-distance trail – it's a hiker headquarters and easily reached by train.

Northern Delights, Kiruna

3 The twin phenomena that have made the north of Sweden so famous – one natural, one artificial – are both found beyond the Arctic Circle. No other natural spectacle compares to the aurora borealis – the shape-shifting lights that dance across the night sky during the Arctic winter (October to March). The Icehotel, humble igloo turned ice palace just outside Kiruna, takes its inspiration from the changeable nature of the northern lights, and is recreated in a slightly different form every winter.

Bohuslän Coast

4 Caught between sky and sea, the coast of Bohuslän is raw and starkly beautiful, its skerries thick with birds and its villages brightly painted specks among the rocks. Choose from myriad quaint seaside bolt-holes. Film star Ingrid Bergman loved pretty Fjällbacka, the bargain-hunting Norwegians flock to Strömstad, and every sailor knows Tjörn is the place to be in August for the round-island regatta. For a real taste of Swedish summer, spread your beach blanket on a smooth rock and tuck into a bag of peel-and-eat shrimp.

ERIK HERMANSSON / SHUTTERSTOCK ©

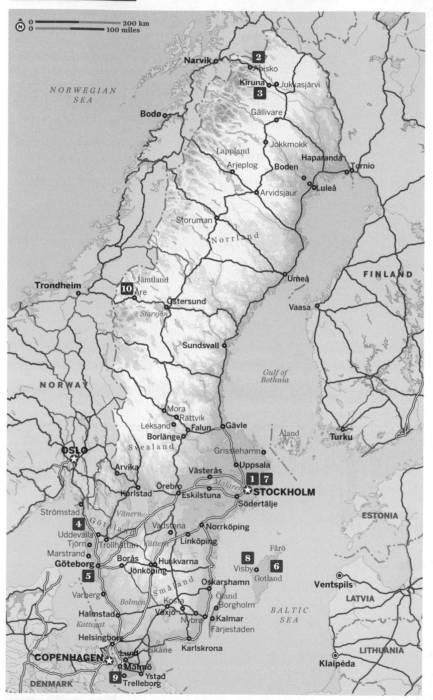

Best on Film

The Seventh Seal (1957) Ingmar Bergman pits man against Death in a cosmic chess game.

Let the Right One In (2008) Tomas Alfredson's icy, preteen take on the vampire romance is palpably set in Norrland.

Together (2000) Lukas Moodysson aims his lens at a Swedish commune in 1975.

Best in Print

Gösta Berling's Saga (1891) Nobel Prize winner Selma Lagerlöf's debut novel.

Faceless Killers (1997) Henning Mankell's detective series, with Kurt Wallander, starts here.

The Great Enigma (2004) The Swedish poet Tomas Tranströmer won the 2011 Nobel Prize for literature.

Food & Drink

Köttbullar och potatis Meatballs and mashed potatoes, served with *lingonsylt* (lingonberry jam).

Gravlax Cured salmon.

Filmjölk Fermented milk, a bit like buttermilk.

Nässelsoppa Nettle soup, traditionally served with hardboiled eggs.

Sill/strömming Herring, eaten smoked, fried or pickled and often accompanied by capers, mustard and onion.

Toast skagen Toast with bleak roe, crème fraiche and chopped red onion.

Brännvin Sweden's trademark spirit, also called aquavit and drunk as *snaps* (vodka).

Göteborg

 5 The edgy alter ego to Stockholm's confident polish, Göteborg is a city of contrasts, with slick museums, raw industrial landscapes, pleasant parks, can-do designers and cutting-edge food. Try delectable shrimp and fish – straight off the boat or at one of the city's five Michelin-rated restaurants. There's the thrill-packed chaos of Sweden's largest theme park, the cultured quiet of the many museums, and you can't leave without window-shopping in Haga and Linné. For a unique way of getting there, jump on a boat and wander the 190km of the Göta Canal.

Gotland & Fårö

 6 Merchants in the 12th and 13th centuries dotted the beautiful island of Gotland with fabulous churches. Today, Gotland's lovely ruins, remote beaches, idyllic bike- and horse-riding paths, peculiar rock formations, excellent restaurants and rousing summer nightlife attract visitors from all over the world. The event of the season is Medieval Week, which brings Visby's old town alive with costumes, re-enactments and markets. Film buffs and nature lovers will want to head north to visit Ingmar Bergman's stomping ground of Fårö.

When to Go

HIGH SEASON (mid-Jun–Aug) Expect warm weather and most sights and accommodation to be open.

SHOULDER (Sep & Oct) Many tourist spots are closed, but you'll have the rest all to yourself.

❄

LOW SEASON (Nov–mid-Jun) Best season for winter-sports adventures, the northern lights and holiday markets.

Kingdom of Crystal

In the Glasriket region you can watch local glass-blowers spin bubbles of molten crystal into fantastic creatures, bowls, vases and sculptures. Try it for yourself in Kosta and Orrefors.

Midsummer

Midsummer's Eve traditionally falls on the Friday between 19 and 25 June; revellers head to the countryside to raise the maypole, sing and dance, drink, and eat pickled herring.

The Sami

Europe's only indigenous people, the ancestors of the Sami, migrated to the north of present-day Scandinavia, following the path of the retreating ice. They lived by hunting reindeer in the area spanning from Norway's Atlantic coast to the Kola Peninsula in Russia, collectively known as Sápmi.

By the 17th century, the depletion of reindeer herds had transformed the Sami's hunting economy into a nomadic herding economy. In Sweden today, the stereotype of the nomadic reindeer herder has been replaced with the multifaceted reality of modern Sami life. The Sami population of Sápmi numbers around 100,000, out of whom around 45,000 live in Norway, 27,000 or so in Sweden, slightly fewer in Finland and some 2000 in Russia. These numbers are approximate, as a census has never taken place. Famous people of Sami descent include Joni Mitchell and Renee Zellweger.

There are many opportunities to learn more about the Sami, be it through a visit to an absorbing museum or an overnight (or longer) stay in a traditional Sami reindeer camp.

Stockholm Archipelago

7 Scattered between the city and the open Baltic Sea, this archipelago is a mesmerising wonderland of small rocky isles, some no more than seagull launch-pads, others studded with deep forests and fields of wildflowers. Most are within easy striking distance of the city, with regular ferry services in summer and several organised tours for easy island-hopping. Hostels, campgrounds and more upmarket slumber options make overnighting a good option, as does the growing number of excellent restaurants.

Medieval Visby

8 It's hard to overstate the beauty of the Hanseatic port town of Visby, in itself justification for making the ferry trip to Gotland. Inside its thick medieval walls are twisting cobblestone streets, fairy-tale cottages draped in flowers and gorgeous ruins atop hills with stunning Baltic views. The walls themselves, with 40-plus towers and the spectacular church ruins within, are a photographer's dream, and the perimeter makes an ideal scenic stroll. The city is also packed with top-notch restaurants accustomed to impressing discriminating diners.

Vikings Village – Foteviken

9 There are still real, live Vikings, and you can visit them at one of Sweden's most absorbing attractions. An evocative 'living' reconstruction of a late–Viking Age village, Foteviken Viking Reserve was built on the coast near the site of the Battle of Foteviken (1134) and contains some 22 reed-roofed houses. The houses you see belong to various tradespeople, like the town's *jarl* (commander of the armed forces), juror and scribe; and the chieftain, whose home has wooden floorboards, fleeces and a Battle of Foteviken tapestry. You can tour all of these, check out the great meeting hall, see a war catapult and buy Viking-made handicrafts. Amazingly, the reserve's residents live as the Vikings did, eschewing most modern conveniences and adhering to old traditions, laws and religions – even after the last tourist has left.

Winter Sports, Åre

10 Winter sports in Lappland are a major draw. To go cross-country skiing, just grab a pair of skis and step outside; for downhill sports, be it heliskiing or snowboarding, Åre is your best bet. Few pastimes are as enjoyable as rushing across the Arctic wasteland pulled by a team of dogs, the sled crunching through crisp snow – but if you want something with a motor, you can test your driving (and racing) skills on the frozen lakes instead. Summer here also brings a bewildering array of mountain-related activities that you can try your hand at.

Getting Around

 Sweden has an extensive and reliable railway network, and trains are almost always faster than buses, although not necessarily cheaper.

 Cars are expensive but ideal if you want to explore smaller roads and remote places.

 There is a comprehensive network of buses throughout Sweden. In general, travelling by bus is cheaper than by train.

 Like most of Scandinavia, Sweden is an extremely bike-friendly country with a well-developed network of cycle paths in and around its towns and cities.

CAPITAL
Bern

POPULATION
8.18 million

AREA
41,277 sq km

OFFICIAL LANGUAGES
German, French,
Italian, Romansch

The Matterhorn, Zermatt

Switzerland

Look past the silk-smooth chocolate, cuckoo clocks and yodelling –
contemporary Switzerland is all about epic journeys and sublime experiences.

Switzerland is a harmonious tableau of beautiful images, a slideshow of epic proportions that is easy to step into. From the intoxicating chink of Verbier glitterati hobnobbing over Champagne to the reassuring bell jangle of silky black Val d'Hérens cattle being mucked out in the Valais, Switzerland mixes rural and urban with astonishing ease, grace and precision. Ride a little red train between peak and pine, soak in mountain spa waters, snowshoe to your igloo or scamper across medieval bridges and know

that this small landlocked country will be picture perfect, with not a hair out of place.

The perfect antidote to rural beauty is a surprise set of cities: capital Bern with its medieval old town and world-class modern art, deeply Germanic Basel and its bold architecture, shopping-chic Geneva astraddle Europe's largest lake, tycoon-magnet Zug and ubercool Zürich with its rooftop bars and atypical Swiss street grit. Beard cutting or stone throwing, Paul Klee art or hip club gig: what a euphoric journey indeed.

Top Experiences

Matterhorn

1 No mountain has so much pulling power, natural magnetism or is so easy to become obsessed with as this charismatic peak – a beauty from birth who demands to be admired, ogled and repeatedly photographed at sunset, sunrise, in different seasons and from every last infuriating angle. And there is no finer place to pander to Matterhorn's every last topographic need than Zermatt, one of Europe's most highly desirable Alpine resorts, in fashion with the skiing, climbing, hiking and hip hobnobbing set since the 19th century.

Hiking in the Swiss National Park

2 No country in Europe is more synonymous with magnificent and mighty hiking beneath eagle-dotted skies than Switzerland, and its high-altitude national park created a century ago is the place to do it. Follow trails through flower-strewn meadows to piercing blue lakes, knife-edge ravines, rocky outcrops and Alpine huts where shepherds make summertime cheese with cows' milk, taken fresh that morning from the herd. It's nature gone wild and on the rampage, and is a rare and privileged glimpse of Switzerland before the dawn of tourism.

Aletsch Glacier

3 One of the world's natural marvels, this mesmerising glacier of gargantuan proportions in the Upper Valais is tantamount to a 23km-long, five-lane highway of ice powering between mountain peaks at altitude. Its ice is glacial-blue and 900m thick at its deepest point. The view of Aletsch from Jungfraujoch will make your heart sing, but for the hard-core adrenaline surge nothing beats getting up close: hike between crevasses with a mountain guide from Riederalp, or ski above it on snowy pistes in Bettmeralp.

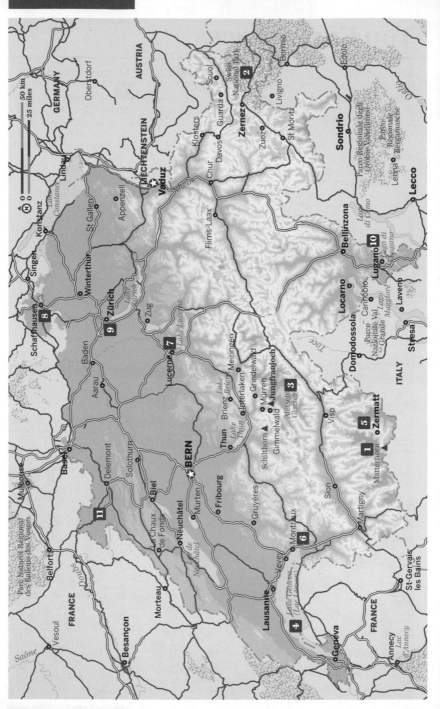

GERMANY

Oberstdorf

AUSTRIA

50 km
25 miles

N

Lindau

Konstanz
Singen
Lake Constance

St Gallen

Appenzell

Schaffhausen 8

Winterthur

Zürich 9

Baden

Aarau

Zug

Lake Zürich

LIECHTENSTEIN

Vaduz

Chur

Flims-Laax

Klosters

Scuol

Guarda

Swiss National Park 2

Davos

Zernez

Livigno

Bormio

Zuoz

St Moritz

Edolo

Sondrio

Parco Regionale delle
Orobie Valtellinesi

Parco
Regionale
Lema-Bergamasche

Lecco

Lago di Como

Bellinzona

Locarno

Lugano 10

Lago di Lugano

Laveno

Delemont

Solothurn

BERN

Thun

Brienz

Lake Brienz
Meiringen

Interlaken

Grindelwald

Mürren

Schilthorn
Gimmelwald
Jungfraujoch 3

Aletsch Glacier

Visp

Zermatt 5

1

Matterhorn

Basel

Mulhouse

Belfort

Vesoul

Besançon

FRANCE

Parc Naturel Régional
des Ballons des Vosges

Doubs

Morteau

La Chaux
de Fonds

Biel

Neuchâtel

Lac de
Neuchâtel

Murten

Fribourg

Gruyères

Lake Thun

Montreux 6

Sion

Martigny

St-Gervais
les Bains

Lausanne

Lake Geneva (Lac Léman)

Vevey

Geneva

Annecy

Lac d'Annecy

FRANCE

Saône

ITALY

Domodossola

Parco
Nazionale Val
Grande

Lago
Maggiore

Cannobio

Stresa

Toce

Lucerne 7

Lake Lucerne

Zug

Best on Film

Puppylove (2013) Coming-of-age story starring Lausanne-born Vincent Perez, directed by Delphine Lehericey.

Sister (2012) Ursula Meier's award-winning film about the complicated dynamics between poor siblings at a Swiss ski resort.

Home (2008) A family unravels as life by an unfinished motorway takes its toll in this Ursula Meier drama.

Journey of Hope (1991) Oscar-winning tale of a Kurdish family seeking a better life in Switzerland.

Breathless (1960) New wave classic by Swiss avant-garde film-maker Jean-Luc Godard.

Classic Dishes

Fondue Switzerland's best-known dish, in which melted emmental and Gruyère cheese are combined with white wine in a large pot and eaten with small bread chunks.

Raclette Another popular artery-hardener of melted cheese served with potatoes.

Rösti German Switzerland's national dish of fried shredded potatoes is served with everything.

Veal Highly rated throughout the country; in Zürich, veal is thinly sliced and served in a cream sauce (*Gschnetzeltes Kalbsfleisch*).

Bündnerfleisch Dried beef, smoked and thinly sliced.

Chocolate Good at any time of day and available seemingly everywhere.

Lake Geneva

 The emerald vines marching uphill in perfect unison from the shores of Lake Geneva in Lavaux are staggering. But the urban viewpoint from which to admire and experience Europe's largest lake is Geneva, French-speaking Switzerland's most cosmopolitan city, where canary-yellow mouettes (seagulls) ferry locals across the water and Mont Blanc peeps in on the action. Strolling Old Town streets, savouring a vibrant cafe society, paddle-boarding on the lake and making the odd dash beneath its iconic pencil fountain is what life's about for the 180 nationalities living here.

The Glacier Express

 It's among the world's most mythical train rides, linking two of Switzerland's glitziest Alpine resorts. Hop aboard the red train with floor-to-ceiling windows in St Moritz or Zermatt, and savour shot after cinematic shot of green peaks, glistening Alpine lakes, glacial ravines and other hallucinatory natural landscapes. Pulled

When to Go

HIGH SEASON
(Jul, Aug & Dec–Apr)
High season for summer and winter outdoor sports.

SHOULDER
(Apr–Jun & Sep)
Look for accommodation deals in ski resorts and traveller hotspots.

LOW SEASON
(Oct–Mar)
Sights and restaurants are open fewer days and shorter hours.

Completely Dada

Antibourgeois, rebellious, nihilistic and deliberately nonsensical, Dada grew out of revulsion to WWI and the mechanisation of modern life. It paved the way for nearly every form of contemporary art by using collage, extracting influences from indigenous art, applying abstract notions to writing, film and performance, and taking manufactured objects and redefining them as art.

Zürich was the movement's birthplace. Hugo Ball, Tristan Tzara and Emmy Jennings' creation of the Cabaret Voltaire in February 1916 kicked off a series of raucous cabaret and performance-art events in a bar at Spiegelgasse 1 (still in place today).

By 1923 the movement was dead, but its spirit lives on in the works of true Dadaists like George Grosz, Hans Arp and Max Ernst and those infected with its ideas, such as Marcel Duchamp (whose urinal-as-art piece conveys the idea succinctly) and Man Ray. See Dadaist works in Zürich's Kunsthaus and Museum für Gestaltung.

Getting Around

Switzerland's compact size and excellent rail transport render internal flights almost unnecessary.

All the larger lakes are serviced by steamers operated by Swiss Federal Railways, or allied private companies for which national travel passes are valid.

Yellow Post Buses supplement the rail network, following postal routes and linking towns to the less accessible mountain regions.

Public transport is excellent in city centres – unlike parking cars, which is usually hard work.

All major train stations are connected to each other by hourly departures, at least between 6am and midnight, and most long-distance trains have a dining car.

by steam engine when it first puffed out of the station in 1930, the Glacier Express traverses 91 tunnels and 291 bridges on its famous journey. Lunch in the vintage restaurant car or bring your own Champagne picnic.

Romance in Montreux

6 As if being host to one of the world's most mythical jazz festivals, with open-air concerts on the shore of Lake Geneva is not enough, Montreux has a castle to add to the French-style romance. From the well-known lakeside town with a climate so mild that palm trees grow, a flower-framed footpath follows the water to Château de Chillon. Historic, sumptuous and among Switzerland's oldest, this magnificent stone château built by the Savoys in the 13th century is everything a castle should be.

Lakeside Lucerne

7 Medieval bridge-strolling is the charm of this irresistible Romeo in Central Switzerland. Throw sparkling lake vistas, an alfresco cafe life, candy-coloured architecture and Victorian curiosities into the cooking pot and, yes, lakeside Lucerne could well be the start of a very beautiful love affair. With the town under your belt, step back to savour the ensemble from a wider perspective: views across the lake of green hillsides, meadows and hidden lake resorts atop Mt Pilatus, Mt Rigi or Stanserhorn will not disappoint.

Splash of the Rheinfall

8 So moved were Goethe and Lord Byron by the wispy waterfalls of Staubbach Falls, their fairy-tale threads of spray ensnaring the cliffside in Lauterbrunnen, that they composed poems exalting their ethereal beauty. Yet it is the theatrical, crash-bang-wallop splash of the thunderous Rheinfall, guarded by a twin set of medieval castles,

in northeastern Switzerland that really takes your breath away. To appreciate the full drama of it all, ride the panoramic lift up to the Känzeli viewing platform in medieval Schloss Laufen.

Zürich Lifestyle

9 One of Europe's most liveable cities, Zürich in German-speaking Switzerland is an ode to urban renovation. It's also hip (yes, this is where Google employees shoot down a slide to lunch). With enough of a rough edge that it resembles Berlin at times, a visit to Zürich means drinking in waterfront bars, dancing until dawn in Züri-West, shopping for recycled fashion accessories in Kreis 5 and boogying with the best of them at Europe's largest street party, the city's wild and wacky, larger-than-life Street Parade in August.

Lago di Lugano

10 An intrinsic part of Switzerland's unique charm is its mixed bag of languages and cultures. And no spot on Swiss earth exalts the country's Italianate soul with such gusto as Lago di Lugano in Ticino, a shimmering Alpine lake fringed with palm-tree promenades and pretty villages of delicate pastel hues. Lugano, the biggest town on the lake and the country's third-largest affluent banking centre to boot, is vivacious and busy with porticoed alleys, cafe-packed piazzas and boats yo-yoing around the lakeside destinations.

Rural Jura

11 Tiptoe off the tourist map and into clover-shaped Jura, a fascinating backwater on the French–Swiss border woven from thick dark forests, gentle rolling hills, medieval villages and a go-slow vibe. No piece of scenery is too large, too high or too racy here. Rather, travel in the rural Jura is an exquisite sensory experience laced with inspirational bike rides, cross-country skiing through silent glades, fragrant nights in hay barns, fabulous farm feasts and cheese cut in the shape of a flower.

Tipping

Tipping is not necessary, given that hotels, restaurants, bars and even some taxis are legally required to include a 15% service charge in bills.

Farmstay

If you are walking in the lowlands and fancy going back to nature, consider spending the night at a farmstay.

10

9

CAPITAL
Damascus

POPULATION
17. 2 million

AREA
185,180 sq km

OFFICIAL LANGUAGE
Arabic

Syria

Due to a civil war that has dominated the news headlines and traumatised a nation, Syria has been off-limits for several years. But in years gone by this gateway to the Middle East was famed for its culture and hospitality.

At the time of writing, you can't go: if you can, you shouldn't. Peaceful protests against the Assad regime that began in early 2011 have evolved into a chaotic and multi-faceted civil war spanning much of the country.

There's violent conflict around Aleppo in the rebel-held north, Homs in central Syria and also around Damascus in the government stronghold of the south. Although organisations such as the UN and the Arab League have attempted to broker peace, events remain unpredictable.

How long this will continue is impossible to guess. When it ends, the wealth of historic sites, from Palmyra in the desert to the crusader castles like Crac des Chevaliers, within sight of the Mediterranean, will lure us back and the gracious hospitality of Syrians will warm us to their country.

Snapshot

Crac des Chevaliers

 Added to Unesco's World Heritage list in 2006, this crusader castle comprises two distinct parts: the outside wall with its 13 towers and main entrance; and the inside wall and central construction, built on a rocky platform. The castle has been damaged during the civil war.

Damascus Old City

 Legend has it that on a journey from Mecca, the Prophet Mohammed cast his gaze upon Damascus but refused to enter the city because he wanted to enter paradise only once – when he died. In this city of legend, which vies for the title of the world's oldest continually inhabited city, this is but one of thousands of stories.

Euphrates River

 Rising in Turkey, the historic Euphrates river, the longest in western Asia, carves its course through north-eastern Syria before joining forces with the Tigris and emptying into the Persian Gulf. From the sixteenth to nineteenth century European travellers in the Syrian Euphrates basin sent back tales of abundant wildlife such as the now-extinct Arabian Ostrich, gazelle and onager.

Seasons

☀ MAY–SEP

⛅ OCT

☂ NOV–MAY

Food & Drink

Tabbouleh and **fattoush** Two of the most well-known Syrian salads. Both use mint, lemon juice and olive oil for flavour, and contain cucumber and tomato.

Shay na'ana Mint tea, the essential complement to Syrian hospitality.

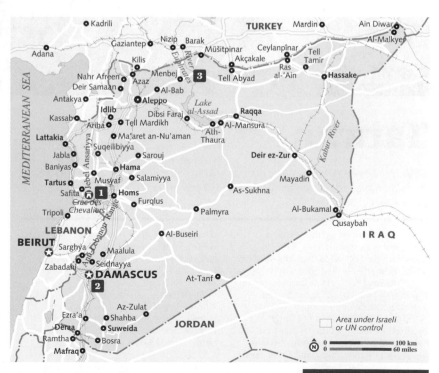

Taroko Gorge

CAPITAL
Taipei

POPULATION
23.5 million

AREA
36,000 sq km

OFFICIAL LANGUAGES
Mandarin, Taiwanese

Taiwan

With legacies as varied as its adventure landscape and spirited traditions thriving alongside the cream of Asian sophistication, Taiwan is a continent on one green island.

Famed for centuries as Ilha Formosa (Beautiful Isle), this is a land with more sides than the 11-headed Guanyin. Towering sea cliffs, marble-walled gorges and tropical forests are just the start of your journey, which could take you as far as Yushan, Taiwan's 3952m alpine roof.

Taiwan offers the gamut of Chinese cuisines, some of the best Japanese outside Japan, and a full house of local specialities from Tainan milkfish and Taipei beef noodles to indigenous barbecued wild boar. Night markets around the island serve endless feasts of snacks including stinky tofu, steamed dumplings, oyster omelettes, shrimp rolls and shaved ice.

The Taiwanese have created Asia's most vibrant democracy and liberal society, with a raucous free press, gender equality, and respect for human rights and, increasingly, animal rights as well.

Top Experiences

Taroko Gorge

 Taiwan's top tourist draw is a walk-in Chinese painting. Rising above the froth of the blue-green Liwu River, the marble walls (yes, marble!) of Taroko Gorge swirl with the colours of a master's palette. Add grey mist, lush vegetation and water falls seemingly tumbling down from heaven, and you have a truly classic landscape. Walk along the Swallow Grotto to see the gorge at its most sublime or brave the Jhuilu Old Trail, a vertigo-inducing path 500m above the canyon floor.

Hiking Snow Mountain

 Don't forget your boots because two-thirds of Taiwan's terrain is mountainous – and what mountains they are. Hundreds soar above 3000m, and well-established hiking routes run everywhere. Everyone wants to tackle Yushan, the highest peak in Northeast Asia, but the second highest, Snow Mountain, is a more scenic climb and leads to the aptly named Holy Ridge, a five-day walk on an exposed ridgeline that never drops below 3000m.

When to Go

🌂 **HIGH SEASON**
(Jul & Aug)

🌂 **SHOULDER**
(Jun, Sep)

⛅ **LOW SEASON**
(Nov–Mar)

National Palace Museum, Taipei

 Taiwan houses the greatest collection of Chinese art in the world. With ancient pottery, bronzes and jade, Ming vases, Song landscape paintings and calligraphy even those who are not art lovers can appreciate, this museum isn't merely a must-visit, it's a

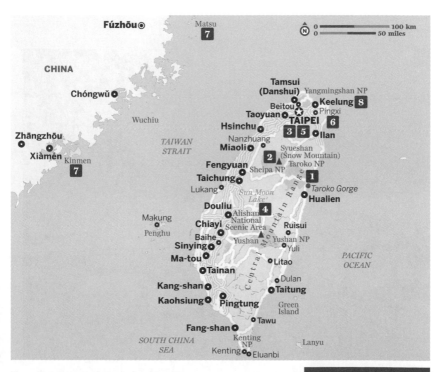

must-repeat-visit. Why? Out of the nearly 700,000 pieces in the museum's collection – spanning every Chinese dynasty – only a tiny fraction is ever on display at the one time.

Sun Moon Lake National Scenic Area

4 Sun Moon Lake is the largest body of water in Taiwan and has a water-colour background, ever-changing with the season. Although the area is packed with tour groups these days, it's still easy to get away from the crowds on the trails and cycling paths. For diverse fun, loop down to the old train depot at Checheng or visit the Chung Tai monastery in nearby Pul. No matter what, don't miss the region's high-mountain oolong tea: it's some of the world's finest.

Bao'an Temple, Taipei

5 Recipient of a Unesco Asia-Pacific Heritage Award for both its restoration and its revival of temple rites and festivities, the Bao'an Temple is a must-visit when in Taipei. This exquisite structure is loaded with prime examples of the traditional decorative arts, and the yearly folk arts festival is a showcase of traditional performance arts.

Pingxi Sky Lantern Festival

6 One of the oldest of the lunar events, the Lantern Festival celebrates the end of the New Year's festivities. The focus of course is light, and everywhere streets and riversides are lined with glowing lanterns, while giant neon

Getting Around

Fast, reliable and cheap, Taiwan has both a high-speed rail and a regular rail link.

Slower but cheaper than trains, buses also connect passengers to more destinations than trains.

Cycling around the island is now a popular tourist activity.

and laser displays fill public squares. Making the mundane surreal and the commonplace magical, the little mountain village of Pingxi takes simple paper lanterns and releases them en masse into the night sky.

Matsu & Kinmen Islands

7 Close enough to see China from, even on a hazy day, Matsu and Kinmen Islands were long the front lines in the propaganda (and occasionally real) wars between the nationalists and communists. These days, with the military presence scaling down,

travellers are discovering islands whose rich history is not limited to recent times – Matsu and Kinmen are treasure troves of preserved old villages. Visitors will also find some fine cycling and bird-watching among the varied landscapes.

Miaokou Night Market, Keelung

8 Taiwan's night markets are as numerous as they are varied.

Fulfilling the need for both food and entertainment (to say nothing of socialising), markets bring happy crowds almost every night of the week to gorge on a bewildering array of snacks and dishes. Check out the Miaokou Night Market in Keelung, in many ways the grandaddy of them all, for the quintessential experience of eating and people-watching.

GRACETHANG2 / SHUTTERSTOCK ©

Food & Drink

Chòu dòufu Stinky tofu, a classic Taiwanese snack.

Fó tiào qiáng ('Buddha Jumps Over the Wall') A stew of seafood, chicken, duck and pork simmered in a jar of rice wine. Allegedly the dish is so tasty that even the Buddha – a vegetarian, of course – would hop over a wall to get a taste.

Gāoliáng jiǔ Kaoliang liquor, made from fermented sorghum.

Kèjiā xiǎo chǎo Stir-fried cuttlefish with leeks, tofu and pork.

Kézǎi tāng Clear oyster soup with ginger.

Tiěbǎn shānzhūròu Fatty wild boar grilled, sliced, and grilled again with onions and wild greens.

Xiǎoyú huāshēng Fish stir-fry with peanuts and pickled vegetables.

Zhà shūcài bǐng Fried, salty balls made from local mushrooms and flour.

Lunar New Year

Celebrated for two weeks in January or February, Lunar New Year is the most cherished holiday of the year. Activities include a thorough clean of the house; decorating doorways with couplets expressing good fortune; and a family reunion dinner on New Year's Eve. On the second day of New Year's, married daughters return to their parents' home. The last days of the public holidays are for visiting friends and travelling. The 15th and final day is the Lantern Festival, which in Taiwan is celebrated with a number of exceptional activities.

CAPITAL
Dushanbe

POPULATION
8.3 million

AREA
143,100 sq km

OFFICIAL LANGUAGE
Tajik

Pamir Highway

Tajikstan

Tajikistan offers the region's most outlandish high-altitude scenery and its most stunning road trips. Fabulous trekking and the region's most humbling hospitality make this the cutting edge of adventure travel.

Where 'Great Game' spies and explorers once ventured, Tajikistan's awesomely dramatic highland landscapes are now testing playgrounds for hardy climbers, trekkers and adventure travellers.

Nascent rural homestay programs mean you might stay in timelessly photogenic rural villages hosted by gold-toothed, white-bearded patriarchs in iridescent robes. The people, predominantly Persian-rather than Turkic-speaking, are enor-mously hospitable, but little English is spoken; also, rural transport is so irregular that you will probably want to fork out for a rented 4WD.

But the marvels of the Wakhan Valley, the starkly beautiful 'Roof of the World' Pamirs and the breathtaking lakes and pinnacles of the Fan Mountains all contribute to making Tajikistan arguably Central Asia's most exciting destination.

Top Experiences

Pamir Highway

1 From the deep, rugged mountain valleys of beautiful Badakhshan, the Soviet-built Pamir Highway climbs up on to the treeless Pamir plateau to the 'wild east' town of Murgab and on past the dramatic azure lake of Karakol in to Kyrgyzstan's stunning Alai Valley. En route you'll pass ancient tombs, hot springs, remote yurt camps and some of the most spectacular mountain scenery in Asia. It's one of the world's great mountain road trips. Tackle it in a rented Soviet 4WD or as a challenging bicycle ride.

Fan Mountains

2 The mountains northwest of Dushanbe rank as Central Asia's premier trekking destination. Dozens of turquoise lakes stud the high mountain valleys. Go on a multiday trek to meet local Tajik shepherds, or drive to the seven lakes (Haft Kul) of the Marguzor Valley and do some delightful day hikes from a chain of homestays. You can even visit the ruined old Sogdian city of Penjikent en route. Check in advance whether the border between Samarkand and Penjikent has reopened.

When to Go

 HIGH SEASON
(Apr–Jul,
Sep–Oct)

 SHOULDER
(Aug)

 LOW SEASON
(Nov–Mar)

Iskander-Kul

3 This opal-blue mountain lake looks almost tropical in strong sunlight. It isn't. At 2195m, don't expect to swim here. But adding greatly to the visual spectacle is the variegated colouration on the superlative mountain backdrop. The scene is especially dramatic around 1.5km before arriving at the lake, but

breathtaking views continue as you drive along the 6km of coast road.

Istaravshan

4 Called Kir by the Parthians, Cyropol by Alexander the Great and Ura-Tyube by the Russians and Soviets, Istaravshan has a small historical core that is a little better preserved than most in Tajikistan. Its gently intriguing maze of lanes hides a handful of mosques and madrasas, while its vast, colourful central bazaar is a town unto itself. On a clear day, the views from Mug Teppe, the city's grassy, flat-topped former fortress hill, show off the city's mountain horizon to great advantage.

Dushanbe

5 Backed by a hazy phalanx of mountains, Dushanbe is a city in rapid transition. Its long, tree-lined central avenue still passes a collection of pastel-hued neoclassical buildings from its original Soviet incarnation. But much is threatened with the demolition ball as a whole new gamut of glitzy, oversized newcomers rise in a style that is often an intriguingly discordant blend of Roman triumphalism and budget futurism. The focus for this curious renaissance is a manicured central park dominated by a vast new museum and the world's tallest flag pole.

Jizeu Valley

6 One of the best short-hike destinations in the region, the Jizeu (Jisev, Geisev) Valley offers idyllic scenes around a series of seasonally over-flowing, treelined river lakes. The prettiest lakes are bracketed by two halves of the tiny traditional hamlet of Jizeu

Getting Around

Domestic flights are limited to Dushanbe–Khojand and the spectacular, but notoriously unreliable Dushanbe–Khorog service.

The bus/minibus network is limited. Shared taxis are the only public transport between Dushanbe and Penjikent or Khojand.

Travellers commonly organise themselves into groups to rent chauffeured 4WD vehicles in the Pamirs and to Khorog and Murgab.

5

(pronounced jee-sao) which has a wonderful, timeless feel. An added thrill of the visit, albeit a potential logistical problem, is that there's no road and the access footpath starts with a remarkable 'cable car' – a wooden contraption looking more like a sentry box that dangles on twin wires and is hand-wound to take up to four people across the gushing river.

Wakhan Valley

MILOSZ MASLANKA / SHUTTERSTOCK ©

7 The Tajik side of the Wakhan Valley feels like a hidden Shangri La. Bordered by the Hindu Kush and a finger of remotest Afghanistan, the valley is dotted with Silk Road forts, Ismaili shrines and village homestays run by welcoming Wakhi Tajik families. It's an essential add-on to a Pamir Highway trip and a potential springboard into Afghanistan. Even Marco Polo was impressed when he passed through. To get the most out of the valley, hire transport or hike the valley.

Food & Drink

Borj A meat-and-grain mix that resembles savoury porridge.

Chakka (known as *yakka* to Tajik speakers around Samarkand and Bukhara) is curd mixed with herbs, typically served with flat-bread.

Kurutob Flat-bread morsels layered with onion, tomato, parsley and coriander and doused in a yoghurt-based sauce.

Shir chai Somewhere between milk tea and Tibetan butter tea.

Pamiri Houses

From outside, a traditional *huneuni chid* (Pamiri house) looks like a poor, low-slung, mud-stone box. Inside things look very different. Guests are received in the large, five-pillared room with raised areas around four sides. The most distinctive feature is the wooden ceiling built in four concentric squares, each rotated 45 degrees then topped with a skylight which provides most of the illumination. Each ceiling level represents one of the elements: earth, fire, air and water. Carpets line the walls and mattresses take the place of furniture. Amid panels of photographs, pride of place almost inevitably goes to a portrait of the Aga Khan.

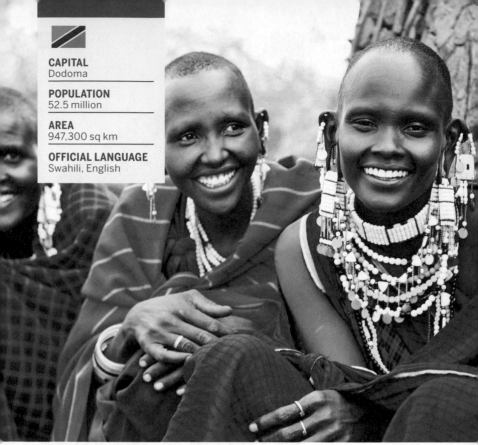

CAPITAL
Dodoma

POPULATION
52.5 million

AREA
947,300 sq km

OFFICIAL LANGUAGE
Swahili, English

Maasai women

Tanzania

*Wildlife, beaches, friendly people, fascinating cultures, Serengeti,
Ngorongoro, Mt Kilimanjaro, Zanzibar – Tanzania has all these and more
wrapped up in one adventurous, welcoming package.*

More than almost any other destination,
Tanzania is *the* land of safaris. Wildebeest
stampede across the plains. Hippos jostle
for space in muddy waterways. Elephants
wander along seasonal migration routes and
chimpanzees swing through the treetops.

Sending its shadow across Tanzania's
northern plains, Mt Kilimanjaro beckons
visitors with its graceful, forested flanks
and stately snow-capped summit. Climbers
by the thousands venture here to challenge

themselves on its muddy slopes, rocky trails
and slippery scree. The reward: the thrill of
standing at the top of Africa.

Above all, it is the Tanzanian people –
with their characteristic warmth and
politeness, and the dignity and beauty of
their cultures – that make visiting Tanzania
so memorable. Chances are you'll want
to come back for more, to which most
Tanzanians will say '*karibu tena*' (welcome
again).

Top Experiences

Serengeti National Park

1 The sound of pounding hooves on the Serengeti plains draws closer. Suddenly, thousands of animals stampede by as the great wildebeest migration – one of earth's most spectacular natural dramas – plays out. Despite the theatrics, time seems to stand still in this superlative park. Lions sit on lofty outcrops, giraffes stride into the sunset, crocodiles bask on riverbanks. Wildlife watching is outstanding year round. Whether you stay for two days or a week, there never seems to be enough time to take in all the Serengeti has to offer.

Zanzibar's Stone Town

2 Whether it's your first visit or your 50th, Stone Town, the atmospheric older section of Zanzibar Town, never loses its touch of the exotic. First, you'll see the skyline, with the spires of St Joseph's Cathedral and the Old Fort. Later, as you wander through narrow alleyways, surprises are revealed at every turn. Linger in dusty shops scented with cloves, watch as men wearing white, robe-like kanzu play a bao (board game) and let island rhythms take over as mainland life slips away.

Ngorongoro Crater

3 On clear days, the magic of Ngorongoro starts while you're still up on the rim, with sublime views over the enormous crater. The descent takes you down to a wide plain cloaked in hues of blue and green and covered with an unparalleled concentration of wildlife. If you're lucky enough to find a quiet spot, it's easy to imagine primeval Africa, with an almost constant parade of animals streaming past against a quintessential East African backdrop. Go as early in the day as possible to maximise viewing time.

GUDKOV ANDREY / SHUTTERSTOCK ©

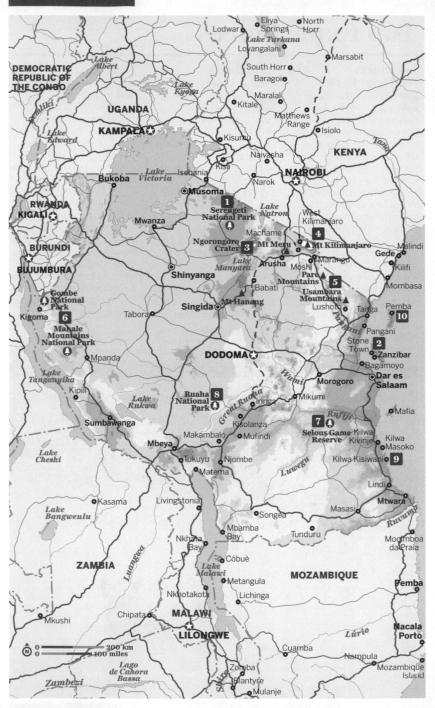

Mt Kilimanjaro

4 It's difficult to resist the allure of climbing Africa's highest peak, with its snowy summit and views over the surrounding plains. Thousands of trekkers complete the climb each year, with a main requirement for success being adequate time for acclimatisation. But there are also other rewarding ways to experience Kilimanjaro. Take a day hike on the mountain's lush lower slopes, learn about local Chagga culture or sip a sundowner from one of many nearby vantage points with the mountain as a backdrop.

Best in Print & Film

The Tree Where Man Was Born (Peter Matthiessen; 1972) Lyrical account of northern Tanzania and Kenya's people, wildlife and landscapes.

The Gunny Sack (MG Vassanji; 1989) Memoir of family and growing up told through the contents of a gunny sack.

Tumaini (2005) The devastation of AIDS in a Tanzanian family.

As Old as My Tongue (2006) Story of legendary Zanzibari singer Bi Kidude.

Memoirs of an Arabian Princess from Zanzibar (Emily Ruete; 1888) Autobiography of a 19th-century Zanzibari princess.

Paradise (Abdulrazak Gurnah; 1994) An East African coming-of age tale.

Local Life

5 Wildlife galore, Kilimanjaro, fantastic beaches and Swahili ruins are but a backdrop to Tanzania's most fascinating resource – its people. Local culture is accessible and diverse: hunt up cultural tourism programs to get acquainted with the Maasai, learn about the burial traditions of the Pare and experience a local market day with the Arusha. The Usambara area, with its lively Sambaa villages and culture, is one of many good places to start your explorations. Wherever you go, Tanzania's rich cultures are fascinating to discover.

When to Go

HIGH SEASON
(Jun–Sep)
Animal-spotting is easiest, as foliage is sparse and animals congregate around dwindling water sources.

SHOULDER
(Oct–Feb)
Hot, especially from December.

LOW SEASON
(Mar–May)
Heavy rains; landscapes are lush and green.

Food

It's easy to travel through Tanzania thinking that the country subsists on *ugali* (the main maize and cassava flour staple) and sauce. But there are some treats to be found. The Zanzibar Archipelago is one of East Africa's culinary highlights. Here, scents of coriander and coconut recall the days when the coast was a port of call on the spice route from the Orient. Elsewhere, lively local atmosphere and Tanzanian hospitality compensate for what can otherwise be a rather bland diet.

Saving the Sea Turtle

Tanzania's sea turtle population is critically endangered, due to nest poaching, subsistence hunting and turtles getting caught in fishing nets. Sea Sense (www.seasense.org) has been working with coastal communities to protect sea turtles, as well as dugongs, whale sharks and other endangered marine species. It has made considerable progress, especially with its community nest protection program, in which locally trained conservation officers assume responsibility for monitoring sea turtle nesting activity, and protecting eggs from poachers and other dangers.

As part of this initiative, local community members are trained as 'turtle tour guides' to take visitors to nesting sites to watch hatchlings emerge and make their way to the sea; sites include include Dar es Salaam's South Beach, Ushongo beach (south of Pangani) and Mafia island. The modest fee is split between Sea Sense, to support its nest protection program, and local village environment funds. In this way, community members are able to benefit directly from their conservation efforts.

Getting Around

 There is a good flight network that's pricey, but often the most feasible option for bridging long distances in limited time.

 Bus travel is inexpensive, often gruelling, risky (due to fast speeds and challenging road conditions), but the main way of getting around for most travellers.

 Car hire is expensive. Self-drive is not common, but well worth it if you have experience driving in Africa. Driving is on the left.

 Trains are inexpensive and slow but scenic and a real cultural experience.

Chimpanzee Tracking

6 Climbing steep muddy paths, stumbling over twisted roots and making your way through dense vegetation – chimpanzee tracking is hard work. But the struggle and sweat is all forgotten when chimpanzees are spotted in a clearing ahead. Tanzania's remote western parks – Mahale Mountains and Gombe – are among the best places anywhere to get close to our primate cousins. Combine chimpanzee tracking with a safari in Katavi National Park or an exploration of the Lake Tanganyika shoreline for an unforgettable adventure well off the beaten track.

Selous Game Reserve

7 Vast Selous, with its tropical climate, profusion of greenery and massive Rufiji River, is completely different to Tanzania's northern parks. Take a boat safari, and as you glide past borassus palms, slumbering hippos, cavorting elephants and the stealthy shapes of motionless crocodiles, watch as well for the many smaller attractions along the river banks. These include majestic African fish eagles, stately Goliath herons and tiny white-fronted bee-eaters – all part of the daily natural symphony in Africa's largest wildlife reserve.

Ruaha National Park

8 Rugged, baobab-studded Ruaha National Park, together with surrounding conservation areas, is home to one of Tanzania's largest elephant populations. An ideal spot to watch for the giant pachyderms is along the Great Ruaha River at sunrise or sundown, when they make their way down to the banks to snack or to swim in the company of hippos, antelopes and over 400 different types of birds. A visit here, together with a journey through nearby areas of southern Tanzania, is far removed from the more popular northern circuit and unfailingly rewarding.

Ruins & Rock Art

9 Tanzania offers a wealth of attractions for history buffs. The most impressive of the many coastal ruins are those at Kilwa Kisiwani – a Unesco World Heritage Site harking back to the days of sultans and far-flung trade routes that linked inland gold fields with Persia, India and China. Standing in the restored Great Mosque, you can almost hear the whispers of bygone centuries. Inland, armed with a sense of adventure and a taste for rugged travel, head for the enigmatic Kondoa Rock-Art Sites, spread throughout Central Tanzania's Irangi hills.

Beaches & Diving in Pemba

10 With exotic archipelagos, inland lakes and over 1000km of Indian Ocean coastline, you'll be spoiled for choice with Tanzania's beaches. Zanzibar's coastline is developed but lovely, with white sand, palm trees and rewarding diving. To get away from the crowds, head to Pemba, with its placid coves and spectacular diving. Much of Pemba's coast is lined with mangroves and lagoons, interspersed with a few good stretches of sand and some idyllic islets. Offshore, coral reefs, the steeply dropping walls of the Pemba Channel and an abundance of fish offer some of East Africa's best diving.

Wildflowers

The blooms of orchids and many other wildflowers carpet Kitulo Plateau come February. It's the rainy, muddy season here, but hardy, well-equipped hikers will be rewarded.

Safaris

Booking and paying for a safari before arriving in Tanzania is recommended if you'll be travelling in popular areas during the high season.

6

8

ANDREW MOLINARO / SHUTTERSTOCK ©

ANDREW MOLINARO / SHUTTERSTOCK ©

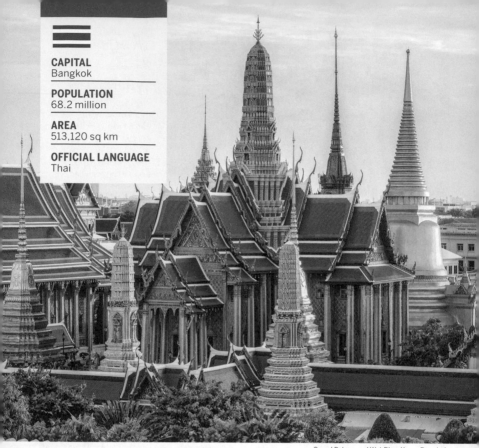

Bangkok

POPULATION
68.2 million

AREA
513,120 sq km

OFFICIAL LANGUAGE
Thai

Grand Palace and Wat Phra Keaw, Bangkok

Thailand

Friendly and fun loving, exotic and tropical, cultured and historic, Thailand radiates a golden hue from its glittering temples and tropical beaches through to the ever-comforting Thai smile.

Adored around the world, Thai cuisine expresses fundamental aspects of Thai culture: it is generous, warm, refreshing and relaxed. Each Thai dish relies on fresh, local ingredients. A varied national menu is built around the four fundamental flavours: spicy, sweet, salty and sour. Roving appetites go on eating tours of Bangkok noodle shacks, seafood pavilions in Phuket and Burmese market stalls in Mae Sot.

With two coastlines and jungle-topped islands anchored in azure waters, Thailand is a tropical getaway for the hedonist and the hermit, the prince and the pauper. This paradise offers a varied menu: playing in the gentle surf of Ko Lipe, diving with whale sharks off Ko Tao, scaling the sea cliffs of Krabi, kiteboarding in Hua Hin, partying on Ko Phi Phi, recuperating at a health resort on Ko Samui and feasting on the beach wherever sand meets sea.

Top Experiences

Bangkok

1 Glittering temples, towering skyscrapers, a cracking nightlife and, oh – the food! What's not to love about Bangkok? Traffic jams, humidity and political instability aside, the Thai capital is now tidier and easier to navigate than ever. Zip between golden shrines, colourful markets, glitzy mega-malls and fascinating museums, stopping to refuel at sizzling streetside food stands and some of Asia's best restaurants. Head up to one of the city's famous skybars on your first night to get your bearings in this heaving, twinkling metropolis, and prepare to dive straight in.

Railay

2 At the tip of the Krabi peninsula are some of Thailand's most famous natural features: the soaring limestone karsts of Railay, anchored in the ocean. The beaches are sugar white and the forested interior is traversed by foot traffic, not cars. No traffic jams, no transport hassles. Visitors come and go by long-tail boats. Come to lounge, swim, dive or rock climb. Beginners can learn basic skills, and some stay so long they can get good enough to do a free solo on a pinnacle then tumble harmlessly into a cobalt sea.

Chiang Rai Province

3 The days of the Golden Triangle opium trade are over, but Chiang Rai still packs intrigue in the form of fresh-air fun, such as hiking and self-guided exploration. It is also a great destination for unique cultural experiences, ranging from a visit to an Akha village to a stay at the Yunnanese hamlet of Mae Salong. From the Mekong River to the mountains, Chiang Rai is arguably Thailand's most beautiful province, and if you've set your sights further, it's a convenient gateway to Myanmar and Laos.

DMITRY MOLCHANOV / SHUTTERSTOCK ©

Chiang Mai

4 The cultural capital of the north, Chiang Mai is beloved by culture geeks, temple-spotters and families. The old city is jam-packed with temples born during the time of the once-independent Lanna kingdom. The winding side-roads are best explored on bicycle while the scenic countryside boasts jungle treks. Cooking schools teach visitors the art of Thai food and the city enjoys fantastic dining thanks to imports such as Japanese sushi and Burmese curries, plus homegrown northern specialities and vegetarian fare. The surrounding areas are rich with traditional handicraft outlets.

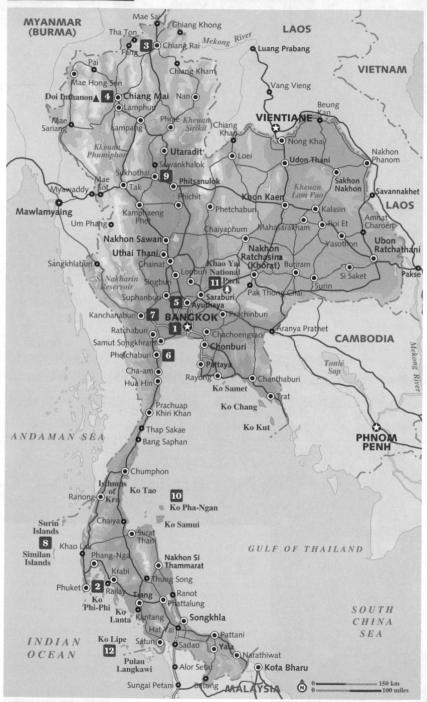

Best on Film

How to Win at Checkers (Every Time) (2015) Based on a short story by Rattawut Lapcharoensap, 11-year-old Oat deals with the military draft of his gay older brother.

Tom-Yum-Goong (2005) Tony Jaa, the Jackie Chan of Thailand, stars in the most successful Thai film ever released in the US.

Last Life in the Universe (2003) A lonely love story that established Thai new wave cinema.

Best in Print

Very Thai (2013) Philip Cornwel-Smith's photos and essays on Thailand's quirks.

A Kingdom in Crisis (2014) Andrew MacGregor Marshall's work on Thailand's Struggle for Democracy in the Twenty-First Century is banned in Thailand, so read it before you go.

Bangkok Days (2010) Lawrence Osborne gives a witty and insightful account of living in Bangkok.

Ayuthaya

5 A once vibrant, glittering capital packed with hundreds of temples, Ayuthaya today only hints at its erstwhile glory. Cycle around the brick-and-stucco ruins, which form part of a Unesco World Heritage Site, and try to imagine how the city must have looked in its prime, when it greeted merchants from around the globe. On the outskirts of the city sit several more attractions, including an enormous handicraft centre and the most eclectic royal palace you will ever see.

Phetchaburi

6 A delightful mix of culture and nature combine in this provincial capital, a close and quiet alternative to the hectic streets of Bangkok. Explore an antique hilltop palace, sacred cave shrines and bustling temples. Wander the old shophouse neighbourhood filled with do-it-yourself businesses run by Thai aunties and grannies. Then head off to the wilds of Kaeng Krachan National Park to spot wild gibbons and exotic birds.

Kanchanaburi

7 Once you've explored this western province's wartime past – the infamous Bridge Over the River Kwai is here – get ready to walk on the wild side in Kanchanaburi, where dragon-scaled limestone mountains gaze down upon dense jungle. Activities from ziplining to kayaking and elephant encounters are all on offer at this popular adventure-traveller hub. Trek past silvery waterfalls and rushing rivers in search of gibbons and some of Thailand's last

When to Go

HIGH SEASON (Nov–Mar) A cool and dry season follows the monsoons.

SHOULDER (Apr–Jun & Sep–Oct) Generally hot and dry.

LOW SEASON (Jul–Aug) Monsoon season ranges from afternoon showers to major flooding.

tigers, then spend the night at a homestay organised through an ethnic group.

Surin & Similan Islands Marine National Parks

8 The world-renowned dive sites off the Surin and Similan Islands have anchored Thailand as a global diving destination.

Sà·nùk

Thais place high value on sà·nùk, which means 'fun'. It is often regarded as a necessary underpinning of anything worth doing. Even work should have an element of sà·nùk, otherwise it automatically becomes drudgery.

Loi Krathong

Also known as Yi Peng, this lunar holiday is celebrated along the Mae Ping with the launching of small lotus-shaped boats honouring the spirit of the river, and the release of thousands of illuminated lanterns into the night sky.

Food & Drink

Ðôm yam Lemon grass, kaffir lime leaf and lime juice give this soup its characteristic tang; fresh chillies or oily chilli paste provide its legendary sting.

Gaang mát·sà·màn 'Muslim curry' is a rich coconut-milk-based dish, which, unlike most Thai curries, gets much of its flavour from dried spices.

Kà·nŏm bêuang The old-school version of these taco-like snacks comes in two varieties: sweet and savoury.

Máh hór With origins in the palace, this appetiser combines chunks of mandarin orange or pineapple and a sweet/savoury/peppery topping that includes pork, chicken, peanuts, sugar, peppercorns and coriander root.

Nám pŏn·lá·mái Fruit juices, often served with a touch of sugar and salt and a whole lot of ice.

Nám prík A spicy chilli dip.

þlah hâang Dried fish combined with sugar and crispy deep-fried shallots, served on top of slices of watermelon.

Roh·đee This crispy fried pancake, drizzled with condensed milk and sugar, is the perfect street dessert.

Yam þlah dùk foo Fried shredded catfish, chilli and peanuts served with a sweet/tart mango dressing.

Live-aboard trips set out from Khao Lak, allowing for more time hanging out with aquatic residents including manta rays and whale sharks. The islands are an attraction in their own right, with jungle-filled interiors and smooth white beaches surrounded by coral reefs.

Sukhothai Historical Park

9 Step back some 800 years at one of Thailand's most impressive historical parks. Exploring the ruins of this former capital by bicycle is a leisurely way to see the crumbling temples, graceful Buddha statues and fish-filled ponds.

Worthwhile museums and some of the country's best-value accommodation round out the package. Sukhothai rarely feels crowded, but for something off the beaten track head to nearby Si Satchanalai-Chaliang Historical Park, where you might be the only one scaling an ancient stairway.

Ko Pha-Ngan

10 Famous for its techno-fuelled Full Moon Parties, Ko Pha-Ngan has long since graduated from a sleepy island to an Asian Ibiza. Comfort seekers have an alternative to Ko Samui thanks to a bevy of boutique bungalows. On the northern and eastern coasts, ascetic hammock hangers can still find castaway bliss. Just offshore is one of the gulf's best dive sites, while much of the island's interior is unspoiled forest.

Khao Yai National Park

11 Wildlife sightings are at the mercy of chance, but your odds are excellent at this vast Unesco-listed reserve, just a few hours out of Bangkok. And even if you don't meet many big animals, the orchids, birds, waterfalls and sense of adventure that inevitably arises when hiking in the jungle guarantee a good day. Khao Yai's mix of scenery and accessibility is hard to beat.

Ko Lipe

12 Where creature comforts meet laid-back island escape, Ko Lipe takes work to reach but the ever-growing devotees agree that it's worth it. The days of desertion are over, especially in the high season when the island is overrun, but it is still a wonderful blend of white-sand beaches, authentic Thai kitchens, groovy guesthouses, boutique resorts and nature adventures in the national park. The diving and living are best here during the early wet season (mid-April to June). But keep that hush-hush.

12

Getting Around

Hopping around Thailand by air continues to be affordable.

The bus network in Thailand is prolific and reliable. The train system connects the four corners of the country and is a scenic, if slow, alternative to buses.

Hiring a motorcycle in Thailand is relatively easy and a great way to independently tour the countryside.

Cars, 4WDs and vans can be hired in most major cities and airports from local companies as well as all the international chains.

CAPITAL
Lhasa

POPULATION
3.2 million

AREA
2.5 million sq km

OFFICIAL LANGUAGE
Tibetan, Mandarin

Mt Kailash

Tibet

Tibet offers fabulous monasteries, breathtaking high-altitude treks, stunning views of the world's highest mountains and some of the most likeable people you will ever meet.

For many people, the highlights of Tibet will be of a spiritual nature: magnificent monasteries, prayer halls of chanting monks, and remote cliffside retreats. Tibet's pilgrims – from local grandmothers murmuring mantras in temples heavy with the aroma of juniper incense and yak butter, to hard-core visitors walking or prostrating themselves around Mt Kailash – are an essential part of this appeal. Tibet has a level of devotion and faith that seems to belong to an earlier, almost medieval age. It's fascinating, inspiring and endlessly photogenic.

Whatever your interests, your lasting memories of Tibet might be the bottle of Lhasa Beer you shared in a teahouse, the yak-butter tea offered by a monk or the picnic enjoyed with a herding family on a lakeshore. Always ready with a smile, and with great openness of heart despite decades of hardship, it is the people that truly make travelling in Tibet such a profound joy.

Top Experiences

Mt Kailash

1 Worshipped by more than a billion Buddhists and Hindus, Asia's most sacred mountain rises from the Barkha plain like a giant four-sided 6714m *chörten* (Buddhist stupa). Throw in the stunning nearby Lake Manasarovar and a basin that forms the source of four of Asia's greatest rivers, and who's to say this place really isn't the centre of the world? Travelling here, to one of the world's most beautiful and remote corners, brings an added bonus: the three-day pilgrim path around the mountain erases the sins of a lifetime.

Barkhor Circuit

2 You never know quite what you're going to find when you join the centrifugal tide of Tibetans circling the Jokhang Temple on the Barkhor Circuit. Pilgrims and prostrators from across Tibet, stalls selling prayer wheels and turquoise, Muslim traders, Khampa nomads in shaggy cloaks, women from Amdo sporting 108 braids, *thangka* (religious painting) artists and Chinese military patrols are all par for the course. It's a fascinating microcosm of Tibet and a place you'll want to come back to again and again.

Potala Palace

3 There are moments in travel that will long stay with you, and your first view of Lhasa's iconic Potala Palace is one such moment. A visit to the former home of the Dalai Lamas is a spiralling descent past gold-tombed chapels, opulent reception rooms and huge prayer halls into the bowels of a medieval castle. It's nothing less than the concentrated spiritual and material wealth of a nation. Finish by joining the pilgrims on a walking *kora* (pilgrim circuit) of the entire grounds.

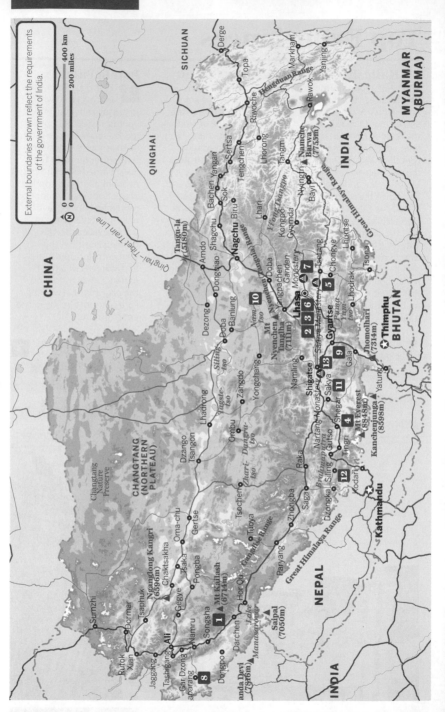

External boundaries shown reflect the requirements of the government of India.

400 km
200 miles

Views of Mt Everest

4 Don't tell the Nepal Tourism Board, but Tibet has easily the best views of the world's most famous mountain from its northern base camp, which was was first used by the 1924 British Everest expedition. While two-week-long trekking routes on the Nepal side offer only fleeting glimpses of the peak, the view of Mt Everest's unobstructed north face framed in the prayer flags of Rongphu Monastery or from a base-camp tent will stop you in your tracks. Now you can even drive all the way here on a paved road. Bring a sleeping bag, some headache tablets and a prayer for clear skies.

Samye Monastery

5 Tibet's first monastery is a heavily symbolic collection of chapels, *chörtens* and shrines arranged around a medieval Tibetan-, Chinese- and Indian-style temple. The 1200-year-old site is where Guru Rinpoche battled demons to introduce Buddhism to Tibet and where the future course of Tibetan Buddhism was sealed in a great debate. The dreamy location on the desert-like banks of the Yarlung Tsangpo is just superb and there are some fine hiking excursions nearby. It's also the end point of Tibet's most popular trekking route.

Jokhang Temple

6 The atmosphere of hushed awe is what hits you first as you inch through the dark, medieval passageways of the Jokhang, Lhasa's most sacred temple. Queues of wide-eyed pilgrims

Best in Print

The Open Road: The Global Journey of the Fourteenth Dalai Lama (Pico Iyer) An engaging look at the warmth and contradictions of the 14th Dalai Lama.

Fire Under the Snow (Palden Gyatso) A moving autobiography of a Buddhist monk imprisoned in Tibet for 33 years.

Tears of Blood (Mary Craig) A riveting and distressing account of the Tibetan experience since the Chinese takeover.

Best on Film

Kundun (1997) Martin Scorsese's beautifully shot depiction of the life of the Dalai Lama.

Vajra Sky Over Tibet (2006) John Bush's Buddhist-inspired cinematic pilgrimage to the principal sites of central Tibet.

Seven Years in Tibet (1997) Yes, it's a bit silly, and, no, it's not the greatest film but it's still great inspiration before a trip to Tibet.

When to Go

HIGH SEASON (May–Sep)
The warmest weather makes travel, trekking and transport easiest.

SHOULDER (Apr & Oct–Nov)
The slightly colder weather means fewer travellers and a better choice of vehicles.

LOW SEASON (Dec–Feb)
Very few people visit Tibet in winter, so you'll have key attractions largely to yourself.

shuffle up and down the stairways, past medieval doorways and millennium-old murals, pausing briefly to stare in awe at golden Buddhas or to top up the hundreds of butter lamps that flicker in the gloom. It's the beating spiritual heart of Tibet. Welcome to the 14th century.

Politics & Permits

There's no getting away from politics here. Whether you see Tibet as an oppressed, occupied nation or an underdeveloped province of China, the normal rules of Chinese travel simply don't apply. Government travel restrictions require foreign travellers to pre-arrange a tour with a guide and transportation for their time in Tibet, making independent travel off-limits. On the plus side, new airports, boutique hotels and paved roads offer a level of comfort unheard of just a few years ago, so if the rigours of Tibet travel have deterred you in the past, now might be the time to reconsider.

Getting Around

Trains are great for getting to and from Tibet but of limited use within the country.

By car is the only way to travel around Tibet at the moment, since foreign travellers have to hire private transport as part of their obligatory tour.

Buses have lots of services, but foreigners are currently not allowed to take buses or shared taxis.

Ganden–Samye Trek

7 Tibet is one of those places you really should experience away from the tour-group circuit, at the pace of one foot in front of the other. This classic four-day trek between two of Tibet's most important monasteries takes you past herders' camps, high alpine lakes and a Guru Rinpoche hermitage, as well as over two 5000m-plus passes. Hire a horse or yaks for a wonderful wilderness trek, with just the marmots for company. May to October are the best months.

Guge Kingdom

8 The spectacular lost kingdom of Guge at Tsaparang is quite unlike anything you'll see in central Tibet; it feels more like Ladakh than Lhasa. There comes a point as you are lowering yourself down a hidden sandstone staircase or crawling through an interconnected cave complex that you can't help but stop and think: 'This is incredible!' What's really amazing is that you'll likely have the half-forgotten ruins to yourself. Rank this as one of Asia's great travel secrets.

Gyantse Kumbum

9 The giant *chörten* at Gyantse ranks as as one of Tibet's great artistic treasures and is unique in the Himalayas. As you spiral around and up the snail-shell-shaped building, you pass dozens of dim alcoves full of serene painted Buddhas and bloodthirsty Tantric demons. It's an unrivalled collection of early Tibetan art. Finally, you pop out onto the golden eaves, underneath all-seeing eyes, for fabulous views of Gyantse fort and old town. An added bonus is the attached monastery complex.

Nam-tso

10 Just a few hours north of Lhasa, spectacular Nam-tso epitomises the dramatic but harsh scenery of northern Tibet. This deep-blue salt lake is fringed by prayer-flag-draped hills, craggy cliffs and nesting migratory birds, all framed by a horizon of snow-capped 7000m peaks. The scenery is breathtaking, but so is the altitude: 1100m higher than Lhasa. Walking the *kora* path at dusk with a band of pilgrims is superb. It's cold, increasingly

developed and devastatingly beautiful. To see the lake at its best, try to minimise your time in the ugly and poorly planned accommodation centre.

Sakya Monastery

11 A 25km detour off the main Friendship Hwy takes you to this brooding, massive, grey-walled fortress-like building. In a land of magnificent monasteries, Sakya's main prayer halls are among the most impressive, lined with towering buddhas, tree-trunk-sized pillars, sacred relics, a three-storey library that ranks as Tibet's finest, and a fine kora path. Pilgrims come here from across western Tibet, adding to the colour and charm. Give yourself most of the day to explore monastery complexes on both side of the river.

Peiku-tso & Shishapangma

12 Tibet is not short on spectacular, remote, turquoise-blue lakes. Of these, none boasts a grander backdrop than little-visited Peiku-tso near Tibet's southern border with Nepal. Rising south of the huge lake is a wall of glaciers and Himalayan peaks crowned by 8027m giant Shishapangma, the tallest mountain wholly inside Tibet. The lake makes a great picnic or camping spot en route to western Tibet or to the planned new border crossing with Nepal's Langtang region at Kyirong. Tibet doesn't get wilder or more scenic than this hidden corner.

Friendship Highway: Lhasa to Kathmandu

13 Organising a 4WD trip across Tibet is the quintessential traveller experience. You'll have to overcome the labyrinthine permit system and brave some terrible toilets, but the rewards are ample: the visually stunning Tibetan countryside, little-visited monasteries such as Nartang, a satisfying sense of journey and a giant slice of adventure. At the end of the trip you finally drop like a stone off the plateau into the green, oxygen-rich and curry-scented jungles bordering Nepal. Figure on at least a week; the hard core can cycle the route.

Travel Tips

Try to patronise as many small Tibetan businesses as possible to ensure that money stays in local hands. If you want to donate to a monastery, leave your offering on the altar.

Losar (New Year Festival)

The first week of the first lunar month (February) is a particularly colourful time to be in Lhasa. During Losar, Tibetan opera is performed and the streets are thronged with Tibetans in their finest cloaks.

CAPITAL
Dili

POPULATION
1.3 million

AREA
14,874 sq km

OFFICIAL LANGUAGES
Tetum, Portuguese

View from Christo Rei

Timor-Leste

With mountains to climb, untouched reefs to dive, and ancient traditions that have survived the ravages of war, Asia's newest country offers some of the world's last great off-the-beaten-track adventures.

Dili is a city on the rise. It is a good place to recharge batteries (literally) between jaunts into the districts. Get an insight into Timor-Leste's dark history in Dili's museums, then venture out of the capital for wild cultural experiences.

Head for the hills to hike to jungle caves, wander misty mountain village markets, and sip local coffee on the terrace of a grand Portuguese *pousada* (hotel). Bump along diabolical roads in search of your own perfect beach, stopping for photos of the stunning seascapes as you grip the rugged cliffs along the north coast road. Strap on a snorkel and marvel at the pristine reefs that fringe the north coast and Atauro Island, or delve deeper with Dili-based dive companies, which have spent the past decade discovering world-class sites. Trailblaze your way through this amazing country, and find out what everyone else has been missing.

Top Experiences

Maubisse

1 Waking up in chilly Maubisse, 70km from Dili, and watching clouds rising to uncover the village below, is a highlight of travelling in Timor-Leste.

Cristo Rei

2 Around 7km east of Dili centre is the hard-to-miss Cristo Rei, a popular morning and evening exercise spot for locals and expats. As you climb the well-marked path up to the statue (590 steps), look for a little path after the last of 14 grottoes. It leads down to often-deserted Jesus Backside Beach. On the way back to town,

stop at the popular Areia Branca, a restaurant-lined beach perfect for taking in the sunset with a beer in your hand and your toes in the sand.

Atauro Island

3 After busy Dili, Atauro Island seems positively deserted. Located 30km from Dili over a section of sea that is 3km deep in parts, it was used as a jail by both the Portuguese and Indonesian governments. Atauro's sandy beaches are gateways to broad fringing reefs and there's great snorkelling all around the island. Walking trails lead through traditional villages,

savannah, and remnants of tropical forest.

When to Go

 HIGH SEASON
(May–Nov)

 LOW SEASON
(Dec–Apr)

Food & Drink

Dili's fresh fish, lobster and prawns will make your mouth water. Sure, there are a few fine-dining places that serve up amazing seafood in Asian, Portuguese and African flavours, but nothing beats the nightly charcoal-grill food stalls on the Av de Portugal beachfront, where the seafood is simple and fresh.

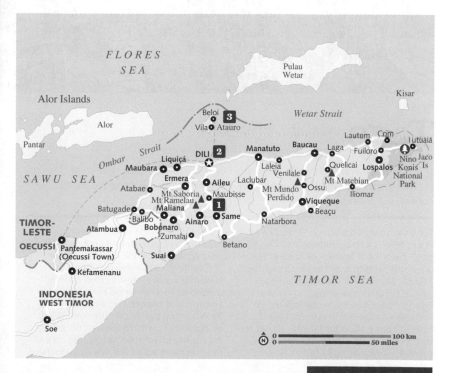

Lomé central market

Togo

With its palm-fringed beaches, verdant hills and savannah, and approximately 40 ethnic groups, Togo crams a whole lot of Africa into a surprisingly small space.

For those fond of travelling off the beaten track, Togo is a rewarding destination. Its great diversity of landscapes ranges from lakes and palm-fringed beaches along the Atlantic coastline to the rolling forested hills in the centre; heading further north, lush forest is replaced by the light-green and yellowy tinges of savannah. It's an excellent playground for hikers – there's no better ecofriendly way to experience the country's savage beauty than on foot.

Another highlight is Togo's melting-pot culture. The compounds of Koutammakou are a reminder that the country's diverse population didn't always get along, but nowadays voodoo, Muslim, Christian and traditional festivals crowd the calendar and are often colourful celebrations for all. The cherry on top is Lomé, the low-key yet elegant capital, with its large avenues, tasty restaurants and throbbing nightlife – not to mention the splendid beaches on its doorstep.

Top Experiences

Lomé

1 Soak up the mellow vibes, jazz clubs and vibrant markets of the coastal capital. Once dubbed 'the pearl of West Africa', Lomé retains a charm and nonchalance that is unique among West African capitals, with unexpected treats and gems: from maquis food to palm-fringed boulevards.

Kpalimé

2 Kpalimé is only 120km from Lomé, but feels like another world. Hidden among the forested hills of the cocoa and coffee region, it offers some of Togo's best scenery and hiking and a lovely waterfall. It's also a busy place thanks to its proximity to the Ghanaian border and an important and lively market.

Lac Togo

3 Relax on the shores of this serene inland lagoon stretching all the way from Lomé to Aného. Swimming in the lake – which is croc- and bug-free – is blissful. It's also a good place to find a pirogue (traditional canoe) to Togoville, which was the former seat of the Mlapa dynasty and Togo's historical centre of voodoo.

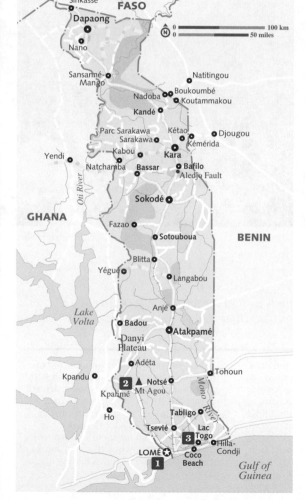

Food & Drink

Pâte A dough-like substance made of corn, manioc or yam.

Fufu Yam with vegetables and meat.

Aloko Snack of fried plantain.

Koliko Yam chips.

Wagasi A mild cheese fried in hot spice.

When to Go

HIGH SEASON (Nov–Feb)

SHOULDER (Mar–Apr)

LOW SEASON (May–Oct)

CAPITAL
Nuku'alofa

POPULATION
106,500

AREA
747 sq km

OFFICIAL LANGUAGES
Tongan, English

Coral reef off Tongatapu

Tonga

Think lush, reef-fringed islands with sandy foreshores that virtually glow in the tropical sunshine. In Tonga you'll need to slow down to the pace of local island life.

Kiss the tourist hype goodbye – and say a warm *Malo e lelei* (hello!) to the Kingdom of Tonga. Resolutely sidestepping flashy resorts and packaged cruise-ship schtick, Tonga is unpolished, gritty and unfailingly authentic. Life here ticks along at its own informal pace: church-life is all pervasive, chickens and pigs have right-of-way, and there's nothing that can't wait until tomorrow. You don't have to seek out a cultural experience in Tonga – it's all around you!

Once you've shifted down into 'Tonga time', you'll find these islands awash with gorgeous beaches, low-key resorts, myriad snorkelling, diving, yachting and kayaking opportunities, hiking trails, rugged coastlines and affable locals (especially the kids!). Gear up for some active pursuits, then wind down with a cool sunset drink to the sound of waves folding over the reef.

Top Experiences

Hiking in 'Eua

1 Rugged 'Eua is an unassuming slice of natural paradise. Known as 'the forgotten island', it's geologically the oldest island in Tonga (40 million years old!) and one of the oldest in the Pacific. There are steep hilly areas, cliff-top lookouts, hidden caves, sinkholes, a limestone arch and jungle-like rainforest to explore. With its own species of plants, trees and the endemic koki (red shining parrot), 'Eua has a growing awareness of itself as a unique ecotourism destination.

Ha'amonga 'a Maui Trilithon

2 The South Pacific's equivalent of Stonehenge, the Ha'amonga

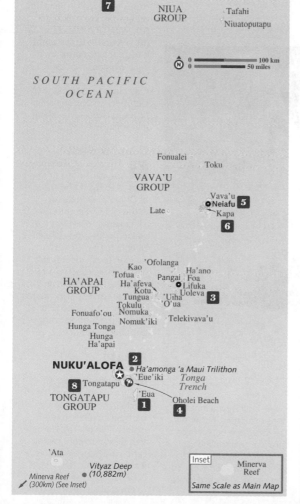

Niuafo'ou **7**

NIUA GROUP

Tafahi

Niuatoputapu

N 0 ━━━━ 100 km
   0 ━━━━ 50 miles

SOUTH PACIFIC OCEAN

Fonualei

Toku

VAVA'U GROUP

Vava'u
Neiafu **5**
Kapa

Late

6

Kao 'Ofolanga
Tofua Ha'ano
HA'APAI Pangai Foa
GROUP Ha'afeva Lifuka
Kotu Uoleva **3**
Tungua 'Uiha
Tokulu 'O'ua
Fonuafo'ou Nomuka
Hunga Tonga Nomuk'iki Telekivava'u
Hunga
Ha'apai

2
NUKU'ALOFA Ha'amonga 'a Maui Trilithon
'Eue'iki Tonga
8 Tongatapu Trench
TONGATAPU 'Eua
GROUP **1** Oholei Beach
4

'Ata

Vityaz Deep
Minerva Reef • (10,882m)
(300km) (See Inset)

Inset | Minerva Reef
Same Scale as Main Map

Food & Drink

Being an island nation, Tonga is surrounded by the sea and Tongans will eat just about anything that comes out of it, from shellfish to shark to sea turtle. 'Ota'ika (raw fish in coconut milk) is an island-wide favourite. Pigs are prized possessions and roam the streets along with chickens. For feasts, smaller pigs are roasted on spits over open fires while bigger ones are cooked in umu (underground ovens).

Root crops such as taro, sweet potato and yams take precedence over other vegetables, which are much harder to produce. Tropical fruits are everywhere, with coconuts, bananas and papaya available year-round. Summer is the season for mango, pineapple, passionfruit and guava.

Tongan men drink kava, made from pepper roots, as a social activity.

When to Go

 HIGH SEASON (Jun-Oct)

 SHOULDER (Apr-May & Nov)

 LOW SEASON (Dec-Mar)

Fakaleiti

One of the most distinctive features of Tongan culture are *faka-leiti,* a modern continuation of an ancient Polynesian tradition, known as *fa'afafine* in Samoa and *mahu* or *rae rae* in French Polynesia.

The term *fakaleiti* is made up of the prefix *faka-* (in the manner of) and *-leiti* from the English word *lady.* Traditionally, if a Tongan woman had too many sons and not enough daughters she would need one of the sons to assist with 'women's work' such as cooking and house cleaning. This child would then be brought up as a daughter. These days, becoming a *fakaleiti* can also be a lifestyle choice. There is little stigma attached to *fakaleiti,* and they mix easily with the rest of society, often being admired for their style. On Tongatapu, the Tonga Leitis' Association (TLA) is an active group – members prefer to call themselves simply *leiti* (ladies).

LIMEWAVE - INSPIRATION TO EXPLORATION / GETTY IMAGES ©

'a Maui (Maui's Burden) trilithon near Niutoua, is one of ancient Polynesia's most intriguing monuments. Archaeologists and oral history credit its construction to Tu'itatui, the 11th Tu'i Tonga. Others say it was built by ancient Chinese explorers. Either way, the structure consists of three large coralline stones, each weighing about 40 tonnes, arranged into a tri-lithic gate. Mortised joints ensure the top stone won't fall off, as per Stonehenge!

Uoleva

3 Robbed a bank? On the run from tax-evasion allegations back home? The island of Uoleva, just south of Lifuka, is the perfect place to hide. Un-inhabited apart from the accommodation providers (there are no villages here), it offers up an uncluttered, unharried South Pacific experience with little to do other than swim, snorkel, fish, read and relax (and fig-ure out your escape route if the cops do come knock-ing). Whales swim close to the shore here during the migration season (June to October) – you can some-times see them breaching just offshore.

Feast & Show

4 The pinnacle of Ton-gatapu entertainment is this fab feast and show at Oholei Beach Resort in the island's southeast. The evening starts with a welcome on sandy Oholei Beach, followed by a hefty Tongan feast, including suckling pig roasted on a spit. The highlight is an tra-ditional dance performance in the open-topped Hina Cave, culminating in an eye-popping fire dance.

Neiafu

5 Strung around the fringes of Port of Refuge, surely one of the world's most photogenic harbours, Neiafu has a dishevelled charm. Home to a slew of decent restau-rants and bars along the waterfront, the town itself is ramshackle and rakish (a great place to drink rum

Getting Around

Flying is by far the easiest, fastest and most comfortable way to get around Tonga.

Interisland ferries sail between Tongatapu and the main island groups and are a good way to get around if you have plenty of time.

Buses run on Tongatapu, and in a more limited capacity on Vava'u and its causeway-linked islands.

and write a novel). Over winter (June to October), with visiting yachties and a steady flow of visitors winging in, the ol' town buzzes with accents and activity.

Swallows' Cave, Kapa

6 Kapa island's big-ticket attraction is Swallows' Cave, cutting into a cliff on the west side of the island. It's actually inhabited by hundreds of swiftlets (not swallows) and you can swim right into it. The water is gin-clear, with the floor of the cave 18m below the surface. A regular inclusion in day tours, the only access is by boat.

Niuafo'ou

7 Remote Niuafo'ou (Tin Can Island), about 100km west of

Niuatoputapu, looks like a huge doughnut floating in the ocean. But it's not fast food for giants – it's a collapsed volcanic cone (caldera), thought to have once topped 1300m in height. Today, the highest point on the caldera is 210m, and the lake it encloses is nearly 5km wide and 23m above sea level.

Ha'atafu Beach

8 On the sunset side of Tongatapu, Ha'atafu Beach is a sandy slice protected by a reef, where some of Tonga's best surf peels in (experienced surfers only need apply). There's sheltered swimming and snorkelling at high tide in the broad lagoon. If your timing is good (from June to November), you can sometimes spy whales cavorting beyond the reef.

MARTIN PROCHAZKACZ / SHUTTERSTOCK ©

6

CAPITAL
Port of Spain

POPULATION
1.2 million

AREA
5128 sq km

OFFICIAL LANGUAGE
English

Carnival, Trinidad

Trinidad & Tobago

Get ready for calypso, cricket and Carnival parties when you hit these twin Caribbean islands that are better known for birdwatching than beaches.

Trinidad and Tobago are an exercise in beautiful contradiction. In Trinidad, pristine mangrove swamps and rainforested hills sit side by side with smoke-belching oil refineries and ugly industrial estates. Tobago has everything you'd expect from a Caribbean island, with palm trees and white sand aplenty, yet it's relatively unchanged by the tourist industry. Combined, this twin-island republic offers unparalleled birdwatching; first-class diving; luxuriant

rainforests perfect for hiking, waterfall swimming and cycling; and electric nightlife, with the fabulous Carnival easily the biggest and best of the region's annual blowouts.

But don't expect anyone to hold your hand. The oil and gas industry leaves tourism low on the priority list, so it's up to you to take a deep breath, jump in and enjoy the mix.

Top Experiences

Port of Spain

1 Spreading back from the Gulf of Paria and cradled by the Northern Range foothills, Port of Spain is a mish-mash of the pretty and the gritty, with the green expanse of the central Queen's Park Savannah and a host of gorgeous fretworked buildings alongside a frenetic, gridlocked downtown area. This isn't a place that kowtows to the tourist dollar, and it's all the richer for it. During Carnival season, huge outdoor 'fetes' rock all corners, steel-pan music fills the air and the atmosphere is electric.

Maracas Bay

2 Maracas Bay is Trinidad's most popular beach. The wide, white-sand shore, dotted with palm trees contrasting against the backdrop of verdant mountains, remains an irresistible lure for both locals and travellers. Despite the curving headland, the sand is often pounded by waves that serve up good body-surfing. On weekends the beach can get pretty crowded, but during the week it can feel almost deserted.

Northern Range

3 Plum in the middle of the lush rainforest that smothers the Northern Range, Brasso Seco is a quiet little village that once made its living from growing cocoa and other crops. Today, it has reinvented itself as a low-key base for nature lovers in search of hiking, birdwatching, cocoa-cultivation tours or just a bit of insight into the slow, slow pace of life in rural Trinidad.

When to Go

 HIGH SEASON (Feb & Mar)

 SHOULDER (Jan, Apr-Jun & Oct-Dec)

 LOW SEASON (Jul-Sep)

Diving at Speyside

4 The small fishing village of Speyside fronts Tyrrel's Bay, and attracts divers and birders. It's the jumping-off point for excursions to uninhabited Little Tobago island, which is a bird sanctuary 2km offshore. Protected waters, high visibility, abundant coral and diverse marine life make for choice diving, and Speyside is home to some of the best scuba sites in the Caribbean. Several dive shops operate in the village and most visitors stay in diver-oriented hotels. Nondivers can take glass-bottom boat/snorkel tours to Little Tobago.

Asa Wright Nature Centre

5 A former cocoa and coffee plantation transformed into an 80-hectare nature reserve, this place blows the minds of birdwatchers. Even if you can't tell a parrot from a parakeet, it's still worthwhile as you can see a great number of colorful specimens from the veranda viewing gallery, as well as lizards and agouti. Located amid the rainforest of the Northern Range, the center has a lodge catering to birding tour groups and a series of hiking trails, open to day visitors via guided tours.

Pigeon Point

6 You have to pay to get access to Pigeon Point, the fine dining of Tobago's beaches, with landscaped grounds, bars, restaurants, toilets and showers spread along plenty of beachfront. The postcard-perfect, palm-fringed beach has powdery white sands and milky aqua water; around the head-

Getting Around

Twenty-minute flights link Trinidad with Tobago.

Fast catamaran ferries shuttle between Port of Spain on Trinidad and Scarborough on Tobago, though the ride can be rough.

Infrequent, air-conditioned buses travel around Trinidad from Port of Spain, and around Tobago from Scarborough, but are not very convenient for wider exploration.

PHBCZ / GETTY IMAGES ©

land, the choppy waters are perfect for windsurfing and kitesurfing.

Grand Riviere

7 The closest the northeast gets to a resort town, Grand Riviere is still a far cry from most Caribbean holiday spots. It's a quiet and peaceful place, rich in natural attractions, including a stunning beach where, between March and August, leatherback turtles lay their eggs; and the surrounding rainforest, which is studded with waterfalls and hiking trails and offers plenty of good birdwatching. A few small-scale hotels have sprung up to cater to lovers of the outdoors, and the village is a fantastic place to get away from it all.

Food & Drink

Callaloo The leaves of the dasheen tuber cooked up with pumpkin, okra and plenty of seasoning.

Carib and Stag The national beers – always served beastly cold.

Doubles Curried *channa* (chickpeas) in a soft-fried *bara* bread.

Roti A split-pea-infused flatbread wrapped around curried meat and vegetables.

Shark and bake Seasoned shark steaks, topped with salad and local sauces and served in a floaty fried bake.

5

VARC GUITARD / GETTY IMAGES ©

Calypso

A medium for political and social satire, calypso hearkens back to the days when African slaves – unable to talk when working – would sing in patois, sharing gossip and news while mocking their colonial masters. Today, risqué lyrics, pointed social commentary and verbal wordplay are still the order of the day.

Mighty Sparrow, long acknowledged the king of calypso, has voiced popular concerns and social consciousness since the 1950s, as did his contemporary, the late, great 'Grandmaster,' Lord Kitchener. Another famous calypsonian, David Rudder, helped revive the musical form in the mid-1980s by adding experimental rhythms, unearthing both the cultural importance and flexibility of calypso. Others to look out for include the distinctive voice of Shadow, and the inimitable Calypso Rose, whose collaboration LP with Manu Chao has brought worldwide success.

CAPITAL	Tunis
POPULATION	11.1 million
AREA	163,610 sq km
OFFICIAL LANGUAGE	Arabic

Fatimid fortifications, Mahdia

Tunisia

From the sands of the Sahara to golden-hued beaches, tangled Tunis alleys to scattered Roman ruins, Tunisia is a country that intrigues and charms at every turn. However, be aware that travel to Tunisia is risky and not recommended.

It may be but a slim wedge of North Africa's vast horizontal expanse, but Tunisia has enough history and diverse natural beauty to pack a country many times its size.

With a balmy, sand-fringed Mediterranean coast, scented with jasmine and sea breezes, and where the fish on your plate is always fresh, Tunisia is all about sun, sand and sea. But beyond the beaches, it's a thrilling, underrated country where distinct cultures and incredible extremes of landscape – forested coastlines along the coast, Saharan sand seas in the south – exist alongside each other.

Sadly, there have been a number of terrorist attacks in Tunisia in recent years and most Western governments currently advise against travel to the country.

Snapshot

Tunis

1 Tunis is cosmopolitan, yet remains charmingly stuck in time. The new city, created by French colonials in the 19th century, is an orderly European grid, with wrought-iron balconies, and cafes bordering the boulevards. The 8th-century medina is the city's historic heart. Here there's a tangled maze of narrow streets with giant keyhole-shaped doors, artisans' workshops and swarming souqs.

Carthage

2 Carthage was a great ancient city, inspiring legend, poetry and envy. Built on a site of great natural beauty, the city boasted walls 34km in length, with houses running from the top of Byrsa Hill down to the waterfront. Sadly, not much is left, however the fragments that remain evoke an epic past of empire, siege and regeneration.

Mahdia

3 This peninsula town's centre has old-world charm thanks to its earlier inhabitants: Romans, Spaniards, Ottomans and Turks have all left their mark.

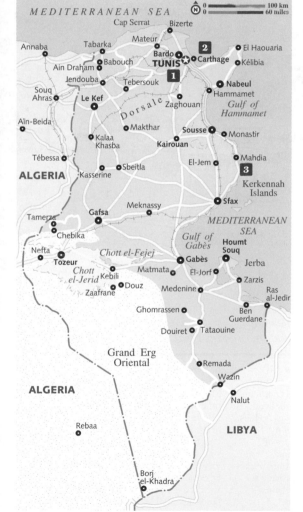

Food & Drink

Tunisians love spicy food, and it's almost impossible to encounter a meal that doesn't involve harissa, a fiery chilli paste. Fresh produce is plentiful and salads form part of most meals. The most popular are *salade tunisienne*, a tomato, onion and cucumber mix, topped with tuna.

Seasons

☀ MAR–OCT

⛅ NOV–FEB

Bosphorus River, İstanbul

Turkey

This richly historical land has some of the best cuisine you will ever taste, scenery from beaches to mountains and the great city of İstanbul.

A succession of historical figures and empires – including the Romans, Byzantines and Ottomans – have all left their mark on this former stopover along the Silk Road. From the ancient port city of Ephesus (Efes) to the soaring Byzantine dome of Aya Sofya, Turkey has more than its fair share of world-famous ruins and monuments.

Turkey's diverse landscapes, from Aegean olive groves to eastern steppe, provide a lyrical setting for its many great ruins. The country's most magical scenery is to be found in Asian Anatolia, where beautiful vistas are provided by the vertiginous Mediterranean coastline, Cappadocia's otherworldly 'fairy chimney' rock formations and wavy valleys, the alpine pastures of the Kaçkar Mountains, and golden beaches such as 18km-long Patara. Whether you settle down with a *çay* to enjoy the view across mountain-ringed Lake Eğirdir or explore the hilly hinterland on the southwest coast's many peninsulas, Turkey's landscape will leave a lasting impression.

CAPITAL
Ankara

POPULATION
89.3 million

AREA
783,562 sq km

OFFICIAL LANGUAGES
Turkish, Kurdish

Top Experiences

Cappadocia

1 Cappadocia's hard-set honeycomb landscape looks sculpted by a swarm of genius bees. The truth – the effects of erosion on rock formed of ash from megalithic volcanic eruptions – is only slightly less cool. Humans have also left their mark here, in the Byzantine frescoes in rock-cut churches and in the bowels of complex underground cities. These days, Cappadocia is all about good times: fine wine, local dishes and five-star caves; horse riding, valley hikes and hot-air ballooning. There's enough to keep you buzzing for days.

Aya Sofya

2 Even in mighty İstanbul, nothing beats the Aya Sofya, or Church of the Divine Wisdom, which was for centuries the greatest church in Christendom. Emperor Justinian had it built in the 6th century as part of his mission to restore the greatness of the Roman Empire; gazing up at the floating dome, it's hard to believe this fresco-covered marvel didn't single-handedly revive Rome's fortunes. Glittering mosaics depict biblical scenes and ancient figures such as Empress Zoe, one of only three standalone Byzantine empresses.

Ephesus

3 Undoubtedly the most famous of Turkey's countless ancient sites, and considered the best-preserved ruins in the Mediterranean, Ephesus (Efes) is a powerful tribute to Greek artistry and Roman architectural prowess. A stroll down the marble-coated Curetes Way provides myriad photo opportunities – not least the Library of Celsus with its two storeys of columns, and the Terrace Houses, their vivid frescoes and sophisticated mosaics giving insight into the daily lives of the city's elite. Much of the ancient port is yet to be unearthed.

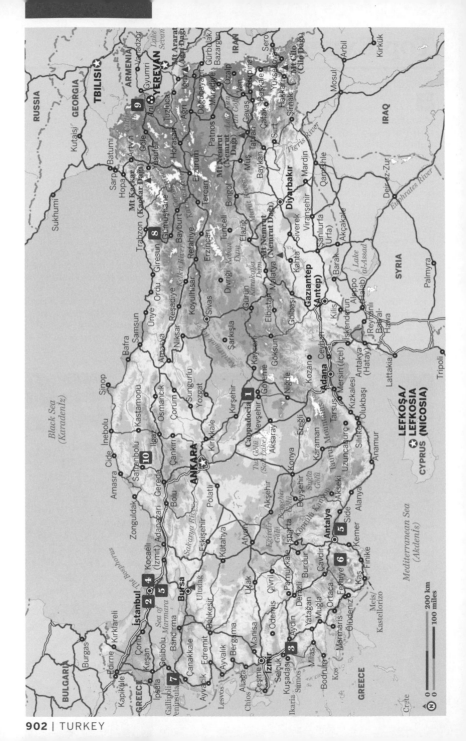

Best on Film

Mustang (2015) Turkish-French film about orphaned sisters in a remote village.

Innocence of Memories (2015) Documentary about Orhan Pamuk's Museum of Innocence.

Winter Sleep (2014) Poignant character study in snowy Anatolia.

The Cut (2014) Drama by Turkish-German director Fatih Akin, set during the Armenian tragedy of 1915.

Once Upon a Time in Anatolia (2011) Night-time search for a corpse on the steppe.

Best in Print

The Architect's Apprentice (Elif Şafak; 2013) The magical realist's tale of Ottoman architect Mimar Sinan.

A Strangeness in My Mind (Orhan Pamuk; 2014) Twentieth-century İstanbul through the eyes of an Anatolian street hawker.

Birds Without Wings (Louis de Bernières; 2004) *Captain Corelli's Mandolin* author covers the Turkish-Greek population exchange.

The Janissary Tree (Jason Goodwin; 2006) First in the Yashim series about a eunuch detective in 19th-century İstanbul.

Turkish Awakening (Alev Scott; 2014) Turkish-British writer's personal discovery of modern Turkey.

Portrait of a Turkish Family (Irfan Orga; 1950) Account of growing up in 20th-century İstanbul.

Crossing Between Continents

4 In İstanbul, you can board a commuter ferry and flit between Europe and Asia in under an hour. Every day, a flotilla takes locals up the Bosphorus and over the Sea of Marmara, sounding sonorous horns as it goes. Morning services share the waterways with diminutive fishing boats and massive container ships, all accompanied by flocks of shrieking seagulls. At sunset, the tapering minarets and Byzantine domes of the Old City are thrown into relief against a dusky pink sky – it's the city's most magical sight.

Hamams

5 At many hamams in Turkey, plenty of extras are on offer: bath treatments, facials, pedicures and so on. However, we recommend you stick with the tried and true hamam experience – a soak and a scrub followed by a good (and optional) pummelling. After this cleansing ritual and cultural experience, the world (and your body) will never feel quite the same again; do leave time to relax with a çay afterwards. For a truly memorable hamam, seek out a soak in Antalya's atmospheric old quarter or historic Sultanahmet, İstanbul.

Lycian Way

6 Acclaimed as one of the world's top 10 long-distance walks, the

When to Go

HIGH SEASON
(Jun–Aug)
Prices and temperatures are their highest.

SHOULDER
(May & Sep)
Warm spring and autumn temperatures, especially in the southwest.

LOW SEASON
(Oct–Apr)
High season in ski resorts; some accommodation in other tourist areas closes or offers discounts.

Culinary Exploration

The best thing about sampling Turkey's delicious specialities – ranging from meze on a Mediterranean harbour to a pension breakfast featuring ingredients fresh from the kitchen garden – is that they take you to the heart of Turkish culture. For the sociable and family orientated Turks, gathering together and eating well is a time-honoured ritual. So get stuck into olive-oil-lathered Aegean vegetables, spicy Anatolian kebaps and dishes from Turkey's many other corners – and as you drink a tulip-shaped glass of çay and contemplate some baklava for dessert, remember that eating is deepening your understanding of Turkey.

Getting Around

Turkey is a vast country and domestic flights are an affordable way of reducing travel time. More route choices if flying to/from İstanbul.

Buses are generally efficient and good value, with frequent services between the major cities and tourist spots. Often fewer services in winter.

Car is a great way to explore rural areas, with rental operators in cities and airports. Drive on the right. Petrol is expensive.

Regular ferry services cross the Sea of Marmara and link parts of the Aegean coast.

The growing network of high-speed train services offers rapid routes across Anatolia, for example between İstanbul and Ankara. The bus is often quicker than normal trains.

Lycian Way follows signposted paths for 500km between Fethiye and Antalya. This is the Teke Peninsula, once the stamping ground of the ancient and mysterious Lycian civilisation. The route leads through pine and cedar forests in the shadow of mountains rising almost 3000m, passing villages, stunning coastal views and an embarrassment of ruins at ancient cities such as Pınara, Xanthos, Letoön and Olympos. Walk it in sections (unless you have plenty of time and stamina).

Gallipoli Peninsula

7 The narrow stretch of land guarding the entrance to the much-contested Dardanelles is a beautiful area, where pine trees roll across hills above Eceabat's backpacker hang-outs and

Kilitbahir's castle. Touring the peaceful countryside is a poignant experience for many: memorials and cemeteries mark the spots where, a century ago, young men from far away fought and died in gruelling conditions. The passionate guides do a good job of evoking the futility and tragedy of the Gallipoli campaign, one of WWI's worst episodes.

Sumela Monastery

8 The improbable cliff-face location of Sumela Monastery is more than matched by the Black Sea hinterland's verdant scenery. The gently winding road to the Byzantine monastery twists past riverside fish restaurants, and your journey from nearby Trabzon may be pleasantly hindered by a herd of fat-tailed sheep en route to fresh pastures. The last

few kilometres afford tantalising glimpses across pine-covered valleys of Sumela's honey-coloured walls, and the final approach on foot leads up a forest path to the rock-cut retreat.

Ani

9 Ani is a truly exceptional site. Historically intriguing, culturally compelling and scenically magical, this ghost city floating in a sea of grass looks like a movie set. Lying in blissful isolation right at the Armenian border, the site exudes an eerie ambience. Before its decline following a Mongol sacking in 1236, Ani was a thriving city, a Silk Road entrepôt and capital of the Armenian kingdom from 961 to 1046. The ruins include several notable churches as well as a cathedral built between 987 and 1010.

Safranbolu

10 Listed for eternal preservation by Unesco in 1994, Safranbolu is Turkey's prime example of an Ottoman town brought back to life. Domestic tourists full of nostalgia descend here to stay in half-timbered houses that seem torn from the pages of a children's storybook. And the magic doesn't end there. Sweets and saffron vendors line the cobblestone alleyways, and artisans and cobblers ply their centuries-old trades beneath medieval mosques. When the summer storms light up the night sky, the fantasy is complete.

Meyhanes

Say *şerefe* (cheers) to Efes-drinking Turks in a *meyhane* (tavern). A raucous night mixing meze with drinks and live music is a time-honoured Turkish activity.

Health

The Turks say *'Afiyet olsun'* ('May it be good for your health') before starting to eat. After the meal, they say *'Elinize sağlık'* ('Health to your hands') to compliment the host on their cooking.

10

5

CAPITAL
Ashgabat

POPULATION
5.3 million

AREA
488,100 sq km

OFFICIAL LANGUAGE
Turkmen

Palace of Happiness, Ashgabat

Turkmenistan

Isolated Turkmenistan is one of the oddest corners of Central Asia yet boasts its own distinctive attractions.

By far the most mysterious and unexplored of Central Asia's s'stans, Turkmenistan became famous for the truly bizarre dictatorship of Saparmyrat Niyazov, who ruled as 'Turkmenbashi' ('leader of the Turkmen') until his death in 2006. Niyazov covered this little-known desert republic with golden statues of himself and grandiose monuments to the achievements of his 'golden age'. But the least-visited of Central Asia's countries is far more than the totalitarian theme park it's often portrayed as being – it is an ancient land of great spirituality, tradition and natural beauty.

The cities of Merv and Konye-Urgench inspire visions of caravans plodding along the ancient Silk Road, while the haunting beauty of the Karakum Desert is equally mesmerising. From underground lakes to dinosaur footprints, almost everything in Turkmenistan is unexpected. The full experience is ultimately about mingling with the warm and fascinating Turkmen people themselves, whose hospitality is the stuff of legend.

Top Experiences

Konye-Urgench

1 Turkmenistan's premier historical site is a Unesco World Heritage Site. Once the capital of the Khorezmshahs and a centre of the Muslim world in the 12th century, the city was pulverised by both Genghis Khan and Timur. The remains include royal mausoleums, Sufi shrines and a 14th-century minaret.

Darvaza Gas Craters

2 One of Turkmenistan's most unusual sights, the Darvaza Gas Craters are the result of Soviet-era gas exploration in the 1950s. Of the three craters, the fire crater is the most impressive, and it's best seen at night, when the blazing inferno can only be compared to the gates of hell.

Ashgabat

3 With its lavish marble palaces, gleaming gold domes and vast expanses of manicured parkland, the Turkmen capital Ashgabat ('the city of love' in Arabic) has reinvented itself as a showcase city for the newly independent republic and is one of Central Asia's strangest places. At its heart it's a surprisingly relaxed city, with a varied dining scene and no shortage of quirky sights.

When to Go

 HIGH SEASON
(Apr–Jun & Sep–Oct)

 SHOULDER
(Jul–Aug)

 LOW SEASON
(Nov–Mar)

Food & Drink

Shashlyk Ubiquitous kebabs of fresh or marinated meat, usually served with nan bread and vinegary onions.

Dograma Soup made from bread and pieces of boiled meat and onions.

Manty Steamed dumplings served with sour cream.

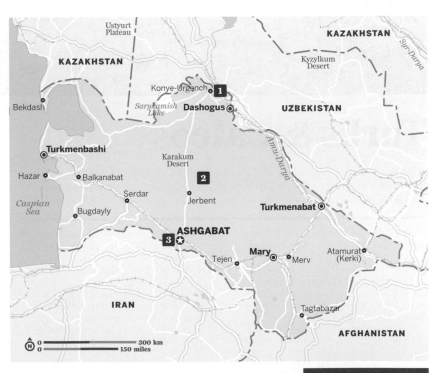

CAPITAL
Cockburn Town

POPULATION
51,430

AREA
948 sq km

OFFICIAL LANGUAGE
English

Cave at Mudjin Harbor

Turks & Caicos

With some of the whitest beaches, the clearest waters and the most varied marine life in the Caribbean, Turks & Caicos will thrill anyone who likes to spend time in or by the water.

Hiding at the southern tip of the Bahamian Archipelago, this string of islands elude most travellers' radars, yet boasts some of the world's most spectacular coral reefs, and has built itself into a true luxury tourism destination. The pace of life is easygoing, the local welcome genuine and the diving truly out of this world.

Providenciales is the bustling epicenter of all this, but beyond its endless beaches and world-class resorts, you'll find local festivals, jungle-wrapped ruins, perfect seaside bars and even traces of Europe's first discovery of the New World. Venture to the less-populated islands, and you'll be enchanted by colorful postcards of fading colonial glories, gobsmacked by the annual migration of thousands of humpback whales, spoiled with your pick of deserted beaches and all but forced to abandon the pace of modern life.

Top Experiences

Grace Bay Beach

1 Several miles long, this world-famous stretch of coast is powdered with icing-sugar white sand and close enough to the reef wall to see the Atlantic breakers. Though it's studded with hotels and resorts, its sheer size means that finding your own square of paradise is a snap.

Mudjin Harbor

2 Five miles west of Bambarra Beach, directly in front of Blue Horizon Resort, is Mudjin Harbor – the rocky shore rears up to form a bit of rare elevation. Walking along the clifftop you'll be surprised to see a staircase appear out of nowhere, leading into the earth. Take it down through the cave and emerge on a secluded cliff-lined beach – this is one of the best beach entrances anywhere in the Caribbean. Looking seaward you'll be entertained by the waves crashing into the offshore rocks in spectacular fashion.

Historic Cockburn Town

3 For a taste of the old Caribbean, look no further. Without knowing beforehand, you'd be hard pressed to guess that this sleepy place is the capital city of the Turks & Caicos. What it lacks in polish and sophistication it more than makes up for in rustic charm. The town itself comprises two parallel streets that are interconnected with narrow laneways. Brightly painted, colonial-era houses line the tiny streets and former salt-storage sheds hark back to a bygone era of

When to Go

 HIGH SEASON (Dec–Apr)

 SHOULDER (May)

 LOW SEASON (Jun–Nov)

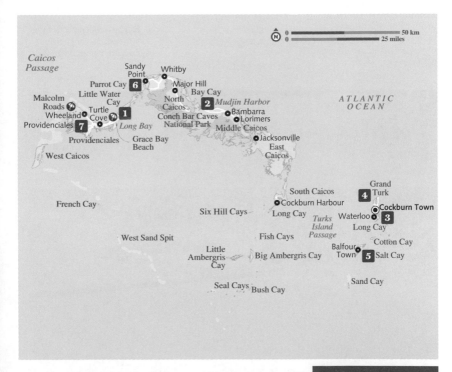

dusty roads and donkey-filled streets. It's hard not to be enchanted by the whitewashed stone walls, traditional streetlamps and creaking old buildings.

Grand Turk

4 Happily lacking the modern development that has enveloped Provo, Grand Turk is a step back in time. At just 6½ miles long, this dot amid the sea is a sparsely populated, brush-covered paradise. Where salt was once the main industry, tourism has taken over and you are blessed with a slew of charming guesthouses to choose from. Beaches rim the land and calm blue water invites you in for a refreshing swim. Diving is the main reason to come to Grand Turk – where the fish are plentiful and the reef pristine. Diving operators will take you snorkeling if you're not a diver, and run courses if you want to learn.

Salt Cay

5 If you can't quite envision what the Turks would have been like in the 19th century, take a trip to Salt Cay. Like stepping into a time machine, this picturesque island is the sort of hideaway that you search your whole life to discover. A few dusty roads interconnect the handful of structures, and donkeys wander aimlessly through the streets intermixed with friendly locals. While the land is quiet, the sea surrounding the island is awash with life. Turtles, eagle rays and the majestic humpback whale all frequent the waters.

Parrot Cay

6 For true indulgence, Parrot Cay is definitely the best hotel in the Turks & Caicos, and one of the very best in the Caribbean. On its own eponymous private island, Parrot Cay is part resort with its infinity

Getting Around

Air Turks & Caicos flies from Providenciales to Grand Turk, North Caicos, Middle Caicos, South Caicos and Salt Cay daily. It also flies from Grand Turk to Salt Cay daily.

TCI Ferry Service is a small passenger-ferry operation taking people from the Leeward Marina on Providenciales to North Caicos. A ferry runs biweekly trips from Grand Turk to Salt Cay.

Bicycles are complimentary for guests at many hotels or can be rented at concessions.

4

MIKOLAJN / GETTY IMAGES ©

pool, water sports, diving school and superb restaurants, and part spa, with a firm emphasis on healthy treatments, yoga and 'wellness.' Of course, if you need to ask about the price, you probably can't afford it, but if you're looking for a once-in-a-lifetime splurge or you happen to be a Wall Street banker, then this is the place for you.

Providenciales

7 Providenciales, or Provo as it's known locally, is the tourism capital of the Turks & Caicos. It's home to a busy international airport, some fairly rampant development and its crowning glory, miles of beautiful white-sand beaches along its northern coast. It's a great place for those wanting to enjoy cosmopolitan pursuits: you can shop in Provo's many malls, eat in its great restaurants and enjoy cocktails on the beach.

Food & Drink

Conch This grilled gastropod remains the dish of choice across the islands, and rigorous controls on the fishing industry mean that its numbers are not declining here.

Lobster Don't miss tasting the fresh lobster during your stay – traditionally served in a butter sauce with lime, it's the culinary highlight of the country.

Turk's Head The local beer is a great way to cool down in the height of the Caribbean afternoon.

3

DANITA DELIMONT / GETTY IMAGES ©

Whale Watching

The annual migration of 2500 to 7000 Atlantic humpback whales through the Columbus Passage, the deep-water channel separating the Caicos and Turks islands, is one of the Caribbean's great sights. Moving through the channel (also known as Turks Islands Passage) between January and March, with the most reliable sightings in February and March, the mighty creatures are on their way to their breeding grounds in Silver Bank in the Dominican Republic, and Mouchoir Bank in Turks & Caicos' southern waters. Scores of local boats take visitors close to the action. If you prefer terra firma, perhaps with a drink in hand, you can also watch from the shores of Grand Turk and Salt Cay, as they are close to the passage.

Funafuti Atoll

Tuvalu

Approaching Tuvalu by plane, after miles of rolling ocean, a dazzling smear of turquoise appears, ringed with coral and studded with palm-topped islets – a vulnerable Pacific paradise.

The landmass of Fongafale, Tuvalu's main island, is so startlingly narrow that as the plane nears the airstrip it seems as if it's about to tip into the ocean. In fact, the airstrip is something of a social hub: kids play ball games on the runway in the late afternoons, young men race up and down it on their motorcycles and, on steamy summer nights, whole families may drag their sleeping mats and pillows out to spend the night.

The major long-term ecological threat to Tuvalu comes from climate change and rising sea levels. As well as shoreline erosion, water bubbles up through the porous coral on which the islands are based, and causes widespread salt contamination of areas used to grow staple crops. If sea levels continue to rise as predicted, much of Tuvalu will be underwater, with the remnants above sea level rendered uninhabitable.

CAPITAL
Funafuti

POPULATION
10,950

AREA
26 sq km

OFFICIAL LANGUAGES
Tuvaluan, English

Top Experiences

Funafuti Conservation Area

1 Live out your desert-island fantasies on the palm-covered islets of the Funafuti Conservation Area. Boat trips here can be booked through the town council in Fongafale and might include some time on one or two of the islets and some snorkelling in the amazing underwater world.

Te Ano

2 While in Tuvalu, try to watch, or better still join in, a game of Tuvalu's unique sport, *te ano*. Almost completely incomprehensible to a first-timer, it's great fun and one of the few games that men and women play together. It's played with two balls made from pandanus leaves. A popular place for playing is the runway at Fongafale's airstrip!

Fongafale

3 Fongafale is Tuvalu's answer to a metropolis, the seat of government, and the largest islet in Funafuti Atoll. Wind down to match the island way of life, take a stroll around town or take in a performance of Tuvalu's national dance, *fatele*. There are also a handful of WWII relics here. Funafuti's must-sees include Funafala Islet, which is lined with talcum-powder beaches.

When to Go

HIGH SEASON
(May–Oct)

SHOULDER
(Nov–Feb)

LOW SEASON
(Feb–Apr)

Food & Drink

Staples of the Tuvaluan diet include coconut, seafood, taro and breadfruit. Most restaurants sell cheap, filling plates of Chinese-style food. Thursday to Saturday is party night on Fongafale, when the old timers go to 'twists' (discos) and the youngsters go 'clubbing'.

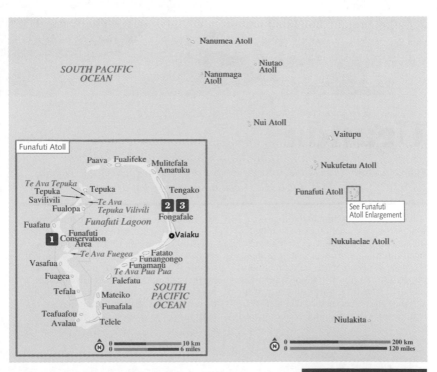

CAPITAL
Kampala

POPULATION
38.3 million

AREA
241,038 sq km

OFFICIAL LANGUAGE
English

Baby gorilla, Bwindi Impenetrable National Park

Uganda

Emerging from the shadows of its dark history, a new dawn of tourism has risen in Uganda, polishing a glint back into the 'pearl of Africa'.

Travellers are streaming in to explore what is basically the best of everything the continent has to offer. For a relatively small country, there's a lot that's big about the place. It's home to the tallest mountain range in Africa (Rwenzori Mountains), the source that feeds the world's longest river and the continent's largest lake. And with half the planet's remaining mountain goril-las residing here, as well as the Big Five to be ticked off, wildlife watching is huge.

While anti-gay sentiments have cast a shadow over an otherwise positive tourism picture, Uganda remains one of the safest destinations in Africa. Other than watching out for the odd hippo at your campsite, there's no more to worry about here than in most other countries.

Top Experiences

Bwindi Impenetrable National Park

1 Home to almost half of the world's surviving mountain gorillas, the World Heritage–listed Bwindi Impenetrable National Park is one of East Africa's most famous national parks. Set over 331 sq km of improbably steep mountain rainforest, the park is home to an estimated 340 gorillas: undoubtedly Uganda's biggest tourist drawcard.

Ssese Islands

2 If you're looking for a place to slow it right down, Ssese's lush archipelago of 84 islands along Lake Victoria's northwestern shore boasts some stunning white-sand beaches. There's not much to do other than grab a good book and relax. There are canoes for hire, but swimming is not advised due to the risks of bilharzia, and some outlying islands have the occasional hippo and crocodile. Most guesthouses on the beach have nightly bonfires, which is a great way to relax with a few drinks after enjoying one of Ssese's famous sunsets.

Murchison Falls

3 Uganda's largest national park is one of its very best; animals are in plentiful supply and the raging Murchison Falls, where the Victoria Nile crashes through the rock and descends dramatically towards Lake Albert, is an unforgettable sight. Despite a decimation of animal numbers during the war years, numbers have recovered well and you can expect to see elephants, Rothschild giraffes, lions,

When to Go

 HIGH SEASON (Jun–Aug)

 SHOULDER (Sep, Jan & Feb)

 LOW SEASON (Oct–Nov, Mar–May)

Ugandan kobs (antelopes), waterbucks, buffaloes, hippos and crocodiles these days, not to mention some 460 species of bird.

Lake Bunyonyi

4 Lake Bunyonyi ('place of many little birds') is undoubtedly the loveliest lake in Uganda. Its contorted shore encircles 29 islands, and the steep surrounding hillsides are intensively terraced, reminiscent of parts of Nepal. A magical place, especially with a morning mist rising off the placid waters, it has supplanted the Ssese Islands as the place for travellers to chill out on their way through Uganda, and has a selection of gorgeously remote and bucolic places to stay on distant islands, where you've only the birds for company. Best of all – unlike many lakes in East Africa – Bunyonyi is bilharzia, croc and hippo free, and so its crystal-clear waters are all yours to swim in. Bliss.

Kidepo Valley National Park

5 Offering some of the most stunning scenery of any protected area in Uganda, Kidepo Valley National Park is hidden away in a lost valley in the extreme northeast of Uganda. The rolling, short-grass savannah of the 1442-sq-km national park is ringed by mountains and cut by rocky ridges. Kidepo is most notable for harbouring a number of animals found nowhere else in Uganda, including cheetahs, bat-eared foxes, aardwolves, caracals, and greater and lesser kudus.

Rwenzori Mountains

6 The legendary, mist-covered Rwenzori Mountains were named a World Heritage Site by

Getting Around

Uganda is the land of shared minibuses (called taxis, or occasionally *matatus*), and there's never any shortage of these blue-and-white minivans. Standard buses and sometimes half-sized 'coasters' connect major towns on a daily basis.

Hiring a 4WD is the best way to get around Uganda. While some people hire a driver, it's not really necessary and is an added expense. There's a pretty good system of sealed roads between most towns in Uganda. As with other transport, avoid travelling at night due to higher risks of accidents and banditry.

4

Unesco in 1994 because of both their beauty and biodiversity. It's the tallest mountain range in Africa and several of the peaks are permanently covered by ice and glaciers. The range stretches for about 110km by 50km wide and is a haven for an extraordinary number of rare plants and animals, and new examples of both are still being discovered.

Nile River

7 The source of the Nile is one of the most spectacular whitewater rafting destinations in the world, and for many visitors to Uganda a rafting trip is the highlight of their visit. Here you can expect long, rollicking strings of Grade IV and V rapids, with plenty of thrills and spills. Most people who venture here are first-time rafters; it's the perfect opportunity to get out of your comfort zone.

Food & Drink

Local food is much the same as elsewhere in the region, except in Uganda *ugali* (a food staple usually made from maize flour) is called *posho*, and is far less popular than *matoke* (mashed plantains). Rice, cassava and potatoes are also common starches. One uniquely Ugandan food is the *rolex*, a chapatti rolled around an omelette.

Popular local beers include the light Bell Beer, infamous for its 'Great night, good morning!' ad-jingle and stronger Nile Special. Waragi (millet-based alcohol) is the local hard stuff and tastes a little like gin, so it's best with a splash of tonic.

ARIACNE VAN ZANDBERGEN / GETTY IMAGES ©

Wildlife

Uganda can't compete with Kenya or Tanzania for sheer density of wildlife, but with 500 species of mammal it has amazing diversity. You have a good chance of spotting all the classic African animals including lions, elephants, giraffes, leopards, hippos, zebras, hyenas, and up north, cheetahs and ostriches. Furthermore, with the opening of the Ziwa Rhino Sanctuary, the Big Five are all here again.

Its main attraction, however, are mountain gorillas. Uganda is home to more than half the world's mountain gorillas, and viewing them in their natural environment is one of the country's highlights. On top of this, Uganda has a good number of chimpanzees and there are several places where you can track them. With well over 1000 species recorded inside its small borders, Uganda is one of the best birdwatching destinations in the world.

CAPITAL
Kyiv

POPULATION
44.2 million

AREA
603,550 sq km

OFFICIAL LANGUAGE
Ukrainian

Chernogorsky Ridge, Carpathian Mountains

Ukraine

Big, diverse and largely undiscovered, Ukraine is one of Europe's last genuine travel frontiers, a nation rich in colourful tradition, warm-hearted people and off-the-map experiences.

Shaped like a broken heart, with the Dnipro River dividing it into two, this Slavic hinterland is a vast swath of sage-flavoured steppe filled with sunflowers and wild poppies. Blessed with a near-ideal climate and the richest soil in Europe, it's one huge garden of a country where flowers are blossoming, fruits are ripening and farmers markets sing hymns of abundance.

If only its history was as idyllic. Just over two decades into a very troubled independence, Ukraine is dogged by a conflict with neighbouring Russia that has left Crimea and a small chunk of its eastern territory off-limits to most travellers. But the country's main attractions, including eclectic and rebellious Kyiv, architecturally rich Lviv and flamboyant Odesa, are well away from the conflict zone. A long stretch of the Black Sea coast invites beach fun, while the Carpathians draw skiers in winter and cyclists in summer.

Top Experiences

Carpathian Landscapes

1 By and large Ukraine is as flat as a topographically challenged *blin* (pancake), which makes its bumpy bits all the more special. Ukraine's slice of the Carpathian arc barely reaches over 2000m, but its soothing wooded slopes, rough stony trails, flower-filled upland pastures and wide, snaking valleys make this prime hiking, biking and skiing territory. Needless to say, the Carpathians are home to Ukraine's highest peak, Mt Hoverla, a fairly easy trek from nearby villages, as well as several ski resorts.

Kyevo-Pecherska Lavra, Kyiv

2 Discover the mysteries of Eastern Orthodoxy and descend into catacombs to see mummies of much-revered saints on an excursion to the holiest of holies for all eastern Slavs. Founded as a cave monastery in 1051, the Lavra is packed with golden-domed churches, baroque edifices and orchards. Religious ceremonies take place in lavishly decorated, icon-filled interiors, accompanied by beautiful choir singing and attended by flocks of pilgrims and monks. Obscure museums in the grounds

When to Go

HIGH SEASON
(Jul & Aug)

SHOULDER
(May, Jun, Sep & Oct)

LOW SEASON
(Nov–Apr)

are dedicated to Scythian gold, micro-miniatures and decorative arts.

Kamyanets-Podilsky

3 Ringed by the dramatic gorge of the Smotrych River, there are few more eye-pleasing spots in Ukraine than this Podillyan town. A stroll from the new bridge takes you through

the cobbled quarters of this once-divided community, past beautifully renovated churches, crumbling palaces and forgotten pieces of the once beefy defences, to the town's impossibly picturesque fortress, surely one of the highlights of any visit to Ukraine.

Kolomyya

4 With its traveller-friendly places to stay, two fascinating museums and effortless access to the surrounding forested hills, Kolomyya is one of the best bases from which to scale the heights of the Carpathian Mountains. The town's central Pysanky Museum, housed in a giant Easter egg, is the obvious highlight, but aimless wandering also bears fruit in the shape of some twirling art nouveau architecture from the town's Austro-Hungarian days.

Danube Delta Biosphere Reserve

5 The Danube Delta Biosphere Reserve is Europe's largest wetland, located in a huge delta in Ukraine's far southwest where the Danube dumps its cargo of water and silt into the Black Sea. Few make the effort to reach this far-flung wedge of fertile Ukrainian territory, but those who do are rewarded with some astoundingly beautiful scenery, colourful bird life, memorable days out on the water and serene evenings in drowsy Vylkovo, fancifully nicknamed the 'Ukrainian Venice' thanks to its network of canals.

Odesa

6 By day Odesa's museums, parks, beaches and, of course, the celebrated Potemkin Steps provide ample distraction. At night the city really comes alive;

Getting Around

Trains are cheap but slow, especially the old-school overnight services. New express trains, which travel by day, connect Kyiv with Ukraine's biggest cities.

Buses are very cheap, with regular services, but sometimes packed to bursting and unbearably hot in summer.

Car is a good and fun way to travel around Ukraine, if you don't mind dire road quality.

6

RINA OLCHOVKA / SHUTTERSTOCK ©

with its imaginatively styled dance temples and chill-out zones just steps from the Black Sea, Arkadia Beach is the place to strut and pose until the wee summer hours. But Odesa also has a stomping alternative scene, with several hip venues serving up cool ales to the sound of guitar-happy indie bands and local DJs.

Lviv's Historical Centre

7 Lviv is the beating cultural heart of Ukraine, and the main square, pl Rynok, is the bustling heart of Lviv. Plonked in the middle is the huge *ratusha* (town hall), around which mill clutches of camera-toting tourists and quick-footed locals. The aroma of freshly milled

---

Food & Drink

Borsch The Ukrainian national soup, which is made with beetroot, pork fat and herbs. There's also an aromatic 'green' variety, based on sorrel.

Kasha Sometimes translated as 'porridge', but usually turns out to be buckwheat swimming in milk and served for breakfast.

Salo Basically raw pig fat, cut into slices and eaten with bread or added to soups and other dishes. Look out for the 'Ukrainian Snickers bar' – *salo* in chocolate.

Varenyky Similar to Polish *pierogi* – pasta pockets filled with everything from mashed potato to sour cherries.

Vodka Also known in Ukraine as *horilka*, it accompanies every celebration, red-letter day and get-together – in copious amounts.

---

coffee beans wafts across the square from the city's legendary coffee houses, and summer tables tumble out across the Habsburg-era cobbles as old Soviet-era trams rumble past.

Sofiyivka Park, Uman

8 Forget boxes of chocolates, bouquets of roses or even diamond rings – how about wowing your loved one with a gift measuring 150 hectares, complete with grottoes, water features and an entire town's worth of architectural follies? That was the grandiose way one 18th-century Polish magnate chose to express adoration for his wife, Sofia, and the legacy of his devotion is this amazing landscaped park intended to resemble the countryside of Sofia's native land. Her response? An affair with his son.

Searching for Lost Ancestors

Brought to the reading public's attention by Jonathan Safran Foer's 2002 novel *Everything is Illuminated*, for the last two decades countless descendents of Ukrainians, Jews, Germans and Poles who left the region in the 19th and 20th centuries have been returning to Ukraine to research their family history. However, as Foer discovers, this is not always an easy task! The secret of finding records, locations and survivors is to do your research before you leave home and hire a reliable guide (especially if you don't speak the language and/or are not familiar with the culture/history/geography of Ukraine).

CAPITAL
Abu Dhabi

POPULATION
9.5 million

AREA
83,600 sq km

OFFICIAL LANGUAGE
Arabic

Burj Khalifa and cityscape, Dubai

United Arab Emirates

Beyond the glitter of Dubai, the sci-fi-esque city of iconic skyscrapers, palm-shaped islands, city-sized malls, indoor ski slopes and palatial beach resorts awaits a diverse mosaic of six more emirates, each with its own allure.

An hour's drive south, oil-rich Abu Dhabi, the UAE capital, is positioning itself as a hub of culture, sport and leisure. Beyond looms the vast Al Gharbia region, which is dominated by the northern reaches of the Rub' Al Khali desert. Its magical silence is interrupted only by the whisper of shifting dunes rolling towards Saudi Arabia.

North of Dubai, Sharjah does art and heritage best, while tiny Ajman and Umm Al Quwain provide glimpses of life in the pre-oil days, and Ras Al Khaimah snuggles against the mighty Hajar Mountains. For the best swimming and diving, though, head across the range to Fujairah to frolic in the clear waters of the Gulf of Oman.

Top Experiences

Dubai

1 Dubai has a stirring alchemy of profound traditions and ambitious futuristic vision. With space-age skyscrapers sprouting across an endless desert hemmed in by a coastline etched with palm-shaped archipelagos, the city is a 21st-century Middle Eastern Shangri-la powered by unflinching ambition and can-do spirit. The motto: if you can think of it, it shall be done. The world's tallest building? Check. Skiing in the desert? Check. Islands shaped like the entire world? Check. Dubai is an exciting place to visit, with lovely beaches, sophisticated restaurants and bars, world-class shopping, ultra-luxe hotels, and awe-inspiring architecture, including the Burj Khalifa, the world's tallest building.

Sheikh Zayed Grand Mosque, Abu Dhabi

2 Rising majestically from beautifully manicured gardens and visible from each of the bridges joining Abu Dhabi Island to the mainland, the Sheikh Zayed Grand Mosque represents an impressive welcome to the city. More than 80 marble domes dance on its roofline, which is held aloft by over 1000 pillars and punctuated by four 107m-high minarets. The interior is a made-to-impress mix of marble, gold, semi-precious stones, crystals and ceramics. It's home to the world's largest Persian carpet (which took 2000 craftsmen two years to complete) and seven massive gold-plated crystal chandeliers.

When to Go

 HIGH SEASON
(Nov–Mar)

 SHOULDER
(Apr–May & Oct)

 LOW SEASON
(Jun–Sep)

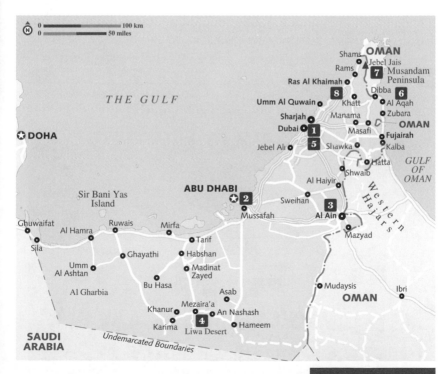

Al Ain Oasis

3 Lose yourself in the labyrinth of Al Ain's shady date-palm oases. Eight gates lead into the great date plantations of this famous oasis, with some 150,000 trees of around 100 varieties fed by a 3000-year-old *falaj* natural irrigation system lacing the grounds. Al Ain's famous camel market is a wonderful immersion in traditional Arabic culture. All sorts of camels are holed up in pens, from wobbly legged babies that might grow up to be racers to imposing studs kept for breeding. The intense haggling is fun to watch.

Liwa Oasis

4 Wonder at the spectacle of undulating sand dunes shimmering in shades from apricot to cinnamon on the edge of the Rub' al-Khali (Empty Quarter). It truly lives up to its name: the odd roaming camel or small verdant oasis magnifies just how magnificent this endless landscape is. Once you visit, you'll understand why the Liwa Oasis has a special place in the hearts of nationals, who come here to get back to their roots, relax and just take in the arid splendour of this glorious landscape.

Dubai Mall

5 With around 1200 stores, Dubai Mall isn't merely the world's largest shopping mall, it's a small city, with a giant ice rink and aquarium, a dinosaur skeleton, indoor theme parks as well as 150 food outlets. There's a strong European-label presence, along with branches of the French Galeries Lafayette department store, the British

Getting Around

A growing fleet of public buses makes inter-emirate travel increasingly convenient.

Having your own wheels is a great way to see the UAE. For off-road driving, you need a 4WD.

Taxis are cheap, metered and ubiquitous and given the dearth of public transportation in some emirates. Most drivers can also be hired by the hour.

Hamley's toy store and the first Bloomingdale's outside the US.

Al Aqah

6 In Fujairah, Al Aqah is known for having the eastern coast's best beaches, which are flanked by high-end hotels. This is prime snorkelling and diving territory, and even beginners can have a satisfying experience thanks to Snoopy Island, named by some clever soul who thought the shape of this rocky outcrop about 100m offshore resembled the Peanuts cartoon character sleeping atop his doghouse. Unfortunately, the 2008–09 red tide killed off much of the coral, but the waters here still teem with all sorts of colourful critters including, if you're lucky, green sea turtles and

(harmless) black-tip reef sharks.

Jebel Jais

7 Take the spectacular drive (almost) to the top of Jebel Jais, the UAE's highest mountain, in Ras Al Khaimah. At 1934m, Jebel Jais is occasionally dusted with snow. Since 2015 a mountain road has corkscrewed almost to the top, delivering great visual drama of artistically eroded cliffs, deep canyons and warped escarpments around every bend.

Jazirat Al Hamra Fishing Village

8 For an authentic glimpse of the pre-oil era, poke around this deliciously spooky ghost town, one of the oldest and best preserved coastal villages in the UAE. First settled in the 14th century, its people subsisted mostly on fishing and pearling until they suddenly picked up and left in 1968. A stroll among this cluster of coral stone houses, wind towers, mosques, schools and shops is at its most atmospheric at sundown.

Food & Drink

Balaleet Vermicelli blends with sugar syrup, saffron, rosewater and sauteed onions in this rich breakfast staple.

Fareed Mutton-flavoured broth with bread; popular at Ramadan.

Hareis Ground wheat and lamb slow cooked until creamy (a bit like porridge); sometimes called the 'national dish'.

Khuzi Stuffed whole roasted lamb on a bed of spiced rice.

Madrooba Salt-cured fish (*maleh*) or chicken mixed with raw bread dough until thick.

Makbous A casserole of spice-laced rice and boiled meat (usually lamb) or fish garnished with nuts, raisins and fried onions.

SANCHAI KUMAR / SHUTTERSTOCK ©

Camel Racing

See the 'ships of the desert' running like mad around a camel race track at the Al Wathba Race Track, 45km southeast of Abu Dhabi. Sporting colourful nose bags and matching blankets, the camels are the stars of the show. Over 100 animals participate in a typical race, each outfitted with 'robo-jockeys' since the use of child jockeys was outlawed in 2005. Races are great fun, even just to watch the enthusiasm of the owners who drive alongside the track cheering their beloved animals along and giving commands by remote.

CAPITAL
Washington, DC

POPULATION
323 million

AREA
9.8 million sq km

OFFICIAL LANGUAGE
English

Brooklyn Bridge, New York City

United States of America

The USA is home to such diverse cities as Los Angeles, Chicago, Miami and New York City – each a brimming metropolis whose name alone conjures a million different notions of culture, cuisine and entertainment.

Look more closely, and the American quilt unfurls in all its surprising variety: the eclectic music scene of Austin, the easygoing charms of antebellum Savannah, the eco-consciousness of free-spirited Portland, the magnificent waterfront of San Francisco and the captivating French Quarter of jazz-loving New Orleans.

The great American experience is about so many things: bluegrass and Hollywood, tradition and rule-breaking, restaurant-loving cities and big open skies. This is a country where four million miles of highways lead past deserts, below towering mountains, through redwood forests and across wheat fields that roll off toward the horizon.

Top Experiences

New York City

1 Home to striving artists, hedge fund moguls and immigrants from every corner of the globe, New York City is constantly reinventing itself. It remains one of the world centers of fashion, theater, food, music, publishing, advertising and finance. A staggering number of museums, parks and ethnic neighborhoods are scattered through the five boroughs. Do as every New Yorker does: hit the streets. Every block reflects the character and history of this dizzying kaleidoscope, and on even a short walk you can cross continents.

New Orleans

2 The things that make life worth living – eating, drinking and the making of merriment – are the air that New Orleans breathes. Caribbean-colonial architecture, Creole cuisine and a riotous air of celebration seem more alluring than ever in the Big Easy. Nights out are spent catching Dixieland jazz, blues and rock amid bouncing live-music joints, and the city's riotous annual fests (Mardi Gras, Jazz Fest) are famous the world over. 'Nola' is a food-loving town that celebrates its myriad culinary influences. Feast on lip-smacking jambalaya, soft-shelled crab and Louisiana *cochon* (pulled pork) before hitting the bar scene on Frenchman St.

Route 66

3 This ribbon of concrete was the USA's original road trip, connecting Chicago with Los Angeles in 1926. You'll find neon signs, motor courts, pie-filled diners and drive-in theaters along the way. The route was bypassed by I-40 in 1984, but many original sites remain and tracing Route 66 today is a journey through small-town America. Whether you do the whole length or just a stretch, you'll come face to face with classic, nostalgic Americana.

5

YUNSUN_KIM / SHUTTERSTOCK ©

Grand Canyon

4 You've seen it on film, and heard about it from all and sundry who've made the trip. Is it worth the hype? The answer is a resounding yes. The Grand Canyon is vast and nearly incomprehensible in age – it took 6 million years for the canyon to form and some rocks exposed along its walls are 2 billion years old. Peer over the edge and you'll confront the great power and mystery of this earth we live on. Once you see it, no other natural phenomenon quite compares.

JAY YUAN / SHUTTERSTOCK ©

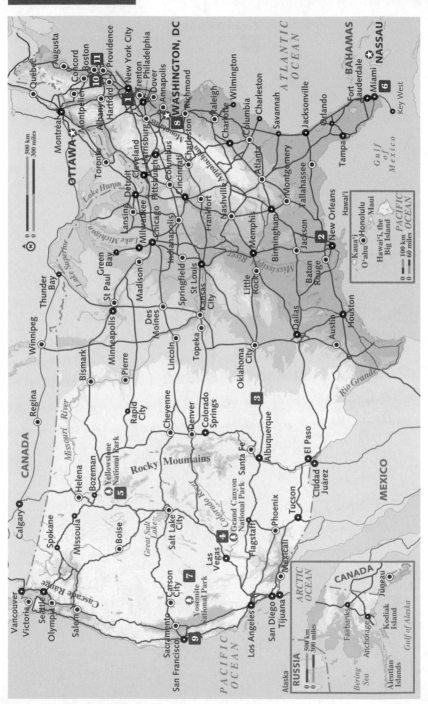

Best on Film

Singin' in the Rain (1952) Among the best in the era of musicals, with an exuberant Gene Kelly and a timeless score.

Annie Hall (1977) Woody Allen's brilliant romantic comedy, with New York City playing a starring role.

North by Northwest (1959) Alfred Hitchcock thriller with Cary Grant on the run across America.

Godfather (1972–90) Famed trilogy that looks at American society through immigrants and organized crime.

Best in Print

On the Road (1957) Jack Kerouac on post-WWII America.

The Great Gatsby (1925) F Scott Fitzgerald's powerful Jazz Age novel.

Beloved (1987) Toni Morrison's searing Pulitzer-prize-winning novel set during the post–Civil War years.

Huckleberry Finn (1884) Mark Twain's moving tale of journey and self-discovery.

Yellowstone National Park

5 Stunning natural beauty, amazing geology and some of the best wildlife watching in North America: these are just a few reasons why Yellowstone has such star power among the world's national parks. Divided into five distinct regions, this place is huge – almost 3500 sq miles – and you could spend many days exploring the park's wonders.

Highlights include massive geysers, waterfalls, fossil forests, rugged mountains, scenic overlooks and gurgling mud pools – with some 1100 miles of hiking trails providing the best way to take it all in.

Miami

6 How does one city get so lucky? Most content themselves with one or two attributes, but Miami seems to have it all. Beyond the stunning beaches and Art Deco Historic District, there's culture at every turn. In cigar-filled dance halls, Havana expats dance to son and boleros, in exclusive nightclubs stiletto-heeled, fiery-eyed Brazilian models shake to Latin hip-hop, and in the park old men clack dominoes. To top it off, street vendors and restaurants dish out flavors from the Caribbean, Cuba, Argentina and Spain.

Sierra Nevada

7 An outdoor adventurer's wonderland, the Sierra Nevada is a year-round pageant of snow sports, white-water rafting, hiking, cycling and rock climbing. With fierce granite mountains standing

When to Go

HIGH SEASON
(Jun–Aug)
Warm days across the country bring the busiest season.

SHOULDER
(Apr, May & Oct)
Spring flowers; fiery autumn colors in many parts.

LOW SEASON
(Nov–Mar)
Snowfall in the north, and heavier rains in some regions.

watch over high-altitude lakes, the eastern spine of California is a formidable but exquisite topographical barrier enclosing magnificent natural landscapes. In the majestic national parks of Yosemite and Sequoia & Kings Canyon, visitors will be humbled by the groves of solemn giant sequoias,

Native Americans

There are more than three million Native Americans from 500 tribes, speaking some 175 languages and residing in every region of the United States.

Hawaii

It's easy to see why Hawaii has become synonymous with holiday paradise. With sugary beaches, crystal waterfall pools and volcanoes it couldn't be more worth the trip.

Food & Drink

Americans have rich variety in their cuisine, based on the bounty of the continent: drawing on the seafood of the North Atlantic, Gulf of Mexico and Pacific Ocean; the fertility of Midwest farmlands; and vast western ranchlands. Some of the treats a visitor might encounter:

Buffalo wings Deep-fried chicken wings glazed with a buttery hot sauce and served with blue cheese dressing; originated in Buffalo, NY.

California roll Fusion sushi made with avocado, crabmeat and cucumbers wrapped in vinegared rice and nori (dried seaweed).

Clam chowder Potato-based soup full of clams, vegetables and sometimes bacon, thickened with milk.

Doughnuts Not just for police officers, seemingly everyone loves doughnuts. Look for gourmet varieties.

Tacos A handheld favorite all across the US. Some of the best are served off street carts and food trucks.

Fried chicken With famed spots in the South, including Prince's Hot Chicken in Nashville and Willie Mae's in New Orleans.

Reuben sandwich Sandwich of corned beef, Swiss cheese and sauerkraut on rye bread.

ancient rock formations and valleys, and the ever-present opportunity to see bears and other wildlife.

Washington, DC

8 The USA's capital teems with iconic monuments, vast museums and the corridors of power where visionaries and demagogues roam. The National Mall – nearly 2 miles long and lined with iconic monuments and hallowed marble buildings – is the epicenter of Washington, DC's political and cultural life. For exploring American history, there's no better place to ruminate, whether tracing your hand along the Vietnam War Memorial or ascending the steps of Lincoln Memorial, where Martin Luther King Jr gave his famous 'I Have a Dream' speech.

San Francisco

9 Grab your coat and a handful of glitter, and enter the land of fog and fabulousness. So long, inhibitions; hello, San Francisco. Amid the clatter of old-fashioned trams and thick fog that sweeps in by night, the diverse hill and valley neighborhoods of San Francisco invite long days of wandering, with colorful Victorian architecture, great indie shops and world-class restaurants. Round a corner to waterfront views and you'll be hooked. If you can tear yourself away, the lush vineyards of Napa, Sonoma and the Russian River Valley lie just north.

New England in Fall

10 It's a major event, one approaching epic proportions in New England: watching the leaves change color. You can do it just about anywhere – all you need is one brilliant tree. But if you're like most people, you'll want lots of trees. From the Litchfield Hills in Connecticut and the Berkshires in Massachusetts to the Green Mountains in Vermont, entire hillsides blaze in brilliant crimsons, oranges and yellows. Covered bridges and white-steeple churches with abundant maple trees put Vermont and New Hampshire at the forefront of leaf-peeping heaven.

Boston

11 You can hardly walk a step of the cobblestone streets in Boston without running into some historic site. The Freedom Trail winds its way around the city, connecting sites from the city's revolutionary history; there are also centuries-old pubs, the esteemed Harvard Univer-

sity and America's oldest baseball park. After all that history, Cape Cod is the

perfect place to cool off on dune-backed beaches and slurp down raw oysters.

Getting Around

 When time is tight, book a flight. The domestic air system is extensive and reliable.

 To save money, travel by bus, particularly between major towns and cities.

 For maximum flexibility and convenience, and to explore rural America and its wide-open spaces, a car is essential.

 Trains are rarely the cheapest, timeliest or most convenient option, but they turn the journey into a relaxing, social and scenic all-American experience.

Carnaval, Montevideo

CAPITAL	Montevideo
POPULATION	3.3 million
AREA	176,215 sq km
OFFICIAL LANGUAGE	Spanish

Uruguay

Uruguay is a backpacker's dream. Travelers come for the wild, surf-pounded beaches, for celeb-spotting at Punta and the history-soaked smugglers' port of Colonia.

Wedged like a grape between Brazil's gargantuan thumb and Argentina's long forefinger, Uruguay has always been something of an underdog. Yet after two centuries living in the shadow of its neighbors, South America's smallest country is finally getting a little well-deserved recognition. Progressive, stable, safe and culturally sophisticated, Uruguay offers visitors opportunities to experience everyday 'not made for tourists' moments, whether caught in a cow-and-gaucho traffic jam on a dirt road to nowhere or strolling with *mate*-toting locals along Montevideo's beachfront.

Short-term visitors will find plenty to keep them busy in cosmopolitan Montevideo, picturesque Colonia and party-till-you-drop Punta del Este. But it pays to dig deeper. Go wildlife watching along the coast, hot-spring-hopping up the Río Uruguay, or horseback riding under the big sky of Uruguay's interior, where vast fields spread out like oceans.

Top Experiences

Montevideo's Carnaval

1 If you thought Brazil was South America's only Carnaval capital, think again! Montevideanos cut loose in a big way every February, with music and dance filling the air for a solid month. Not to be missed is the early February Desfile de las Llamadas, a two-night parade of *comparsas* (neighborhood Carnaval societies) through the streets of Palermo and Barrio Sur districts. Neighborhood rivalries play themselves out as wave after wave of dancers whirl to the electri-fying rhythms of traditional Afro-Uruguayan candombe drumming.

Punta del Diablo

2 Once a sleepy fishing village, Punta del Diablo has long since become a prime summer getaway for Uruguayans and Argentines, and the epicenter of Uruguay's backpacker beach scene. Waves of uncontrolled development have pushed further inland and along the coast in recent years, but the stunning shoreline and laid-back lifestyle still exert their age-old appeal.

When to Go

 HIGH SEASON (Nov–Feb)

 SHOULDER (Mar–May, Sep & Oct)

 LOW SEASON (Jun–Aug)

Thermal Baths around Salto

3 A whole slew of hot springs bubbles up around Salto. Termas San Nicanor, surrounded by a pastoral landscape of cows, fields and water vaguely reminiscent of a Flemish painting, is the most tranquil of Salto's hot-springs

resorts. It has two gigantic outdoor thermal pools, a restaurant, and accommodations for every budget. Termas de Daymán, about 8km south of Salto, is a heavily developed Disneyland of thermal baths complete with kids' water park. Termas de Arapey, about 90km northeast of Salto, is Uruguay's oldest hot-springs resort and offers multiple pools surrounded by gardens, fountains and paths to the Río Arapey Grande.

Cabo Polonio

4 Northeast of La Paloma, Cabo Polonio is one of Uruguay's wildest areas and home to its second-biggest sea-lion colony, near a tiny fishing village nestled in sand dunes on a windswept point crowned by a lonely lighthouse. In 2009 the region was declared a national park. Despite a growing influx of tourists, Cabo Polonio remains one of Uruguay's most rustic coastal villages.

Punta del Este

5 OK, here's the plan: tan it, wax it, buff it at the gym, then plonk it on the beach at 'Punta.' Once you're done here, go out and shake it at one of the town's clubs. Punta del Este – with its many beaches, elegant seaside homes, yacht harbor, high-rise apartment buildings, pricey hotels and glitzy restaurants – is one of South America's most glamorous resorts, popular with Argentines and Brazilians. Celebrity watchers have a full-time job here. Punta is teeming with big names, and local gossip-mongers keep regular tabs on who's been sighted where.

Getting Around

Buses are comfortable, fares are reasonable and distances are short.

Uruguayan drivers are extremely considerate, and even bustling Montevideo is quite sedate compared with cities such as Buenos Aires.

Taxis are metered; between 10pm and 6am, and on Sundays and holidays, fares are 20% higher.

4

Colonia del Sacramento

6 On the east bank of the Río de la Plata, 180km west of Montevideo, but only 50km from Buenos Aires by ferry, Colonia is an irresistibly picturesque town enshrined as a Unesco World Heritage Site. Its Barrio Histórico, an irregular colonial-era nucleus of narrow cobbled streets, occupies a small peninsula jutting into the river. Pretty rows of sycamores offer protection from the summer heat, and the riverfront is a venue for spectacular sunsets (it's a Uruguayan custom to applaud the setting sun).

Food & Drink

Asado Uruguay's national gastronomic obsession, a mixed grill cooked over a wood fire, featuring various cuts of beef and pork, chorizo, morcilla (blood sausage) and more.

Buñuelos de Algas Savory seaweed fritters, a specialty along the coast of Rocha.

Chajá A terrifyingly sweet concoction of sponge cake, meringue, cream and fruit, invented in Paysandú.

Chivito A cholesterol bomb of a steak sandwich piled high with bacon, ham, fried or boiled egg, cheese, lettuce, tomato, olives, pickles, peppers and mayonnaise.

Medio y medio A refreshing blend of half white wine, half sparkling wine, with ties to Montevideo's historic Café Roldós.

Ñoquis The same plump potato dumplings the Italians call gnocchi, traditionally served on the 29th of the month.

Tacuarembó

7 In the rolling hills along the Cuchilla de Haedo, Tacuarembó is gaucho (cowboy) country. Not your 'we pose for pesos' types, but your real-deal 'we tuck our baggy pants into our boots and slap on a beret just to go to the local store' crew. It's also the alleged birthplace of tango legend Carlos Gardel.

LUCOP / GETTY IMAGES ©

Oxo Cubes

In 1865 the Liebig Extract of Meat Company located its pioneer South American plant near the river town of Fray Bentos. It soon became Uruguay's most important industrial complex. British-run El Anglo took over operations in the 1920s and by WWII the factory employed 4000 people.

Looking at the abandoned factory today, you'd never guess that its signature product, the Oxo beef cube, once touched millions of lives on every continent. Oxo cubes sustained WWI soldiers in the trenches, Jules Verne sang their praises in his book *Around the Moon*, they went with Scott to Antarctica and with Hillary to Everest. More than 25,000 people from over 60 countries worked here, and at its peak the factory exported nearly 150 different products, using every part of the cow except its moo.

Enshrined as a Unesco World Heritage Site in 2015, the former factory is now a museum – the Museo de la Revolución Industrial. Dozens of colorful displays, ranging from the humorous to the poignant, bring the factory's history vividly to life: a giant cattle scale where school groups are invited to weigh themselves; and the old company office upstairs, left exactly as it was when the factory closed in 1979.

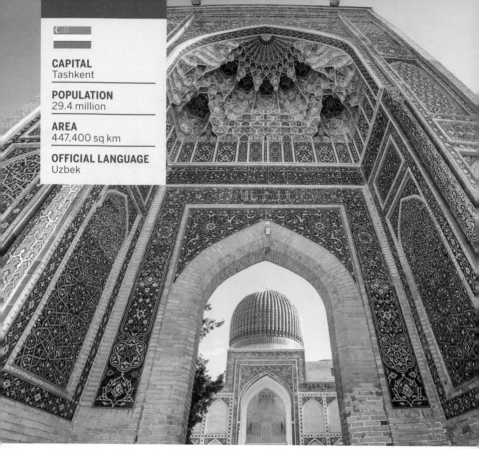

CAPITAL
Tashkent

POPULATION
29.4 million

AREA
447,400 sq km

OFFICIAL LANGUAGE
Uzbek

Gur-E-Amir, Samarkand

Uzbekistan

A Silk Road destination of the highest order, Uzbekistan is a centre of culture, trade and architecture that has drawn travellers for centuries.

The region's cradle of culture for more than two millennia, Uzbekistan is the proud home to a spellbinding arsenal of architecture and ancient cities, all deeply infused with the bloody, fascinating history of the Silk Road. In terms of sights alone, Uzbekistan is Central Asia's biggest draw and most impressive showstopper.

Samarkand, Bukhara and Khiva never fail to impress visitors with their fabulous mosques, medressas and mausoleums, while its more eccentric attractions, such as the fast disappearing Aral Sea, the fortresses of desperately remote Karakalpakstan, its boom town capital Tashkent and the ecotourism opportunities of the Nuratau Mountains, mean that even the most diverse tastes can be catered for.

Despite being a harshly governed police state, Uzbekistan remains an extremely friendly country where hospitality remains an essential element of daily life and you'll be made to feel genuinely welcome by the people you meet.

Top Experiences

Samarkand

1 Although already an important oasis town, it was Timur (Tamerlane) who turned Samarkand into one of the most beautiful cities in Asia. Visit Timur's own mausoleum, the Gur-E-Amir, followed by the spectacular street of tombs of his Timurid relatives. For epic and audacious architecture it's hard to beat the crumbling remains of the epic Bibi Khanum Mosque, built for Timur's wife. Then throw in the breathtaking Registan Square (one of the Islamic world's greatest architectural ensembles), some great bazaars and the 2000-year-old remains of Afrosiab, the original Silk Road trading town.

Bukhara

2 Central Asia's most interesting town, Bukhara is the one urban space that best rewards some serious exploring. Visit the medieval Ark, from where Emirs ruled with a cruel, vice-like grip; sip green tea beside the Lyabi-Hauz pool; and then start at the towering Kalon Minaret for a stroll through the surrounding network of bazaars, bathhouses and trade halls. Best of all are the labyrinthine backstreets, home to hidden synagogues, Sufi shrines and half-forgotten medressas. Bukhara also boasts the region's most stylish B&Bs, many in converted merchants' houses.

Khiva

3 The former khanate of Khiva is an entire walled city of traditional mud-baked architecture, frozen in time in the desert

When to Go

 HIGH SEASON (Apr–Jun & Sep–Oct)

 SHOULDER (Jul–Aug)

 LOW SEASON (Nov–Mar)

wastes of Khorezm. It may lack the lived-in backstreet life of Bukhara but in return you get the best preserved medieval city in Central Asia, if not the Islamic world. You can wander city walls, former slave markets and extensive royal palaces, where khaki walls burst with green and blue tilework.

Savitsky Collection in Nukus

4 The isolated, Soviet creation of Nukus is definitely one of Uzbekistan's least appealing cities, however its Savitsky Museum houses one of the most remarkable art collections in the former Soviet Union. About half of the paintings were brought here in Soviet times by renegade artist and ethnographer Igor Savitsky, who managed to preserve an entire generation of avant-garde work that was proscribed and

destroyed elsewhere in the country for not conforming to the socialist realism of the times. The paintings found protection in these isolated backwaters and it's interesting to hear how this nonconformist museum survived during the Soviet era.

Bazaars

5 Central Asia's bazaars have been fuelling Silk Road trade for two millennia. Shopping for melons, carpets and silly hats is perhaps the quintessential activity and we'd even say that the local bazaars offer the most direct route to Uzbekistan's soul. Every town has its own bazaar lined with *chaikhanas* (teahouses), smoking *shashlyk*, fruit stalls and even animal markets. Our favourite is possibly the Kumtepa bazaar outside Margilon, in the Fergana Valley, though

Getting Around

Clapped-out state buses are fast disappearing from Uzbek roads, undercut by a boom in private buses that do not keep schedules and leave when full.

Shared taxis save tons of time but are more costly than buses. They ply all the main intercity routes.

Trains are perhaps the most comfortable and safest method of intercity transport.

MIHTIANDER / GETTY IMAGES ©

Silk Shopping in Margilon

6 Margilon's main attraction is the fascinating Yodgorlik Silk Factory, which can be explored on a tour where you'll witness traditional methods of silk production from steaming and unravelling the cocoons to the weaving of the dazzling khanatlas (hand-woven silk, patterned on one side) fabrics for which Margilon is famous. After the tour (available in English, French, Russian or German), you can buy silk by the metre and offset your purchases against your entry fee. There is also premade clothing, carpets and embroidered items for sale.

Tashkent

7 Sprawling Tashkent is Central Asia's hub and the place where everything in Uzbekistan happens. It's one part newly built national capital, thick with the institutions of power, and one part leafy nearby Andijon's Jahon Bazaar is also excellent.

Soviet city, and yet another part sleepy Uzbek town, where traditionally clad farmers cart their wares through a maze of mud-walled houses to the grinding crowds of the bazaar. Tashkent is a fascinating jumble of contradictions that's well worth exploring over several days. Like most places that travellers use mainly to get somewhere else, Tashkent doesn't always immediately charm visitors, but it's a surprisingly fun and interesting place, with the best restaurants, museums and nightlife in the country.

Food & Drink

Plov A Central Asian pilaf consisting of rice and fried vegetables, is the national staple and every region prepares its own distinct version.

Naryn Horse meat sausage with cold noodles.

Somsa Puff pastry stuffed with lamb meat and onion.

Katyk A thin yoghurt drink that comes plain but can be sweetened if you have some sugar or jam handy.

The Silk Road

For centuries, the great civilisations of East and West were connected by the Silk Road, a fragile network of shifting intercontinental trade routes that threaded across Asia's highest mountains and bleakest deserts. The heartland of this trade was Central Asia, whose cosmopolitan cities grew fabulously wealthy. Its native beasts – horses and two-humped Bactrian camels – kept the goods flowing in both directions.

Silk was certainly not the only trade on the Silk Road but it epitomised the qualities – light, valuable, exotic and greatly desired – required for such a long-distance trade. Bukhara and Samarkand marked the halfway break, where caravans from Aleppo and Baghdad met traders from Kashgar and Yarkand. A network of *rabat* (caravanserais) grew up along the route, offering lodgings, stables and stores.

CAPITAL
Port Vila

POPULATION
281,500

AREA
12,189 sq km

OFFICIAL LANGUAGES
Bislama, English,
French

Tanna Island

Vanuatu

Tropical weather, sandy beaches and turquoise waters await you. Locals welcome visitors with dazzling grins and a chance to peek into their unique Melanesian cultures.

Vanuatu is a Pacific island adventure far beyond any notions of cruise-ship ports and flashy resorts. Deserted beaches, ancient culture, remote and rugged islands and world-class diving are just a small part of the magnetism of this scattered 80-plus island archipelago.

Where else can you hike up a crater to stare down into a magma-filled active volcano then ashboard back down, snorkel in a blue hole and drink kava with the local village chief – all in the same day? The resorts and restaurants of Port Vila have little in common with traditional *kastom* (custom) village life in the outer islands, but it's contrasts like these that make Vanuatu a surprise and a challenge.

It takes a little time, effort and a healthy sense of adventure to truly explore Vanuatu's islands, but it's worth every bit of it.

Top Experiences

Mt Yasur

 Staring down into the real-life, lava-spouting mouth of a volcano is exactly the nerve-wracking experience you might expect it to be. And Mt Yasur in Vanuatu is one of the most accessible places in the world to do it. Set yourself up in a bungalow or tree house at the volcano's base, then climb the crater in the evening to watch the volcano light up the night. For more adventure, visit Ambrym island.

Espiritu Santo

 Vanuatu's largest island offers a lively main town, island resorts, dazzling white-sand beaches and a rugged interior where mountain treks and caving adventures await. Scuba diving and snorkelling are major attractions.

Malekula

 One of Vanuatu's wildest islands, Malekula abounds with stories of tribal warfare and cannibalism. Visit the intriguing Big Nambas and Small Nambas tribes, burial sites of chiefs or trek with a local guide deep into the highlands of the Dog's Head.

Food & Drink

Laplap Grated manioc, taro roots or yams soaked in coconut cream (often with pork, beef, poultry, fish, prawns or flying fox) and wrapped in leaves before cooking in a ground oven.

Tahitian fish salad With fish marinated in lime juice, then sweetened with coconut milk.

Coconut An ubiquitous staple, used for drinking, eating and its fibre.

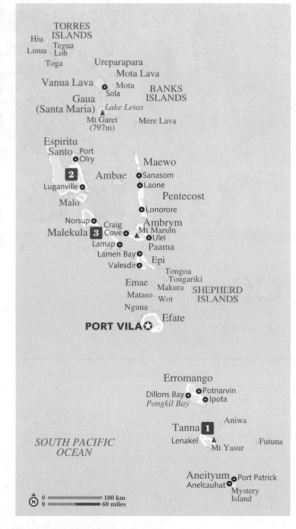

TORRES ISLANDS
Hiu
Linua — Tegua
Loh
Toga
Ureparapara
Mota Lava
Vanua Lava — Mota
Sola — BANKS
Gaua — ISLANDS
(Santa Maria) — Lake Letas
Mt Garet (797m) — Mere Lava
Espiritu Santo — Port Olry
Ambae — Maewo
Luganville — Sanasom
Laone
Malo — Pentecost
Norsup — Lonorore
Craig — Ambrym
Malekula — Cove — Mt Marum
Lamap — Ulei
Lamen Bay — Paama
Valesdir — Epi
Emae — Tongoa
Mataso — Tongariki
Nguna — Makura — SHEPHERD
Wot — ISLANDS
PORT VILA
Efate
Erromango
Dillons Bay — Potnarvin
Pongkil Bay — Ipota
Aniwa
Tanna — 1
Lenakel — Mt Yasur — Futuna
SOUTH PACIFIC OCEAN
Aneityum — Port Patrick
Anelcauhat — Mystery Island
0 — 100 km
0 — 60 miles

When to Go

☼ **HIGH SEASON** (May–Aug)

⛅ **SHOULDER** (Sep & Oct)

☂ **LOW SEASON** (Nov–Apr)

CAPITAL
Vatican City

POPULATION
1000

AREA
0.44 sq km

OFFICIAL LANGUAGE
Italian

St Peter's Square

Vatican City

The Vatican, at a mere 0.44 sq km, may be the world's smallest sovereign state, but it boasts some of Italy's most celebrated masterpieces.

Ensconced in the centre of the Italian capital Rome and enshrined in a bevy of sacrosanct traditions and rituals, the Vatican City is one of those rare places that must be visited to be believed. This is the seat of the Catholic Church, ruled with absolute authority by the Pope, who lives in a palace with over a thousand rooms and is protected by a hundred single Swiss men in ceremonious red, yellow and blue costume.

Established under the terms of the 1929 Lateran Treaty, the Vatican is the modern vestige of the Papal States, the papal fiefdom that ruled Rome and much of central Italy until Italian unification in 1861. The Vatican's association with Christianity dates to the 1st century, when St Peter was crucified head down in Nero's Circus. To commemorate this, Emperor Constantine commissioned a basilica to be built on the site where the saint was buried. The glory of St Peter's Basilica, however, is only the beginning of the wealth of treasures that await deep inside the Vatican Museums.

Top Experiences

Sistine Chapel

1 Home to two of the world's most famous works of art – Michelangelo's ceiling frescoes and his *Giudizio Universale* (Last Judgment) – the Sistine Chapel is the one part of the Vatican Museums that everyone wants to see. Michelangelo's ceiling design, best viewed from the chapel's main entrance, covers the entire 800-sq-m surface.

St Peter's Basilica

2 In this city of outstanding churches, none can hold a candle to St Peter's (Basilica di San Pietro), Italy's largest, richest and most spectacular basilica. Its lavish interior contains many spectacular works of art, including three of Italy's most celebrated masterpieces: Michelangelo's *Pietà*, his soaring dome, and Bernini's 29m-high baldachin over the papal altar.

Vatican Museums

3 The Vatican Museums boast one of the world's greatest art collections, which are displayed along some 7km of halls and corridors. Highlights include the spectacular collection of classical statuary in the Museo Pio-Clementino, a suite of rooms frescoed by Raphael, and the Michelangelo-painted Sistine Chapel.

When to Go

 HIGH SEASON (Jul–Aug)

SHOULDER (Apr–Jun)

LOW SEASON (Sep–Mar)

Food & Drink

Try Roman pasta such as creamy carbonara (egg yolk, parmesan and bacon), and fiery alla matriciana (tomato, bacon and chilli).

Sample local wines such as Frascati and Torre Ercolana.

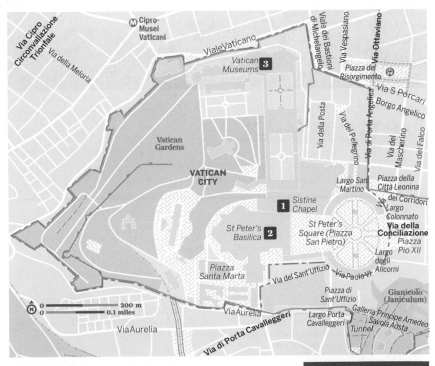

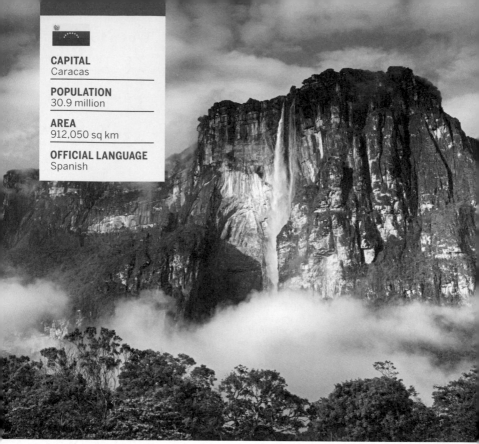

CAPITAL
Caracas

POPULATION
30.9 million

AREA
912,050 sq km

OFFICIAL LANGUAGE
Spanish

Salto Ángel (Angel Falls)

Venezuela

'La Tierra de Gracia' (Land of Grace), as Christopher Columbus called Venezuela in 1498, is nothing if not strangely beautiful and beautifully strange.

Spectacular Venezuela, home to some of South America's most incredible landscapes, rightly has a terrible image problem at the moment. Hyperinflation has led to a dramatic drop in living standards and issues with the supply of basic goods, while personal safety, particularly in Caracas, is worse than anywhere else on the continent. And yet, visiting Venezuela is both possible and remarkably cheap, with dollars instantly making even backpackers feel wealthy. Safety is a serious concern, of course, but sensibly managed it should be no deterrent to a trip.

The rewards if you do go are frankly immense. Few countries in the world have this degree of natural beauty: Andean peaks, Caribbean coastline, idyllic islands, grasslands teeming with wildlife, the steamy Orinoco Delta and the world's highest waterfall, Angel Falls. This is true trip-of-a-lifetime stuff, and right now you'll have it pretty much all to yourself.

Top Experiences

Salto Ángel (Angel Falls)

1 Salto Ángel is the world's highest waterfall and Venezuela's number-one tourist attraction. Its total height is 979m, with an uninterrupted drop of 807m – about 16 times the height of Niagara Falls. The cascade pours off the towering Auyantepui, one of the largest of the tepuis. The waterfall is in a distant, lush wilderness with no road access. The village of Canaima, about 50km northwest, is the major gateway to the falls – most tourists fly here then take a boat. You can opt to stay overnight in hammocks at one of the camps near the base of the falls. The trip upriver, the surrounding area and the experience of staying at the camp are as memorable as the waterfall itself. An alternative is to take a flight over Auyantepui and the falls. If you have time, do both, as the experiences are both unforgettably spectacular and offer very different perspectives on this most extraordinary chunk of nature.

Mérida

2 The adventure-sports capital of Venezuela, progressive Mérida is an affluent Andean city with a youthful energy and a spectacular mountain position. It has an unhurried, friendly and cultured atmosphere derived from the massive university, its outdoor-sports presence and its wonderful climate, which attracts lowlanders for its bright but breezy days and cool nights. Active visitors will be spoiled for choice, with myriad options for hiking, canyoning, rafting, mountain biking and Mérida's specialty: paragliding.

Roraima

3 A stately table mountain towering into churning clouds, Roraima (2810m) lures hikers and nature-lovers looking for Venezuela at its natural and rugged best. Unexplored

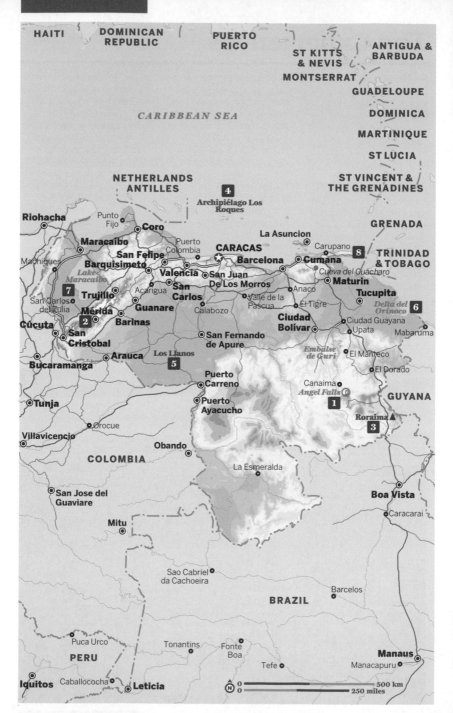

HAITI

DOMINICAN
REPUBLIC

PUERTO
RICO

ST KITTS
& NEVIS

ANTIGUA &
BARBUDA

MONTSERRAT

GUADELOUPE

CARIBBEAN SEA

DOMINICA

MARTINIQUE

ST LUCIA

NETHERLANDS
ANTILLES

4

Archipiélago Los
Roques

ST VINCENT &
THE GRENADINES

Riohacha

Punto
Fijo

Coro

GRENADA

La Asuncion

Carupano

8

TRINIDAD
& TOBAGO

Maracaibo

Puerto
Colombia

CARACAS

Cumana

Cueva del Guácharo

San Felipe

Barcelona

Machiques

Barquisimeto

Valencia

Lake
Maracaibo

**San Juan
De Los Morros**

Maturin

Tucupita

7

Trujillo

Acarigua

**San
Carlos**

Anaco

Delta del
Orinoco

6

San Carlos
del Zulia

Mérida

Valle de la
Pascua

El Tigre

2

Guanare

Calabozo

**Ciudad
Bolívar**

Ciudad Guayana

Cúcuta

Barinas

Upata

Mabaruma

**San
Cristobal**

**San Fernando
de Apure**

Embalse
de Guri

El Manteco

Arauca

Los Llanos

Bucaramanga

5

El Dorado

Canaima

GUYANA

Tunja

**Puerto
Carreno**

Angel Falls

1

Orocue

**Puerto
Ayacucho**

Roraima ▲

Villavicencio

3

Obando

COLOMBIA

La Esmeralda

**San Jose del
Guaviare**

Boa Vista

Caracarai

Mitu

Sao Gabriel
da Cachoeira

Barcelos

BRAZIL

Puca Urco

Tonantins

Fonte
Boa

Manaus

PERU

Tefe

Manacapuru

Iquitos

Caballococha

Leticia

0   500 km
0   250 miles

Food & Drink

Pabellón criollo The Venezuelan national dish of shredded beef, black beans, rice and plantains.

Arepa Small, grilled corn pancake stuffed with a variety of fillings.

Casabe Huge, flat bread made from yucca; a staple in indigenous communities.

Hallaca Maize dough with chopped meat and vegetables, wrapped in banana leaves and steamed.

Chocolate Not widely exported, Venezuelan chocolate is some of the best in the world.

Batidos Fresh fruit juice, either pure or cut with water (merengadas is the same thing with milk).

Polar beer If there was a national beverage, it would be these icy minibottles of brew.

Coffee Aromatic espresso shots of homegrown liquid heaven, served in little plastic cups at the *panadería* (bakery).

Best on Film

Secuestro Express (2005) Takes a cold look at crime, poverty, violence, drugs and class relations in the capital.

Oriana (1985) Recounts a pivotal childhood summer at a seaside family hacienda.

Huelepega (1999) A portrayal of Caracas street children using real street youth.

Amaneció de golpe (1999) The story of how Chávez burst onto the political scene.

Manuela Saenz (2000) Depicts the War of Independence through the eyes of Bolívar's mistress.

until 1884, and studied extensively by botanists ever since, the stark landscape contains strange rock formations and graceful arches, ribbon waterfalls, glittering quartz deposits and carnivorous plants. The frequent mist only accentuates the otherworldly feel. Although it's one of the easier tepuis to climb and no technical skills are required, the trek is long and demanding. However, anyone who's reasonably fit and determined can reach the top.

Archipiélago Los Roques

4 Island-hopping is the primary activity on Los Roques, a group of nearly 300 shimmering, sandy islands that lie in aquamarine waters some 160km due north of Caracas. It's far pricier than the mainland because everything is imported, but for those who love undeveloped beaches, snorkelling and diving, the trip is worth every bolívar. There is just one settlement on the main island of Gran Roque, and even that is limited to a few sandy and car-free streets, a charming contrast to the relentless

When to Go

HIGH SEASON
(Dec–Apr)
The whole country vacations during Christmas and Carnaval.

SHOULDER
(May–Sep)
Salto Ángel is swollen with rainy-season flow.

LOW SEASON
(Oct & Nov)
Beaches are empty before the Christmas holidays.

traffic and overcrowding of most other towns in the country. The whole archipelago, complete with the surrounding waters (2211 sq km), was made a national park in 1972.

Los Llanos

5 One of Venezuela's best destinations is the wildlife-rich Los Llanos, an immense savanna

Chamos

Regardless of national ills and social tensions, Venezuelans are full of life and humor. People are open, willing to talk and not shy about striking up conversations with a stranger who becomes an instant *chamo* (pal or friend). The nature of the current moribund political and economic situation is something locals are always willing to discuss (and if you can find a single person with anything good to say about the government, consider yourself to have made a serious anthropological find). Wherever you are, you're unlikely to be alone or feel isolated, especially if you can speak a little Spanish: in Venezuela there's always a rumba brewing somewhere.

Getting Around

We recommend using a travel agency in Venezuela, however independent and experienced a traveller you may be.

Flights should be reserved several weeks in advance due to overbooking and enormous demand.

Long-distance buses are generally safe, but tickets are not always available at short notice.

Many travellers go between cities using taxis as fuel prices are so low and it's also the safest method to get around over land. Taxis don't have meters, so always fix the fare with the driver before getting into the cab. It's a good idea to find out the correct fare beforehand from an independent source.

Venezuela has a number of islands, but only Isla de Margarita is serviced by regular scheduled ferries.

a book at night. Various hypotheses have been put forth to explain the lightning, but so far none have been proven. The theory that stands out is based on the topography of the region, characterized by the proximity of 5000m-high mountains (the Andes) and a vast sea-level lake (Lago de Maracaibo) – a dramatic configuration found nowhere else in the world. The clash of the cold winds descending from the freezing highlands with the hot, humid air evaporating from the lake is thought to produce the ionization of air particles responsible for the lightning.

plain south of the Andes that's also the home of Venezuela's cowboys and the twangy harp music of *joropo* (traditional music of Los Llanos). With Venezuela's greatest repository of wildlife found here, you'll be flat-out dazzled by caimans, capybaras, piranhas, anacondas and anteaters, plus an enormous variety of birds.

Delta del Orinoco

6 Roaring howler monkeys welcome the dawn. Piranhas clamp onto anything that bleeds. Screaming clouds of parrots gather at dusk, and weaving bats gobble insects under the blush of a million stars. For wildlife-viewing on the water's edge, it's hard to outshine the Delta del Orinoco. A deep-green labyrinth of islands, channels and mangrove swamps engulfing nearly 30,000 sq km – the size of Belgium – this is one

of the world's great river deltas and a mesmerizing region to explore. Mixed forest blankets most of the land, which includes a variety of palms. Of these, the moriche palm is the most typical and important, as it is the traditional staple food for the delta's inhabitants, the Warao people, and provides material for their crafts, tools, wine and houses.

Relámpago de Catatumbo

7 Centered on the mouth of the Río Catatumbo, where it runs into the vast Lago de Maracaibo, the Relámpago de Catatumbo (Catatumbo Lightning) is an amazing phenomenon that consists of frequent flashes of lightning with little or no accompanying thunder. The eerie, silent electrical storm can be so strong and constant that you will often be able to read

Península de Paria

8 The Península de Paria – the only place in South America where Colombus actually set foot – has some of the most gorgeous and least-visited spots in the country, all backed by the thick jungle-covered mountains of the peninsula's largely untouched interior. Dozens of white- and gold-sand beaches await travellers on the 50km coastal stretch between Río Caribe and San Juan de Unare, the last seaside village accessible by road. Beyond San Juan de Unare you can only continue by boat, making a trip to futher flung villages such as Santa Isabel a real adventure. Bring insect repellent if you stay overnight, and always check with locals before swimming, as some beaches have treacherous currents.

Latin Pop

Caracas is a center of Latin pop and the *rock en español* movement, which combines the rhythm and energy of Latin beats with international rock trends.

Sports

In Venezuela, *béisbol* (baseball) rules supreme. The next most popular sport is basketball, followed by *fútbol* (soccer), which is the sport of choice among the country's indigenous population.

CAPITAL
Hanoi

POPULATION
95.3 million

AREA
331,210 sq km

OFFICIAL LANGUAGE
Vietnamese

Floating village in Halong Bay

Vietnam

Astonishingly exotic and utterly compelling, Vietnam is a country of breathtaking natural beauty with a unique heritage, where travel quickly becomes addictive.

Unforgettable experiences are everywhere in Vietnam. There's the sublime: gazing over a surreal seascape of limestone islands from the deck of a traditional junk in Halong Bay. The ridiculous: taking 10 minutes just to cross the street through a tsunami of motorbikes in Hanoi. The inspirational: exploring the world's most spectacular cave systems in Phong Nha-Ke Bang National Park. The comical: watching a moped loaded with honking pigs weave a wobbly route along

a country lane. And the contemplative: witnessing a solitary grave in a cemetery of thousands of war victims.

Vietnam has thrills and chills, beaches, outstanding spas and excellent food. Up and down the country you can mingle with villagers, sample local dishes and sip rice wine in regional markets.

Forty years after the carnage of an epoch-defining conflict, Vietnam a dynamic nation on the move.

Top Experiences

Halong Bay

1 Halong Bay's stunning combination of karst limestone peaks and sheltered, shimmering seas is one of Vietnam's top tourist draws, but with more than 2000 different islands, there's plenty of superb scenery to go around. Definitely book an overnight cruise and make time for your own special moments on this World Heritage wonder – rise early for an ethereal misty dawn, or pilot a kayak into grottoes and lagoons. If you're hankering for more karst action, move on to the less touristy but equally spectacular Lan Ha Bay.

Hoi An

2 Vietnam's most cosmopolitan and civilised town, this beautiful ancient port is bursting with gourmet restaurants, hip bars and cafes, quirky boutiques and expert tailors. What's more, the 21st-century curses of traffic and pollution are noticeably absent. Immerse yourself in history in the warren-like lanes of the Old Town, and tour the temples and pagodas. Dine like an emperor on a peasant's budget (and even learn how to cook like the locals). Then hit glorious An Bang Beach, wander along the riverside and bike the back roads. Yes, Hoi An has it all.

Phong Nha-Ke Bang National Park

3 With hills shrouded in verdant rainforest, and mountain rivers coursing through impressive ravines, above ground this is one of Vietnam's most spectacular national parks. Head underground for even more proof that the area should be part of any Vietnamese itinerary. A fortunate selection of travellers can experience the cathedral-like chambers of Hang Son Doong, the world's largest cave, but more accessible are the ziplining and kayaking thrills of Hang Toi (Dark Cave), and the ethereal beauty of aptly named Paradise Cave.

Sapa Trekking

4 Undulating rice terraces cascade down to valleys inhabited by Hmong, Red Dzao and Giay villages. Up above, the sinuous ridges of the Hoang Lien Mountains (dubbed the Tonkinese Alps by the French) touch the sky. Brushed with every shade of green in the palette, the countryside surrounding Sapa is a showcase of northern Vietnam's most superb rural vistas and a fascinating glimpse into the country's astounding cultural diversity. This is prime territory for digging out your walking boots and hitting the trails.

CHAN SRITHAWEEPORN / GETTY IMAGES ©

CHINA

Ha Giang **9**
Ba Be National Park
13 Cao Bang
Lai Chau (Tam Duong)
4 Lao Cai
Sapa
Muong Lay (Lai Chau)
Fansipan
Yen Bai
Tuyen Quang
Viet Tri
Lang Son
Thai Nguyen
Mong Cai
Dien Bien Phu
Tay Trang
Tuan Giao
Son La
7 HANOI
Hai Duong
Haiphong
Halong City
Mai Chau
Hoa Binh
Thai Binh
1
Halong Bay
Nam Xoi
Na Meo
Ninh Binh
Thanh Hoa

Nanning
Pingxiang
Zhanjiang

Gulf of Tonkin

Hainan Island (China)

LAOS

Phonsavan
Nam Can
Nam Phao
Vinh
Ha Tinh
Cha Lo
Na Phao
3
Dong Hoi
Tha Khaek
Phong Nha-Ke Bang National Park
Dansavanh
Dong Ha
Savannakhet
Khe Sanh
5 Hue
Bach Ma National Park
Danang
2 Hoi An
Tam Ky
Quang Ngai

VIENTIANE

Mekong River

Pakse
Attapeu

THAILAND

Kon Tum
Pleiku
Quy Nhon
Tuy Hoa

CAMBODIA

Siem Reap
Battambang
Tonlé Sap
Mekong River

Buon Ma Thuot

Nha Trang
Dalat **12**
Phan Rang & Thap Cham

PHNOM PENH

Tay Ninh
8 Cat Tien National Park
Bien Hoa
Gulf of Thailand

Takeo
Kampot
HO CHI MINH CITY (SAIGON)
Chau Doc
Long Xuyen
My Tho
Vung Tau
Phan Thiet
Mui Ne **14**

10 Ha Tien
Phu Quoc Island
Rach Gia
Can Tho
Tra Vinh
Soc Trang
Bac Lieu
Ca Mau
Mekong Delta
11

6 Con Dao Islands

SOUTH CHINA SEA

Central Highlands

N
0   200 km
0   120 miles

Best on Film

Apocalypse Now (1979) The American War depicted as an epic 'heart of darkness' adventure.

The Deer Hunter (1978) Examines the emotional breakdown suffered by small-town servicemen.

Cyclo (Xich Lo; 1995) Visually stunning masterpiece that cuts to the core of HCMC's underworld.

Vertical Ray of the Sun (2000) Exquisitely photographed family saga set in Hanoi by a Vietnamese-French director.

Best in Print

The Quiet American (Graham Greene; 1955) Classic novel set in the 1950s as the French empire is collapsing.

The Sorrow of War (Bao Ninh; 1990) The North Vietnamese perspective, retold in novel form via flashbacks.

Vietnam: Rising Dragon (Bill Hayton; 2010) A candid, highly insightful assessment of the nation.

Catfish & Mandala (Andrew X Pham; 1999) Beautifully written and thought-provoking biographical tale of a Vietnamese-American who returns to his homeland.

Hue

5 The capital of the nation for 150 years in the 19th and early 20th centuries, Hue is perhaps the easiest Vietnamese city to love and spend time in. Its situation on the banks of the Perfume River is sublime, its complex cuisine justifiably famous, and its streets are relatively traffic free. And that's without the majesty of the Hue Citadel, its royal residences and elegant temples, formidable walled defences and gateways to explore. On the city's fringes are some of Vietnam's most impressive pagodas and royal tombs, many in wonderful natural settings.

Con Dao Islands

6 The furious energy that characterises Vietnamese cities can be intoxicating, but when you need an urban detox, these idyllic tropical islands make the perfect escape. Once hell on earth for a generation of political prisoners, Con Dao is now a heavenly destination of remote beaches, pristine dive sites and diverse nature. It's a wonderful place to explore by bike in search of that dream beach, while the main settlement of Con Son is one of Vietnam's most charming towns.

Hanoi

7 Ancient but dynamic, the nation's capital hurtles towards modernity, cautiously embracing visitors. Sample Hanoi's heady mix of history and ambition by wandering the streets of the Old Quarter, sipping drip-coffee, slurping on

When to Go

HIGH SEASON
(Jul & Aug)
All Vietnam, except the far north, is hot and humid, with the summer monsoon bringing downpours.

SHOULDER
(Dec–Mar)
North of Nha Trang can get cool weather. In the south, clear skies and sunshine are the norm.

LOW SEASON
(Apr–Jun & Sep–Nov)
Typhoons can lash the central and northern coastline until November.

Cooking Courses

The best way to tackle Vietnamese cuisine head-on is to sign up for a cooking course during your stay. Courses have really taken off in recent years, and many courses also incorporate a market visit to purchase essential ingredients.

Battle Sites

In the centre of Vietnam, the Demilitarized Zone (DMZ) has the greatest concentration of battle sites from the American War. Down south the Cu Chi Tunnels are a popular day trip from Ho Chi Minh City. In the far north, Dien Bien Phu shouldn't be missed.

Food & Drink

Locally-sourced and seasonal, complex and refined, Vietnamese food is perhaps Asia's greatest culinary secret. Essentially it's all about the freshness of the ingredients – chefs shop twice daily to collect just-picked herbs from the market. The result? Incomparable texture and flavour combinations. For the Vietnamese, a meal should balance sour and sweet, crunchy and silky, fried and steamed, soup and salad. Wherever you are, you'll find exquisite local specialities – the 'white rose' of Hoi An, the *canh chua* (a fish and vegetable soup) of the Mekong Delta or the good ol' *pho* of the north.

a hearty bowl of bun rieu cua and scoring souvenirs for next to nothing. When you're done, check out the crumbling decadence of the French Quarter then zip up to cosmopolitan Tay Ho for finer dining and the low-down on Hanoi's burgeoning art scene.

Cat Tien National Park

8 An accessible and impressive protected area, Cat Tien lies conveniently midway between Ho Chi Minh City and Dalat. It is set on a bend in the Dong Nai River, and there is something vaguely *Apocalypse Now* about arriving here. Popular activities include trekking, cycling and wildlife spotting: the Wild Gibbon Trek is a must. The park is also home to a primate centre, where gibbons and langurs are coaxed back into their natural environment.

Extreme North

9 The extreme north of Vietnam is all about raw adventure travel. Ha Giang province is Vietnam's spectacular emerging destination for the intrepid, with dizzying ascents up the Quan Ba Pass (Heaven's Gate), towering karsts and granite outcrops, and jaw-dropping vistas on the epic trip between Dong Van and Meo Vac. And with improved roads, new trekking routes, minority markets and a wider choice of guesthouses, Vietnam's final frontier – now a Unesco-listed geopark – is really opening up.

Phu Quoc Island

10 Lapped by azure waters and edged with the kind of white-sand beaches that make sun seekers sink to their weak knees, Phu Quoc – way down in the south of Vietnam – is ideal for slipping into low gear, reaching for a seaside cocktail and toasting a blood-orange sun as it dips into the sea. And if you want to notch it up a tad, grab a motorbike and hit the red-dirt roads: the island's the size of Singapore.

Ho Chi Minh City

11 Increasingly international but still unmistakably Vietnamese, the former Saigon's visceral energy will delight big-city devotees. HCMC doesn't inspire neutrality: you'll either be drawn into its thrilling vortex and hypnotised by the perpetual whir of its orbiting motorbikes, or you'll find the whole experience overwhelming. Dive in and you'll be rewarded with a wealth of history, delicious food and a vibrant nightlife that sets the standard for Vietnam. The heat is always on in Saigon; loosen your collar and enjoy.

Dalat

12 Dalat is the queen of the southwest highlands and has been popular with international tourists since the days of the French colonialists. Grand Gallic villas are dotted amid pine groves and the whole town is centred on a pretty lake, with numerous nearby waterfalls adding to its natural appeal. Dalat is also fast becoming one of Vietnam's key adventure-sport hubs, with abseiling, canyoning, mountain-biking, hiking and rafting all on offer. The temperate climate here will be quite a relief if you've been suffering in Saigon.

Ba Be National Park

13 Detour off the regular Vietnam tourist trail in Ba Be National Park, an essential destination for adventurous travellers, with towering limestone mountains, plunging valleys and evergreen forests. Waterfalls, caves and lakes combine in a landscape that sustains over 550 different plants and hundreds of different bird and animal species. Explore Ba Be's natural spectacle by boat or on trekking and mountain-biking excursions, before relaxing in the rustic homestays and village guesthouses of the local Tay ethnic minority.

Mui Ne

14 The relaxed, prosperous beach resort of Mui Ne is a kitesurfing capital with world-class wind and conditions, and excellent schools for professional training. For those who prefer dry land, sandboarding and golf are popular alternatives.

DAVID BOKUCHAVA / SHUTTERSTOCK ©

Getting Around

 Train travel is reasonably priced and comfortable enough in air-conditioned carriages (and sleepers). But note there are no real express trains.

 Vietnam has good domestic flight connections, with new routes opening up all the time, and very affordable prices (if you book early).

 Having your own set of wheels gives you maximum flexibility to visit remote regions and stop when and where you please. Car hire always includes a driver.

 On the main highways bus services are very frequent, although it's not a particularly relaxing way to travel. Open-tour buses are inexpensive and worth considering.

CAPITAL
Charlotte Amalie
(USVI), Road Town
(BVI)

POPULATION
103,000 (USVI),
28,000 (BVI)

AREA
1910 sq km (USVI),
151 sq km (BVI)

OFFICIAL LANGUAGE
English

Trunk Bay, St John

Virgin Islands, US & British

Balmy weather, ridiculously white sand shores, diving and snorkeling, and calypso-wafting beach bars: the Virgin Islands have the tropical thing down.

Although considered one archipelago, the Virgin Islands are divided between two countries: the British Virgin Islands (BVI) and the United States Virgin Islands (USVI). With more than 90 little landmasses bobbing in a triangular patch of sea, steady trade winds, calm currents and hundreds of protected bays, it's easy to see how the Virgins became a tropical fantasyland.

Believe it or not, a day will come during your Virgin stay when you decide enough with the beach lounging. Then it's time to snorkel with turtles and spotted eagle rays, dive to explore a 19th-century shipwreck, hike to petroglyphs and sugar-mill ruins and kayak through a bioluminescent bay.

Top Experiences

Virgin Islands National Park, USVI

1 Virgin Islands National Park covers two-thirds of St John, plus 5650 acres underwater. It's a tremendous resource, offering miles of shoreline, pristine reefs and 20 hiking trails. The park visitors center sits on the dock across from the Mongoose Junction shopping arcade. It's an essential first stop to obtain free guides on hiking, birdwatching, petroglyph sites and ranger-led activities. Green iguanas, geckos, hawksbill turtles and wild donkeys roam the landscape. A couple of good trails leave from behind the center.

The Baths, BVI

2 This collection of sky-high boulders marks a national park and the BVI's most popular attraction. The rocks – volcanic lava leftovers from some 70 million years ago – form a series of grottoes that flood with sea water. The area makes for unique swimming and snorkeling, but the coolest part is the trail through the 'Caves' to Devil's Bay. During the 20-minute trek, you'll clamber over boulders, slosh through tidal pools, squeeze into impossibly narrow passages, then drop on to a sugar-sand beach.

Christiansted, USVI

3 Christiansted evokes a melancholy whiff of the past. Cannon-covered Fort Christiansvaern rises up on the waterfront. It abuts Kings Wharf, the commercial landing where, for more than 250 years,

When to Go

 HIGH SEASON (Dec–Apr)

 SHOULDER (May–Jul)

 LOW SEASON (Aug–Nov)

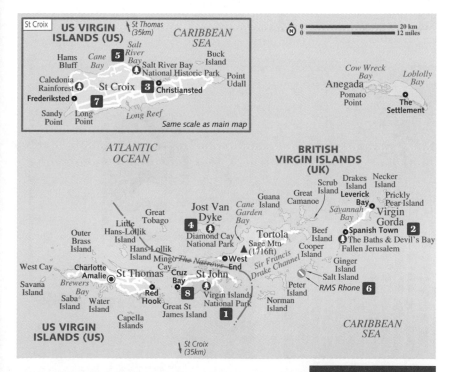

ships landed with slaves and set off with sugar or molasses. Today the wharf is fronted by a boardwalk of restaurants, dive shops and bars. It all comes together as a well-provisioned base from which to explore St Croix.

White Bay, BVI

4 This gorgeous long white crescent lies pressed to the sea by steep hills. A barrier reef shelters the water from swells and waves, which makes for good swimming and a protected anchorage. Lots of day trippers arrive by charter boat. The beach's main activities are drinking, wriggling your toes in the sand and people-watching.

Salt River Bay, USVI

5 Luminescent bays, Chris Columbus' landing pad and hot dive sites await along the north shore. Kayaking through the glowing water of Salt River Bay at night is a St Croix highlight.

Wreck of the Rhone, BVI

6 T-shaped Salt Island is a forlorn place. The salt making (which gave the island its name) still goes on here, but the RMS *Rhone* is the big attraction. The Rhone crashed against the rocks off the southwest coast during a hurricane in 1867. Now a national park, the steamer's remains are extensive, making it one of the Caribbean's best wreck dives. The stern lies in shallower water, so snorkelers can get in on the action, too.

Cruzan Rum Distillery, USVI

7 To find out how the islands' popular elixir gets made, stop by

Getting Around

A few commercial services fly within the Virgins, especially between St Thomas and St Croix. Other than that, you'll need to charter a plane to fly between islands.

Frequent and inexpensive public ferries connect the main islands in the Virgins, as well as several of the smaller islands. For trips between USVI and BVI, a passport is required. The major islands have marinas where you can charter sailing yachts or powerboats, either bareboat or with a crew.

RICHARD CUMMINS / GETTY IMAGES ©

this historic distillery for a tour. The journey through gingerbread-smelling (from molasses and yeast), oak-barrel-stacked warehouses takes 20 minutes, after which you get to sip plenty of the good stuff. The Nelthropp family, Cruzan Rum's owners, have been perfecting the recipes since 1760.

Cruz Bay, USVI

8 Nicknamed 'Love City,' St John's main town indeed wafts a carefree, spring-break party vibe. Hippies, sea captains, American retirees and reggae worshipers hoist happy-hour drinks in equal measure, and everyone wears a silly grin at their great good fortune for being here. Cruz Bay is also the place to organize your hiking, snorkeling, kayaking and other activities, and to fuel up in the surprisingly good restaurant mix. Everything grooves within walking distance of the ferry docks.

ROMONA ROBBINS PHOTOGRAPHY / GETTY IMAGES ©

Food & Drink

Anegada lobster Hulking crustaceans grilled on the beach in converted oil drums.

Callaloo Spicy soup stirred with okra, various meats, greens and hot peppers.

Cruzan Rum St Croix' happy juice since 1760, from light white rum to banana, guava and other tropical flavors.

Fungi (*foon*-ghee) A polenta-like cornmeal cooked with okra, typically topped with fish and gravy.

Painkiller Jost Van Dyke's Soggy Dollar Bar supposedly invented this mix of rum, coconut, pineapple, orange juice and nutmeg.

Pate (*paw*-tay) Flaky fried dough pockets stuffed with spiced chicken, fish or other meat.

Roti Fiery chutney sets off the curried chicken, beef, conch or vegetable fillings in these burrito-like flat-bread wraps.

Local Sounds

Reggae and calypso tunes blast from USVI vehicles and emanate from shops, restaurants and beach bars. *Quelbe* and *fungi* (*foon*-ghee, also an island food made of cornmeal) are two types of folk music. *Quelbe* blends jigs, quadrilles, military fife and African drum music, with lyrics (often biting satire) from slave field songs. *Fungi* uses homemade percussion such as washboards, ribbed gourds and conch shells to accompany a singer. The best time to experience island music is during the 'jump up' parades and competitions associated with major festivals such as Carnival on St Thomas and St John, or at St Croix' Cruzan Christmas Fiesta.

Snowdonia National Park

Wales

The phrase 'good things come in small packages' may be a cliché, but in the case of Wales it's undeniably true.

Compact but geologically diverse, Wales offers myriad opportunities for escaping into nature. It may not be wild in the classic sense – humans have been shaping this land for millennia – but there are plenty of lonely corners to explore, lurking behind mountains, within river valleys and along surf-battered cliffs. An extensive network of paths makes Wales a hiker's paradise. Things are even more untamed on the islands scattered just off the coast, some of which are important wildlife sanctuaries.

Castles are an inescapable part of the Welsh landscape. They're absolutely everywhere. You could visit a different one every day for a year and still not see them all. There's also an altogether more inscrutable and far older set of stones to discover – the stone circles, dolmens and standing stones erected long before castles were ever dreamt up, before even histories were written.

Beyond the scenery, it's the interactions with Welsh people that will remain in your memory the longest.

Top Experiences

Wales Coast Path

1 Since 2012, all of Wales' famously beautiful coastal paths have been linked up in one continuous 1400 km route. Walk for two months or for two days – there's no rule that you have to do it all in one go. The best stretches take in the Gower's beautiful beaches, Pembrokeshire's multicoloured cliffs and limestone arches, the remote edges of the Llŷn Peninsula and the ancient vistas of Anglesey. And if you link it up with Offa's Dyke Path, you can circle the entire country!

Snowdonia

2 The rugged northwest corner of the country has rocky mountain peaks,

Map legend (selected labels):
- 0 — 50 km / 0 — 25 miles
- Irish Sea
- Liverpool Bay
- Blackpool
- Preston
- Liverpool
- Holyhead
- Anglesey
- Llandudno
- Conwy
- Rhyl
- Dee Estuary
- Colwyn Bay
- Chester
- Bangor
- Caernarfon
- **2** Snowdon
- **3**
- **5**
- Wrexham
- Blaenau Ffestiniog
- Porthmadog
- Portmeirion
- Berwyn Mountains
- Snowdonia National Park
- Dolgellau
- Cader Idris
- Welshpool
- Shrewsbury
- Cardigan Bay
- Newtown
- Llanidloes
- Aberystwyth
- ENGLAND
- Elan Valley
- Cambrian Mountains
- Llandrindod Wells
- Pembrokeshire Coast National Park
- **1** **4** Cardigan
- Mynydd Epynt
- **7** Hereford
- St Davids
- Cwmcerwyn
- Llandovery
- Carreg Cennen
- Hay-on-Wye
- **8**
- St Brides Bay
- **6** Carmarthen
- Brecon Beacons National Park
- Abergavenny
- Haverfordwest
- Llanelli
- Pembroke
- Tenby
- Merthyr Tydfil
- Gower Peninsula
- Swansea
- Port Talbot
- Mumbles
- CARDIFF
- Newport
- Bristol Channel
- ATLANTIC OCEAN
- Barry
- Barnstaple
- ENGLAND
- Taunton
- Yeovil

Food & Drink

Historically, Welsh cuisine was based on what could be grown locally and cheaply. Food was functional and needed to satisfy the needs of labourers on the farm or workers down the mine. It was hearty and wholesome but not exactly haute cuisine.

The most traditional Welsh dish remains *cawl*, the hearty, one-pot soupy stew of bacon, lamb, cabbage, swede and potato. It's one of those warm, cosy dishes that you long for when you're walking in the hills. Another famous favourite is Welsh rarebit, a kind of cheese on toast, generously drizzled with a secret ingredient tasting suspiciously like beer. For breakfast, there's nothing more Welsh than laverbread. It's not actually bread at all, but a surprisingly delicious concoction of boiled seaweed mixed with oatmeal and served with bacon or cockles.

When to Go

HIGH SEASON (Jul & Aug)

SHOULDER (Apr–Jun, Sep & Oct)

LOW SEASON (Nov–Mar)

Merlin the Magician

This great Welsh wizard is probably modelled upon Myrddin Emrys (Ambrosius), a 6th-century holy man who became famous for his prophecies. It was probably Geoffrey of Monmouth who changed Myrddin's name to Merlin and presented him as the wise, wizardly advisor to Arthur's father King Uther Pendragon. One of Merlin's seminal acts was to disguise Uther as Duke Gorlois, allowing him to spend the night with the duke's wife, Ygerna, who duly conceived Arthur. Merlin also predicted that Uther's true heir would draw a sword from a stone and acquired the sword Excalibur from a Lady of the Lake. Merlin's own end appears to have come courtesy of this same lady when she trapped the wizard in a cave on Bryn Myrddin (Merlin's Hill), east of Carmarthenshire, where wind-carried groans and clanking chains are part of local lore even today.

towering over it. None has a more symbiotic relationship with its settlement than Conwy. The castle still stretches out its enfolding arms to enclose the historic town in a stony embrace, originally designed to keep a tiny English colony safe from the populace they displaced. Even today it's awe-inspiring.

Pembrokeshire

4 Whether you come armed with hiking boots, a bucket and spade, or a surfboard, Wales' western extremity won't disappoint. Famous in Britain for its beaches and coastal walks, Pembrokeshire is a small sampler of all that Wales has to offer. Pembroke has one of Britain's finest Norman castles, and there are smaller versions at nearby Tenby, Manorbier, Carew and Haverfordwest. The Preseli Hills offer upland walking and ancient standing stones. Add to that wildlife reserves, cute villages and an ancient cathedral, and all bases are covered.

Ffestiniog & Welsh Highland Railways

5 Once you could only get views this good if you were a hunk of slate on your way to the port. This twin set of narrow-gauge train lines now shuttles rail enthusiasts from Porthmadog up into the mountains of Snowdonia, with the Welsh Highland Railway slicing right past Snowdon to the coast at Caernarfon. The Ffestiniog Railway heads to the former industrial heartland of Blaenau Ffestiniog, where you can take a whistle stop to delve into the depths of the slate caverns.

glacier-hewn valleys and lakes, sinuous ridges, sparkling rivers and charm-infused villages in abundance. The busiest part is around Snowdon itself, where hordes hike to the summit and many more take the less strenuous cog railway from Llanberis. Elsewhere in Snowdonia's rugged mountains are rarely trodden areas perfect for off-the-beaten-track

exploration. Glorious under the summer sun and even better under a blanket of snow, Snowdonia is one of Wales' absolute treasures.

Conwy Castle

3 The golden age of castle building happened to coincide with the golden age of 'let's show the Welsh what's what'. There's barely a town in Wales of any note that doesn't have a castle

Getting Around

Driving will get you to remote corners of Wales not connected to public transport.

Bus is the most useful form of public transport, with routes connecting most towns and villages. National Express coaches only stop in major destinations.

The train network isn't extensive, but it's handy for those towns connected to it. Trains are comfortable and reliable, but more expensive than the buses.

Brecon Beacons

6 Not as wild as Snowdonia nor as spectacular as the Pembrokeshire Coast, Wales' third national park manages quite a feat – and that's to be simultaneously bleak and beautiful. Walkers will delight in its unpopulated moors and bald hills, while history buffs can seek out hill forts and barrows, and the enigmatic ruins of abbeys and castles. The towns within the park's confines are some of Wales' most endearingly idiosyncratic, including Hay-on-Wye and Abergavenny – hallowed names for book lovers and food fans respectively.

Hay-on-Wye

7 When a former US president describes your annual festival as the 'Woodstock of the mind', you know you're doing something right. This unselfconsciously pretty border town has assumed near mythic proportions among both the worldwide literati and lit-loving Brits as the most book-imbued place in the world. Hay is like a bizarro world version of tabloid culture, where intellectuals are admired, poets are praised and librarians are the new Kardashians. Oh, and there's good beer and food to be had, too.

St Davids

8 Some places have a presence all of their own, and that's certainly true of precious little St Davids. Officially a city but more like a large village, the peaceful home of Wales' patron saint has attracted the spiritually minded for centuries. Whether you come seeking salvation in the surf, hoping to commune with the whales in the Celtic Deep, or genuinely wishing to embrace the grace of Wales' patron saint, St Davids is a strangely affecting place.

6

CAPITAL
Sana'a

POPULATION
23 million

AREA
527,968 sq km

OFFICIAL LANGUAGE
Arabic

Dragon's blood trees, Socotra Island

Yemen

Short of the glitz of many of the Gulf states, Yemen compensates with the depth of its history and attachment to traditions and rich culture. Today, travellers do not have the privilege of experiencing these, as the country is in crisis, with civil war taking a desperate toll on most of the population. Needless to say, it is not safe to travel here at the moment.

In days past, the sons of Noah knew it as the land of milk and honey, Gilgamesh came here to search for the secret of eternal life, wise men gathered frankincense and myrrh from its mountains and, most famously, the Queen of Sheba called Yemen her home.

Yemen is home to some awe-inspiring places and while it may be the Arabian Peninsula's poor cousin, therein lies its charm. With none of the oil wealth of its neighbours, the country is like a time capsule preserving the traditions and texture of old Arabia.

Snapshot

Socotra Island

 Socotra is home to the strange and unique dragon's blood tree, so called because of its dark red resin, much sought after in ancient times as a dye. The four islands that make up this tiny, isolated archipelago are listed by Unesco as a World Natural Heritage Site due to their incredible biodiversity, with almost 700 species found here and nowhere else on earth.

Haraz Mountains

 A trail weaves through a tapestry of fortresses and fields in these mountains which rise abruptly off the steamy Red Sea coastal plains. The sheer-sided Haraz Mountains have, for centuries, acted as a cultural fortress protecting the Yemeni heartland from interfering foreigners.

Wadi Hadramawt

 Giants once roamed and scorpions line the entrance to Hell at the weird and wonderful sandcastle cities of Wadi Hadramawt. This dry river valley lined with lush oases is like another world. In an instant, sterility is replaced by fertility and ochre browns give way to disco greens.

Seasons

☀ NOV–FEB

⛅ MAR–MAY & OCT

☁ JUN–SEP

Food & Drink

Bread More than 40 mouth-watering kinds of bread exist in Yemen.

Fuul A paste made from beans, tomatoes, onions and chilli.

Shai Sweet tea.

Shurba wasabi Lamb soup.

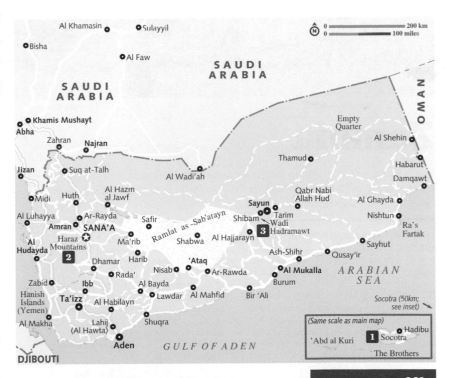

CAPITAL
Lusaka

POPULATION
15.5 million

AREA
752,614 sq km

OFFICIAL LANGUAGES
English, Bemba, Lozi,
Nyanja, Tonga

Southern carmine bee-eaters, South Luangwa National Park

Zambia

*The rewards of travelling in Zambia are those of exploring remote,
mesmerising wilderness as full of an astonishing diversity of wildlife as any
part of Southern Africa.*

Adventures undertaken here will lead
you deep into the bush where animals,
both predators and prey, wander through
unfenced camps, where night-time means
swapping stories around the fire and where
the human footprint is nowhere to be seen.
Where one day you can canoe down a wide,
placid river and the next raft through the
raging rapids near world-famous Victoria
Falls.

Though landlocked, three great rivers –
the Kafue, the Luangwa and the Zambezi –
flow through Zambia, defining both its
geography and the rhythms of life for many
of its people. For the independent traveller,
however, Zambia is a logistical challenge,
because of its sheer size, dilapidated road
network and upmarket facilities. For those
who do venture here, the relative lack of
crowds means an even more satisfying
journey.

Top Experiences

South Luangwa National Park

1 For scenery, variety and density of animals, South Luangwa National Park is one of the best parks in Zambia, if not Africa. Impalas, pukus, waterbucks, giraffes and buffaloes wander on the wide-open plains; leopards, of which there are many in the park, hunt in the dense woodlands; herds of elephants wade through the marshes; and hippos munch serenely on Nile cabbage in the Luangwa River. The bird life is a highlight: about 400 species have been recorded.

Zambezi River

2 One of the country's premier wildlife-viewing areas, the Lower Zambezi National Park covers a large stretch of wilderness area along the northeastern bank of the Zambezi River. Several smaller rivers flow through the park, which is centred on a beautiful flood plain alongside the Zambezi, dotted with acacias and other large trees, and flanked by a steep escarpment on the northern side, covered with thick miombo woodland. On the opposite bank, in Zimbabwe, is Mana Pools National Park, and together the parks constitute one of Africa's finest wildlife areas.

Victoria Falls

3 Taking its place alongside the Pyramids and the Serengeti, Victoria Falls (Mosi-oa-Tunya – the 'smoke that thunders') is one of Africa's original blockbusters. And although Zimbabwe and Zambia share it, Victoria Falls is a place all of its own. As a

When to Go

 HIGH SEASON (May–Aug)

 SHOULDER (Sep–Oct)

 LOW SEASON (Nov–Apr)

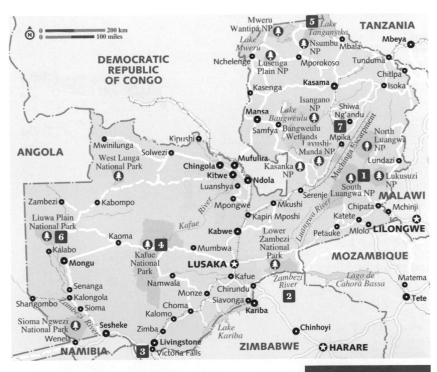

magnet for tourists of all descriptions – backpackers, tour groups, thrill seekers, families, honeymooners – Victoria Falls is one of earth's great spectacles. View it directly as a raging mile-long curtain of water, in all its glory, from a helicopter ride or peek precariously over its edge from Devil's Pools; the sheer power and force of the falls is something that simply does not disappoint.

Kafue National Park

4 Covering more than 22,500 sq km, this is the largest park in Zambia and one of the biggest in the world. With terrain ranging from the lush riverine forest of the Kafue River to the vast grassland of the Busanga Plains, the park rewards wildlife

enthusiasts with glimpses of various carnivores and their nimble prey. This is the only major park in Zambia that's easily accessible by public transport, with a handful of camps just off the highway.

Lake Tanganyika

5 Spreading over a massive 34,000 sq km, and reaching almost 1500m deep, cavernous Lake Tanganyika is the second-deepest lake in the world and contains about 15% of the earth's fresh water. Believed to be up to 15 million years old and lying in the Great Rift Valley, the shores of the lake reach Tanzania, Burundi, the Democratic Republic of the Congo and Zambia. The climate here is always very hot, especially at the end of the dry season.

Getting Around

There are a number of domestic airports and several airlines.

Recent years have seen the conditions of Zambia's roads improve out of sight.

Distances are long, buses are often slow and some (but not many these days) roads are badly potholed.

3

Liuwa Plain National Park

6 About 100km northwest of Mongu near the Angolan border, Liuwa Plain National Park is 3600 sq km of true wilderness. The remote park is characterised by expanses of flat, grassy flood plains, and most famous for the second-largest wildebeest migration in Africa in the wet season, when wall-to-wall herds gather at the beginning of November. Liuwa is also notable for having one of the highest population densities of hyena in the world and a stunning variety of bird life.

Shiwa Ng'andu

7 Deep in the northern Zambian wilderness sits Shiwa Ng'andu, a grand country estate and labour of love of eccentric British aristocrat Sir Stewart Gore-Brown. The estate's crowning glory is Shiwa Ng'andu manor house, which is a magnificent English-style mansion. Driving up to the house through farm buildings, settlements and workers' houses it almost feels like an old feudal domain: there's a whole community built around it, including a school and a hospital, and many of the people now working at Shiwa Ng'andu are the children and grandchildren of Sir Stewart's original staff. Today Gore-Brown's grandchildren live on and manage the estate, which is a working farm.

MICHAEL D. KOCK / GETTY IMAGES ©

Food & Drink

Although food isn't generally considered a highlight of travel in Zambia, you'll eat very well, particularly in the national park lodges, which offer the highest standards of culinary options.

Don't miss the opportunity to sample traditional Zambian food either, including the locals' staple *nshima*, a thick maize porridge that's bland but filling. It's eaten with your hands and accompanied by beans or vegetables and a hot relish, and sometimes meat or fish.

Local and imported beer, spirits, wine and soft drinks are widely available across the country from supermarkets, bars and lodges at far cheaper prices than in Western countries. An increasing number of cafes are serving Zambian coffee, which makes a good brew.

Wildlife

Because of Zambia's diverse landscape, plentiful water supplies, and position between Eastern, Southern and Central Africa, the diversity of animal species is huge. The rivers support large populations of hippos and crocs, and the associated grasslands provide plenty of fodder for herds of zebras, impalas and pukus. These animals naturally attract predators, so most parks contain lions, leopards, hyenas (which you'll probably see) and cheetahs (which you probably won't). Elephants, another big drawcard, are also found in huge herds in South Luangwa, Lower Zambezi and some other national parks. Bird lovers will love Zambia, where about 750 species have been recorded.

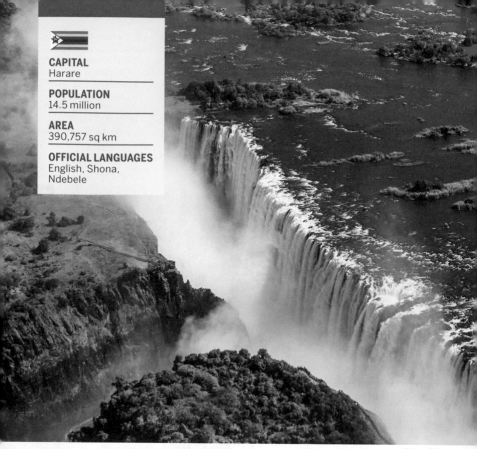

CAPITAL
Harare

POPULATION
14.5 million

AREA
390,757 sq km

OFFICIAL LANGUAGES
English, Shona,
Ndebele

Victoria Falls

Zimbabwe

A journey in Zimbabwe will take you through an attractive patchwork of landscapes, from highveld, balancing boulders and flaming msasa trees, to laid back towns, lush mountains and lifeblood rivers up north.

Here you can spot the Big Five strut their stuff around spectacular parks, discover World Heritage–listed archaeological sites and stand in awe of one of the natural wonders of the world, Victoria Falls.

Along the way you'll receive a friendly welcome from locals, famous for their politeness and resilience in the face of hardship. After almost two decades of political ruin, violence and economic disaster, Zimbabweans continue to hold on to the hope that a new dawn will soon rise upon this embattled nation.

While from afar Zimbabwe's plight doesn't paint a rosy picture, the reality is different on the ground for tourists – most insist it's hands down one of the safest, friendliest and most spectacular countries in Africa. Zimbabwe is ready and waiting. All it's missing is you..

Top Experiences

Victoria Falls

1 This is what you're here for, the mighty Victoria Falls. The 1km-long viewing path stretches along the top of the gorge, with various vantage points opening up to extraordinary front-on panoramas of the powerful curtain of water. One of the most dramatic spots is the westernmost point known as Cataract View. Another track leads to the aptly named Danger Point, where a sheer, unfenced 100m drop-off will rattle your nerves. From there, you can follow a side track for a view of the Victoria Falls Bridge.

Great Zimbabwe

2 The greatest medieval city in sub-Saharan Africa, the World Heritage–listed Great Zimbabwe is one of the nation's most treasured sights. So much so, that the country was named after it! These wonderfully preserved ruins of the Bantu civilisation and fabled capital of the Queen of Sheba provide evidence that ancient Africa reached a level of civilization not suspected by earlier scholars. As a religious and political capital, this city of 10,000 to 20,000 dominated a realm that stretched across eastern Zimbabwe and into modern-day Botswana, Mozambique and South Africa. Trade of gold and ivory was rampant, with goods coming from and going to places as far reaching as Arabia and China.

Mana Pools National Park

3 This magnificent 2200-sq-km national park is a Unesco World Heritage–listed site and its magic stems from its

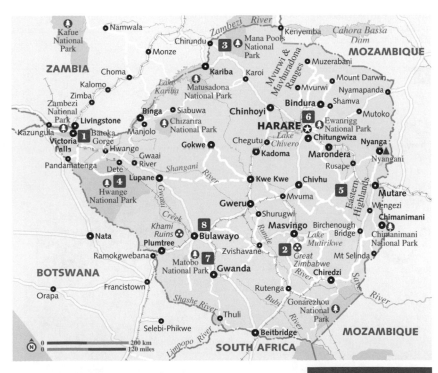

remoteness and pervading sense of the wild and natural. This is one park in Zimbabwe where you're guaranteed plenty of close encounters with hippos, crocs, zebras and elephants and are *almost* guaranteed to see lions and possibly wild dogs, leopards and cheetahs. What sets Mana Pools apart from just about any other park in the world is that you're allowed to walk around on foot without a guide.

Hwange National Park

4 One of the 10 largest national parks in Africa, and the largest in Zimbabwe, at 14,651 sq km, Hwange National Park, pronounced 'Wang-ee', has a ridiculous amount of wildlife. Some 400 species of bird and 107 types of animal can be found in the park, including lions, giraffes, leopards,

cheetahs, hyenas and wild dogs. But the elephant is what really defines Hwange, being home to one of the world's largest populations of around 40,000 tuskers.

Eastern Highlands

5 This narrow strip of mountain country that makes up Manicaland province isn't the Africa that normally crops up in armchair travellers' fantasies. The Eastern Highlands more resembles Great Britain, with verdant hills cloaked in mists, and pine forests and botanical gardens taking the place of the usual arid landscapes and game plains. It's where well-heeled Harare residents used to head away to their weekend holiday homes to fish for trout, and sit by the fireplace in between meanders into the countryside. The region has always had huge tourism

Getting Around

New to Zimbabwe is FastJet, a popular budget airline offering cheap flights to Victoria Falls from Harare.

Major train services connect Harare, Bulawayo, Mutare and Victoria Falls. Definitely opt for 1st class.

Buses operate according to published timetables. Most bus companies have both local and luxury coaches.

PAULA FRENCH / SHUTTERSTOCK ©

potential; during the 1990s it was a backpacker hub, but these days it only gets a fraction of the visitors it deserves. Come to hike in its spectacular national parks – it offers easily the best walks in the country, taking you past tranquil rivers, waterfalls and stunning vistas overlooking Mozambique.

Harare

6 More attractive than most other Southern African capitals, Harare gets a bad rap and unjustly so. While it's certainly not without its problems, overall it's a safe and laid-back city where wide avenues are lined with dusty red earth, and indigenous plants and blooming jacarandas provide a lovely African summertime feel. While it's tempting to rush off to your safari, it's worth hanging around in Harare to sample its fine dining, museums, craft markets and varied bars.

Food & Drink

Food in Zimbabwe is generally good and typically comprises charcoal-grilled meats such as T-bone steaks, chicken or Zambezi bream served with greens and a starch.

The staple for locals is *sadza*, a white maize meal made into either porridge or something resembling mashed potato, which is eaten with your fingers and served with tomato-based relishes, meat and/or gravy.

In the cities and tourist towns you'll get a good assortment of multicultural cuisine, as well as exotic game meats such as crocodile, kudu and warthog. Sandwiches, pies and other cafe fare are also widely available.

Matobo National Park

7 Home to some of the most majestic granite scenery in the world, the Matobo National Park is one of the unsung highlights of Zimbabwe. This Unesco World Heritage Site is a stunning and otherworldly landscape of balancing *kopjes* – giant boulders unfeasibly teetering on top of one another. When you see it, it's easy

to understand why Matobo is considered the spiritual home of Zimbabwe.

Bulawayo

8 Wide tree-lined avenues, parks and charming colonial architecture make Bulawayo, Zimbabwe's second city, an attractive one. It has a lovely historic feel to it, and it's worth visiting to soak up the superb architecture, art galleries and history.

JEZ BENNETT / SHUTTERSTOCK ©

The Arts

Zimbabwe's festivals, fairs and street-side stalls, live music and poetry, dance, art and sculpture are great expressions of its people and a wonderful way for visitors to meet the locals and learn about their lives. Most Zimbabweans are creative in some way: whether they bead, embroider, weave, sculpt or carve. The word 'Zimbabwe' means 'great stone house', so it is fitting that stone sculpture – also referred to as Shona sculpture – is the art form that most represents the people of Zimbabwe. The exuberance of the work, the vast varieties of stone and the great skill and imagination of the sculptors has led to many major, critically acclaimed exhibitions worldwide over the years.

Index

Hiroshima (Japan) 469
Ho Chi Minh City
(Vietnam) 958
Hobart (Australia) 74-5
Hoi An (Vietnam) 953
Hollókő (Hungary) 402
Hope Town, Elbow Cay
(Bahamas) 89
Hsipaw (Myanmar)
612
Hue (Vietnam) 957
Hvar (Croatia) 227
Inhambane
(Mozambique) 607
Istaravshan (Tajikistan)
864
Jazirat Al Hamra
Fishing Village
(United Arab
Emirates) 925
Jeddah (Saudi Arabia)
752
Jeonju Hanok Maeul
(South Korea) 802
Johannesburg (South
Africa) 796
Juba (South Sudan)
805
Kabul (Afghanistan) 33
Kaikoura (New
Zealand) 644
Kampong Ayer
(Brunei) 147
Kamyanets-Podilsky
(Ukraine) 919-20
Kandy (Sri Lanka)
819-20
Kassala (Sudan) 835
Katara, Doha (Qatar)
725
Kazbegi (Georgia) 337
Kecskemét (Hungary)
402
Khartoum (Sudan) 835
Khiva (Uzbekistan)
939-40
Kibuye (Rwanda) 740
Kigali (Rwanda) 741
Kilkenny City (Ireland)
440
Kingstown (St Vincent
& the Grenadines)
833
Kinshasa (Democratic
Republic of Congo)
209
Kisangani (Democratic
Republic of Congo)
209
Kolomyya (Ukraine)
920

Kotor (Montenegro)
593
Kpalimé (Togo) 889
Kraków (Poland) 705
Kratie (Cambodia) 168
Kutná Hora (Czech
Republic) 250
Lagos (Nigeria) 655
Lahıc (Azerbaijan)
84-5
Lambaréné (Gabon)
329
Lamu (Kenya) 481-2
Las Galeras (Domini-
can Republic) 264
Las Terrazas (Cuba)
239
Las Terrenas (Domini-
can Republic) 264
Laura (Marshall
Islands) 563
Libreville (Gabon) 330
Liepāja (Latvia) 504-5
Limbe (Cameroon) 171
Ljubljana (Slovenia)
783
Lobamba (Swaziland)
840
Lomé (Togo) 889
London (England) 281
Luang Prabang (Laos)
497
Lucerne (Switzerland)
854
Lüderitz (Namibia) 617
Luxembourg City
(Luxembourg) 528
Luxor (Egypt) 273
Lviv (Ukraine) 921
Maastricht
(Netherlands) 632
Madaba (Jordan)
473-4
Magome (Japan) 467
Mahdia (Tunisia) 899
Malbun (Liechtenstein)
519
Male (Maldives) 553
Maletsunyane Falls
(Lesotho) 511-12
Maputo (Mozambique)
605-6
Maubisse
(Timor-Leste) 887
Medellín (Colombia)
204
Melbourne (Australia)
69
Mérida (Mexico) 579
Mérida (Venezuela)
947

Mexico City (Mexico)
575
Miami (USA) 931
Minsk (Belarus) 101
Monrovia (Liberia) 515
Montezuma (Costa
Rica) 222
Montreux
(Switzerland) 854
Moroni (Comoros &
Mayotte) 207
Mui Ne (Vietnam) 959
Munich (Germany) 341
Nanortalik (Greenland)
362
Naples (Italy) 455
Navala village (Fiji)
305
Nebaj (Guatemala) 378
Negril (Jamaica) 457
Neiafu (Tonga) 892-3
New Orleans (USA)
927
New York City (USA)
927
Niš (Serbia) 766
Nkhata Bay (Malawi)
545
North Nicosia (Cyprus)
244
Nosara (Costa Rica)
221-2
Nuremberg (Germany)
347
Oaxaca City (Mexico)
575
Odesa (Ukraine) 920-1
Old Dhaka
(Bangladesh) 94
Old Kathmandu
(Nepal) 623
Old San Juan (Puerto
Rico) 719
Olomouc (Czech
Republic) 249-50
Osh (Kyrgyzstan)
494-5
Oshogbo (Nigeria) 655
Otepää (Estonia) 294
Ouro Prêto (Brazil) 143
Oxford (England) 285
Panama City (Panama)
681
Paramaribo
(Suriname) 837
Pärnu (Estonia) 294-5
Patan (Nepal) 626
Pécs (Hungary) 402
Perast (Montenegro)
595

Phetchaburi (Thailand)
877
Phnom Penh
(Cambodia) 163
Piran (Slovenia) 783-4
Plovdiv (Bulgaria) 153
Plzeň (Czech Republic)
250
Pointe-Noire (Republic
of the Congo) 213
Port of Spain (Trinidad
& Tobago) 895
Port Royal (Jamaica)
460
Porto (Portugal) 711
Potosí (Bolivia) 126
Prague (Czech
Republic) 247
Prizren (Kosovo) 489
Providenciales (Turks
& Caicos) 911
Ptuj (Slovenia) 784
Punta del Este
(Uruguay) 936
Pyongyang (North
Korea) 659
Qassiarsuk
(Greenland) 362
Québec City (Canada)
178
Quetzaltenango
(Guatemala) 378
Quito (Ecuador) 267
Rabaul (Papua New
Guinea) 687
Rhodes (Greece) 357
Ribe (Denmark) 255
Rīga (Latvia) 503
Robertsport (Liberia)
515
Rome (Italy) 450
Roseau (Dominica) 261
Rothenburg ob der
Tauber (Germany)
347
Rotorua (New Zealand)
643
Safed (Israel) 446
Safranbolu (Turkey)
904
Saint-Louis (Senegal)
762
Salamanca (Spain) 813
Salamis (Cyprus) 245
Salta (Argentina) 61
Salvador (Brazil) 141
Samaipata (Bolivia) 126
Samarkand
(Uzbekistan) 939
San Cristóbal (Mexico)
579

The World

This Book

This 2nd edition of Lonely Planet's *The World* guidebook was produced by the following:

Product Editors Catherine Naghten, Tracy Whitmey

Assisting Product Editors Carolyn Boicos, Hannah Cartmel, Bridget Blair

Senior Cartographer Alison Lyall

Assisting Cartographers Julie Dodkins, Wayne Murphy, Anthony Phelan, Diana Von Holdt

Book Designer Katherine Marsh

Cover Designer Campbell McKenzie

Assisting Book Designers Cam Ashley, Nicholas Colicchia, Clara Monitto, Virginia Moreno, Mazzy Prinsep, Wibowo Rusli

Thanks William Allen, Imogen Bannister, Ani Bartoszek, Michelle Bennett, Meri Blazevski, Kate Chapman, Katie Connolly, Gwen Cotter, Joel Cotterell, Melanie Dankel, Grace Dobell, Sasha Drew, Shona Gray, Liz Heynes, Kate Kiely, Indra Kilfoyle, Jodie Martire, Anne Mason, Kate Mathews, Jenna Myers, Darren O'Connell, Lauren O'Connell, Susan Paterson, Martine Power, Rachel Rawling, Kirsten Rawlings, Alison Ridgway, Jessica Rose, Kathryn Rowan, Dianne Schallmeiner, Victoria Smith, John Taufa, Tony Wheeler, Amanda Williamson, Juan Winata

STAY IN TOUCH LONELYPLANET.COM/CONTACT

AUSTRALIA
The Malt Store, Level 3, 551 Swanston St, Carlton, Victoria 3053

IRELAND Unit E, Digital Court. The Digital Hub, Rainsford St, Dublin 8, Ireland

USA 124 Linden Street, Oakland, CA 94607

UK 240 Blackfriars Road, London SE1 8NW

 twitter.com/ lonelyplanet

 facebook.com/ lonelyplanet

 instagram.com/ lonelyplanet

 youtube.com/ lonelyplanet

 lonelyplanet.com/ newsletter

The adventure continues on
lonelyplanet.com

Explore
Thorn Tree, the
biggest and best
online travel
community

Share
with Lonely Planet
on Instagram,
Facebook, Twitter,
YouTube and more

Shop
for guidebooks,
eBooks, gift books
and more

Book
flights, hotels,
tours and travel
insurance

lonelyplanet.com

Download our free app – Guides by Lonely Planet
City guides with offline maps, essential tips and
top experiences curated by our experts.

MIX
Paper from
responsible sources
FSC™ C021741
www.fsc.org

Paper in this book is certified
against the Forest Stewardship
Council™ standards. FSC™ promotes
environmentally responsible, socially
beneficial and economically viable
management of the world's forests.

Published by Lonely Planet Global Limited
CRN 554153
2nd edition – Oct 2017 ISBN 978 1 78657 653 8
© Lonely Planet 2017 Photographs © as indicated 2017
10 9 8 7 6 5 4 3 2 1   Printed in Malaysia